MICHELANGELO

This edition published by Barnes & Noble Inc.,
by arrangement with Parragon Publishing

2005 Barnes & Noble Books

M 10 9 8 7 6 5 4 3 2 1

ISBN 0-7607-6793-9

Printed and bound in Indonesia

The right of Kirsten Bradbury to be identified as the author
of this work has been asserted in accordance with Section 77
of the Copyright, Designs and Patents Act of 1988.

The right of Lucinda Hawksley to be identified as the
author of the introduction to this book has been asserted
in accordance with Section 77 of the Copyright, Designs
and Patents Act of 1988.

MICHELANGELO

KIRSTEN BRADBURY

Introduction by Lucinda Hawksley

BARNES & NOBLE BOOKS

NEW YORK

CONTENTS

CONTENTS

INTRODUCTION

Michelangelo Buonarroti was born on March 6 1475. He lived for almost a full century and died on February 18 1564; he was still working six days before his death. During his life, the western world underwent what was perhaps the most remarkable period of change since the decline of the Roman Empire. The Renaissance saw changes in all aspects of life and culture, with dramatic reforms sweeping through the worlds of religion, politics, and scientific belief. Michelangelo was one of the most fervent advocates of this exciting new philosophy, working with a remarkable energy that was mirrored by contemporary society.

He was born at Caprese, in Tuscany, the second of five sons of Lodovico di Leonardo (a civil servant) and Francesca Buonarroti. The family had two homes: one in the Tuscan countryside, and a much smaller one in the city of Florence. In 1481, when Michelangelo was six years old, his mother died. 1481 was to be a portentous year in more ways than one, as it was also the year in which he had his first drawing lesson from a local artist named Francesco Granacci.

In 1488, at the age of 13, Michelangelo moved to Florence and began working as an assistant to Domenico Ghirlandaio (1449–94), who had recently started work on Florence's Santa Maria Novella church. In 1489, after completing just one year of his apprenticeship, Michelangelo came to the attention of Lorenzo de' Medici, who summoned the boy to his court. There, he was free to wander the gardens at will, drinking in all the fine examples of Classical statuary owned by the Medicis. It was there that he began to learn the secrets of sculpting, teaching himself by making drawings of the statues and attempting to recreate them in clay. He was aided in his studies by the elderly curator of the gardens, Bertoldo di Giovanni (*c.* 1420–91), who had formerly studied under the master sculptor Donatello (*c.* 1386–1466).

Through his association with the court of Lorenzo, Michelangelo was in contact with the most brilliant thinkers, artists, and writers of his day. This experience was to enrich his life and consciousness. He was not only an artist, architect, and sculptor; he also wrote proficiently, producing countless poems and letters in his lifetime. Other influences on his young mind included two members of the church: one was his local priest, who, in return for the gift of a crucifix the young sculptor had carved, allowed him access to the bodies kept at the church so that he could study anatomy; the other formative influence was an articulate and opinionated monk named Fra Girolamo Savonarola (1452–98). He was a zealous reformer and an outspoken preacher; he was later to become the moral dictator of Florence for several months after the flight of the Medicis in 1494. He ruled by instilling religious fear into the Florentine people, foretelling great disaster if God was offended. His blistering sermons scalded many facets of Renaissance society and implicated many of the most powerful people of the day. This led to his eventual excommunication and execution in 1498; he was burnt at the stake in the Piazza della Signoria, where Michelangelo's *David* was later to stand.

Michelangelo first heard Savonarola preach in 1492, the year in which his first patron, Lorenzo de' Medici, died and Michelangelo returned to his father's home. The monk's sermons and his subsequent violent death had a lifelong effect on the artist and many of his works; the loss of Lorenzo also deeply affected his artistic consciousness.

By the age of 16, Michelangelo had begun to produce his own works. These included *Madonna of the Steps* (1491–92) and the *Battle of Hercules with the Centaurs* (1491–92). These two pieces, although of a similar date, are vastly different from one another: the *Battle* abounds with aggression and vitality, it teems with writhing, undulating shapes filling every section of the marble with boundless energy; in contrast, the *Madonna* is serenely tranquil, containing little movement within an unfinished relief created to invoke an atmosphere of gentleness.

In 1494, Florence suffered severe political upheaval. Until that time, it had been a separate city state led by the powerful Medici family, but in 1494 the city was invaded by the French king, Charles VIII. The political climate for intimates of the Medici circle became troubled, and when news of the forthcoming French invasion reached Florence, Michelangelo, like many other prominent Florentines, fled the city before the troops arrived. First, he traveled to Venice and then to Bologna, before he felt able to return home in 1495. While in Bologna, he was commissioned to complete a sculpture that had remained unfinished for 200 years, the tomb of St Dominic, Bologna's patron saint. The piece was begun by the sculptor Nicola Pisano (*c.* 1284–1314), but three figures needed adding. These were freestanding statues—the first of Michelangelo's career: St Proculus, St Petronius, and an angel.

Michelangelo's work for the Medici family continued after the invasion of Florence. At the age of 21, he made his first trip to Rome—a city that was both to play a prominent part in his life and create many frustrations for him. This time he spent five years in the city, creating some of his best-known works. In 1496–97, he completed his first important commission, Bacchus. As was his wont, the sculptor depicted the god of wine in a way never seen before. In place of the usual vision of *Bacchus*, an omnipotent force, genial but capable of brutality if crossed, Michelangelo sculpted a decadent, stupefied, almost effeminate drunk. Typically of his work, Bacchus's anatomy is executed superbly, the fluidity of the back muscles suggesting he has only just slipped into his drunken posture. It is a world away from previous depictions of the god and from the attractive, youthful *Bacchus* of Jacopo Sansovino (1486–1570), created just 15 years later, which reverts to the traditional Classical method that Michelangelo had considered outdated.

In 1497–98, Michelangelo created the *Pietà*, a masterpiece of sculpture that could not be farther removed in content from the witty *Bacchus*. The *Pietà* is heralded as one of his greatest achievements. The sorrowing face of Mary, contemplating the lifeless body of her eldest child, still wrings the heart today. He took the subject out of a religious context and placed it in a humanist light, emphasizing the grief of Mary and the mortality of her dead son.

On August 4 1501, the turbulence of previous years seemed to come to an end and the city of Florence was declared a republic. On August 16, the new republic commissioned Michelangelo to make the statue of *David*. He was asked to sculpt it from a single block of marble; one that had been worked on 40 years previously by Agostino di Duccio, but had been left unfinished.

David is perhaps the world's most famous statue and a cult has grown up around it. When one views this sixteenth-century masterpiece, it is apparent what all the fuss is about. Michelangelo's command of anatomy is superb; every muscle is painstakingly defined, every movement understood by the artist. Traditionally, works on this subject show a diminutive David standing by the severed head of the defeated Goliath; Michelangelo chose to change the perspective of this time-honored myth. His *David*, his face determined and thoughtful, stands strongly and pensively waiting to attack the giant. His hand holds the shot, his sling hangs over his back. Michelangelo captures the brief moment of reflection on the hero's face, showing tremendous concentration as he decides how to save his people. The subject matter was apt for the Florentines, themselves on the brink of a new era having recently been freed from a political dinosaur.

On September 8 1504, the completed sculpture was taken to the Piazza della Signoria in the centre of Florence, where it was placed in front of the Palazzo Vecchio. Such was the impact of Michelangelo's creation that it changed Florentine law—becoming the first naked statue to be allowed on public display since Classical times. Today, the original is housed in the Galleria della Accademia, but a copy also remains in the Piazza della Signoria in the heart of Florence.

In 1505, Michelangelo was summoned to Rome on the orders of Pope Julius II, who ruled between 1503 and 1513. He was a member of one of the most important families in Italy—the della Rovere family, political rivals of the Medicis. Hungry for earthly immortality, Julius commissioned Michelangelo to make his tomb; a monument of vast and expensive proportions, which was intended to be finished within five years.

The next few years were to be the most frustrating and miserable of Michelangelo's life, in which he found himself at the mercy of an inconsistent, temperamental authoritarian. The power of the pope forbade Michelangelo to leave Rome, even though he was unable to begin working on the tomb: Julius stalled the project through his indecision as to where the great edifice was to be placed. In preparation for his own death, the pope began an extensive recreation of St Peter's cathedral, intending to rest in supreme state for eternity – meanwhile Michelangelo was left in a state of limbo.

Relations with the pope eased when, on May 10 1508, Julius

gave Michelangelo a new commission, which drastically changed the way in which he saw himself and his art. Until now he had been, by definition, a sculptor, yet the pope commissioned him to fresco the ceiling of the Sistine Chapel. Michelangelo had to learn the art of painting, just as he had had to do with sculpture as a teenager. He found this arduous and disheartening; a letter sent to his father in 1509 records his extreme frustration:

"… my work does not seem to go ahead [as I would like it to] … This is due to the difficulty of the work and also because it is not my profession. In consequence, I lose my time fruitlessly. May God help me."

The frustrated artist looked to his former master, Ghirlandaio, for assistance with the technique of fresco painting, in 1481–82. Ghirlandaio had begun the task of painting the Sistine Chapel ceiling in 1481 before his death in 1494. Between 1508 and 1512, Michelangelo painted over 300 figures onto the ceiling. As with *David* and *Bacchus*, the scenes were not always depicted in the expected, conventional, and traditional manner of the time. This is most notable in his *Garden of Eden* fresco, where both Adam and Eve are seen as equally culpable for their downfall after eating from the Tree of Knowledge. The ceiling was eventually completed on 21 October 1512; a task that was arduous in the extreme.

In 1513, Pope Julius III died—his magnificent tomb still unfinished—leaving Michelangelo to continue discussions about the tomb with his more agreeable heirs. However, the tomb was to suffer further setbacks for much of the sculptor's life. After the death of Pope Julius II, Giovanni de' Medici was ordained as Pope Leo X. He remained in power for ten years. Michelangelo's links with the Medici family had remained strong and Pope Leo determined to keep the association going —not least to prevent the harried artist from having any free time in which to work on the tomb of a della Rovere.

The reign of Leo X was liberating to Michelangelo. Within a couple of years of Leo's election, he was back in his beloved Florence, free to live where he chose and still to undertake prestigious projects for the new pope. Meanwhile, Julius II's tomb was planned and replanned several times—each new drawing diminishing the tomb in size from previous plans and becoming less and less ornate.

Michelangelo made his home in Florence from 1515 until 1534. During this time, the city once again suffered massive upheavals. Since the time of Charles VIII's invasion and the city's subsequent republican status, the Medici family had returned. Although originally supported by the Medicis, Michelangelo was a fervent supporter of the republic. In 1527, the Medicis were driven from Florence once more, and the city declared a republic for a second time. Michelangelo was among several prominent Florentines who foresaw great political times ahead. He was appointed Governor of the Fortifications, a position that he took great pride in, although the rapid return to power of the Medicis thwarted his political ambitions. In 1530, the Medicis, aided by King Charles V of Spain, were restored to long-term power in Florence.

The year 1530 also saw a new commission for Michelangelo, given by Baccio Valori, the hugely unpopular governor of the Florentine republic. The result of this commission was the work that has become known as *David (Apollo)*, owing to uncertainty about which figure it represents. There are arguments for both and, with no concrete evidence, the art world will never be able to decide for certain. If it was intended as David—some critics suggest this because the crude round shape on which the figure's foot rests may have been intended as an unfinished head of Goliath—it is significantly inferior to his earlier masterpiece. This has often been cited as indicative of Michelangelo's dislike of his patron Valori; he often used his art as a medium to express his opinions of people. For instance, he incorporated recognisable portraits in the ceiling of the Sistine Chapel, using the character of the painted figure to suggest his like or dislike of the person intimated. He also incorporated his own face into his work at times—his self-portrait can be discerned in several of his works.

In 1532, Michelangelo paid one of his frequent visits to Rome. Here, at the age of 57, he fell in love with a young nobleman called Tommaso de' Cavalieri. Two years later, he decided to leave Florence and settle in Rome. Cavalieri was extremely handsome, and as one who strove to create beauty in his art, Michelangelo saw his lover as God's most perfect artwork, describing him as the "paragon of all the world." Much of their correspondence survives, as does the poetry that the sculptor wrote to his lover. His creative energy now had a new outlet, which complemented his prolific output. The two men remained close until Michelangelo's death.

Another important friend of the artist was a widow named Vittoria Colonna, Marchioness of Pescara. She was a deeply religious woman and a Catholic reformer, whose forward-thinking views held abundant interest for Michelangelo. He wrote her some of his most evocative poetry and, until her death in 1547, the two were extremely close—some sources suggest they were lovers, while others see it as an impassioned friendship. Michelangelo, as a poet, was strongly influenced by the work of yet another famous Florentine, the revered Dante Alighieri (1265–1321). During his early exile from Florence, in the time of King Charles VIII's invasion, and subsequently, during his enforced time in Rome under Pope Julius II, Michelangelo must have felt kinship with Dante, who had also been exiled. In his poetry to and about Vittoria, Michelangelo often compared her to Beatrice Portinari, the eulogized object of Dante's love. He also produced some of his finest religious drawings for Vittoria, in particular a masterful *Pietà*, drawn in 1546, just one year before she died. The distraught but powerful mother of Christ sits with her arms outstretched, embodying the cross from which her son has just been removed. The dead Christ is slumped between her knees—supported on either side by a robust, sorrowful *putto*—his head bowed with the sins of the world, his limbs loose in death. Both mother and son are powerfully drawn, with Christ's figure utilising Michelangelo's fine command of anatomy. From the start of his friendship with Vittoria Colonna, Michelangelo's work became more religious in content, and his poetry and art also became more concerned with death.

Michelangelo's time in Rome was filled with commissions —alongside which he was still attempting to finish the long-term project of the tomb of Pope Julius II. This was eventually unveiled in 1547; it had taken 42 years to reach completion. While in Rome, he was appointed Chief Architect of St Peter's in the Vatican and was commissioned to paint the frescoes in the Vatican's Pauline Chapel (Pope Paul III's private chapel).

The works of Michelangelo are an intimate insight into the superb mind of a remarkable man; a man who, even in his own lifetime, was revered as a genius. His contemporary and biographer, Giorgio Vasari (1511–74), wrote of him as "the divine Michelangelo," describing him as a "master" who "surpasses and excels" not only the artists of his own time, but also all artists who came before, including the great sculptors of antiquity. Michelangelo was a deeply spiritual man, whose genius came in part from his observations of the many different forces to which he was exposed throughout his extraordinary life. It came from the teenage years spent at the court of Lorenzo de' Medici—who was a prominent humanist and forward-thinking leader of Renaissance philosophy—and from Lorenzo's brilliant circle of acquaintances; from Michelangelo's admiration for the fervor of Savonarola; via the traditional religious views of the Vatican under two very different popes; and from the passionate religious beliefs of Vittoria Colonna.

Michelangelo lived for almost 89 years—an unusually long life span for a man of his era. In 1557 he had been forced to leave Rome because of the threat of invasion by Spain; he spent several of the last years of his life traveling in much the same way as he had started his adult years. He returned to Rome after the threat had passed and it was there that his life ended; he was buried at the church of Saint Apostoli in a huge formal ceremony. However, the story of his remarkable life was not over even in death: after burial, his body was secretly reclaimed and smuggled back to Florence, on the orders of Duke Cosimo de' Medici. There it was laid to rest in the church of Santa Croce. It remains there today, in a magnificent marble tomb designed by Vasari in 1570. The tomb bears a bust of Michelangelo, below which are sculptures of three sorrowing women: *Architecture*, *Painting*, and *Sculpture*.

LUCINDA HAWKSLEY

COPY OF THE SAGRA DEL CARMINE (C. 1490)

Celimage.sa / Scala Archives

This was Michelangelo's copy of Masaccio's *Sagra del Carmine*. Michelangelo's version is dated to around 1490 and is one of his earliest sketches. The copy shows a draped figure; the folds of his attire are formed with a careful crosshatching technique.

Florence, the undoubted nursery of the Renaissance, was the starting point for the genius, and would characterize Michelangelo. As a boy in this city Michelangelo was influenced by the works of the old masters, including frescoes by Masaccio and Giotto, of which he made several copies to develop his skills. Against his father's wishes, Michelangelo started an apprenticeship at the studio of Ghirlandaio. After one year he left Ghirlandaio in order to specialize in sculpture.

The quality of Michelangelo's draftsmanship was very high, considering his youth. His cross-hatching technique, especially in the forms and spaces of the drapery, is notable. A number of Michelangelo's early surviving works (he is known to have destroyed many such drawings) are copies based on earlier Italian masters such as Giotto or Masaccio. Others are drawn from ancient statuary.

Michelangelo went on to study at the sculpture school in the Medici gardens at Florence. There he attracted the patronage of Lorenzo de' Medici, the Magnificent.

Two Figures after Giotto (1490)

Celimage.sa / Scala Archives

In 1488 Michelangelo was apprenticed for a term of three years to Domenico Ghirlandaio and must have learnt the elements of fresco technique from his master. After the death of the young artist's patron Lorenzo de' Medici in 1492 the political situation in Florence deteriorated, and in October 1494, Michelangelo left for Bologna. Here, he carved three small figures for the tomb of Sa. This figure is part of the whole extraordinary series of the Madonna and Child, with the different variations of Michelangelo's constant meditation on that great theme. The subject is always part of the salvation process. Here it functions specifically as the crucial point of the Resurrection.

Giotto's 1320 fresco at the Peruzzi Chapel in Santa Croce, Florence, has two figures at the left of the painting. These two figures are reproduced in a Michelangelo drawing of 1490, now held at the Louvre, Paris.

Reflecting the poses in Giotto's work, these figures are shown as supplicants at the adoration. They carry themselves with the patrician demeanor of a Florentine noble and his compatriot. Their robes are thick and heavy. Yet despite their obvious power there is a humility discernible in their expressions. This work is an excellent example of the young and very talented Michelangelo during the period of his apprenticeship.

MADONNA OF THE STEPS (1491–92)

Celimage.sa/Scala Archives

Madonna of the Steps dates from 1491–92, during the period of Michelangelo's apprenticeship to the Florentine sculptor Bertoldo di Giovanni (*c.* 1420–91) at the Medici Palace. At that time the head of the Medici family was Lorenzo the Magnificent, the most powerful and influential man in Florence, an important patron of the arts and leader of the Renaissance. His vast collection of ancient sculpture and artefacts was housed in the garden of San Marco, a nearby monastery. Michelangelo had unlimited access to this treasure trove of antiquities and the influence of his studies there is apparent in this piece.

For this marble rectangular relief, Michelangelo has chosen the popular religious scene of the Madonna with the baby Jesus, to which he would return in later years with his sculpture *Madonna and Child* (1520–34). He departed from the traditional treatment of this theme by placing the Madonna sideways, a position often used in ancient Greek funerary decorations, which gives the piece a somber air.

The strong influence of Donatello (*c.* 1386–1466) is evident in the shallow pale-yellow marble relief, and although there are several faults in perspective, as well as in form, the work is representative of the development of an incredible talent in the young Michelangelo.

BATTLE OF HERCULES WITH THE CENTAURS (1491–92)

Celimage.sa/Scala Archives

Along with *Madonna of the Steps* (1491–92), the marble relief of *Battle of Hercules with the Centaurs* is counted among Michelangelo's earliest surviving pieces. Thought to have been started in 1491–92, but never completed, the piece presents a theme that was to dominate Michelangelo's work throughout his career—the male nude in movement. Here, as with his later cartoon *Battle of Cascina* (1504), Michelangelo created a consolidated expanse of male nudes frozen in a violent and turbulent struggle. Arms grab, push, or throw punches and both pieces focus on the men's interlocking limbs and the gestures forming this compact mass. Some of the figures are in relief while others, in the foreground of the sculpture, appear to be almost freestanding.

The theme of *Battle of Hercules with the Centaurs* was a popular choice in Classical sculpture, and the artist found inspiration for the work amongst the artefacts kept in the Medici garden. The piece is based on a tale in Ovid's (43 BC –18 AD) *Metamorphoses*, in which a wedding feast is disrupted by centaurs attempting to kidnap the women present, including the bride. Michelangelo has depicted all the figures as human, despite the centaurian subject of the relief, focusing mainly upon the muscular torsos of the men.

BACCHUS (C. 1496–97)

Celimage.sa/Lessing Archive

Bacchus in Greek and Roman mythology was the god of the vine, wine, and mystic ecstasy, and Michelangelo chose to represent the two former qualities of the god. Bacchus, his head crowned with grapevines, stands with his cup held aloft as if about to offer a toast. His expression is one of vague puzzlement, as though he has forgotten what he intended to do. His head is tilted and his mouth open, while his eyes appear glazed and unfocused. The unsteady stance of the god furthers his drunken appearance; one leg is partly lifted while his body tilts backward, making him seem unsure of his footing, almost staggering in his drunken stupor.

The piece was commissioned by wealthy Roman banker Jacopo Galli between 1497–98, while Michelangelo was living in Rome. The piece was placed in his garden and at one point the raised arm was broken off deliberately to increase the statue's Classical appearance. *Bacchus* is the earliest surviving life-size statue by Michelangelo. The perfection of the natural, realistic form that Michelangelo achieved here shows, as does *David* (1501–04), that despite his youth, he was far beyond the reach and ability of other sculptors of his time.

SATYR (DETAIL FROM BACCHUS) (C. 1496–97)

Celimage.sa/Lessing Archive

In Classical mythology the satyr was a demon of nature, representing the animal elements of humanity with its half-man and half-animal form. The satyr was sometimes represented as a horse, but more commonly as having the legs and hindquarters of a goat, cloven hoofs, and budding horns. Traditionally satyrs were the attendants of Bacchus, following him around and joining in with his festivities and sybaritic excesses.

This diminutive satyr hides behind the back of Bacchus, who is swaying drunkenly, and he nibbles at the grapes he steals from the leopard skin that Bacchus holds loosely. It was with this statue, and in particular along the edges of limbs such as the satyr's leg, that Michelangelo started to perfect his use of the drill to create textured surfaces. This effect would not have been possible with his preferred tools—the claw, toothed, and flat chisels.

Bacchus was created to be viewed from every angle; to be a freestanding statue. When viewed from the front, the satyr can only be partially glimpsed and it is necessary to walk around the statue to see it fully. The two figures are not attached by their bodies but by the leopard skin and the grapes; the satyr's body, however, curves suggestively, mirroring the form of Bacchus.

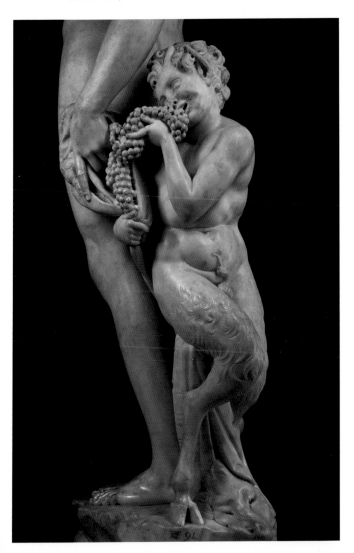

PIETÀ, ST PETER'S (1498–99)

Celimage.sa / Scala Archives

Pietà (1497–99) established Michelangelo as a master sculptor beyond comparison with any of his contemporaries. The sculpture now stands in St Peter's, on a high pedestal and protected by bulletproof glass, following a recent attack.

The pietà, a scene in which the Virgin Mary supports the dead body of Jesus in her lap, was a popular subject matter in other areas of Europe but had rarely been depicted in Italy. The composition of the pietà had caused other artists much difficulty in creating a realistic position that allowed Mary to support the body of an adult man. Michelangelo solved this problem by making Mary's robes heavy and large, creating an area in which the body of Christ could lie across her lap.

Pietà shows a reversal of the popular theme of Madonna with Child that Michelangelo explored in his early work *Madonna of the Steps* (1491–92). In *Pietà*, Mary holds the lifeless body of her only son, her left hand stretched palm upward, as if she is questioning the fate of Jesus. This gesture draws the viewer in to the scene emphatically, reiterating the Christian belief that Jesus died for humanity's salvation.

THE VIRGIN'S HEAD
(DETAIL FROM PIETÀ) (1498–99)

Celimage.sa/Scala Archives

During Michelangelo's lifetime, the face of the Virgin in this statue was criticized for appearing too young to be that of the mother of the adult Christ. Michelangelo defended his creation by saying: "Don't you know that women who are chaste remain much fresher than those who are not? How much more so a virgin who was never touched by even the slightest lascivious desire ...." He went on to add that he portrayed Jesus as older to emphasize his humanity; that he had subjected himself to the effects of mortality.

"Pietà" is the Italian word for pity. Despite its youthful appearance, the face of Mary still manages to convey the tragedy of the scene. Her eyes are downcast, almost shut. There is a quiet stillness in her expression, as if she is accepting of the death of her son.

Across Mary's chest is a sash upon which Michelangelo carved the words "Michaelangelo Buonarroti Florentine made this." *Pietà* was the only work Michelangelo signed in this manner, and his biographers recorded that he overheard some people credit *Pietà* to another artist, so that night he carved his name across the piece. The manner in which the sash follows the shape of Mary's body underneath the drapes would indicate that this story is fiction. Nonetheless, the prominent positioning of his signature is evidence of Michelangelo's pride in his work.

DAVID (1501–04)

Celimage.sa / Lessing Archive

Michelangelo's *David* (1501–04) sealed his reputation as the greatest living sculptor of the time. The piece was commissioned by Piero Soderini, the first chancellor of the Florentine republic, after the sculptor returned to Florence flushed with success from Rome.

The marble for *David* was a huge block that Renaissance sculptor Agostino di Duccio had abandoned about 40 years previously, and it had been lying disused ever since. Several other sculptors wanted the commission but Michelangelo was the only one to achieve a design of such enormous dimensions that used only this marble block, requiring no additional parts. Owing to the limitations of the damaged marble from which Michelangelo worked, the statue is much broader than it is deep, and so *David* was intended to be viewed from the front or back rather than the side.

For the Florentines, the Biblical character of David was an exemplar of strength and enormous courage in the face of adversity. Upon its completion the statue became a centerpiece of civic pride in the city, and Michelangelo would later draw upon this victory scene in the Sistine Chapel. His portrayal of David differs from other versions in form as well as in position —he uses developed, more muscular forms and creates a powerful physical presence in the spirit of a giant-slaying hero and future king.

FACE (DETAIL FROM DAVID) (1501–04)

Celimage.sa/Scala Archives

As the Republicans had beaten the Medici family to gain ruling power in Florence, the subject of David was chosen as a reminder to the republican government that David had beaten mighty Goliath and that he had ruled his people well and fairly thereafter. The face of *David* emphasizes this idea through its watchful and expectant expression, frowning with intense concentration. This expression is matched by the almost stationary pose; he seems pensive yet alert with the loaded slingshot held lightly over one shoulder as he gazes into the distance, waiting for his foe to come within range.

Some critics have noted that the head and hands of *David* are slightly too large for the body. Given that the statue is almost 17 ft high, only photographs enable us to have a direct view of the youth's face, an experience not possible for a contemporary viewer. The model for the statue was an adolescent boy and these slightly over-defined features ring true in their natural rendering of a boy not quite fully grown.

The face itself is classically ideal, with perfect features. Upon completion of *David*, Piero Soderini told Michelangelo that the nose was too large. To appease him the sculptor climbed up the statue and carefully pretended to chisel at the nose, letting some marble dust fall to the ground to enforce his deceit.

THE DONI TONDO
(THE HOLY FAMILY) (1504)

Celimage.sa/Lessing Archive

The Holy Family is known as the *Doni Tondo*, since it was commissioned by Michelangelo's friend Angelo Doni in 1503–04. Michelangelo rarely worked in the medium of panel painting and the *Doni Tondo* is the only piece that can undeniably be attributed to him; other surviving paintings, such as *The Entombment* (*c.* 1506), have a more questionable status.

The three figures are closely linked together by their positions and their movements, forming a compact, almost sculptural whole. The round frame is set off by the triangular configuration and the delineation of the figures is crisp, almost harsh, with a sharp, clear definition. This is a technique that, while necessary in tempera painting, further increases the sculptural quality of the figures by making the three stand out against the background, as if they have been superimposed.

The colors are bold and brightly vivid; the orange-gold material of Joseph's clothes seems to have a satin sheen. Michelangelo used color in a similar way throughout the Sistine Chapel frescoes, as can be seen in *The Delphic Sibyl* (1508–12). The contrasting colors also create blocks within the figures that emphasize their movements.

St John the Baptist
(Detail from The Holy Family) (1504)

Celimage.sa / Lessing Archive

St John the Baptist appears in the middle ground of the *Doni Tondo*, as he does in the later *Pitti Tondo* (*c.* 1504). With his animal skin draped round him, he gazes adoringly at the baby Jesus held aloft, symbolically, between his parents. A celestial light that seems to emanate from the family itself falls onto St John.

The distant landscape is barren, with a rocky mountain that can be seen at the top of this detail. Between the family and the mountains are five young male nudes. One of the nudes has his arm around the youth in front of him, while to their right another playfully tries to pull off the cloth that is draped over him. The significance of these nudes has been generally taken to be that they denote the pagan world from which St John has turned away to face the Holy Family, as if he can already sense their importance. Michelangelo created symbolic layers within this picture, representing the path of man: from the harsh natural world, to his naked paganism, to the intermediary St John, and to the Christian world, newly formed and represented by the child in the foreground.

STUDY FOR THE DONI MADONNA (1503)

Celimage.sa/Scala Archives

Madonna and Child (*Study for the Doni Tondo Madonna*) is a preliminary drawing for the *Doni Tondo* (1504). Michelangelo chose not to use the positioning seen here, opting for a triangular configuration. Michelangelo's preferred medium for this type of work was red chalk, which had been introduced by Leonardo da Vinci (1452–1519) during the year this work was executed. His confident depiction of the child demonstrates the ease with which he mastered new media, and he went on to use it frequently, as in his *Study of Adam* (1511).

From 1503, both Leonardo and Michelangelo were living in Florence. The two great artists were both later to receive a commission for battle scenes which were to be placed next to each other. There is said to have been great rivalry between the two; Leonardo had long been acknowledged as a genius, while Michelangelo was still building his reputation, although his success with *Pietà* and *Bacchus* had considerably strengthened his fame. Michelangelo also derived the notion of a triangular configuration—which he used for the Holy Family in his *Doni Tondo*—from Leonardo's work, but it was an idea that he developed and made his own.

St Peter (1501–04)

Celimage.sa / Scala Archives

St Peter is one of several statues of saints that Michelangelo made for the Cardinal Francesco Piccolomini. Piccolomini went on to become Pope Pius III in 1503 but died after only three weeks. On Michelangelo's return to Florence in 1501, flushed with the success of his *Pietà* in Rome, he received a three-year commission from the future Pope to carve 15 statues of saints. Each statue was to be 4.5 ft high and they were to be situated in the Piccolomini altar in Siena Cathedral. Following the death of the Pope, the contract was renewed by his heirs, but Michelangelo was never to fulfill its terms completely, delivering only four of the saints in 1504—*St Peter*, *St Pius*, *St Paul*, and *St Gregory*.

St Peter leans slightly to one side with his knee bent and raised, giving the appearance of being caught in mid-step. His head is lowered, his eyes humbly kept to the ground. The statue is a conventional treatment of the saint, unlike the St Peter seen in the fresco of *The Crucifixion of St Peter*.

THE MADONNA OF BRUGES (1501–04)

Celimage.sa / Scala Archives

Set within the decorative high altar of the richly decorated Church of Our Lady of Notre Dame in Bruges, Belgium, this masterpiece is an extraordinary and reverential work. Also known as the *Bruges Madonna*, this statue was carved by Michelangelo at about the same time that he was working on the colossal statue of David. During the same time period Michelangelo produced several Madonna paintings and sculptures, including the painting of the Holy Family known as the *Doni Madonna*. From about 1505 onward Michelangelo devoted nearly all of his time to large-scale projects.

This work focuses on the seated Madonna, who has the nude Christ Child standing between her knees. The Madonna figure has a haunting and ethereal beauty. The richly detailed folds of her drapery lend an astonishing realism to this High Renaissance work.

THE PITTI TONDO (*C.* 1504)

Courtesy of Edimedia

The *Pitti Tondo* (1504–05) and the *Taddei Tondo* (*c.* 1504) were named after the Florentine families that commissioned them. By the time these two marble reliefs were made, Michelangelo was a very famous artist and his work was highly sought after. Both of these pieces were left unfinished, and it has been suggested that this is because Michelangelo returned to Rome in 1505. Others believe, however, that he left them in this state deliberately; the *Pitti Tondo* appears to be a finished work in which Michelangelo quite consciously used the effects of the unfinished surfaces as an aesthetic device.

"Tondo" means a round framed picture or relief. The *Pitti Tondo* was one of three tondi Michelangelo worked on in the space of two years, seeking different ways to make use of circular space. Here Michelangelo has broken the constraints of the circle by placing Mary's head outside it. To the left of Mary is the vague figure of St John, who also appears in the other tondi.

The *Pitti Tondo* relief is less deep than that of the *Taddei Tondo*. To create the illusion of perspective in the placement of St John, the relief is very shallow; he is ghost-like, being only lightly defined.

THE TADDEI TONDO (C. 1504)

Courtesy of the Bridgeman Art Library

In the *Taddei Tondo* Michelangelo further explores the theme of the Madonna and Child which he worked on in his teenage years with *Madonna of the Steps* (1491–92). As in the earlier relief, Michelangelo portrays Mary in a protective role while the Christ Child is shown as fearful or wary, clinging to his mother. Both pieces evince a somber atmosphere.

The Christ Child is cowering away in fear from St John on the left. He shelters in Mary's lap as she gently holds the other child at a distance from him. The cause of Christ's fear is a goldfinch held by St John, a bird that supposedly feeds on thorns and symbolizes his Passion (passion meaning the suffering of Christ).

The placement of the figures in this scene is circular, thus echoing the round frame. Although the piece appears to be incomplete, it is more likely that Michelangelo meant his strokes to be expressive; his roughly hewn chisel marks show clearly in the background. Parts of the scene are missing in entirety: the feet of the Christ Child and one of Mary's arms have yet to be carved.

STUDY FOR THE BATTLE OF CASCINA (1504)

Celimage.sa / Scala Archives

In 1504 Piero Soderini commissioned Michelangelo to create a huge fresco depicting a battle scene. This was to be placed in the Signoria Palace alongside *The Battle of Anghiari*, to be produced by Leonardo da Vinci. Michelangelo's invitation to the Vatican by Pope Julius II meant that the painting was never executed, although several studies survive.

The fresco shows the story of a surprise attack by Pisan forces on the Florentine army, who were caught unawares while bathing in the river Arno. In *Study for The Battle of Cascina* we can discern a group of writhing figures, a mixture of vanquished victims and desperate survivors.

The study is a seminal example of Michelangelo's evolving style and contains clear examples of the artist's rigid, sculptural approach to figurative subjects. Through examination of his epic drawings, such as *Study for The Battle of Cascina*, we begin to comprehend the processes that led to his large-scale paintings. We can discern the internal dynamism of the overall work, which belies its softly etched tones

STUDY FOR A FIGURE FROM THE BATTLE OF CASCINA (1504)

Celimage.sa / Scala Archives

The *Battle of Cascina* cartoon was highly influential, and studied by many contemporary artists who visited Florence. Several effusive descriptions of the cartoon exist from renowned artists such as Benvenuto Cellini (1500–71). Many claimed that the cartoon was superior even to Michelangelo's painting of the Sistine Chapel.

The cartoon's significance stems not just from the influence it exerted but also from its signaling the development of Michelangelo's exclusive focus on the male nude in motion. The story of the Florentine captain raising alarm among his soldiers bathing in the river Arno provided an excellent opportunity to explore the many postures and poses of the body and gave a pretext for nudity. As in all his work the background is simple, the intensity of his focus directed purely on the human form.

This study shows the superb naturalism of the muscles working in the youth's back and gives an idea of what the original cartoon must have been like in the hands of the master. Bastiano da Sangallo's work often presents an anatomically inaccurate portrayal of the human body; this is evident when comparing Michelangelo's study with the same figure at the top of the da Sangallo cartoon.

St Matthew (1505)

Celimage.sa/Scala Archives

The Florentine Wool Guild and the Opera del Duomo commissioned Michelangelo to carve 12 statues of the apostles for Florence Cathedral in 1503. The Guilds were important patrons of the arts and the commission was a prestigious one for Michelangelo. Patronage of the arts had developed alongside the increase in wealth within the city and in turn had greatly improved the standing of the artist in society.

It was agreed that Michelangelo would produce one apostle statue a year, but *St Matthew* was the only piece that Michelangelo had begun. By the end of 1505, following his return to Rome, the contract was canceled before his work had been completed.

The statue of *St Matthew* is significant, since it indicates the emergence of an important stage in Michelangelo's career; the study of the body in contorted movement. The figure has one smooth, almost completed knee raised while his opposite arm grips the side of the huge marble block, as if he were about to push himself up and out of the marble constraint. Michelangelo was to continue exploring this new area of movement in his frescoes in the Sistine Chapel, especially the *Ignudi* (1508–12).

MALE NUDE (FULL FACING) (1502–06)

Celimage.sa/Lessing Archive

The *Male Nude* uses a medium of red chalk, often employed by Michelangelo as it was softer than black chalk. The artist has drawn the sketch with great attention to detail, yet it appears uncompleted. Michelangelo emphasized the torso, arms, and legs, leaving the head vague and ill-defined.

Through foreshortening, the artist has effectively established mobility and perspective within this figure. Muscle shape and shaded areas create the realistic illusion of the leg and body in motion. This is a preparatory study for a fullscale work. There is no suggestion of context or background.

Male Nude's posture is dramatic and extreme. Michelangelo's use of such postures influenced the art style known as Mannerism (*c.* 1515–1610), which employed artistic tricks such as elongating a figure to heighten its dramatic impact.

Two Nude Men Raising a Third Man (1502–06)

Celimage.sa/Lessing Archive

Michelangelo has been quoted as saying that an "artist must have his measuring tools, not in the hand, but in the eye, because the hands do but operate, it is the eye that judges...." He was a superb draftsman, a skill that he believed was paramount to all the arts in which he excelled, whether it was sculpture, painting, or architecture.

Two Nude Men Raising a Third Man shows the artist's skill at handling the human figure in movement. The men's torsos appear to be pushing forward out of the frame, half staggering toward the viewer. The absence of facial features adds to this rough quality, as does the balancing of the body and the arm thrust up from the central figure. The men are thickset, muscular, and reminiscent of representations of figures that appear in Michelangelo's later paintings. The heavier forms that filled his final works have been described as evidence of his disillusionment with the portrayal of the perfect male form, once so prevalent in his sculpture, painting, and drawings. There is the suggestion of a struggle to achieve a goal in which the three men are playing an interdependent role.

The Virgin, St Anne, and Male Nude (1502–06)

Celimage.sa/Lessing Archive

This work, embellished with quotes from Petrarch, is a finely detailed rendition of two biblical figures. The additional male figure appears as a footnote to the main portrait.

This is an especially penetrative portrayal. We are reminded of Leonardo da Vinci's work *Virgin, Infant, and St Anne*, which offers a more empathetic treatment of the subject. The two artists shared similar family backgrounds and early childhood experiences.

Michelangelo (1475–1564) was born in Tuscany, Italy, and was raised by a wet nurse until the age of two, because his mother was ill. His mother died when he was six, and his father remarried. His childhood is usually described as lacking affection, and he retained a grim and taciturn demeanor throughout his life.

Leonardo (1452–1519) was also born in Tuscany, the illegitimate son of a wealthy notary and a peasant woman. His father took custody of the boy, and each of Leonardo's parents married other people, eventually providing him with 17 half-sisters and half-brothers. Leonardo's first stepmother died when he was 12, and his second stepmother died when he was 21.

Perhaps fueled by their early loss of a strong maternal figure, the art of both men is infused with a wish to reunite with the mother, and these "conflicts of masculine and feminine forces show in the sublime genius of their art," according to the distinguished art historian, Dr Simons.

Like Leonardo, Michelangelo crafted many renditions of the Virgin Mary and her mother, St Anne, many of them depicting mother figures who are aloof.

DIFFERENT STUDIES OF FIGURES, WITH AN INSCRIPTION AFTER A SONNET BY PETRARCH (1506)

Celimage.sa/Lessing Archive

Francis Petrarch (Francesco Petrarca) was born in Arezzo, the son of a notary, but he spent his early childhood in a village near Florence. The Black Guelfs, who had seized power in Florence, expelled his father, Ser Petracco. In Avignon Petrarch composed numerous popular sonnets. In his search for old Latin classics and manuscripts, he traveled through France, Germany, Italy, and Spain.

Petrarch was regarded as the greatest scholar of his age. He wrote most of his works in Latin, although his sonnets and *canzoni*, written in Italian, were equally influential. Petrarch was known as a devoted student of antiquity. He combined an interest in classical culture with Christianity and had a deep influence on literature throughout western Europe.

In *Different Studies of Figures*, Michelangelo demonstrates his abiding deference to classical form in art. In this ink sketch he combines several anatomical and figurative elements. The arm set to the foreground establishes a distance behind which a tall androgynous figure stands. Other elements such as the helmeted head appear as visual references in the form of an *aide-mémoire* for the artist who is perhaps making quick notes for some future work.

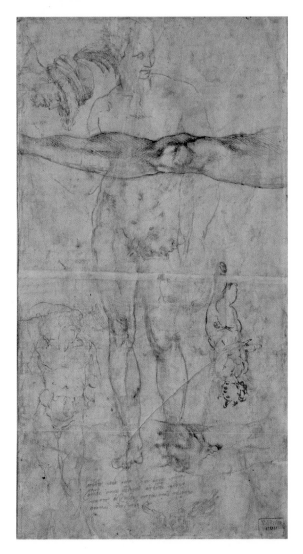

SISTINE CHAPEL (1508–12)

Celimage.sa/Scala Archives

The Sistine Chapel creates an overwhelming impression, with a barrage of highly ornate and decorative images that surround the visitor. The chapel was named after Pope Sixtus IV (1471–84) and is used for meetings of the Conclave (the papal council that runs the elections). It has dense walls, the remnant of a past when sieges were a real threat to the papacy. The ceiling has a shallow barrel-vault design and the only natural light to come into the chapel enters through the windows that are just underneath it.

The walls of the chapel are horizontally separated into three tiers, with the top tier housing the windows and their surmounting lunettes, which were decorated by Michelangelo. Beside the windows there are paintings of the popes of the past by Sandro Botticelli (1444/5–1510). Beneath these, in the middle tier, Pope Sixtus had frescoes painted by three outstanding and highly influential artists—Botticelli, Ghirlandaio, and Pietro Perugino (*c.* 1445–1523). These frescoes depict the life of Christ and Moses with the symbolic intention of underlining the concept that the papacy descended from the apostle of Christ, St Peter. The bottom tier contains painted curtains.

SISTINE CHAPEL CEILING (1508–12)

Celimage.sa/Lessing Archive

Given the continuing respect and admiration for Michelangelo's epic masterpiece of the Sistine Chapel ceiling, it is ironic that the artist did not want to accept the colossal commission for the fresco. He believed that his rival, Pope Julius II's chief architect Donato Bramante (1444–1514), had convinced Julius to commission Michelangelo for the ceiling, believing that he would either refuse the pope, making himself dangerously unpopular with the most crucial of patrons, or that his fresco painting would be disastrous. Although he saw himself as a sculptor and not a painter, Michelangelo reluctantly gave in to the pope's wishes and accepted the commission in 1508.

The original ceiling was based on a simple star motif which Julius II wished to replace with a fresco of the 12 Apostles. Michelangelo believed this would appear "rather meanly" and eventually persuaded Julius to grant "commission to do what I liked best," ensuring that he had control of the design.

Michelangelo created an architectural framework to establish an order within the complex frescoes and also to link them with the real architecture of the chapel, such as the lunettes, spandrels, and curves of the vault. The ceiling is divided into nine narrative panels by the painted pilasters.

THE SEPARATION OF LIGHT FROM DARKNESS (1508–12)

Celimage.sa/Scala Archives

Chronologically the first panel in the narrative scheme, *The Separation of Light from Darkness* is seen last if entering the Sistine Chapel through the lay entrance. Michelangelo chose to begin painting here and worked back toward the altar wall. The first five panels depict the creations of God, beginning here with the *Creation of Form from Chaos* (*Separation of Light from Darkness*). The narrative then moves on to highlight the Biblical history of mankind, starting with *The Fall of Man*, followed by three panels that show stories of *Noah and The Flood*. The narrative panels end with a panel that alludes to the re-emergence of sin amongst mankind, thus announcing the coming of Christ which links the panels to the earlier frescoes within the chapel.

Michelangelo was the first artist to attempt the illustration of such an ethereal and intangible subject as the beginning of the universe and he chose a literal translation of the Bible, focusing solely on the recognizable: the figure of God. God fills almost the entire panel as he reaches ahead, the appearance of movement created by the swirling colors about him.

THE CREATION OF THE PLANETS, THE SUN, AND THE MOON (1508–12)

Celimage.sa / Lessing Archive

Following on from *The Separation of Light from Darkness* is *The Creation of the Planets, the Sun, and the Moon*. This painting is a continuous narrative depicting God in two acts of creation, so He appears twice within the one panel.

On the right of the scene, at God's outflung hand, is the vague, gray outline of the moon at which one of His fingers is pointing. Beside the outstretched right hand, God's finger points to the huge globe of the sun, a burnt orange in color as if seen at dawn. The expression of concentration created by His furrowed brow and piercing stare gives God a stern, fierce appearance; a God of action, immensely powerful and with the potential for a dangerous anger. Under His outstretched arms and amongst His swirling robes are naked cherubs or angels, which gaze up at God in awe at His incredible powers.

The second part of this narrative panel depicts God from a most unusual viewpoint: from the back. We see the soles of His feet as He flies through the air, one arm reaching toward the green land below.

THE SEPARATION OF THE EARTH FROM THE WATERS

Celimage.sa/Scala Archives

The Separation of the Earth from the Waters, as with *The Separation of Light from Darkness*, is a difficult concept to express visually. This is one of the five smaller panels and like the first panel, Michelangelo has used the figure of God to fill the space, employing extreme foreshortening so that He appears to fly out from the frame. This effect is exaggerated by the formation of God's robes, which create an oval-shaped, darker area for Him to emerge from. Beneath God is a murky sea and above an equally blurred, misty sky.

God's features are similar to those of Pope Julius II, possibly as an attempt to appease the fiery pope. He was an old man and worried that he would not live to see the completed fresco, frequently visiting Michelangelo to check on his progress. On one such occasion when the Pope queried the timescale of the project, Michelangelo replied, "When it shall be done." This surly reply angered Julius so much that he struck the artist, causing the equally hot-tempered Michelangelo to leave the chapel. He returned only after the pope had sent him money by way of apology.

THE CREATION OF ADAM (1508–12)

Celimage.sa/Lessing Archive

The notion of God creating Man had been represented in art before Michelangelo began working on the Sistine Chapel, but never with the majesty and vitality that he achieved. This treatment is not reserved purely for the figure of God but is equally abundant in Adam, fittingly so for a being made in God's image. Adam has been painted nude, a massive figure reclining against a rocky mountain amid an otherwise barren landscape. He is gracefully poised, a perfection of form—muscular yet beautifully proportioned—a heroically Classical image.

God is shown in movement, as He is in the preceding three panels, which portray images of Creation. The gestures and expressions of the angels and cherubs clinging to His side emphasize His movement; some are watching expectantly as the two hands draw close.

The scale within *The Creation of Adam* is larger than in the preceding panels. The scaffolding had been removed from the completed half of the ceiling by this time and upon viewing it, Michelangelo decided to increase the size of the figures and decrease the detail, making the paintings more impressive and startling to the audience below.

THE CREATION OF ADAM
(1508–12) (RESTORED)

Celimage.sa / Lessing Archive

The Creation of Adam is depicted in the large field of the vault of the sixth bay, between the triangular spandrels. It represents perhaps the most complex composition in Western art. The space contains an intricate *trompe l'oeil* architecture surrounding classical figures drawn from the Bible. Out of nine narrative scenes depicting events from Genesis, probably the most sublime is this Creation of Adam, in which Michelangelo's new vision of humanity is represented pictorially.

Michelangelo experiences the stages of creation within himself, retracing the way to the divine source by the double path of religion and art. God creates Adam through the slightest touch. It is this gesture between God and man that sets forth the human experience. The painting focuses on the naked male torso, with great attention devoted to muscle and skin tone. This is a seminal study of the male form painted under harrowing conditions. Michelangelo was to make numerous studies, sculptures, and paintings of the male torso, seeking to create balance and perfection.

THE HAND OF GOD
(DETAIL FROM THE CREATION OF ADAM)
(1508–12)
Celimage.sa / Lessing Archive

The Hand of God is perhaps the most enduring of Michelangelo's paintings. Almost five centuries later this image remains prevalent and is still being used in advertising and on posters and T-shirts. This is particularly true of the detail that shows the two hands as they reach toward each other, tantalizingly close, almost touching.

The panel illustrates the moment when life is instilled in Adam by God. Michelangelo has placed the central focus upon the hands of God and of Adam, not just by the placement of the figures, but also by the lines of form that flow within the painting between the two outstretched arms.

Adam, who is only half sitting up against the mountainside, seems weak and languid, with his arm resting upon one bent knee as if it is too heavy for him to hold up without some support. The hand is limp, the fingers are drooping as if they are without energy, awaiting the vital spark of life.

THE CREATION OF EVE (1508–12)

Celimage.sa/Lessing Archive

The figure of Eve has none of the majesty or heroic form of Adam in *The Creation of Adam*. Eve's body is hunched, her hands are clasped tightly together and she reaches up toward God, appearing almost obsequious as he blesses her. The *Creation of Eve* is a small panel and Michelangelo has painted the figure of God as an immense form, clothed in heavy robes, with his head slightly bent forward so that he fits just within the panel.

In the bottom left-hand corner a fiery-headed Adam lies unconscious against a dead tree, reminding the viewer of how Eve was formed (from one of Adam's ribs) and also that she will bring about the fall of man and the loss of paradise.

The colors used within this panel are repeated in the objects that the surrounding *Ignudi* hold and are themselves echoes of the hues from *The Fall of Man and the Expulsion from Paradise*. The recent problematic restoration of the Sistine Chapel ceiling revealed Michelangelo's original intense use of color once the dirt of almost 500 years had been removed.

THE CREATION OF EVE AND THE PROPHET EZEKIEL (1508–1512)

Celimage.sa/Lessing Archive

Michelangelo painted a complex architectural structure, resembling that used for the tomb of Pope Julius II, to give his mammoth fresco structural order. The panel of *The Creation of Eve* is blocked off by two of the 10 painted pilasters that separate the huge ceiling into the nine sections used for the central narrative panels. On either side of the small panel are two of the four larger narrative panels.

Figures of naked men perch at the base of the pilasters, and they are often shown twisted in movement, demonstrating Michelangelo's skill at handling the male nude. Pairs of these figures, known as *Ignudi*, appear at either side of the smaller panels and hold medallions between them containing scenes from Biblical history.

Underneath the *Ignudi*, carved into the columns, are small cherubic figures, also known as caryatids, who appear to prop up the cornice above them. Darkly painted nudes appear besides the caryatids in the triangular spaces created by the spandrels, beneath the larger narrative panels. They seem crammed into their tiny spaces, pushing against their confinement. Underneath the medallion that the *Ignudi* hold sits the prophet Ezekiel.

THE FALL OF MAN AND THE EXPULSION FROM PARADISE (1508–12)

Celimage.sa / Lessing Archive

Michelangelo used the same device of continuous narrative for this large panel of *The Fall of Man and the Expulsion from Paradise* that he used in *The Creation of the Planets, the Sun, and the Moon*. The tale begins on the left, with the figure of Adam grabbing the branches of a tree while Eve sits beneath him. Eve reaches behind her to take the apple from the serpent, while Adam stretches to grasp one of the forbidden fruits. The narrative continues its flow through the serpent in the tree on to the right, where the couple can be seen as they are cast out of Paradise.

The landscape is barren, almost inhospitable, with only a few rocks surrounding the figures, with the exception of the one tree where the serpent lurks. This is an unusual depiction of Paradise, contrasting with the verdant foliage and lush vegetation that can be seen in traditional representations of the story, or even in the fifteenth-century frescoes that line the second tier of the Sistine chapel. Throughout the work there is a noticeable lack of detailed background or landscapes; Michelangelo's priority was always the natural and realistic depiction of the human form.

THE SNAKE AND THE EXPULSION (DETAIL FROM THE FALL OF MAN) (1508–12)

Celimage.sa / Lessing Archive

The snake from the Garden of Eden is usually portrayed as male or genderless. Michelangelo chose a feminine depiction for his serpent, tempting the eagerly awaiting Eve with the forbidden fruit while also focusing her gaze on the nearby Adam. Her lower half, in the form of a snake, is painted in lurid, bright colors whilst her top half takes the form of a voluptuous and tempting woman. This means that pictorially, woman is blamed twice for the Fall and the Expulsion.

On the right of the fresco, Adam and Eve are shown leaving Eden. Adam looks away from the scene of their disgrace, his hands sheltering his eyes from the sight as they are pushed out of their paradise by the angel hovering above. Eve looks back, her body hunched forward with her hand against her face as if trying to hide herself in shame. There are interesting comparisons to be drawn between Adam's tortured body and the majestic figure in *The Creation of Adam. The Expulsion* leans heavily on Masaccio's famous *Expulsion from Paradise*, in the Brancacci Chapel in Florence, a piece with which Michelangelo was certainly familiar.

THE SACRIFICE OF NOAH (1508–12)

Celimage.sa / Scala Archives

Chronologically the story of Noah's sacrifice belongs to the period after the Flood, but the story of the Flood required a large panel owing to the number of figures it was to contain. This smaller panel was Michelangelo's last before he changed the scale within his fresco: the following panel, *The Fall of Man*, shows fewer and larger figures, which enhanced visibility.

In the background, behind the table, is the figure of Noah, one arm raised as if preaching to his family, trying to gain some order. On his right his daughter-in-law raises a hand and turns her head away, unwilling to hear his words. Noah's wife stands on his left, whispering words into his ear. In front of Noah and the table, his three sons are busy with their preparations for the sacrifice they are to make in praise of God. They grapple with the animals to be slaughtered, one sitting astride a ram, or carry wood. The scene is tumultuous and the two women, seemingly mid-argument, infuse the painting with a dangerous and sinister quality.

THE FLOOD (1508–12)

Celimage.sa/Lessing Archive

Believed to have been the first narrative panel that Michelangelo painted, *The Flood* offers a wealth of images crowded together. It is the smallest of the nine panels and when viewed from the floor of the chapel it is difficult to make out the finer points of the piece. It is thought that he changed the scale after seeing *The Flood* from the ground, as all the subsequent panels have larger and fewer figures.

Given the similarities in their subject matter, *The Flood* bears a great resemblance to the later fresco, *The Last Judgment*, with its mass of troubled bodies. In the foreground of the picture, a woman lies despondent on the hillside. Behind her a long line of people, some bearing children, women or belongings, struggle up the hill, in an attempt to gain sanctuary from the rising water. One figure clings frantically to a tree, bent almost double in the wind. To the right, a man carries the lifeless body of another toward a tent full of huddled people, who reach out their arms to help him. This compassionate portrayal dissolves in the background, where figures can be seen beating one another on the boat, and again on the ark.

THE DRUNKENNESS OF NOAH (1508–12)

Celimage.sa / Lessing Archive

In terms of the overall theme of the ceiling, this panel is the final chapter of the story. Having depicted the glorious creations of God, the subsequent Fall of Man, and finally the Flood God sent to wipe out mankind in order to begin again with his chosen few, Michelangelo chose to conclude with the tale of *The Drunkenness of Noah.*

The naked figure of an old and pathetic Noah, unwittingly drunk from the vines that he has grown, lies in the foreground. To emphasize Noah's pitiful state, a figure is shown hard at work in a field. The young nudes standing to the right of Noah are his sons, Shem, Japheth, and Ham. Two of his sons avert their eyes so they do not see the shame represented by his nudity. Regardless of this fact, Michelangelo portrays all the men nude.

This story is integral to the ceiling's theme: it is linked with the mocking of Christ (Ham mocks Noah and is later cursed by his father) and it is the tale that, by showing the reversion to sin, foretells the coming of Christ.

IGNUDI BETWEEN THE DRUNKENNESS OF NOAH AND THE FLOOD (1508–12)

Celimage.sa/Scala Archives

Among the many nude figures that can be seen within and upon the painted architectural frame of the fresco, there are 20 *Ignudi*, placed in pairs on either side of the small narrative panels. They share delicate, almost feminine facial features and active figures. Their symbolism, or whether they actually have any, has been greatly debated and many theories for their inclusion in the ceiling have been expressed. Some believe that the *Ignudi* represent the ideal of man; others argue that they represent ancient pagan societies.

The first two sets of *Ignudi* to be painted surround *The Drunkenness of Noah*. For these first two pairs, Michelangelo used a cartoon for one of the *Ignudi* and then reversed it for the *Ignudo* placed opposite, so that they acted as mirrors to each other; the only difference between the paired *Ignudi* was to be in tone and minor details. This technique was quickly abandoned, however. It was initially devised in order that Michelangelo could pass on work to assistants, but he soon became dissatisfied with their work and dismissed them, continuing to work alone. The subsequent *Ignudi* were individually drawn.

IGNUDO BETWEEN THE DRUNKENNESS OF NOAH AND THE FLOOD (1508–12)

Celimage.sa/Scala Archives

This *Ignudo* shares many similarities with the *Libyan Sibyl* (1508–12) on page 121; like her he twists in his seat with his legs bent to one side, holding the pedestal with his free arm as he half turns to reveal his back. As with the *Libyan Sybil*, Michelangelo has positioned the *Ignudo* in such a way that the muscles in his back and arms are naturally taut and sharply defined. His skin tone is dark, almost bronze, in contrast to the golden paleness of the sibyl, which is enhanced by the burnt-orange glow of her dress. Both figures display the same facial features, indicating that they were based upon the same model.

Michelangelo had been working on sculptures for the *Tomb of Pope Julius II* (1505–45) at the time that the pope requested him to take on the immense task of painting the ceiling, and the *Ignudi* clearly demonstrate his sculptor's eye for position and form. The position of this *Ignudo* suggests he is straining to keep hold of the medallion that hangs between him and his partner; however, his relaxed, almost despondent expression negates this idea.

IGNUDO NEAR THE SACRIFICE OF NOAH

Celimage.sa/Scala Archives

Moving along the ceiling from *The Drunkenness of Noah* through to *The Separation of Light from Darkness*, the *Ignudi* take on various extreme postures, becoming increasingly animated. This *Ignudo*, with his arm thrown across his face, seems to be trying to hide his eyes from the sight of the events taking place in the panel above him. He is precariously placed on the edge of his pedestal and his torso leans forward and to the right, as if he is trying to escape. The panel is *The Sacrifice of Noah*, and Noah's son is seen holding a bundle of wood.

The placement of the *Ignudi* beneath the four corners of the panels, and their frontal positioning, draws the viewer's eye into the narrative panel. The expressions of fear or agitation that some of the *Ignudi* have adds to this, causing the viewer to wonder what it is they are pulling away from.

Once again, this *Ignudo* recalls Michelangelo's love of contorted sculptural poses, as shown in the *Dying Slave* (1513–16), one of the sculptures he worked on for the *Tomb of Pope Julius II* (1505–43), before and after the Sistine Chapel.

IGNUDO BY THE DRUNKENNESS OF NOAH (1508–12)

Celimage.sa / Scala Archives

Sitting in a relaxed pose, the *Ignudo* leans back against the pilaster, one hand languidly holding on to the material that contains his medallion. The other Ignudi that surround *The Drunkenness of Noah* also share an air of despondency, with sad, downcast eyes, as if reflecting upon the event of mankind's return to sin that is depicted within the panel. The medallion, showing a scene from ancient Biblical history, has a piece missing and a crack that also runs through the *Ignudo*. The other *Ignudo* in this panel is missing; only his head and the calves remain following an explosion at the nearby Castel Sant'Angelo in 1797, which damaged the top left corner of *The Flood*.

This was not the first time *The Flood* had been damaged. Shortly after completing the panel Michelangelo was dismayed to find a fine mold growing from the plaster. He quoted the mold as evidence to the Pope that he knew too little of the techniques of fresco painting to complete the ceiling successfully. This attempt to get himself removed from the project was ignored: his mistake at leaving the plaster too damp was pointed out to him and he was commanded to continue in his work.

IGNUDO BY THE LIBYAN SIBYL (1508–12)

Celimage.sa/Scala Archives

As well as serving to draw the viewer's eye into the panel, the *Ignudi* perform another important and practical purpose within the ceiling in camouflaging the increase in scale that occurs from the central narrative panels to the statuesque proportions of the prophets and sibyls. By placing these intermediary *Ignudi* between the prophets or sibyls and the narrative panels, Michelangelo has cleverly focused the viewer's attention away from the discontinuity in perspective that developed within the ceiling and onto the graceful figures of the *Ignudi*.

This *Ignudo* sits beneath the panel of *The Separation of Light from Darkness*, but he faces away from the events of the panel to look over his shoulder. His eyes are focused downward, nearly closed, onto the heads of the viewer beneath.

The rounded form and the feminine face of the *Ignudo* is reminiscent of the *Delphic Sibyl*, indeed it could almost be the mirror reflection of the sibyl's pose. It is possible that Michelangelo based this *Ignudo* on the same cartoon that he used for the *Delphic Sibyl*, merely reversing their position and decreasing the scale.

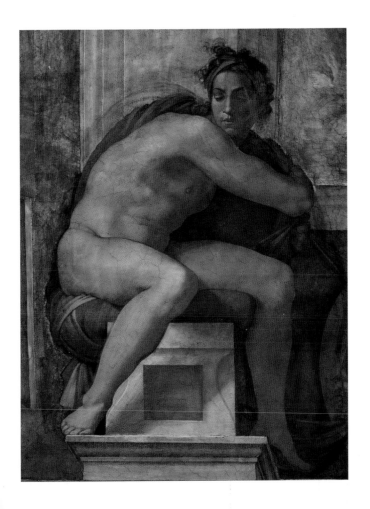

THE ANCESTORS OF CHRIST (VAULTED PANEL SHOWING THE FAMILY OF KING JOSIAH)(1508–12)

Celimage.sa/Scala Archives

Around the edge of the ceiling, where the vault meets the walls, spandrels are formed over the lunettes that rise above the windows. There are 12 spandrels; the four corner ones are double the size of the side ones and are used to illustrate stories in the same way as the central narrative panels. The side spandrels and the lunettes beneath them are filled with portraits of the ancestors of Christ. The idea of showing the genealogy of Christ links the spandrels to the running theme within the narrative panels—from the Genesis through to Noah's drunkenness—of events in the history of Man that anticipate the coming of Christ.

Although the figurative composition used here is the same as in the *Doni Tondo (The Holy Family)* (1514), Michelangelo's treatment differs greatly. The compact and united position of the trio in the tondo, portraying the love and closeness of the family, is missing. Instead we see the three from a side view, slumped and disconnected from each other, appearing desolate and depressed. All the ancestors of Christ appear dejected and despondent, their attitude in sharp contrast to the glory and hope that Christ will bring.

ANCESTOR OF CHRIST (1508–12)

Celimage.sa / Scala Archives

The arched windows of the chapel are on the upper tier of the building. A semicircular space, or lunette, is formed between each window arch and the top of the vaulted ceiling. The top of these lunettes forms the bottom of the spandrels (the top of one spandrel can be seen in the left corner of the detail), so it was fitting that the lunettes should share the same theme as the spandrels, which was the Ancestors of Christ.

The lunette ancestors share the same despondent, hopeless attitude that the spandrel ancestors portray; suggested mostly by their apathetic postures. In the lunettes, most of the ancestors of Christ appear alone, as opposed to the family groupings of the spandrels.

This old man seems both frail and weary. He has heavily rounded shoulders with a hunched back and leans on the stone with a hand and foot placed to steady himself. He is holding a staff, which suggests that he is a shepherd; a wind blows his beard out in front of him, giving an impression of harsh weather. The man rests one foot against the decorative plaster that surmounts the window in a gesture that continues the architectural conceit of the illusionary setting in the ceiling.

ESTHER AND HAMAN (1508–12)

Celimage.sa / Scala Archives

One of four corner spandrels, *Esther and Haman* tells the story of Esther, the wife of a Persian king who denied her Jewish heritage until Haman, the king's minister, planned to slaughter all Jews. Esther appealed to her king on behalf of the Jews and Haman was subsequently hanged. The tale of Esther augurs Mary's pleading for mankind on Judgment Day, connecting this panel with the later fresco *The Last Judgment* (1536–41) positioned on the right.

Esther and Haman is another continual narrative: to the left of the scene Esther denounces Haman, to the right the king lies awake in bed. Next Haman is seen greeting Mordecai, whom he plots to have hanged. Finally, the central, dominant image of the piece is of the contorted figure of Haman being crucified.

Michelangelo has painted the figure of Haman as if he were running; the cross he is on is twisted so that his limbs are flung out and in front of his body rather than in the more usual side position, shown in *The Crucifixion of Christ* (*c.* 1541) on page 225. The suggestion of movement in the trapped body is symbolic of Haman's desperate struggle to free himself.

JUDITH CARRYING THE HEAD OF HOLOFERNES (1508–12)

Celimage.sa/Scala Archives

At the corners of the ceiling are four spandrels which Michelangelo used to illustrate stories of the saviors of the Jews. In the two spandrels over the lay entrance of the chapel, near the final narrative panel *The Drunkenness of Noah*, Michelangelo painted two stories of the weak overcoming their rivals: *Judith and Holofernes* and *David and Goliath*.

This scene shows Judith making her escape after killing Holofernes, the leader of the attacking forces of the Assyrians, who were holding the Israelites under siege. In the center of the painting two women leave a bedchamber in which the body of a naked man lies, with his knees bent and torso stretching away from the viewer so that his neck cannot be seen. Judith looks at Holofernes' body as she lifts a sheet to cover the head that her maid carries in a tray.

The scene within the spandrel, and in *David and Goliath* opposite it, is relatively simple in form by comparison with the other two spandrels at the opposite end of the ceiling, such as *Esther and Haman*.

THE PERSIAN SIBYL (1508–12)

Celimage.sa / Lessing Archive

Appearing at opposite sides of each of the five smaller narrative panels are the massive figures of the prophets and the sibyls. There are five sibyls and seven prophets overall, with two prophets at either end of the ceiling and the rest alternating with the sibyls. The sibyls sit on the opposite side of a panel to a prophet; the old *Persian Sibyl* sits opposite the young *Prophet Daniel*.

The sibyls were female prophets from ancient times, so their appearance here could seem at odds with the Christian theme of the ceiling. They were included because they foretold the coming of Christ and so are symbolic links between the ancient pagan civilizations and the Christian world. The inclusion of the sibyls also represented the non-Jewish tradition of oracles, ensuring that the ceiling was not dominated by Jewish symbols and stories such as the prophets.

The Persian sibyl is credited with the prophecy of the Virgin Mary conquering the Beast of the Apocalypse. Very little of her face can be seen as she turns away to study her predictions in the book she holds.

THE CUMAEAN SIBYL (1508–12)
Celimage.sa/Lessing Archive

The *Cumaean Sibyl* illustrates a failing of Michelangelo's that many critics have highlighted: although he was a master of the male nude, his skill at handling the female form was not parallel to this. In *The Creation of Eve* the figure of Eve seems bulky, servile and somewhat misshapen compared with the grace, poise and dignity of Adam in the preceding panel.

The *Cumaean Sibyl* shares this awkward portrayal; she has the heavily, muscular body of a man, with a head too small for her massive body. Her breasts, seen through the sheerness of her clothes, do not seem realistic for such a masculine frame. This inability of the artist to portray the female form may be attributed to his lack of knowledge of women: at the time it was hard to recruit female models for fear of their being regarded as prostitutes, so he used male models only. In addition, it is likely that he was homosexual; Michelangelo once opined in a poem that the grace of the male body was superior to that of the female. Despite the flaws, the *Cumaean Sibyl* is still an impressive figure as she leans over her book of prophecies, her face frowning with apprehension at what she foresees.

THE ERITHRAEAN SIBYL (1508–12)

Celimage.sa / Lessing Archive

The *Erithraean Sibyl*, placed beneath the narrative panel of *The Sacrifice of Noah*, reiterates the fact that she was Noah's daughter-in-law; it was she who foresaw the coming of Judgment Day. As well as symbolizing the link between the ancient Classical and Christian worlds, the sibyls also function as representatives of the ancient civilizations from which they came: Erithraea represents Ionia, Delphica Greece, Persica the Persian Empire, Cumaea Rome and Libya the continent of Africa.

Erithraea sits with her legs crossed and her face toward that of the neighboring prophet, Ezekiel. With one muscular arm, she reaches forward to turn the pages of her book, whilst the other is relaxed by her side. This posture leaves the upper half of her body in an open, frontal position in contrast with the twisted, closed lower half of her body.

Above her book are two genii, one hidden in shadow. These genii appear in pairs next to all of the prophets and sibyls. Their significance is believed to be related to the neo-platonic philosophy that every person is born with two such spirits that reflect the dual nature of their spiritual and material sides. The genii blow upon the flames of a torch to enable the sibyl to read her book.

THE DELPHIC SIBYL (1508–12)

Celimage.sa/Lessing Archive

The Delphic sibyl foretold the coming of a great prophet who would be born to a virgin who knew nothing of the corruption of man. A wind is blowing over the prophetess; her hair trails out behind her and her cloak billows out round her shoulders. The hair of her two genii that stand behind her, mimicking her actions, also seems ruffled by this wind. This sense of the blowing wind together with the sibyl's wide-eyed and fearful expression, with her mouth ajar as she looks out past the viewer to see the future that approaches, gives the Delphic Sibyl a grave air of import.

Like the *Cumaean Sibyl*, the *Delphic Sibyl* is placed in a frontal position, while the other sibyls are all seen in varying degrees of a twisted, half-turned position. The *Delphic Sibyl* is a far more confident rendering of the female form: she has delicate, feminine features and a well-proportioned body.

Michelangelo used startling colors in the robes of the *Delphic Sibyl*, creating a vivid contrast of burnt orange and lime green.

THE LIBYAN SIBYL (1508–12)

Celimage.sa/Lessing Archive

The *Libyan Sibyl* is placed beneath the panel of *The Separation of Light from Darkness* and opposite the morose figure of the prophet Jeremiah. In Classical mythology Libya was the daughter of Zeus and Lamia, the prophetess who foretold the "coming of the day when that which is hidden shall be revealed."

The *Libyan Sibyl* sits in a very complicated pose with her feet showing under her dress, perching forward with her weight on her toes as she twists her body to lean backward to lift up the huge book from behind her. Michelangelo has used foreshortening techniques in the sibyl's arms to create the impression that they move farther away from us as she reaches ahead of her. The genius to her left mirrors her position with his turned head and twisted shoulder—a reminder to us that he is one part of a dual reflection of the sibyl's nature.

The features of the sibyl are similar to those in the *Ideal Head* (*c.* 1533) on page 192, completed almost 20 years later. In addition to sharing the same features, the two have a similar posture; looking over one shoulder with downcast eyes.

THE PROPHET ZACHARIAH

Celimage.sa / Scala Archives

The prophets appear in the Old Testament. They are the inspired men of Israel, through whom the Holy Spirit tells of the coming of Christ and of the Christian era. Of the seven prophets that appear in the Sistine Chapel, four are major prophets and three are minor. *Zachariah* is one of the three minor prophets and is positioned at the end over the lay entrance to the chapel; at the altar end is the prophet *Jonah*. Zachariah had eight apocalyptical visions, one of which was of four chariots colored red, black, white, and piebald, that represented the four winds carrying God's judgment to the four corners of the earth. Zachariah also predicted the coming of the Messiah and the crucifixion.

Gold paint has been used on the decorations adorning the pilasters on either side of the prophets. Originally it was planned that there would be much more gilding within the ceiling fresco, but Michelangelo stopped painting following an argument with Pope Julius II. Julius wanted Michelangelo to carry out further gilding, saying that the fresco would look "poor" without it. Michelangelo replied that "those who are painted there were poor men," and so the gilding was left as it now stands.

THE PROPHET EZEKIEL (1508–12)

Celimage.sa / Scala Archives

Of all the prophets and sibyls, it is *Ezekiel* that is charged with the most energy and movement. A wind is apparent in the painting that blows the prophet's hair and robes, adding to his animated appearance. Clutching his scroll of prophecies in one hand, he twists in his seat, turning his head to one side as his massive body leans forward. One hand is held open in a gesture of questioning as he gazes with a severe intensity to his right. *Ezekiel* appears beneath the panel *The Creation of Eve*, opposite the *Cumaean Sibyl*, but he faces toward the *Erithraean Sibyl*. While the Erithraean sibyl foresaw the Judgment Day, in a vision Ezekiel saw the skeletal dead rising to assume flesh and clothing, which was interpreted as the resurrection of the dead on Judgment Day. Michelangelo later illustrated this vision in his *Last Judgment* fresco.

With his wild, gray beard and dominating presence, Ezekiel bears much resemblance to the figure of God as Michelangelo portrayed him in his narrative panels. The intense frown here is especially reminiscent of God's fierce expression in the panel *The Creation of the Planets, the Sun, and the Moon.*

THE PROPHET JOEL

Celimage.sa / Lessing Archive

Joel is one of the 12 minor prophets. His predictions included the arrival of Judgment Day and a plague of locusts devouring the earth, blotting out the sun, moon, and the stars. Michelangelo portrayed Joel as an old man: his face is lined, his expression serious and attentive as he reads from the scroll that he holds. The genius behind him on the left is mimicking his pose and also reading from the scroll with a solemn face. The other genius carries a book of prophecies while he points to the distance, his mouth open as if he himself is uttering a prophecy. The two nearest caryatids on the pilasters also turn to read the scroll that Joel carries.

Joel appears beneath the panel of *The Drunkenness of Noah* as well as opposite the *Delphic Sibyl*, and so was one of the first prophets to be painted. The increase in scale that Michelangelo employed in the later panels of the ceiling can also be seen in the prophets and sibyls. Joel sits in a simple, relaxed pose, easily fitting within the confines of his setting, whilst the later prophet Jeremiah leans forward out of his throne.

THE PROPHET JEREMIAH (1508–12)

Celimage.sa / Lessing Archive

Jeremiah appears under the panel of *The Separation of Light from Darkness* and opposite the *Libyan Sibyl*. One of the four major prophets, Jeremiah wrote the "Lamentations" and is often referred to as the "dismal" prophet, being renowned for his despondent manner. Jeremiah repeatedly complained to the various kings of Israel, threatening them with disaster and pestilence if they were to go against the praise of one God alone. He was also known for his repeated diatribes against evil. To reflect his supposed character of gloom, Michelangelo gave Jeremiah a suitably despondent pose. He sits forward in his throne, leaning his head on his right hand, which is covering his mouth. This gesture was used again by Michelangelo in his sculpture *Lorenzo de' Medici* (1520–34) on page 167. As here, the pensive gesture was used to give the impression that Lorenzo was in deep thought.

Unusually, Jeremiah's genii are clothed women, differing from the cherubic genii that appear behind most of the prophets and sibyls. One genius has the same depressed stance as the prophet, while the other looks to the distance, symbolic of his prophetic nature.

THE PROPHET ISAIAH (1508–12)

Celimage.sa / Scala Archives

Isaiah is a major prophet and has an Old Testament book that bears his name. His prophecies refer to the coming of Christ, the inauguration of the Messianic age and the Virgin Birth. Through his prophecies Isaiah gave the assurance of universal peace.

It has been suggested that besides their prophecies, the seven prophets are also illustrations of the Seven Gifts of the Holy Spirit. Isaiah described these as Wisdom, Understanding, Counsel, Fortitude, Knowledge, Compassion, and Fear of God. The various expressions and poses of the seven prophets can indeed be seen to reflect these attributes. Isaiah turns to listen to the genius that whispers in his ear, suggesting that he is considering the genius's counsel or advice. The mighty figure of Ezekiel is easily interpreted as Fortitude, while Zachariah's studious pose evokes Wisdom. A fearful Jonah looks up toward the figure of God creating light from darkness, illustrating the Fear of God. The gloomy prophet Jeremiah, with his air of despair, can be seen as representative of Compassion or Pity, leaving the figures of Daniel and Joel to portray Knowledge and Understanding respectively.

THE PROPHET DANIEL (1508–12)

Celimage.sa/Scala Archives

Daniel is one of the four major prophets, along with Ezekiel, Isaiah and Jeremiah, and here represents Justice, one of the four cardinal virtues. During his lifetime, Daniel's prophetic gifts brought him much success and honor at the courts of kings. One of his most famous prophecies came from the interpretation of the writing that mysteriously appeared upon the walls during a feast at Belshazzar's court, the prediction of Belshazzar's death and the subsequent division of his kingdom. This incident has passed into everyday use with the saying "seen the writing on the wall."

Of all the prophets in the fresco, *Daniel* has been given the most youthful appearance and his pose and expression, like that of Ezekiel, suggests energy and movement. He leans forward from his throne, and the curve of the ceiling means that he appears to be looking down onto the chapel floor. He writes with one hand while holding his book of prophecies in the other. Placed between Daniel's legs is his genius, who bears the weight of the large book upon his head and shoulders. His other genius hides in shadow behind him, barely seen.

THE ANCESTORS OF CHRIST (DETAIL SHOWING DAVID AND GOLIATH) (1508–12)

Celimage.sa/Lessing Archive

Between each prophet and sibyl are the spandrels that Michelangelo filled with his illustrations of the Ancestors of Christ. Above each spandrel, leaning against the steeply sloping sides, are two figures. The symbolism of these figures is unclear. They are painted in deep golden or bronze colors and display a variety of complicated, dramatic poses. Most of the figures seem to be imprisoned within their niches, straining against the walls with their bodies. The niches in which they sit are shadowy and their features are difficult to see. It has been suggested that these dark, foreboding figures are intended to be representative of pre-Christian societies.

With their contorted positions and cramped attitudes these figures could also be reflective of the artist's working conditions in the Sistine Chapel. The ceiling fresco took over four years to complete, during which time Michelangelo spent many of his days in convoluted contortions upon the scaffolding. He made a joke of the physical trials that he had endured in a poem to a friend:

> *"My beard turns up to heaven; my nape falls in,*
> *Fixed on my spine: my breast-bone visibly*
> *Grows like a harp: a rich embroidery*
> *Bedews my face from brush-drops thick and thin."*

THE RISEN CHRIST (1519–20)

Celimage.sa/Scala Archives

The Risen Christ was commissioned in 1514 by three of Michelangelo's patrons. The sculpture is also known as *Christ of the Minerva* because it is located in the Santa Maria sopra Minerva church, in Rome. Upon nearly completing the piece, Michelangelo realized the marble was flawed by veins of black, so the piece had to be started again from scratch.

In 1921, the artist sent *The Risen Christ* to his assistant Pietro Urbano in Rome to install in the church and make some finishing touches. He damaged the toes, fingers, hair, and face of the sculpture; in a letter to Michelangelo, Urbano's touch was likened to that of a baker rather than a sculptor. Consequently, Michelangelo gave the statue to the sculptor Federigo Frizzi to complete. Deeply dissatisfied with the results, he offered to carve another *Risen Christ*, but the patrons refused, saying they were satisfied with the sculpture.

The figure of Christ here resembles the warrior-like figure of Christ in *The Last Judgment* (1536–41) and has been criticized for being too much like a heroic fighter and too little like the gentle son of God.

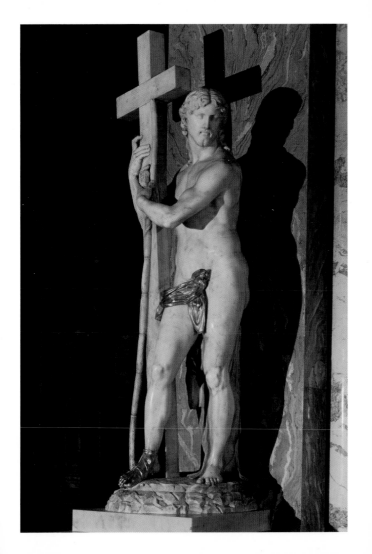

TOMB OF POPE JULIUS II (1505–45)

Celimage.sa/Scala Archives

St Julius II, known as the Warrior Pope after his campaigns to reclaim lost papal states and fiefdoms, was a great patron of the arts. Julius wanted a suitably grand design to commemorate his tomb and so he called Michelangelo to Rome in March 1505 to discuss possible designs. From the beginning, the relationship between Michelangelo and Julius was a tempestuous one, peppered by many arguments between two equally volatile and determined men. A deep-rooted respect for each other eventually grew between the two men and this survived in Michelangelo long after the death of Julius II.

The tomb project proved to be a millstone about Michelangelo's neck. He had hoped that it would be a grand and astonishing masterpiece, a magnificent reminder—not just of a great and powerful pope but also of his own genius. Michelangelo was never to be allowed to dedicate himself to the tomb; he was repeatedly taken off the project to work on others. The first such occasion was by Julius' own insistence that he should work on the Sistine Chapel, temporarily abandoning the tomb. The later uprisings in Florence also contributed to Michelangelo's inability to fulfil the contract.

DESIGN FOR THE TOMB OF POPE JULIUS II (1505–45)

Celimage.sa/Scala Archives

The original design for the tomb of Julius was for a free-standing block about 50 ft high, with three stories containing niches that were to house more than 40 statues. There was to be an internal room for the remains of the pope. The top storey was to have gigantic statues, twice life-size, of figures such as *Moses* (1513–16).

Condivi, one of Michelangelo's biographers, called the project "the tragedy of the tomb" and Michelangelo himself felt that he wasted his youth over it, intermittently spending 40 years on the project. Following the pope's death in 1513, the contract for the tomb was taken up by his family and there were allegations that Michelangelo had cheated Julius out of a substantial amount of money. This upset Michelangelo deeply, particularly as the fate of the tomb had largely been taken out of his hands; often one of his patrons would wrangle with another over which project he was to take on next.

After several revisions, arguments, and court cases, the tomb was completed with only three statues by Michelangelo: *Moses, Rachel,* and *Leah*, the last two produced between 1542 and 1559.

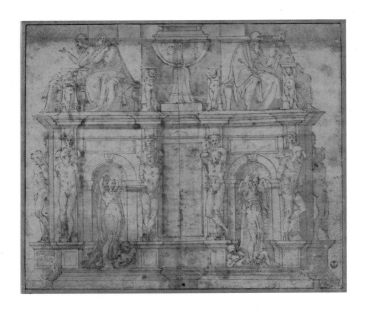

MOSES (DETAIL FROM THE TOMB OF POPE JULIUS II) (1513–16)

Celimage.sa/Lessing Archive

Easily the most impressive piece on the tomb of Pope Julius II is the majestic *Moses*. Reminiscent of *The Prophet Ezekiel* (1508–12) with his fierce expression and gigantic proportions, *Moses* stands out against the other more diminutive and tame statues on the tomb. Completed between 1513 and 1516, this huge statue is more than twice life-size. In the earlier designs for the tomb, Moses was initially intended to take a place on the second tier of what was to be a three-tier, 50-ft structure among five other statues of the same size. This intention explains the incongruous size and the fierce expression of *Moses*: he was meant to be seen at a distance, from below, which would have made these factors less apparent.

Moses was the greatest figure of the Old Testament, deliverer of the Children of Israel out of Egypt to the Promised Land. Under his right arm he holds the tablets of law given to him by God. On his head are two horns; this convention dates from medieval times as a result of a mistranslation of Hebrew text. He should have rays of light emanating from his head.

RACHEL AND LEAH (DETAIL FROM THE TOMB OF POPE JULIUS II) (1542–55)

Celimage.sa/Scala Archives

In the Old Testament, Rachel was the younger and more attractive daughter of Laban. Jacob loved her and worked for seven years under Laban in order to marry her. He was deceived into marrying her sister, Leah, and served Laban for a further seven years before being finally allowed to marry Rachel, only to find that she was barren. After persuading Jacob to sleep with both Leah and her servant Bilhah, Rachel prayed to God, who heard her pleas and "opened her womb." She died in childbirth.

Aside from the Biblical description of this story, Michelangelo derived much from the interpretation that Dante Alighieri (1265–1321) gave the two sisters in *Purgatorio*; that of Active and Contemplative life. To illustrate the idea of contemplation, Michelangelo shows a serene Rachel gazing up toward heaven with her hands clasped in prayer. He also used the notion of Active life in his sculpture of *Giuliano de' Medici*. With *Leah*, the Active element is portrayed by the mirror she holds, symbolizing the sentiment with which we must contemplate our actions. While *Giuliano de' Medici* embodies the idea of the Active life through his expression and posture, Leah's posture seems more to embody the Contemplative life, as she is slightly slumped and seems deep in thought.

DYING SLAVE (1513–16)

Celimage.sa/Lessing Archive

The *Dying Slave* was one of twelve sculptures of slaves that Michelangelo originally intended to be housed in the *Tomb of Pope Julius II*. This statue, together with the *Rebellious Slave* (1513–16), are the only two that appear near completion; both sculptures are now in the Louvre in Paris.

The *Slaves*, in much the same way as the *Ignudi* in the Sistine Chapel, were designed to be decorative figures along the base of the tomb as it was originally designed. They were to be placed against columns and pilasters or on the corners of the tomb, but after many revisions and rescalings, the figures were found to be too big for their planned niches. The figures of *Rachel* and *Leah* (1542–55) were carved and the rest, such as the *Young Slave* (1520–30), were abandoned in what may be their incomplete state, although many critics believe that Michelangelo intended them to be left freely carved.

The sculpture of the *Dying Slave* has a sensual, erotic quality. Michelangelo has created the semblance of a reclining figure in a vertical position. The left arm is held above the tilted head and the other arm lies limply upon the breast—the figure appears to be in a dreamlike state rather than actually dying.

REBELLIOUS SLAVE
(1513–16)

Celimage.sa / Scala Archives

Pope Julius II summoned Michelangelo to Rome to commission him to design his tomb. What should have been the most prestigious commission of his career, a freestanding tomb with some 40 figures, to be located in St Peter's, became the "tragedy of the tomb." Julius died in 1513, the contract was redrawn several times over the following years with ever-diminishing funding, other demands were made on Michelangelo by successive popes, and the project was finally cobbled together in 1545, a shadow of its original conception, with much help from assistants, in S. Pietro in Vincoli (Julius's titular church). The tomb is now principally famous for the colossal figure of Moses (c. 1515), one of Michelangelo's greatest sculptures.

Two slave figures, *Dying Slave* and *Rebellious Slave* (c.1513), intended for the tomb, are now in the Louvre, in Paris. These unfinished slaves reveal Michelangelo's sculptural process, in which the figure would be outlined on the front of the marble block and then worked steadily inward from one side of the block. Those parts that projected farthest were brought to a fairly finished state, with those parts farther back remaining rough-hewn. In this way the figures of the slaves appear to be struggling to be free.

Rebellious Slave, originally intended for the tomb of Pope Julius II, is an evocative and poignant testimony to the sculptor's ability to convey emotion through the medium of stone.

AWAKENING SLAVE (1520–30)

Celimage.sa/Scala Archives

In their various stages of completion, the slave sculptures are perfect examples of Michelangelo's techniques in sculpture, as is the *Taddei Tondo* (*c.* 1504). Several of this series are now in the Galleria dell' Accademia in Florence, where they are keenly studied by students. The *Awakening Slave* is barely formed: only his heavy torso and one giant leg have been worked on to any extent, and the rest of the figure appears to have sunk within the marble. Michelangelo described the process of sculpture as releasing a form that was trapped within the block of marble; when viewing the *Awakening Slave* this observation seems especially apt.

He would first make a wax lifesize model of his sculpture, then draw an outline of this onto the marble in charcoal. He chiseled from the front of the marble block, then chipped from all sides. For the carving of the *Slaves*, it is recorded that the wax model was sunk horizontally in a bath of water so that just the highest parts of it would emerge. He would then decrease the water level little by little so that he could see more and more of the figure appearing, as if it were the *Slave* freed from the marble block.

BEARDED SLAVE (1520–30)

Celimage.sa / Scala Archives

Another of the Accademia *Slaves*, the *Bearded Slave* has been given a similar pose to that of the *Dying Slave* (1513–16), but expresses a potently different quality. This sculpture has been left in a much lesser state of completion; the hands are still sunk into the marble, giving him the appearance of struggling, not against his bonds, but against the marble itself. He is thick-set and muscular compared with the *Dying Slave*, who seems lithe by comparison. Because of his beard and furrowed brow, the *Bearded Slave* seems older than the others; his solidity of form adds to this illusion.

As well as an excellent opportunity for Michelangelo to show his advanced skill at handling the male nude, the *Slaves* were intended to symbolize the Arts. As Pope Julius II had been a strong patron of the arts during his lifetime, the sculptures were created to represent the idea that the Arts had become enslaved by the death of such a vital patron. Above the *Slaves*, on the top tier of the original design for the tomb, were to have been the figures of Heaven and Earth; the latter mourning the passing of Julius and the former rejoicing in his arrival in eternity.

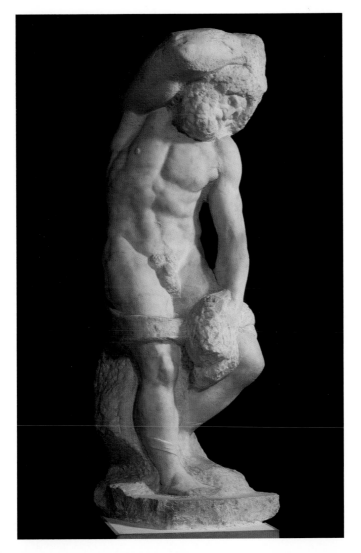

YOUNG SLAVE (1520–30)

Celimage.sa / Scala Archives

Like the *Dying Slave* (1513–16), the *Young Slave* seems to be slumbering. His head is hidden in the crook of his arm, with his hand loosely clenched, appearing to be softly described within the rough marble. Michelangelo's method of working from the front of the block of marble first is demonstrated here by the protrusion of the *Young Slave's* bent leg. The angle of the leg means that the calf is behind the knee, and therefore still within the block of marble, waiting for Michelangelo's chisel to bring it into being.

By the positioning of his raised arm, the *Young Slave* appears to be struggling, as if held behind his back by unseen forces. His torso twists with the movement of his arm so that it is slightly off-center.

Although the *Slaves* share the similarly contorted poses of the *Ignudi* (1508–12), this particular statue lacks the elegance of the latter; the limbs of the figure are thick and heavy. Whether this is to do with the incomplete state of the figure or with Michelangelo's attempt to represent a slave trapped in marble is a question for endless debate.

VICTORY (1519–30)

Celimage.sa / Scala Archives

The *Victory* statue may have been intended as another *Slave* for the *Tomb of Julius II* (1505–45), but was carved later than the others, after another revision of the contract for the tomb with Pope Leo X. *Victory* is one Michelangelo's most influential sculptures; the spiral form and the unnatural, self-conscious pose were much simulated among the Mannerist artists that he helped to inspire.

The sculpture has a triangular configuration like that of the *Doni Tondo (Holy Family)* (1504). The spiral movement can be seen starting with the defeated, crouched figure, rising through the knee of the victor and carrying on through his twisted torso to his turned head. This mimics the form and movement of a serpent and gained the name *figura serpentinata*.

A spiraling form in sculpture encourages the creation of a free-standing piece that can be viewed from every angle. However, with *Victory*, this was not to be the case. It was planned to stand against the tomb of Julius II. Michelangelo may have intended his sculpture to be viewed from the front only, but now it can be viewed freely all round and stands up well to that scrutiny.

HEAD (DETAIL FROM VICTORY) (1519–1530)

Celimage.sa / Scala Archives

As with much of Michelangelo's work, many opinions have been offered as to the meaning behind the *Victory* statue. The victorious, but curiously mild-looking, youth has been put forward as the soul who has conquered the old man, thus representing mortality. Other opinions suggest that the old man is Michelangelo himself and that the young man symbolizes the suffocating demands of his patrons. The head of the old man does indeed bear some resemblance to the Michelangelo we see in portraits and he did suffer endless problems with demanding patrons changing their minds about his commissions or fighting among themselves and with him.

Another suggestion from critics is that the statue may symbolize youth conquering the progress of age. Michelangelo was approaching middle age when this piece was carved; the youth's arrogant and overly self-confident appearance, with his vacuous stare and conceited pose, have been used to back up this theory.

THREE VIRILE NUDES (DATE UNKNOWN)
Celimage.sa/Scala Archives

During the High Renaissance, the three outstanding artists were Leonardo da Vinci, Raphael (1483–1520), and, of course, Michelangelo. All three Italian artists worked within similar areas, shared the same patrons and, often, the same locations. In his *Study for the Doni Madonna* (1503), Michelangelo successfully recreated the manner and techniques of Leonardo da Vinci and this study is a reproduction of work by Raphael.

While Michelangelo worked on the Sistine Chapel ceiling, Raphael was painting frescoes for one of the papal rooms in the Vatican, the Stanza della Segnatura (1508). Michelangelo viewed Raphael as an enemy; he was the nephew of his professional rival, Bramante, and, with his sociable, extravagant lifestyle, was the antithesis of Michelangelo's meager, isolated life; during this period the latter claimed "I have no friends, nor do I want any."

After Michelangelo had completed the narrative panels in the Sistine Chapel, Bramante sought permission for his nephew Raphael to complete the work; a request that both distressed and angered Michelangelo. In a letter dated 1542, more than 20 years after the death of Raphael, Michelangelo claimed that all the arguments between himself and Julius II were caused by Bramante and Raphael, blaming them for his inability to complete the pope's tomb, and saying of Raphael "all he had of art he owed to me."

INTERIOR OF THE MEDICI CHAPEL (1519–34)

Celimage.sa/Scala Archives

In 1520, Michelangelo began work, at the request of Pope Leo X, on the interior of the New Sacristy of the San Lorenzo Chapel in Florence. San Lorenzo was the private chapel of the Medici family and the New Sacristy was built to house the bodies of four of the Medici clan, of which Leo X himself was a member. Michelangelo kept the design for the New Sacristy in line with Filippo Brunelleschi's (1377–1446) design of the Old Sacristy in the same church, built about 100 years earlier.

The chapel has eight doors, two on each wall, of which five are façades that were added to make the remarkable symmetry of the interior possible. Above each door is a niche created purely for decoration. The windows in the second storey of the chapel have been given heavy pediments and are narrower at the top than at the bottom; this gives them an increased perspective to make the walls appear higher than they are.

The pilasters, cornices and pediments are all a dark-gray *pietra serena*, a fine-grained sandstone, to accentuate the white marble of the walls. The contrast between the two is enhanced by the light that enters through the many windows of the three-tiered building.

STUDY FOR THE MEDICI CHAPEL (c. 1520)

Celimage.sa / Scala Archives

Work on the Medici Chapel, like the *Tomb of Julius II* (1505–45), was interrupted and redesigned several times; the Republican uprisings in Florence halted work, as did changes in popes. The Medicean Pope Leo X died in 1521, to be replaced by Pope Adrian VI who had no interest in the arts, but he was succeeded by another Medici, Giulio, who became Pope Clement VII, and work on the chapel was recommenced.

Michelangelo's plans developed and changed over the years. As originally designed, the chapel was to house the bodies of four of the Medicis: Michelangelo's first patron, Lorenzo the Magnificent, and his brother Giuliano, as well as Giuliano, Duke of Nemours, and Lorenzo, Duke of Urbino. The tombs of Lorenzo the Magnificent and his brother were never made and the chapel houses only the tombs of the two Medici dukes. The sketch shown is for a double tomb; it is possibly an early design for the one that now houses their remains.

With his plans for the Medici Chapel, Michelangelo was hoping to achieve his longstanding ambition of creating the perfect fusion of architecture, painting, and sculpture.

TOMB OF LORENZO DE' MEDICI (1520–34)

Celimage.sa/Scala Archives

In 1534, Michelangelo left Florence and returned to Rome, thereby abandoning any further work on the Medici Chapel. Some time after this, the unfinished statues were placed upon the sarcophagi of the two dukes. It is unclear what was intended to fill the niches on either side of Lorenzo of Urbino, although it is mentioned that for Giuliano of Nemours, the niches were to be filled with representations of Heaven and Earth. Earth was to mourn Giuliano's passing and Heaven rejoice in his arrival— an idea taken from the *Tomb of Pope Julius II* (1505–45).

One of the earlier designs for the tombs included the figures of river gods to be placed on both of the sarcophagi. These river gods were to represent the underworld and also important Italian rivers, such as the Arno. The statues on top of the sarcophagi, *Twilight* and *Dawn*, were to symbolize human mortality and the corporeal state, leaving the statue of the Duke to represent Heaven, or the afterworld to which he had now gone. This symbolic layering of sculptures is reminiscent of the original plans for the *Tomb of Pope Julius II*. The Medici tombs mix both pagan and Christian symbolism, elements of Classical architecture, and Michelangelo's own innovative touch.

MADONNA AND CHILD (1520–34)

Celimage.sa/Lessing Archive

The *Madonna and Child* statue sits opposite the altar in the Medici Chapel, flanked by statues of the Medici family's patron saints, *Cosmas* and *Damian*, which were not carved by Michelangelo. *Madonna and Child* is a larger work than the two saints beside it, and the figures of the two dukes, because it was originally designed to go on the double tomb of Lorenzo the Magnificent and his brother Giuliano. It was abandoned when Michelangelo returned to Rome, and the marks of his chisel are still clear.

The Madonna is seated with her left leg crossed over her right, leaning back on her right arm as if to counterbalance the weight of her struggling child. She shares the same resigned, despondent expression as the Madonna of the *Pietà* in St Peter's (1497–99). She stares sadly past her son toward the floor, almost appearing unaware of the child. The child turns in his mother's lap so that his face cannot be seen. This is a symbolic pose implying that Jesus hides his face so that he does not see the mortality that surrounds him in this funeral chapel.

GIULIANO DE' MEDICI (1520–34)

Celimage.sa/Scala Archives

Perched in an alcove above the figures of *Night* and *Day*, *Giuliano de' Medici* stares across to the *Madonna and Child* that sits opposite the altar. Michelangelo was criticised for not creating a more recognizable likeness; Giuliano is given curled hair and handsome features which have an idealized Classical origin. Of all the sculptures within the chapel, Giuliano is the only one that has been finished to such a high degree—his body armor was carved to the finest detail in every tassel and ribbon.

Giuliano has the same pose as *Moses* in the *Tomb of Pope Julius II* (1505–45), with his head turned to one side while his body faces forward, the limbs positioned to leave the body open. This alert position gives the statue the impression that he is poised for action and ready to move from his niche.

Giuliano, the Duke of Nemours, died in 1516. Along with Lorenzo, Duke of Urbino, he was the last direct ancestor of the patriarch Cosimo Medici, and so the connection to an illustrious past and years of patronage of the arts died with him.

NIGHT (1520–34)

Celimage.sa/Lessing Archive

The figure of *Night* sits on the sarcophagus of Giuliano de' Medici. She lies with her eyes closed, as if asleep, her head bowed, resting against her hand. She wears a crown decorated with a moon and stars. Crouched in the crook of her leg is an owl, a further allusion to the state of night. Nighttime and sleep have long been poetically linked to—and used as euphemisms for—death, so the sculpture of *Night* is particularly apt for a funeral chapel.

This figure, although graceful and exquisitely poised, again shows Michelangelo's misunderstanding of the female form through the unrealistic, misshapen breasts of the statue, which are too far apart. As with the *Cumaean Sibyl* (1508–12), the flaw in his depiction of the female form can be blamed on the fact that he did not use female models in his work and probably never slept with a woman.

In response to admiration of the statue, Michelangelo wrote the following poem:

> *"Dear to me is sleep, and better to be stone,*
> *So long as shame and sorrow is our portion.*
> *Not to see, not to feel is my great fortune;*
> *Hence, do not wake me; hush, leave me alone."*

DAY (1520–34)

Celimage.sa/Lessing Archive

The partner to the statue of the slumbering *Night* is the ponderous figure of *Day*. With his huge head raised to look over one muscular shoulder, *Day* echoes the impression of alertness that *Giuliano* above him gives. His posture is the opposite of his partner *Night*: where her legs are closed to the viewer and her chest is open, *Day's* legs are open and the chest is closed. These postures reflect the different attributes of the sculptures; in sleep we are exposed and vulnerable while awake we can control our vulnerabilities.

Day is sitting in a complicated, crossed, and twisted position; his left arm can be seen behind his back, the hand pointed toward the viewer. This huge figure seems impossibly balanced upon the sarcophagus, as if he is in danger of sliding off. As with all of the statues on top of the tombs, *Day's* feet hang precariously over the edge. The base of the statue remains rough and unfinished, in contrast to the smooth limbs and torso. A further more noticeable contrast lies in the unfinished head of the piece, only barely formed, seeming to suggest in stone the vagaries of light and the ambiguity of time, reminiscent of the face of the *Bearded Slave* (1520–30).

LORENZO OF URBINO (1520–34)

Celimage.sa / Scala Archives

Lorenzo of Urbino, like *Giuliano of Nemours*, sits in his niche with his gaze directed toward the *Madonna and Child* (1520–34). As Giuliano is alert and appearing ready to move toward the Madonna, Lorenzo's pose is somber and introverted. He has one hand to his mouth and his head is bowed, as if he is deep in thought as he gazes at the Madonna. The *Madonna and Child* was originally planned to adorn the tombs of Lorenzo the Magnificent, the grandfather of the two dukes, and his brother Giuliano, so the fact that they are both gazing in that direction may have as much to do with deference toward their ancestors as religious piety.

Michelangelo again used Classical idealized features on the statue, rather than attempting a likeness of the duke. The slightly larger figure of Lorenzo sits less easily than Giuliano within the confines of his niche; his posture means that he takes up more space. *Lorenzo of Urbino* also shares the Roman body armor of his counterpart. His helmet is positioned low on his head so that his eyes are almost lost within the shadows of the niche he occupies.

Dawn (1520–34)

Celimage.sa / Scala Archives

To reflect the representation of *Lorenzo of Urbino* as contemplative, Michelangelo placed the figures of *Dawn* and *Dusk* underneath the statue. The personification of these indeterminate, hazy times of day acts to symbolize the hesitant, inactive nature of Lorenzo as Contemplative life. To emphasize the aspects of *Dawn* and *Dusk*, the original lighting in the chapel was dimmed by the use of shaded windows on the side of Lorenzo's tomb. These shadings have since been removed so that light in the chapel is now consistent.

Dawn exudes a most sorrowful air. Seemingly full of woe, she also appears confused, as if she has just awoken and is bitterly disappointed to be in a conscious state again. The band round *Dawn's* chest and the veil on her head were both signs of mourning which, together with her expression of dismay, gives us the impression that she is in the throes of grief. Perhaps *Dawn* is grieving over the death of Lorenzo, whose sarcophagus she reclines upon, or maybe she grieves over the existence and inevitability of death itself. *Dawn* opens her eyes from her disturbed dreams to see the symbol of death, *Night*, as she lies asleep on the tomb opposite her.

DUSK (1520–34)

Celimage.sa / Scala Archives

Dusk, like the statue of *Day*, may be incomplete. The body has been highly finished and the smooth marble is polished, but his face is still pitted with the marks of Michelangelo's chisel. This lack of finish does nothing to detract from the magnificence of Michelangelo's creation.

Dusk lies with his legs stretched out in front of him and his arms relaxed down by his sides in an open posture, leaving his body softened and exposed. His partner *Dawn* shares this position and both figures act to contrast the contorted poses of *Night* and *Day* that appear opposite them. Both *Dawn* and *Dusk* seem even more precariously balanced upon the sarcophagus than the figures of *Night* and *Day* do, as their relaxed legs extend farther over the edge.

The age of *Dusk* reflects the time of day he represents, while the figure of *Dawn* is young. *Dusk's* head is bowed, *Dawn's* uplifted—alluding to the rising and setting of the sun. The four statues represent the inexorable passing of time and the inevitability of death.

LAURENTIAN LIBRARY, READING ROOM (C. 1524–34)

Celimage.sa / Scala Archives

The Medici family were not only great collectors of art, between them they had also compiled an extensive library of precious books and rare manuscripts. In 1519, the Medicean Pope Clement VII decided that a suitably grand library should be built to house this collection, which had been started by Cosimo de' Medici during the fifteenth century.

The design of the Laurentian Library above the refectory in the San Lorenzo monastery followed that of the library in San Marco convent, also in Florence. Situating a library on the upper floor of the building meant that the natural lighting was improved and any potential damage from damp was limited.

As the library was to be built on top of the existing refectory as an extra storey, it was necessary to make the structure as light as possible in order to minimize the strain on the building below. The walls of the reading room are very thin, painted in a white stucco. Michelangelo used the same *pietra serena* sandstone for the supporting structures, pilasters, cornices ,and window frames of the reading room that he used in the Medici Chapel (1519–34). The tilted, ornate wooden desks were also designed by Michelangelo.

LAURENTIAN LIBRARY, STAIRCASE
(C. 1524–34)
Celimage.sa / Scala Archives

The entrance hall, or vestibule, of the Laurentian Library is higher than the long, narrow reading room. Michelangelo chose the same *pietra serena* sandstone to accentuate the supporting structures and the same contrasting white stucco walls that he used for the reading room. The thick columns set into niches along the walls and beside the entry door may look purely decorative but are in fact essential, weight-bearing structures.

Work on the library began in 1524, but the staircase was completed much later. There are studies by Michelangelo which record the development of his ideas for the staircase, which was originally planned as two side stairs that would meet centrally, similar to the grand staircase that he later designed for the Senate in the *Piazza del Campidoglio* (*c.* 1538) in Rome.

The staircase could easily have been just the one central flight; the addition of the two rectangular flanking flights of stairs that stop abruptly two-thirds of the way up, gives the staircase the illusion of spilling, or flowing freely from the entry door to the floor below. The three middle-bottom steps are oval and the steps above curve along their outer edge so that they echo this unusual oval design.

APOLLO (C. 1530)

Celimage.sa / Lessing Archive

Michelangelo began this statue of Apollo, sometimes called *David*, between 1528 and 1530, for Baccio Valori, who was a political nominee of the Medici family. In 1530 they fought to regain power over the city of Florence from the republican government that had formed after they were expelled in 1527. Michelangelo had allied with the Florentine republicans and helped their cause by building fortifications for the besieged city and consequently was not popular with the Medici. *Apollo* may have been a diplomatic commission to appease any feelings of resentment that Valori held against Michelangelo. The piece was left in an unfinished state when he returned to Rome after the death of his father in 1534; it was never completed.

The sculpture employs a twisting form, a lesser *figura serpentinata* than *Victory* (1519–34), but still evidently serpentine —from the bent leg through to the tilt of the torso and the turn of the head. The artist had explored bodies in twisted movement with the *Ignudi* (1508–12) in the Sistine Chapel and in much of his sculpture.

DETAIL FROM APOLLO (C. 1530)

Celimage.sa/Lessing Archive

Giorgio Vasari, a biographer of Michelangelo, claimed that the unfinished *Apollo* has one arm raised to reach and pull out an arrow from a quiver that was to be positioned on his back. Seen from this angle, there is a noticeable block of marble still remaining unformed but unremoved across and down Apollo's shoulder, which could possibly have been intended to be a quiver of arrows.

When *Apollo* is seen in entirety, the lack of finish of the sculpture does not detract from the graceful, liquid stance and the perfect naturalism used for the body of the god. Observed in detail, however, the lack of finish becomes more obtrusive. The head of *Apollo* is pitted with Michelangelo's chisel marks. His features are lacking in expression and character, his eyes sealed blindly shut.

The face of the bearded man in the statue of *Victory* (1519–30) has been completed to a much higher degree than *Apollo*. In comparison, it becomes clear that the facial expressions of Michelangelo's marble statues were created at a late stage in their metamorphosis.

HERCULES AND CACUS (1525–28)

Celimage.sa/Scala Archives

In Classical mythology, Cacus, the son of Vulcan, stole Hercules' cattle, hiding their destination by dragging them by their tails. Upon finding his herd, Hercules fought and strangled Cacus. This is a classic tale of good triumphing over evil, and the piece was commissioned by the Signoria (republican governors) of Florence following the ousting of the Medici family in 1527. Likewise *David* had been commissioned after the republican uprisings of 1494, and it was intended that the two pieces should be placed together as a permanent reference to the might of the republic over the fallen Medici.

The block of marble intended for the piece had been quarried in Carrara before 1508 and was assigned to Michelangelo. He never used this marble, since it was later given to Baccio Bandinelli (1493–1560), an arch-rival of Michelangelo, who made the flawed *Hercules and Cacus* that now stands in front of the Palazzo Vecchio in Florence.

Michelangelo usually used small, three-dimensional models in wax and clay as part of his sketching process. This figure of *Hercules and Cacus* shows that Michelangelo intended to create a statue to be viewed from every angle. The arm of Cacus wraps round the legs of Hercules, whose legs point in the same direction, encouraging the viewer to walk round the piece.

IDEAL HEAD (C. 1533)

Celimage.sa/Scala Archives

The *Ideal Head* is one of many drawings made by Michelangelo for his friend and probable lover, Tommaso de' Cavalieri, a beautiful young nobleman. He was one of the few people Michelangelo drew, claiming that most people's features were too imperfect, but Cavalieri's beauty made him exceptional. The drawings were intended to help Cavalieri as an artist, so that he could study the master's hand. *Ideal Head* is a black-and-red chalk drawing of Michelangelo's concept of the ideal of beauty. The features are drawn from his imagination, as with the similar drawing of *Zenobia* (*c.* 1533).

During Michelangelo's lifetime, love (platonic or otherwise) between men was not deemed as subversive as it was by the end of the century; even so, there were caustic comments about his affections for the young nobleman. His poems to Cavalieri were altered by later publishers to decrease the amorous affection within them, in lines such as:

> *"Your will includes and is the lord of mine;*
> *Life to my thoughts within your heart is given;*
> *My words begin to breathe upon your breath:*
> *Like to the moon am I, that cannot shine*
> *Alone."*

STUDY OF A MAN SHOUTING (C. 1533)

Celimage.sa / Scala Archives

The *Study of a Man Shouting* is a good example to art students on how to create vivid and intense expressions. The sketch shows in great detail the movement of every muscle that takes place when shouting. The veins on the man's neck stand out angrily, as does his Adam's apple. The muscles on his forehead are clenched together in a frown. Michelangelo evoked the form of the face using charcoal as a medium.

By drawing material and hair swirling as if they are being blown around the man's face, Michelangelo has given the impression that he is attempting to shout into a violent wind. This is a simple device that was used on the Sistine Chapel ceiling to create the illusion of movement or, as with the *Delphic Sibyl* (1508–12), to give the idea of a forbidding wind blowing through the scene.

The fierce facial expression that many of Michelangelo's older men wear, also seen in the *The Creation of the Planets, the Sun, and the Moon* (1508–12), has been characterized as the *terribilità*, and is generally interpreted as a reflection of Michelangelo's own tormented, turbulent emotions.

THE FALL OF PHAETON (C. 1533)

Celimage.sa / Scala Archives

Like the *Ideal Head* (*c.* 1533) this sketch is another Cavalieri drawing. *The Fall of Phaeton* illustrates the Classical myth of Phaeton, seen here tumbling out of his cart, as told in Ovid's *Metamorphoses*. Michelangelo drew three versions of *The Fall of Phaeton* and each is given three layers of figures that form a triangle against a blank background.

Phaeton was the son of Phoebus, the god who mistakenly allowed his son to ride the Chariot of the Sun. Phaeton drove the cart so badly that he was in danger of destroying Heaven and Earth. To stop the impending disaster Zeus, seen at the top of the drawing riding upon a great bird, had to kill Phaeton with a thunderbolt.

The three women at the bottom are Phaeton's sisters, the weeping Heliades. Zeus transformed these three into poplar trees; their legs have taken the shape of tree trunks, while their arms are changing into branches. Phaeton's friend Cygnus has already been transformed into a swan, flapping his huge wings behind the sisters. At the bottom of the sketch, the reclining figure of the river god Eridanus calmly looks up to see the body of Phaeton hurtling toward him.

THE DEAD CHRIST (BASED UPON A STUDY FOR THE PIETÀ FOR THE GOVERNOR OF MILAN) (1533–54)

Celimage.sa / Lessing Archive

Knowledge of human anatomy was greatly limited in the sixteenth century and information that any art student can take for granted today was not available. Studies of medicine and anatomy increased throughout the Renaissance but were still uncommon. Much of what isolated Michelangelo as a genius and artist beyond compare, was the supreme naturalism that he displayed in his depiction of nudes. As can be seen in this sketch, and in the *Studies for a Flying Angel* (1536–41), every muscle was intently studied and perfected before he began to paint or sculpt his chosen image.

Michelangelo's outstanding representation of the human form was not derived simply from an astute observation of his models. In his late teenage years, following the death of Lorenzo the Magnificent, Michelangelo studied human anatomy. A prior at a local hospital allowed him access to the corpses, and Michelangelo spent many grim hours dissecting these bodies to gain an understanding of the muscles, ligaments, and frame that make human movement possible. It was study that, according to his biographer Ascanio Condivi, left Michelangelo with a damaged appetite: "He gave up dissecting corpses because long handling of them had so affected his stomach that he could neither eat nor drink salutarily."

SKETCH OF A MALE HEAD AND TWO LEGS (C. 1536)

Celimage.sa/Scala Archives

This charcoal sketch demonstrates Michelangelo's frugality. As with all his material possessions, he was very careful with the amount of paper he used, making as much use as possible out of any one piece. Here he has taken up the main part of the paper with a sketch of a grizzled old man in profile, while beneath are two brief sketches of legs, bent at the knee as if the leg is in a lunging position.

The face has sunken cheeks, insinuated by a dab of shading. The protruding frown of the brow, the heavy bags underneath the small eyes and the downturned mouth with a slight overbite all create a disgruntled, irritated expression on the man's face. It is thought that this might be a self-portrait. All these facial features, together with the misshapen nose, are reminiscent of a description of Michelangelo, and the face does indeed bear more than a passing resemblance to him. As a teenager, his nose was broken by a fellow apprentice at the Medici court after being taunted by him. Michelangelo added a few self-portraits within some of his works, such as *Study for the Holy Family* (*c.* 1553).

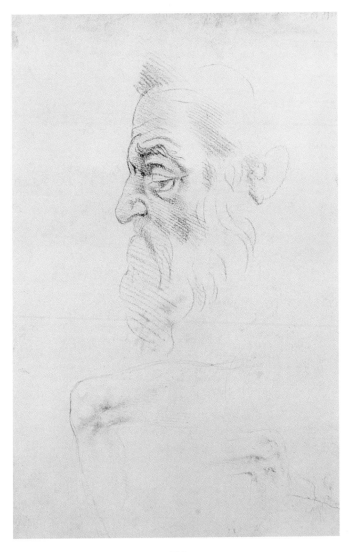

THE LAST JUDGMENT (1536–41)

Celimage.sa / Scala Archives

Pope Julius II had originally conceived the idea of covering the altar wall of the Sistine Chapel in St Peter's, Rome, with a depiction of the Resurrection of Christ, a theme that would have complemented the ceiling's overall theme of the creation and downfall of Man. The plans for the altar wall re-emerged following a fire that damaged the altarpiece by Pietro Perugino. Pope Paul III, who appointed Michelangelo as his chief painter, sculptor, and architect, gave him the commission for the fresco in 1534. At the time, Michelangelo was yet again trying to complete the doomed project of the *Tomb of Pope Julius II* (1505–45), but Paul III intervened, insisting that the artist should work on his projects instead.

The altar wall is 40 ft wide by 45 ft high, making *The Last Judgment* the largest undivided work of art to be undertaken by a single individual. At what point the theme of the Resurrection became *The Last Judgment* is unclear, although it is most probable that Pope Paul III, a strong reformist, influenced the change. The theme was a fitting one for Rome, recovering as it was from several murderous attacks both on the city and on the papacy, that had led to famine, poverty, and plague.

Detail of Christ (from The Last Judgment) (1536–41)

Celimage.sa / Scala Archives

Throughout the many representations of Christ that Michelangelo produced, most were either scenes of the crucifixion or of his death, as with the thin, bearded figure in the *Duomo Pietà* (*c.* 1547–55). In *The Last Judgment* we are shown neither a gentle nor a suffering Christ. Here, on the last day of the world, he has returned to earth to pronounce his judgment upon humanity as a muscular, beardless young man. Charged with a powerful energy, which glows about him, he epitomizes the idea of a vengeful God.

Michelangelo has placed Christ centrally, near the top of the painting with the circular movement in the piece revolving around him. A dense ring of figures has formed about Christ; these are the souls that have already risen and are bound for Heaven. The massive figures closest to him are the saints and apostles. Those on the right of the picture underneath the saints are the damned, and on the left the blessed. Almost hiding against Christ, beneath his right arm sits Mary, who is turning her head away as he raises one robust arm in the gesture of making his final judgment.

DETAIL OF THE BLESSED (FROM THE LAST JUDGMENT) (1536–41)

Celimage.sa / Scala Archives

Within the mass of crowded figures in *The Last Judgment* there is much movement; bodies are seen struggling, fighting, and tumbling in various directions, but the whole painting has a definite sweeping circular movement which is clearly visible. The main motion within the piece begins on the bottom left, with the dead rising up from their graves, floating up to join the blessed on their ascent to Heaven, circling the figure of Christ, then swarming down with the sinners as they descend into Hell. This gives the huge fresco a sense of order.

Among the crowd of the blessed, some figures float upwards with no apparent effort, while most have to struggle to make their ascent or are pulled up by the figures standing on the clouds. On the right, a figure pulls two people up using a rosary, an obvious allusion to the salvation of prayer. The varying efforts of the blessed, while ensuring that the left side of the fresco did not appear static in comparison with the violent movement on the right, illustrates the belief that the path to Heaven is a difficult one, although for a few it seems naturally easy.

DETAIL OF ANGELS (FROM THE LAST JUDGMENT) (1536–41)

Celimage.sa/Scala Archives

At the very top of *The Last Judgment* are two lunettes that once contained frescoes of the *Ancestors of Christ* by Michelangelo, but these were removed to gain more space for the dramatic vision of *The Last Judgment* to unfold. The lunettes now show flying angels that carry the objects of Christ's suffering. In the left lunette, an angel carries Christ's crown of thorns as he looks over his shoulder toward the angels that struggle to keep a hold of the cross. The angels' difficulty with carrying the cross serves as a reminder to the congregation of Christ's burden and strength in carrying the cross alone.

Above the lunettes are the two end spandrels of Michelangelo's ceiling fresco, the left illustrating *Esther and Haman* (1508–12) and on the right-hand side *The Brazen Serpent* (1508–12). Viewed from this angle, Michelangelo's staggering understanding of perspective becomes evident.

In between the spandrels is the massive figure of the prophet *Jonah* (1508–12), leaning back to stare up in awe at the sight of *The Separation of Light from Darkness* (1508–12). The original idea of a Resurrection fresco for the altar wall was apt as the figure of *Jonah* above was himself resurrected after his encounter with the whale.

STUDY FOR THE LAST JUDGMENT (DATE UNKNOWN)

Celimage.sa / Scala Archives

Michelangelo employed the same preparatory habits for *The Last Judgment* fresco that he used while painting the ceiling frescoes. Several studies have survived that demonstrate his habit of sketching a figure in the position envisioned, before copying this outline on to fresh plaster and then painting. He studied the movement of muscles that occurred in the chosen pose, as well as the perspective and shading necessary to portray the body in that position realistically.

The Christ figure dominates the study as it stands powerfully above the melange of bodies. Desperation and reverence combine within the skillfully drawn scene to convey an evocative detail from the Last Judgment. The subsequent adaptation of the final painted work is faithful to the chaotic intertwining of the human forms depicted in this study.

The theme of *The Last Judgment* as Michelangelo has handled it, with the mass of flying, tumbling, twisting bodies, gave the artist an ideal arena to explore the varying movements and postures of a body in motion. Michelangelo once claimed that he never used the same pose twice, and the huge variety of figures in *The Last Judgment* would seem to back up this claim.

DETAIL OF THE SINNERS (FROM THE LAST JUDGMENT) (1536–41)

Celimage.sa/Scala Archives

On the far left, isolated from the throng of the damned, a man holds one hand to his face as he is clasped by devils and dragged down to Hell. While the nearby figures fight with each other and the devils as they tumble toward the ground, this man offers no resistance, his anguished face showing the recognition of his fate. Beneath the man is a golden trumpet that belongs to the Seven Angels of the Apocalypse, who herald the arrival of the Judgment Day and hold the books that record the life of every individual so that all sinners can read and judge their sins for themselves. *The Last Judgment* shows a change in Michelangelo's compositions; the figures are heavy, bulky, and far removed from the beauty of form that he strove to achieve in earlier works in the Sistine Chapel such as the *Ignudi* (1508–12). Michelangelo's chief concern had become the sharing of his religious vision.

From the moment of its unveiling in 1541, *The Last Judgment* had proved to be controversial, with criticism raised over the nudity of most figures. Shortly before Michelangelo's death, the decision was made to paint coverings on the figures.

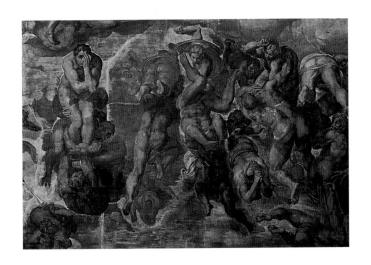

DETAIL OF ST BARTHOLOMEW (FROM THE LAST JUDGMENT) (1536–41)

Celimage.sa / Scala Archives

The saints appear huge, looming over the twisted masses beneath them. Their appearance is partly due to techniques of perspective: as they were painted higher up the wall, their size was increased so they would not appear too small to the viewer on the floor. Each of the saints holds the instruments of their martyrdom; here St Bartholomew sits astride a cloud holding his own skin—he was flayed to death.

As the saints look up toward Christ they thrust the tools of their martyrdom toward him, demanding recognition for their suffering. Although they are already among the blessed, it appears that the saints are fearful of Christ's judgments. Their expressive angst serves to increase the tensions within the piece.

The flayed, gray skin that St Bartholomew holds contains a self-portrait of Michelangelo. This ironic gesture proves to be prophetic when viewed in the light of the arguments that surrounded *The Last Judgment*. When asked by Pope Paul III to make the fresco "more suitable," following comments that it would be more fittingly displayed in a brothel, Michelangelo replied, "make the world a suitable place and the painting will follow suit."

DETAIL OF CHARON (FROM THE LAST JUDGMENT) (1536–41)

Celimage.sa/Scala Archives

Michelangelo's affection for the literature of Dante Alighieri (1265–1321) is seen in the bottom right of *The Last Judgment*. On the far left of this detail is the figure of Charon, portrayed as Dante described him, standing in his boat with an oar raised about to strike. In Classical mythology, he was the ferryman of the dead over the marsh of Acheron; here he is the herder of the damned into Hell.

The devils in *The Last Judgment* are not portrayed as inhuman or demonic monsters; instead those that appear here have human form, albeit with the traditional horns and clawed feet. These devils, seen dragging struggling bodies down toward Charon, retain human form to emphasize the human failings of the sinners.

Before the fresco was completed, Pope Paul III's Master of Ceremonies, Biagio da Cesana, visited the fresco and complained upon seeing the amount of nudity, reporting that the work was obscene and unfitting for the chapel. In an act of revenge, Michelangelo painted a portrait of Cesana among the sinners in the far bottom right, with horns on his head and a snake entwined around him.

Piazza del Campidoglio (c. 1538)

Celimage.sa/Scala Archives

The Piazza del Campidoglio sits upon the Capitoline Hill in Rome. While St Peter's is the heart of the religious center of the city, the Campidoglio is the heart of the civic center. Michelangelo's designs for the Campidoglio reclaimed Rome's glorious past; the Capitoline Hill was the center of the Roman Empire, but by the Renaissance it had fallen into ruins.

Michelangelo began work on the Piazza del Campidoglio in 1537–38. He was initially asked by Pope Paul III to create a new pedestal for the Classical statue of Emperor Marcus Aurelius. The statue was then placed in the center of the piazza and became the central focus of Michelangelo's plans, with an oval of patterned pavement spreading out around it, although the pavement was not completed to Michelangelo's design until the twentieth century.

At the back of the piazza is the Senate building which was the Roman Tabularium; on the right is the fifteenth-century Palazzo Conservatori. To create symmetry within the piazza, Michelangelo designed a third palace on the left and façades for the Senate and the Conservatori. This idea of a symmetrical, balanced town center was novel at the time, yet it was perhaps Michelangelo's most influential architectural design and has been widely copied throughout the world.

BUST OF BRUTUS (C. 1542)

Celimage.sa / Lessing Archive

While still working on *The Last Judgment*, Michelangelo began work on a marble bust in the Classical Roman Imperialist style that had previously been reserved for emperors and the wealthy. The bust was commissioned by a friend of Michelangelo who, like himself, had helped defend the city of Florence from the siege by the Medicis. It is thought that the bust may have been made to commemorate the murder of tyrannical Alessandro de' Medici by his cousin Lorenzino in 1537. Alessandro was hated by the Florentine exiles in Rome, who fled the city after the Medicis regained their power, and his murder was likened to that of Caesar by Brutus in 44 BC. An alternative inspiration is noted as an imperial portrait bust of the Roman emperor Caracalla, who reigned from 211 to 217 AD.

The features for the face were taken either from an ancient portrait believed to be of Brutus or from the bust of Caracalla. The piece is unfinished and as a result the thick neck appears strangely large if viewed from the front, set as it is against such finely draped robes. With the Classical Roman features and side profile, the bust bears some resemblance to the statue of *Giuliano de' Medici* (1520–34), but Brutus appears stronger, more determined and lacks the slight arrogance seen in the face of Giuliano.

SACRIFICE OF ISAAC (DATE UNKNOWN)

Celimage.sa/Scala Archives

God told Abraham to take his son Isaac to the land of Moriah and offer him as a burnt offering. So Abraham cut the wood for the burnt offering, and took two men to accompany him and Isaac close to the place of sacrifice. Then he built an altar, bound Isaac and laid him upon it, and covered him with wood. He was just about to slay his son with the knife, but was stopped by the angel of the Lord. Abraham's dutiful willingness to sacrifice his son secured his reputation as the first Jewish patriarch.

In this evocative sketch the artist captures the dramatic biblical episode and poignantly depicts the fear and blind faith of the subjects. Michelangelo gives a sensitive treatment to a highly charged episode through fine line and soft tones.

The Crucifixion of Christ (c. 1541)

Celimage.sa/Lessing Archive

The Crucifixion of Christ is another of the religious pictures made for Vittoria Colonna in the 1540s that are collectively known as presentation drawings. They were made *c.* 1541 using the medium of black chalk on paper. Michelangelo used a stippling, or dabbling, effect with the chalk, which he also employed in the other presentation drawings. The stippling technique means that the delineation round the figure of Christ is darker and He therefore seems to stand out against the background. Stippling is also used to create shadows. The techniques used in the presentation drawings differ greatly from those in later drawings such as *Study for a Crucifixion* (*c.* 1540–55).

There are few signs of life in the figure of Christ; the skull seen at the foot of the cross symbolizes his approaching death. Under Christ's outstretched arms are the figures of two angels. One angel looks worriedly at Christ, while the other looks despondently to the ground. Their expressions indicate that Christ is about to die. His face, as He gazes upward to Heaven, shows signs of intense suffering and this portrayal was greatly admired by Vittoria Colonna for the profound religious sentiments it portrayed.

HEAD OF CHRIST (C. 1540)

Celimage.sa / Scala Archives

This *Head of Christ* is a partial fragment of a sculpture that Michelangelo worked on during the 1540s. The sculpture was of a *Pietà* scene with a similar structure to that of the later *Rondanini Pietà* (*c.* 1556–64), which shows the body of Christ being supported by the Madonna standing behind him. This was a vision of the *Pietà* that Michelangelo was never able to successfully portray in marble, although sketches survive that show us his intentions for this unusual rendering of the scene.

There are many unfinished sculptures by Michelangelo. As was evident in the *Tomb of Pope Julius II* (1505–45), his patrons would often disrupt his work on particular projects and his own life often interrupted his work too. Many scholars have suggested that Michelangelo would abandon a piece when he found that he had achieved the intimation of the expression he had been searching for; that pieces such as the *Abandoned Slaves* (1520–30) embody within their unfinished form the heart of the artist's vision. Unlike his contemporaries, Michelangelo rarely made use of assistants. Despite this, he accepted many large commissions that overlapped, leaving their completion a physical impossibility for himself.

STUDY OF MADONNA AND CHILD (WITH ST JOSEPH) (DATE UNKNOWN)

Celimage.sa / Scala Archives

The last works of Michelangelo were invariably religious in content, reflecting his deepening sense of spirituality. From his work as an architect at St Peter's in Rome, through to his final Pietà sculptures and drawings, Michelangelo seems to have been seeking redemption through his art. It was as though he were trying to find some visual expression of intense religious and personal beliefs. This drawing revisits the theme of the Madonna and Child, treated in his famous sculpture at Bruges, and other works such as his *Pitti Tondo* and the *Taddei Tondo*.

Michelangelo's treatment of the Madonna and Child with St Joseph offers an unusually intimate group portrait. All three figures are loosely connected in a touching intimacy, which nevertheless pays attention to the formalities of anatomical drawing. The Virgin Mary offers protection to an unusually plausible infant, who seems to play nonchalantly as he rests upon her knee.

MARY MAGDALENE CONTEMPLATING THE CROWN OF THORNS (DATE UNKNOWN)

Celimage.sa/Lessing Archive

This lovely drawing is astonishing for its sheer beauty. It represents Mary Magdalene, who had supported Mary the Mother of Christ after the deposition following the crucifixion.

Mary Magdalene is obscured by the legends that surrounded her following the Resurrection and there is considerable difference of opinion as to her identity. She was the woman exorcised of seven devils, she ministered to the Lord in Galilee, and was among the women present at the crucifixion of Christ. With Joanna and Mary, the mother of James, and Salome, she discovered the empty tomb and heard the angelic announcement of the Resurrection of Christ. She was said to be the first person to see Christ later that same day.

Mary Magdalene Contemplating the Crown of Thorns is an intense and moving portrayal of despair as the young woman grieves, clutching the fallen crown. The natural pose lends an authenticity to this work.

THE CONVERSION OF ST PAUL (1542–45)

Celimage.sa/Lessing Archive

Upon completion of *The Last Judgment* (1536–41) in the Vatican, Pope Paul III asked Michelangelo to decorate his private chapel, the Capella Paolina, which was adjacent to the Sistine Chapel and in which popes were selected at that time. Michelangelo began in 1542 with *The Conversion of St Paul*, a theme chosen in deference to Paul III. Before his vision of God and subsequent conversion to Christianity, Paul was a Pharisee named Saul who was traveling along the road to Damascus to murder the Christians who lived there. Although historically St Paul was young, here he is depicted as an old man of a similar age to the pope.

The *Conversion* fresco was begun shortly after the unveiling of *The Last Judgment*, but the coloring within the piece shares more with that used in the ceiling of the Sistine Chapel. In the *Conversion*, the colors are bright and varied, with none of the drabness that invades *The Last Judgment*. The whole fresco is infused with the light that the figure of Christ directs at St Paul.

Despite the many figures within the work, the viewer's attention is focused on two figures: that of St Paul as he lies on the ground, and on Christ as he hurls himself down from the Heavens, with a blazing light in his path. Michelangelo reverted to a more traditional portrayal of Christ here than in *The Last Judgment*.

THE CRUCIFIXION OF ST PETER
(1542–50)

Celimage.sa/Lessing Archive

The *Crucifixion of St Peter* was chosen as decoration for Pope Paul III's private chapel in the Vatican because in Christian tradition Peter was the first pope and therefore father of the new Church.

There is a circular motion within *The Crucifixion of St Peter* akin to that in *The Last Judgment* (1536–41). The figures are all placed in a wide circle round the central figure of Peter. People point to Peter to emphasize the focus on him and the women in the near foreground direct the gaze to him with turned heads and wide-eyed stares. Michelangelo increased the intensity of the light within the center of the picture to further focus the viewer's attention on the figure of St Peter.

Four men are preparing to stand the cross that bears the saint. St Peter chose to be crucified upside down, and in order to avoid compositional difficulties, Michelangelo chose to show the cross as it is about to be erected so that St Peter is able to pull himself up to glare fiercely out at the viewer. The impact of his accusatory stare outward enhances the fact that he is the focus of everybody else in the painting.

INNER COURTYARD, PALAZZO FARNESE (BEGUN 1547)

Celimage.sa / Scala Archives

The Farnese Palace in Rome was mainly built to the designs of Antonio da Sangallo the Younger, who also worked on St Peter's. He began work on the Palace in 1517 and by his death in 1534, the building had reached the second storey, with the façade almost complete. The completion of the palace was thrown open to a public design competition in 1547; Michelangelo's successful design included an additional third storey for the inner courtyard of the palace and the large cornice that now surmounts the façade.

In the courtyard, Sangallo's middle storey is clearly much more traditional than the ornate, grandiose style Michelangelo employed for his third storey. The windows are surmounted by heavy, arched pediments, decorated with a ram's head placed centrally in each and garlands flowing from either side. These pediments do not connect with the windows but rest upon the capitals that crown the pilasters. On top of the window frames are lion's heads. The columns that flank the windows of the second storey have become dominating pilasters by the third storey. Michelangelo also altered the second storey by adding triangular pediments and the entablature decorated with a garland motif.

INTERIOR OF THE DOME OF THE BASILICA OF ST PETER'S (DATE UNKNOWN)

Celimage.sa / Scala Archives

The original Basilica of St Peter dates from 324 AD. It was built in honor of St Peter on top of his burial site. In the early fifteenth century the original cathedral was torn down and replaced by the church we see today. The construction was a slow, lengthy process. Julius II sought out the artist Bramante, who didn't complete his work on the structure. Raphael, Antonio da Sangallo, Petuzzi, and Michelangelo were selected to continue constructing the basilica. They incorporated their ideas with some of those of Bramante and Rosselli.

In 1547 Pope Paul III entrusted the design of the dome on St Peter's Basilica to the 72-year-old Michelangelo, who had turned down the job half a century earlier. Though he didn't finish the project, he played a large role in making St Peter's the magnificent home of art and beauty that it is today. Domenico Fontana and Guglielmo Della Porta finished the job between 1585 and 1590.

The architectural makeup of St Peter's Basilica is one of grandiose proportions. Five entrance portals lead into the church. Michelangelo projected a dome in a slightly pointed form. As with Brunelleschi's Florence dome, the pointed shape exerts less thrust. It is believed that the dome's astounding size is greater than Michelangelo had planned. It sweeps to an awesome height and allows a cycle of light to stream through the windows inset below the Cupola.

DUOMO PIETÀ (*C.* 1547–55)

Celimage.sa/Lessing Archive

Michelangelo worked on the *Duomo Pietà* intermittently for seven years. He carved it for his family tomb as a fitting memorial for himself and the family he loved so well. By 1547 he was 70 years old and the knowledge of his own mortality was evidently important in this work. The sculpture is housed in the Museo dell' Opera del Duomo in Florence and is sometimes called *The Deposition of Christ*, as is the painting of *The Entombment*, which illustrates a similar scene.

The man at the back supporting the body of Christ is Nicodemus, who was a follower of Jesus and, together with Joseph, helped take down his body from the cross. He was also a sculptor who carved the visions that God sent him; poignantly Michelangelo has given Nicodemus his own features.

The deformed left arm of Christ has clearly been broken in several places and his left leg is missing altogether. According to Vasari, Michelangelo was deeply discouraged both by the *Pietà* and his own failing abilities, and attacked the statue in a fit of frustration. He later gave the *Pietà* to his assistant Tiberio Calcagni, who attempted to finish it; the incongruous figure on the right, Mary Magdalen, is attributed to his weak craftmanship.

STUDY FOR THE HOLY FAMILY (EPIFANIA) (C. 1553)

www.heritage-images.com/The British Museum

There is much mystery surrounding the cartoon of the *Holy Family (Epifania)*; it is unclear why this large preparatory drawing was produced and equally uncertain what the cartoon is depicting. It was later used by Ascanio Condivi, Michelangelo's friend and biographer, as the basis for his version of the painting.

The central figure is the Virgin Mary, who shelters Christ beneath her legs. The other child is St John the Baptist. On her left, Mary pushes away Joseph, whose features are clearly a self-portrait by Michelangelo. Mary is in deep discussion with the androgynous figure on her right, who leans toward her. There are several other outlines of faces within the cartoon, which are also leaning toward Mary, as if straining to hear the discussion.

One explanation of the cartoon's subject is that the surrounding vague outlines are the half-brothers and half-sisters of Christ, who were Joseph's children from an early marriage. The androgynous figure may be St Julian, who was renowned for his chastity and may be encouraging Mary's continuing chastity, hence her pushing Joseph away.

STUDY FOR CHRIST ON THE CROSS
(WITH THE VIRGIN AND ST JOHN)
(1562–64)

Celimage.sa/Lessing Archive

This crucifixion scene is one of several that Michelangelo worked on during his final years. It uses the medium of pencil and black chalk on paper. At one point Michelangelo intended to make a fitting memorial to his great friend Vittoria Colonna, who died in 1547, and it is possible that some of the crucifixion drawings are designs made for this purpose.

On the right is the hazy figure of St John, his mouth agape, eyes wide as if in dismay, much like the expressions of some of the sinners in *The Last Judgment* (1536–41). All three figures have been sketched and reworked as Michelangelo strived for the ideal postures that he was seeking. As a result of this reworking, their outlines are blurred and both the Virgin, who stands on Christ's right, and St John appear to have double images behind them, giving the picture a haunting quality.

The design of the cross means that Jesus' arms are high above his head. This placement is echoed by the form of Mary, who stands with her arms crossed protectively against her chest. Michelangelo altered the picture to make this possible and the original position of her arm is easily seen.

PALESTRINA PIETÀ (C. 1556)

Celimage.sa/Scala Archives

The *Palestrina Pietà* is so named because it was originally placed in Palestrina, having been cut from a marble that was found only close to this small town. Michelangelo is believed to have made the statue around 1556, although its authenticity has been questioned. The *Pietà* was first documented in Palestrina in the seventeenth century. At the least, it is probable that other sculptors added their own touches to the piece, or that Michelangelo started the sculpture, which was then carried on in his style by an apprentice.

The composition of the *Palestrina Pietà* bears a great resemblance to that of the earlier *Duomo Pietà* (*c.* 1547–55). Both pieces are unusual in that the *Pietà* traditionally depicts the Madonna and Christ alone. In both statues, the body of Christ leans heavily against the figures that try to support him; his head is tilted and his legs fold underneath him.

The *Palestrina Pietà* is in a lesser state of completion than the *Duomo Pietà*. Only the body of Christ has been partially completed; as was common with Michelangelo, the torso and upper limbs are almost finished, while the lower limbs are still barely freed from the marble.

HEAD OF CLEOPATRA (C. 1553)

Celimage.sa / Scala Archives

During the Ptolemaic Period there were several queens in Egypt named Cleopatra; the most famous and influential in history was the seventh. Cleopatra's beauty was surpassed only by her charm and ambition. Despite her political acumen, she had notably contributed to the fall of both Julius Caesar and Marc Antony. After her defeat by Octavius, Egypt came under Roman domination.

Cleopatra was that last sovereign of the Macedonian dynasty, and although she had no Egyptian blood, she proclaimed herself Daughter of Ra, the Sun God of Egypt. She dedicated her efforts to enforcing her royal status as queen of Egypt, restoring the glories of Ptolemy and recovering Egypt's dominions in southern Syria and Palestine, as well as sharing in the central Roman authority.

Head of Cleopatra is a powerful aristocratic portrait. It evinces the seductive and vulnerable beauty of the legendary queen whose death by suicide is a theme touched on by artists and writers alike. This classical study of the female head allows us to see the natural evolution from portrait sketch to sculpted stone used to great effect by the artist. The pose and the vacant eyes give a sculptural quality rather than a formal portrait effect to the image.

THE RONDANINI PIETÀ (C. 1556–64)

Celimage.sa/Scala Archives

The *Rondanini Pietà* (named after the palace where it was housed) was the final sculpture on which Michelangelo worked. He was working on the sculpture up to six days before his death. Working with marble takes considerable strength; although Michelangelo was almost 90 by this time, he was in the habit of carving a little of the *Pietà* each day.

The *Rondanini Pietà* differs from other of Michelangelo's *Pietàs* in that the figure of the Madonna is standing on a raised level, the body of Christ leans back against her, and she supports his body from behind. Michelangelo's frustration with the erosion of his sight and skills is keenly felt within the piece. The bodies and scale of the two figures bear no relation to the lower legs of Christ or to the dismembered right arm that can be seen on the left. It is possible Michelangelo became unhappy with the sculpture and began decreasing the scale, starting from the top, to create smaller figures from the block.

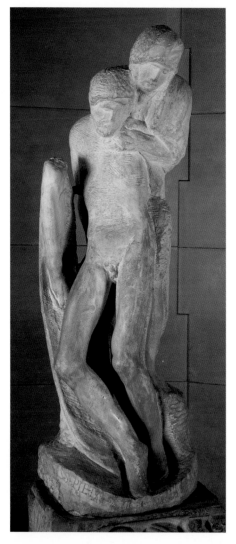

St Peter's Basilica (begun 1546)

Celimage.sa / Scala Archives

Emperor Constantine (*c.* 288–337 AD) built the original St Peter's church over his tomb in the fourth century. Pope Julius II initially commissioned Michelangelo's great rival Bramante to renovate the building, but as the structure had deteriorated, the architect began to demolish the old building and created designs for a new, grand church. Bramante died in 1514 and was replaced by several successive architects, including his nephew Raphael. Pope Paul III approached Michelangelo in 1546 following the death of Sangallo the Younger; although reluctant, Michelangelo accepted the commission in 1547.

Bramante died leaving incomplete plans for St Peter's, which were modified by later architects. Despite his intense dislike of Bramante, Michelangelo chose to return to much of his original design, rejecting Sangallo's later plans. The workers on St Paul's held allegiance to Sangallo, having worked under him for many years, and Michelangelo's changes made him unpopular. He justified himself by saying that Bramante's designs were "not full of confusion, but clear, pure, and full of light, so that it did not in any way damage the palace...whoever departs from this order of Bramante's, as Sangallo has done, departs from the truth."

St Peter's Basilica (1546–1564)

Celimage.sa / Scala Archives

Michelangelo once remarked lightheartedly that "one could expect to see the last day of the world sooner than see St Peter's finished." He would accept no payment for his work on the basilica, and viewed the project as spiritually redeeming. During the 17 years he spent working on St Peter's, the building work was considerably progressed and by the time of his death in 1564, a large part of the drum that the cupola rests on had already been erected.

Following Michelangelo's death, Pope Paul III set a brief that his designs for St Peter's were still to be adhered to, but as few clear or instructive plans were left by the artist to show his intentions, later architects made various changes to the building. One major change in design was the form of the nave being changed from the Greek cross plan of Michelangelo's and Bramante's to the Latin cross design that can now be seen.

Overall, however, Michelangelo did succeed in setting the style of the building. The cupola was completed after his death, largely to his design. The columns and rectangular windows with their arched pediments are reminiscent of his work in the Piazza del Campidoglio.

Auditing

Auditing:

An

Integrated Approach

ALVIN A. ARENS, PH.D., C.P.A.

Associate Professor
Michigan State University

JAMES K. LOEBBECKE, C.P.A.

Partner
Touche Ross & Co.

PRENTICE-HALL, INC., Englewood Cliffs, New Jersey

Library of Congress Cataloging in Publication Data

ARENS, ALVIN A
   Auditing, an integrated approach.

   1. Auditing. I. Loebbecke, James K., joint author.
II. Title.
HF5667.A69   657'.45   76-7451
ISBN 0-13-051698-8

Printed in the United States of America

10 9 8 7 6 5 4 3 2 1

Prentice-Hall International, Inc., *London*
Prentice-Hall of Australia Pty. Limited, *Sydney*
Prentice-Hall of Canada, Ltd., *Toronto*
Prentice-Hall of India Private Limited, *New Delhi*
Prentice-Hall of Japan, Inc., *Tokyo*
Prentice-Hall of Southeast Asia Pte. Ltd., *Singapore*

Contents

Preface

OBJECTIVES

This book is an introduction to auditing for students who have not had significant experience in auditing. It is intended for either a one quarter or one semester course at the undergraduate or graduate level. The book is also appropriate for introductory professional development courses for CPA firms, internal auditors, and governmental auditors.

The primary emphasis in this text is on the auditor's decision-making process. We believe the most fundamental concepts in auditing relate to determining the nature and amount of evidence the auditor should accumulate after considering the unique circumstances of each engagement. If a student of auditing understands the objectives to be accomplished in a given audit area, the circumstances of the engagement, and the decisions to be made, he or she should be able to determine the appropriate evidence to gather and how to evaluate the evidence obtained.

Thus, as the title of the book reflects, our purpose is to integrate the most important concepts of auditing as well as certain practical aspects in a logical manner to assist students in understanding audit decision-making and evidence accumulation. For example, internal control is integrated into each of the chapters dealing with a particular functional area and is related to tests of transactions; tests of transactions are in turn related to the direct tests of financial statement balances of the accounts for the area; and statistical sampling is applied to the accumulation of audit evidence rather than treated as a separate topic.

ORGANIZATION

It is convenient to think of the book as consisting of seven parts.

Part One includes Chapters 1 through 3 and provides background information and concepts that every auditor must understand. Chapter 1 defines and describes auditing, different types of audits and auditors, and types of evidence. The chapter includes an overview of the audit process to aid students in understanding how the concepts discussed in subsequent chapters fit into the total audit. Chapters 2 and 3 are a study of the most important considerations affecting auditors' actions and the accumulation of audit evidence. The chapters include such subjects as the Code of Professional Ethics, the SEC, legal liability, the factors affecting auditors' expectation of errors in the financial statements, and factors affecting the likelihood of sanctions against the auditor.

Part Two is made up of Chapters 4 through 7. These chapters relate to the accumulation of audit evidence and the documentation of results. Chapter 4 considers the importance of obtaining an understanding of the client and its business and discusses the means of doing this, including: discussions with client personnel, reference to industry data, examining legal records, calculating ratios, comparing financial information with previous years, and investigating the likelihood of material management fraud. The need to understand the client's business and the environment in which the audit is being conducted is emphasized throughout the book. The study and evaluation of internal control is discussed in Chapter 5, and emphasizes the most important elements in any system, a proper methodology for studying and evaluating the system, and the implications of the results of the study. A unique aspect of Chapter 5 is a set of internal control objectives that relates internal control evaluation to tests of the system. Chapter 6 summarizes the first five chapters and integrates them with the remainder of the text. The chapter examines the interrelationship of different types of tests, and establishes a general framework for studying tests of transactions and direct tests of balances. It focuses on the importance of the interaction of all tests and the need for specific audit objectives. Chapter 7 examines the documentation of audit tests through the use of audit working papers.

Part Three applies the concepts from the first two parts of the book to the audit of sales, cash receipts, and the related income statement and balance sheet accounts. In Chapter 8, the appropriate audit procedures for sales and cash receipts are related to the system of internal control and a set of audit objectives common to all tests of transactions. Determination of an appropriate sample size and deciding which sample items should be tested are considered in Chapter 9, primarily through the use of attributes statistical sampling. Chapter 10 is the study of accounts receivable and the allowance for uncollectible accounts, with emphasis on the relationship of those accounts to the evaluation of internal control and tests of sales and cash receipts transactions. The audit procedures for accounts receivable and all other balance sheet accounts included in the remainder of the text are studied using the audit framework developed in Chapter 6. Chapter 11 discusses the concepts of variables sampling and illustrates their application to accounts receivable.

Part Four includes only Chapter 12, which covers the evaluation of internal control for EDP systems, the audit of systems that include significant EDP processing, and auditing with and without the use of the computer. The emphasis in this chapter is on the impact of EDP on the way an audit is conducted.

Part Five includes Chapters 13 through 18. Each of these chapters deals with a specific transaction cycle or part of a transaction cycle in much the same manner as Chapters 8 through 11 deal with the sales and collection cycle. The cycles in Part Five are as follows:

- Payroll and personnel—Chapter 13
- Acquisitions and disbursements—Chapters 14 and 15
- Inventory and warehousing—Chapter 16
- Capital acquisitions and repayments—Chapter 17
- Cash in the bank—Chapter 18 (This chapter indicates the interaction of all of the preceding transaction cycles as they affect cash.)

Each chapter in Part Five is meant to clearly demonstrate the relationship of internal control evaluation and tests of transactions for each broad category of transactions (e.g. general cash disbursements) to the related balance sheet and income statement accounts (e.g. accounts payable and insurance expense). Cash in the bank is studied late in the text to demonstrate how the audit of cash balances is related to most other audit areas.

Part Six (Chapter 19) is concerned with summarizing all of the audit tests, reviewing working papers, and other aspects of completing the audit.

Part Seven (Chapter 20) covers the various types of reports issued by auditors. The emphasis in this chapter is on the conditions affecting the type of report the auditor must issue and the type of audit report applicable to each condition under varying levels of materiality.

ASSIGNMENT OF CHAPTERS

The book has been designed to provide maximum flexibility in assigning chapters. Certain chapters can be omitted completely without significantly sacrificing effectiveness. The omitted chapters will reduce the applications of the concepts by studying fewer individual audit areas, but the most important concepts themselves will not be bypassed if the first ten and last two chapters are studied.

The following are suggestions for assigning chapters:

Chapters 1–10. These chapters include the fundamental concepts in auditing, and, except as modified below, should be studied sequentially. Some instructors may want to delete working papers, but the other chapters include important fundamental concepts that are interrelated with the remaining chapters of the book.

Chapter 11. The study of variables sampling can be conveniently deleted by instructors who are not committed to a heavy emphasis on the use of statistical sampling in auditing. Attributes sampling (Chapter 9) is used more extensively in auditing practice than variables sampling and is such an integral part of the book that it should not be bypassed in ordinary circumstances.

Chapter 12. The study of EDP can be conveniently studied after Chapter 5 (internal control) or any time after Chapter 11. It can also be deleted entirely or supplemented with other materials.

Chapters 13–18. One or more of these chapters can be eliminated if the instructor believes that it is unnecessary to study every major audit area in a typical audit. Chapter 13 (payroll) and Chapter 17 (issue and repayment of capital) are likely candidates for omission, but alternative or additional chapters might be deleted. Chapter 15 (accounts payable) should not be studied unless Chapter 14 (acquisitions and disbursements) is assigned first, but it is practical to study Chapter 14 without 15. Certain audit areas in Chapter 15 can also be easily deleted. Chapter 16 (inventory and warehousing) is a useful chapter to demonstrate the interrelationships between different parts of the audit, but it should not be assigned unless either Chapter 14 or 15, or both, have been studied.

Chapter 19. Completing the audit is an essential part of the book and should be assigned late in the course.

Chapter 20. Audit reports can be assigned at any point in the course. Those instructors who believe audit reports should be studied early can assign it immediately after Chapter 2. It would also be acceptable to study the material after Chapters 10, 12, 18, or 19.

ACKNOWLEDGMENTS

We acknowledge the American Institute of Certified Public Accountants for permission to quote extensively from Statements on Auditing Standards, the Code of Professional Ethics, Accounting Principles Board Opinions, Uniform CPA Examinations, and other publications. The willingness of this major accounting organization to permit the use of their materials is a significant contribution to the book.

We also gratefully acknowledge the contributions of the following reviewers for their suggestions: Andrew D. Bailey, Jr., Purdue University;

William C. Boynton, University of Virginia; Darwin J. Casler, Northern Illinois University; Geraldine Dominiak, Texas Christian University; William L. Felix, University of Washington; Joe R. Fritzemeyer, Arizona State University; Shane Moriarity, University of Kansas; Michael B. Sheffey, Wittenberg University; and Doyle Williams, Texas Tech University.

A special note of thanks is appropriate to Geraldine Dominiak of Texas Christian University who did an unusually detailed and helpful review, and to Donald Bear and Gary Burgher of Touche Ross & Co. who assisted with the solutions manual.

Finally, the assistance of Irene Arens, Rita Grant, and Margaret W. Jones at various stages of the book, and the support of our families throughout the entire project, are acknowledged.

A.A.A. and J.K.L.

1

An Overview
of
Auditing

This chapter is intended to present an overview of auditing to the reader, and in effect represents an overview of the entire text. The chapter contains seven topics:

1. The need for reliable information
2. Nature of auditing
3. Types of audits
4. Types of auditors
5. Audit evidence decisions
6. Types of audit evidence
7. An overview of the audit process

The first four topics provide background information about all types of audits and auditors, whereas the last three are directed primarily at the audit of financial statements by certified public accountants. Types of evidence are discussed in some detail at this early juncture due to their importance throughout the remainder of the text. The overview of the audit process is intended to help the reader see how the parts of the audit fit together before each part is discussed in subsequent chapters. In this text, a strong emphasis is placed on not only the individual parts of the audit, but on the *integration* of the parts. It is this integration that binds the parts into a workable *process,* as contrasted with a series of disconnected steps.

THE NEED FOR RELIABLE INFORMATION

Economic decisions in every society must be based upon the information available at the time the decision is made. For example, the decision of a bank to make a loan to a business is based upon previous financial relationships with that business, the financial condition of the company as reflected by its financial statements, and other factors.

If decisions are to be consistent with the intentions of the decision makers, the information used in the decision process must be *reliable*. Unreliable information can cause inefficient use of resources to the detriment of society and to the decision makers themselves. In the lending decision example, assume that the bank makes the loan on the basis of misleading financial statements and the borrower company is ultimately unable to repay. As a result, the bank has lost both the principal and the interest. In addition, another company that could have used the funds effectively was deprived of the money.

As society becomes more complex, there is an increased likelihood that unreliable information will be provided to decision makers. There are several reasons for this: remoteness of information, voluminous data, and the existence of complex exchange transactions.

Remoteness of Information

In the modern world it is virtually impossible for a decision maker to have much firsthand knowledge about the organization with which he does business. He therefore has to rely upon information provided by others. Whenever that information is provided by someone whose goals are inconsistent with those of the decision maker, the information will at times be *biased* in favor of the provider of the information. The reason could be an honest optimism about future events or an intentional emphasis designed to influence users in a certain manner. In either case, the result is a misstatement of information. For example, in a lending decision where the borrower provides financial statements to the lender, there is considerable likelihood that the statements will be biased in favor of the borrower to enhance his chance of obtaining the loan. The misstatement could be in the form of outright incorrect dollar amounts being included in the statements or inadequate or incomplete disclosures of information.

Voluminous Data

As organizations become larger, the volume of their exchange transactions increases. This increases the likelihood that improperly recorded information will be included in the records—perhaps buried in a large amount of other information. For example, if a check by a large governmental agency in payment of a vendor's invoice is overstated by two hundred dollars, there is a fairly good chance it will not be uncovered unless the agency has instituted reasonably complex procedures to check for this type of error. If a large number of minor errors remain undiscovered, the combined total could be significant.

Complex Exchange Transactions

In the past few decades, exchange transactions between organizations have become increasingly complex and hence more difficult to properly record. For example, the correct accounting treatment of the trade-in of manufacturing equipment or the replacement of the roof of a building poses relatively difficult and important problems. Even more difficult is the proper combining and disclosing of the results of operations of subsidiaries in different industries, or the calculation of earnings per share under Accounting Principles Board Opinion No. 15 (APB 15) when there are convertible bonds or other similar financing arrangements.

Need for Independent Verification

As a means of overcoming the problem of unreliable information, the decision maker must develop a method of assuring himself that the information is sufficiently reliable for his decisions. In doing this, he must weigh the cost of obtaining more reliable information against the expected benefits.

A common way to obtain such reliable information is to have some type of verification (*audit*) performed by independent persons. The audited information is then used in the decision-making process on the assumption that it is reasonably complete, accurate, and unbiased. If more than one decision maker uses a particular type of information, it is usually less expensive to have someone perform the audit for all of the users than to have each user verify the information individually. However, even if only one user relies on the information, it is desirable to have someone with special skills perform the audit function.

NATURE OF AUDITING

Auditing Defined

Auditing is an integrated process of accumulating and evaluating evidence by a competent independent person about quantifiable information of a specific economic entity for the purpose of determining and reporting upon the degree of correspondence between the quantifiable information and established criteria.

This definition includes several key words and phrases that are worth examining briefly at this time. Each of these terms is analyzed more extensively in later chapters. For ease of understanding, the terms are discussed in a different order than they are included in the definition.

Determining the Degree of Correspondence between Quantifiable Information and Established Criteria

Before an auditor can provide useful information to decision makers, it is necessary to have the information in a *verifiable form* and there must be some standards (*criteria*) by which he can determine whether the information is proper. The quantifiable information can and does take many different forms. It is possible to audit such things as canceled checks and vendor's invoices, the amount of time it takes for an employee to complete an assigned task, the total cost of a government construction contract, and an individual's tax return. In each case there must be some criteria to determine whether the quantifiable information is stated in an appropriate manner. For example, in auditing a vendor's invoice for the acquisition of raw materials, it is possible to determine whether materials of the quantity and stated description were actually received, whether the proper raw material was acquired considering the production needs of the company, or whether the price charged for the goods was reasonable. Naturally, the criteria used depend upon the objectives of the audit.

A Specific Economic Entity

Whenever an audit is conducted, it is necessary to set boundaries to clarify the scope of the auditor's responsibility. The primary method involves defining the *economic entity* and the *time period*. In most instances the economic entity is also a legal entity such as a corporation, unit of government, partnership, or proprietorship. But in some types of audits the entity is defined as a division, a department, or even an individual. The time period for conducting an audit is typically one year, but there are also audits for a month, a quarter, several years, and in some cases the lifetime of an entity.

It is not possible to evaluate whether quantifiable information corresponds to established criteria until the economic entity is defined, since one of the primary criteria for evaluating information is whether it is proper for the entity being audited. A simple example is the sole proprietorship, in which the entity under audit is the owner's business. A proper business expense in this situation would be repairs to equipment or the acquisition of raw materials. On the other hand, if the proprietor used funds from the business to buy food for his family or took them on a vacation to the Bahamas, the expenditures would not likely be a proper business expense.

Accumulating and Evaluating Evidence

Evidence can be defined as any information used by the auditor to determine whether the quantifiable information being audited is stated in accordance with the established criteria. Evidence takes many different forms, including oral testimony of the auditee (client), written communication with outsiders, and observations by the auditor. It is important to obtain a sufficient quality and volume of evidence in an audit to satisfy the audit objectives. The process of determining the amount of evidence necessary and evaluating whether the quantifiable information corresponds to the established criteria is a critical part of every audit. It is the primary subject of this book.

Integrated Process

The term *integrated* is included here to emphasize that every part of the audit is related to some other part. The emphasis throughout this text is on the most significant interrelationships.

A *process,* as the term is used here, denotes a continuous series of actions leading to some kind of a conclusion. A good audit is a systematic, well-planned series of steps leading to a logical conclusion about the correspondence of the quantifiable information to the established criteria.

Competent Independent Person

Before audited information can be regarded as reliable, the auditor must be *qualified* to understand the criteria in use, and he must have the *competence* to know the types and amount of evidence to accumulate to reach the proper conclusion after the evidence has been examined.

It is also necessary that the auditor have an *independent mental attitude.* It does little good to have a competent person who is biased performing the evidence accumulation when unbiased information is needed for decision making. Independence is not an absolute concept by any means; there are different degrees of independence. For example, even though an auditor is paid a fee by the company he audits, he may still be sufficiently independent to conduct audits that can be relied upon by users if he is not also an employee of the company.

In addition to actually being independent, the auditor must also be perceived to be independent *(independence in appearance).* Even if the auditor maintains and carries out all of his responsibilities properly, users will not be satisfied if they believe the auditor is biased.

Reporting

The final stage in the audit process is the *audit report*—the communication of the findings of the audit to users. Reports differ in nature, but in all cases they must inform readers of the degree of correspondence between quantifiable information and established criteria. Reports also differ in form and can vary from a highly technical one of the type usually associated with financial statements to a simple oral report in situations where an audit is conducted for a particular individual. The form and content of any particular report will depend upon the nature of the audit, its purpose, its findings, and the needs of the decision makers who receive it.

Distinction between Auditing and Accounting

Many financial statement users and members of the general public confuse *auditing* and *accounting*. The confusion results because most auditing is concerned with accounting information and many auditors have considerable expertise in accounting matters. The confusion is increased by giving the title "certified public accountant" to individuals who are primarily responsible for performing the audit function.

Accounting is the process of recording, classifying, and summarizing economic events in a logical manner for the purpose of providing financial information for decision making. The function of accounting, to an entity and to society as a whole, is to provide certain types of quantitative information that management and other recipients of the information can use to make decisions. To provide relevant information, accountants must have a thorough understanding of the principles and rules that provide the basis for preparing the accounting information. In addition, accountants must develop a system to make sure that the entity's economic events are properly recorded on a timely basis and at a reasonable cost.

In *auditing* accounting data, the concern is with determining whether the recorded accounting information for the entity properly reflects the economic events that occurred during the accounting period. Since the accounting rules are the criteria for evaluating whether the accounting information is properly recorded, any auditor involved with accounting data must also thoroughly understand the rules. In the context of the audit of financial statements, these are generally accepted accounting principles. Throughout this text the assumption is made that the reader has already studied generally accepted accounting principles.

In addition to understanding accounting, the auditor must also possess expertise in the accumulation and interpretation of audit evidence. This skill is the major characteristic that distinguishes auditors from accountants. Determining the proper audit procedures, sample size, particular items to examine, timing of the tests, and evaluating the results are problems unique to the auditor.

TYPES OF AUDITS

The three types of audits discussed in this section are the audit of financial statements, the compliance audit, and the operational audit.

Audit of Financial Statements

An *audit of financial statements* is conducted to determine whether the *overall* financial statements—which are the quantifiable information being verified—are stated in accordance with specified criteria. Normally, the criteria are generally accepted accounting principles, although it is also common to conduct audits of financial statements prepared using the cash basis or some other basis of accounting appropriate for the organization. The financial statements most commonly included are the statement of financial position, the income statement, and the statement of changes of financial position, including accompanying footnotes.

The underlying assumption in auditing financial statements is that they will be used by different groups for different purposes. Therefore, it is more efficient to have one audit firm perform an audit and draw conclusions that can be relied upon by all users than to have each user perform his own audit. If any individual user feels that the general audit does not provide sufficient information for his purposes, he has the option of obtaining more data, but of course there might be an additional audit cost to him. For example, a general audit of a business may provide sufficient accounting information for a banker who is considering making a loan to the company, but a corporation considering a merger with that business may also wish to know the replacement cost of fixed assets and other information relevant to the decision.

Although auditing of financial statements is now restricted primarily to financial statements based on *historical costs,* there have been recommendations from many sources to expand the audit function to cover other financial information. One type frequently mentioned is *forecast financial statements.* A major problem in auditing forecasts is establishing criteria to determine whether they are properly stated. It would certainly be more difficult for an auditor to determine whether forecast information was properly stated than it would be for him to determine this for historical information. On the other hand, audited forecast financial statements may be much more useful for decision making than historical information and therefore worth the effort and risks involved. Other areas where the audit function might be expanded include *all* financial information in published annual reports that is not currently audited, information on the outstanding *backlog of sales* and *quarterly historical statements.*

Compliance Audit

The purpose of a *compliance audit* is to determine whether the auditee is following specific procedures or rules set down by some higher authority. A compliance audit for a private business could include determining whether accounting personnel are following the procedures prescribed by the company controller, reviewing wage rates for compliance with minimum wage laws, or examining contractual agreements with bankers and other lenders to be sure the company is complying with legal requirements. In the audit of governmental units such as school districts, there is increased compliance auditing due to extensive regulation by higher government authorities. In virtually every private and not-for-profit organization, there are prescribed policies, contractual agreements, and legal requirements that may call for compliance auditing.

Results of compliance audits are generally reported to someone within the organizational unit being audited rather than to a broad spectrum of users. Management, as opposed to outside users, is the primary group concerned with the extent of compliance with certain prescribed procedures and regulations. Hence, a significant portion of all work of this type is done by auditors employed by the organizational units themselves. There are exceptions to this. Whenever an organization wants to determine whether individuals or organizations who are obligated to follow its requirements are actually complying, the auditor is employed by the organization issuing the requirements. An example is the auditing of taxpayers for compliance with the federal tax laws—the auditor is hired by the government to audit the taxpayers' records.

Operational Audit

An *operational audit* is a review of any part of an organization's operating procedures and methods for the purpose of evaluating efficiency and effectiveness. At the completion of an operational audit, recommendations to management for improving operations are normally expected.

The conduct of an operational audit and the reported results are normally less well defined than for either compliance or financial statement audits. Efficiency and effectiveness of operations are far more difficult to evaluate objectively than compliance or the presentation of financial statements in accordance with generally accepted accounting principles.

Due to the many different areas in which operational effectiveness can be evaluated, it is impossible to characterize the conduct of a typical operational audit. In one organization the auditor might evaluate the relevancy and sufficiency of the information used by management in making decisions to acquire new fixed assets, while in a different organization he might evaluate the efficiency of the paper flow in processing sales. In operational auditing, the reviews are not limited to accounting. They can include the evaluation of organizational structure, computer operations, production methods, marketing, and any other area where the auditor is qualified.

Establishing criteria for evaluating the quantifiable information in an operational audit is an extremely *subjective* matter. In practice, operational auditors are usually more concerned with making recommendations for improving performance than with attempting to assess the effectiveness of existing performance. In this sense, operational auditing is more similar to management consulting than to what is generally regarded as auditing.

TYPES OF AUDITORS

In this section the four most widely known types of auditors are discussed briefly. They are: certified public accountants, general accounting office auditors, internal revenue agents, and internal auditors.

Certified Public Accountants

Certified public accountants (CPAs) have as their primary responsibility the performance of the audit function on published financial statements of all publicly traded companies and most other reasonably large companies. Due to the important role of published financial statements in the U.S. economy, as well as businessmen's and statement users' familiarity with these statements, it is common to use the terms *auditor* and *CPA* synonymously even though there are many different types of auditors.

Because of their responsibility for the audit of financial statements, it is essential that CPAs have a high level of *independence* and *competence.* Independence is important to encourage auditors to remain unbiased in drawing conclusions about the financial statements. Both independence and competence in conducting an audit are necessary to enable users to rely upon the statements. The large number of CPAs in the United States makes it impossible for users to evaluate the independence and competence of individual CPAs. Consequently, an organizational structure for CPAs has emerged that encourages, but certainly does not guarantee, both independence and competence.

The organizational form used by CPA firms is that of a partnership or a professional corporation. In a typical firm organized as a partnership, several CPAs join together to practice as partners, offering auditing and other services to interested parties. The partners normally hire professional staff persons to assist them in their work. These assistants are, or aspire to become, CPAs.

Thus, the organizational hierarchy in a typical CPA firm includes partners, managers, supervisors, seniors or in-charge auditors, and assistants, with a new employee usually starting as an assistant and spending two or three years in each classification before achieving partner status. The titles of the positions vary from firm to firm, but the structure is basically the same in all firms. When we refer in this text to the *auditor,* we mean the particular person performing some aspect of an audit. It is common to have one or more auditors from each level on larger engagements.

The existence of a separate entity to perform audits encourages independence by avoiding an employee-employer relationship between the CPAs and their clients. A separate entity also enables CPA firms to become sufficiently large to prevent any one client from representing a significant portion of a partner's total income and thereby endangering the firm's independence. Competence is encouraged by having a large number of professionals with related interests associated in one firm, which facilitates a professional attitude and makes continuing professional education more feasible.

Competence is also encouraged by each state's requiring that an individual pass a national standardized examination to qualify as a CPA. The two and one-half day written examination is prepared and graded by the American Institute of Certified Public Accountants (AICPA), the national professional organization. Since the examination is a one-time-only hurdle that must be passed by practitioners, rather than a periodic requirement, it does not ensure continuing professional competence. But an individual who passes it does demonstrate a certain level of competence at the entry level. Passing the CPA examination is also indicative of an ability to grasp complex accounting and auditing concepts. In addition to the CPA examination, many states require qualifying experience of two or three years in the profession before an individual becomes a CPA.

Continued professional education is encouraged by the AICPA, the individual state professional organizations of CPAs, and most CPA firms. Although only some states currently require continuing education for retaining certification, an increasing percentage of the members of the profession take part in development programs each year as a means of maintaining professional competence. Many members feel that continuing professional development should be required of all practicing CPAs.

Although the organizational form of CPA firms, the requirement for a CPA certificate, and continuing education programs were developed primarily because of CPAs' responsibility for the audit of published financial statements, CPAs are also actively involved in compliance and operational audits and other services to clients. The latter include such diverse activities as counseling on tax matters, providing assistance in installing computer systems, and performing executive searches. The reason for providing the other services is that the partners desire to increase income and the clients desire additional services that CPAs are competent to perform.

General Accounting Office Auditors

The United States General Accounting Office (GAO) is a nonpartisan agency in the legislative branch of the federal government. The GAO, which is headed by the controller general, reports to and is responsible solely to Congress. The primary responsibility of the audit staff is to conduct the audit function for Congress.

Many of the GAO's audit responsibilities are basically the same as the

CPA's. Much of the financial information prepared by various government agencies is audited by the GAO before it is submitted to Congress. Since the authority for expenditures and receipts of governmental agencies is defined by law, there is considerable emphasis on compliance in these audits.

An increasing portion of the GAO's audit efforts has been devoted to evaluating the *operational efficiency and effectiveness* of various federal programs. A typical example is the evaluation of the computer operations of a particular governmental unit. The auditor can review and evaluate any aspect of the computer system, but he is likely to emphasize the adequacy of the equipment, the efficiency of the operations, the adequacy and usefulness of the output, and similar matters, with the objective of identifying means of providing the same services for less cost.

Due to the immense size of many federal agencies and the similarity of their operations, the GAO has made significant advances in developing better methods of auditing. For example, the use of statistical sampling and computer auditing techniques has been widespread and highly sophisticated for several years.

In many states experience as a GAO auditor qualifies as experience required to become a CPA. In those states, if an individual passes the CPA examination and fulfills the experience stipulations for becoming a GAO auditor, he may then obtain a CPA certificate.

As a result of their great responsibility for auditing the expenditures of the federal government, their use of advanced auditing concepts, their eligibility to be CPAs, and their opportunities for performing operational audits, GAO auditors are highly regarded in the auditing profession.

Internal Revenue Agents

The Internal Revenue Service (IRS), under the direction of the commissioner of Internal Revenue, has as its responsibility the enforcement of the *federal tax laws* as they have been defined by Congress and interpreted by the courts. A major responsibility of the IRS is to audit the returns of taxpayers to determine whether they have complied with the tax laws. The auditors who perform these examinations are referred to as internal revenue agents. These audits can be regarded as solely compliance audits.

It might seem that the audit of returns for compliance with the federal tax laws would be a simple and straightforward problem, but nothing could be further from the truth. The tax laws are highly complicated, and there are hundreds of volumes of interpretations. The tax returns being audited vary from the simple returns of individuals who work for only one employer and take the standard tax deduction to the highly complex returns of multinational corporations. There are taxation problems involving individual taxpayers, gift taxes, estate taxes, corporate taxes, trusts, and so forth. An auditor involved in any of these areas must have considerable knowledge to conduct an audit.

Internal Auditors

Internal auditors are employed by private industry to audit for management much as the GAO does for Congress. The internal audit group in some large firms includes over a hundred persons and typically reports directly to the president or another high executive officer.

Internal auditors' responsibilities vary considerably, depending upon the employer. Some internal audit staffs consist of only one or two employees who may spend most of their time doing routine compliance auditing. Other internal audit staffs consist of numerous employees who have diverse responsibilities including many outside the accounting area. In recent years many internal auditors have become involved in operational auditing or have developed expertise in evaluating computer systems.

The major difference between internal auditors and CPAs is the degree of independence. To operate effectively, an internal auditor must be independent of the line functions in an organization, but he cannot be independent of the entity so long as an employer-employee relationship exists. Internal auditors can provide management with valuable information for making decisions concerning effective operation of its business. Users from outside of the entity are unlikely to want to rely on information audited by internal auditors due to their lack of independence.

AUDIT EVIDENCE DECISIONS

A major judgment problem facing every auditor is determining the appropriate *amount of evidence* to accumulate. This problem exists for certified public accountants attesting to financial statements, internal revenue agents auditing tax returns, internal auditors evaluating the efficiency of an operating unit—in fact, for any auditor in any audit situation.

Auditors must make a decision about the appropriate amount of evidence mainly because of the prohibitive cost of examining and evaluating all available evidence. It is necessary to restrict the evidence accumulated to an amount sufficient to provide reasonable satisfaction that the information being reported upon is consistent with the audit report being issued. For example, in an audit of financial statements of most organizations it is impossible for the CPA to examine all canceled checks, vendor's invoices, documents evidencing the receipt of goods, sales invoices, shipping documents, customer orders, payroll time cards, and the many other types of documents and records.

The auditor's evidence accumulation process can be broken into four interrelated *decisions:*

1. The audit procedures to use
2. The sample size to select for a given procedure
3. The particular items to select from the population
4. The appropriate time to perform the procedures

Audit Procedures

An *audit procedure* is the description of a particular type of audit evidence that is to be obtained at some time during the audit. For example, such evidence as counting the physical inventory, comparing the canceled checks with the cash disbursements journal for proper payee and amount, and examining a shipping document for proper approval are all audit procedures.

In using audit procedures, it is common to spell them out in sufficiently specific terms to permit their use as instructions during the audit. For example, the following is an audit procedure for the verification of cash receipts:

> Obtain a listing of daily incoming cash receipts and compare the amount with the postings in the cash receipts journal.

The list of audit procedures for an entire audit is called the *audit program*. Generally, the program also states the sample size and timing of the procedures.

Sample Size

Once an audit procedure is selected, it is possible to vary the sample size from one to all the items in the population being tested. The decision of how many items to test must be made by the auditor for each audit procedure. The sample size for any given procedure is likely to vary from audit to audit and procedure to procedure.

The Particular Items To Select

After the sample size has been determined for a particular audit procedure, it is still necessary to decide upon the particular items to examine. If the auditor decides, for example, to select two hundred canceled checks from a population of ten thousand for comparison with the cash disbursements journal, he can use several different methods to select the specific checks to be examined. Three possible methods are: select a week and examine the first two hundred checks, select the two hundred checks with the largest amounts, or select the checks randomly.

Timing

Since an audit of financial statements normally covers a period of time such as a year, the auditor could start to accumulate evidence soon after the beginning of the accounting period. Because an audit is usually not completed until several weeks or months after the end of the period, the timing of audit procedures can vary from early in the accounting period to long after it has ended. In the audit of financial statements, the client normally desires that the audit be completed from one to three months after year-end, but it is common for internal revenue agents to conduct audits several years after the taxpayer's tax return has been filed.

TYPES OF AUDIT EVIDENCE

There are seven types of evidence used in conducting audits. These are listed below and defined and discussed in this section:

1. Physical examination
2. Confirmation
3. Documentation
4. Observation
5. Inquiries of the client
6. Mechanical accuracy
7. Comparisons and relationships

The appropriate type of evidence to select for a given situation depends upon the nature of the *information being verified,* the *applicability* of the evidence to that information, the *availability* of other types of evidence, and the *cost.*

Audit procedures are distinguished from types of evidence in that procedures are the detailed instructions for the collection of a particular type of evidence. For example, an audit procedure for one type of audit evidence, physical examination, might instruct the auditor to count all marketable securities on hand on a specified date.

Physical Examination

Physical examination is the inspection or count by the auditor of a tangible asset. This type of evidence is most often associated with inventory and cash, but it is also applicable to the verification of securities, notes receivable, and tangible fixed assets. The distinction between the physical examination of assets, such as marketable securities and cash, and the examination of documents, such as canceled checks and sales documents, is important for auditing purposes. If the object being examined, such as a sales invoice, has no inherent value, the evidence is called *documentation.* For example, before a check is signed, it is a document; after it is signed, it becomes an asset; and when it is canceled, it becomes a document again. Technically, then, physical examination of the check can only occur while the check is an asset.

Physical examination, which is a direct means of verifying that an asset actually exists, is regarded as one of the most reliable and useful types of audit evidence. Generally, physical examination is an objective means of ascertaining both the quantity and the description of the asset. In some cases it is also a useful method for evaluating an asset's condition or quality. On the other hand, physical examination is not sufficient evidence to verify that existing assets are owned by the client. And in many cases the auditor is not qualified to judge such qualitative factors as obsolescence or authenticity.

Confirmation

Confirmation describes the receipt of a written response from an independent third party verifying the accuracy of information that was requested by the auditor. Since confirmations come from sources independent of the client, they are a highly regarded and often used type of evidence. However, confirmations are relatively costly to obtain and may cause some inconvenience to those asked to supply them. Therefore they are not used in every instance in which they are applicable.

Whether or not confirmations should be used depends on the reliability needs of the situation as well as the alternative evidence available. Traditionally, confirmations are not used to verify individual transactions between organizations, such as sales transactions, because the auditor can use documents to determine the adequacy of the client's system of recording information. Similarly, confirmations are seldom used in the audit of fixed asset additions because these can be adequately verified by documentation and physical examination.

Whenever practical and reasonable, the confirmation of a sample of accounts receivable is *required* of CPAs. This requirement, which is imposed by the AICPA, exists because accounts receivable usually represent a significant balance on the financial statements, and confirmations are a highly reliable means of verifying the fairness of the balance.

Although confirmation is not required for any account other than accounts receivable, this type of evidence is useful in verifying many types of information. The major types of information that are frequently confirmed, along with the source of the confirmation, are indicated in Figure 1-1 on page 16.

To be considered reliable evidence, confirmations must be controlled by the auditor from the time their preparation is completed until they are returned. If the client controls the preparation of the confirmation, performs the mailing, or receives the responses, the auditor has lost control; hence independence is lost, and the reliability of the evidence is reduced.

Documentation

Documentation, which is commonly referred to as *vouching,* is the auditor's examination of the client's documents and records to substantiate the information that is or should be included in the financial

FIGURE 1-1

INFORMATION FREQUENTLY CONFIRMED

Information Confirmed	*Confirmation Obtained from*
Assets	
Cash in bank	Bank
Accounts receivable	Debtor
Notes receivable	Maker
Owned inventory out on consignment	Consignee
Inventory held in public warehouses	Public warehouse
Cash surrender value of life insurance	Insurance company
Liabilities	
Accounts payable	Creditor
Notes payable	Lender
Advances from customers	Customer
Mortgages payable	Mortgagor
Bonds payable	Bondholder
Owner's Equity	
Shares outstanding	Registrar and transfer agent
Other Information	
Insurance coverage	Insurance company
Contingent liabilities	Company attorneys, bank, etc.
Bond indenture agreements	Bondholder
Collateral held by creditors	Creditor

statements. The documents examined by the auditor are the records used by the client to provide information for conducting its business in an organized manner. Since each transaction in the client's organization is normally supported by at least one document, there is a large volume of this type of evidence available for the auditor's use. For example, the client normally retains a customer order, a shipping document, and a duplicate sales invoice for each sales transaction. These same documents are useful evidence for verification by the auditor of the accuracy of the client's records for sales transactions. Documentation is a widely used form of evidence in every audit because it is usually readily available to the auditor at a relatively low cost. Sometimes it is the only reasonable type of evidence available.

Documents can be conveniently classified as internal and external. An *internal document* is one that has been prepared and used within the client's organization and is retained without its ever going to an outside party such as a customer or a vendor. Examples of internal documents include duplicate sales invoices, employees' time reports, and inventory receiving reports. An *external document* is one that has been in the hands of someone outside the client's organization who is a party to the transaction being documented, but which is either currently in the hands of the client or readily accessible. In some cases, external documents originate outside the client's organization and end up in the hands of the client. Examples of this type of external document are vendor's invoices, canceled notes payable, and insurance policies. In other cases, such as canceled checks, the documents originate with the client, go to an outsider, and are finally returned to the client.

The primary determinant of the auditor's willingness to accept a document as reliable evidence is whether it is an internal or an external document. Since external documents have been in the hands of both the client and another party to the transaction, there is some indication that both members are in agreement about the information and the conditions stated on the document. External documents are therefore regarded as more reliable evidence than internal ones.

Observation

Observation is the use of the senses to assess certain activities. Throughout the audit there are many opportunities to exercise the sensory mechanisms of sight, hearing, touch, and smell to evaluate a wide range of things. For example, the auditor may tour the plant to obtain a general impression of the client's facilities; he may observe whether inventory has rust to evaluate whether it is likely to be obsolete; and he may watch individuals perform accounting tasks to determine whether the person assigned a responsibility is actually doing it. Observation is rarely sufficient by itself—it is necessary to follow up initial impressions with other kinds of corroborative evidence. Nevertheless, observation is useful in most parts of the audit.

Inquiries of the Client

Inquiry is the obtaining of *written* or *oral* information from the client in response to questions from the auditor. Although considerable evidence is obtained from the client through inquiry, it cannot usually be regarded as conclusive because it is not from an independent source and may be biased in the client's favor. Therefore, when the auditor obtains evidence through inquiry, it is normally necessary to obtain further corroborating evidence by other procedures. As an illustration, when the auditor wants to obtain information about the client's method of recording and controlling of accounting transactions, he usually begins by asking the client how the accounting system operates. Later, he performs tests of the system to determine if the transactions are recorded and authorized in the manner stated.

Mechanical Accuracy

Testing of *mechanical accuracy* involves rechecking a sample of the computations and transfers of information made by the client during the period under audit. The rechecking of computations consists of testing the client's arithmetical accuracy. It includes such procedures as extending sales invoices and inventory, adding journals and subsidiary ledgers, and checking the calculation of depreciation expense and prepaid expenses. The rechecking of transfers of information consists of tracing amounts to be confident that when the same information is included in more than one place, it is recorded at the same amount each time. For example, the auditor normally makes limited tests to ascertain that the information in the sales journal has been included for the proper customer and at the correct amount in the subsidiary accounts receivable ledger and accurately summarized in the general ledger.

Comparisons and Relationships

Comparisons and *relationships* are useful primarily as a means of isolating accounts or transactions that should be intensively investigated. An example of this type of evidence is to compare the current period's total repair expense with previous years and to investigate the difference to determine the cause of the increase or decrease. The auditor's own calculations generally comprise the information used for comparisons and relationships. The tests should be performed early in the audit to aid in determining which audit areas should be more thoroughly investigated, and reviewed again at the end of the audit to corroborate the tentative conclusions reached on the basis of the other evidence.

OVERVIEW OF THE AUDIT PROCESS

This section of the chapter is an overview of the *audit of financial statements* by CPAs. It is included to provide a frame of reference for understanding the entire audit process. A major problem in the study of auditing is the tendency to become so involved in individual parts and complexities that it is difficult to maintain a proper perspective about the overall investigation and the general audit process.

Overall Objective

The overall objective of the ordinary audit of financial statements by CPAs is to determine whether the statements are presented in accordance with generally accepted accounting principles applied on a basis consistent with that of the preceding year. The auditor evaluates whether the financial statements are fairly presented by accumulating audit evidence in a thorough and conscientious manner. When, on the basis of adequate evidence, he reaches the conclusion that the financial statements are unlikely to mislead a prudent user, he gives an audit opinion on their fair presentation and associates his opinion with the statements. If facts subsequent to the issuance of the statements indicate that they were actually not fairly presented, the auditor is likely to have to demonstrate to the courts or regulatory agents that he conducted the audit in a proper manner and drew reasonable conclusions. Although the auditor is not an insurer or a guarantor of the fairness of the presentations in the statements, he has considerable responsibility for notifying users as to whether or not the statements are properly stated. If he believes the statements are not fairly presented or if he is unable to reach a conclusion because of insufficient evidence or prevailing conditions, he has the responsibility for notifying the users of the statements through an auditor's report.

Audit conclusions about whether financial statements are fairly presented are not reached in a precisely defined manner. Instead, evidence is obtained and conclusions are reached by bits and pieces. The auditor starts with relatively little information about whether the client's statements are fairly presented. He has the results of previous audits on a repeat engagement and impressions about integrity and competency, but little else. As the audit proceeds, each additional piece of evidence either confirms or contradicts his initial impression. At the completion of the audit, the auditor should have strong beliefs about the fairness of the presentation, which will lead to his opinion. Even though audit conclusions are not reached in a precisely defined manner, the audit tests should be carefully designed and organized to ensure their effective and timely completion.

Obtain a General Understanding of the Client and Its Circumstances

Each audit is in one sense a replication of all other audits and in another sense a unique experience. Every audit is the same in the sense that a minimum amount of information must be obtained and evaluated and certain audit procedures are carried out on practically every audit engagement. On the other hand, such audit procedures as the sample size, the particular items in the population to select for testing, and the timing of the tests depend upon the unique characteristics of the client. To identify the unique characteristics that affect the accumulation of evidence, the auditor must understand the client and its circumstances.

The general understanding of the client includes four general categories of information:

1. *Background information for the audit.* Background information enables the auditor to better understand the client's industry and the peculiarities of the business.

2. *Analytical tests.* Analytical tests include the calculations and comparisons by the auditor of ratios and trends in the client's records as a test of reasonableness of the account balances.

3. *Information concerning the client's legal obligations.* The legal commitments of the client, including such items as government regulations, the corporate charter and bylaws, corporate minutes, and contracts of all types, must be understood before it is possible to evaluate whether the financial statements are fairly stated.

4. *Information for evaluation of the possibility of management involvement in fraud.* In recent years there has been an increasing incidence

of involvement by management in fraudulent activities. These include the massive theft of company assets and the issuance of intentionally misleading financial statements. A well-known example is the Equity Funding fraud. An evaluation of the environmental factors affecting the predictability of these frauds is useful in helping the auditor decide upon the proper evidence to accumulate.

The process of obtaining a general understanding of the client and its circumstances is studied in depth in Chapter 4. The information described above must be gathered as early in the audit as possible to enable the auditor to decide on the evidence to accumulate. As the audit progresses, a clearer understanding of the client will gradually emerge.

Study and Evaluate the System of Internal Control

One of the most widely accepted concepts in the theory and practice of auditing is the importance of the client's accounting system (system of internal control) in generating reliable financial information. If the auditor is convinced the client has an excellent system, which includes controls for providing reliable data and for safeguarding assets and records, the amount of audit evidence to be accumulated can be significantly less than if the system is not adequate. On the other hand, in some instances the controls may be so inadequate as to preclude conducting an effective audit.

The first step in the study and evaluation of the client's system of internal control is to *determine how it operates*. This is done by means of the auditor's review of organizational charts and procedural manuals, by discussions with client personnel, and by completing internal control questionnaires and flowcharts.

The second step is to make a *preliminary evaluation* of whether the system has been designed to effectively accomplish the objectives of good control, including the prevention of errors. This evaluation involves identifying specific controls that provide substance to the system which the auditor may be willing to rely upon to reduce certain audit tests, and identifying areas of the system where errors are more likely to occur due to the absence of controls. This process is referred to by auditors as *identifying the strengths and weaknesses of the system*. The study and evaluation of internal control is covered in general terms in Chapter 5 and in detail in several other chapters as a part of the study of different audit areas. The effect of electronic data processing on the system of internal control and how differences in controls affect the audit are discussed in Chapter 12.

Test the Effectiveness of the System

Where the auditor has identified an effective control, or strength, in the system, he is entitled to rely on this control to enhance the reliability of financial information. Hence he can reduce the extent to which the accuracy of that information must be validated through the accumulation of evidence related directly to it. To justify this reliance, however, the auditor must test the effectiveness of the controls. The procedures involved in this type of testing are commonly referred to as either *tests of compliance* or *tests of transactions.* Tests of transactions for various types of controls are studied throughout the text. Specifically, tests of controls in the area of sales and collections are studied in Chapters 8 and 9, payroll and personnel in Chapter 13, acquisitions and payments in Chapter 14, inventory and warehousing in Chapter 16, and capital acquisitions and repayments in Chapter 17.

Directly Test the Financial Statement Accounts

The ending balances in the balance sheet and income statement accounts are verified by physical observation, confirmation, documentation, and other types of evidence. Examples include the confirmation of accounts and notes receivable, physical observation of inventory, and the examination of vendor's statements for accounts payable. These tests of ending balances are essential to the conduct of the audit because for the most part the evidence is obtained from a source independent of the client, and thus is considered to be of high quality.

There is a close relationship between the general review of the client's circumstances, the results of the evaluation and tests of the system of internal control, and the direct tests of the financial statement accounts. If the auditor has obtained a reasonable level of confidence about the fair presentation of the financial statements through the general review of internal control and tests of its effectiveness, the direct tests can be significantly decreased. In all instances, however, some tests of the financial statement accounts are necessary. The direct test of the balance sheet is discussed primarily in Chapters 10 and 11 and Chapters 15 through 18.

As part of conducting an audit, *working papers* are prepared to provide a frame of reference for planning the audit and to demonstrate that an adequate audit was completed. The working papers include a permanent file, which contains information and records of continuing importance on repeat engagements, and current working papers pertaining to the current year's audit. Current working papers are maintained by most firms for at least ten years before being destroyed. Working papers are studied in Chapter 7.

Complete the Audit, Combine the Results of All of the Tests, and Draw Conclusions

In addition to direct tests of the financial statement accounts, the auditor must carry out such procedures as testing for material subsequent events and reviewing the working papers.

After the auditor has completed all the procedures, it is necessary to combine the information obtained in some manner to reach an *overall conclusion* as to whether the financial statements are fairly presented. This is a highly subjective process which relies heavily upon the auditor's professional judgment. In practice the auditor continuously combines the information obtained as he proceeds through the audit. The final combination is only a summation at the completion of the engagement. The combining of information for making evidence decisions is studied in Chapters 3 and 19.

Issue an Audit Report

At the completion of the audit, the CPA must issue an audit report which accompanies the client's published financial statements. The report must meet well-defined technical requirements that are affected by the scope of the audit and the nature of the findings. Audit reports are studied briefly in Chapter 2 and extensively in Chapter 20.

Summary

The overview of the audit process and the most important concepts discussed up to this point are presented schematically in Figure 1-2.

REVIEW QUESTIONS

1. Discuss the major factors in today's society that have made the need for independent audits much greater than it was fifty years ago.
2. In providing information to a bank for a loan, list three types of information, other than financial statements, that might affect the loan officer's decision to grant the loan. How could the loan officer verify each type of information?
3. Under what circumstances is the loan officer likely to grant a loan to a company on the basis of financial statements that have not been audited by an auditor who is independent of the organization requesting the loan?
4. List five specific quantifiable events that an auditor can verify, and state specific criteria for evaluating the events.
5. How would the conduct of an audit of a medium-sized company be affected by the company's being a small part of a large conglomerate as compared with its being a separate entity?
6. What methods do auditors use to obtain a better understanding of the unique characteristics of the client?
7. Explain why the auditor must study and evaluate the system of internal control and test the effectiveness of the system as a part of the ordinary audit.
8. Distinguish between tests of the effectiveness of the system of internal control and direct tests of the ending balances in the financial statements.
9. Distinguish between internal documentation and external documentation as audit evidence and give three examples of each.
10. Explain the importance of comparisons and relationships as evidence in determining the fair presentation of the financial statements.

FIGURE 1-2

AN OVERVIEW OF THE AUDIT PROCESS

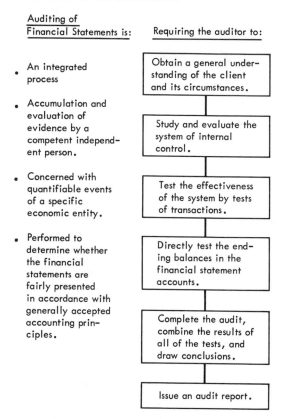

Auditing of
Financial Statements is:

- An integrated process

- Accumulation and evaluation of evidence by a competent independent person.

- Concerned with quantifiable events of a specific economic entity.

- Performed to determine whether the financial statements are fairly presented in accordance with generally accepted accounting principles.

Requiring the auditor to:

Obtain a general understanding of the client and its circumstances.

Study and evaluate the system of internal control.

Test the effectiveness of the system by tests of transactions.

Directly test the ending balances in the financial statement accounts.

Complete the audit, combine the results of all of the tests, and draw conclusions.

Issue an audit report.

11. Distinguish between the audit of financial statements for a governmental agency and accounting for the economic events of a for-profit company.
12. In the conduct of audits of financial statements it would be a serious breach of responsibility if the auditor did not thoroughly understand accounting. On the other hand, many competent accountants do not have an understanding of the auditing process. What causes this difference?
13. List the four major audit evidence decisions that must be made on every audit.
14. List five audit procedures the auditor could use in the verification of accounts receivable.
15. List the seven types of audit evidence included in this chapter and give two examples of each type.
16. Distinguish between confirmation and inquiries of the client. When should each of these be used?
17. What are the major differences in the scope of the audit responsibilities for CPAs, GAO auditors, IRS agents, and internal auditors?
18. What major characteristics of the organization and conduct of CPA firms permit them to fulfill their social function competently and independently?

19. The conduct of all audits of publicly held companies by auditors reporting to an independent branch of government such as the Securities and Exchange Commission rather than by CPAs would have certain advantages and disadvantages. List the advantages or disadvantages to society as a whole.
20. What are the differences and similarities in audits of financial statements, compliance audits, and operational audits?
21. List five examples of specific operational audits that could be conducted by an internal auditor in an insurance company.

DISCUSSION QUESTIONS AND PROBLEMS

22. Consumers Union is a nonprofit organization that provides information and counsel on consumer goods and services. A major part of its function is the testing of different brands of consumer products that are bought on the open market and the reporting on the results of the tests in *Consumer Reports,* a monthly publication. Examples of the types of products it tests are middle-sized automobiles, residential dehumidifiers, canned tuna, and boys' jeans.

    Required:

    a. Compare the need for the information provided by Consumers Union with the need for audited financial statements by investors and other statement users.
    b. In what ways is the service provided by Consumers Union similar to audit services, and in what ways does it differ?
    c. In setting criteria for evaluating the brands of a product, what major problems does Consumers Union face? How does this compare with the problems of setting criteria for auditing?
    d. Compare the four audit evidence decisions made by auditors with the "information decisions" Consumers Union must make.
23. A large conglomerate is considering the possibility of acquiring a medium-sized manufacturing company in a closely related industry. A major consideration by the management of the conglomerate in deciding whether to pursue the merger is the operational efficiency of the company. Management has decided to obtain a detailed report, based on an intensive investigation, of the operational efficiency of the sales department, production department, and research and development department.

    Required:

    a. Whom should the conglomerate engage to conduct the operational audit?
    b. What major problems are the auditors likely to encounter in conducting the investigation and writing the report?
24. The following are examples of documentation typically obtained by auditors:
    a. Vendors' invoices
    b. General ledgers
    c. Bank statements
    d. Canceled payroll checks
    e. Payroll time cards
    f. Purchase requisitions

g. Receiving reports (document prepared when merchandise is received)
h. Minutes of the board of directors
i. Remittance advices
j. Signed W-4s (Employees' Withholding Exemption Certificate)
k. Signed lease agreements
l. Duplicate copies of bills of lading
m. Subsidiary accounts receivable records
n. Canceled notes payable
o. Duplicate sales invoices
p. Articles of incorporation
q. Title insurance policies for real estate
r. Notes receivable

Required:

a. Classify each of the preceding items according to types of documentation: (1) internal or (2) external.
b. Explain why external evidence is more reliable than internal evidence.

25. The following are examples of audit procedures:

a. Reviewing the accounts receivable with the credit manager to evaluate their collectibility
b. Standing by the payroll time clock to determine whether any employee "punches in" more than one time
c. Counting inventory items and recording the amount in the audit working papers
d. Obtaining a letter from the client's attorney addressed to the CPA firm stating the attorney is not aware of any existing lawsuits
e. Extending the cost of inventory times the quantity on an inventory listing to test whether it is accurate
f. Obtaining a letter from an insurance company to the CPA firm stating the amount of fire insurance coverage on building and equipment
g. Examining an insurance policy stating the amount of the fire insurance coverage on buildings and equipment
h. Calculating the ratio of cost of goods sold to sales as a test of overall reasonableness of gross margin relative to the preceding year.
i. Obtaining information about the system of internal control by requesting the client to fill out a questionnaire
j. Tracing the total on the cash disbursements journal to the general ledger
k. Watching employees count inventory to determine whether company procedures are being followed
l. Examining a piece of equipment to make sure a major acquisition was actually received and is in operation
m. Calculating the ratio of sales commissions expense to sales as a test of sales commissions
n. Examining corporate minutes to determine the authorization of the issue of bonds
o. Obtaining a letter from management stating there are no unrecorded liabilities
p. Reviewing the total of repairs and maintenance for each month to determine whether any month's total was unusually large
q. Comparing a duplicate sales invoice with the sales journal for customer name and amount

r. Adding the sales journal entries to determine whether they were correctly totaled

s. Making a petty cash count to make sure the amount of the petty cash fund is intact

t. Obtaining a written statement from a bank stating the client has $2,671 on deposit and liabilities of $10,000 on a demand note

Required:

Classify each of the preceding items according to the seven types of audit evidence: (1) physical examination, (2) confirmation, (3) documentation, (4) observation, (5) inquiries of the client, (6) mechanical accuracy, and (7) comparisons and relationships.

26. Four college seniors with majors in accounting are discussing alternative career plans. The first senior plans to become an internal revenue agent because his primary interest is income taxes. He believes the background in tax auditing will provide him with a better exposure to income taxes than will any other available career choice. The second senior has decided to go to work for a CPA firm for at least five years, possibly as a permanent career. She feels the wide variety of experience in auditing and related fields offers a better alternative than any other available choice. The third senior has decided upon a career in internal auditing with a large industrial company because of the many different aspects of the organization with which internal auditors become involved. A fourth senior plans to pursue some aspect of auditing as a career but has not decided upon the particular type of organization to enter. He is especially interested in an opportunity to continue to grow professionally, but meaningful and interesting employment is also an important consideration.

Required:

a. What are the major advantages and disadvantages of each of the three types of auditing careers?

b. What other types of auditing careers are available to those who are qualified?

27. The following two statements are representative of attitudes and opinions sometimes encountered by CPAs in their professional practice:

a. Today's audit consists of test checking. This is a dangerous practice because test checking depends upon the auditor's judgment, which may be defective. An audit can be relied upon only if every transaction is verified.

b. An audit by a CPA is essentially negative and contributes to neither the gross national product nor the general well-being of society. The auditor does not create; he merely checks what someone else has done.

Required:

Evaluate each of the above statements and indicate

a. Areas of agreement with the statement, if any.

b. Areas of misconception, incompleteness, or fallacious reasoning included in the statement, if any.   (AICPA adapted)

28. In his examination of financial statements, an auditor must judge the validity of the audit evidence he obtains.

Required:

Assume that you have evaluated internal control and found it satisfactory.

a. In the course of his examination, the auditor asks many questions of client officers and employees.

(1) Describe the factors the auditor should consider in evaluating oral evidence provided by client officers and employees.

(2) Discuss the validity and limitations of oral evidence.

b. An auditor's examination may include computation of various balance sheet and operating ratios for comparison with previous years and industry averages. Discuss the validity and limitations of ratio analysis.

c. In connection with his examination of the financial statements of a manufacturing company, an auditor is observing the physical inventory of finished goods, which consists of expensive, highly complex electronic equipment. Discuss the validity and limitations of the audit evidence provided by this procedure. (AICPA adapted)

29. A CPA accumulates various kinds of evidence upon which he will base his auditor's opinion as to the fairness of financial statements he examines. Among this evidence are confirmations from third parties.

Required:

a. What is an audit confirmation?

b. What characteristics should an audit confirmation possess if a CPA is to consider it as valid evidence? (AICPA adapted)

30. As auditor of the Star Manufacturing Company, you have obtained

1. a trial balance taken from the books of Star one month prior to year-end:

	Dr. (Cr.)
Cash in bank	$ 87,000
Trade accounts receivable	345,000
Notes receivable	125,000
Inventories	317,000
Land	66,000
Buildings, net	350,000
Furniture, fixtures, and equipment, net	325,000
Trade accounts payable	(235,000)
Mortgages payable	(400,000)
Capital stock	(300,000)
Retained earnings	(510,000)
Sales	(3,130,000)
Cost of sales	2,300,000
General and administrative expenses	622,000
Legal and professional fees	3,000
Interest expense	35,000

2. There are no inventories consigned either in or out.

3. All notes receivable are due from outsiders and held by Star.

Required:

Which accounts should be confirmed with outside sources? Briefly describe from whom they should be confirmed and the information that should be confirmed. Organize your answer in the following format:

Account Name	*From Whom Confirmed*	*Information to Be Confirmed*

(AICPA adapted)

31. In the normal course of performing their responsibilities, auditors frequently conduct examinations or reviews of
    a. Federal income-tax returns of an officer of the corporation to determine whether he has included all taxable income in his return.
    b. Disbursements of a branch of the federal government for a special research project to determine whether it would have been feasible to accomplish the same research results at a lower cost to the taxpayers.
    c. Computer operations of a corporation to evaluate whether the computer center is being operated as efficiently as possible.
    d. Annual statements for the use of management.
    e. Operations of the Internal Revenue Service to determine whether the internal revenue agents are using their time efficiently in conducting audits.
    f. Statements for bankers and other creditors when the client is too small to have an audit staff.
    g. Financial statements of a branch of the federal government to make sure the statements present fairly the actual disbursements made during a period of time.
    h. Federal income-tax returns of a corporation to determine whether the tax laws have been followed.
    i. Financial statements for the use by stockholders when there is an internal audit staff.
    j. A bond indenture agreement to make sure a company is following all requirements of the contract.
    k. The computer operations of a large corporation to evaluate whether the internal controls are likely to prevent errors in accounting and operating data.
    l. Disbursements of a branch of the federal government for a special research project to determine whether the expenditures were consistent with the legislative bill that authorized the project.

Required:

For each of the above examples, state the most likely type of auditor (CPA, GAO, IRS, or internal) and type of audit (audit of financial statements, compliance audit, or operational audit).

32. List two examples of audit evidence the auditor can use in support of each of the following:
    a. Recorded value of entries in the purchase journal
    b. Physical existence of inventory
    c. Valuation of accounts receivable
    d. Ownership of permanent assets
    e. Liability for accounts payable
    f. Obsolescence of inventory
    g. Existence of petty cash

2

The Environment of Auditing

This chapter considers the major influences on the development of auditing in the United States. As in every environment, the various influences are interdependent; thus it is not possible to state which of the following is predominant:

1. Structure of the CPA profession
2. The Code of Professional Ethics
3. AICPA professional pronouncements in auditing
4. Generally accepted accounting principles
5. Securities and Exchange Commission
6. Legal liability of CPAs

STRUCTURE OF THE CPA PROFESSION

Certified public accountants have had a greater influence on the practice of auditing than any other group of auditors. There are several reasons for this, the most important being the close involvement of CPAs with external users of financial statements. Investors, creditors, and the many other people who depend heavily on financial statements for decision making exert considerable pressure on CPAs to develop reasonable standards of auditing and rules of conduct so that reliable financial information will be available. There can be direct pressures on the

AICPA by user groups such as the Securities and Exchange Commission (SEC) or industry associations, and pressures on individual CPA firms through lawsuits that allege that an inadequate audit was performed.

The existence of many CPA practitioners with reasonably common interests also contributes to their influence. Due to the large demand for auditing services from various users, more than one hundred thousand CPAs practice public accounting in the United States. Their common goal—providing auditing services on a fee basis—enables them to exert considerable influence in developing new audit tools and techniques, auditing standards, and ethical standards for all auditors.

Another reason for the increasing influence of CPAs is the size of the larger CPA firms. Included among the several thousand CPA firms practicing public accounting are approximately fifteen extremely large firms which audit most of the publicly held companies and many of the private companies. Each of these firms has offices in most major cities in the United States, as well as international offices. Some of the firms have more than five thousand professionals on their staff. These firms are able to justify the expenditure of large sums on research for new approaches to auditing and new standards of performance. Hence they have a strong influence on the development of standards and regulations for the entire profession.

The services other than auditing provided by CPAs also significantly influence auditing practice. These include the following:

Tax Services. CPA firms prepare corporate and individual tax returns for both audit and nonaudit clients. In addition, estate tax, gift tax, tax planning, and other aspects of tax services are provided by most CPA firms. Tax services are now a part of almost every CPA firm, and for many small firms such services are far more important to their practice than auditing.

Management Advisory Services. Most CPA firms provide certain services that enable their clients to operate their businesses more effectively. These services range from simple suggestions for improving the client's accounting system to aids in marketing strategies, executive searches, and computer installations. Many large firms now have departments involved exclusively in management advisory services with little interaction with the audit or tax staff.

Accounting Services. Many small clients who may have a limited accounting staff rely upon CPA firms to prepare their financial statements. Generally, in this type of engagement a large number of adjustments are made by the CPA to properly reflect transactions throughout the period and to adjust for valuation changes or allocations at the end of the period. In many instances the CPA prepares these adjustments as part of an audit. In other instances only accounting services are performed. When this occurs, the resulting statements are called *unaudited financial statements.*

Bookkeeping. Some small clients lack the personnel or expertise to prepare even their own journals and ledgers. Many small CPA firms spend most of their time performing this type of work, termed "write-up" work. In recent years some firms have utilized electronic data-processing systems to provide bookkeeping services to clients. In some instances the CPA firm also conducts an audit after the bookkeeping services have been provided; in other instances unaudited financial statements are prepared.

The CPAs' most important influence has been through their national professional organization, the American Institute of Certified Public Accountants. The AICPA conducts research and publishes materials on many different subjects related to accounting, auditing, management advisory services, and taxes. Some of the major periodicals and other publications in accounting and auditing issued by the AICPA are the following:

PERIODIC JOURNALS

- The Journal of Accountancy (monthly)
- Management Adviser (bimonthly)
- The Tax Adviser (monthly)

ACCOUNTING RELATED

- Accounting Research Studies (1 through 15)
- Opinions of the Accounting Principles Board (1 through 31)
- Accounting Trends and Techniques (annual)

AUDITING RELATED

- Statement on Auditing Standards No. 1 and beyond
- An Auditor's Approach to Statistical Sampling (vols. 1–6)
- Auditing and EDP
- Internal Control
- Case Studies in Internal Control
- Industry Audit Guides (several volumes in different fields)
- Audit Research Monographs

GENERAL

- Code of Professional Ethics
- Semiannual CPA examination questions and unofficial answers

Included in the above are two publications that will be discussed in greater detail in this chapter: the Code of Professional Ethics and Statement on Auditing Standards No. 1.

THE CODE OF PROFESSIONAL ETHICS

The underlying philosophy for a code of ethics for any profession is the need for *public confidence* in the quality of the service, regardless of the individual providing it. For the CPA, it is essential that the client and external financial statement users have confidence in the quality of audits and other services. Since it is virtually impossible for these users to evaluate the performance of different auditors, it is desirable that the profession encourage high standards of performance and conduct on the part of all practitioners. The AICPA Code of Professional Ethics is meant to assist practitioners in achieving a reasonable level of conduct.

The emphasis in the Code is on identifying those practices and relationships that could be damaging to the image of CPAs in the minds of users. The Code follows a highly pragmatic approach to ethics that emphasizes the implementation and enforceability of the Code by setting forth reasonably well defined rules of conduct and their interpretations. Ideally a practitioner should be able to read the Code and have an understanding of unacceptable behavior.

Parts of the Code

The AICPA Code of Professional Ethics comprises three distinct parts:

Concepts of Professional Ethics. The concepts section of the Code contains a general discussion of the importance of certain characteristics required of a CPA. Independence receives the most attention, but competence, responsibility to clients and colleagues, and other matters are also discussed. In addition to stating the importance of different parts of the Code, the reasons for including each major requirement are brought out. Relevant portions of the concepts section, as well as the two other sections of the Code, will be included in this and subsequent chapters as individual topics are discussed. The Code in its entirety can be found in Appendix A.

Rules of Conduct. This part of the Code includes the explicit rules that must be followed by every CPA in the practice of public accounting. (Those individuals holding the CPA certificate, but not actually practicing public accounting, must only follow certain requirements.) Because the Rules of Conduct section is the *only enforceable part* of the Code, it is for the most part stated in more precise language than the section on concepts.

An example of the precision found in the Rules of Conduct is Rule 402:

> *Rule 402—Offers of Employment.* A member in public practice shall not make a direct or indirect offer of employment to an employee of another public accountant on his own behalf or that of his client without first informing such accountant. This rule shall not apply if the employee of his own initiative or in response to a public advertisement applies for employment.[1]

Rule 402 is meant to support a congenial and cooperative spirit among CPAs by explicitly prohibiting CPA firms from pirating employees from each other. The underlying assumption is that cooperation and com-

---

1 *Code of Professional Ethics*, AICPA (New York, 1972), p. 24.

munication enhance both the performance of auditing and the public confidence in CPAs in general. The rule is straightforward in that it prohibits one CPA firm from contacting an employee of another in any way without first informing the employer of the intent.

On the other hand, certain concepts do not lend themselves to so close a definition. An example is Rule 501:

> *Rule 501—Acts Discreditable.* A member shall not commit an act discreditable to the profession.[2]

In interpreting Rule 501, do traffic tickets, excessive drinking, and rowdiness qualify as discreditable acts? Although the rule is not specific, a "discreditable act" has been interpreted as covering only a convicted criminal offense.

Failure to follow the Rules of Conduct can result in *expulsion* from the institute. This by itself would not prevent a CPA from practicing public accounting, but it would certainly be a weighty social sanction. More important is the existence of rules of conduct, similar to the AICPA's, that have been enacted by the professional CPA associations of each of the individual states. Since each state grants the individual practitioner a license to practice as a CPA, a significant breach of a state society's code of ethics can result in the *loss of the CPA certificate and the license to practice.* Although it happens infrequently, this loss removes the practitioner from public accounting.

Interpretation of Rules of Conduct. The need for published interpretations of the Rules of Conduct arises when there are frequent questions from practitioners about a particular rule. The Division of Professional Ethics of the AICPA prepares each interpretation based upon a consensus of a committee made up mostly of public accounting practitioners. At the present time there are twenty-five interpretations of the Rules of Conduct (see Appendix A).

Although the prohibitions of advertising, solicitation, and encroachment on the practice of another practitioner are probably not the most important parts of the Rules of Conduct for protecting the CPA's image in the minds of users, nearly two-thirds of the interpretations of the rules deal with these topics. The emphasis on these areas of the Code reflects the fact that most of the questions arise from practitioners, who in the short run are likely to be more concerned about losing their clients to other firms than about the other matters in the Code.

Independence, Solicitation, and Forecasts

All parts of the Concepts, Rules of Conduct, and Interpretation of the Rules are relevant to the practice of public accounting, but three issues

[2] Code, p. 24.

have the greatest effect: independence, obtaining clients, and restrictions on forecasts. Independence is given the most attention in this text because it is essential to the long-run health of the profession, while the other two are discussed briefly at this time. Competence, technical standards, responsibilities to clients, and other parts of the Code are integrated into other chapters.

Independence. Independence in auditing means taking an *unbiased viewpoint* in the performance of audit tests, the evaluation of the results, and the issuance of the audit report. If the auditor is an advocate for the client, a particular banker, or anyone else, he cannot be considered independent. Independence must certainly be regarded as one of the auditor's most critical characteristics. The reason that many diverse users are willing to rely upon the CPA's reports as to the fairness of financial statements is their expectation of an unbiased viewpoint.

Not only is it essential that CPAs maintain an independent attitude in fulfilling their responsibility, but it is also important that the users of financial statements have confidence in that independence. These two objectives are frequently identified as *independence in fact* and *independence in appearance*. Independence in fact exists when the auditor is actually able to maintain an unbiased attitude throughout the audit, whereas independence in appearance is dependent on others' interpretations of this independence. If auditors are independent in fact, but users believe them to be advocates for the client, most of the value of the audit function will be lost.

Although it is possible to take the extreme position that anything affecting either independence in fact or in appearance must be eliminated to ensure a high level of respect in the community, it is doubtful whether this would solve as many problems as it would create. The difficulty with this position is that it is likely to significantly restrict the services offered to clients, the freedom of CPAs to practice in the traditional manner, and the ability of CPA firms to hire competent staff. At this point it will be helpful to examine some of the conflicts of independence that have arisen, evaluate the significance of the conflicts, and determine how the profession has resolved them.

1. *Ownership of stock by a CPA.* Although it was once acceptable for CPAs to own a limited amount of stock in a client, it is now regarded as potentially damaging to actual audit independence, and it certainly is likely to affect the users' perceptions of the auditor's independence. Stock ownership and similar investments are specifically prohibited in Rule 101 of the Rules of Conduct:

> *Rule 101—Independence.* A member or a firm of which he is a partner or shareholder shall not express an opinion on financial statements of an enterprise unless he and his firm are independent with respect to such enterprise. Independence will be considered to be impaired if, for example:

A. During the period of his professional engagement, or at the time of expressing this opinion, he or his firm
   1. Had or was committed to acquire any direct or material indirect financial interest in the enterprise; or
   2. Had any joint closely held business investment with the enterprise or any officer, director or principal stockholder thereof which was material in relation to his or his firm's net worth; or
   3. Had any loan to or from the enterprise or any officer, director or principal stockholder thereof. This latter proscription does not apply to the following loans from a financial institution when made under normal lending procedures, terms and requirements:
      (a) Loans obtained by a member or his firm which are not material in relation to the net worth of such borrower.
      (b) Home mortgages.
      (c) Other secured loans, except loans guaranteed by a member's firm which are otherwise unsecured.[3]

2. *Directorship or officer of a company.* If a CPA is a member of the board of directors or an officer of a client company, his ability to make independent evaluations of the fair presentation of financial statements could easily be affected. Even if holding one of these positions did not actually affect the auditor's independence, the frequent involvement with management and the decisions it makes is likely to affect how statement users would perceive the CPA's independence. To eliminate this possibility, Rule 101 specifically prohibits this and similar practices.

3. *Performance of management advisory services and audits for the same client.* What is the effect on actual independence and the appearance of independence when an auditor recommends a computer installation or some other improvement in the client's system and at a later date audits the output of the computer installation? If the recommended system turns out to be ineffective, will the auditor evaluate the system as harshly as he would have if someone else had made the recommendation? There are no clear-cut answers to these questions, but the profession has decided to permit the CPA to audit clients for which he has also provided management advisory services. The determining factor in this decision is the impact on independence compared with the effect of restrictions on services needed by clients. Some CPA firms have all management advisory services performed by staff members other than the auditors as a means of reducing the problem of independence.

4. *Performance of bookkeeping services and audits for the same client.* If a CPA records transactions in the journals for the client, posts monthly totals to the general ledger, makes adjusting entries, and subsequently does an audit, there is some question as to whether he can be independent in his audit role. The AICPA permits a CPA firm to do both bookkeeping and auditing for the same client; nevertheless it cannot be done for clients listed with the SEC because it prohibits this dual role. The

[3] Code, pp. 20–21.

AICPA's conclusion is presumably based upon a comparison of the need for bookkeeping services or audits by many small clients with the effect on independence if both services are provided simultaneously.

5. *Dependence upon a client for a large percentage of audit fees.* Nothing in the Code specifically requires a diversification of clients, but there is pressure from the SEC to discourage the audit of listed companies by a CPA firm that depends heavily upon a particular client. It is doubtful whether there can be independence in both fact and appearance if the fees from one client make up a significant part of the total income of the firm.

6. *Engagement of the CPA and payment of audit fees by management.* Can an auditor be truly independent in fact and appearance if the payment of fees is dependent upon the management of the audited entity? There is probably no satisfactory answer to this question, but it does demonstrate the difficulty of obtaining an atmosphere of complete independence of auditors. The alternative to engagement of the CPA and payment of audit fees by management would probably be either the use of governmental or quasi-governmental auditors. All things considered, it is questionable whether the audit function would be performed better or cheaper by the public sector.

Regardless of the rules set forth by the Code of Professional Ethics, it is essential that the CPA maintain an unbiased relationship with the client and all other parties affected by the performance of the CPA's responsibilities. In every engagement, including those involving management advisory and tax services, the CPA must refuse to subordinate his professional judgment to that of others. Even though pressures on the CPA's objectivity and integrity are frequent, the long-run standing of the profession in the financial community demands resisting these pressures. If the conflicts are sufficiently great to compromise the CPA's objectivity, it may be necessary for the CPA firm to resign from the engagement.

Obtaining Clients. A significant aspect of public accounting is the restrictions imposed upon CPAs in obtaining new clients. With minor exceptions, the only acceptable way to obtain a new client is by a request for services without any inducement from the CPA. The following are explicitly prohibited by the Rules of Conduct or related interpretations:

1. Any means of solicitation of any kind of clients of other CPA firms, including sending unsolicited firm literature or invitations to seminars.
2. Advertising of any kind, including any designation of specialties of the firm, undignified business stationery, and the inclusion of the firm's name in help-wanted advertisements.
3. The payment of a commission or fee to obtain a client.
4. The concurrent practice of public accounting and another business or occupation that serves to provide clients to the public accounting practice.

The basis for these prohibitions is the belief on the part of the profession that advertising and other methods of solicitation could result in *excessive competition* and the simultaneous reduction in the quality of audits. In addition, advertising is regarded by many as being undignified and unprofessional. The argument can also be advanced that since it is not possible for laymen to distinguish between the quality of audits, advertising would not serve a useful economic function. The reader should be aware, however, that the legality of restrictions against advertising by all professions is currently being questioned in the courts.

The Code of Professional Ethics formerly included a rule against *competitive bidding,* but it was declared void by a U.S. District Court in an antitrust suit in 1972. Bidding is now common practice by CPAs, especially in audits of governmental agencies requiring competitive bids. Nevertheless, bidding is still prohibited in some states.

With the exception of situations where competitive bids are requested, CPA firms are expected to acquire new clients through friends, referrals, and contacts made through memberships in associations. Critics of the restrictions imposed upon CPAs believe the purpose of the existing rules is to protect existing practitioners from losing clients to other CPA firms.

Restrictions on Forecasts. The following Rule of Conduct with respect to forecasts has had an important effect on the practice of auditing in the United States:

> *Rule 204—Forecasts.* A member shall not permit his name to be used in conjunction with any forecast of future transactions in a manner which may lead to the belief that the member vouches for the achievability of the forecast.[4]

This restriction on auditing forecast information prevents CPAs from providing a service that many members of the profession believe is needed and wanted by statement users. Certainly forecasts of information are relevant for users' decision-making purposes, and audited forecasts would presumably be more reliable than those submitted by management without verification.

The prime concern over the involvement of CPAs with forecasts is the protection of their credibility in attesting to historical statements. Even if an auditor were to attest to only the reasonableness of the underlying assumptions and to the mechanical accuracy of the forecasts (and thus be in compliance with Rule 204), there might be a deterioration of the respect for CPAs whenever a forecast failed. Since forecasts, by their very nature, are often likely to be wrong, the well-established reputation of CPAs for accuracy and reliability in historical financial statements could be adversely affected. There is no simple way to measure the pros and cons of attesting to forecasts, and it is a matter of continuing discussion within the profession.

[4] Code, p. 22.

AICPA PROFESSIONAL PRONOUNCEMENTS IN AUDITING

Generally Accepted Auditing Standards

An *auditing standard* is a general guideline to aid auditors in fulfilling their professional responsibilities. Standards are much broader than procedures. They include consideration of professional qualities such as competence and independence, reporting requirements, and evidence, whereas procedures are specific and related to a particular audit.

The broadest guidelines available are the ten *Generally Accepted Auditing Standards*, which were developed by the AICPA in 1947 and have, with minimum changes, remained the same. Although these standards are not sufficiently specific to provide any meaningful guidance to practitioners, they represent a framework upon which the AICPA can provide interpretations. These ten standards are as follows:

GENERAL STANDARDS

1. The examination is to be performed by a person or persons having adequate technical training and proficiency as an auditor.
2. In all matters relating to the assignment, an independence in mental attitude is to be maintained by the auditor or auditors.
3. Due professional care is to be exercised in the performance of the examination and the preparation of the report.

STANDARDS OF FIELD WORK

1. The work is to be adequately planned and assistants, if any, are to be properly supervised.
2. There is to be a proper study and evaluation of the existing internal control as a basis for reliance thereon and for the determination of the resultant extent of the tests to which auditing procedures are to be restricted.
3. Sufficient competent evidential matter is to be obtained through inspection, observation, inquiries, and confirmations to afford a reasonable basis for an opinion regarding the financial statements under examination.

STANDARDS OF REPORTING

1. The report shall state whether the financial statements are presented in accordance with generally accepted accounting principles.
2. The report shall state whether such principles have been consistently observed in the current period in relation to the preceding period.
3. Informative disclosures in the financial statements are to be regarded as reasonably adequate unless otherwise stated in the report.
4. The report shall either contain an expression of opinion regarding the financial statements, taken as a whole, or an assertion to the effect that an opinion cannot be expressed. When an overall opinion

cannot be expressed, the reasons therefor should be stated. In all cases where an auditor's name is associated with financial statements, the report should contain a clear-cut indication of the character of the auditor's examination, if any, and the degree of responsibility he is taking.

The *general standards* stress the important personal qualities the auditor should possess. The first standard is normally interpreted as requiring the auditor to have formal education in auditing and accounting, adequate practical experience for the work being performed, and continuing professional education. Recent court cases clearly demonstrate that the auditor must be technically qualified and experienced in those industries in which his audit clients are engaged.

The Rules of Conduct of the Code of Professional Ethics also recognize the importance of the first general standard in Rule 201:

> *Rule 201—Competence.* A member shall not undertake any engagement which he or his firm cannot reasonably expect to complete with professional competence.[5]

In any case where the CPA or his assistants are not qualified to perform the work, a professional obligation exists to acquire the requisite knowledge and skills, suggest someone else who is qualified to perform the work, or decline the engagement.

The second general standard, maintaining an independence in mental attitude, was discussed in the preceding section and should require no further elaboration. The third standard involves *due care* in the performance of all aspects of auditing. Simply stated, this means that the auditor is a professional who is responsible for adequately fulfilling his duties diligently and carefully. As an illustration, "due care" includes consideration of the completeness of the working papers, the sufficiency of the audit evidence, and the adequacy of the audit report. As a professional, the auditor must avoid negligence and bad faith; but he is not expected to make perfect judgments in every instance.

The *standards of field work* concern the performance of the audit. Most of this text involves meeting the requirements of these three standards.

The *standards of reporting* deal with the issuance of the proper audit report upon completion of the audit. Reporting standards are considered briefly in this chapter and again in Chapter 20.

Statements on Auditing Standards

The 1973 Statement on Auditing Standards No. 1 (SAS 1) and all subsequent statements on auditing standards are the most *authoritative references* available for auditors. These statements are issued by the

---

5 Code, p. 22.

AICPA and are interpretations of generally accepted auditing standards. Frequently these interpretations are referred to as auditing standards or simply as standards, but they should not be called generally accepted auditing standards. Only the ten Generally Accepted Auditing Standards bear that designation.

Statements on Auditing Standards are successors to the Statements on Auditing Procedure of the AICPA. SAS 1 is a codification of fifty-four previous statements on auditing procedure dating from 1939 to 1972, while subsequent SASs are new pronouncements. New statements are issued whenever an auditing problem arises of sufficient importance to warrant an official interpretation by the AICPA.

The Generally Accepted Auditing Standards and the Statements on Auditing Standards are regarded as authoritative literature because *every member of the profession is required to follow their recommendations.* They obtain their status of authoritative literature through the Code of Professional Ethics, Rule of Conduct 202.

Even though the Generally Accepted Auditing Standards and the Statements on Auditing Standards are the authoritative auditing guidelines for members of the profession, they provide less direction to auditors than might be suspected. There are almost no specific audit procedures required by the standards; and there are no specific requirements for determining sample size, selecting sample items from the population for testing, or evaluating results. Many practitioners believe the standards should provide more clearly defined guidelines for determining the extent of evidence to be accumulated. Such specificity would eliminate some of the difficult audit decisions and provide a line of defense if a CPA were charged with conducting an inadequate audit. On the other hand, highly specific requirements could turn auditing into mechanistic evidence gathering, void of professional judgment. From the point of view of both the profession and the users of auditing services, there is probably a greater harm in defining authoritative guidelines too specifically than too broadly.

Certain points about the general and field work auditing standards are worth brief discussion. First, these AICPA pronouncements should be looked upon by practitioners as *minimum standards* of performance rather than as maximum standards or ideals. Any professional auditor who is constantly seeking means of reducing the scope of the audit by relying only on the standards, rather than evaluating the substance of the situation, fails to satisfy the spirit of the standards. Second, the existence of auditing standards does not mean the auditor must always follow them blindly. If the auditor sincerely believes the requirement of a standard is impractical or impossible to perform, he is justified in following an alternative course of action. Similarly, if the issue in question is immaterial in amount, it is also unnecessary to follow the standard. It is important to note, however, that the burden of justifying departures from the standards falls upon the practitioner. As an example, SAS 1 requires the confirmation of accounts receivable in an ordinary audit. The auditor should confirm accounts receivable in virtually every audit; but if the balance in accounts receivable is immaterial, or if confirmation is not practical considering all the circumstances of the audit, there is justification for verifying accounts receivable in a different manner.

When auditors desire more specific guidelines, they must turn to less authoritative sources. These include textbooks, journals, and technical publications. The materials published by the AICPA, mentioned earlier in the chapter, such as the *Journal of Accountancy* and Industry Audit Guides, are particularly useful in furnishing assistance on specific questions.

The Standard Short-Form Report

The profession has defined and enumerated the types of audit reports that should be included with financial statements. Standards for reporting are more precise and well defined than for any other aspect of auditing; the profession recognized the need for uniformity in reporting as a means of avoiding confusion. Users would have considerable difficulty interpreting the meaning of an auditor's report if each report were an original creation. As a result, the wording of audit reports is quite uniform, but there are different audit reports for different circumstances.

The most common type of audit report is the *standard short-form report,* used when the following conditions have been met:

1. Sufficient evidence has been accumulated by the CPA to enable him to evaluate whether the financial statements are fairly stated.
2. The financial statements are presented in accordance with generally accepted accounting principles applied on a basis consistent with that of the preceding period.
3. Adequate disclosures have been included in the footnotes and other parts of the financial statements.
4. There are no unusual uncertainties concerning future developments which cannot be reasonably estimated or satisfactorily resolved.

When these conditions are met, the following standard short-form audit report is issued:

To the Stockholders
ABC Corporation

We have examined the balance sheet of ABC Corporation as of December 31, 1977, and the related statements of income, retained earnings and changes in financial position for the year then ended. Our examination was made in accordance with generally accepted auditing standards, and accordingly included such tests of the accounting records and such other auditing procedures as we considered necessary in the circumstances.

In our opinion, the financial statements mentioned above present fairly the financial position of ABC Corporation at December 31, 1977, and the results of its operations and the changes in its financial position for the year then ended, in conformity with generally accepted accounting principles applied on a basis consistent with that of the preceding year.

Martin Blaine & Co., CPAs
March 6, 1978

Each standard short-form report includes five distinct parts:

1. *The audit report address.* The report is usually addressed to the company, its stockholders, or the board of directors. In recent years it has become customary to address the report to the *stockholders,* to indicate that the auditors are independent of the company and the board of directors.

2. *The scope of the audit.* In the first paragraph of the audit report, which is referred to as the *scope paragraph,* the auditor lists the financial statements he has examined and informs readers in very general terms about what was done on the audit. The scope paragraph intentionally states the work performed in general terms, rather than enumerating the details, because no reader is in a position to evaluate the adequacy of the evidence unless he has professional experience and knows all the facts about the audit. Several important aspects of the scope paragraph may not be apparent without careful examination:

   a. The entire paragraph is a factual statement about the performance of the audit.
   b. The titles of the financial statements and accounting periods included in the audit report are the same as those used on the accompanying financial statements. It is inappropriate to refer to the "balance sheet" in the audit report if it is called a "statement of financial position" in the financial statements.
   c. The first sentence refers to the statements "of ABC Corporation." This brief phrase is meant to indicate that the financial statements were prepared by management and are its representations. The primary responsibility for the fair presentation of the statements rests with management, not the auditor. The auditor's responsibility is to conduct an audit of the statements and form an opinion on the basis of his findings.
   d. There is specific reference to the adherence to generally accepted auditing standards, which includes the interpretations of the ten standards as they are found in the SASs.
   e. The reader is informed that the audit procedures and sample sizes *were limited* to the type considered necessary for this particular client, *based upon the professional judgment of the CPA.*

3. *The opinion of the auditor.* The second paragraph in the short-form report, which is directly related to the four generally accepted auditing standards of reporting, is called the *opinion paragraph.* This part of the report is so important that frequently the entire audit report is re-

ferred to simply as the *auditor's opinion*. Here the auditor states his conclusions about the financial statements based upon the results of his audit procedures. Several phrases and parts of the opinion paragraph merit a closer examination:

a. By the first words, "in our opinion," the reader is put on notice that this is an expression of professional judgment based upon a reasonable examination of the financial statements and underlying records rather than a certification or a guarantee of the accuracy and correctness of the statements. This is not meant to imply that the auditor takes no responsibility for the fair presentation of the financial statements. The extent of his responsibility will be discussed further in the section on legal liability.

b. Reporting Standard 4 requires an expression of an overall opinion about the financial statements. If the auditor conducts any part of an audit or is associated with the financial statements, some type of opinion must be expressed. In the case of the standard short-form report, this indicates that an audit was performed and no material misstatements or omissions were discovered.

c. Reporting Standard 1 requires the opinion to state whether the financial statements were prepared in accordance with generally accepted accounting principles. For the purpose of the auditor's opinion, this means that the financial statements are not considered fairly presented unless they are in accordance with generally accepted accounting principles.

d. When the auditor expresses an opinion on fair presentation, it includes consideration of material misstatements of information, inadequate disclosure, and omission of financial data or other information. Reporting Standard 4 makes this a reporting requirement.

4. *The date of the audit report.* The appropriate date for the report is the one on which the auditor has completed the most important auditing procedures in the field. This date is important to users because it indicates the last day of the auditor's responsibility for the review of significant events that occurred after the date of the financial statements. For example, if the balance sheet is dated December 31, 1977, and the audit report is dated March 6, 1978, this indicates that the auditor has searched for material unrecorded transactions and events that occurred up to March 6, 1978.

5. *The signature of the auditor.* This signature identifies the CPA or CPA firm that has performed the audit. Typically, the signature will be that of the CPA firm, since it has the responsibility for making sure the quality of the audit meets its standards.

Reports Other Than the Standard Short-Form Report

The scope paragraph of the report is important as a means of revealing when the auditor has not followed generally accepted auditing standards or has failed to accumulate the evidence he believes was appropriate for the audit. Whenever this occurs, the auditor must specifically state the shortcoming in the scope paragraph and the effect that it has on his opinion.

The opinion paragraph also becomes particularly pertinent when the auditor lacks sufficient information to form an overall opinion or believes, on the basis of the evidence, that the financial statements are not fairly presented. Under these conditions it is necessary for the auditor to express an opinion as to the overall fairness of the statements or state that it is not possible to give an opinion. It is also necessary to indicate any reservations the auditor has about the statements.

Whenever sufficient evidence has not been accumulated or the results of the tests lead the auditor to believe the statements are not fairly presented, it is necessary to issue some type of report other than the standard short-form. At the present time three other types of audit reports are available to auditors: an adverse opinion, a disclaimer of opinion, and a qualified opinion. These are described briefly at this time and in depth in Chapter 20.

1. *Adverse opinion.* This type of report is used only when the auditor believes the overall financial statements are so *materially misstated or misleading* that they do not present fairly the financial position or results of operations in accordance with generally accepted accounting principles. The adverse report can arise only when the auditor has knowledge, after an adequate investigation, that the financial statements are not fairly stated. This is not a common occurrence and, thus, the adverse opinion is rarely employed.

2. *Disclaimer of opinion.* A disclaimer is issued whenever the auditor has been *unable to satisfy himself* that the overall financial statements are fairly presented. The necessity for disclaiming an opinion may arise because of (a) a *severe limitation on the scope* of the audit examination, (b) the *existence of unusual uncertainties* concerning the amount of an item or the outcome of a matter materially affecting the financial position or the results of operations, or (c) a *nonindependent relationship* under the Code of Professional Ethics between the auditor and the client. Any one of these situations prevents the auditor from forming an opinion on the financial statements as a whole.

The disclaimer is distinguished from an adverse opinion in that it can arise only from a *lack* of knowledge by the auditor, whereas to express an adverse opinion the auditor must have knowledge that the financial statements are not fairly stated.

3. *Qualified opinion.* The qualified report can result from a *limitation on the scope* of the audit, the *lack of fairly presented information* in the financial statements, or the *existence of unusual circumstances* that prevented the auditor from knowing whether certain information in the statement was fairly presented. *This type of report can be used only when the auditor believes that the overall financial statements are fairly presented.* A disclaimer or an adverse report must be used if the auditor believes the exceptions being reported are extremely material. For this

reason the qualified report is considered the least severe type of report for disclosing exceptions.

GENERALLY ACCEPTED ACCOUNTING PRINCIPLES

Even though auditing is a discipline separate from accounting, auditors involved with financial statements must thoroughly understand generally accepted accounting principles. When the auditor gives his opinion on the fairness of the financial statements, *fairness* specifically means that the statements are in accordance with generally accepted accounting principles.

Given the similarity in terminology between the phrases "generally accepted auditing standards" and "generally accepted accounting principles," one might be inclined to believe they are actually similar in nature. Nothing would be further from reality. The ten Generally Accepted Auditing Standards are very general, but clearly identifiable by the profession. In contrast, generally accepted accounting principles are much more like rules than principles, and they tend to be more specific than general. For example, APB 15 deals with the subject of computing earnings per share. This lengthy publication defines in minute detail the proper method of calculation of earnings per share under various circumstances.

A major difficulty, from an auditing point of view, is the existence of alternative accounting principles for a given set of circumstances. In any particular situation the auditor must decide whether an alternative selected by the client is satisfactory for the existing conditions. This is a difficult decision for the auditor because the criteria for selecting among the alternatives are often ambiguous. Regardless of the principle selected by the client, the auditor could have difficulty defending the position that the proper principles were used.

Although the profession has not yet been able to resolve the problem of alternative accounting principles, an attempt has been made by taking the responsibility for setting accounting principles out of the hands of the AICPA. The Financial Accounting Standards Board succeeded the Accounting Principles Board in 1972 and has as one of its major objectives the elimination of some of the alternative principles of accounting.

Rule 203 of the Code of Professional Ethics requires the auditor to evaluate the fairness of the financial statements on the basis of accounting principles established by a properly designated body, except in unusual circumstances.

This requirement prevents an auditor from endorsing an unusual accounting principle as being generally accepted unless it has been designated as acceptable by the Financial Accounting Standards Board or its predecessor, the Accounting Principles Board. Auditors have references available that designate generally accepted accounting principles.

SECURITIES AND EXCHANGE COMMISSION

The overall purpose of the Securities and Exchange Commission (SEC), an agency of the federal government, is to assist in providing investors with reliable information upon which to make investment decisions. The Securities Act of 1933 contributes to fulfilling this purpose by requiring most companies planning to issue *new securities* to the public to submit a registration statement to the SEC for approval. The Securities Act of 1934 provides additional protection by requiring the same companies and others to file detailed annual reports with the commission. The commission examines these statements for completeness and adequacy before permitting the company to sell its securities through the securities exchanges.

Although the SEC requires considerable information that is not of direct interest to CPAs, the Securities Acts of 1933 and 1934 require financial statements, accompanied by the opinion of an independent certified public accountant, as part of a registration statement and subsequent reports.

Of special interest to auditors are several specific reports that are subject to the reporting provisions of the Securities Acts. The most important of these are as follows:

1. *Forms S-1, S-7, or S-16.* These forms must be completed and registered with the SEC whenever a company plans to issue new securities to the public.

2. *Form 8-K.* This report is filed at the end of any month in which significant events have occurred which are of interest to public investors. Such events include the acquisition or sale of a subsidiary, a change in officers or directors, an addition of a new product line, or a change in auditors.

3. *Form 10-K.* This report must be filed annually within ninety days after the close of each fiscal year. Extensive detailed financial information is included in this report.

Since large CPA firms usually have clients that must file one or more of these reports each year, and the rules and regulations affecting filings with the SEC are extremely complex, most CPA firms have specialists who spend a large portion of their time making sure their clients satisfy all the SEC requirements.

The SEC has considerable influence in setting generally accepted accounting principles and disclosure requirements for financial statements as a result of its authority for specifying reporting requirements considered necessary for fair disclosure to investors. The Accounting Principles Board followed the practice of working closely with the SEC, and the Financial Accounting Standards Board (FASB) has continued this tradition. In addition, the SEC has power to establish rules for any CPA associated with audited financial statements submitted to the commission. Even though the commission has taken the position that accounting principles and auditing standards should be set by the profession, the SEC's attitude is generally considered in any major change proposed by the FASB.

The most important SEC requirements of interest to CPAs are set forth in the commission's *Regulation S-X* and *Accounting Series Releases.* These two publications constitute important basic regulations, as well as decisions and opinions on accounting and auditing issues affecting any CPA dealing with publicly held companies. It is worthwhile to examine briefly some of the major influences the SEC has had on auditors in the past few decades, even though it is not feasible to study the SEC regulations in this text in depth. The discussion in this section will focus on the SEC's impact on audit reports, generally accepted auditing standards, and professional ethics. The legal liability of auditors under the Securities Acts of 1933 and 1934 is covered in the next section.

The Audit Report and Generally Accepted Auditing Standards

Rule 2-02 of Regulation S-X specifies the nature of the accountant's report (auditor's report) to accompany the financial statements. In reading Rule 2-02, keep in mind that this requirement existed before the current wording of the standard short-form report or the existence of generally accepted auditing standards. In fact, the inclusion of requirement *b*-1 was a major impetus for developing generally accepted auditing standards, since it would be impossible for auditors to conclude that "the audit was made in accordance with generally accepted auditing standards" if there were no formal standards. A careful examination of requirements *c* and *d* reveals the similarity between the reporting standards and the opinion paragraph of the short-form report to Rule 2-02. The SEC rule now reads as follows:

RULE 2-02: ACCOUNTANTS' REPORTS

a. Technical requirements—
The accountant's certificate (1) shall be dated; (2) shall be signed manually; (3) shall indicate the city and state where issued; and (4) shall identify without detailed enumeration the financial statements covered by the report.

b. Representations as to the audit—
The accountant's report (1) shall state whether the audit was made in accordance with generally accepted auditing standards; and (2) shall designate any auditing procedures deemed necessary by the accountant under the circumstances of a particular case, which have been omitted, and the reason for their omission.

Nothing in this rule shall be construed to imply authority for the omission of any procedure which independent accountants would ordinarily employ in the course of an audit made for the purpose of expressing the opinions required by paragraph (c) of this rule.

c. Opinion to be expressed—

The accountant's report shall state clearly: (1) the opinion of the accountant in respect to the financial statements covered by the report and the accounting principles and practices reflected therein; and (2) the opinion of the accountant as to the consistency of the application of the accounting principles, or as to any changes in such principles which have a material effect on the financial statements as required to be set forth in Rule 3-07 (a).

d. Exceptions—

Any matters to which the accountant takes exception shall be clearly identified, the exception thereto specifically and clearly stated, and, to the extent practicable, the effect of each such exception on the related financial statements given.

Independence of the Auditor

Prior to 1964 the AICPA Code of Professional Ethics was far less stringent with regard to independence than the SEC. Under the AICPA Code it was permissible to be a member of a client's board of directors and to have a financial interest in the business of a client if the ownership was not material relative to the total assets of either the client or the CPA. Although there was significant reluctance on the part of some CPAs, the rule was finally changed to be consistent with SEC requirements.

One SEC requirement involving independence which is still inconsistent with the AICPA Code of Professional Ethics is a rule *prohibiting the auditor from doing bookkeeping work* for any client filing reports with the SEC if the work involves making management decisions. The most likely management decision in bookkeeping is deciding upon the proper amount to record for a transaction and its account classification; therefore, the auditor cannot perform this function for SEC clients. Even under the existing rule it may still be permissible to post transactions to general ledgers or provide computer services to audit clients filing with the SEC, so long as all decisions are made by the client.

The SEC also requires a report by management on the 8-K report if there is a *change in the CPA firm* conducting the audit. This report must state the reason for the change of auditors, and the company must also inform the SEC of all resolved and unresolved disagreements on accounting principles during the previous eighteen months which might have caused the CPA firm to qualify the audit opinion. The reason for this requirement is to strengthen the independence of CPAs by discouraging clients from changing auditors over disputes on accounting methods. If the client has to justify changing auditors to the SEC, there is less likelihood of pressuring a CPA into accepting a particular accounting principle by threatening to change to a more cooperative CPA firm.

LEGAL LIABILITY

One attribute common to all professionals is the acceptance of the responsibility for performing high-quality services in good faith. Every professional offering services to the public is potentially liable if he fails to live up to his professional responsibilities. Just as it is not uncommon for a physician to be sued for malpractice, so also the CPA can be sued for failure to adequately perform an audit.

Since the early 1960s, lawsuits against all professionals have increased dramatically, and CPAs are no exception to this trend. In the United States, there have been more lawsuits against public accountants in the past decade than in the entire previous history of the profession. There are no simple reasons for this trend, but the following are major factors:

1. The greater complexity of auditing and accounting due to such factors as the increasing size of business, the existence of the computer, and the intricacies of business operations.
2. The growing awareness of the responsibilities of public accountants on the part of users of financial statements.
3. An increased consciousness on the part of the SEC regarding its responsibility for protecting investors' interests.
4. Society's increasing acceptance of lawsuits by injured parties against anyone who might be able to provide compensation, regardless of who was at fault.
5. Large civil court judgments against CPA firms in a few cases, which have encouraged attorneys to provide legal services on a contingent fee basis. This arrangement offers the injured party a potential gain when the suit is successful, but minimal loss when it is unsuccessful.
6. The willingness of CPA firms to settle out of court in an attempt to avoid legal fees and adverse publicity rather than resolve through the judicial process the legal problems facing the profession.
7. The many alternative accounting principles from which clients can elect to present their financial statements, and the lack of clear-cut criteria for the auditor to evaluate whether the proper alternative was selected.
8. The increasing number of business failures directly related to the dishonesty of management.
9. The willingness of some CPAs to succumb to management's pressures to ensure their retention as auditors.

The CPA can have liability for every aspect of his public-accounting work, including auditing, taxes, management advisory services, and bookkeeping. Since most of the major lawsuits have dealt with auditing, the following discussion is restricted to that aspect of public accounting. The areas of liability in auditing can be classified as (a) liability to clients, (b) civil liabilities to third parties under common or statutory law, and (c) criminal liability.

Liability to Clients

Legal action by a client against the auditor can result from the auditor's failure to properly fulfill his contract for services. The lawsuit can be for *breach of contract,* which is a claim that the contract was not performed in the manner agreed upon, or it can be a *tort action for negligence.* Most lawsuits involving clients are tort rather than breach of contract actions because the amount recoverable under tort is normally larger.

The most common type of lawsuit by clients is for the failure to detect fraud during the course of an audit. The suit arises when the fraud is discovered, either by the auditor or by someone else at a subsequent date. The plaintiff (client) claims the auditor had a duty to discover the defalcation and failed due to negligence in auditing. The amount of the claim is likely to be the audit fee plus the amount of the defalcation between the time the auditor should have discovered the defalcation and the time it was actually discovered.

The auditor's defense to claims of negligence for the failure to discover defalcation will normally be the lack of responsibility for such discovery. SAS 1 specifically expresses this position:

> In making the ordinary examination, the independent auditor is aware of the possibility that fraud may exist. Financial statements may be misstated as the result of defalcations and similar irregularities, or deliberate misrepresentations by management, or both. The auditor recognizes that fraud, if sufficiently material, may affect his opinion on the financial statements, and his examination, made in accordance with generally accepted auditing standards, gives consideration to this possibility. However, the ordinary examination directed to the expression of an opinion on financial statements is not primarily or specifically designed, and cannot be relied upon, to disclose defalcations and other similar irregularities, although their discovery may result. Similarly, although the discovery of deliberate misrepresentation by management is usually more closely associated with the objective of the ordinary examination, such examination cannot be relied upon to assure its discovery. The responsibility of the independent auditor for failure to detect fraud (which responsibility differs as to clients and others) arises only when such failure clearly results from failure to comply with generally accepted auditing standards.[6]

Unless the case is settled out of court, the ultimate decision as to whether the auditor had responsibility for discovering fraud in any situation will be determined by the judge or jury on the basis of the facts. The normal procedure is for both the plaintiff and the defendant to call *expert witnesses* to express their professional opinion as to the responsibility of the auditor and the adequacy of the evidence in the circumstances

---

[6] *Statement on Auditing Standards,* No. 1, AICPA (New York, 1973), p. 2.

in question. The standard of due care to which the auditor is expected to be held is expressed in *Cooley on Torts,* as follows:

> Every man who offers his service to another and is employed assumes the duty to exercise in the employment such skill as he possesses with reasonable care and diligence. In all these employments where peculiar skill is prerequisite, if one offers his service, he is understood as holding himself out to the public as possessing the degree of skill commonly possessed by others in the same employment, and, if his pretentions are unfounded, he commits a species of fraud upon every man who employs him in reliance on his public profession. But no man, whether skilled or unskilled, undertakes that the task he assumes shall be performed successfully, and without fault or error. He undertakes for good faith and integrity, but not for infallibility, and he is liable to his employer for negligence, bad faith, or dishonesty, but not for losses consequent upon pure errors of judgment.[7]

To protect against lawsuits by clients for the failure to discover defalcations, most CPA firms follow the procedure of obtaining an engagement letter and a letter of representation. The *engagement letter* from the auditor to the client specifies the responsibilities of the auditor and the client in the engagement. It includes such matters as the deadlines for completion of the audit, fee arrangements, and assistance to be provided by the client. It is also common for the auditor to include a statement specifying that the client has responsibility for the prevention of fraud and the audit cannot be relied upon for its discovery. The *letter of representation* is a letter from the client to the auditor stating that the primary responsibility for the fair presentation of the financial statements rests with management rather than with the auditor. Generally, specific references are included concerning the fair presentation of inventories, liabilities, and other account balances and disclosures. Here again, it is common for the auditor to insist that the letter include a statement to the effect that the client recognizes that management rather than the auditor has responsibility for the prevention and discovery of fraud. The letter is specially prepared by the auditor on the client's stationery and is signed by the client.

When the client is protected from embezzlement losses by a surety insurance company, the surety company can sue the auditor on the same basis as the client. Unless the loss is reasonably large, however, most surety companies are unlikely to take legal action.

Liability to Third Parties under Common Law

Public accountants may be liable to third parties if a loss was incurred by the claimant due to reliance upon misleading financial statements. Third parties include actual and potential stockholders, vendors, bankers

[7] SAS 1, p. 10.

and other creditors, employees, and customers. A typical suit might occur when a bank is unable to collect a major loan from an insolvent customer. The bank can claim that misleading audited financial statements were relied upon in making the loan. Assuming the judge or the jury is convinced the statements were not properly presented and the bank would not have granted the loan if the statements had been presented differently, there is a high likelihood that the auditor of the statements will be held liable. The three significant parts of this example are (1) existence of misleading financial statements, (2) incurrence of a financial loss on the part of the claimant, and (3) that reliance upon the statements was the cause of the loss. All three of these elements must exist before a third party has a claim against the auditor.

The liability to third parties is more restricted than the liability to clients due to the lack of a contractual agreement between the auditor and third parties. The courts have generally held that the auditor is liable to third parties only for fraud or gross negligence. *Fraud* is the willful misstatement or omission of a material fact with the intent to deceive, whereas *gross negligence* is the unintentional but flagrant violation of generally accepted auditing standards. Gross negligence is frequently referred to as *constructive fraud*. Naturally, when a third party incurs a loss, there is a tendency to charge the auditor with negligence so severe as to constitute gross negligence rather than ordinary negligence.

In recent years common law seems to be moving in the direction of granting relief to claimants for ordinary negligence if the claiming party is clearly identifiable to the auditor. For example, the auditor could be held responsible for being able to identify all significant existing creditors and perhaps even major stockholders as known users of the financial statements. This trend toward increasing the auditor's responsibility for ordinary negligence could have an important impact on legal liability in the future.

Civil Liability under the Securities Laws

Any auditor filing with the SEC under either the 1933 or the 1934 Securities Act faces exposure to legal action beyond common law. Many CPAs now feel that the risk of significant lawsuits for certain clients is greater from the SEC than from any other source. In addition, the amount of potential damages is extremely large.

The Securities Act of 1933, which deals with information in registration statements and prospectuses, can impose an unusual burden upon the auditor. Section 11(a) of the 1933 act outlines the right of third parties to sue the auditor for damages if the registration statement contains an untrue statement of a material fact or if the omission of a material fact results in misleading financial statements. Under Section 11(a), any investor can sue the auditor for alleged misleading misstatements in the financial statements without having the burden of proving reliance upon the statements or even showing that his loss resulted from the misstatement. An even greater hardship is imposed upon the auditor by requiring him to demonstrate the absence of negligence or fraud in the conduct of the audit. Fortunately for the profession, there have been only rare instances of suits under the 1933 act.

The liability of auditors under the 1934 act, which is concerned primarily with information included in the annual 10-K reports for publicly traded companies, is more similar to that under common law than to the liability under the 1933 act. Under the 1934 act the burden of proof is on third parties to show that they relied upon the 10-K information and that the erroneous misleading financial statements were the cause of the loss incurred. There is only liability for gross negligence and fraud under the 1934 act. Since there are far more annual reports filed under the 1934 act than there are registration statements under the 1933 act, there are also more legal actions under the 1934 act.

Criminal Liability

It is possible for public accountants to be found guilty for criminal action under both federal and state laws. The most likely statutes to be used under state law are the Uniform Securities Acts, which are similar to parts of the SEC rules. The 1933 and 1934 Securities Acts, as well as the Federal Mail Fraud Statute and the Federal False Statements Statute, are the most relevant federal laws affecting auditors. All of these make it a criminal offense to defraud another person through knowingly being involved with false financial statements.

Fortunately for the accounting profession, there have been few criminal actions involving public accountants. The public's reaction to extensive criminal action would be highly damaging to the integrity of the profession.

The most celebrated case involving criminal action is *United States* v. *Simon,* better known as the *Continental Vending* case, which took place in the late 1960s. This highly complex case involved the company's failure to properly disclose in a footnote the nature of material loans to an affiliated company. The conclusion of the court was that the partners and staff involved in the audit had conspired with the client to deceive the users of the financial statements. The senior partner, a junior partner, and a manager were convicted and heavily fined. Even though there were no prison sentences imposed, these three individuals all left the profession.

The determination of the extent to which auditors should be legally responsible for financial statements is relevant to both the professional and to society. Clearly, the existence of legal responsibility is an important deterrent to inadequate and even dishonest activities of some auditors. No reasonable CPA would want the profession's legal responsibility for fraudulent or incompetent performance eliminated. The maintenance of public trust in the competent performance of the auditing function is essential to the profession's self-interest. At the other extreme, it is unreasonable for auditors to be held legally responsible for every misstatement in financial statements. The audit costs to society that would be required to achieve such high levels of assurance would exceed the benefits. Even with increased audit costs, well-planned collusive frauds would frequently not be discovered. In between these two extremes, it is necessary for the profession and society to determine a reasonable trade-off between the degree of responsibility the auditor should take for fair presentation and the audit cost to society. The courts have the major influence in shaping the final solution.

In addition to the discussion of legal liability in this section, specific lawsuits against CPAs are discussed in Chapter 4 and other parts of the text.

Appendix A:

Code of Professional Ethics

CONCEPTS OF PROFESSIONAL ETHICS

A distinguishing mark of a professional is his acceptance of responsibility to the public. All true professions have therefore deemed it essential to promulgate codes of ethics and to establish means for ensuring their observance.

The reliance of the public, the government and the business community on sound financial reporting and advice on business affairs, and the importance of these matters to the economic and social aspects of life imposed particular obligations on certified public accountants.

Ordinarily those who depend upon a certified public accountant find it difficult to assess the quality of his services; they have a right to expect, however, that he is a person of competence and integrity. A man or woman who enters the profession of accountancy is assumed to accept an obligation to uphold its principles, to work for the increase of knowledge in the art and for the improvement of methods, and to abide by the profession's ethical and technical standards.

The ethical Code of the American Institute emphasizes the profession's responsibility to the public, a responsibility that has grown as the number of investors has grown, as the relationship between corporate managers and stockholders has become more impersonal and as government increasingly relies on accounting information.

8 American Institute of Certified Public Accountants, *Code of Professional Ethics.* American Institute of Certified Public Accountants, New York, 1972. *Code of Professional Ethics* reproduced with permission of the American Institute of Certified Public Accountants.

The Code also stresses the CPA's responsibility to clients and colleagues, since his behavior in these relationships cannot fail to affect the responsibilities of the profession as a whole to the public.

The Institute's Rules of Conduct set forth minimum levels of acceptable conduct and are mandatory and enforceable. However, it is in the best interests of the profession that CPAs strive for conduct beyond that indicated merely by prohibitions. Ethical conduct, in the true sense, is more than merely abiding by the letter of explicit prohibitions. Rather, it requires unswerving commitment to honorable behavior, even at the sacrifice of personal advantage.

The conduct toward which CPAs should strive is embodied in five broad concepts stated as affirmative Ethical Principles:

Independence, integrity and objectivity. A certified public accountant should maintain his integrity and objectivity and, when engaged in the practice of public accounting, be independent of those he serves.

Competence and technical standards. A certified public accountant should observe the profession's technical standards and strive continually to improve his competence and the quality of his services.

Responsibilities to clients. A certified public accountant should be fair and candid with his clients and serve them to the best of his ability, with professional concern for their best interests, consistent with his responsibilities to the public.

Responsibilities to colleagues. A certified public accountant should conduct himself in a manner which will promote cooperation and good relations among members of the profession.

Other responsibilities and practices. A certified public accountant should conduct himself in a manner which will enhance the stature of the profession and its ability to serve the public.

The foregoing Ethical Principles are intended as broad guidelines as distinguished from enforceable Rules of Conduct. Even though they do not provide a basis for disciplinary action, they constitute the philosophical foundation upon which the Rules of Conduct are based.

The following discussion is intended to elaborate on each of the Ethical Principles and provide rationale for their support.

Independence, Integrity and Objectivity

A certified public accountant should maintain his integrity and objectivity and, when engaged in the practice of public accounting, be independent of those he serves.

The public expects a number of character traits in a certified public accountant but primarily integrity and objectivity and, in the practice of public accounting, independence.

Independence has always been a concept fundamental to the accounting profession, the cornerstone of its philosophical structure. For no matter how competent any CPA may be, his opinion on financial statements will be of little value to those who rely on him—whether they be clients or any of his unseen audience of credit grantors, investors, governmental agencies and the like—unless he maintains his independence.

Independence has traditionally been defined by the profession as the ability to act with integrity and objectivity.

Integrity is an element of character which is fundamental to reliance on the CPA. This quality may be difficult to judge, however, since a particular fault of omission or commission may be the result either of honest error or a lack of integrity.

Objectivity refers to a CPA's ability to maintain an impartial attitude on all matters which come under his review. Since this attitude involves an individual's mental processes, the evaluation of objectivity must be based largely on actions and relationships viewed in the context of ascertainable circumstances.

While recognizing that the qualities of integrity and objectivity are not precisely measurable, the profession nevertheless constantly holds them up to members as an imperative. This is done essentially by education and by the Rules of Conduct which the profession adopts and enforces.

CPAs cannot practice their calling and participate in the world's affairs without being exposed to situations that involve the possibility of pressures upon their integrity and objectivity. To define and proscribe all such situations would be impracticable. To ignore the problem for that reason, however, and to set no limits at all would be irresponsible.

It follows that the concept of independence should not be interpreted so loosely as to permit relationships likely to impair the CPA's integrity or the impartiality of his judgment, nor so strictly as to inhibit the rendering of useful services when the likelihood of such impairment is relatively remote.

While it may be difficult for a CPA always to appear completely independent even in normal relationships with clients, pressures upon his integrity or objectivity are offset by powerful countervailing forces and restraints. These include the possibility of legal liability, professional discipline ranging up to revocation of the right to practice as a CPA, loss of reputation and, by no means least, the inculcated resistance of a disciplined professional to any infringement upon his basic integrity and objectivity. Accordingly, in deciding which types of relationships should be specifically prohibited, both the magnitude of the threat posed by a relationship and the force of countervailing pressures have to be weighed.

In establishing rules relating to independence, the profession uses the criterion of whether reasonable men, having knowledge of all the facts and taking into consideration normal strength of character and normal behavior under the circumstances, would conclude that a specified relationship between a CPA and a client poses an unacceptable threat to the CPA's integrity or objectivity.

When a CPA expresses an opinion on financial statements, not only the fact but also the appearance of integrity and objectivity is of particular importance. For this reason, the profession has adopted rules to prohibit the expression of such an opinion when relationships exist which might pose such a threat to integrity and objectivity as to exceed the strength of countervailing forces and restraints. These relationships fall into two general categories: (1) certain financial relationships with clients and (2) relationships in which a CPA is virtually part of management or an employee under management's control.

Although the appearance of independence is not required in the case of management advisory services and tax practice, a CPA is encouraged to avoid the proscribed relationships with clients regardless of the type of services being rendered. In any event, the CPA, in all types of engagements, should refuse to subordinate his professional judgment to others and should express his conclusions honestly and objectively.

The financial relationships proscribed when an opinion is expressed on financial statements make no reference to fees paid to a CPA by a client. Remuneration to providers of services is necessary for the continued provision of those services. Indeed, a principal reason for the development and persistence in the professions of the client-practitioner relationship and of remuneration by fee (as contrasted with an employer-employee relationship and remuneration by salary) is that these arrangements are seen as a safeguard of independence.

The above reference to an employer-employee relationship is pertinent to a question sometimes raised as to whether a CPA's objectivity in expressing an opinion on financial statements will be impaired by his being involved with his client in the decision-making process.

CPAs continually provide advice to their clients, and they expect that this advice will usually be followed. Decisions based on such advice may have a significant effect on a client's financial condition or operating results. This is the case not only in tax engagements and management advisory services but in the audit function as well.

If a CPA disagrees with a client on a significant matter during the course of an audit, the client has three choices—he can modify the financial statements (which is usually the case), he can accept a qualified report or he can discharge the CPA. While the ultimate decision and the resulting financial statements clearly are those of the client, the CPA has obviously been a significant factor in the decision-making process. Indeed, no responsible user of financial statements would want it otherwise.

It must be noted that when a CPA expresses an opinion on financial statements, the judgments involved pertain to whether the results of operating decisions of the client are fairly presented in the statements and not on the underlying wisdom of such decisions. It is highly unlikely therefore that being a factor in the client's decision-making process would impair the CPA's objectivity in judging the fairness of presentation.

The more important question is whether a CPA would deliberately compromise his integrity by expressing an unqualified opinion on financial statements which were prepared in such a way as to cover up a poor business decision by the client and on which the CPA had rendered advice. The basic character traits of the CPA as well as the risks arising from such a compromise of integrity, including liability to third parties, disciplinary action and loss of right to practice, should preclude such action.

Providing advice or recommendations which may or may not involve skills logically related to a client's information and control system, and which may affect the client's decision-making, does not in itself indicate lack of independence. However, the CPA must be alert to the possibility that undue identification with the management of the client or involvement with a client's affairs to such a degree as to place him virtually in the position of being an employee, may impair the appearance of independence.

To sum up, CPAs cannot avoid external pressures on their integrity and objectivity in the course of their professional work, but they are expected to resist these pressures. They must, in fact, retain their integrity and objectivity in all phases of their practice and, when expressing opinions on financial statements, avoid involvement in situations that would impair the credibility of their independence in the minds of reasonable men familiar with the facts.

Competence and Technical Standards

> *A certified public accountant should observe the profession's technical standards and strive continually to improve his competence and the quality of his services.*

Since accounting information is of great importance to all segments of the public, all CPAs, whether in public practice, government service, private employment or academic pursuits, should perform their work at a high level of professionalism.

A CPA should maintain and seek always to improve his competence in all areas of accountancy in which he engages. Satisfaction of the requirements for the CPA certificate is evidence of basic competence at the time the certificate is granted, but it does not justify an assumption that this competence is maintained without continuing effort. Further, it does not necessarily justify undertaking complex engagements without additional study and experience.

A CPA should not render professional services without being aware of, and complying with, the applicable technical standards. Moreover, since published technical standards can never cover the whole field of accountancy, he must keep broadly informed.

Observance of the rule on competence calls for a subjective determination by a CPA with respect to each engagement. Some engagements will require a higher level of knowledge, skill and judgment than others. Competence to deal with an unfamiliar problem may be acquired by research, study or consultation with a practitioner who has the necessary competence. If a CPA is unable to gain sufficient competence through these means, he should suggest, in fairness to his client and the public, the engagement of someone competent to perform the needed service, either independently or as an associate.

The standards referred to in the rules are elaborated and refined to meet changing conditions, and it is each CPA's responsibility to keep himself up to date in this respect.

Responsibilities to Clients

> *A certified public accountant should be fair and candid with his clients and serve them to the best of his ability, with professional concern for their best interests, consistent with his responsibilities to the public.*

As a professional person, the CPA should serve his clients with competence and with professional concern for their best interests. He must not permit his regard for a client's interest, however, to override his obligation to the public to maintain his independence, integrity and objectivity. The discharge of this dual responsibility to both clients and the public requires a high degree of ethical perception and conduct.

It is fundamental that the CPA hold in strict confidence all information concerning a client's affairs which he acquires in the course of his engagement. This does not mean, however, that he should acquiesce in a client's unwillingness to make disclosures in financial reports which are necessary to fair presentation.

Exploitation of relations with a client for personal advantage is improper. For example, acceptance of a commission from any vendor for recommending his product or service to a client is prohibited.

A CPA should be frank and straightforward with clients. While tact and diplomacy are desirable, a client should never be left in doubt about the CPA's position on any issue of significance. No truly professional man will subordinate his own judgment or conceal or modify his honest opinion merely to please. This admonition applies to all services including those related to management and tax problems.

When accepting an engagement, a CPA should bear in mind that he may find it necessary to resign if conflict arises on an important question of principle. In cases of irreconcilable difference, he will have to judge whether the importance of the matter requires such an action. In weighing this question, he can feel assured that the practitioner who is independent, fair and candid is the better respected for these qualities and will not lack opportunities for constructive service.

Responsibilities to Colleagues

> *A certified public accountant should conduct himself in a manner which will promote cooperation and good relations among members of the profession.*

The support of a profession by its members and their cooperation with one another are essential elements of professional character. The public confidence and respect which a CPA enjoys is largely the result of the cumulative accomplishments of all CPAs, past and present. It is, therefore, in the CPA's own interest, as well as that of the general public, to support the collective efforts of colleagues through professional societies and organizations and to deal with fellow practitioners in a manner which will not detract from their reputation and well-being.

Although the reluctance of a professional to give testimony that may be damaging to a colleague is understandable, the obligation of professional courtesy and fraternal consideration can never excuse lack of complete candor if the CPA is testifying as an expert witness in a judicial proceeding or properly constituted inquiry.

A CPA has the obligation to assist his fellows in complying with the Code of Professional Ethics and should also assist appropriate disciplinary authorities in enforcing the Code. To condone serious fault can be as bad as to commit it. It may be even worse, in fact, since some errors may result from ignorance rather than intent and, if let pass without action, will probably be repeated. In situations of this kind, the welfare of the public should be the guide to a member's action.

While the Code proscribes certain specific actions in the area of relationships with colleagues, it should be understood that these proscriptions do not define the limits of desirable intraprofessional conduct. Rather, such conduct encompasses the professional consideration and courtesies which each CPA would like to have fellow practitioners extend to him.

It is natural that a CPA will seek to develop his practice. However, in doing so he should not seek to displace another accountant in a client relationship, or act in any way that reflects negatively on fellow practitioners.

A CPA may, of course, provide services to those who request it, even though they may be served by another practitioner in another area of service, or he may succeed another practitioner at a client's request. In such circumstances it is desirable before accepting an engagement that the CPA who has been approached should advise the accountant already serving the client. Such action is indicated not only by considerations of professional courtesy but by good business judgment.

A client may sometimes request services requiring highly specialized knowledge. If the CPA lacks the expertise necessary to render such services, he should call upon a fellow practitioner for assistance or refer the entire engagement to another. Such assistance or referral brings to bear on the client's needs both the referring practitioner's knowledge of the client's affairs and the technical expertise of the specialist brought into the engagement. The rules encourage referrals by helping to protect the client relationships of the referring practitioner.

Other Responsibilities and Practices

> *A certified public accountant should conduct himself in a manner which will enhance the stature of the profession and its ability to serve the public.*

In light of the importance of their function, CPAs and their firms should have a keen consciousness of the public interest and the needs of society. Thus, they should support efforts to achieve equality of opportunity for all, regardless of race, religious background or sex, and should contribute to this goal by their own service relationships and employment practices.

The CPA is a beneficiary of the organization and character of his profession. Since he is seen as a representative of the profession by those who come in contact with him, he should behave honorably both in his personal and professional life and avoid any conduct that might erode public respect and confidence.

Solicitation to obtain clients is prohibited under the Rules of Conduct because it tends to lessen the professional independence toward clients which is essential to the best interests of the public. It may also induce an unhealthy rivalry within the profession and thus lessen the cooperation among members which is essential to advancing the state of the art of accounting and providing maximum service to the public.

Advertising, which is a form of solicitation, is also prohibited because it could encourage representations which might mislead the public and thereby reduce or destroy the profession's usefulness to society. However, a CPA should seek to establish a reputation for competence and character, and there are many acceptable means by which this can be done. For example, he may make himself known by public service, by civic and political activities, and by joining associations and clubs. It is desirable for him to share his knowledge with interested groups by accepting requests to make speeches and write articles. Whatever publicity occurs as a natural by-product of such activities is entirely proper. It would be wrong, however, for the CPA to initiate or embellish publicity.

Promotional practices, such as solicitation and advertising, tend to indicate a dominant interest in profit. In his work, the CPA should be motivated more by desire for excellence in performance than for material reward. This does not mean that he need be indifferent about compensation. Indeed, a professional man who cannot maintain a respectable standard of living is unlikely to inspire confidence or to enjoy sufficient peace of mind to do his best work.

In determining fees, a CPA may assess the degree of responsibility assumed by undertaking an engagement as well as the time, manpower and skills required to perform the service in conformity with the standards of the profession. He may also take into account the value of the service to the client, the customary charges of professional colleagues and other considerations. No single factor is necessarily controlling.

Clients have a right to know in advance what rates will be charged and approximately how much an engagement will cost. However, when professional judgments are involved, it is usually not possible to set a fair charge until an engagement has been completed. For this reason CPAs should state their fees for proposed engagements in the form of estimates which may be subject to change as the work progresses.

Other practices prohibited by the Rules of Conduct include using any firm designation or description which might be misleading, or practicing as a professional corporation or association which fails to comply with provisions established by Council to protect the public interest.

A member, while practicing public accounting, may not engage in a business or occupation which is incompatible therewith. While certain occupations are clearly incompatible with the practice of public accounting, the profession has never attempted to list them for in most cases the individual circumstances indicate whether there is a problem. For example, there would be a problem of incompatibility if a practicing CPA were to sell insurance or securities because these occupations involve solicitation and promotional activities which might be used to promote a public accounting practice. Moreover, they might, under some circumstances, jeopardize the CPA's independence.

Paying a commission is prohibited in order to eliminate the temptation to compensate anyone for referring a client. Receipt of a commission is proscribed since practitioners should look to the client, and not to others, for compensation for services rendered. The practice of paying a fee to a referring CPA irrespective of any service performed or responsibility assumed by him is proscribed because there is no justification for a CPA to share in a fee for accounting services where his sole contribution was to make a referral.

Over the years the vast majority of CPAs have endeavored to earn and maintain a reputation for competence, integrity and objectivity. The success of these efforts has been largely responsible for the wide public acceptance of accounting as an honorable profession. This acceptance is a valuable asset which should never be taken for granted. Every CPA should constantly strive to see that it continues to be deserved.

RULES OF CONDUCT

Definitions

The following definitions of terminology are applicable wherever such terminology is used in the rules and interpretations.

    Client. The person(s) or entity which retains a member or his firm, engaged in the practice of public accounting, for the performance of professional services.

Council. The Council of the American Institute of Certified Public Accounts.

Enterprise. Any person(s) or entity, whether organized for profit or not, for which a CPA provides services.

Firm. A proprietorship, partnership or professional corporation or association engaged in the practice of public accounting, including individual partners or shareholders thereof.

Financial statements. Statements and footnotes related thereto that purport to show financial position which relates to a point in time or changes in financial position which relate to a period of time, and statements which use a cash or other incomplete basis of accounting. Balance sheets, statements of income, statements of retained earnings, statements of changes in financial position and statements of changes in owners' equity are financial statements.

Incidental financial data included in management advisory services reports to support recommendations to a client, and tax returns and supporting schedules do not, for this purpose, constitute financial statements; and the statement, affidavit or signature of preparers required on tax returns neither constitutes an opinion on financial statements nor requires a disclaimer of such opinion.

Institute. The American Institute of Certified Public Accountants.

Interpretations of Rules of Conduct. Pronouncements issued by the Division of Professional Ethics to provide guidelines as to the scope and application of the Rules of Conduct.

Member. A member, associate member or international associate of the American Institute of Certified Public Accountants.

Practice of public accounting. Holding out to be a CPA or public accountant and at the same time performing for a client one or more types of services rendered by public accountants. The term shall not be limited by a more restrictive definition which might be found in the accountancy law under which a member practices.

Professional services. One or more types of services performed in the practice of public accounting.

Applicability of Rules

The Institute's Code of Professional Ethics derives its authority from the bylaws of the Institute which provide that the Trial Board may, after a hearing, admonish, suspend or expel a member who is found guilty of infringing any of the bylaws or any provisions of the Rules of Conduct.

The Rules of Conduct which follow apply to all services performed in the practice of public accounting, including tax and management advisory services except (a) where the wording of the rule indicates otherwise and (b) that a member who is practicing outside the United States will not be subject to discipline for departing from any of the rules stated herein so long as his conduct is in accord with the rules of the organized accounting profession in the country in which he is practicing. However, where a member's name is associated with financial statements in such a manner as to imply that he is acting as an independent public accountant and under circumstances that would entitle the reader to assume that United States practices were followed, he must comply with the requirements of Rules 202 and 203.

A member may be held responsible for compliance with the Rules of Conduct by all persons associated with him in the practice of public accounting who are either under his supervision or are his partners or shareholders in the practice.

A member engaged in the practice of public accounting must observe all the Rules of Conduct. A member not engaged in the practice of public accounting must observe only Rules 102 and 501 since all other Rules of Conduct relate solely to the practice of public accounting.

A member shall not permit others to carry out on his behalf, either with or without compensation, acts which, if carried out by the member, would place him in violation of the Rules of Conduct.

Independence, Integrity, and Objectivity

Rule 101—Independence. A member or a firm of which he is a partner or shareholder shall not express an opinion on financial statements of an enterprise unless he and his firm are independent with respect to such enterprise. Independence will be considered to be impaired if, for example:

    A. During the period of his professional engagement, or at the time of expressing his opinion, he or his firm
        1. Had or was committed to acquire any direct or material indirect financial interest in the enterprise; or
        2. Had any joint closely held business investment with the enterprise or any officer, director or principal stockholder thereof which was material in relation to his or his firm's net worth; or
        3. Had any loan to or from the enterprise or any officer, director or principal stockholder thereof. This latter proscription does not apply to the following loans from a financial institution when made under normal lending procedures, terms and requirements:
           (a) Loans obtained by a member or his firm which are not material in relation to the net worth of such borrower.
           (b) Home mortgages.

(c) Other secured loans, except loans guaranteed by a member's firm which are otherwise unsecured.

B. During the period covered by the financial statements, during the period of the professional engagement or at the time of expressing an opinion, he or his firm

1. Was connected with the enterprise as a promoter, underwriter or voting trustee, a director or officer or in any capacity equivalent to that of a member of management or of an employee; or

2. Was a trustee of any trust or executor or administrator of any estate if such trust or estate had a direct or material indirect financial interest in the enterprise; or was a trustee for any pension or profit-sharing trust of the enterprise.

The above examples are not intended to be all-inclusive.

Rule 102—Integrity and objectivity. A member shall not knowingly misrepresent facts, and when engaged in the practice of public accounting, including the rendering of tax and management advisory services, shall not subordinate his judgment to others. In tax practice, a member may resolve doubt in favor of his client as long as there is reasonable support for his position.

Competence and Technical Standards

Rule 201—Competence. A member shall not undertake any engagement which he or his firm cannot reasonably expect to complete with professional competence.

Rule 202—Auditing standards. A member shall not permit his name to be associated with financial statements in such a manner as to imply that he is acting as an independent public accountant unless he has complied with the applicable generally accepted auditing standards promulgated by the Institute. Statements on Auditing Procedure issued by the Institute's committee on auditing procedure are, for purposes of this rule, considered to be interpretations of the generally accepted auditing standards, and departures from such statements must be justified by those who do not follow them.

Rule 203—Accounting principles. A member shall not express an opinion that financial statements are presented in conformity with generally accepted accounting principles if such statements contain any departure from an accounting principle promulgated by the body designated by Council to establish such principles which has a material effect on the statements taken as a whole, unless the member can demonstrate that due to unusual circumstances the financial statements would otherwise have been misleading. In such cases his report must describe the departure, the approximate effects thereof, if practicable, and the reasons why compliance with the principle would result in a misleading statement.

Rule 204—Forecasts. A member shall not permit his name to be used in conjunction with any forecast of future transactions in a manner which may lead to the belief that the member vouches for the achievability of the forecast.

Responsibilities to Clients

Rule 301—Confidential client information. A member shall not disclose any confidential information obtained in the course of a professional engagement except with the consent of the client.

This rule shall not be construed (a) to relieve a member of his obligation under Rules 202 and 203, (b) to affect in any way his compliance with a validly issued subpoena or summons enforceable by order of a court, (c) to prohibit review of a member's professional practices as a part of voluntary quality review under Institute authorization or (d) to preclude a member from responding to any inquiry made by the ethics division or Trial Board of the Institute, by a duly constituted investigative or disciplinary body of a state CPA society, or under state statutes.

Members of the ethics division and Trial Board of the Institute and professional practice reviewers under Institute authorization shall not disclose any confidential client information which comes to their attention from members in disciplinary proceedings or otherwise in carrying out their official responsibilities. However, this prohibition shall not restrict the exchange of information with an aforementioned duly constituted investigative or disciplinary body.

Rule 302—Contingent fees. Professional services shall not be offered or rendered under an arrangement whereby no fee will be charged unless a specified finding or result is attained, or where the fee is otherwise contingent upon the findings or results of such services. However, a member's fees may vary depending, for example, on the complexity of the service rendered.

Fees are not regarded as being contingent if fixed by courts or other public authorities or, in tax matters, if determined based on the results of judicial proceedings or the findings of governmental agencies.

Responsibilities to Colleagues

Rule 401—Encroachment. A member shall not endeavor to provide a person or entity with a professional service which is currently provided by another public accountant except:

1. He may respond to a request for a proposal to render services and may furnish service to those who request it. However, if an audit client of another independent public accountant requests a member to provide professional advice on accounting or auditing matters in connection with an expression of opinion on financial statements, the member must first

consult with the other accountant to ascertain that the member is aware of all the available relevant facts.

2. Where a member is required to express an opinion on combined or consolidated financial statements which include a subsidiary, branch or other component audited by another independent public accountant, he may insist on auditing any such component which in his judgment is necessary to warrant the expression of his opinion.

A member who receives an engagement for services by referral from another public accountant shall not accept the client's request to extend his service beyond the specific engagement without first notifying the referring accountant, nor shall he seek to obtain any additional engagement from the client.

Rule 402—Offers of employment. A member in public practice shall not make a direct or indirect offer of employment to an employee of another public accountant on his own behalf or that of his client without first informing such accountant. This rule shall not apply if the employee of his own initiative or in response to a public advertisement applies for employment.

Other Responsibilities and Practices

Rule 501—Acts discreditable. A member shall not commit an act discreditable to the profession.

Rule 502—Solicitation and advertising. A member shall not seek to obtain clients by solicitation. Advertising is a form of solicitation and is prohibited.

Rule 503—Commissions. A member shall not pay a commission to obtain a client, nor shall he accept a commission for a referral to a client of products or services of others. This rule shall not prohibit payments for the purchase of an accounting practice or retirement payments to individuals formerly engaged in the practice of public accounting or payments to their heirs or estates.

Rule 504—Incompatible occupations. A member who is engaged in the practice of public accounting shall not concurrently engage in any business or occupation which impairs his objectivity in rendering professional services or serves as a feeder to his practice.

Rule 505—Form of practice and name. A member may practice public accounting, whether as an owner or employee, only in the form of a proprietorship, a partnership or a professional corporation whose characteristics conform to resolutions of Council.

A member shall not practice under a firm name which includes any fictitious name, indicates specialization or is misleading as to the type of organization (proprietorship, partnership or corporation). However, names of one or more past partners or shareholders may be included in the firm name of a successor partnership or corporation. Also, a partner surviving the death or withdrawal of all other partners may continue to practice under the partnership name for up to two years after becoming a sole practitioner.

A firm may not designate itself as "Members of the American Institute of Certified Public Accountants" unless all of its partners or shareholders are members of the Institute.

INTERPRETATIONS OF RULES OF CONDUCT

Interpretations under Rule 101—Independence

101-1—Directorships. Members are often asked to lend the prestige of their name as a director of a charitable, religious, civic or other similar type of nonprofit organization whose board is large and representative of the community's leadership. An auditor who permits his name to be used in this manner would not be considered lacking in independence under Rule 101 so long as he does not perform or give advice on management functions, and the board itself is sufficiently large that a third party would conclude that his membership was honorary.

101-2—Retired partners and firm independence. A retired partner having a relationship of a type specified in Rule 101 with a client of his former firm would not be considered as impairing the firm's independence with respect to the client provided that he is no longer active in the firm, that the fees received from such client do not have a material effect on his retirement benefits and that he is not held out as being associated with his former partnership.

101-3—Accounting services. Members in public practice are sometimes asked to provide manual or automated bookkeeping or data processing services to clients who are of insufficient size to employ an adequate internal accounting staff. Computer systems design and programming assistance are also rendered by members either in conjunction with data processing services or as a separate engagement. Members who perform such services and who are engaged in the practice of public accounting are subject to the by-laws and Rules of Conduct.

On occasion members also rent "block time" on their computers to their clients but are not involved in the processing of transactions or maintaining the client's accounting records. In such cases the sale of block time constitutes a business rather than a professional relationship and must be considered together with all other relationships between the member and his client to determine if their aggregate impact is such as to impair the member's independence.

When a member performs manual or automated bookkeeping services, concern may arise whether the performance of such services would impair his audit independence—that the performance of such basic accounting services would cause his audit to be lacking in a review of mechanical accuracy or that the accounting judgments made by him in recording transactions may somehow be less reliable than if made by him in connection with the subsequent audit.

Members are skilled in, and well accustomed to, applying techniques to control mechanical accuracy, and the performance of the record-keeping function should have no effect on application of such techniques. With regard to accounting judgments, if third parties have confidence in a member's judgment in performing an audit, it is difficult to contend that they would have less confidence where the same judgment is applied in the process of preparing the underlying accounting records.

Nevertheless, a member performing accounting services for an audit client must meet the following requirements to retain the appearance that he is not virtually an employee and therefore lacking in independence in the eyes of a reasonable observer.

1. The CPA must not have any relationship or combination of relationships with the client or any conflict of interest which would impair his integrity and objectivity.

2. The client must accept the responsibility for the financial statements as his own. A small client may not have anyone in his employ to maintain accounting records and may rely on the CPA for this purpose. Nevertheless, the client must be sufficiently knowledgeable of the enterprise's activities and financial condition and the applicable accounting principles so that he can reasonably accept such responsibility, including, specifically, fairness of valuation and presentation and adequacy of disclosure. When necessary, the CPA must discuss accounting matters with the client to be sure that the client has the required degree of understanding.

3. The CPA must not assume the role of employee or of management conducting the operations of an enterprise. For example, the CPA shall not consummate transactions, have custody of assets or exercise authority on behalf of the client. The client must prepare the source documents on all transactions in sufficient detail to identify clearly the nature and amount of such transactions and maintain an accounting control over data processed by the CPA such as control totals and document counts. The CPA should not make changes in such basic data without the concurrence of the client.

4. The CPA, in making an examination of financial statements prepared from books and records which he has maintained completely or in part, must conform to generally accepted auditing standards. The fact that he has processed or maintained certain records does not eliminate the need to make sufficient audit tests.

When a client's securities become subject to regulation by the Securities and Exchange Commission or other federal or state regulatory body, responsibility for maintenance of the accounting records, including accounting classification decisions, must be assumed by accounting personnel employed by the client. The assumption of this responsibility must commence with the first fiscal year after which the client's securities qualify for such regulation.

Interpretation under Rule 201—Competence

201-1—Competence. A member who accepts a professional engagement implies that he has the necessary competence to complete the engagement according to professional standards, applying his knowledge and skill with reasonable care and diligence, but he does not assume a responsibility for infallibility of knowledge or judgment.

Competence in the practice of public accounting involves both the technical qualifications of the member and his staff and his ability to supervise and evaluate the quality of the work performed. Competence relates both to knowledge of the profession's standards, techniques and the technical subject matter involved, and to the capability to exercise sound judgment in applying such knowledge to each engagement.

The member may have the knowledge required to complete an engagement professionally before undertaking it. In many cases, however, additional research or consultation with others may be necessary during the course of the engagement. This does not ordinarily represent a lack of competence, but rather is a normal part of the professional conduct of an engagement.

However, if a CPA is unable to gain sufficient competence through these means, he should suggest, in fairness to his client and the public, the engagement of someone competent to perform the needed service, either independently or as an associate.

Interpretation under Rule 203—Accounting Principles

203-1—Departures from established accounting principles. Rule 203 was adopted to require compliance with accounting principles promulgated by the body designated by Council to establish such principles. There is a strong presumption that adherence to officially established accounting principles would in nearly all instances result in financial statements that are not misleading.

However, in the establishment of accounting principles it is difficult to anticipate all of the circumstances to which such principles might be applied. The rule therefore recognizes that upon occasion there may be unusual circumstances where the literal application of pronouncements on accounting principles would have the effect of rendering financial statements misleading. In such cases, the proper accounting treatment is that which will render the financial statements not misleading.

The question of what constitutes unusual circumstances as referred to in Rule 203 is a matter of professional judgment involving the ability to support the position that adherence to a promulgated principle would be regarded generally by reasonable men as producing a misleading result.

Examples of events which may justify departures from a principle are new legislation or the evolution of a new form of business transaction. An unusual degree of materiality or the existence of conflicting industry practices are examples of circumstances which would not ordinarily be regarded as unusual in the context of Rule 203.

Interpretation under Rule 204—Forecasts

204-1—Forecasts. Rule 204 does not prohibit a member from preparing, or assisting a client in the preparation of, forecasts of the results of future transactions. When a member's name is associated with such forecasts, there shall be the presumption that such data may be used by parties other than the client. Therefore, full disclosure must be made of the sources of the information used and the major assumptions made in the preparation of the statements and analyses, the character of the work performed by the member, and the degree of the responsibility he is taking.

Interpretation under Rule 301—Confidential Client Information

301-1—Confidential information and technical standards. The prohibition against disclosure of confidential information obtained in the course of a professional engagement does not apply to disclosure of such information when required to properly discharge the member's responsibility according to the profession's standards. The prohibition would not apply, for example, to disclosure, as required by Statement on Auditing Procedure No. 41 (now section 561 of Statement on Auditing Standards No. 1), of subsequent discovery of facts existing at the date of the auditor's report which would have affected the auditor's report had he been aware of such facts.

Interpretations under Rule 401—Encroachment

401-1—Relations with clients also served by other public accountants. The unsolicited sending to clients of firm literature or invitations to seminars which cover services that are currently being rendered to the client by another public accountant is considered a violation of Rule 401.

401-2—Reliance on work of others. Rule 401-2 makes clear that it is not improper for a member expressing his opinion on combined or consolidated financial statements to insist on auditing such components as in his judgment are necessary to warrant the expression of his opinion. However, the auditor's exercise of judgment in this regard is subject to review. For example, insistence upon auditing an unreasonably large percentage of consolidated net assets or net income may lead to the conclusion that the auditor's judgment had been made as part of a plan or design to solicit an engagement, which action would be a violation of the rule against encroachment.

Interpretations under Rule 502—Solicitation and Advertising

502-1—Announcements. Publication in a newspaper, magazine or similar medium of an announcement or what is technically known as a "card" is prohibited. Also prohibited is the issuance of a press release regarding firm mergers, opening of new offices, change of address or admission of new partners.

Announcements of such changes may be mailed to clients and individuals with whom professional contacts are maintained, such as lawyers and bankers. Such announcements should be dignified and should not refer to fields of specialization.

502-2—Office premises. Listing of the firm name in lobby directories of office buildings and on entrance doors solely for the purpose of enabling interested parties to locate an office is permissible. The listing should be in good taste and modest in size.

The indication of a specialty such as "income tax" in such listing constitutes advertising.

502-3—Directories: telephone, classified and trade association. A listing in a telephone, trade association, membership or other classified directory shall not:

1. Appear in a box or other form of display, or in a type or style which differentiates it from other listings in the same directory.
2. Appear in more than one place in the same classified directory.
3. Appear under a heading other than "Certified Public Accountant" or "Public Accountant" where the directory is classified by type of business occupation or service.
4. Be included in the yellow pages or business section of a telephone directory unless the member maintains a bona fide office in the geographic area covered. Determination of what constitutes an "area" shall be made by referring to the positions taken by state CPA societies in the light of local conditions.

Such listing may:

1. Include the firm name, partners' names, professional title (CPA), address and telephone number.
2. Be included under both the geographical and alphabetical section where the directory includes such sections.

502-4—Business stationery. A member's stationery should be in keeping with the dignity of the profession and not list any specialty.

The stationery may include the firm name, address and telephone number, names of partners, names of deceased partners and their years of service, names of professional staff when preceded by a line to separate them from the partners, and cities in which other offices and correspondents or associates are located. Membership in the Institute or state CPA society or associated group of CPA firms whose name does not indicate a specialty may also be shown. In the case of multi-office firms, it is suggested that the words "offices in other principal cities" (or other appropriate wording) be used instead of a full list of offices. Also, it is preferable to list only the names of partners resident in the office for which the stationery is used.

502-5—Business cards. Business cards may be used by partners, sole practitioners and staff members. They should be in good taste and should be limited to the name of the person presenting the card, his firm name, address and telephone number(s), the words "Certified Public Accountant(s)," or "CPA" and such words as "partner," "manager" or "consultant" but without any specialty designation.

Members not in the practice of public accounting may use the title "Certified Public Accountant" or "CPA" but shall not do so when engaged in sales promotion, selling or similar activities.

502-6—Help wanted advertisements. A member shall not include his name in help-wanted or situations-wanted display advertising on his own behalf or that of others in any publication. In display advertising, the use of a telephone number, address, or newspaper box number is permissible.

In classified advertisements other than display, the member's name should not appear in boldface type, capital letters or in any other manner which tends to distinguish the name from the body of the advertisement.

502-7—Firm publications. Newsletters, bulletins, house organs, recruiting brochures and other firm literature on accounting and related business subjects prepared and distributed by a firm for the information of its staff and clients serve a useful purpose. The distribution of such material outside the firm must be properly controlled and should be restricted to clients and individuals with whom professional contacts are maintained, such as lawyers and bankers. Copies may also be supplied to job applicants, to students considering employment interviews, to nonclients who specifically request them and to educational institutions.

If requests for multiple copies are received and granted, the member and his firm are responsible for any distribution by the party to whom they are issued.

502-8—Newsletters and publications prepared by others. A member shall not permit newsletters, tax booklets or similar publications to be imprinted with his firm's name if they have not been prepared by his firm.

502-9—Responsibility for publisher's promotional efforts. It is the responsibility of a member to see that the publisher or others who promote distribution of his writing, observe the boundaries of professional dignity and make no claims that are not truthful and in good taste. The promotion may indicate the author's background including, for example, his education, professional society affiliations and the name of his firm, the title of his position and principal activities therein. However, a general designation referring to any specialty, such as "tax expert" or "tax consultant," may not be used.

502-10—Statements and information to the public press. A member shall not directly or indirectly cultivate publicity which advertises his or his firm's professional attainments or services. He may respond factually when approached by the press for information concerning his firm, but he should not use press inquiries as a means of aggrandizing himself or his firm or of advertising professional attainments or services. When interviewed by a writer or reporter, he is charged with the knowledge that he cannot control the journalistic use of any information he may give and should notify the reporter of the limitations imposed by professional ethics.

Releases and statements made by members on subjects of public interest which may be reported by the news media, and publicity not initiated by a member such as that which may result from public service activities, are not considered advertising. However, press releases concerning internal matters in a member's firm are prohibited.

502-11—Participation in educational seminars. Participation by members in programs of educational seminars, either in person or through audiovisual techniques, on matters within the field of competence of CPAs is in the public interest and is to be encouraged. Such seminars should not be used as a means of soliciting clients. Therefore, certain restraints must be observed to avoid violation of the spirit of Rule 502 which prohibits solicitation and advertising. For example, a member or his firm should not:

1. Send announcements of a seminar to nonclients or invite them to attend. However, educators may be invited to attend to further their education.
2. Sponsor, or convey the impression that he is sponsoring, a seminar which will be attended by nonclients. However, a member or his firm may conduct educational seminars solely for clients and those serving his clients in a professional capacity, such as bankers and lawyers.

In addition, when a seminar is sponsored by others and attended by nonclients, a member or his firm should not:

1. Solicit the opportunity to appear on the program.
2. Permit the distribution of publicity relating to the member or his firm in connection with the seminar except as permitted under Interpretation 502-9.
3. Distribute firm literature which is not directly relevant to a subject being presented on the program by the member or persons connected with his firm.

502-12—Solicitation of former clients. Offers by a member to provide services after a client relationship has been clearly terminated, either by completion of a nonrecurring engagement or by direct action of the client, constitute a violation of Rule 502 prohibiting solicitation.

502-13—Soliciting work from other practitioners. Rule 502 does not prohibit a member in the practice of public accounting from informing other practitioners of his availability to provide them or their clients with professional services. Because advertising comes to the attention of the public, such offers to other practitioners must be made in letter form or by personal contact.

502-14—Fees and professional standards. The following statement is required to be published with the Code of Professional Ethics pursuant to the Final Judgment in the court decision referred to below:

> The former provision of the Code of Professional Ethics prohibiting competitive bidding, Rule 3.03, was declared null and void by the United States District Court for the District of Columbia in a consent judgment entered on July 6, 1972, in a civil antitrust suit brought by the United States against the American Institute. In consequence, no provision of the Code of Professional Ethics now prohibits the submission of price quotations for accounting services to persons seeking such services; and such submission of price quotations is not an unethical practice under any policy of the Institute. To avoid misunderstanding it is important to note that otherwise unethical conduct (e.g., advertising, solicitation, or substandard work) is subject to disciplinary sanctions regardless of whether or not such unethical conduct is preceded by, associated with, or followed by a submission of price quotations for accounting services. Members of the Institute should also be aware that neither the foregoing judgment nor any policy of the Institute affects the obligation of a certified public accountant to obey applicable laws, regulations or rules of any state or other governmental authority.

Interpretation under Rule 503—Commissions

503-1—Fees in payment for services. Rule 503, which prohibits payment of a commission to obtain a client, was adopted to avoid a client's having to pay fees for which he did not receive commensurate services. However, payment of fees to a referring public accountant for professional services to the successor firm or to the client in connection with the engagement is not prohibited.

Interpretation under Rule 505—Form of Practice and Name

505-1—Investment in commercial accounting corporation. A member in the practice of public accounting may have a financial interest in a commercial corporation which performs for the public services of a type performed by public accountants and whose characteristics do not conform to resolutions of Council, provided such interest is not material to the corporation's net worth, and the member's interest in and relation to the corporation is solely that of an investor.

REVIEW QUESTIONS

1. List the five primary services offered by CPA firms.
2. What role is played by the American Institute of Certified Public Accountants for its members?
3. Explain the need for a code of professional ethics for CPAs. In which ways should the CPAs' code of ethics be similar to and different from that of other professional groups such as attorneys or dentists?
4. List the three parts of the Code of Professional Ethics and state the purpose of each part.
5. Distinguish between independence in fact and independence in appearance. State three activities that may not affect independence in fact but are likely to affect independence in appearance.
6. What is the purpose of the AICPA's Code of Professional Ethics restriction on the association of the CPA's name with forecasts?
7. Distinguish between generally accepted auditing standards and generally accepted accounting principles and give two examples of each.
8. The first standard of field work requires the performance of the examination by a person or persons having adequate technical training and proficiency as an auditor. What are the various ways auditors can fulfill the requirement of the standard?
9. List the five parts of the standard short-form report and state the purpose of each part.
10. Carefully review the wording of the standard short-form report and explain in layman's terms the meaning of each sentence.
11. Distinguish between an unqualified opinion, a disclaimer of opinion, an adverse opinion, and a qualified opinion. Describe a situation that is appropriate for each type of opinion.
12. Describe the role of the Securities and Exchange Commission in society and discuss its relationship with and influence on the practice of auditing.
13. Lawsuits against CPA firms have increased dramatically in the past decade. State your opinion of the positive and negative effects of the increased litigation on CPAs and society as a whole.
14. Distinguish between the auditor's potential legal liability to the client,

liability to third parties under common law, civil liability under the securities laws, and criminal liability. Describe one situation for each type of liability where the auditor could be held legally responsible.

15. Generally Accepted Auditing Standards have been criticized from different sources for failing to provide useful guidelines for conducting an audit. The critics believe the standards should be more specific to enable practitioners to improve the quality of their performance. As the standards are now stated, they provide little more than an excuse to conduct inadequate audits. Evaluate this criticism of the ten Generally Accepted Auditing Standards.

16. If an auditor makes an agreement with one of his clients that the amount of his audit fee will be contingent upon the number of days required to complete the engagement, is it a violation of the Code of Professional Ethics? What is the essence of the rule of professional ethics dealing with contingent fees, and what are the reasons for the rule? (AICPA adapted)

17. On February 17, 19X7, a CPA completed the field work on the financial statements for the Buckheizer Corporation for the year ended December 31, 19X6. The audit is satisfactory in all respects except for the existence of a change in accounting principles from FIFO to LIFO inventory valuation, which results in a qualified audit opinion as to consistency. On February 26 the auditor completed the tax return and the pencil draft of the financial statement. The final audit report was completed, attached to the financial statements, and delivered to the client on March 7. What is the appropriate date on the auditor's report?

DISCUSSION QUESTIONS AND PROBLEMS

18. For each of the following questions concerning generally accepted auditing standards, select the best answer:

    a. Triolo, CPA, has a small public accounting practice. One of Triolo's clients desires services that Triolo cannot adequately provide. Triolo has recommended a larger CPA firm, Pinto and Company, to his client, and in return, Pinto has agreed to pay Triolo 10 percent of the fee for services rendered by Pinto for Triolo's client. Who, if anyone, is in violation of the AICPA's Code of Professional Ethics? *RULES OF PROFESSIONAL CONDUCT*
       (1) Both Triolo and Pinto
       (2) Neither Triolo nor Pinto
       (3) Only Triolo
       (4) Only Pinto

    b. The CPA who regularly examines Viola Corporation's financial statements has been asked to prepare forecast income statements for the next five years. If the statements are to be based upon the corporation's operating assumptions and are for internal use only, the CPA should
       (1) Reject the engagement because the statements are to be based upon assumptions
       (2) Reject the engagement because the statements are for internal use
       (3) Accept the engagement provided full disclosure is made of the assumptions used and the extent of the CPA's responsibility
       (4) Accept the engagement provided Viola certifies in writing that the statements are for internal use only

c. The Code of Professional Ethics considers Statements on Auditing Standards (formerly Statements on Auditing Procedure) issued by the institute's Auditing Standards Executive Committee (formerly the Committee on Auditing Procedures) to
(1) Supersede generally accepted auditing standards
(2) Be separate and independent of generally accepted auditing standards
(3) Not be part of the Code, since specific rules pertaining to technical standards are established by the Code itself
(4) Be interpretations of generally accepted auditing standards

(AICPA adapted)

19. Sara Fretwell, CPA, has worked three years for a national CPA firm. Her responsibilities have been restricted primarily to working on retail store audits and their related tax problems, but she has also spent several months in the tax department. Due to the resignation of several staff members in the past year and the addition of several new clients, the firm is badly understaffed.

Sara is sent on the audit of a construction company, which is a publicly held company and has always received an unqualified opinion. She is given relatively little guidance by the audit partner because the latter's recent illness has forced him to devote less time to his professional responsibilities. Sara is conscientious in her responsibilities, but she feels uncomfortable and uneasy throughout the entire engagement because of the technical difficulties she encounters. To add to her problems, she is pressured from the controller to meet the deadline the partner had agreed to, even though the audit did not start until a week later than scheduled. By working long days and weekends, Sara is able to complete the job in time to meet the deadline. She feels the audit is far from perfect, but considering the circumstances, she is fairly well satisfied with the quality of the performance.

Required:

a. State which generally accepted auditing standards were violated in this situation.
b. What is the firm's potential legal liability in this audit?
c. How could the firm have avoided this situation?
d. Put yourself in Sara's position. What course of action would you have followed?

20. Watts and Williams, a firm of certified public accountants, audited the accounts of Sampson Skins, Inc., a corporation that imports and deals in fine furs. Upon completion of the examination, the auditors supplied Sampson Skins with twenty copies of the certified balance sheet. The firm knew in a general way that Sampson Skins wanted that number of copies of the auditor's report to furnish to banks and other potential lenders.

The balance sheet in question was in error by approximately $800,000. Instead of having a $600,000 net worth, the corporation was insolvent. The management of Sampson Skins had doctored the books to avoid bankruptcy. The assets had been overstated by $500,000 of fictitious and nonexisting accounts receivable and $300,000 of nonexisting skins listed as inventory when in fact Sampson Skins had only empty boxes. The audit failed to detect these fraudulent entries. Martinson, relying on the certified balance sheet, loaned Sampson Skins $200,000. He seeks to recover his loss from Watts and Williams.

Required:

State whether each of the following is true or false and give your reasons:
a. If Martinson alleges and proves negligence on the part of Watts and Williams, he will be able to recover his loss.
b. If Martinson alleges and proves constructive fraud—i.e., gross negligence on the part of Watts and Williams—he will be able to recover his loss.
c. Martinson does not have a contract with Watts and Williams.
d. Unless actual fraud on the part of Watts and Williams could be shown, Martinson could not recover.
e. Martinson is a third-party beneficiary of the contract Watts and Williams made with Sampson Skins.   (AICPA adapted)

21. The Mobile Home Manufacturing Company is audited by Rossi and Montgomery, CPAs. Mobile Home has decided to issue stock to the public and wants Rossi and Montgomery to perform all the audit work necessary to satisfy the requirements of filing with the SEC. The CPA firm has never had a client go public before.

Required:

a. What are the ethical implications of Rossi and Montgomery's accepting the engagement?
b. List the additional problems confronting the auditors when they file with the SEC as compared with dealing with a regular audit client.

22. The Dandy Container Corporation engaged the accounting firm of Adams and Adams to examine financial statements to be used in connection with a public offering of securities. The audit was completed, and an unqualified opinion was expressed on the financial statements which were submitted to the Securities and Exchange Commission along with the registration statement. Two hundred thousand shares of Dandy Container common stock were offered to the public at $11 a share. Eight months later the stock fell to $2 a share when it was disclosed that several large loans to two "paper" corporations owned by one of the directors were worthless. The loans were secured by the stock of the borrowing corporation which was owned by the director. These facts were not disclosed in the financial report. The director involved and the two corporations are insolvent.
a. The Securities Act of 1933 applies to the above-described public offering of securities in interstate commerce.
b. The accounting firm has potential liability to any person who acquired the stock in reliance upon the registration statement.
c. An investor who bought shares in Dandy Container would make a prima facie case if he alleges that the failure to explain the nature of the loans in question constituted a false statement or misleading omission in the financial statements.
d. The accountants could avoid liability if they could show they were neither negligent nor fraudulent.
e. Accountants' responsibility as to the fairness of the financial statements is determined as of the date of the financial statements and not beyond.
f. The accountants could avoid or reduce the damages asserted against them if they could establish that the drop in price was due in whole or in part to other causes.
g. The Dandy investors would have to institute suit within one year after discovery of the alleged untrue statements or omissions.

h. It would appear that the accountants were negligent in respect to the handling of the secured loans in question—if they discovered the facts regarding the loans to the "paper" corporations and failed to disclose them in their financial statements.

i. The Securities and Exchange Commission would defend any action brought against the accountants in that the SEC examined and approved the registration statement.

Required:

State whether each of the above items (a through i) is true or false. For each false item, rephrase the sentence to make it correct.   (AICPA adapted)

23. The CPA firm of Bigelow, Barton, and Brown was expanding very rapidly. Consequently, it hired several junior accountants, including a man named Small. The partners of the firm eventually became dissatisfied with Small's production and warned him that they would be forced to discharge him unless his output increased significantly.

At that time Small was engaged in audits of several clients. He decided that to avoid being fired, he would reduce or omit entirely some of the standard auditing procedures listed in audit programs prepared by the partners. One of the CPA firm's clients, Newell Corporation, was in serious financial difficulty and had adjusted several of the accounts being examined by Small to appear financially sound. Small prepared fictitious working papers in his home at night to support purported completion of auditing procedures assigned to him, although he in fact did not examine the adjusting entries. The CPA firm rendered an unqualified opinion on Newell's financial statements, which were grossly misstated. Several creditors, relying upon the audited financial statements, subsequently extended large sums of money to Newell Corporation.

Required:

Would the CPA firm be liable to the creditors who extended the money because of their reliance upon the erroneous financial statements if Newell Corporation should fail to pay them? Explain.   (AICPA adapted)

24. Rod Williams, a CPA, was engaged by Jackson Financial Development Company to audit the financial statements of Apex Construction Company, a small closely held corporation. Rod was told when he was engaged that Jackson Financial needed reliable financial statements which would be used to determine whether or not to purchase a substantial amount of Apex Construction's convertible debentures at the price asked by the estate of one of Apex's former directors.

Rod performed his examination in a negligent manner. As a result, he failed to discover substantial defalcations by Brown, the Apex controller. Jackson Financial purchased the debentures but would not have if the defalcations had been discovered. After discovery of the fraud, Jackson Financial promptly sold the debentures for the highest price offered in the market—at a $70,000 loss.

Required:

a. What liability does Rod Williams have to Jackson Financial? Explain.
b. If Apex Construction also sues Rod for negligence, what legal defenses would his attorney probably raise? Explain.
c. Will the negligence of a CPA as described above prevent him from

recovering on a liability insurance policy covering the practice of his profession? Explain. (AICPA adapted)

25. A careful reading of the short-form unqualified report indicates several important phrases. Explain why each of the following phrases or clauses is used rather than the alternative provided:

   a. "In our opinion, the financial statements present fairly" rather than "The financial statements present fairly."

   b. "Our examination was made in accordance with generally accepted auditing standards" rather than "Our audit was performed to detect material errors in the financial statements."

   c. "The financial statements mentioned above present fairly the financial position" rather than "The financial statements mentioned above are correctly stated."

   d. "In conformity with generally accepted accounting principles applied on a basis consistent with that of the preceding year" rather than "are properly stated to represent the true economic conditions on a basis consistent with that of the preceding year."

   e. "Brown & Phillips, CPAs (firm name)" rather than "James E. Brown, CPA (individual partner's name)."

26. The auditor's report must contain an expression of opinion or a statement to the effect that an opinion cannot be expressed. Four types of opinions that meet these requirements are generally known as

   a. An unqualified opinion

   b. A qualified opinion

   c. An adverse opinion

   d. A disclaimer of opinion

Required:

For each of the following situations, indicate which type of opinion you would render and give your reasons. Select the *best* answer choice and mark only one answer for each item.

Unless there is an implication to the contrary in the situation as stated, you may assume that the examination was made in accordance with generally accepted auditing standards, that the financial statements present fairly the financial position and results of operations in conformity with generally accepted accounting principles applied on a consistent basis, and that the statements include adequate informative disclosure necessary not to be misleading.

   a. During the course of his examination, the CPA suspects that a material amount of the assets of his client, Ash Corporation, has been misappropriated through fraud. The corporation refuses to allow the auditor to expand the scope of his examination sufficiently to confirm these suspicions.

   b. The CPA is examining the Chestnut Corporation's financial statements for the first time. Former financial statements carry the unqualified opinion of a CPA who is unknown to the CPA currently conducting the examination. The CPA believes the balance sheet presents fairly the corporation's financial position, but the CPA was not authorized to test the activity of previous periods and is unwilling to assume any responsibility for the work performed by the prior CPA.

   c. The CPA was engaged to examine the Fig Wholesale Corporation's financial statements after the close of the corporation's fiscal year. On the completion of his examination, the CPA is satisfied that the corporation's financial statements are presented fairly except that he is not satisfied that the Fig Wholesale Corporation's inventory is fairly stated on the balance sheet date. The amount of the inventory is material.

d. On the basis of an examination made in accordance with generally accepted auditing standards, the independent auditor formed the opinion that the financial statements present fairly the financial position and results of operations in conformity with generally accepted accounting principles applied on a consistent basis and that the statements include all informative disclosures necessary to make the statements not misleading.

e. The CPA has examined Ginkgo Corporation's financial statements for many years. During the year just ended a service bureau was employed to process the corporation's financial data by computer. The CPA knows very little about computers and does not wish to conduct the audit for the year just ended. The CPA and the president of the corporation are old friends, however, and the president persuaded the CPA that he should not withdraw from the engagement. After glancing at the records and comparing the current year's statements with those of previous years, the CPA believes that the statements prepared by the service bureau are stated fairly.

f. Subsequent to the close of Holly Corporation's fiscal year, a major debtor was declared bankrupt because of a deteriorating financial condition. The debtor had confirmed the full amount due to Holly Corporation at the balance sheet date. Since the account was confirmed at the balance sheet date, Holly Corporation refuses to disclose any information in relation to this subsequent event.

g. A satisfactory audit is performed of the Wholesale Hardware Company, and in the opinion of the auditors, the financial statements are fairly presented. On the last day of the field work, the audit partners discover that the auditor in charge of the engagement has a substantial investment in the client's stock.

h. Linden Corporation has material investments in stocks of subsidiary companies. Stocks of the subsidiary companies are not actively traded on the market, and the CPA's engagement does not extend to any subsidiary company. The CPA is able to satisfy himself that all investments are carried at original cost, and he has no reason to suspect that the amounts are not stated fairly.   (AICPA adapted)

27. During the year ended December 31, 19X6, Yolly Corporation had its fixed assets appraised and found that they had substantially appreciated in value since the date of their purchase. The appraised values have been reported in the balance sheet as of December 31, 19X6; the total appraisal increment has been included as an extraordinary item in the income statement for the year then ended; and the appraisal adjustment has been fully disclosed in the footnotes. If a CPA believes that the values reported in the financial statements are reasonable, what type of opinion should he issue? Why?

(AICPA adapted)

28. A CPA is completing her examination of the financial statements of the Juneau Service Company for the year ended April 30, 19X6. During the year Juneau's employees were granted an additional week's vacation, and this had a material effect upon vacation pay expense for the year and the accrued liability for vacation pay at April 30, 19X6. In the opinion of the

CPA, this occurrence and its effects have been adequately disclosed in a footnote to the financial statements. What effect should this have on the auditor's report? (AICPA adapted)

29. Upon completion of the examination of his client's financial statements, the CPA, in his report, must either express an opinion or disclaim an opinion on the statements taken as a whole. His opinion may be unqualified, qualified, or adverse.

Required:

a. Under what general conditions may a CPA express an unqualified opinion on his client's financial statements?
b. Define and distinguish between (1) a qualified opinion, (2) an adverse opinion, and (3) a disclaimer of opinion on the statements taken as a whole. (AICPA adapted)

30. Fred Browning, CPA, has examined the financial statements of Grimm Company for several years. Grimm's president has now asked Browning to install an inventory system for the company.

Required:

Discuss the factors that Browning should consider in determining whether to accept the engagement. (AICPA adapted)

31. Your client, Nuesel Corporation, requested that you conduct a feasibility study to advise management of the best way the corporation can utilize electronic data-processing equipment and which computer, if any, best meets the corporation's requirements. You are technically competent in this area and accept the engagement. Upon completion of your study, the corporation accepts your suggestions and installs the computer and related equipment that you recommended.

Required:

a. Discuss the effect the acceptance of this management services engagement would have upon your independence in expressing an opinion on the financial statements of the Nuesel Corporation.
b. Instead of accepting the engagement, assume that you recommended Ike Mackey, of the CPA firm of Brown and Mackey, who is qualified in specialized services. Upon completion of the engagement, your client requests that Mackey's partner, John Brown, perform services in other areas. Should Brown accept the engagement? Discuss.
c. A local printer of data-processing forms customarily offers a commission for recommending him as a supplier. The client is aware of the commission offer and suggests that Mackey accept it. Would it be proper for Mackey to accept the commission with the client's approval? Discuss.
(AICPA adapted)

32. The following questions relate to auditors' independence:
a. Why is independence so essential for auditors?
b. Compare the importance of independence of CPAs with that of other professionals, such as attorneys.
c. Explain how an auditor can be independent in fact but not in appearance.
d. Discuss how each of the following could affect independence in fact and independence in appearance, and evaluate the social consequence of prohibiting auditors from doing each one.

    (1) Ownership of stock in a client company

    (2) Having bookkeeping services for an audit client performed by the same person who does the audit

    (3) Recommending adjusting entries to the client's financial statements and preparing financial statements, including footnotes, for the client

    (4) Having management services for an audit client performed by individuals in a department that is separate from the audit department.

    (5) Having the annual audit performed by the same audit team except for assistants for five years in a row

    (6) Having the annual audit performed by the same CPA firm for ten years in a row

    (7) Having management select the CPA firm

  e. Which of the above are prohibited by the AICPA Code of Professional Ethics? Which are prohibited by the SEC?

33. The Lakeland Milk Products Company is a medium-sized company engaged in purchasing unpasteurized milk and processing it into different dairy products. For the past six years Lakeland has had services performed by a CPA firm, which includes an audit, tax services, and management consulting services. Since Lakeland lacks a competent controller, a major part of the fee has consisted of correcting the accounting records, making adjusting entries, and preparing the annual financial statements. The president of Lakeland has approached the CPA in charge of the Lakeland audit for the past three years about the possibility of becoming the full-time combination controller and internal auditor for the company.

Required:

  a. Which services currently being provided by the CPA firm could be done by the CPA acting in his new capacity, assuming he is qualified to perform them?

  b. Which services must the CPA firm continue to perform, even if the new controller is qualified? Why must they be done by the CPA firm?

  c. Explain specific ways the controller can help reduce the CPA's audit fee if he is knowledgeable about the way the audit is conducted.

34. A CPA's report on financial statements includes his opinion as to whether the statements are presented in accordance with generally accepted accounting principles. In evaluating the general acceptability of an accounting principle, the CPA must determine whether the principle has substantial authoritative support.

Required:

  a. Describe the procedure that a CPA should follow in forming an opinion as to whether he should accept an accounting principle proposed by a client for use in preparing the current year's financial statements. Assume that the principle has been consistently applied.

  b. Cite primary sources and authorities that a CPA might consult in determining whether an accounting principle has substantial authoritative support. (A source is primary if it is sufficient evidence by itself to constitute substantial authoritative support.)

  c. Cite secondary sources and authorities that the CPA might consult in determining whether an accounting principle has substantial authoritative support. (A source is secondary if it must be combined with one or more

other secondary sources to constitute substantial authoritative support.)
(AICPA adapted)

35. The following situations each involve a possible violation of ~~Rule 502,~~ *rule dealing with* solicitation and advertising, of the Code of Professional Ethics:

a. Johnson, CPA, has been invited to participate in the tax seminar for industry by the National Association of Accountants. During the seminar, he hands out materials published by his firm, which are relevant to the subject matter under discussion, and includes his business card.

b. Marvin Collins, CPA, sends all existing clients monthly newsletters concerning new developments in taxes and management services. Annually, Collins sends each client brochures describing the nature of the firm's tax and management services capabilities. Included in the list of clients are several who engage other CPA firms for part of their tax or management services.

c. Runckle, CPA, has an office on the first floor of a downtown building. The following is printed on the window of his office in small letters: "R. J. Runckle, CPA, Income Tax Returns Prepared."

d. Every year Oris, CPA, does the annual audit of a church he does not attend. On the month in which the financial statements are issued, the weekly church bulletin acknowledges the CPA firm and thanks it for its outstanding contribution.

e. The East City State Bank has made arrangements for Patricia Clyde, CPA, to be available in the bank lobby to prepare tax returns for its customers on a fee basis. The bank mails a notice of the service and the hours Mrs. Clyde is available with each customer's monthly bank statement.

f. George and Gordon, CPAs, have recently become partners in the practice of public accounting. They ran an advertisement in the city newspaper under the announcement section stating that they had joined together to practice public accounting at 71262 Norell Street. The ad was in fine print, and the only other information included was their phone number.

g. Frederick, CPA, includes his name in the yellow pages in fine print with his firm name and the statement that he limits his practice to taxes and bookkeeping services for physicians and dentists.

h. In a help-wanted ad for new employees, Grant, CPA, included the required qualifications of prospective employees, starting salary, travel requirements, and the name, address, and telephone number of his CPA firm in the city newspaper. No information was included in bold print.

i. Alexander, CPA, buys several hundred copies of an abbreviated income-tax guide from a publishing company specializing in tax-related materials. The name of the CPA firm and its address are imprinted on the cover of the tax guide and mailed to all existing tax clients.

Required:

a. State whether each of these situations is a violation of Rule 502.

b. Discuss the desirable and undesirable aspects of Rule 502 on society, the auditing profession as a whole, existing practitioners who have well-established practices, and newly emerging practitioners who do not have well-established practices.

36. The following each involve a possible violation of the AICPA's Code of Professional Ethics. For each situation, state the applicable section of the Rules of Conduct and whether it is a violation.

a. John Brown is a CPA, but not a partner, with three years of professional experience with Lyle and Lyle, CPAs. He owns twenty-five shares of stock in an audit client of the firm, but he does not take part in the audit of the client and the amount of stock is not material in relation to his total wealth.

b. In preparing the personal tax returns for a client, Phyllis Allen, CPA, observed that the deductions for contributions and interest were unusually large. When she asked the client for backup information to support the deductions, she was told, "Ask me no questions, and I will tell you no lies." Allen completed the return on the basis of the information acquired from the client.

c. A client requests assistance of J. Bacon, CPA, in the installation of a computer system for maintaining production records. Bacon had no experience in this type of work, so he obtained assistance from a computer consultant. The consultant is not in the practice of public accounting, but Bacon is confident of his professional skills.

d. Five small Chicago CPA firms have become involved in an information project by taking part in an intrafirm working paper review program. Under the program, each firm designates two partners to review the working papers, including the tax returns and the financial statements of another CPA firm taking part in the program. At the end of each review, the auditors who prepared the working papers and the reviewers have a conference to discuss the strengths and weaknesses of the audit. They do not obtain the authorization from the audit client before the review takes place.

e. Shirley Morris, CPA, applies to Apple and George, CPAs, for a permanent job as a senior auditor. Ms. Morris informs Apple and George that she works for another CPA firm in the same city but will not permit them to contact her present employer. Apple and George hire Ms. Morris without contacting the other CPA firm.

f. James Thurgood, CPA, stayed longer than he should have at the annual Christmas party of Thurgood and Thurgood, CPAs. On his way home he drove through a red light and was stopped by a policeman, who observed that he was intoxicated. In a jury trial, Thurgood was found guilty of driving under the influence of alcohol. Since this was not his first offense, he was sentenced to thirty days in jail and his driver's license was revoked for one year.

g. Bill Wendal, CPA, set up a casualty and fire insurance agency to complement his auditing and tax services. He does not use his own name on anything pertaining to the insurance agency and has a highly competent manager, Frank Jones, who runs it. Wendal frequently requests Jones to review the adequacy of a client's insurance with management if it seems underinsured. He feels he provides a valuable service to clients by informing them when they are underinsured.

h. Rankin, CPA, provides tax services, management advisory services, and bookkeeping services and conducts audits for the same client. Since the firm is small, the same person frequently provides all of the services.

37. The following each involve possible violations of the AICPA's Code of Professional Ethics. For each situation, state whether it is a violation of the code. In those cases where it is a violation, explain the nature of the violation and the rationale for the existing rule.

a. Ralph Williams is the partner on the audit of a nonprofit charitable organization. He is also a member of the board of directors, but this position is honorary and does not involve performing a management function.

b. Pickens and Perkins, CPAs, are incorporated to practice public accounting. The only shareholders in the corporation are existing employees of the organization including partners, staff members who are CPAs, staff members who are not CPAs, and office personnel.

c. Fenn and Company, CPAs, has time available on a computer which it uses primarily for its own record keeping. Aware that the computer facilities of Delta Equipment Company, one of Fenn's audit clients, are inadequate for company needs, Fenn maintains on its computer certain routine accounting records for Delta.

d. Godette, CPA, has a law practice. Godette has recommended one of his clients to Doyle, CPA. Doyle has agreed to pay Godette 10 percent of the fee for services rendered by <u>Doyle</u> to Godette's client. *IS IN BREACH.*

e. Theresa Barnes, CPA, has an audit client, Smith Inc., which uses another CPA for management services work. Miss Barnes sends her firm's literature covering its management services capabilities to Smith on a monthly unsolicited basis. *BREACH.*

f. A bank issued a notice to its depositors that it was being audited and requested them to comply with the CPA's effort to obtain a confirmation on the deposit balances. The bank printed the name and address of the CPA in the notice. The CPA had knowledge of the notice. *OK*

g. Myron Jones, CPA, is a member of a national CPA firm. His business card includes his name, the firm's name, address, and telephone number, and the word *consultant*. *OK*.

h. Gutowski, a practicing CPA, has written a tax article which is being published in a professional publication. The publication wishes to inform its readers about Gutowski's background. The information, which Gutowski has approved, includes his academic degrees, other articles he has had published in professional journals, and a statement that he is a tax expert. *BREACH.*

i. Poust, CPA, has sold his public accounting practice, which includes bookkeeping, tax services, and auditing, to Lyons, CPA. Poust obtained permission from all audit clients for audit-related working papers before making them available to Lyons. *OK,*

j. Murphy and Company, CPAs, is the principal auditor of the consolidated financial statements of Lowe, Inc., and subsidiaries. Lowe accounts for approximately 98 percent of consolidated assets and consolidated net income. The two subsidiaries are audited by Trotman and Company, CPAs, a firm with an excellent professional reputation. Murphy insists on auditing the two subsidiaries because he deems this necessary to warrant the expression of an opinion. *OK,* (AICPA adapted)

3

The Auditor's
Decision Process

Determining the appropriate amount of evidence to accumulate is an important decision the auditor must make every time an audit is conducted. The decision is based primarily on two interrelated considerations: the degree of responsibility the auditor takes for the fair presentation of financial statements and the unique circumstances in a particular audit. These two considerations, and the way they influence evidence accumulation, are the primary subjects of this chapter.

In general terms, it is possible to determine the proper evidence by referring to the third standard of field work, which states:

> *Sufficient competent evidential* matter is to be obtained through inspection, observation, inquiries, and confirmations to afford a *reasonable basis for an opinion* regarding the financial statements under examination (italics added).[1]

The relevance of this standard is certainly difficult to dispute, but like most of the standards it provides little in the way of practical guidelines. What is meant by *sufficient competent evidential matter?* What is a *reasonable basis for an opinion?* These must be understood before the auditor can begin to conduct an audit.

---

[1] SAS 1, p. 5.

DEGREE OF RESPONSIBILITY

As a first step in establishing the amount of evidence to accumulate, it is important to understand the auditor's responsibility for the fairness of the representations made in the financial statements. The professional literature makes it clear that this responsibility rests with management rather than with the auditor:

> Management has the responsibility for adopting sound accounting policies, for maintaining an adequate and effective system of accounts, for the safeguarding of assets, and for devising a system of internal control that will, among other things, help assure the production of proper financial statements. The transactions which should be reflected in the accounts and in the financial statements are matters within the direct knowledge and control of management. The auditor's knowledge of such transactions is limited to that acquired through his examination. Accordingly, the fairness of the representations made through financial statements is an implicit and integral part of management's responsibility.[2]

If auditors were responsible for making certain that all representations in statements were correct, it would be necessary to accumulate far more evidence than is generally obtained. The cost of an audit would be increased to such an extent that audits would not be economically feasible.

Management's responsibility for the fairness of the representations in the financial statements carries with it the privilege of determining which disclosures it considers necessary, but it is acceptable for an auditor to prepare a draft of the statements for the client or to offer suggestions for clarification. If management refuses to permit a particular financial statement disclosure that the auditor considers necessary, the auditor can either issue an adverse or qualified opinion or withdraw from the engagement.

The profession has been especially emphatic that the auditor is *not responsible* for the failure to discover fraud if the examination has been performed in accordance with generally accepted auditing standards. The profession has concluded that the prevention and detection of fraud can be more economically accomplished by an adequate accounting system with appropriate internal controls. However, if the auditor has sound reasons to suspect the existence of fraud that may materially affect the reliability of financial statements, he has a responsibility to determine whether the fraud actually exists. The investigation can be made by the client under the auditor's supervision, or by the auditor himself.

If it is the client's responsibility to make proper representations in the financial statements and to establish controls for the prevention of fraud,

---

[2] SAS 1, p. 1.

what is the auditor's responsibility? The profession has taken the position that *the auditor's responsibility is limited to performing the audit investigation and reporting the results in accordance with generally accepted auditing standards.* But as a practical matter, if significant errors or omissions exist in the financial statements, the likelihood of the auditor's having to defend the adequacy of his performance in the audit is reasonably high. The auditor is likely to have to defend the audit regardless of whether the errors are due to misrepresentation by management, employee fraud, or unintentional omissions. Therefore, the standard of evidence accumulation used by most competent auditors is to proceed until the likelihood of material errors existing in the financial statements is fairly low.

REASONABLE LEVELS OF ASSURANCE

The decision about how much evidence to accumulate comprises two basic steps:

1. The overall level of assurance the auditor feels he needs in the existing circumstances
2. The evidence necessary to achieve that overall level of assurance, considering the existing circumstances

First we will discuss the problem of setting a reasonable level of overall assurance. In the last part of the chapter we will examine the decision process used in determining how much evidence is needed to satisfy the overall level of assurance.

The *overall level of assurance* is the subjectively determined level of confidence that the auditor has of the fair presentation of the financial statements after the audit is completed. The higher the level of assurance attained, the more confident the auditor is that the financial statements contain no material misstatements or omissions. One hundred percent assurance would be certainty, and zero assurance would be complete uncertainty. Complete assurance of the accuracy of the financial statement is not possible, but reasonably high levels can be obtained.

The higher the level of assurance the auditor demands, the more evidence he must obtain. This is true because the auditor achieves assurance by gathering evidence. Since the greater the amount of evidence, the greater the cost, the basic audit decision of the proper level of assurance boils down to a cost-benefit equation. The important question is, at what point does the additional cost of acquiring more evidence exceed the benefit obtained from the additional information? When that level of assurance is reached, the auditor should stop accumulating evidence. If the auditor believes the additional cost of the evidence exceeds the additional benefit from continuing to accumulate, but the level of assurance is still not satisfactory, he has several options. He can negotiate for a

denial *discuss*

higher audit fee; he can issue a ~~disclaimer~~ of opinion; he can bear the additional costs himself; or he can withdraw from the engagement. ✗

It is *not possible to quantify* the overall level of assurance achieved in an audit. It is practical to obtain a measure of the level of assurance for some individual audit procedures by using statistical sampling techniques, but there is no objective measurement method for most audit tests. Furthermore, auditors presently have no means of objectively combining levels of assurance obtained from individual procedures into an overall level of assurance. There are too many different audit procedures and considerations in the audit to make this possible. The idea of a reasonable level of assurance is highly subjective and is determined by the auditor's professional judgment. It is possible to think in terms of high levels of assurance in some circumstances or reasonable levels of assurance and even low levels, but a precise measure is not realistic.

There have been few studies within the profession to determine whether different auditors strive for approximately the same level of assurance for similar audit clients, but there are several considerations that encourage reasonably uniform standards of assurance:

1. *Competition among CPA firms.* If a firm chooses extraordinarily high levels of assurance relative to other CPA firms, the billing submitted to the client will have to reflect the additional time needed to complete the audit. If the total bill is significantly higher than what another CPA firm would charge, the client may change to a less expensive auditor. Competitive forces, then, help to prevent auditing beyond reasonable levels of assurance.

2. *Lawsuits and other sanctions.* If auditors in a CPA firm fail to achieve adequate levels of assurance, they may be financially successful in the short run, but they are also likely to fail to discover material errors in the financial statements. When material errors are not detected, lawsuits by users who have been harmed, sanctions by the SEC, and even censure for substandard practice by state societies of CPAs will negatively affect the firm financially and will discredit the firm's professional reputation. Fear of these sanctions has the effect of encouraging CPAs to attain reasonable levels of assurance for all audits.

3. *Professionalism.* Even without the lawsuits and other sanctions, most auditors want to do high-quality audits, even at some personal financial sacrifice. Most professionals take pride in their work and the quality of the services performed by their firm. Generally, the practitioners who maintain a high degree of professionalism also develop a reputation in their community that pays off in terms of both professional pride and excellent financial rewards.

There are also several conditions that cause different auditors to achieve different levels of assurance in similar audit situations. The most important of these are as follows:

1. *The difficulty of measuring levels of assurance.* As long as it is difficult to measure levels of assurance, it is unreasonable to expect that all auditors will end up with the same level of evidence under similar circumstances. Such differences might be partially avoided if the profession were to set precise requirements for evidence accumulation, but the result would probably be inflexibility and the failure of auditors to adequately modify evidence under different circumstances.

2. *Different levels of risk avoidance.* The level of assurance an auditor selects must take into account the trade-off between the cost of evidence and the risk the auditor is willing to take that material errors exist in the statements. Naturally, auditors differ as to the risks they are willing to accept. Some are highly conservative and constantly fear a lawsuit or loss of professional reputation. Others are more interested in a high level of income and less concerned with sanctions. The former type of auditor could be expected to seek higher levels of assurance than the latter.

3. *Different levels of competence.* Unfortunately, in every profession some practitioners do not properly perform their responsibilities. Even requiring a CPA certificate and continuing education cannot eliminate incompetent practitioners. Incompetent practitioners are likely to arrive at lower levels of assurance than competent ones.

It is hoped that competition, legal liability, other sanctions, and professionalism will tend to minimize the differences in levels of assurance. Nevertheless, it must be recognized that the level of assurance sought by different auditors in similar circumstances is unlikely to be exactly the same.

Changing Levels of Assurance for Different Circumstances

The interests of society are better served when all auditors strive for approximately the same level of assurance for all clients operating under similar circumstances. This practice provides users with the same level of assurance regardless of the particular auditor. However, when the circumstances of the audit change, the level of assurance should also change. In other words, in certain situations the overall level of assurance should be higher than in others. These circumstances fall into two categories:

1. *The degree to which external users rely upon the statements.* When external users place heavy reliance upon the financial statements, it is appropriate that the auditor's overall level of assurance be increased. When the statements are extensively relied upon, a great social harm could result if a significant error were to remain undetected in the financial statements. The cost of additional evidence can be more easily justified when the loss to users from material errors is substantial. Several factors are good indicators of the degree to which statements are relied upon by external users:

a. *Client's size.* Generally speaking, the larger a client's operations, the more widely used the statements will be. The client's size, measured by total assets or total revenues, will have an effect on the overall level of assurance desired.

b. *Distribution of the client's ownership.* The statements of publicly held corporations are normally relied upon by many more users than those of closely held corporations. For these companies, the interested parties include the SEC, financial analysts, and the general public.

c. *Nature and amount of the client's liabilities.* When statements include a large amount of liabilities, the statements are more likely to be used extensively by actual and potential creditors than when there are few liabilities.

2. *The likelihood of the client's filing bankruptcy subsequent to the audit.* If a client is forced to file bankruptcy or even just suffers a significant loss subsequent to the completion of the audit, there is a much greater chance of the auditor's being required to defend the quality of the audit than if the client were under no financial strain. There is a natural tendency for those who lose money in a bankruptcy or because of a stock price reversal to file suit against the auditor. This can result from the honest belief that the auditor failed to conduct an adequate audit or from the users' desire to recover part of their loss regardless of the adequacy of the audit work.

In those situations where the auditor believes the chance of bankruptcy or loss is high, the overall level of assurance should be increased. If a subsequent challenge does occur, the auditor will then be in a much better position to successfully defend the audit results. The total audit evidence and the audit costs will increase in this circumstance, but this is justifiable because of the additional risk of lawsuits that the auditor faces.

It is difficult for an auditor to predict a bankruptcy before it occurs, but certain factors are good indicators of an increased probability of bankruptcy:

a. *Liquidity position.* If a client is constantly short of cash and working capital, this is one indication of a future problem in paying bills. The auditor must assess the likelihood and significance of a weak liquidity position getting worse.

b. *Profits (losses) in previous years.* When a company has rapidly declining profits or increasing losses for several years, the auditor should recognize the future solvency problems the client is likely to encounter. It is also important to consider the changing profits relative to the balance remaining in retained earnings.

c. *Method of financing growth.* The more a client relies on debt as a means of financing, the greater the risk of financial difficulty if the client's operations become less successful. It is also important to evaluate whether permanent assets are being financed with short-term or long-term loans. Large amounts of required cash outflows during a short period of time can force a company into bankruptcy.

     d. *Nature of the client's operations.* Certain types of businesses are in-
herently riskier than others. For example, other things being equal,
there is a much greater likelihood of bankruptcy of a stockbroker
than of a utility.

     e. *Competence of management.* Competent management is constantly
alert for potential financial difficulties and modifies its operating
methods to minimize the effects of short-run problems. The ability
of management must be assessed as a part of the evaluation of the
likelihood of bankruptcy.

The auditor must investigate his client and assess the importance of
each of the factors affecting the degree to which external users rely upon
the statements, and the likelihood of the client's filing bankruptcy subsequent to the audit. Based upon this investigation and assessment, the
auditor should be able to set a tentative and highly subjective level of
the risk that he is willing to take that the financial statements will include a material error after the audit is completed. As the audit progresses, additional information about the client is obtained and the
desired level of assurance may be modified. In an ideal world, different
auditors would set the same level of assurance for any one particular
audit, and the differing levels of assurance would reflect only differing
circumstances.

The Need To Segment the Audit

As stated in Chapter 1, four basic audit decisions must be made on
each audit engagement:

    1. The audit procedures to use
    2. The sample size to select for each audit procedure
    3. The particular items to select from each population
    4. The appropriate time to perform the audit procedures

In making these four decisions, the auditor must divide the evidence
accumulation task into smaller segments. It would be impractical to
determine the proper audit procedures for the entire audit without in
some way segmenting the task. Furthermore, auditors perform the audit
segments in sequence over time, so it is convenient to develop them in
that manner.

The two broadest segments of tests are *tests of transactions* and *direct
tests of financial statement balances,* but each of these is also subdivided.
The tests of transactions are divided into tests of the various subparts of
the client's accounting system, such as the sales and cash receipts area,
payroll, and cash disbursements. Similarly, the tests of financial statement
balances accounts are typically subdivided into types of accounts such as
cash, accounts receivable, inventories, prepaid expenses, fixed assets, and
accounts payable. The number of subdivisions depends primarily on the
nature of the client's system and the account classifications used in the
chart of accounts. Once the segments (audit areas) have been selected,

the auditor must make the four evidence accumulation decisions for each segment. For example, in the tests of sales transactions for a given client, the auditor must decide which procedures are appropriate and when they should be performed. For each audit procedure selected, the number of sample items to test must be decided upon. Next, the particular items for testing from the population must be selected. This same decision process must be repeated for cash receipts, accounts receivable, notes payable, and every other audit area being tested.

In assessing whether an adequate level of overall assurance for the financial statements taken as a whole has been obtained, it is necessary for the auditor to subjectively combine the level of assurance achieved for each of the individual parts of the audit. It is impossible to achieve a high level of overall assurance if the auditor is uncertain about any one material part of the statements, such as inventory or the adequacy of the disclosure of a significant lawsuit against the client.

A higher overall level of assurance is achieved by obtaining an increased level of assurance in one or more of the components of the financial statements. This increased level of assurance in the individual components is in turn accomplished by accumulating more evidence in certain audit areas. As an illustration, if a partner on an audit feels there is a reasonably high chance of the bankruptcy of a client listed on the New York Stock Exchange, he is likely to test inventory, accounts receivable, accounts payable, and other significant audit areas more carefully than usual.

THE EVIDENCE NEEDED TO ACHIEVE A GIVEN LEVEL OF ASSURANCE

It is now possible to turn to the problem of deciding upon the amount of evidence needed to achieve a given level of assurance. In analyzing this decision, the assumption is made that the auditor has already decided upon the proper overall level of assurance. If the level of assurance changes, this means the evidence needed must also be modified.

It is more convenient at times to refer to assurance in terms of *risks*. This is not a change in concept because the overall level of risk is simply 100 percent minus the overall level of assurance. The auditor's evaluation of when the acceptable overall level of risk has been reached is accomplished by assessing two closely related considerations:

1. *The risk that the client makes errors* that are individually or collectively material enough to make the financial statements misleading. The errors can be intentional or unintentional, and they can be errors affecting the dollar balance in accounts or disclosure errors. The risk of the client's making these errors can be low in some instances and extremely high in others.
2. *The risk that the audit tests fail to uncover the material errors.* Assuming the audit tests are made with due care, the more evidence

the auditor accumulates, the less risk there is of failing to uncover material errors.

The *combination* of these two risks must be lower than the acceptable overall risk level before the auditor should be willing to issue an unqualified opinion.

At the time the audit starts, which is usually fairly near the end of the year or after year-end, there is not much that can be done about changing the first risk. Instead, the auditor must *assess the factors* making up the risk and *modify his audit evidence* to take them into consideration. If the auditor believes the risk of error is high, the amount of evidence collected must be increased to reduce the overall risk. When the first risk is low, the amount of evidence to be collected can be greatly reduced to arrive at the same overall risk.

Auditors do not now and probably never will quantify these two risk factors and combine them into an overall risk. There are too many complex factors affecting each risk factor to reduce it to a single quantification. Nevertheless, the decision process that auditors follow is of the nature described, except that it is subjective rather than objective and is frequently carried out informally.

Factors Affecting the Auditor's Expectation of Errors

The auditor should consider several major factors when assessing the risk of the financial statements' including errors:

- The system of internal control
- Materiality
- Population size
- Makeup of the population
- Initial versus repeat engagement
- Results of the current and previous audits
- Others

The factors discussed in this section are similar to those previously considered as factors affecting levels of assurance in that both groups affect the *amount* of evidence that should be accumulated. Both sets of factors are of the utmost importance in the process of professional judgment. Without considering them, the evidence would be the same for each audit.

The major difference between the factors affecting the levels of assurance and those affecting the auditor's expectation of errors is the more *specific nature* of the latter. Evaluating the factors affecting the proper level of assurance has the effect of requiring higher or lower levels of overall assurance; by implication, additional or less evidence is needed in *all* audit areas. For example, the widespread distribution of client ownership implies the need for increased evidence in most facets of the audit because a higher level of overall assurance is desired. The factors affecting the expectation of errors, on the other hand, guide the auditor toward emphasizing particular parts of the audit. For example, if there were numerous errors in the confirmation of accounts receivable in the preceding year's audit, accounts receivable should ordinarily be heavily emphasized in the current year.

In dealing with the individual factors affecting the expectation of errors, it is the auditor's responsibility to *identify* the factors in a given audit, *evaluate* the significance of each, and *modify* the evidence to take each significant factor into account. Due to the lack of a precise measurement system, the impact of each factor is evaluated subjectively. We shall identify the most important factors the auditor should keep in mind throughout the engagement, explain them in general terms, and show how they affect audit procedures and sample size.

System of Internal Control

The system of internal control is one of the most important determinants of the audit procedures to be performed, the sample size for each procedure and the timing of the procedures. A thorough evaluation of the system must be completed before the audit can be regarded as adequate, and the results of this evaluation will aid the auditor in determining what evidence is to be accumulated throughout the audit. Internal control is such an important factor in evidence accumulation that it is discussed separately in Chapter 5, as well as being integrated into most subsequent chapters.

The client's system of internal control greatly affects the auditor's expectation of errors and therefore the evidence the auditor accumulates. If the auditor believes the client's controls are sufficient to provide reasonable assurance that there are likely to be no material errors in the records, it is possible to keep the evidence accumulation to a reasonably low level. On the other hand, if the auditor believes the controls are so weak as to significantly increase the expectation of errors, it will be necessary to expand the audit tests accordingly to determine whether material errors actually exist.

Materiality of Account Balances

The concept of materiality as it relates to auditing is simply that the auditor should concentrate on the financial statement information that is important and put less emphasis on the less significant accounts and transactions. This attitude is justified because auditors are concerned that the financial statements be reasonably stated, not necessarily correct to the penny. For example, in most cases the auditor will have a higher level of overall assurance if the verification of a small supplies account is limited to a brief review, and the primary audit emphasis is placed on verifying accounts receivable and inventory, than he would if he devoted an equal amount of time to each of these accounts.

In deciding on materiality in a given situation, the auditor must establish whether the account or transaction under consideration contains errors or omissions that, when combined with other possible errors in the statements, will make the overall financial statements misleading. Several important facets of materiality make it difficult for the auditor to decide whether any particular item is material:

1. *Materiality is a relative concept rather than an absolute one.* An error of a given magnitude might be material for a small company, whereas the same dollar error could be immaterial for a large one. For example, a total error of $100,000 would be extremely material for a company with $200,000 total assets, but it would be immaterial for a company such as General Motors. Hence it is not possible to establish any dollar-value guidelines applicable to all audit clients.

2. *A basis is needed for evaluating materiality.* Since materiality is relative, it is necessary to have a basis for establishing whether an error is material. *Net income* is normally the most important basis for deciding what is material, because it is regarded as a critical item of information for users; but it also is important to learn whether the item in question could materially affect the reasonableness of such subtotals as current assets, total assets, current liabilities, and owner's equity, and how it affects longer-run trends. It is the responsibility of the individual auditor to decide whether the item in question contains errors that would be material when compared with any one of these bases.

3. *The combined errors are more important than errors in individual accounts.* It is not sufficient for the auditor to consider the materiality of the errors in just a particular account. The auditor must ultimately decide whether *all the errors combined* are sufficient to make the overall financial statements misleading. It is possible for individual errors to be immaterial when they are considered separately and for the overall financial statements to be misleading because of their combined effect. Evaluation of the reliability of the overall financial statements becomes especially difficult because the auditor, having only sampled the population, does not know the exact extent of all errors.

4. *Accounts with small recorded balances can contain material errors.* In judging whether an account is material enough to justify extensively verifying the balance, it is not sufficient to make the decision on the basis of the recorded account balance. It is possible for an account with a small balance, or even a zero balance, to contain significant errors.

Certain factors influence the auditor's decision about whether an account with a small recorded balance potentially contains material errors. First, he should consider the materiality of the transactions that affected the balance in the current period. For example, the balance in the cash account may be small, but there usually are material cash receipt and cash disbursement transactions during the year. Second, he should consider the maximum potential size of the account. As an illustration, if the income-tax liability from previous years is recorded at zero, it is still necessary to examine the internal revenue agent's reports for those years, since the unrecorded liability could be material. On the other hand, it is unlikely in most situations that the correct balance of certain accounts (e.g., prepaid insurance) would be material even if the errors relative to the account balances were reasonably large. Finally, the auditor should consider such other factors as the system of internal control and the results of previous audits in deciding whether an account with a small balance is likely to contain a material error.

When an account balance is immaterial and the auditor decides there is little likelihood of a significant error, it may be acceptable to reduce the audit tests to a review of the account. The Canadian Institute of Chartered Accountants has suggested the following procedures for reviewing such accounts:

1. Learn what the item represents.
2. Decide that it appears reasonable.
3. Check the amount to the general ledger ' scrutinize the relevant accounts.
4. Decide that in comparison to similar items for the previous year it is reasonable.
5. Decide that there are no special circumstances that would render material this otherwise immaterial item.[3]

Materiality is also a consideration in performing tests of transactions. In most cases, tests of transactions areas such as cash receipts, sales, purchases, payroll, and cash disbursements are highly material and require significant audit attention. Certain transactions areas such as sales returns and allowances are frequently immaterial and can be de-emphasized. Also, in multifirm or multibranch operations, the segments with the most significant operations should usually receive the greatest audit attention. Naturally, other factors such as the system of internal control will affect the amount of auditing in the various transactions areas and business segments.

Population Size

Population size is closely related to materiality, but it is of sufficient importance to be considered as a separate factor. In general it is reasonable to expect more errors to exist in a large population than in a small one unless there are compensating factors. Therefore, the population size has traditionally been an important determinant of the auditor's sample size. For example, it was traditionally common to audit transactions for a certain period of time such as a month for tests of cash disbursements, or to confirm a certain percentage of the accounts receivable outstanding. In these cases the sample size would be in direct proportion

---

[3] Study Group on Audit Techniques, *Materiality in Auditing* (Toronto: Canadian Institute of Chartered Accountants, 1965), pp. 8–9.

to the population size. The advent of statistical sampling in auditing has dramatically changed this approach. In using statistical sampling, the population size still affects the sample size, but only to a certain point; a doubling of the population, for example, might have little effect on the number of items in the sample where statistical sampling is used.

Makeup of the Population

The individual items making up the total of a population also frequently affect the auditor's expectation of a material error's being included. For example, most auditors would be more concerned about the possibility of a material misstatement in a population of accounts receivable containing a small number of large customer balances than if there were a large number of small accounts. To compensate for the greater possibility of a significant error, a larger percentage of the accounts with bigger customer balances would normally be confirmed and a different type of confirmation would be used. The nature and the source of individual transactions within a total balance also affect the audit tests. Transactions with affiliated companies, amounts due from officers, cash disbursements made payable to cash, and accounts receivable outstanding for several months are examples of situations requiring greater investigation because there is usually a higher likelihood of errors than in more typical transactions.

Initial versus Repeat Engagement

Evidence accumulation is different when the audit is being performed for a new client rather than for one that has been an audit client in previous years. There are three primary reasons for this:

1. *It is necessary to verify the details making up those balance sheet accounts that are of a permanent nature, such as fixed assets, patents, and retained earnings.* On an initial audit it may be necessary to verify transactions that occurred several years earlier in order to establish that the current balance in the account is reasonable, whereas on repeat engagements it is necessary only to audit the transactions that took place in the current period.

2. *It is necessary to verify the beginning balances in the balance sheet accounts on an initial engagement.* This step is essential even if comparative financial statements are not issued because the accuracy of the current year's income statement is dependent on the accuracy of the beginning balances in the balance sheet accounts. In a repeat engagement this step is unnecessary because the prior year-end balances, which were verified in the audit of the preceding year, are the current year's beginning balances.

3. *The auditor is less familiar with the client's operations in an initial audit.* The lack of knowledge about a client's operations includes such

considerations as unfamiliarity with the system of internal control, absence of reliable historical ratios and balances with which to compare the current year's results, and nonexistence of previous years' audit evidence and conclusions as a basis for developing a current year's audit program. As a consequence of the lack of knowledge, it is often necessary to perform more audit procedures for an initial engagement than for a repeat audit. Similarly, larger sample sizes are usually appropriate in new audits.

If a new client has had audits performed in previous years by a reputable CPA firm in which the current auditor has a high degree of confidence, it is acceptable to place some reliance on the previous auditor's results. The extent to which the current auditor should rely on a previous audit depends on his knowledge of the previous auditor, but it is always necessary to at least review the previous auditor's working papers and to perform sufficient procedures on beginning balances to establish that the current-period transactions are recorded on a basis consistent with that of the preceding year.

Results of the Current and Previous Audits

An auditor would be considered negligent if the results of the preceding year's examination were ignored during the development of the current year's audit program. If the auditor found a significant number of errors in the preceding year in an audit area such as inventory pricing, extensive testing would have to be done in the current audit as a means of determining whether the deficiency in the client's system had been corrected. On the other hand, if the auditor has found no errors for the past several years in his tests of an audit area, he is justified in reducing the audit tests provided that the internal control review indicates that the system has not deteriorated.

If, during the current-year audit, the auditor finds errors that lead him to believe the total population being tested may be improperly stated, he must ultimately establish whether the population contains material errors. Before the auditor completes his tests, he must either (a) satisfy himself by additional testing that the original sample was not representative of an essentially satisfactory population or (b) take corrective action regarding the population.

Other Factors

Several other factors also affect the expectation of errors. Following are some of the important situations in which the auditor can expect a high probability of errors:

1. *The transaction is an unusual one for the client.* Unusual transactions are more likely to be incorrectly recorded by the client than

routine transactions because the client lacks experience in recording them. Therefore, transactions that occur with relative infrequency for a particular client should be carefully scrutinized by the auditor. Examples include fire losses, major property acquisitions, disposals of assets, and lease agreements.

2. *The account being verified contains transactions or information that requires considerable accounting judgment to record properly.* Transactions for major repairs or partial replacement of assets are examples of this type of situation. It is common for inexperienced accountants to record these transactions as repairs when in many cases company policy dictates that they should be recorded as assets, or vice versa. When fixed assets are replaced by similar assets, it also requires an adequate knowledge of accounting theory to record the new asset at the correct amount. Another example is the expensing of legal fees which should actually be classified as a patent cost, a part of a property acquisition cost, or a comparable asset.

3. *The asset being verified is highly susceptible to defalcation.* The auditor should be concerned about the risk of possible defalcation in situations where it is relatively easy to convert company assets to personal use. Such is the case when currency or highly marketable inventory is not closely controlled.

4. *There is some motivation for the client to misstate the financial statements.* In many situations, managements may believe that it would be advantageous to misstate the financial statements. For example, if management receives a percentage of total profits as a bonus, there may be a tendency to overstate net income. Similarly, if a bond indenture requirement includes a specification that the current ratio must remain above a certain level, the client may be tempted to overstate current assets or to understate current liabilities by an amount sufficient to meet the requirement. Also, there may be considerable motivation for intentional understatement of income when management wants the company to pay less income taxes. The auditor should constantly be alert to all of these possibilities and adjust his evidence accumulation accordingly.

5. *The client lacks basic integrity.* When management is dominated by a few individuals who lack the integrity to obey the law, the likelihood of significantly misrepresented financial statements is greatly increased. This important area is considered in more detail in Chapter 4.

Factors Affecting the Risk of Failing To Discover Existing Material Errors

In addition to the previously discussed factors affecting the expectation of errors, the auditor must keep three other considerations in mind as he conducts the audit: the scope of the engagement, the reliability of the evidence, and the nature of the industry. None of these factors affect the expectation of errors in the statements, but they bear directly upon the likelihood of whether the errors will be discovered through the audit.

Scope of the Engagement

The auditor must have complete freedom in selecting the procedures he believes necessary and the sample size he considers appropriate; otherwise there would be little sense in having an independent person perform the audit function. Nevertheless, occasionally some clients request that the auditor omit certain procedures or not test specific accounts. When the client does impose restrictions on the procedures that can be performed or the extent of the application of the procedures, the auditor must either find satisfactory alternative means of verifying the account in question or qualify his audit report.

Any restrictions imposed by the client or additions to the responsibilities agreed to by the auditor should be clearly understood by both the auditor and the client before the audit actually begins. This understanding will aid the auditor in modifying the audit procedures and sample size whenever it is possible. In the case where a client has imposed restrictions, this understanding will facilitate the acceptance of a modified report if the auditor cannot satisfy himself about the fairness of the financial statements by other audit evidence. Any modifications of the normal audit contract should be included as part of the formal *letter of engagement* between the client and the auditor. The letter could become important evidence in a later dispute over the auditor's responsibilities.

Reliability of the Available Evidence

Not all the evidence accumulated by the auditor is equally reliable. Its reliability can vary from nearly useless in the case of a rumor to near certainty in some kinds of physical examination. The following three considerations are the most important determinants of the reliability of audit evidence:

1. *The independence of the provider of the evidence.* Evidence obtained from a source outside of the entity is more reliable than that obtained from within the entity. For example, external evidence such as that received by confirmations from banks, attorneys, or customers is generally regarded as more reliable than answers obtained from inquiries of the client and from internal documents that do not leave the client's organization.

2. *The qualifications of the individuals providing the information.* Although the source of information is independent, the evidence will not be reliable unless the individual providing it is qualified to provide it. For this reason, confirmations from attorneys and banks are typically more highly regarded than accounts receivable confirmations from persons who are not familiar with the business world. Even evidence obtained directly by the auditor may not be reliable if the auditor lacks the qualifications to obtain the evidence. For example, the physical observa-

tion of an inventory of diamonds by an auditor untrained in distinguishing between diamonds and glass would not provide reliable evidence of the existence of diamonds.

3. *The degree of objectivity of the evidence.* Evidence that is objective in nature, compared with evidence that requires considerable judgment to determine whether it is correct, is more believable and therefore more reliable. Examples of objective types of evidence include confirmation of accounts receivable and bank balances, the physical count of securities and cash, and adding (footing) a list of accounts payable to determine if it adds to the balance on the general ledger. Examples of subjective evidence include confirmation by a client's attorney of the likely significance of outstanding lawsuits against the client, observation of obsolescence of inventory during physical examination, and inquiring of the credit manager about the collectibility of noncurrent accounts receivable. In evaluating the reliability of subjective evidence, the qualifications of the person providing the evidence become increasingly important.

The reliability of the evidence affects the audit procedures performed and, in some cases, the sample size. Less reliable evidence must be combined with other information to provide a level of competent evidence sufficient to satisfy the auditor. If the type of evidence being collected is highly reliable, the overall level of assurance can usually be increased by testing additional sample items. On the other hand, it does no good to increase sample size if the evidence is extremely low in reliability in the first place.

Nature of the Client's Industry

A major consideration affecting the audit procedures used by auditors is the industry in which the client is engaged. In most cases it is undesirable for the auditor to use the same audit procedures for widely differing industries. For example, many of the audit procedures for testing revenue for a life insurance company will be significantly different from those for an automobile manufacturer. Similarly, many of the procedures for the valuation of inventory for a building contractor will be different from those for a department store using the retail method. However, it is important to keep in mind that even for different industries a considerable portion of the audit is similar in nature. For example, the audit of cash in the bank is likely to be almost identical for most clients, regardless of the type of industry.

The AICPA has recognized the differences in auditing in various industries by publishing specific audit guides for somewhat unusual types of audits. The categories covered by these audit guides include the following:

1. Banks
2. Brokers and dealers in securities

3. Colleges and universities
4. Construction contractors
5. State and local governmental units
6. Voluntary health and welfare organizations

THE FOUR AUDIT DECISIONS

Now that the factors that determine the amount of evidence for the auditor to accumulate have been discussed, it is appropriate to turn directly to the four decisions the auditor must make and discuss each of them briefly.

Appropriate Audit Procedures

There are some procedures for each audit area that will almost always be used. These are the *minimum audit procedures*. If many actual audit programs of highly regarded CPA firms for many different clients were examined, those audit procedures common to all of them would be the minimum audit program. Neither the AICPA nor any other group serving more than one firm has ever specified a set of minimum audit procedures for each audit area. It is the responsibility of every firm to decide for itself its minimum standard of performance. Fortunately, the communication system between CPA firms is sufficient to provide some agreement as to what these minimum procedures should be.

The minimum audit program is insufficient for most audits. The auditor must perform other audit procedures beyond these to take into account unusual situations in the engagement. Professional judgment comes into play in recognizing such situations and modifying the procedures accordingly. In making this judgment, the factors of interest to the auditor include all those previously discussed in this chapter.

A Proper Sample Size

Sample size should vary depending upon the same circumstances in the audit that affect the adequacy and selection of audit procedures. In most cases the same factors that determine whether additional audit procedures should be used will have a major influence on the actual sample size. For example, an inadequacy in the system of internal control requires an increase in the number of audit procedures; it is also likely to cause a need for an increased sample size for some tests.

For most audits, determining the proper sample size is a more difficult decision than selecting the proper audit procedures because most of the procedures are likely to be a part of the minimum audit program. In such situations it is only necessary to decide whether to add one or two more procedures. It would be rare, even in those audit areas where the minimum audit program is not extensive, to add more than four or five. On the other hand, in selecting the proper sample size, the variation can be anywhere from a small number to all the items in the population. Since population sizes for different clients can vary in certain audit areas, such as cash disbursements and inventory, from a few dozen to hundreds of thousands, the sample size decision is indeed difficult. The problem is further complicated by the fact that a minimum sample size has not been well defined by either the organized profession or individual practitioners.

Wherever it is applicable, the use of statistical sampling is desirable in helping the auditor select the appropriate sample size. Statistical sampling techniques do not change the basic sample size decision, but they do help the auditor formalize his judgment. This will become apparent in Chapters 9 and 11, where the use of statistical sampling is discussed in detail.

The Timing of the Procedures

The decision as to when to perform audit procedures is less difficult and less important than the decisions about proper audit procedures and sample size. Nevertheless, timing cannot be ignored. As a means of better understanding the audit-timing decision, it is necessary to be familiar with the time framework in which the auditor operates.

Figure 3-1 shows points of time and time periods of special significance in the audit. The time period from 1-1-76 to 12-31-76 is the reporting period of the income statement and statement of changes of financial position and is therefore the most important period shown. The most important single date is 12-31-76, since the statement of financial position is at that point of time. For continuing audits, the 1-1-76 date has already been verified in the previous year. The last day of field work is important because it signifies that the auditor has reviewed for important subsequent events from 12-31-76 to 2-27-77. The date the audit report is sent to the client is important only for the relationship between the client and the auditor. In normal circumstances, the report will be delivered on or before a date specified in a preliminary discussion between a representative of management and the partner responsible for the audit.

Certain audit procedures should normally be *done as close to the*

FIGURE 3-1

SIGNIFICANT POINTS OF TIME AND TIME PERIODS

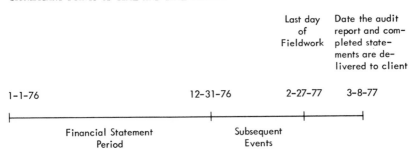

balance sheet date as possible. These are primarily tests of the most important current assets, such as the physical count of cash, securities, and inventory, and the confirmation of accounts receivable. The reason for testing these types of assets near year-end is their relatively fast turnover. If the assets are not tested at that time, it is often difficult to verify them at a later date. When the client's system of internal control is considered highly reliable, it is possible to perform the tests somewhat earlier or later than the balance sheet date.

The tests of transactions of the client's system of internal control should be done *for the entire period under audit,* and they should be done before the direct tests of balances. This is because the results of the tests of transactions are a major determinant of the remaining audit evidence needed to reach a conclusion about the fair presentation of the financial statements.

The timing of audit tests other than tests of transactions and certain direct tests of current assets depends upon when the client has the records and documents prepared. After the end of the client's fiscal year, such *accounting tasks* as the pricing of inventory, computation of depreciation, and adjustment of prepaid expenses must be completed before the financial statements are ready for audit. It typically takes several weeks before the client's financial records are sufficiently complete to perform many of the necessary audit tests.

A major consideration affecting the timing of audit tests is the CPA firm's difficulty of *scheduling personnel.* Scheduling would not be a significant problem if the year-end dates of a firm's clients were evenly distributed throughout the year. Since this is not the case for most CPA firms, there is a shortage of personnel during certain periods of the year and an excess at other times. To overcome this problem, CPA firms schedule audit tests earlier than the end of the year to the extent that it is practical. It is usually possible to update the permanent asset records maintained in the auditor's working papers, examine new loan agreements and other legal records, analyze changes in the client's system, and perform other similar procedures throughout the accounting period. These tests have to be finalized after the end of the year, but some early testing will aid in spreading the audit work throughout the year. As already mentioned, it may also be possible to perform some direct tests of balances earlier than the end of the year if the client has an adequate system of internal control.

The timing of the audit tests for a typical audit is shown in Figure 3-2. Each of these parts of the audit will be studied in greater depth as we proceed through the text.

The Particular Items Selected for Testing

The most important considerations in selecting the sample items from a population are (1) obtaining a representative sample of the entire population and (2) emphasizing those items most likely to be in error.

FIGURE 3-2

TIMING OF THE AUDIT TESTS

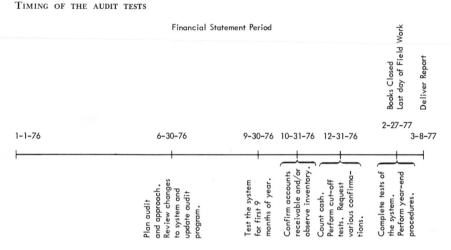

These can both be accomplished by taking a larger portion of certain types of items, and at the same time making sure that some of each type of item is included. For example, in confirming accounts receivable, the auditor is likely to want to test the large balances and the balances that have been outstanding for a long period of time more extensively than the small and current balances. If the combined total of all the small balances is material, a representative sample of these accounts should also be selected. More will be said about this decision in Chapter 10.

SUMMARY

This chapter examines the process the auditor goes through in deciding upon the appropriate evidence to accumulate. The emphasis is on the nature of these decisions in every audit and the most important factors the auditor considers in determining the proper level of evidence.

The underlying concept throughout the chapter is the auditor's need to consider the underlying risk of failing to discover material errors if they exist in the financial statements. Even though the auditor is not a guarantor of the financial statements, the risk must be kept to a reasonable level if the profession is to retain credibility in the financial community.

The proper level of assurance or overall level of risk for which the auditor should strive in a given audit is dependent upon two major considerations: the degree to which users rely upon the statements and the likelihood of the client's filing bankruptcy subsequent to the audit. In determining the permissible overall level of risk, the factors affecting these two considerations should be carefully assessed before a decision is made. The desired overall level of risk has a direct effect on accumulation of sufficient competent evidence.

In conducting the audit, it is necessary to evaluate several factors that enable the auditor to perceive the overall risk of the financial statements' including a material error. These factors include the system of internal control, materiality, the results of previous audits, and so forth. The auditor must modify his evidence to take such factors into consideration because the greater the risk of error in the statements, the greater the need for more extensive evidence. These factors must be evaluated early in the audit if the evidence is to be effectively modified. As the auditor obtains the additional information from the audit, he may change his assessment of the factors.

Figure 3-3 on page 110 summarizes and integrates the most important concepts presented in the first three chapters. A careful review of the figure at this point will clarify the interrelationship of the concepts.

Starting with Chapter 4 the approach followed by auditors is studied in greater depth. Chapter 4 investigates the first item in the flowchart: obtain a general understanding of the client and its circumstances.

REVIEW QUESTIONS

1. Select the best response for each of the following questions:
   a. The primary responsibility for the adequacy of disclosure in the financial statements and footnotes rests with the
      (1) Partner assigned to the engagement.
      (2) Auditor in charge of field work.
      (3) Staffperson who drafts the statements and footnotes.
      (4) Client.
   b. When a CPA expresses an opinion on financial statements, his responsibilities extend to
      (1) The underlying wisdom of the client's management decisions.
      (2) Whether the results of the client's operating decisions are fairly presented in the financial statements.
      (3) Active participation in the implementation of the advice given to the client.
      (4) An ongoing responsibility for the client's solvency.
   c. The strongest criticism of the reliability of audit evidence that the auditor physically observes is that
      (1) The client may conceal items from the auditor.
      (2) The auditor may *not* be qualified to evaluate the items he is observing.
      (3) Such evidence is too costly in relation to its reliability.
      (4) The observation must occur at a specific time, which is often difficult to arrange.
   d. The concept of materiality will be least important to the CPA in determining the
      (1) Scope of his audit of specific accounts.
      (2) Specific transactions that should be reviewed.
      (3) Effects of audit exceptions upon his opinion.

Figure 3-3

An expanded overview of the audit process

Major influences on the way audits are conducted

The structure of the profession

The Code of Professional Ethics

Generally Accepted Accounting Principles

AICPA Professional Pronouncements in Auditing

Securities and Exchange Commission

Legal Liability of CPAs

Auditing is:

An integrated process

The accumulation and evaluation of evidence by a competent independent person

Concerned with quantifiable events of a specific economic entity.

Performed to determine whether the financial statements are fairly presented in accordance with generally accepted accounting principles.

Obtain a general understanding of the client and its circumstances.

↓

Evaluate the factors affecting the overall acceptable level of risk.

↓

Evaluate the factors affecting the likelihood of error.

↓

Study and evaluate the system.

↓

Test the balance in the balance sheet account.

↓

Combine the results of all tests and draw conclusions about the overall level of risk.

↓

Issue an audit report.

Types of Evidence

Physical examination
Confirmation
Documentation
Inquiries of the client
Mechanical accuracy
Comparisons and relationships
Observation

Evidence Decisions

Audit procedures
Sample size
The particular items to select
Timing

Major Determinants of the Evidence Decision

Factors affecting the proper level of assurance:

The degree to which users rely on the statements:

Client size
Distribution of ownership
Nature of the client's business

The likelihood of bankruptcy:

Liquidity
Profits (losses) in previous years
Method of financing growth
Nature of the client's operation
Competence of management

Factors affecting the auditor's expectation of errors:

System of internal control
Materiality of account balances
Makeup of the population and its size
Initial versus repeat engagement
Results of the current and previous audits
Others

Factors affecting the risk of failing to discover existing material errors:

Scope of the engagement
Reliability of the available evidence
Nature of the client's industry

---

(4) Effects of his direct financial interest in a client upon his independence. (AICPA adapted)

2. Distinguish between the auditor's responsibility for fraud and his responsibility for unintentional errors.

3. For a considerable portion of the audit of small clients, the auditor makes adjustment entries for errors and misstatements in the records, prepares the financial statements, and writes the footnotes. Frequently, the management of these clients does not have a sufficient understanding of generally accepted accounting principles to properly prepare the statements even if it wanted to. How do you reconcile this relationship between the client and the

auditor with the statement in the professional literature that the fairness of the representations made through financial statements is management's responsibility?

4. Describe what is meant by an overall level of assurance. Explain why each of the following statements is true:

   a. A CPA firm should attempt to achieve the same overall level of assurance for all audit clients with approximately the same circumstances.

   b. A CPA firm should increase the overall level of assurance for audit clients where external users rely heavily upon the statements.

   c. A CPA firm should increase the overall level of assurance for audit clients where there is a reasonably high likelihood of a client's filing bankruptcy.

   d. Different CPA firms should attempt to achieve reasonably uniform overall levels of assurance for clients with similar circumstances.

5. When an auditor issues an unqualified opinion, it is the same for a publicly held company and a small closely held firm. What justification is there for providing lower levels of assurance for closely held companies than for listed companies if the audit report is the same? Justify it from the point of view of auditors and users of financial statements.

6. Explain the relationship between the desired level of assurance and the legal liability of auditors.

7. State the two categories of circumstances that determine the overall level of assurance and list the factors that the auditor can use to indicate the degree to which each category exists.

8. Auditors have not been successful in measuring the levels of assurance achieved in different audits. How is it possible to think in terms of obtaining increased or decreased levels of assurance without a precise means of measuring the level achieved?

9. Explain the relationship between the factors affecting the expectation of error, the desired overall level of assurance, and the accumulation of audit evidence.

10. List the factors affecting the auditor's expectation of error and explain why each factor should affect the evidence needed to achieve a given level of assurance.

11. Assume that the client's internal controls over the recording and classifying of permanent assets additions are considered weak because the individual responsible for recording new acquisitions has inadequate technical training and limited experience in accounting. How would this situation affect the evidence you should accumulate in auditing permanent assets as compared with another audit where the controls are excellent? Be as specific as possible.

12. Each of the following questions concerns the concept of materiality in auditing:

    a. What criteria should the auditor use in deciding whether an estimated error in inventory, based on a sample, is sufficiently material to require an adjustment to the financial statements?

    b. What criteria should the auditor use in deciding whether an account balance is sufficiently immaterial to justify performing minimal tests rather than extensive procedures? Using your criteria, state the conditions when extensive audit procedures are required for cash in the bank, federal income taxes payable, petty cash, and unexpired insurance.

    c. Assume the auditor has decided to perform no detailed tests of factory supplies on hand in the audit of a manufacturing company. List the overall reasonableness tests the auditor should use.

13. Brad Jackson was assigned to the audit of a client that had not been audited by any CPA firm in the preceding year. In conducting the audit, he did no testing of the beginning balance of accounts receivable, inventory, or accounts payable on the grounds that the audit report is being limited to the ending balance sheet, the income statement, and the statement of changes in financial position. No comparative financial statements are to be issued.
    a. Explain the error in Jackson's reasoning.
    b. Suggest an approach Jackson can follow in verifying the beginning balance in accounts receivable.
    c. Why doesn't the same problem exist in the verification of beginning balances on continuing audit engagements?
14. Define what is meant by reliability of audit evidence and list the characteristics of evidence that affect its reliability.
15. Why do auditors frequently consider it desirable to perform audit tests throughout the year rather than wait until year-end? List several examples of evidence that can be accumulated prior to the end of the year.
16. Distinguish between a minimum audit program and the minimum evidence for a particular engagement that must meet the requirements of the third Generally Accepted Auditing Standard of field work. Under what circumstances could these two be the same?
17. Select the best response for each of the following questions:
    a. Although the discovery of fraud is not the objective of the CPA's ordinary audit engagement, the CPA would be responsible for the detection of fraud if he failed to detect the fraud because
        (1) Of management's failure to disclose an unrecorded transaction. The documents pertaining to the transaction are kept in a confidential file.
        (2) Of management's description of the system of internal control.
        (3) Of management's misstatement of the value of an inventory of precious gems.
        (4) The amount of fidelity bond coverage for certain employees is not compatible with the amount of potential defalcation that might be committed.
    b. What is the independent auditor's responsibility prior to completion of field work when he believes that a material fraud may have occurred?
        (1) Notify the appropriate law enforcement authority.
        (2) Investigate the persons involved, the nature of the fraud, and the amounts involved.
        (3) Reach an understanding with the appropriate client representatives as to the desired nature and extent of subsequent audit work.
        (4) Continue to perform normal audit procedures and write the audit report in such a way as to disclose adequately the suspicions of material fraud. (AICPA adapted)
18. State whether each of the following statements is true or false, and give your reason:
    a. The audit evidence accumulated for every client should be approximately the same, regardless of the circumstances.
    b. If the audit evidence accumulated for two different clients is approximately the same, the overall level of assurance achieved is approximately the same.
    c. If the desired level of assurance is the same for two different clients, the audit evidence for the two clients should be approximately the same.
    d. If the desired level of assurance, the factors affecting the expectation of

error, and the factors affecting the auditor's likelihood of failing to discover existing errors are approximately the same for two different clients, the audit evidence for the two clients should be approximately the same.

DISCUSSION QUESTIONS AND PROBLEMS

19. Jordan Finance Company opened four personal loan offices in neighboring cities on January 2, 19X6. Small cash loans are made to borrowers who repay the principal with interest in monthly installments, over a period not exceeding two years. Ralph Jordan, president of the company, uses one of the offices as his headquarters and visits the other offices periodically for supervision and internal auditing purposes.

Mr. Jordan is concerned about the honesty of his employees. He came to your office in December 19X6. "I want to engage you to install a system to prohibit employees from embezzling cash," he stated. "Until I went into business for myself I worked for a nationwide loan company with five hundred offices, and I am familiar with that company's system of accounting and internal control. I want to describe that system so you can install it for me because it will absolutely prevent fraud."

Required:

a. How would you advise Mr. Jordan on his request that you install the large company's system of accounting and internal control for his firm? Discuss.
b. How would you respond to the suggestion that the new system would prevent embezzlement? Discuss.
c. Assume that in addition to undertaking the system's engagement in 19X7, you agreed to examine Jordan Finance Company's financial statements for the year ended December 31, 19X6. No scope limitations were imposed.
    (1) How would you determine the scope necessary to satisfactorily complete your examination? Discuss.
    (2) Would you be responsible for the discovery of fraud in this examination? Discuss.   (AICPA adapted)

20. You have examined Hagren Appliance Corporation's financial statements for several years and have always rendered an unqualified opinion. To reduce its current auditing cost, Hagren limited the scope of your examination of its financial statements for the year just ended to exclude accounts receivable and commissions payable. Hagren's officers stated that the type of auditor's opinion you would render was not important because your report would be used for internal management purposes only and would not be distributed externally. The materiality of the accounts not examined required you to disclaim an opinion on the fairness of the financial statements as a whole.

Required:

a. Why does a CPA prefer that the scope of his auditing engagement not be limited? Discuss.

b. How would a client's assurance to a CPA that his auditor's report will be used only for internal purposes affect the scope of the CPA's examination and the kind of opinion rendered? Discuss.   (AICPA adapted)

21. Frequently, questions have been raised ". . . regarding the responsibility of the independent auditor for the discovery of fraud (including defalcations and other similar irregularities), and concerning the proper course of conduct of the independent auditor when his examination discloses specific circumstances which arouse his suspicion as to the existence of fraud."

Required:

a. What are (1) the function and (2) the responsibilities of the independent auditor in the examination of financial statements? Discuss fully, but in this part do not include fraud in the discussion.
b. What are the responsibilities of the independent auditor for the detection of fraud? Discuss fully.
c. What is the independent auditor's proper course of conduct when his examination discloses specific circumstances that arouse his suspicion as to the existence of fraud?   (AICPA adapted)

22. The concept of materiality is important to the CPA in his examination of financial statements and expression of opinion upon these statements.

Required:

Discuss the following:
a. How are materiality (and immateriality) related to the proper presentation of financial statements?
b. In what ways will consideration of materiality affect the CPA in
   (1) Developing his audit program?
   (2) Performing his auditing procedures?
c. What factors and measures should the CPA consider in assessing the materiality of an exception to financial statement presentation?
d. How will the materiality of a CPA's exceptions to financial statements influence the type of opinion he expresses? (The relationship of materiality to *each type* of auditor's opinion should be considered in your answer.)   (AICPA adapted)

23. Rank each of the following five examples of audit evidence in terms of its reliability relative to the other four items in the group, and state the reasons for your ranking. The ranking should be *most reliable, second most reliable,* etc.
   a. Vendor's invoice
   b. Bank confirmation
   c. Client's list of permanent asset acquisitions
   d. Vendor's invoice with a receiving report attached
   e. Duplicate sales invoice

24. In Chapter 1 seven different types of evidence were discussed. The following questions concern the reliability of that evidence:
   a. Explain why confirmations are normally more reliable evidence than inquiry from the client.
   b. Describe a situation where confirmation would be considered highly reliable and another where it would not be reliable.
   c. Under what circumstances is the physical observation of inventory considered relatively unreliable evidence?

    d. Explain why mechanical accuracy tests are highly reliable, but of relatively limited usefulness.

    e. Give three examples of relatively reliable documentation and three examples of less reliable documentation. What characteristics distinguish the two?

    f. Give several examples where the qualifications of the respondent or the qualifications of the auditor affect the reliability of the evidence.

    g. Explain why comparisons and relationships are important evidence even though they are relatively unreliable by themselves.

25. Kim Bryan is confused by the inconsistency of the three audit partners she has been assigned to on her initial three audit engagements. On the first engagement she spent a considerable amount of time in the audit of cash disbursements by examining canceled checks and supporting documentation, but almost no testing was done in the verification of permanent assets. On the second engagement a different partner had her do less intensive tests in the cash disbursements area and take smaller sample sizes than in the first audit even though the company was much larger. On her most recent engagement under a third audit partner, there was a thorough test of cash disbursement transactions, far beyond that of the other two audits, and an extensive verification of permanent assets. In fact, this partner insisted on a complete physical examination of all permanent assets recorded on the books. The total audit time on the most recent audit was longer than that of either of the first two audits in spite of the smaller size of the company. Bryan's conclusion is that the amount of evidence to accumulate depends on the audit partner in charge of the engagement.

Required:

    a. State several factors that could explain the difference in the amount of evidence accumulated in each of the three audit engagements as well as the total time spent.

    b. What could the audit partners have done to help Bryan understand the difference in the audit emphasis on the three audits?

    c. Explain how these three audits are useful in developing Bryan's professional judgment. How could the quality of her judgment have been improved on the audits?

26. The following are different types of errors that can be encountered on an audit:

    a. The use of a method of valuing inventory that is not in accordance with generally accepted accounting principles

    b. Failure to disclose a lawsuit for patent infringement where the amount of the liability is unknown

    c. The recording of expenditures as permanent assets which should have been recorded as repairs and maintenance

    d. The inclusion of invalid amounts in accounts receivable by preparing fictitious sales invoices to nonexisting customers

Required:

    a. Assuming the amounts are equally material, rank the above types of errors in terms of the difficulty of uncovering the error. (*Most difficult is* first.) Give reasons to support your answers.

b. Discuss whether auditors should have the same responsibility for uncovering the most difficult error as for discovering the least difficult one. Consider this from the point of view of the auditors and the users of financial statements.

27. A competent auditor has done a conscientious job of conducting an audit, but due to a clever fraud by management, a material fraud is included in the financial statements. The fraud, which is an overstatement of inventory, took place over several years, and it covered up the fact that the company's financial position was rapidly declining. The fraud was accidentally discovered in the latest audit by an unusually capable audit senior, and the SEC was immediately informed. Subsequent investigation indicated the company was actually near bankruptcy, and the value of the stock dropped from $26 per share to $1 in less than one month. Among the losing stockholders were pension funds, university endowment funds, retired couples, and widows. The individuals responsible for perpetrating the fraud were also bankrupt.

After making an extensive investigation of the audit performance in previous years, the SEC was satisfied that the auditor had done a high-quality audit and had followed generally accepted auditing standards in every respect. The commission concluded that it would be unreasonable to expect auditors to uncover this type of fraud.

Required:

State your opinion as to who should bear the loss of the management fraud. Include in your discussion a list of potential bearers of the loss, and state why you believe they should or should not bear the loss.

28. Gale Brewer, CPA, has been the partner in charge of the Merkle Manufacturing Company, a client listed on the Midwest Stock Exchange for thirteen years. Merkle has had excellent growth and profits in the past decade, primarily as a result of the excellent leadership provided by Bill Merkle and other competent executives. Brewer has always enjoyed a close relationship with the company and prides himself on having made several constructive comments over the years which have aided in the success of the firm. Several times in the past few years Brewer's CPA firm has considered rotating a different audit team on the engagement, but this has been strongly resisted by both Brewer and Merkle.

For the first few years of the audit, the system of internal control was inadequate and the accounting personnel had inadequate qualifications for their responsibilities. Extensive audit evidence was required during the audit, and numerous adjusting entries were necessary. However, because of Brewer's constant prodding, the system of internal control improved gradually and competent personnel were hired. In recent years there were normally no audit adjustments required, and the extent of the evidence accumulation was gradually reduced. During the past three years Brewer was able to devote less time to the audit because of the relative ease of conducting the audit and the cooperation obtained throughout the engagement.

In the current year's audit, Brewer decided the total time budget for the engagement should be kept approximately the same as in recent years. The senior in charge of the audit, Phil Warren, was new on the job and highly competent, and he had the reputation of being able to cut time off of the budget. The fact that Merkle had recently acquired a new division through merger would probably add somewhat to the time, but Warren's efficiency would probably compensate for it.

The interim tests of the system of internal control took somewhat longer than expected because of the use of several new assistants, a change in the accounting system to computerize the inventory and several other aspects of the accounting records, a change in accounting personnel, and the existence of a few more errors in the tests of the system. Neither Brewer nor Warren was concerned about the budget deficit, however, because they could easily make up the difference at year-end.

At year-end Warren assigned the responsibility for inventory to an assistant who had also not been on the audit before but was competent and extremely fast at his work. Even though the total value of inventory increased, he reduced the size of the sample from that of other years because there had been few errors the preceding year. He found several items in the sample that were overstated due to errors in pricing and obsolescence, but the combination of all of the errors in the sample was immaterial. He completed the tests in 25 percent less time than the preceding year. The entire audit was completed on schedule and in slightly less time than the preceding year. There were only a few adjusting entries for the year, and only two of them were material. Brewer was extremely pleased with the results and wrote a special letter to Warren and the inventory assistant complimenting them on the audit.

Six months later Brewer received a telephone call from Merkle and was informed that the company was in serious financial trouble. Subsequent investigation revealed that the inventory had been significantly overstated in the preceding audit. The major cause of the misstatement was the inclusion of obsolete items in inventory (especially in the new division), errors in pricing due to the new computer system, and the inclusion of nonexistent inventory in the final inventory listing. The new controller had intentionally overstated the inventory to compensate for the reduction in sales volume from the preceding year.

Required:

a. List the major deficiencies in the audit and state why they took place.
b. What things should have been apparent to Brewer in the conduct of the audit?
c. If Brewer's firm is sued by stockholders or creditors, what is the likely outcome of the suit?

29 In a preliminary discussion before beginning your audit of the Mark Company, the president states that he would like to ascertain whether any key employees have interests that conflict with their duties at the company. He asks that, during your regular audit, you be watchful for signs of these conditions and report them to him.

Required:

Briefly discuss your professional position in this matter. Include the following aspects in your discussion:

a. The responsibility of the CPA for the discovery of conflicts of interest. Give reasons for your position.
b. At the same time that you are conducting the audit of Mark Company

you are also conducting the audit of Timzin Company, a supplier of Mark Company. During your audit of Timzin Company you determine that an employee of Mark Company is receiving kickbacks.

(1) Discuss your responsibility, if any, to reveal this practice to the president of Mark Company.
(2) Discuss your professional relationship with Timzin Company after discovering the kickbacks.   (AICPA adapted)

4

Understanding
the Client and Its Business

In achieving the overall objective of determining whether the financial statements are fairly presented in accordance with generally accepted accounting principles, it is necessary to obtain *general information* about the organization, as well as to perform detailed tests of individual audit areas. The detailed tests receive the greatest emphasis in the auditing literature, but the more general information is equally important in the audit.

It was stated in Chapter 1, and it is worth repeating here, that it is impossible to conduct an adequate audit without an understanding of the client's business. After detailed evidence is gathered, a judgment must be made regarding the overall fairness of the financial statements. This can only be done in the context of the business environment. For example, it is necessary to evaluate the fairness of the valuation of assets in the context of the economic conditions of the client's industry and unique circumstances, such as liquidity problems.

The careful review and examination of certain types of general information are useful in predicting the likelihood of errors in different audit areas and evaluating whether sufficient evidence has been accumulated. Detailed tests can then be modified to provide adequate assurance of the discovery of all material errors. Internal control is viewed as a critical, but not singular, aspect of the client's organization affecting the expectation of errors. Subsequent material is devoted entirely to the study of internal control. At this time attention is given to other important general considerations that affect the auditor's understanding of the client's organization and his ability to determine the proper audit evidence to accumulate. The following categories of general information are covered:

1. Background information for the audit
2. Analytical tests
3. Information about the client's legal obligations
4. Evaluation of the possibility of management involvement in material fraudulent transactions

BACKGROUND INFORMATION FOR THE AUDIT

Background information should help the auditor to thoroughly understand the client's industry, the nature of the client's business, and past relationships and existing agreements between the auditor and the client. Some of the information is useful in deciding upon the appropriate evidence to accumulate, whereas other information is useful in interpreting the evidence, planning the audit, and making constructive comments to the client.

Obtain Knowledge of the Client's Industry

To adequately interpret the meaning of information obtained throughout the audit, an understanding of the *client's industry* is essential. Certain unique aspects of different industries must be reflected in the financial statements. An audit for a life insurance company could not be performed with due care without an understanding of the unique characteristics of the life insurance business. And imagine attempting to audit a client in the bridge construction industry without understanding the construction business and the percentage-of-completion method of accounting.

There are also relevant differences the auditor needs to understand for different *lines of business* within the general classifications of "manufacturing," "retail," or "other industry." As an illustration, assume that a client has included a highly material amount of technologically obsolete inventory in its financial statements at original cost. If the auditor completely understands the client's line of business, there is a reasonable chance of discovering the error.

Knowledge of the client's industry can be obtained in different ways. These include discussions with the auditor who was responsible for the engagement in previous years and auditors currently on similar engagements, as well as conferences with the client's personnel. There are textbooks and technical magazines available for the auditor to study in most major industries. Some auditors follow the practice of subscribing to specialized industry journals for those industries in which they spend a large amount of time. Considerable knowledge can also be obtained by participating actively in industry associations and training programs.

Obtain General Information about the Client's Business

A knowledge of the important aspects of the business that differentiate it from other firms in its industry is needed by the auditor in making industry comparisons. Similarly, information such as organizational structure, marketing and distribution practices, method of inventory valuation, and other unique characteristics of the client's business should be understood before the audit is started because such facts are continuously used in interpreting auditing information as it is obtained.

The auditor's *permanent file* frequently includes the history of the company, a listing of the major lines of business, and a record of the most important accounting policies in previous years. The study of this information and discussions with the client's personnel aid in understanding the business.

Tour the Plant and Offices

A *tour of the facilities* is helpful in obtaining a better understanding of the client's business and operations because it provides an opportunity to meet key personnel. Discussions with nonaccounting employees during the tour and throughout the audit are useful in maintaining a broad perspective. The actual viewing of the physical facilities aids in understanding physical safeguards over assets and in interpreting accounting data providing a frame of reference in which to visualize such assets as inventory in process and factory equipment. A knowledge of the physical layout also facilitates getting answers to questions later in the audit.

Review the Permanent File for Company Policies

Regardless of the quality of the system of internal control, many company policies and authorizations reflected in the financial statements are outside the scope of the accounting system. These include such things as authorization for disposal of a portion of the business, credit policies, loans to affiliates, and accounting policies for recording assets and recognizing revenue. Basic policy decisions must always be carefully evaluated as part of the audit to determine whether management has authorization from the board of directors to make certain decisions, and to be sure the decisions of management are properly reflected in the statements.

A useful approach followed by many CPA firms is to include a record in the *permanent file* of the most important policies followed by the client and the name of the person or group authorized to change the policy. The inclusion in the permanent file of the primary generally accepted accounting principles, such as the costs to be included in inventory valuation, is especially useful in helping the auditor determine whether the client has changed accounting principles. A review of the permanent file for this information before the audit begins can be a valuable aid in understanding the client's operations and the policies the client should be following.

Investigate the Results of the Previous Audits

An important source of information in determining the parts of the current audit that are likely to cause the auditor difficulty is the results of previous years. Two major indicators of problem areas from previous years are the *amount of time* that was spent on each audit area and the *errors discovered* during the audit. If a particular audit area received unusual attention, the reasons for the emphasis should be obtained. If the conditions have not changed, increased attention may also be warranted in the current audit. Similarly, consideration should be given to heavy emphasis in the current year on those parts of the audit where significant errors were discovered in the past.

The best source of information for reviewing the results of a previous audit is that year's *working papers.* For at least the preceding year a careful study should be made of key memoranda, the audit program, the records of the time spent on each audit area, and the auditor's adjusting entries; however, all the working papers are normally reviewed. Excellent information is available in these sources indicating how the audit was approached, the evidence that the auditor considered necessary, the nature of the errors discovered in the testing, and the follow-up efforts by the auditor to resolve the errors.

Although the preceding year's working papers are an excellent source of information, the current year's audit should not automatically be developed along the same lines. Changed conditions require a different approach to the audit, and means of improving the quality of the audit should always be sought.

Engagement Letter with the Client

The *engagement letter* is the agreement between the CPA firm and the auditor for the conduct of the audit and related services (see Figure 4-1). It should specify whether the auditor will prepare the client's tax returns and also a letter recommending improvements in the client's system based upon observations made during the audit (*management letter*). It should also state whether any restrictions will be imposed on the auditor's work, deadlines for completing the audit, assistance to be provided by the client's personnel for obtaining records and documents and schedules to be prepared for the auditor. The engagement letter is also a means of informing the client that the auditor is not responsible for the discovery of fraud. The engagement letter does not affect the

FIGURE 4-1

ENGAGEMENT LETTER

Berger and Wild, CPAs
Gary, Indiana

6-11-77
Merchant's Steel
2146 Willow St.
Gary, Indiana

Dear Mr. Hocking:

We are pleased to serve as independent accountants for Merchant's Steel.

Mr. Wild will be the partner in charge of
all work we perform for you. Examining and reporting
on your annual financial statements is to be our
recurring basic assignment. We would like also to be
helpful to you on current problems as they arise
throughout the year. Hence, we hope you will call
him whenever you feel he can be of assistance.

The purpose of our engagement is to examine
the Company's financial statements for the year
ended 12-31-77 and evaluate the fairness of presentation
of the statements in conformity with generally accepted
accounting principles applied on a basis consistent
with that of the preceding period.

Our examination will be conducted in accordance with generally accepted auditing standards which
will include a review of the system of internal control
and tests of transactions to the extent we believe
necessary. Accordingly, it will not include a detailed
audit of transactions to the extent which would be
required if intended to disclose defalcations or other
irregularities, although their discovery may result.

We direct your attention to the fact that
management has the responsibility for the proper recording of transactions in the books of account, for
the safeguarding of assets, and for the substantial
accuracy of the financial statements. Such statements
are the representations of management.

FIGURE 4-1 (cont.)

The timing of our examination will be scheduled for performance and completion as follows:

	Begin	Complete
Preliminary tests	9-11-77	9-24-77
Internal control letter		10- 3-77
Year-end closing	2-3-78	2-18-78
Delivery of report		3-10-78

Assistance to be supplied by your personnel, including the preparation of schedules and analyses of accounts, is described on a separate attachment. Timely completion of this work will facilitate the conclusion of our examination.

Our fees are based on the amount of time required at various levels of responsibility, plus actual out-of-pocket expenses (travel, typing, telephone, etc.), payable upon presentation of our invoices. We will notify you immediately of any circumstances we encounter which could significantly affect our initial estimate of total fees of $23,000.

If the foregoing is in accordance with your understanding, please sign and return to us the duplicate copy of this letter.

We very much appreciate the opportunity to serve you and trust that our association will be a long and pleasant one.

Yours very truly,

John Wild

Accepted:

By: *Virgil Hockang*
Date: 6-21-77

auditor's responsibilities to external users of audited financial statements, but the responsibility to the client can be modified by the agreement.

Engagement letter information is important in planning the audit principally because it affects the timing of the tests and the total amount of time the audit and other services will take. If the deadline for submitting the audit report is soon after the balance sheet date, a significant portion of the audit must be done before the end of the year. When the auditor is preparing tax returns and a management letter, or if client assistance is not available, arrangements must be made to extend the amount of time on the engagement. Restrictions on the audit imposed by the client could affect the audit procedures performed and possibly even the type of audit opinion issued.

ANALYTICAL TESTS

Analytical tests are calculations by the auditor of ratios and key totals from data in the client's records for use as a basis of comparison with the client's experience in prior years, other companies in the same industry, and predetermined standards set by the client. Significant differences or unusual fluctuations noted in these comparisons are signals of the need for more detailed investigation.

One of the difficulties in using analytical tests is the frequent change in the results as the auditor makes adjustments to the client's statements for errors or omissions discovered during the audit. If the auditor makes the calculations early in the audit when they will be useful as an indicator of areas where errors might be expected, the results are likely to be incorrect by the end of the audit. On the other hand, if calculations are not made until the end of the audit, it may be inconvenient and time consuming to investigate those aspects of the audit where material differences between the data and the basis of comparison exist. In most audits, analytical data are of sufficient importance to merit calculation early in the audit and recalculation after material audit adjustments have been made.

Industry Ratios and Percentages

Dun and Bradstreet, Robert Morris Associates, and other publishers accumulate financial information for thousands of companies and compile the data for different lines of business. Many CPA firms purchase these publications for use as a basis for industry comparisons in their audits.

Robert Morris Associates, for example, publishes *ratios and percentages* for manufacturing, wholesaling, retailing, contractors, finance, and miscellaneous industries. Within the manufacturing category alone there are approximately 110 different lines of business included in such diverse areas as men's work clothing, poultry-dressing plants, and iron and steel forgings. There are also numerous diverse business lines for the other categories. For each industry area, the publication includes several different calculations for different sizes of businesses. Figure 4-2 contains the data shown for one business line in the retail section of the Robert Morris Associates Annual Statement Studies.

The most important benefits of industry comparisons are as follows:

1. *A better understanding of the client and its industry.* A better understanding of the client's industry can be accomplished by comparing current period industry ratios with the same industry for prior years and determining the reasons for any changes in the industry. Another useful approach is to compare the current period industry average with other industries as a means of better understanding the unique financial characteristics of the client's line of business. Once the auditor understands the nature of the industry and the changes that are taking place in the industry, the comparison of the client's ratios with the industry averages and the investigation of the differences can provide a better understanding of the client's operations.

2. *Indication of financial difficulty.* If the ratios for the client are unfavorable relative to the average firm of its size in the same industry, this may indicate the inability to adequately fund current operations, repay debt in the future, and possible financial failure. For example, if a higher than normal ratio of long-term debt to net worth is coupled with a lower than average ratio of profits to total assets, a relatively high risk of financial failure is indicated.

3. *Recommendations to the client.* When the auditor discovers areas where the client's ratios are significantly different from those of other firms in its industry, these areas can be discussed with the client. In some instances the client may be unaware of the differences between its practices and those of the other firms in the same industry. For example, if the ratio of sales to accounts receivable is higher than that of the average firms in the industry, it could indicate the client is losing sales because of an overly restrictive credit policy.

4. *Indication of errors in the financial statements.* It is possible for a difference between the ratios for a client and the industry averages to indicate a potential material error in the statements. If a difference is large, the auditor should determine the reason and investigate the possibility of one or more of the client's account balances being materially wrong. This is certainly an important aspect of ratio analysis and will be discussed more fully in the next section.

A major *weakness* of using industry ratios for auditing is the differences between the nature of the client's financial information and that of the firms making up the industry totals. Since no two companies are the same, the comparisons may not be meaningful in some cases. Many times the client's line of business is not the same as the industry standards. For example, in Figure 4-2, if the audit client being compared with the Robert Morris Associates' ratios for retailers of family clothing stores is a highly exclusive family store, the comparisons with the industry standards might not yield much relevant information. In addition, different companies follow different accounting methods, and this affects the comparability of data. If most companies in the industry use FIFO inventory valuation and straight-line depreciation, while the audit client uses LIFO and double-declining balance, the results are not too significant. This does not mean that industry comparisons should not be made. Rather, it is an indication of the need for great care in interpreting the results.

FIGURE 4-2

RETAILERS OF—FAMILY CLOTHING

35 STATEMENTS
ENDED ON OR ABOUT JUNE 30, 1972
78 STATEMENTS
ENDED ON OR ABOUT DECEMBER 31, 1972

ASSET SIZE	UNDER $250M	$250M & LESS THAN $1MM	$1MM & LESS THAN $10MM	$10MM & LESS THAN $50MM	ALL SIZES
NUMBER OF STATEMENTS	28	48	26	11	113
ASSETS	%	%	%	%	%
Cash	7.6	9.1	9.2	6.8	7.5
Marketable Securities	.2	1.4	.2	3.9	2.8
Receivables Net	21.3	22.8	23.3	21.4	21.9
Inventory Net	47.3	45.9	42.2	42.2	42.6
All Other Current	.4	1.2	1.5	1.2	1.3
Total Current	76.8	80.4	76.4	75.5	76.1
Fixed Assets Net	19.9	13.3	17.7	19.9	18.9
All Other Non-Current	3.3	6.4	5.9	4.6	5.0
Total	100.0	100.0	100.0	100.0	100.0
LIABILITIES					
Due To Banks-Short Term	13.6	10.8	6.2	2.0	3.8
Due To Trade	15.9	17.2	16.0	18.9	18.1
Income Taxes	1.5	1.6	2.4	3.4	3.0
Current Maturities LT Debt	2.2	1.2	3.3	1.9	2.2
All Other Current	8.4	5.9	9.2	6.8	7.3
Total Current Debt	41.5	36.6	37.1	33.1	34.4
Non-Current Debt, Unsub.	12.5	9.6	13.8	11.5	11.9
Total Unsubordinated Debt	54.0	46.2	50.9	44.6	46.3
Subordinated Debt	1.1	.6	1.2	.3	.5
Tangible Net Worth	44.9	53.2	47.8	55.1	53.1
Total	100.0	100.0	100.0	100.0	100.0
INCOME DATA					
Net Sales	100.0*	100.0*	100.0*	100.0*	100.0*
Cost Of Sales	61.6	65.1	61.1	69.3	66.7
Gross Profit	38.4	34.9	38.9	30.7	33.3
All Other Expense Net	36.2	31.9	35.0	25.3	28.6
Profit Before Taxes	2.2	3.0	3.9	5.3	4.7

RATIOS	UNDER $250M	$250M & LESS THAN $1MM	$1MM & LESS THAN $10MM	$10MM & LESS THAN $50MM	ALL SIZES
Quick	1.6	1.2	1.4	1.1	1.3
	.7	.7	.9	.9	.8
	.3	.5	.4	.6	.5
Current	2.8	3.0	2.6	3.1	2.8
	2.1	2.1	2.2	2.1	2.1
	1.5	1.5	1.4	1.8	1.5
Fixed/Worth	.0	.1	.2	.2	.1
	.3	.2	.3	.4	.3
	.7	.4	.6	.5	.5
Debt/Worth	.6	.4	.6	.4	.5
	1.1	.9	1.2	.8	1.0
	3.0	1.7	2.3	1.4	2.1
Unsub. Debt/Capital Funds	.6	.5	.6	.4	.5
	1.1	.9	1.1	.8	1.0
	2.4	1.8	1.9	1.4	1.8
Sales/Receivables	17 21.2	23 15.6	29 12.6	14 25.1	20 18.3
	50 7.2	42 8.5	49 7.4	45 8.0	43 8.3
	257 1.4	64 5.6	72 5.0	106 3.4	72 5.0
Cost Sales/Inventory	92 3.9	84 4.3	86 4.2	84 4.3	86 4.2
	120 3.0	116 3.1	97 3.7	113 3.2	116 3.1
	164 2.2	164 2.2	139 2.6	139 2.6	157 2.3
Sales/Working Capital	9.4	8.4	7.9	7.1	8.4
	7.3	5.7	6.3	4.9	5.9
	3.0	3.8	4.3	3.4	3.6
Sales/Worth	9.0	7.3	7.2	5.1	7.2
	4.2	4.1	4.9	3.9	4.2
	3.3	2.9	3.7	2.0	3.2
% Profit Bef. Taxes/Worth	20.5	19.1	34.5	25.3	21.8
	8.6	11.7	17.3	12.3	12.3
	.0	5.9	4.7	7.7	4.7
% Profit Bef. Taxes/Tot. Assets	8.9	9.6	11.9	16.4	10.2
	3.5	6.9	7.9	6.9	6.3
	.9	3.4	2.8	2.4	2.5
Net Sales	$8668M	$55403M	$163107M	$390389M	$617587M
Total Assets	3701M	23639M	68922M	202747M	299009M

Internal Ratios, Percentages, and Other Comparisons

Another approach to analytical testing as a means of isolating areas where error potential is high is to calculate important relationships from the client's accounting records and compare the results with previous years, standards, or other available information. There are several advantages in emphasizing this approach:

1. There are no restrictions on the number and type of calculations to make. For most comparisons to industry sources there are a limited number of ratios published.
2. The ratios can be much more specific and directly related to the auditor's areas of interest. For example, when the auditor wants to calculate sales returns and allowances on a monthly basis, it is possible to do so if the data are available in the records.
3. The comparisons are made only within the firm; therefore, there is no problem of determining the client's industry.
4. There is little difficulty encountered in comparing data based upon different methods of accounting. In fact, one of the uses of analytical testing is discovering instances where the client has changed accounting methods without disclosing this fact in the financial statements.

There are many different *types of internal analytical tests* available for auditors to compute. The appropriate ones to use depend upon the auditor's information needs and his personal preferences. Following are five categories of internal analytical tests which are potentially useful in different situations:

1. *Comparison of budgets with actual operating results.* Since budgets represent the client's expectations for the period, an investigation of the most significant areas where differences exist between budget and actual results may disclose errors in the financial statements. The starting point for the investigation should be a discussion with management as to why the differences exist. In many instances, additional evidence is also necessary to satisfy the auditor that the explanations provided by management are a reasonable interpretation rather than a rationalization of the differences.

2. *Comparison of the current-year absolute total balance with the balance of the preceding year.* One of the easiest ways to make this test is to include the preceding year's adjusted trial balance results in a special column of the current year's trial balance worksheet. This gives the auditor an opportunity to find out early in the audit whether a particular account should receive more than the normal amount of attention because of a significant change in the balance. For example, if the auditor observes a substantial increase in supplies expense, this would indicate the need to determine whether the cause of the increase was the increased use of supplies, a misstatement in the account due to a misclassification, or an error in the supplies inventory.

3. *Comparison of the detail of a total balance with similar detail for the preceding year.* If there have been no significant changes in the client's operations in the current year, much of the detail making up the totals in the financial statements should also remain relatively unchanged. By briefly comparing the detail of the current period with similar detail of the preceding period, it is often possible to isolate information that needs further examination. A common example is comparing the monthly totals for the current and preceding year for sales, repairs, and other accounts. The auditor should perform a more detailed analysis and in-

vestigation of any month that shows a significantly different total. Another example is in the physical examination of inventory where the auditor can compare the current year physical inventory quantities and unit cost for specific items with the preceding years.

4. *Calculation of the approximate balance in an expense or revenue account using relationships to other accounts.* In this type of calculation the auditor makes an estimate of what an account balance should be by relating it to some other balance sheet or income statement balance. If the auditor's estimate of the balance is materially different from the actual balance, detailed investigaion of the reason for the difference is necessary. An example of this is the independent calculation of interest expense on long-term notes payable by multiplying the ending monthly balance in notes payable by the average monthly interest rate. This total should approximate the total balance of interest expense. (See Figure 4-3.) In some instances it is also possible to estimate commission expense in the same manner, but if commission rates vary substantially on different types of sales, this would not be feasible. Similarly, it may be possible by overall calculations to make a useful estimate of total sales, depreciation expense, interest income, and similar account balances.

5. *Computation of ratios and percentage relationships for comparison with previous years.* The computation of ratios and percentage relationships for comparison with previous years is another way to obtain an indication of whether an account is materially misstated. This is commonly done in the case of industry comparisons. For example, one of the most important percentage relationships is the gross margin percentage. A significant change in this amount could be due to an error either in sales or in cost of goods sold. An error in the cost of goods sold could be caused by errors in the quantities or pricing of physical inventory, inadequate cutoff of accounts payable, or other factors. Sales could be misstated due to improper cutoff, the failure to bill, and other reasons. A large change in the gross margin percentage would indicate to the auditor the need for a detailed investigation to determine the cause of the difference. Of course, a major change in gross margin percentage might not be the result of an error; a change in product mix or selling price could also be responsible for the change. It is the auditor's responsibility to determine the cause of the change so he can be sure it did not result from misstated financial statements.

A few of the *types of ratios and internal comparisons* are included in the following list to show the usefulness of ratio analysis. In all cases the comparisons should be made with calculations made in previous years for the same client.

Obtaining Meaningful Results

In making calculations using analytical techniques, certain procedures are helpful in obtaining more meaningful results:

FIGURE 4-3

THE MILFORD COMPANY—OVERALL TESTS OF INTEREST EXPENSE, 12-31-76

The Milfred Company		Schedule N-3 Date	
Overall Test of Interest Expense		Prepared by GL 3/6/77	
12/31/76		Approved by FA 3/12/77	

Interest expense per general ledger — 1753 ①

Computation of estimate:

Short-term loans:

Balance outstanding at month-end: ②

Jan.	47500
Feb.	59200
Mar.	70600
Apr.	70800
May	61200
June	43700
July	20000
Aug.	—0—
Sept.	—0—
Oct.	12700
Nov.	26400
Dec.	35600
Total	447700

Average (÷ 12)   37300   @ 14.5% ③   5410

Long-term loans:

Beginning balance   137500 ②
Ending balance   121700 ②
                   259200

Average (÷ 2)   129600   @ 9.7% ④   12570

Estimated total interest expense   17980

Difference   (441) ⑤

Legend and Comments

① Agrees with general ledger and working trial balance.
② Obtained from general ledger.
③ Estimated, based on examination of several notes throughout the year with rates ranging from 14% to 15%.
④ Agrees with permanent file schedule of long-term debt.
⑤ Difference not significant. Indicates that interest expense per books is reasonable.

Ratio or Comparison	Possible Errors in Statement
a. Raw material turnover for a manufacturing company	Misstatement of inventory or cost of goods sold or obsolescence of raw material inventory
b. Sales commissions ÷ Net sales	Misstatement of sales commissions
c. Sales returns and allowances ÷ Gross sales	Misclassified sales returns and allowances or unrecorded returns or allowances subsequent to year-end
d. Cash surrender value of life insurance (current year) ÷ Cash surrender value of life insurance (preceding year)	Failure to record the change in cash surrender value or an error in recording the change
e. Each of the individual manufacturing expenses as a percentage of total manufacturing expense	Significant misstatement of individual expenses within the total

1. To determine trends that enable meaningful analysis, it is normally desirable to compare ratios, percentages, and absolute amounts with more periods than just the preceding one. Ideally, at least *four periods* should be included for each ratio and percentage used. To facilitate this, carry-forward schedules of ratio and trend calculations should be included in the permanent file.
2. It is desirable to compute *separate ratios* for different divisions, products, or types of expenses. Aggregation of data seldom enhances the meaningfulness of ratio and trend analysis.
3. Ratio and trend analysis should be concerned only with significant differences. This tool is meant to isolate significant differences relative to previous periods or other totals. In most uses, analytical techniques are not able to distinguish small differences.
4. It is important that the auditor know when the current period's calculations *should be different* from those of previous periods *because of changed conditions*. If conditions within the organization change, such as a major decrease in the selling price of its products or the obsolescence of inventory due to change in technology, affected ratios and comparisons should also change. The auditor is unlikely to recognize situations where ratios should change unless he has a good knowledge of the client's business and industry.
5. Ratio and trend analysis requires considerable *professional judgment* both in deciding upon the appropriate ratios to use and in interpreting their results. It is essential that an experienced professional be responsible for determining the appropriate ratios to compute. As much care should be taken in selecting ratios and comparisons for a given client as in the case of any other audit procedure.
6. It is imperative that there be *follow-up* on all material differences discovered through analytical techniques. It would be regarded as a failure to fulfill the requirement of due care if a comparison indicated the possibility of a material error and the auditor failed to investigate the cause of the difference.

INFORMATION ABOUT THE CLIENT'S LEGAL OBLIGATIONS

The fair presentation of financial statements in accordance with generally accepted accounting principles requires compliance with governmental regulations and other legal commitments in which the organization has become involved. Information about the client's legal obligations, if material, must be disclosed in the financial statements; however, even those not requiring direct disclosure are relevant to the auditor. If a client fails to fulfill its legal obligations, a lawsuit could result or a fine could be levied against the organization.

It is important to understand the most important legal requirements and agreements affecting the client *before* the audit begins. This will enable the auditor to properly interpret evidence obtained throughout the audit. If knowledge of a legal requirement is not obtained until the end of the engagement, it will be difficult to recall transactions or events encountered early in the audit that might have been affected by the requirement. It is also more convenient and efficient to evaluate the legal effect of transactions and events as a part of the audit rather than subsequently. An understanding of the legal requirements and agreements is also helpful in obtaining a better knowledge of the client's overall business environment.

A distinction should be made between providing *legal advice* or interpreting legal documents and obtaining a reasonable understanding of the meaning of legal requirements from an audit point of view. The Code of Professional Ethics *prohibits CPAs from providing legal advice and making legal interpretations* if they are also acting as the independent auditor. On the other hand, it is essential that auditors be familiar with the client's legal requirements to the extent that they directly or indirectly affect the financial statements. If any difficulties arise in interpreting legal documents, either the client's legal counsel or the auditor's own attorney should be consulted.

Four general types of legal documents are discussed in this section:

1. Governmental regulations affecting the client
2. Corporate charter and bylaws
3. Minutes of directors' and stockholders' meetings
4. Contracts

Governmental Regulations Affecting the Client

Every organization's operations are affected in some way by local, state, or federal laws. These laws are frequently complex, and in some instances it may be impractical for CPAs to evaluate them. As an illustration, the determination of whether a company is living within the legal requirement of local zoning laws is outside of the CPA's scope of responsibility. On the other hand, many regulations directly affect the financial statements and are within the CPA's domain. The auditor should be familiar with the following:

Federal and state securities acts. The SEC Acts of 1933 and 1934 have special significance to both the client and the auditor. For an auditor involved with publicly held companies, a thorough understanding of these requirements is essential. Most clients rely heavily upon their auditor in complying with SEC regulations. State laws regulating publicly held companies are normally less difficult to comply with than the federal laws, but nevertheless must be understood.

Regulations relating to labor. Numerous regulations affect matters relating to employees. Of special significance are the laws relating to payroll taxes. These include requirements for withholding federal, state, and local income taxes and FICA taxes, as well as the client's tax requirements for federal and state unemployment taxes and the employer's share of FICA taxes. Minimum wage laws, regulations for payment of overtime rates, and nondiscrimination laws should also be understood. The requirements of the 1974 pension reform act are important for the fair presentation of financial statements.

Antitrust laws. Price discrimination in interstate commerce is prohibited by the Robinson-Patman Act. Although it is difficult to determine when a violation of this federal law has taken place, the auditor should at least be familiar with the regulations.

Wage and price controls. At various times the federal government institutes controls on such things as prices, wages, interest, and dividends. A violation of these regulations during the time they are in effect can result in significant fines, including the possibility of a payment to individuals or businesses harmed by the violation of the law. Excess profits taxes are another example of this type of government regulation. The auditor must understand the nature of these regulations and know the periods to which the regulations apply.

Income tax laws. It is essential that auditors involved with businesses for profit understand the state and federal tax laws affecting the business. Even though the study of taxes can be a separate career in itself, auditors must know the tax implications of various accounting transactions and business decisions. Most CPA firms expect their auditors to understand the tax regulations well enough to recognize the possibility of a tax problem. Otherwise it would be difficult to determine whether federal income tax expense and the related liability account are fairly stated. Once a tax problem is recognized, the CPA firm's tax department is typically responsible for resolving the issues and advising the auditor of the proper solution. Many clients also rely on the CPA firm to provide tax advice.

Industry regulations. Many clients in specialized industries are regulated by state and federal regulatory commissions. Examples include banks, railroads, insurance companies, brokers, and dealers in securities. The audits of municipal governments and state and federal governmental agencies also require an understanding of specialized regulations.

Corporate Charter and Bylaws

The *corporate charter* is granted by the state in which the company is incorporated and is the legal document necessary for recognizing a corporation as a separate entity. It includes the exact name of the corporation, the date of incorporation, the kinds and amounts of capital stock the corporation is authorized to issue, and the types of business activities the corporation is authorized to conduct. In specifying the kinds of capital stock, there is also included such information as the voting rights of each class of stock, par or stated value of the stock, preferences and conditions necessary for dividends, and prior rights in liquidation.

The *bylaws* include the rules and procedures adopted by the stockholders of the corporation. They specify such things as the fiscal year of the corporation, the frequency of stockholder meetings, the method of voting for directors, and the duties and powers of the corporate officers.

The auditor must understand the requirements of the corporate charter and the bylaws in order to determine whether the financial statements are properly presented. The correct disclosure of the stockholders' equity, including the proper payment of dividends, depends heavily upon these requirements.

It is common for the auditor to obtain *copies* of the corporate charter and bylaws during the initial audit and *retain them in the permanent file*. In subsequent audits it is then possible to review these documents without obtaining them from the client. Any changes in the requirements will be stated in the corporate minutes.

Minutes of Directors' and Stockholders' Meetings

The *corporate minutes* are the official record of the meetings of the board of directors and stockholders. They include summaries of the most important topics discussed at these meetings and the decisions made by the directors and stockholders. A considerable portion of the information in the minutes has no direct relationship to the fair presentation of the financial statements and is useful to the auditor only as a means of obtaining a better understanding of the client's business. On the other hand, there is some essential information the audior could easily overlook if he failed to examine the minutes. Information such as the following is usually included in the minutes:

1. Declaration of dividends
2. Authorized compensation of officers
3. Acceptance of contracts and agreements
4. Authorization for the acquisition of property
5. Approval of mergers
6. Authorization of long-term loans
7. Approval to pledge securities
8. Authorization of individuals to sign checks
9. Reports on the progress of operations

While examining the corporate minutes, the auditor normally obtains information about those portions having significance to the fair presentation of the financial statements for inclusion in the working papers. This can be done by making an *abstract* of the minutes or obtaining a *copy* and underlining significant portions. At some time before the audit is completed, there must be a follow-up of this information to be sure management has complied with actions taken by the stockholders and the board of directors. As an illustration, the authorized compensation of officers should be traced to each individual officer's payroll record as a test of whether the correct total compensation was paid. Similarly, the auditor should compare the authorizations for the acquisition of equipment in the minutes with the equipment records if the board of directors must approve all new acquisitions of equipment over a specified amount, such as $100,000.

Contracts

Clients become involved in many different types of contracts that are of interest to the auditor. These contracts can include such diverse items as long-term notes and bonds payable, stock options, pension plans, contracts with vendors for future delivery of supplies, government contracts for completion and delivery of manufactured products, royalty agreements, union contracts, and leases.

Most of these contracts are of primary interest in individual parts of the audit and, in practice, receive special attention during the different phases of the detailed tests. As an example, the provisions of a pension plan would receive substantial emphasis as a part of the audit of the unfunded liability for pensions. The auditor should review and abstract the documents early in the engagement to gain a better perspective of the organization and to familiarize himself with potential problem areas. Later these documents can be examined more carefully as a part of the tests of individual audit areas.

In examining contracts, primary attention should focus on any aspect of the legal agreement affecting financial disclosure. Contracts can have an important effect on the statements when the subject of the contract must be directly included at a specific dollar value on the statements, as in the case of a mortgage or bond liability. The potential effect of a contract on the statements will naturally depend upon the nature of the contract. A long-term note has a completely different kind of disclosure requirement than a government contract for the delivery of finished goods.

In *abstracting contracts* to which the client is a party, great care should be taken to accurately include all relevant information. In many cases the abstract will be included in the permanent working papers and be used in several future audits. The contract title and number and the names and addresses of the parties to the contract, as well as the beginning and ending dates of the contract, should be included in the abstract. The provisions of the contract that affect financial statement disclosure must be clearly specified. Emphasis should also be put on any conditions affecting the terms of the contract, as well as penalties for failure to meet the contract's specifications. This information should be stated in a manner that facilitates reference to the key provisions as the audit of specific areas progresses.

In some instances the information included in contracts is too technical for auditors to completely understand. When this occurs, the auditor has a responsibility to consult with an attorney, engineer, or other specialist for assistance in interpreting the contract's contents.

EVALUATION OF THE POSSIBILITY OF MANAGEMENT INVOLVEMENT IN MATERIAL FRAUDULENT TRANSACTIONS

Nature of the Problem

In recent years there have been several known instances of *deliberate management action to materially misrepresent financial statement information* for the personal benefit of various members of management. In some cases the motive was to cover up a massive fraud; in other cases management attempted to portray significantly more favorable financial statements than actually existed in order to prevent undesirable effects such as bankruptcy, a significant decline in value of securities, or the termination of employment. Misstated financial statements can result from intentional failure to record transactions, intentional misstatement of recorded transactions, or recording of invalid transactions. In virtually every instance of management fraud, the misstatement is difficult for the auditor to uncover because of extensive efforts by management to misrepresent or withhold the pertinent information. A few of the major legal cases involving management misrepresentations are briefly summarized below to illustrate the nature of the fraudulent activity and the significance of the problem.

U.S. Financial, Inc.—The chief executive officer of the company did not disclose his personal guarantees of down payment funds used by purportedly independent parties to purchase real property from the company. The SEC's suit against this officer and the company also alleged the "manufacturing" of transactions in an endeavor to stimulate or maintain the price of the company's stock on which his personal fortune may have been dependent.

National Student Marketing—Among the many issues in this complex case, at least two fall into the management involvement area. First, revenues were prematurely recorded and subsequently proved not to have been realized. The reporting of favorable results at the earliest possible time ostensibly stimulated the market valuation of the company's stock, making it attractive for acquisition purposes. Second, the chairman of National Student Marketing also used his own stock in the company as an inducement for employment or as additional compensation, without disclosing such activities.

Equity Funding—The activities in this case were of three types: creation and inflation of assets, failure to record liabilities for borrowed cash, and creation of bogus insurance which was coinsured with other insurance companies. The effect of these practices was to inflate earnings and assets and to create the appearance of sustained growth at a substantial but measured rate. The insurance fraud also provided funds for critical cash needs. Equity Funding has incorrectly been referred to as the "great computer fraud," and although electronic data processing was substantial, a rational analysis leads to the conclusion that persons, not computers, perpetrate fraud.

A common way in which fraudulent transactions by management take place is by management's involvement in *non-arm's-length bargaining* with related parties. The existence of arm's-length bargaining, where each party to a transaction is pursuing his own self-interest without restrictions, is fundamental to financial reporting. When the client's management is able to exert undue influence on the other party to a transaction, the possibility of management fraud is greatly enhanced. For example, if the client sells products to an affiliated company, in the short run management may be able to dictate the selling price on a quantity of goods delivered to the affiliate. This has the effect of potentially permitting management to reflect any level of sales and net earnings desired if consolidated financial statements are not issued. Another type of management fraud is a non-arm's-length loan to an officer or affiliated company in which there is little or no likelihood of being able to collect the loan when it becomes due. In many cases the collateral supporting the loan is inadequate or overvalued. Still another example of this type of management fraud is the setting of excessive salaries for management by a board of directors dominated by the management group. Other types of management fraud include a massive diversion of company assets to personal use, the intentional failure to disclose loans, warranty liabilities and lawsuits against the company, and the fraudulent misstatement of assets through accounting entries.

There is nothing inherently wrong with management's being involved in non-arm's-length transactions. They are a normal part of business activity. Nevertheless, their existence implies a careful evaluation of the increased possibility of fraud.

Auditor's Responsibility

What is the auditor's responsibility for the discovery of material fraud perpetrated by management? In answering this question, *a clear distinction should be made between deliberate fraudulent actions by management and a defalcation by an employee because of inadequate internal control.* There is general agreement that adequate controls and fidelity bonds are a less expensive means than auditing of detecting and preventing employee fraud. Unfortunately, adequate internal accounting controls and fidelity bonds are not likely to uncover or prevent management fraud. In spite of this, the AICPA has taken the position that an ordinary audit cannot be relied upon to discover deliberate misrepresentations by management. The AICPA's position is that the auditor has responsibility for the failure to detect fraud only when the failure results from the inadequate performance of auditing procedures. In recent years, however, the courts, the SEC, and even some CPA firms are beginning to recognize the need for auditors to make *reasonable efforts* to discover management fraud. The cost to society for the losses caused by management frauds and the effect on the CPA's image in the financial community when the auditor fails to discover the fraud are too significant to ignore. How far the responsibility should extend has not yet been established, and none of these groups are willing to go so far as to make auditors responsible for the discovery of all material management frauds.

Evaluation of Environmental Considerations

Before the auditor begins an investigation of the possibility of management fraud, there are four environmental considerations he should evaluate:

1. *Motivation of management.* Management is unlikely to become involved in fraudulent transactions without a strong reason. It is difficult to assess the likelihood that personal reasons, such as heavy gambling or alcoholism, will cause one or two individuals in management to commit fraud. Certain *economic factors,* however, may motivate management to intentionally misrepresent the statements. These factors are basically similar to the factors affecting the likelihood of filing bankruptcy—the lack of sufficient capital to continue business, the urgent desire for a continued favorable earnings record in the hope of supporting the price of the stock, numerous unsuccessful business acquisitions and significant obsolescence dangers because the company is in a high-technology industry.

2. *Business structure.* Experience has shown that the structure and style of operating a business may be *deliberately designed* by management to facilitate management fraud. Of course, in the vast majority of

cases, the business structure and style adopted are meant to be responsive to the abilities of management as well as business geography and product diversification, but an evaluation should be made of the effect of the business structure on the likelihood of management fraud.

Following are a number of factors involved in the business structure that increase the opportunity for management fraud:

    a. The management is dominated by one or a few individuals.

    b. Key financial positions, such as those of the controller and treasurer, do not seem to stay filled very long.

    c. The accounting and financial functions appear to be understaffed, resulting in constant crisis conditions.

    d. The company seems to need, but lacks, an adequate internal audit staff.

    e. The company follows the practice of using different auditors for major subsidiaries or branches.

    f. The auditor must make numerous significant adjusting entries as a part of the audit.

    g. The business locations of the company are widely dispersed, key documents are created at outlying locations, and evidence of a material transaction must be obtained from more than one location.

    h. The company relies on special legal counsel for individual matters rather than retaining general counsel.

3. *Integrity of management.* An analysis of recent court cases involving management fraud shows that in most instances the individuals responsible for the fraud had also been previously involved in illegal or unethical business practices. It should not be surprising to anyone that a member of management who deceives customers, suppliers, and other company employees will also be willing to deceive the users of financial statements and the independent auditor.

Since CPA firms are often able to predict the likelihood of future dishonest actions by one or more members of management on the basis of their past behavior, the *investigation of the background of new clients* has become increasingly important. Most CPA firms are no longer willing to accept new clients without an investigation of the past history of the firm and its management. This invesigation usually includes discussions with the preceding auditor, management, and employees. In many cases the CPA firm hires a professional investigator to obtain information about the reputation and background of the key members of management. If the investigation indicates the likelihood of dishonest management, many firms will not accept the client. If such a client is accepted, a more intensive audit of the possibility of misrepresentation is implied.

4. *Reliance on computers.* While the basic objectives of accounting control do not actually change with the method of data processing used, organization and control procedures utilized in EDP applications may differ significantly from those utilized in manual or mechanical applications. There are risks inherent in business activities involving massive

volumes of individual transactions when total reliance is placed on computer operations. The impact of computers on auditing is discussed in Chapter 12.

Types of Procedures to Apply

Some types of management fraud can be uncovered by normal audit procedures. There is, for example, a good chance of discovering intentional overstatements of assets as a result of failing to charge off uncollectible accounts receivable or obsolete inventory, failing to record the liability for product warranties, and failing to disclose existing lawsuits. The major reason certain types of misstatements are frequently discovered is that the procedures required to detect them are performed as a part of the normal search for unintentional errors.

Other types of fraud require extended procedures, especially for massive fraud where great efforts are made by management to deceive the auditor. In discussing the audit procedures appropriate for uncovering management fraud, we will make no distinction between those necessary as an ordinary part of the audit and those used specifically for the discovery of management fraud. Furthermore, the audit procedures discussed here are meant to be illustrative rather than exhaustive. The procedures are presented in the order in which they will probably be performed on an audit.

1. Obtain background information about the audit in the manner discussed earlier to ensure understanding the client's industry and business.
2. Perform analytical tests of the type discussed earlier to evaluate the possibility of business failure and assess areas where management fraud is likely.
3. Review and understand the client's legal obligations in the manner discussed earlier to become conversant with the legal environment in which the client operates.
4. Review the information available in the audit files—such as permanent files, audit programs, and the preceding year's working papers—for the existence of material non-arm's-length transactions. Also discuss with tax and management service personnel assigned to the client their knowledge of management involvement in material transactions.
5. Discuss the possibility of management fraud with company counsel after obtaining permission to do so from management.
6. When more than one CPA firm is involved in the audit, exchange information with them about the nature of material transactions and the possibility of management fraud.
7. Investigate whether material transactions occurred close to year-end.
8. For *all* material transactions, evaluate whether the parties are economically independent and have negotiated the transaction on an arm's-length basis and whether each transaction was for a valid business purpose.

9. Evaluate each material non-arm's-length transaction to determine its nature and the possibility of its being recorded at the improper amount. The evaluation should consider whether the transaction was for a valid business purpose, was not unduly complex, and was presented in conformity with its substance.

10. When management is indebted to the company in a material amount, evaluate whether management has the financial ability to settle the obligation. If collateral for the obligation exists, evaluate its acceptability and value.

11. Inspect entries in public records as a test of the proper recording of real property transactions and personal property liens.

12. Make inquiries of related parties to determine the possibility of inconsistencies between the client's and the related parties' understanding and recording of transactions that took place between them.

13. When a material transaction is recorded by the client in a questionable manner, inspect the records of the related party.

14. When independent parties such as attorneys or banks are significantly involved in a material transaction, ascertain their understanding of the nature and purpose of the transaction.

REVIEW QUESTIONS

1. For each of the following questions, state the one best response:
   a. With respect to proceedings of the meetings of the board of directors of a client corporation, the normal auditing procedure is to
      (1) Obtain from the company secretary a minutes representation letter that summarizes actions pertinent to the financial statements
      (2) Discuss proceedings of the board with its chairman or his designated representative
      (3) Review the minutes of all meetings
      (4) Obtain tapes or written transcripts of all meetings or attend all meetings
   b. An auditor should examine minutes of board of directors' meetings
      (1) Through the date of his report
      (2) Through the date of the financial statements
      (3) On a test basis
      (4) Only at the beginning of the audit
   c. Your independent examination of the Dey Company reveals that the firm's poor financial condition makes it unlikely that it will survive as a going concern. Assuming that the financial statements have otherwise been prepared in accordance with generally accepted accounting principles, what disclosure should you make of the company's precarious financial position?
      (1) You should issue an unqualified opinion, but in a paragraph between the scope and opinion paragraphs of your report, direct the reader's attention to the poor financial condition of the company.
      (2) You should insist that a note to the financial statements clearly indicate that the company appears to be on the verge of bankruptcy.
      (3) You need not insist on any particular disclosure, since the company's

poor financial condition is clearly indicated by the financial statements themselves.

(4) You should provide adequate disclosure and appropriately modify your opinion because the company does not appear to be a going concern.

d. Which potential error or questionable practice will most likely be discovered by a tour of the plant when the auditor is accompanied by the production manager?

(1) Depreciation expense was recognized in the current year for a machine that is fully depreciated.

(2) Overhead has been underapplied

(3) Necessary plant maintenance was not performed during the year.

(4) Insurance coverage on the plant has been allowed to lapse.

(AICPA adapted)

2. a. When a CPA has accepted an engagement from a new client who is a manufacturer, it is customary for the CPA to tour the client's plant facilities. Discuss the ways in which the CPA's observations made during the course of the plant tour will be of help to him as he plans and conducts his audit.

b. An auditor often tries to acquire background knowledge of his client's industry as an aid to him in his audit work. How does the acquisition of this knowledge aid the auditor in distinguishing between obsolete and current inventory? (AICPA adapted)

3. Gale Gordon, CPA, has found ratio and trend analysis relatively useless as a tool in conducting audits. For several engagements he computed the industry ratios included in publications by Robert Morris Associates and compared them with industry standards. For most engagements the client's business was significantly different from the industry data in the publication and the client would automatically explain away any discrepancies by attributing them to the unique nature of its operations. In cases where the client had more than one branch in different industries, Gordon found the ratio analysis no help at all. How could Gordon improve the quality of his analytical tests?

4. At the completion of every audit, Roger Morris, CPA, calculates a large number of ratios and trends for comparison with industry averages and prior year calculations. He believes the calculations are worth the relatively small cost of doing them because they provide him with an excellent overview of the client's operations. If the ratios are out of line, Morris discusses the reasons with the client and frequently makes suggestions on how to bring the ratio back in line in the future. In some cases these discussions with management have been the basis for management services engagements. Discuss the major strengths and shortcomings in Morris's use of ratio and trend analysis.

5. Explain why the statement "Analytical tests are essential in every part of an audit, but these tests are rarely sufficient by themselves for any audit area" is correct or incorrect.

6. List the five types of information the auditor should obtain or review as a part of gaining background information for the audit, and provide one specific example of how the information will be useful in conducting the audit.

7. Jennifer Bailey is an experienced senior who is in charge of several important

audits for a medium-sized firm. Her philosophy of conducting audits is to ignore all previous years and permanent working papers until near the end of the audit as a means of keeping from prejudicing herself. She believes this enables her to perform the audit in a more independent manner because it eliminates the tendency of simply doing the same things in the current audit that were done on previous audits. Near the end of the audit Bailey reviews the working papers from the preceding year, evaluates the significance of any items she has overlooked, and modifies her evidence if she considers it necessary. Evaluate Bailey's approach to conducting an audit.

8. The following questions refer to the use of industry ratios, internal ratios, percentages, and other comparisons:
   a. List five industry ratios the auditor can compute, explain how to calculate each one, and state the most important information provided by each ratio.
   b. List five types of internal comparisons the auditor can make, state the purpose of each one, and provide two examples for each comparison.
   c. What are the primary advantages of internal comparison over industry ratios?
   d. What are the primary advantages of industry ratios over internal comparison?

9. Your client, Harper Company, has a contractual commitment as a part of a bond indenture to maintain a current ratio of 2.0. If the ratio falls below that level on the balance sheet date, the entire bond becomes payable immediately. In the current year the client's financial statements show that the ratio has dropped from 2.6 to 2.05 over the past year. How should this situation affect your audit plan?

10. Your firm has performed the audit of the Rogers Company for several years and you have been assigned the audit responsibility for the current audit. How would your review of the corporate charter and bylaws for this audit differ from that of the audit of a client that was audited by a different CPA firm in the preceding year?

11. For the audit of Radline Manufacturing Company, the audit partner asks you to carefully read the new mortgage contract with the First National Bank and abstract all pertinent information. List the information that is likely to be relevant to the auditor in a mortgage.

12. List five federal or state regulations the auditor should be familiar with, and state how they would affect the fair presentation of the financial statements.

13. Distinguish between management fraud and employee fraud. Discuss the likely difference between these two types of fraud on the fair presentation of financial statements.

14. "It is well accepted in auditing that throughout the conduct of the ordinary examination, it is essential to obtain large amounts of information from management and to rely heavily on management's judgments. After all, the financial statements are management's representations, and the primary responsibility for their fair presentation rests with management, not the auditor. For example, it is extremely difficult, if not impossible, for the auditor to evaluate the obsolescence of inventory as well as management can in a highly complex business. Similarly, the collectibility of accounts receivable and the continued usefulness of machinery and equipment is heavily dependent on management's willingness to provide truthful responses

to questions." Reconcile the auditor's responsibility for discovering material misrepresentations by management with the above comments.

15. List three major considerations that are useful in predicting the likelihood of management fraud in an audit. For each of the considerations, state two things the auditor can do to evaluate its significance in the engagement.

DISCUSSION QUESTIONS AND PROBLEMS

16. The inspection of the minutes of meetings is an integral part of a CPA's examination of a corporation's financial statements.

   Required:

   a. A CPA should determine if there is any disagreement between transactions recorded in the corporate records and actions approved by the corporation's board of directors. Why is this so and how is it accomplished?

   b. Discuss the effect each of the following situations would have on specific audit steps in a CPA's examination and on his audit opinion:
      (1) The minute book does not show approval for the sale of an important manufacturing division which was consummated during the year.
      (2) Some details of a contract negotiated during the year with the labor union are different from the outline of the contract included in the minutes of the board of directors.
      (3) The minutes of a meeting of directors held after the balance sheet date have not yet been written, but the corporation's secretary shows the CPA notes from which the minutes are to be prepared when the secretary has time.

   c. What corporate actions should be approved by stockholders and recorded in the minutes of the stockholders' meetings?   (AICPA adapted)

17. You are engaged in the annual audit of the financial statements of Maulack Company, a medium-sized wholesale company that manufactures light fixtures. The company has twenty-five stockholders. During your review of the minutes you observe that the president's salary has been increased substantially over the preceding year by action of the board of directors. His present salary is much greater than salaries paid to presidents of companies of comparable size and is clearly excessive. You determine that the method of computing the president's salary was changed for the year under audit. In previous years, the president's salary was consistently based on sales. In the latest year, however, his salary was based on net income before income taxes. The Maulack Company is in a cyclical industry and would have had an extremely profitable year except that the increase in the president's salary siphoned off much of the income that would have accrued to the stockholders. The president is a substantial stockholder.

   Required:

   a. What is the implication of this condition on the fair presentation of the financial statements?

   b. Discuss your responsibility for disclosing this situation.

   c. Discuss the effect, if any, that the situation has upon your auditor's opinion as to

(1) The fairness of the presentation of the financial statements

(2) The consistency of the application of accounting principles

(AICPA adapted)

18. You are meeting with executives of Cooper Cosmetics Corporation to arrange your firm's engagement to examine the corporation's financial statements for the calendar year ending December 31. One executive suggested that the audit work be divided among three audit staff members so that one member would examine asset accounts, a second would examine liability accounts, and a third would examine income and expense accounts to minimize audit time, avoid duplication of staff effort, and curtail interference with company operations.

Advertising is the corporation's largest expense, and the advertising manager suggested that a staff member of your firm whose uncle owns the advertising agency be assigned to examine the advertising expense account. The staff member has a thorough knowledge of the rather complex contract between Cooper Cosmetics and the advertising agency on which Cooper's advertising costs are based.

Required:

a. To what extent should a CPA follow his client's suggestions for the conduct of an audit? Discuss.

b. List and discuss the reasons why audit work should not be assigned solely according to asset, liability, and income and expense categories.

c. Should the staff member of your CPA firm whose uncle owns the advertising agency be assigned to examine advertising costs? Discuss.

(AICPA adapted)

19. In late spring you are advised of a new assignment as in-charge accountant of your CPA firm's recurring annual audit of a major client, the Lancer Company. You are given the engagement letter for the audit covering the current calendar year, and a list of personnel assigned to this engagement. It is your responsibility to plan and supervise the field work for the engagement.

Required:

Discuss the necessary preparation and planning for the Lancer Company annual audit *prior to* beginning field work at the client's office. In your discussion include the sources you should consult, the type of information you should seek, the preliminary plans and preparation you should make for the field work, and any actions you should take relative to the staff assigned to the engagement.   (AICPA adapted)

20. You have been assigned by your firm to complete the examination of the financial statements of Carter Manufacturing Corporation because the senior accountant and his inexperienced assistant who began the engagement were hospitalized due to an accident. The engagement is about one-half completed. Your auditor's report must be delivered in three weeks as agreed when your firm accepted the engagement. You estimate that by utilizing the client's staff to the greatest possible extent you can complete the engagement in five weeks. Your firm cannot assign an assistant to you.

The working papers show the status of the examination as follows:

a. *Completed*—Cash, accounts receivable confirmation, fixed assets, depreciation, mortgage payable, and stockholders' equity
b. *Completed except as noted later*—Inventories, accounts payable, tests of purchase transactions, and payrolls
c. *Nothing done*—Review of internal control, tests of disbursements transactions, tests of sales and collection transactions, inventory receiving cutoff and price testing, accrued expenses payable, unrecorded liability tests, payroll deductions tests and observation of payroll check distribution, other expenses, analytical tests, auditor's report, internal control letter, reading of minutes, preparation of tax returns, examination of controls, review of the correspondence file, and tour of the physical facilities

Your review discloses that the assistant's working papers are incomplete and were not reviewed by the senior accountant. For example, the inventory working papers present incomplete notations, incomplete explanations, and no cross-referencing.

Required:

a. What field work standards have been violated by the senior accountant who preceded you on this assignment? Explain why you feel the work standards you list have been violated.
b. In planning your work to complete this engagement, you should scan working papers and schedule certain work as soon as possible and also identify work that may be postponed until after the report is rendered to the client.
   (1) List the areas on which you should plan to work first, say in your first week of work, and for each item explain why it deserves early attention.
   (2) State which work you believe should be postponed until other parts of the audit have been completed. (AICPA adapted)

21. A major written understanding between a CPA and his client, in connection with an examination of financial statements, is the engagement letter.

Required:

a. What are the objectives of the engagement letter?
b. Who should prepare and sign the engagement letter?
c. When should the engagement letter be sent?
d. Why should the engagement letter be renewed periodically?
(AICPA adapted)

22. The CPA firm of Whipple and White is defending its audit of the Merkle Construction Company, a builder of apartments, in a legal liability case. The firm had audited the client for several years and had observed a gradual deterioration of the client's financial position, but it was surprised when the client filed for bankruptcy three months after the completion of the audit. Several major issues are involved in the lawsuit, including the following:
a. The construction in process on the balance sheet included an overhead rate based upon all construction overhead and 40 percent of all administrative costs. Management contended that this is normal practice for

the industry. There are more buildings in progress in the current year than in any previous year. The same practice was followed in previous years.

b. Two weeks after the balance sheet date, Merkle repurchased an apartment building from a customer for the same amount as the original sale price, which was $10,500,000. One month later the apartment building was resold to a syndicate for $8,200,000 cash. The original sale was included in the audited financial statements at $10,500,000. The audit report was dated eighty-seven days after the balance sheet date.

c. One of the apartment buildings has been included as a completed building available for rent at year-end. This same building was also included as a contract receivable and a sale. Thirty apartments were completed during the year, but only one was recorded more than once.

d. A major mortgage on one of the apartments for the amount of $2,400,000 was not included as a liability. The auditor had confirmed all mortgages, but the unrecorded mortgage was owed to a bank the client had not done business with before. All of the twenty-six apartments owned and operated by the company were mortgaged, and all but the unrecorded one were properly valued.

Required:

a. How could each of the above errors have been discovered in the audit?
b. What appears to be the primary weakness in the auditor's approach to the audit?

23. During the audit of the Railine Manufacturing Company, you observe that the net sales and manufacturing operations have increased tremendously relative to the preceding year. Despite this apparently healthy expansion, the client's net income decreased significantly. In the course of the engagement, the auditor did not find any explanation for the decrease in net income. During the ensuing discussion, one of the staff members on the engagement suggested the need to perform additional tests to explain the decline in profits. Another staff member disagreed with this point of view. He felt that additional testing to discover the cause of the decline was beyond the audit responsibilities required by generally accepted auditing standards. "Our audit fees do not include troubleshooting a client's operating efficiency problems," he remarked. "I will not agree to an extension of auditing procedures if I am satisfied a client's financial statements are presented fairly."

Required:

a. State five possible causes of the decline in profits when volume has expanded.
b. Discuss the auditor's responsibility for determining the cause of the decline in profits when the detailed tests of the records do not indicate the existence of material errors.
c. Ordinarily, when should the auditor determine the cause of a decline in profits? Why?

24. Your comparison of the gross margin percentage for Jones Drugs for the years 19X3 through 19X6 indicates a significant decline. This is shown by the following information:

	19X6	19X5	19X4	19X3
Sales (in thousands)	$14,211	$12,916	$11,462	$10,351
CGS (in thousands)	9,223	8,266	7,313	6,573
Gross margin	$ 4,988	$ 4,650	$ 4,149	$ 3,778
Percent	35.1%	36.0%	36.2%	36.5%

A discussion with Marilyn Adams, the controller, brings to light two possible explanations. She informs you that the industry gross profit percentage in the retail drug industry declined fairly steadily for three years, which accounts for part of the decline. A second factor was the declining percentage of the total volume resulting from the pharmacy part of the business. The pharmacy sales represent the most profitable portion of the business, yet the competition from discount drugstores prevents it from expanding as fast as the non-drug items such as magazines, candy, and the many other items sold. Adams feels strongly that these two factors are the cause of the decline.

The following additional information is obtained from independent sources and the client's records as a means of investigating the controller's explanations:

	Drug Sales	Non-Drug Sales	Drug Cost of Goods Sold	Non-Drug Cost of Goods Sold	Industry Gross Profit Percent for Retailers of Drugs and Related Products
19X6	$5,126	$9,085	$3,045	$6,178	32.7%
19X5	$5,051	$7,865	$2,919	$5,347	32.9%
19X4	$4,821	$6,641	$2,791	$4,522	33.0%
19X3	$4,619	$5,732	$2,665	$3,908	33.2%

Required:

a. Evaluate the explanation provided by Adams. Show calculations to support your conclusions.

b. Which specific aspects of the client's financial statements require intensive investigation in this audit?

25. In the audit of the Worldwide Wholesale Company, you performed extensive ratio and trend analysis. No material exceptions were discovered except for the following:

a. Commission expense as a percentage of sales has stayed constant for several years but has increased significantly in the current year. Commission rates have not changed.

b. The rate of inventory turnover has steadily decreased for four years.

c. Inventory as a percentage of current assets has steadily increased for four years.

d. The number of days sales in accounts receivable has steadily increased for three years.

e. Allowance for uncollectible accounts as a percentage of accounts receivable has steadily decreased for three years.
f. The absolute amount of depreciation expense and depreciation expense as a percentage of gross fixed assets is significantly smaller than in the preceding year.

Required:

a. Evaluate the potential significance of each of the above for the fair presentation of financial statements.
b. State the follow-up procedures you would use to determine the possibility of material errors.

26. You have been making annual audits of the XYZ Sales Company. During the past few years, earnings have shown a slight but steady decline.

At the beginning of this year's audit, you obtain company-prepared financial statements which show a significant increase in earnings for this year over the preceding three years. The company is engaged in a wholesaling operation and resells to retailers the products purchased from various manufacturers. There have been no unit price changes in either purchases or sales. The method of operation remains the same, so that increased efficiency does not account for the increase in income. The company's other sources of revenue remain the same. In short, the business has been run on the same basis as in the past. In addition, you are aware that management is anxious to present a favorable statement of income, since it is facing a struggle for control with a group of stockholders who charge that income has declined due to mismanagement. You conclude that net income may be overstated by understating expired costs and expenses or liabilities, or overstating assets.

The company is on a FIFO inventory basis. A physical inventory was taken at year-end. A tag system was used and all tags were accounted for.

Required:

Draw a line down the middle of a lined sheet(s) of paper.
a. To the left of the line, state the ways that expired costs or liabilities may have been understated, or assets overstated.
b. To the right of the line, for each item mentioned in part *a,* list the audit steps that would reveal each understatement or overstatement.

(AICPA adapted)

27. In auditing the financial statements of a manufacturing company that were prepared by electronic data-processing equipment, the CPA has found that his traditional "audit trail" has been obscured. As a result, the CPA may place increased emphasis upon overall checks of the data under audit. These overall checks, which are also applied in auditing visibly posted accounting records, include the computation of ratios, which are compared with prior year ratios or with industry-wide norms. Examples of such overall checks or ratios are the computation of the rate of inventory turnover and the computation of the number of days in receivables.

Required:

a. Discuss the advantages to the CPA of the use of ratios as overall checks in an audit.

b. In addition to the computations given above, list the ratios that a CPA may compute during an audit as overall checks on balance sheet accounts and related nominal accounts. For each ratio listed, name the two (or more) accounts used in its computation.

c. When a CPA discovers that there has been a significant change in a ratio when compared with the preceding year's ratio, he considers the possible reasons for the change. Give the possible reasons for the following significant changes in ratios:

(1) The rate of inventory turnover (ratio of costs of sales and average inventory) has decreased from the preceding year's rate.

(2) The number of days sales in receivables (ratio of average daily accounts receivable and sales) has increased over the prior year.

(AICPA adapted)

28. Wholesale Gourmet, Inc., is a highly successful wholesaler in the gourmet food supply industry. The company sells all types of bottled and canned gourmet foods to small, medium, and large sized grocery stores and other retailers throughout the Midwest. At this point the client has twenty-six different wholesale grocery subsidiaries operating out of various midwestern regions under different names. In some cases the subsidiaries compete against each other, but for the most part they operate in different sales territories.

The success of the firm is primarily due to the majority owner of the business, Cecil VanDowen. He permits each subsidiary to operate somewhat independently under a manager. The manager is permitted to buy his own products from any source, set sales policies, and hire and discharge employees. At the same time, VanDowen frequently advises the managers and is able to get them to follow similar policies because of his excellent management skills. Sales policies, inventory policies, accounts receivable policies, and most other business practices are amazingly similar between the subsidiaries. Each subsidiary is treated somewhat as a franchise by the main store inasmuch as accounting policies, physical facilities, and records of all kinds are identical. This enables VanDowen to keep better control over the operations.

No store is completely dominant in the operation, but four stores do make up about 40 percent of the total inventory and 45 percent of the sales. Fourteen stores, including the four biggest, account for about 75 percent of the sales and inventory.

The audit is conducted out of Chicago by a single-office, medium-sized CPA firm. A major problem it faces is deciding how many of those subsidiaries must be visited annually. The subsidiaries are spread out widely and most of the records are kept in the subsidiary offices, but monthly statements are sent to the home office in Chicago and retained.

This is the fourth year of the audit of the client. Previous audits have indicated outstanding results. There is rarely an adjusting entry of any kind, and the client is cooperative. The client is not publicly listed, has few loans outstanding, and is highly profitable. In the past every subsidiary has been audited as if it were a separate company, but the client is now putting some pressure on the CPA firm to reduce audit fees. The client feels strongly that previous results warrant a significant reduction in testing, since only a consolidated opinion is issued. The CPA firm discussed the possibility of reducing the audit tests with two larger firms in the Chicago area, and they agree the situation merits a reduction in the number of subsidiaries audited if conditions within the client's organization remain stable.

The most significant assets by far are accounts receivable and inventory. Accounts receivable are collected quickly, but due to the nature of the product, inventory turnover is low. The most significant expense is cost of goods sold. Expenses are well controlled by managers, with strong pressures from VanDowen. Internal control is considered excellent.

Required:

a. Must the CPA firm visit each subsidiary annually? What conditions exist that reduce the need for a test of every subsidiary?
b. Discuss how ratio analysis could be used effectively in this situation.
c. Assume the decision is made to visit twelve subsidiaries. How could ratio analysis help the auditor in this situation to decide which subsidiaries to visit?
d. State several ratios the auditor should calculate for all twenty-six subsidiaries.

29. Solomon is a highly successful closely held Houston, Texas, company that manufactures and assembles specialty parts for automobiles that are sold in auto parts stores in the South. Sales and profits have expanded rapidly in the past few years, and the prospects for future years are every bit as encouraging. In fact, the Solomon brothers are currently considering either selling out to a large company or going public to obtain additional capital.

The company originated in 1955 when Frank Solomon decided to manufacture tooled parts. In 1970 the company changed over to the auto parts business. Fortunately, it has never been necessary to expand the facilities, but space problems have recently become severe and expanded facilities will be necessary. Land and building costs in Houston are currently extremely inflated.

Management has always relied upon you for help in its problems inasmuch as the treasurer is sales oriented and has little background in the controllership function. Salaries of all officers have been fairly modest in order to reinvest earnings in future growth. In fact the company is oriented toward long-run wealth of the brothers more than toward short-run profit. The brothers have all of their personal wealth invested in the firm.

A major reason for the success of Solomon has been the small but excellent sales force. The sales policy is to sell to small auto shops at high prices. This policy is responsible for fairly high credit losses, but the profit margin is high and the results have been highly successful. The firm has every intention of continuing this policy in the future.

Your firm has been auditing Solomon since 1965, and you have been the senior on the job for the past three years. The client has an excellent system of internal control and has always been very cooperative. In recent years the client has attempted to keep net income at a high level because of borrowing needs and future sellout possibilities. Overall, the client has always been pleasant to deal with and willing to help in any way possible. There have never been any major audit adjustments, and an unqualified opinion has always been issued.

In the current year you have completed the tests of the sales and collection area. The tests of the transactions for sales and sales returns and allowances were excellent, and an extensive confirmation yielded no material errors. You have carefully reviewed the cutoff for sales and for sales returns and allowances and find these to be excellent. All recorded bad debts appear reasonable, and a review of the aged trial balance indicates that conditions seem about the same as in past years.

Required:

a. Do you anticipate any trouble for Solomon?
b. Do you agree that sales and accounts receivable are probably fairly stated? Show calculations to support your conclusion.

Balance Sheet	12-31-X7	12-31-X6	12-31-X5	12-31-X4
Cash	$ 49,615	$ 39,453	$ 51,811	$ 48,291
Accounts receivable	2,366,938	2,094,052	1,756,321	1,351,470
Allowance for doubtful accounts	(250,000)	(240,000)	(220,000)	(200,000)
Inventory	2,771,833	2,585,820	2,146,389	1,650,959
Current assets	$4,938,386	$4,479,325	$3,734,521	$2,850,720
Total assets	8,698,917	8,223,915	7,233,451	5,982,853
Current liabilities	$2,253,422	$2,286,433	$1,951,830	$1,625,811
Long term liabilities	4,711,073	4,525,310	4,191,699	3,550,481
Owners equity	1,734,422	1,412,172	1,089,922	806,561
	$8,698,917	$8,223,915	$7,233,451	$5,982,853
Income Statement				
Sales	$6,740,652	$6,165,411	$5,313,752	$4,251,837
Sales return and allowances	207,831	186,354	158,367	121,821
Sales discounts allowed	74,147	63,655	52,183	42,451
Bad debts	248,839	245,625	216,151	196,521
Net sales	6,209,835	5,669,777	4,887,051	3,891,044
Gross margin	1,415,926	1,360,911	1,230,640	1,062,543
Net income after taxes	335,166	322,250	283,361	257,829
Aged Accounts Receivable				
0– 30 days	$ 942,086	$ 881,232	$ 808,569	$ 674,014
31– 60 days	792,742	697,308	561,429	407,271
61–120 days	452,258	368,929	280,962	202,634
>–120 days	179,852	146,583	105,361	67,551
Total	$2,366,938	$2,094,052	$1,756,321	$1,351,470

30. You are engaged in your second annual examination of the financial statements of the Claren Corporation, a medium-sized company that manufactures optical instruments. During the audit it came to your attention that a new controller was employed six months ago. He also serves as office manager but apparently exercises little disciplinary control over his fifteen subordinates, who include a cashier, two bookkeepers, a supply room attendant, and two technicians who show the company products in a factory salesroom attached to the office. The office staff seems to be continually talking about social matters, visiting, or making personal telephone calls or is engaged in other private matters that are generally indicative of inefficiency. You know that the office has fallen about three weeks behind in its accounting work for the year. On numerous occasions you have been unable to obtain answers to questions that arose during the audit because the person who could supply the information was out of the office.

Required:

   a. Discuss what you would do when you found that you were frequently unable to obtain answers to questions because the person who could supply the information was out of the office.

   b. Discuss your responsibility for drawing attention to the apparent inefficiency of the office operations.

   c. What effect would these conditions have on the scope of your audit?

                                                  (AICPA adapted)

31. One of the major means of perpetrating management fraud is for a company to become involved in non-arm's-length transactions for the personal benefit of management. When an auditor is attempting to evaluate whether management has been involved in fraudulent transactions, it is possible to think of the problem at two levels: determining whether there have been any significant transactions with related parties, and evaluating whether any of the transactions resulted in a personal benefit to any individual in management to the detriment of the entity being audited.

Required:

   a. Distinguish between a valid and proper non-arm's-length transaction and a fraudulent transaction.

   b. List several different types of legal or illegal non-arm's-length transactions that could take place in a company.

   c. List the most important related parties who are likely to be involved in non-arm's-length transations involving management.

   d. Discuss different ways the auditor can determine the existence of legal or illegal material transactions with related parties.

   e. For each type of non-arm's-length transaction in part *b,* discuss different ways the auditor can evaluate whether any are fraudulent, assuming he knows the transactions exist.

32. In the audit of Whirland Chemical Company, a large publicly traded company, you have been assigned the responsibility for obtaining background information for the audit. Your firm is auditing the client for the first time in the current year as a result of a dispute between Whirland and the previous auditor over the proper valuation of work in process inventory and the inclusion of sales of inventory that has not been delivered but has for practical purposes been completed and sold.

    Whirland Chemical has been highly successful in its field in the past two decades, primarily because of many successful mergers negotiated by Bert Randolph, the president and chairman of the board. Even though the industry as a whole has suffered dramatic setbacks in recent years, Whirland continues to prosper, as evidenced by its constantly increasing earnings and growth. Only in the last two years have the company's profits turned downward. Randolph has a reputation for having been able to hire an aggressive group of young executives by the use of relatively low salaries combined with an unusually generous profit-sharing plan.

    A major difficulty you face in the new audit is the lack of highly sophisticated accounting records for a company the size of Whirland. Randolph believes that profits come primarily from intelligent and aggressive action based on forecasts, not by relying on historical data that come after the fact. Most of the forecast data are generated by the sales and production department rather than by the accounting department. The personnel in the accounting department do seem competent, but somewhat overworked and underpaid relative to other employees. One of the recent changes that will potentially improve the record keeping is the installation of sophisticated computer techniques. All the accounting records are not computerized yet, but such major areas as inventory and sales are included in the new system. Most of the computer time is being reserved for production and marketing on the grounds that these areas are more essential to operations than the record-keeping function.

The first six months' financial statements for the current year include a profit of approximately only 10 percent less than the first six months of the preceding year, which is somewhat surprising considering the reduced volume and the disposal of a segment of the business, Mercury Supply Co. The disposal of this segment was considered necessary because it had become increasingly unprofitable over the past four years. At the time of its acquisition from Roger Randolph, who is a brother of Bert Randolph, the company was highly profitable and it was considered a highly desirable purchase. The major customer of Mercury Supply Co. was the Mercury Corporation, which is owned by Roger Randolph. Gradually the market for its products declined as the Mercury Corporation began diversifying and phasing out its primary products in favor of more profitable business. Even though Mercury Corporation is no longer buying from Mercury Supply Company, it compensates for it by buying a large volume of other products from Whirland Chemical.

The only major difficulty Whirland faces right now, according to financial analysts, is a fairly severe underfinancing. There is an excessive amount of current debt and long-term debt because of the depressed capital markets. Management is reluctant to obtain equity capital at this point because the increased number of shares would decrease the earnings per share even more than 10 percent. At the present time Randolph is negotiating with several cash-rich companies in the hope of being able to merge with them as a means of overcoming the capital problems.

Required:

    a. List the major concerns you should have in the audit of Whirland Company and explain why they are potential problems.

    b. State the appropriate approach to investigating the significance of each item you listed in part *a*.

33. As part of the analytical review of Mahogany Products, Inc., you perform calculations of the following ratios:

Ratio	Industry Averages 19X6	Industry Averages 19X5	Mahogany Products 19X6	Mahogany Products 19X5
1. Current ratio	3.3	3.8	2.2	2.6
2. Days to collect receivables	87	93	67	60
3. Days to sell inventory	126	121	93	89
4. Purchases÷accounts payable	11.7	11.6	8.5	8.6
5. Inventory÷current assets	.56	.51	.49	.48
6. Operating earnings÷ tangible assets	.08	.06	.14	.12
7. Operating earnings÷net sales	.06	.06	.04	.04
8. Gross margin percent	.21	.27	.21	.19
9. Earnings per share	$14.27	$13.91	$2.09	$1.93

For each of the above ratios:

a. State whether there is a need to investigate the results further and the reason for further investigation.

b. State the approach you would use in the investigation.

c. Explain how the operations of Mahogany Products appear to differ from those of the industry.

34. Following are the auditor's calculations of several key ratios for Cragston Star Products. The primary purpose of this information is to assess the risk of financial failure, but any other relevant conclusions are also desirable.

Ratio	19X6	19X5	19X4	19X3	19X2
Current ratio	2.08	2.26	2.51	2.43	2.50
Quick ratio	.97	1.34	1.82	1.76	1.64
Earnings before taxes÷ interest expense	3.5	3.2	4.1	5.3	7.1
Accounts receivable turnover	4.2	5.5	4.1	5.4	5.6
Days to collect receivables	108.2	83.1	105.2	80.6	71.6
Inventory turnover	2.03	1.84	2.68	3.34	3.36
Days to sell inventory	172.6	195.1	133.9	107.8	108.3
Net sales÷tangible assets	.68	.64	.73	.69	.67
Operating earnings÷net sales	.13	.14	.16	.15	.14
Operating earnings÷tangible assets	.09	.09	.12	.10	.9
Net earnings÷common equity	.05	.06	.10	.10	.11
Earnings per share	$4.30	$4.26	$4.49	$4.26	$4.14

a. What major conclusions can be drawn from this information for the company's future?

b. What additional information would be helpful in your assessment of this company's financial condition?

c. Based on the above ratios, which particular aspects of the company do you believe should receive special emphasis in the audit?

5

The Study and Evaluation
of
Internal Control

In 1949 the AICPA Committee on Auditing Procedure defined *internal control* as follows:

> Internal control comprises the plan of organization and all of the coordinate methods and measures adopted within a business to safeguard its assets, check the accuracy and reliability of its accounting data, promote operational efficiency, and encourage adherence to prescribed managerial policies.[1]

This chapter focuses on the meaning and objectives of internal control from both the client's and the auditor's point of view. The elements of internal control are examined, along with the auditor's methodology for fulfilling the requirement of the second standard of field work.

OBJECTIVES

Objectives from the Client's Point of View

The reason companies establish a system of internal control is to aid the organization in more effectively meeting its own goals. The types of controls adopted are selected by comparing the cost to the organization

[1] Internal control (Committee on Auditing Procedure), AICPA (New York, 1949), p. 6.

relative to the benefit expected. One of the benefits to management, but certainly not the most important one, is the reduced cost of an audit when the auditor evaluates the controls as good or excellent.

The objectives of a good system of internal control, as it is frequently perceived by management, can be categorized as follows:

1. *To provide reliable data.* Management must have accurate information for carrying out its operations. A wide variety of information is used for making critical business decisions. For example, the price to charge for products is based in part on information about the cost of the products; compensation of salesmen is affected by the number of units sold by each salesman and the dollar value of the sales; and the production of finished goods is influenced by the quantity of goods currently on hand and the unfilled orders awaiting shipment.

2. *To safeguard assets and records.* The physical assets of a company can be stolen, misused, or accidentally destroyed unless they are protected by adequate controls. The same is true of nonphysical assets such as accounts receivable, important documents (e.g., confidential government contracts), and records (e.g., the general ledger and journals). The safeguarding of certain assets and records has become increasingly important since the advent of computer systems. Large amounts of information stored on computer media such as magnetic tape can be destroyed permanently if care is not taken to protect them.

3. *To promote operational efficiency.* The controls within an organization are meant to prevent unnecessary duplication of effort, protect against waste in all aspects of the business, and discourage other types of inefficient use of resources.

4. *To encourage adherence to prescribed policies.* Management institutes procedures and rules to provide a means of meeting the goals of the company. The system of internal control is meant to provide reasonable assurance that these are followed by company personnel.

There may at times be a conflict between operational efficiency and the safeguarding of assets and records or the providing for reliable information. There is a cost of fulfilling the first two objectives, and to the extent the cost exceeds the benefits, the results may be operationally inefficient. However, if there is a reasonable trade-off of the costs and benefits of the controls, no real conflict exists.

Objectives from the Auditor's Point of View

The study and evaluation of the client's system of internal control are important to auditors and are specifically included as a generally accepted auditing standard. The second standard of field work is:

> There is to be a *proper study and evaluation of the existing internal control* as a basis for reliance thereon and for the *determination of*

the resultant extent of the tests to which auditing procedures are to be restricted (italics added).[2]

The key phrases in the above standard are now expanded upon briefly for a better understanding of the meaning and importance of the standard.

1. *Proper study and evaluation.* The auditor must have a thorough understanding of the system. A superficial review of the controls fails to meet the standard of due care.

2. *Existing internal control.* Frequently there is a difference between the system that is supposed to be in operation and the one actually being used. It is not sufficient to obtain an understanding of the system by asking questions of management, reviewing the organization chart, and studying procedure manuals. These are important parts of reviewing the system, but to obtain an adequate understanding, the system must also be tested.

3. *Determination of the resultant extent of the tests.* This is the most important phrase in the standard. The client's system of internal control is an essential consideration affecting the audit procedures, sample size for each procedure, timing of the tests, and selection of particular items for inclusion in the sample.

In complying with this standard, the auditor is concerned primarily with the first two of management's internal control objectives: the reliability of data and the safeguarding of assets and records. This emphasis stems from the auditor's need to determine whether the financial statements are fairly presented in accordance with generally accepted accounting principles. The financial statements are unlikely to be correct if the controls affecting the reliability of financial data and the safeguarding of assets and records are inadequate, but the statements can still be properly stated even if the company's controls do not promote efficiency in its operations and the employees fail to follow prescribed policies.

The auditor should emphasize controls concerned with the reliability of data for *external reporting purposes,* but he should not completely ignore controls affecting internal management information, such as statistical analyses, budgets, and internal performance reports. These are important in helping the auditor decide whether the financial statements are fairly presented. If the controls over these internal reports are considered inadequate, the value of the reports as evidence is diminished.

The auditor's interest in the client's controls also should not be limited to those directly affecting the reliability of financial data and the safeguarding of assets. It is inappropriate to disregard controls concerned with operational efficiency and adherence to prescribed policies. If a company fails to follow the rules and procedures set forth by management or is highly inefficient, it is less likely to have accurate financial records. Even though the auditor should be alert for operational efficiency and

2 SAS 1, p. 13.

adherence to prescribed policy controls, the remainder of this chapter is devoted primarily to controls directly related to the reliability of financial data and the physical safeguard of assets and records.

There are three ways in which the study and evaluation of the client's system of internal control is used. A brief examination of these is useful in understanding how the auditor approaches internal control evaluation. They are:

1. *To determine whether an audit is possible.* The adequacy of the system of internal control is crucial to the client's accumulation of accounting data for preparation of the financial statements. If the system is inadequate or nonexistent, it is virtually impossible for the auditor to evaluate whether the financial statements are fairly presented. The major problem arising from inadequate internal control is the possibility of material unrecorded amounts, such as sales made by the company but not recorded, loans made in the company name but not included in the records, and permanent assets used in the business without their being included as assets.

A second problem is the impracticality of assessing the proper valuation of some assets without relying on the client's internal control. An extreme example is construction in process for a bridge builder using the percentage-of-completion method of accounting. An adequate cost accumulation system must exist for the auditor to reach conclusions about the valuation of this asset.

If the internal control is so inadequate as to prohibit basic reliance, the auditor must either *refuse to conduct an audit* or *disclaim an opinion* on the financial statements.

2. *To determine the scope of the audit.* This aspect of internal control is the primary subject of this chapter. It was also discussed in Chapter 3.

3. *To make recommendations to management.* When the auditor identifies weaknesses in the system affecting the control over assets or any other aspect of internal control, including instances of inefficiency in production and clerical operations, there is a professional responsibility to inform the client of the findings. Management can assess the importance of the auditor's information and improve the controls if it believes the potential benefits exceed related costs. Failure to inform the client of problems in its system is a waste of valuable information. Even without a professional responsibility to do so, most auditors are anxious to furnish this information to clients as a means of demonstrating a level of service beyond the audit and to build a strong relationship.

The usual vehicle for making recommendations to management about improving internal controls and operations in general is the *management letter.* It is desirable to put the suggestions in writing to avoid the possibility of misunderstandings. Management letters are discussed in Chapter 19.

ELEMENTS OF INTERNAL CONTROL *relates to total concept.*

It is necessary that a system have certain elements or characteristics if the four objectives of internal control previously discussed are to be fulfilled. The following seven elements are discussed in this section:

1. Competent, trustworthy personnel with clear lines of authority and responsibility
2. Adequate segregation of duties
3. Proper procedures for authorization
4. Adequate documents and records
5. Proper procedures for record keeping
6. Physical control over assets and records
7. Independent checks on performance

Competent, Trustworthy Personnel with Clear Lines of Authority and Responsibility

The most important element of any system of internal control is personnel. If employees are competent and trustworthy, some of the other elements can be absent and reliable financial statements can still result. Honest, efficient people are able to perform at a high level even when there are few other controls to support them. On the other hand, even if the other six elements of control are strong, incompetent or dishonest people can reduce the system to a shambles.

Still, the employment of competent and trustworthy personnel is not by itself sufficient to make a system completely adequate. People have a number of innate shortcomings due to their highly complex nature. They can, for example, become bored or dissatisfied, personal problems can disrupt their performance, or their goals may change. From an audit standpoint, it is important to make a judgment of the competence and integrity of employees, even though it is difficult to do, and to use this as a part of the total evaluation of the system.

Specific responsibility for the performance of duties must be assigned to specific individuals if the system is to operate effectively and work is to be properly performed. If a duty is not adequately performed, it is then possible to place responsibility with the person who did the work. The one assigned is thus motivated to work carefully, and corrective action by management is made possible.

Adequate Segregation of Duties

There are four general types of segregation of duties for the prevention of both intentional and unintentional errors that are of special significance to auditors. These are as follows:

1. *Separation of operational responsibility from record keeping responsibility.* If each department or division in an organization was responsible for preparing its own records and reports, there would be a tendency to bias the results to improve its reported performance. In order to ensure unbiased information, record keeping is typically included in a separate department under the controllership function.

2. *Separation of the custody of assets from accounting.* The reason for not permitting the person who has temporary or permanent custody of an asset to account for that asset is to protect the firm against fraud. When one person performs both functions, there is an excessive risk of his disposing of the asset for personal gain and adjusting the records to relieve himself of responsibility for the asset. If the cashier, for example, receives cash and maintains both the cash and accounts receivable records, it is possible for him to take the cash received from a customer and adjust the customer's account by failing to record a sale or by recording a fictitious credit to the account. Other examples of inadequate segregation of the custodial function include the distribution of payroll checks by the payroll clerk and the maintenance of inventory records by storeroom personnel.

In an EDP system, any person with custody of assets should be prevented from performing the programming function, and be denied access to punched cards or other input records. As a general rule it is desirable that any person performing an accounting function, whether it be in an EDP or in a manual system, be denied access to assets that can be converted to personal gain.

3. *Separation of the authorization of transactions from the custody of related assets.* It is desirable, to the extent that it is possible, to prevent persons who authorize transactions from having control over the related asset. For example, the same person should not authorize the payment of a vendor's invoice and also sign the check in payment of the bill. Similarly, the authority for adding newly hired employees to the payroll or eliminating those who have terminated employment should be performed by someone other than the person responsible for distributing checks to the employees. Nor should anyone who handles incoming cash receipts have the authority to determine which accounts should be charged off as uncollectible. As illustrated, the authorization of a transaction and the handling of the related asset by the same person increases the possibility of fraud within the organization.

4. *Separation of duties within the accounting function.* The least desirable accounting system is one in which one employee is responsible for recording a transaction from its origin to its ultimate posting in the general ledger. This enhances the likelihood that unintentional errors will remain undetected, and it encourages sloppy performance of duties.

There are many opportunities for automatic cross-checking of different employees' work in a manual system by simply segregating the recording in journals from the recording in related subsidiary ledgers. It is also possible to segregate the responsibility for recording in related journals, such as the sales and cash receipts journals. In most cases adequate segregation of accounting duties, where each person performs his work independently, substantially increases control over errors without any duplication of effort.

In an EDP system, segregation of duties is of a different nature than in manual systems, but it is of equal importance. Because the need for frequent cross-checking is unnecessary due to the computer's ability to perform consistently and uniformly, the segregation of duties within the EDP operation puts greater emphasis on control over lost records, improper programming, and fraudulent transactions. For these reasons, the responsibility for processing of data by computer operators, for custody of transactions and library files, and for programming should be separated.

The overall organization structure of a business must provide proper segregation of duties, yet still promote operational efficiency and effective communication. Figure 5-1 shows one typical *organization chart* where these objectives could be achieved. This is not a complete organization chart, but it does indicate the broad segregation of duties. Three of the most important segregations should be apparent:

1. Accounting is completely isolated under the controller, who has no custodial or operating responsibility.
2. The custodianship of cash, including receipts and disbursements, is the responsibility of the secretary-treasurer.
3. The internal auditor reports directly to the president.

Proper Procedures for Authorization

Every transaction must be properly authorized if control is to be satisfactory. If any person in an organization could acquire or expend assets at will, complete chaos would result.

Authorization can be either *general* or *specific*. In performing its function of general authorization, management establishes policies for the organization to follow. Subordinates are instructed to implement these general authorizations by approving all transactions within the limits set by the policy. Examples of general authority are the issuance of fixed price lists for the sale of products, credit limits for customers, and fixed automatic reorder points for making purchases.

Specific authority has to do with individual transactions. For some transactions, management is unwilling to establish a general policy of authorization. Instead, it prefers to make authorizations on a case-by-case basis. An example is the authorization of a sales transaction by the sales manager for a used-car company.

The individual or group who can grant either specific or general authority for transactions should hold a position commensurate with the nature and significance of the transactions, and the policy for such

FIGURE 5-1

ORGANIZATION CHART

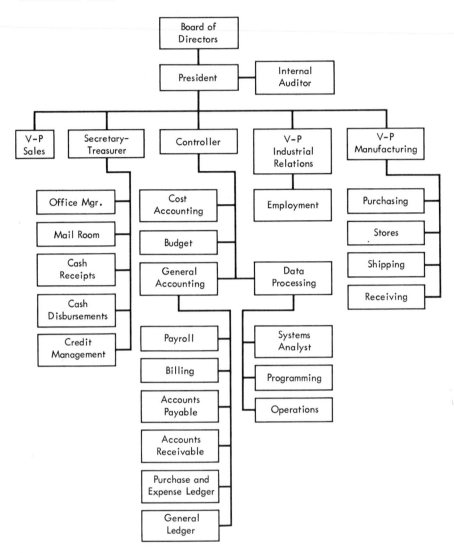

authority should be established by top management. For example, a common policy is to have all acquisitions of capital assets over a set amount authorized by the board of directors.

Approval of a transaction should be distinguished from *authorization*. Approval is only an indication that the conditions required by authorization have apparently been met. For example, the initials of approval on a vendor's invoice do not necessarily mean the goods were ordered or received by the company. Because of this, a prudent auditor often looks beyond approval to other evidence of authorization.

Adequate Documents and Records

Documents and records are the physical objects upon which transactions are entered and summarized. They include such diverse items as sales invoices, purchase orders, subsidiary ledgers, sales journals, time cards, and bank reconciliations. Both documents of original entry and records upon which transactions are entered are important elements of a system, but the inadequacy of documents normally causes greater control problems.

Documents perform the function of transmitting information throughout the client's organization and between different organizations. The documents must be adequate to provide reasonable assurance that all assets are properly controlled and all transactions correctly recorded. For example, if the receiving department fills out a receiving report when material is obtained, the accounts payable department can verify the quantity and description on the vendor's invoice by comparing it with the information on the receiving report.

Certain relevant principles dictate the proper design and use of documents and records. Documents and records should be

1. Sufficiently simple to make sure that they are clearly understood.
2. Designed for multiple uses whenever possible, to minimize the number of different forms. For example, a properly designed and used sales invoice can be the basis for recording sales in the journals, the authority for shipment, the basis for developing sales statistics, and the support for salesmen's commissions.
3. Constructed in a manner that encourages correct preparation. This can be done by providing a degree of internal check within the form or record. For example, a document might include instructions for proper routing, blank spaces for authorizations and approvals, and designated column spaces for numerical data. These help ensure proper inclusion of all required information.
4. Prenumbered consecutively to facilitate control over missing documents, and as an aid in locating documents when they are needed at a later date.
5. Prepared at the time a transaction takes place, or as soon thereafter as possible. When there is a longer time interval, records are less credible and the chance for error is increased.

A control closely related to documents and records is the *chart of accounts,* which classifies transactions into individual balance sheet and income statement accounts. The chart of accounts is an important control because it provides the framework for determining the information presented to management and other financial statement users. It must contain sufficient information to permit the presentation of financial statements in accordance with generally accepted accounting principles, but in addition the classification of the information should help management make decisions. Information by divisions, product lines, responsibility centers, and similar breakdowns should be provided for. The chart of accounts is helpful in preventing misclassification errors if it accurately and precisely describes which type of transactions should be in each account. It is especially important that the descriptions clearly distinguish between capital assets, inventories, and expense items, since these are the major categories of concern to external users of the financial statements.

Proper Procedures for Record Keeping

If the financial statements are to properly reflect the actual transactions during the period, there must be procedures to ensure the proper recording of all transactions. This aspect of control is especially significant to auditors because it relates directly to the objective of providing reliable data. Like many of the elements of control, this one is closely related to each of the others. If the other elements of control are proper, the likelihood of having accurate and adequate record keeping is enhanced. For example, the presence of competent, trustworthy personnel with well-defined responsibilities for keeping the records, but without access to assets, greatly increases the likelihood of proper record keeping. Similarly, the existence of adequate documents and records and adequate internal verification is also beneficial in providing adequate record keeping.

The procedures for proper record keeping should be spelled out in *procedures manuals* to encourage consistent application. The manuals should define the flow of documents throughout the organization and should provide for sufficient information to facilitate adequate record keeping and the maintenance of proper control over assets. For example, to ensure the proper recording of the purchase of raw materials, a copy of the purchase order for acquiring the merchandise and a copy of the receiving report when the raw materials are received should be sent to accounts payable. This procedure aids in properly recording purchases in the accounts payable journal, and it facilitates the determination of whether the vendor's invoice from the supplier should be paid. If both purchase orders and receiving reports are prenumbered, the accounts payable clerk can account for the numerical sequence of these documents as a means of determining whether all purchases have been recorded.

Physical Control over Assets and Records

The most important type of protective measure for safeguarding assets and records is the use of physical precautions. An example is the use of storerooms for inventory to guard against pilferage. When the storeroom is under the control of a competent employee, there is also further assurance that obsolescence is minimized. Fireproof safes and safety deposit vaults for the protection of assets such as currency and securities are other important physical safeguards.

Physical safeguards are also necessary for records and documents. The redevelopment of lost or destroyed records is costly and time consuming. Imagine what would happen if an accounts receivable master file were destroyed. The considerable cost of backup records and other controls can be justified to prevent this loss. Similarly, such documents as insurance policies and notes receivable should be physically protected.

Mechanical protective devices can also be used to obtain additional assurance that accounting information is currently and accurately recorded. Cash registers and certain types of automatic data-processing equipment are all potentially useful additions to the system of internal control for this purpose.

Independent Checks on Performance

The last specific element of control is the careful and continuous review of the other six elements in the system. The need for a system of *internal checks* arises because a system tends to change over time unless there is a mechanism for frequent review. Personnel are likely to forget procedures, become careless, or intentionally fail to follow them unless someone is there to observe and evaluate their performance. In addition, both fraudulent and unintentional errors are always possible, regardless of the quality of the controls.

An essential characteristic of the persons performing internal verification procedures is *independence* from the individuals originally responsible for preparing the data. A considerable portion of the value of checks on performance is lost when the individual doing the verification is a subordinate of the person originally responsible for preparing the data, or lacks independence in some other way.

The least expensive means of internal verification is the separation of duties in the manner previously discussed. For example, when the accounts receivable subsidiary records, the sales journal, and the general ledger are maintained by different people, each of them automatically verifies a part of the work of the others. Similarly, when the bank reconciliation is performed by a person independent of the accounting records and handling of cash, there is an opportunity for verification without incurring significant additional costs.

Some important types of verification can only be accomplished by a duplication of effort. For example, the counting of inventory by two different teams to make certain that the count is correct is costly, but frequently necessary. Another example is the use of a keypunch verifier in an EDP system. In this control procedure a second person keypunches the same information as was originally keypunched, and the results of these two independent activities are automatically compared for differences. Even though the cost of performing the same work more than once may seem excessive, it is sometimes the only practical way of ensuring accurate and reliable results.

The existence of an *internal audit staff* is usually a highly effective method of verifying the proper recording of financial information. If the internal audit staff is independent of both the operating and the accounting departments, and if it reports directly to top management, there is an excellent opportunity for extensive verification within the client's organization.

Although the independent outside auditor is not permitted to rely entirely on evidence obtained by the internal audit staff, the existence of an adequate internal audit staff can greatly reduce the evidence he must gather during the external audit. For example, it is inappropriate for the CPA to completely forgo the confirmation of accounts receivable even if it has already been done by internal auditors. However, it is proper for him to review and evaluate the internal auditors' confirmation procedures and working papers, and significantly reduce the sample size for the audit confirmations if the internal audit results are satisfactory.

UNDERSTANDING THE SYSTEM

Now that the objectives and basic elements of internal control have been discussed, it is possible to investigate the methodology used for the study and evaluation of internal control. The study and evaluation is necessary as a basis for deciding upon the appropriate audit procedures, sample size, selection of the particular items for testing, and timing of the tests. An understanding of the objectives and elements will aid in this process.

Divide the System into Transaction Cycles

As a means of understanding the system and making a meaningful internal control evaluation, it is necessary for the auditor to divide the overall system into a number of major segments called *transaction cycles*. This enables the auditor to manage the engagement without separating parts of the system that are closely intertwined. Every industry has its own set of major transaction cycles consistent with the nature of the economic events that affect it. In this text we consider the following five major cycles that are common to most commercial and manufacturing enterprises, although those of a bank or an insurance company could just as well be used:

1. Sales and collection cycle
2. Payroll and personnel cycle
3. Acquisition of goods and services and payment cycle
4. Inventory and warehousing cycle
5. Capital acquisition and repayment cycle

Transaction cycles are of major importance in the conduct of the audit. For the most part, auditors treat each transaction cycle separately as the audit is being performed. Internal control questionnaires and flowcharts, used in gaining a preliminary understanding of the system, are normally prepared independently for each transaction cycle. Similarly, a preliminary evaluation of the controls and the tests of the controls and account balances in one cycle can be made with relatively little regard for the other cycles. Although care should be taken to interrelate different cycles at different times, the auditor must treat the cycles somewhat independently in order to effectively manage complex audits.

Obtain Information from the Organization

A thorough understanding of the client's system will enable the auditor to identify existing controls, which is an essential part of internal control evaluation. If the auditor understands the way documents and records flow through a transaction cycle, he can identify the procedures employed for processing and recording each transaction. If he knows which person performs each procedure, the existing controls can be easily identified. Although the existence of controls does not necessarily mean that they are effective, their identification is the first step in the process of internal control evaluation.

The starting point for developing an understanding of the client's system is to interview the chief accounting officer and other key personnel and to review the formal procedures the organization has established. A detailed *organization chart* and the *procedures manuals* are key information for understanding the system. As a part of reviewing these documents, it is desirable to obtain a job description for the most important individuals involved in any aspect of record keeping and the custody of assets. The procedures manuals should be studied and discussed with company personnel to ensure an understanding of the prescribed procedures. If the company is small and has no organization chart or procedures manuals, a description of the system should be obtained through discussion with management.

In an EDP system, the documentation of the system is ordinarily more extensive and frequently more formalized than in a manual system. A good starting point for a general review of the EDP system is a tour of the computer facilities conducted by the EDP manager. General impressions can be obtained of the orderliness of the operation and the quality of the facilities. It is also necessary to make a comprehensive review of existing documentation, including system and program flowcharts, information on the programs, and files in the system. A more detailed study of the evaluation of internal control of an EDP system is included in Chapter 12.

After obtaining an overview of the system, it is necessary to obtain more specific information about the flow of documents and records and the nature of specific controls. *Flowcharts* and *internal control question-*

naires are useful for this purpose. These two topics and their relationship to the audit as a whole are discussed in the following sections. It is desirable to use the client's flowcharts and have the client fill out the internal control questionnaire, but this often has the disadvantage of depriving the auditor of the opportunity to interview client personnel and observe procedures. When understandable and reliable flowcharts and questionnaires are not available, which is frequently the case, the auditor must prepare his own.

Flowcharting

A *flowchart* of internal control is a symbolic, diagrammatic representation of the client's documents and their sequential flow in the organization. An adequate flowchart shows the origin of each document and record in the system, the subsequent processing, and the final disposition of any document or record included in the chart. In addition, it is possible for the flowchart to show the separation of duties, authorizations, approvals, and internal verifications that take place within the system.

Flowcharting is advantageous primarily because it can provide a concise overview of the client's system, which is useful to the auditor as an analytical tool in his evaluation. A well-prepared flowchart aids in identifying inadequacies by facilitating a clear understanding of how the system operates. For most uses, it is superior to written descriptions as a method of communicating the characteristics of a system. It is simply easier to follow a diagram than to read a description. It is also usually easier to update a flowchart than a narrative description.

Elements of Flowcharting. The three basic elements of a flowchart are symbols, flow lines, and areas of responsibility. Each of these three elements is examined briefly.

Symbols are used to show predefined items, steps, and actions. No matter what symbols are used, the concept of flowcharting remains unchanged, but naturally the symbols must be defined. Different audit firms use different symbols, but most of them have been derived from the United States of America Standards Institute symbols and are similar in form. Figure 5-2 shows the basic symbols that have been adopted for this textbook and gives an example of each symbol.

Flow lines are used to show how documents and records are related. There are two types of flow lines:

———— document flow (solid line)
-------- information flow (broken line)

Arrowheads are used to indicate the direction of the flow. The flowcharting convention for arrowheads is that they should be used for all directions of flow except down and to the right. We recommend the use of arrowheads whenever it adds clarification.

FIGURE 5-2

BASIC FLOWCHARTING SYMBOLS

Document – paper documents and
reports of all types

Example: a sales invoice

Process Symbol – any processing function;
defined operation causing a change in
value, form, or location of information

Example: a billing clerk prepares a sales invoice

Off-Line Storage – off-line storage of
documents, records, and EDP files

Example: a duplicate sales invoice is
filed in numerical order

Transmittal Tape – a proof or adding machine
tape used for control purposes

Example: an adding machine tape of sales invoices

Input/Output Symbol – used to indicate
information entering or leaving system

Example: a receipt of order from customer

Annotation – the addition of descriptive
comments or explanatory notes as clarification

Example: a billing clerk checks credit
before preparing an invoice

Directional flow lines – the direction
of processing or data flow

Connector – exit to, or entry from, another
part of chart; keyed in by using numbers

Example: a document transfer from one department
into another department

Symbols unique to EDP Systems

Punched Card	Punched Tape	Magnetic Tape	Disk or Drum Storage

Areas of responsibility are established on flowcharts as vertical columns or sections through which the flow of documents takes place horizontally (from left to right). This technique enables the reader to clearly identify changes in responsibility as the documents flow through the system. An example of separation by areas of responsibility is given in Figure 5-3.

Guidelines for Preparation. The overall objectives of a flowchart are to help the preparer understand the system, to communicate a description of a system to all subsequent readers, and to aid in evaluating internal control. Following are a few general guidelines to help accomplish these objectives:

1. Use notations in addition to symbols to make the flowchart more understandable.
2. Where the information on the flowchart is not completely self-explanatory, use supplementary information and refer specifically to its source.
3. Show the source and disposition of every document included in the flowchart.

Illustration. A brief flowcharting illustration is useful at this point. Figure 5-3 furnishes a flowchart for the following narrative description of the sales, billing, and shipping departments of a small wholesale company (accounting is excluded for purposes of simplification). A more extensive illustration is given in Figure 8-6.

The sales department prepares a six-part sales invoice form from the customer's sales order. The sales order is filed alphabetically by customer after the sales invoice is prepared. Credit approval is indicated on copy 2, which is then filed with the customer's order. Parts 1 (sales invoice) and 3 (ledger) are sent to billing; part 4 (packing slip) and part 5 (shipping order) are sent to shipping; and part 6 is sent to the customer as acknowledgment of the order.

Shipping physically collects the items for shipment and notes that the goods were shipped on the shipping order. The packing slip is sent to the customer with the goods, and the shipping order is sent to billing.

Billing enters the shipped items marked on the shipping order on the sales invoice and ledger copy, makes extensions and checks them, compares the prices with the price list, and runs a tape of the amounts on the ledger copy. The shipping order is then filed numerically. The sales invoice is sent to the customer, and the ledger copy and the tape are sent to accounting.

Obtaining Information. Frequently, flowcharts are initially prepared in rough form only because as the review progresses the auditor is likely to need to redraw and refine them. It may be convenient to base the rough charts on the client's manuals and information already included in

FIGURE 5-3

ILLUSTRATION OF A FLOWCHART

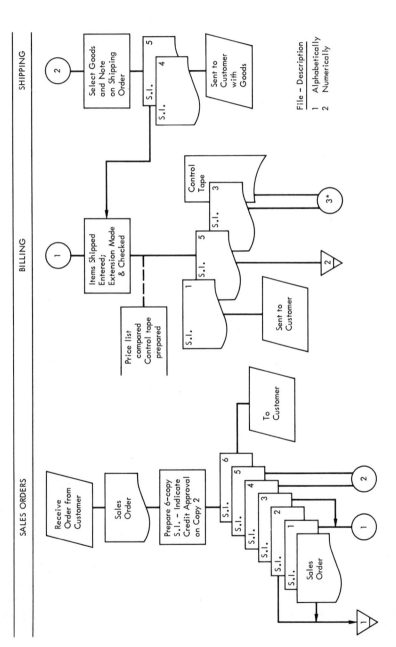

the current or previous audit working papers. Ultimately, the flowcharts must describe the system and procedures *actually in force:* these may differ materially from those management believes to be in effect. The information for the final flowchart can come either from the personnel responsible for performing the work or from the observations of the auditor. A combination of these two can be accomplished by asking the responsible individuals questions and requesting to actually see the documents and records.

After the flowcharting is completed, it is desirable to follow an example of every document described in the chart from its origin to its final disposition. Common terminology to describe this procedure is a *cradle-to-grave test, a sample of one,* or a *walk-through test.* This not only provides a better understanding of the system but also helps to disclose errors or incomplete parts of the flowchart. The tracing of one or two transactions through the system should not be confused with testing the system. To meet the standards of the profession, a test of the system requires a larger sample size than one or two transactions.

Internal Control Questionnaires

An *internal control questionnaire* is designed to ask a series of questions about the controls in each audit area as a means of indicating to the auditor aspects of the system that may be inadequate. In most instances it is designed to require a yes or a no response, with "no" responses indicating potential internal control deficiencies. Figure 5-4 illustrates a part of an internal control questionnaire for sales and credit memoranda.

The primary advantage of the questionnaire approach is the relative completeness of coverage of each audit area that a good instrument affords. Furthermore, a questionnaire can usually be prepared reasonably quickly at the beginning of the audit engagement. The primary disadvantage is that individual parts of the client's system are examined without providing an overall view of the entire cycle. In addition, a standard questionnaire is often inapplicable to some audit clients, especially the smaller ones.

In using questionnaires, it is important to determine whether the controls believed by management to exist are actually being followed. Questioning the personnel actually performing each procedure, observation, and verification by examining documents and records are convenient methods of obtaining information for completing the questionnaire.

We believe the use of both questionnaires and flowcharts is highly desirable for understanding the client's system. The flowcharts provide an overview of the entire system, and the questionnaire is a useful checklist to remind the auditor of many different types of controls that should exist. A combination of these two approaches when properly used should provide the auditor with an excellent description of the system.

FIGURE 5-4

INTERNAL CONTROL QUESTIONNAIRE FOR SALES AND CREDIT

                                                                  N/A Yes No

1. Sales and credit memoranda:

   a. Sales invoices are independently checked to customer's orders for prices, quantities, extensions, and footings and credit discount, and freight terms.   — — —

   b. Sales orders, invoices, and credit memoranda are prepared and promptly recorded in a sales register.   — — —

      (1) Sales orders, invoices, and credit memoranda are issued and filed in numerical sequence and sequence is accounted for periodically.   — — —

      (2) Sales register is balanced monthly and agreed to the general ledger by personnel independent of sales order and invoice posting function.   — — —

   c. The selling function and sales register preparation are independent of cash receipts, shipping, delivery, and billing functions.   — — —

   d. Credit memoranda are supported by evidence of receipt of returned merchandise, adequate explanation of price adjustments, etc.   — — —

      (1) All credit memoranda are reviewed and approved by a responsible official.   — — —

   e. COD, employee, scrap, equipment and cash sales are accounted for in the same manner as charge sales by being recorded independently of the collection procedure.   — — —

2. Credit and collection functions:

   a. The amount of credit which may be extended to a customer without approval and investigation by the credit department is established (at $_____).   — — —

PRELIMINARY EVALUATION

Once the auditor understands how management and other personnel believe the system operates, he is in a position to make a preliminary evaluation of the controls in the system and those aspects of the system that are likely to permit errors due to the absence of adequate controls. The evaluation is only preliminary because a final evaluation cannot take place until the actual operation of the system is tested for congruence with the apparent system.

To evaluate the controls systematically, it is necessary to develop some kind of framework. The following is a summary of the framework used in this book as an aid for the evaluation of internal control and for performing tests of the system:

1. Divide the system of recording transactions into major *transaction cycles* as described earlier in this chapter.
2. Define detailed *internal control objectives* that are applicable to the transaction cycles. These will be developed in the next section for use in the remaining chapters.
3. Identify and evaluate the *specific controls* in existence to fulfill each of the detailed internal control objectives within each transaction cycle.
4. Identify and evaluate the *weaknesses* that result from the absence of controls within each transaction cycle.

Define Detailed Internal Control Objectives

There are seven detailed internal control objectives which embrace the primary concerns the auditor has for the prevention of errors in the recording of transactions in the journals and records. The client's system of internal control in every transaction cycle must be sufficient to provide reasonable assurance that

1. *Recorded transactions are valid.* The system cannot permit the inclusion of fictitious or nonexistent transactions in the system.
2. *Transactions are properly authorized.* If a transaction that is not authorized takes place, it could result in a fraudulent transaction, and it could also have the effect of wasting or destroying company assets.
3. *Existing transactions are recorded.* The procedures must provide controls to prevent the omission of actual transactions from the records.
4. *Transactions are properly valued.* An adequate system includes procedures to avoid errors in calculating, recording, and summarizing transactions at various stages in the recording process.
5. *Transactions are properly classified.* The proper account classification must be made in the journals if the financial statements are to be properly stated. Classification also includes such categories as division and product.
6. *Transactions are recorded at the proper time.* The recording of transactions either before or after the point of time they actually took place increases the likelihood of failing to record transactions, or recording them at the improper amount. If late recording occurs at year-end, the financial statements can be misstated.
7. *Transactions are properly included in subsidiary records and correctly summarized.* In many instances individual transactions are summarized and totaled before they are recorded in the journals. The journals are then posted to the general ledger, and the general ledger is summarized and used to prepare the financial statements. Regardless of the method used to enter transactions in the subsidiary records and to summarize transactions, the procedures must provide for adequate controls to make sure this is properly handled.

These seven internal control objectives can be related to any of the five transaction cycles previously specified as a part of internal control evaluation. For example, if the internal controls over purchases of goods and services are adequate to provide reasonable assurance of fulfilling each of the seven objectives, the likelihood of errors in that system is small.

Identify and Evaluate Existing Controls

For each of the detailed internal control objectives, the auditor must identify the existing controls to prevent errors. Where such controls exist, they are referred to as the *strengths in the system*. Most of these controls should have been identified as a part of understanding the system. The identification of strengths is the association of these controls with each detailed objective. If a control providing strength exists and is functioning properly, the auditor's expectation of certain types of errors is reduced, which means he can reduce the extent of tests for the substance of the error. For example, in the audit of purchase journal transactions there are several controls a client can use to fulfill the "recorded transactions are valid" objective. These include the following:

1. Approval of all purchase requisitions and purchase orders by an authorized person.
2. Issuance of a receiving report at the time goods are received.
3. Matching and comparing of vendor's invoices, receiving reports, and purchase orders before entries are made in the purchases journal.
4. Internal verification by the internal audit staff to determine whether the three above controls are being properly followed.

If the auditor plans to rely upon the strengths, the pertinent controls must be tested through *tests of compliance*. These tests are intended to provide assurance that the controls believed to exist do exist and are functioning properly. An example of a strength which might be relied upon is a clerk examining and initialing all vendor's invoices and other supporting documents after they have been paid. If the clerk is properly performing his duties, the likelihood of errors in recording purchases is significantly reduced. As a compliance test of whether the clerk is performing his duties, a sample of documents can be examined for the clerk's initials. If, as a result of this and other tests, the independent auditor concludes that the clerk is competent and conscientious, the extent of the verification of the propriety and proper classification of recorded purchase transactions could be reduced (but not eliminated). Tests of the strengths of the system are studied in Chapter 8.

Identify and Evaluate Weaknesses

Weaknesses are defined as the *absence of controls*. If there are inadequate controls to prevent a specific type of error, the auditor's expectation of such an error increases. Therefore the audit evidence must be modified to make sure the potential error is not material. For example, if no internal verification of the recording of purchase transactions is taking place, the auditor must test recorded transactions more extensively than he would if adequate internal verification did exist.

Two companies with significantly different types of controls can have equally effective systems if the particular controls used by each company prevent errors from taking place. For example, an effective control to prevent the failure to bill customers for shipments of merchandise is for an independent person to account for all shipping documents and trace the amounts to related duplicate sales invoices. A different company could accomplish the same objective by requiring a copy of the sales invoice as a shipping authorization form and accounting for all sales invoice numbers in the sales journal.

Overall Control Considerations

In addition to the controls in each transaction area, several overall controls within the system should be evaluated. These include the following:

1. Adequate budgets and other reports prepared with sufficient frequency to meet management's needs.
2. A satisfactory chart of accounts.
3. Bonding of employees in a position of trust as a deterrent to fraud and a means of recovering the loss if one should occur.
4. A mandatory vacation policy. If every employee is required to take a vacation, and have his normal duties performed by someone else, the likelihood of a defalcation is reduced.
5. A well defined conflict-of-interest policy strictly adhered to as a means of reducing temptation to employees in their relationship with the organization. Personnel in a position of trust who are related, employees having personal business dealings with the client's major customers or suppliers, and transactions between the company and officers, directors, or major stockholders are common examples where conflicts of interest can occur.
6. Reasonable record retention policies in accordance with state and federal laws.

Usually these controls can be easily evaluated at an early stage in the audit to determine their impact on the accumulation of audit evidence.

Relationship between Size of Business and Controls

An adequate system of internal control is important for small companies as well as for large ones. If there are inadequate controls, the likelihood of errors in the records is enhanced. This can be highly damaging to the effective operation of the company inasmuch as unreliable information frequently leads to poor decisions. Similarly, the safeguarding of assets and operational efficiency is as important for small companies as for large ones.

The size of a company does have a significant effect on the nature of the controls likely to exist. Obviously it is more difficult to establish adequate separation of duties in a small company. It would also be unreasonable to expect a small firm to have internal auditors. On the other hand, if the seven elements of internal control that were previously discussed are examined, it becomes apparent that most of the controls are applicable to both large and small companies. Even though it may not be common to formalize policies in manuals, it is certainly possible for a small company to have competent, trustworthy personnel with clear lines of authority; proper procedures for authorization, execution, and recording of transactions; adequate documents, records, and reports; physical controls over assets and records; and, to a limited degree, checks on performance.

A major control available in a small company is the knowledge and concern of the top operating person, who is frequently an *owner-manager*. His interest in the organization and close relationship with the personnel enable him to evaluate the competence of the employees and the effectiveness of the overall system. For example, the system can be significantly strengthened if the owner conscientiously performs such duties as signing all checks after carefully reviewing supporting documents, reviewing bank reconciliations, examining accounts receivable statements sent to customers, approving credit, examining all correspondence from customers and vendors, and approving bad debts.

Due to the frequent lack of sufficient segregation of duties and other important controls, the auditor must recognize that usually less reliance can be placed on controls in a small company. This generally results in more extensive direct tests of dollar balances and less emphasis on tests of the effectiveness of the system. Even though the lack of controls may dictate more testing for small companies than for large ones, certain other considerations often reduce the amount of testing needed. First, the auditor is likely to have a better understanding of the business and the individuals operating the business for a smaller client. Second, the overall level of assurance needed in the audit is usually less for a smaller client because noninvolvement with the SEC and other variables significantly reduce the auditor's risk. Smaller population sizes also frequently reduce the testing needed.

REVIEW QUESTIONS

1. Select the best response for each of the following questions:
   a. What is the independent auditor's principal purpose for conducting a study and evaluation of the existing system of internal control?
      (1) To comply with generally accepted accounting principles.
      (2) To obtain a measure of assurance of management's efficiency.
      (3) To maintain a state of independence in mental attitude in all matters relating to the audit.

(4) To determine the nature, timing, and extent of subsequent audit work.
b. When evaluating internal control, the auditor's primary concern is to determine
    (1) the possibility of fraud occurring.
    (2) compliance with policies, plans, and procedures.
    (3) the reliability of the accounting information system.
    (4) the type of an opinion he will issue.
c. In evaluating internal control, the first step is to prepare an internal control questionnaire or a flowchart of the system. The second step should be to
    (1) determine the extent of audit work necessary to form an opinion.
    (2) gather enough evidence to determine if the internal control system is functioning as described.
    (3) write a letter to management describing the weaknesses in the internal control system.
    (4) form a final judgment on the effectiveness of the internal control system.   (AICPA adapted)

2. Frequently management is more concerned about internal controls that promote operational efficiency than about obtaining reliable financial data. How can the independent auditor persuade management to devote more attention to controls affecting the reliability of accounting information when management has this attitude?

3. Give an illustration of a situation where the controls are so inadequate as to preclude the possibility of conducting an adequate audit. What are the auditor's options under these circumstances?

4. Frank James was a highly competent employee of Brinkwater Sales Corporation who had been responsible for accounting-related matters for two decades. His devotion to the firm and his duties had always been exceptional, and over the years he had been given increased responsibility. Both the president of Brinkwater and the partner of the independent CPA firm in charge of the audit were shocked and dismayed to discover that James had embezzled more than $500,000 over a ten-year period by not recording billings in the sales journal and subsequently diverting the cash receipts. What major factors permitted the defalcation to take place?

5. The separation of duties within the accounting department is meant to prevent different types of errors than the separation of the custody of assets from accounting. Explain the difference in the purposes of these two types of segregation of duties.

6. In recent years there has been an increased tendency of the internal audit staff to report directly to the president rather than to the controller. What is the major shortcoming of having the internal auditor report to the controller?

7. List the seven elements of internal control and provide one specific illustration of a control in the payroll area for each element.

8. Distinguish between general and specific authorization of transactions and give one example of each type.

9. Define what is meant by a chart of accounts and explain how it relates to an adequate system of internal control.

10. For each of the following, give an example of a physical control the client can use to protect the asset or record:
    a. Petty cash

    b. Cash received by retail clerks

    c. Accounts receivable records

    d. Raw material inventory

    e. Perishable tools

    f. Manufacturing equipment

    g. Marketable securities

11. Explain what is meant by internal checks on performance and give five specific examples of internal checks.

12. Distinguish between the objectives of an internal control questionnaire and the objectives of a flowchart for obtaining information about a client's system. State the advantages and disadvantages of each of these two methods.

13. Jeanne Maier, CPA, believes it is appropriate to review the system of internal control about halfway through the audit, after she is familiar with the client's operations and the way the system actually works. She has found through experience that filling out internal control questionnaires and flowcharts early in the engagement is not beneficial because the system rarely functions the way it is supposed to. Later in the engagement, it is feasible to prepare flowcharts and questionnaires with relative ease because of the knowledge already obtained on the audit. Evaluate her approach to internal control review.

14. Distinguish between the auditor's gaining an understanding of the system of internal control and the auditor's preliminary evaluation of the system. Also explain the methodology the auditor uses for each of them.

15. Explain what is meant by a transaction cycle and discuss the need to separate different cycles as a part of the study and evaluation of internal control.

16. Define what is meant by a strength and a weakness in a system of internal control. Give three examples of each in the sales and collection cycle.

DISCUSSION QUESTIONS AND PROBLEMS

17. Adherence to generally accepted auditing standards requires, among other things, a proper study and evaluation of the existing internal control. The most common approaches to reviewing the system of internal control include the use of a questionnaire, preparation of a memorandum, preparation of a flowchart, and combinations of these methods.

    Required:

    a. What is a CPA's objective in reviewing internal control for an opinion audit?

    b. Discuss the advantages to a CPA of reviewing internal control by using

        (1) An internal control questionnaire

        (2) A flowchart

    c. If the CPA, after completing his evaluation of internal control for an opinion audit is satisfied that no material weaknesses in the client's internal control system exist, is it necessary for him to test transactions? Explain.   (AICPA adapted)

18. A company's system of internal control is strengthened by including procedures in the system that have specific purposes. For example, the controls

may include a voucher system, that provides that all invoices be checked for accuracy, approved for propriety, and recorded before being paid. The system reduces the likelihood that (a) an invoice will be mislaid, (b) the discount will be lost, and (c) improper or unauthorized disbursements will be made.

Required:

Give the purposes of each of the following procedures or techniques that may be included in a system of internal control, and *explain* how each purpose or function is helpful in strengthening internal control:

a. Fidelity bonding of employees
b. Budgeting of capital expenditures
c. Listing of mail remittances by the mail department when the mail is opened.
d. Maintaining a plant ledger for fixed assets   (AICPA adapted)

19. For each of the following errors or inefficiencies, provide a control procedure the client could institute to reduce its likelihood of occurrence:

a. The incorrect price is used on sales invoices for billing shipments to customers.
b. A vendor's invoice is paid twice for the same shipment. The second payment arose because the vendor sent a duplicate copy of the original two weeks after the payment was due.
c. Employees in the receiving department for a retail meat market take sides of beef for their personal use. When a shipment of meat is received, the receiving department fills out a receiving report and forwards it to the accounting department for the amount of goods actually received. At that time, one or two sides of beef are put in an employee's pickup truck rather than in the storage freezer.
d. Assembly workers in a furniture shop go to the raw materials wood bin whenever a piece of wood they are using to make furniture doesn't fit properly. Even though company policy requires the employee to correct the deficiency in the original piece by planing it, he usually throws it away and gets a new piece.
e. The factory foreman of a medium-sized manufacturing company is responsible for delivering weekly paychecks to the employees under his supervision. Last September when his brother-in-law quit working without informing anyone, the factory foreman continued to punch his daily time card. The foreman approves the time card and submits it to the payroll department. On the weekend the foreman delivers the check to his brother-in-law's house and they split the money.

20. Select the best response for each of the following questions and explain the reason for your choice:

a. Which of the following is a responsibility that should *not* be assigned to only one employee?
(1) Access to securities in the company's safe deposit box
(2) Custodianship of the cash working fund
(3) Reconciliation of bank statements
(4) Custodianship of tools and small equipment
b. A company holds bearer bonds as a short-term investment. Custody of these bonds and submission of coupons for interest payments is normally the responsibility of the

(1) treasury function.
(2) legal counsel.
(3) general accounting function.
(4) internal audit function.

c. Operating control of the check-signing machine normally should be the responsibility of the
(1) general accounting function.
(2) treasury function.
(3) legal counsel.
(4) internal audit function.

d. Matching the supplier's invoice, the purchase order, and the receiving report should normally be the responsibility of the
(1) warehouse-receiving function.
(2) purchasing function.
(3) general accounting function.
(4) treasury function. (AICPA adapted)

21. The division of the following duties is meant to provide the best possible controls for the Meridian Paint Company, a small wholesale store:

*a. Assemble supporting documents for disbursements and prepare checks for signature.
*b. Sign general disbursement checks.
*c. Record checks written in the cash disbursements and payroll journal.
d. Mail disbursement checks to suppliers.
e. Cancel supporting documents to prevent their reuse.
*f. Approve credit for customers.
*g. Bill customers and record the invoices in the sales journal and subsidiary ledger.
*h. Open the mail and prepare a prelisting of cash receipts.
*i. Record cash receipts in the cash journal and subsidiary ledger.
*j. Prepare daily cash deposits.
*k. Deliver daily cash deposits to the bank.
*l. Assemble the payroll time cards and prepare the payroll checks.
*m. Sign payroll checks.
n. Post the journals to the general ledger.
o. Reconcile the accounts receivable subsidiary account with the control account.
p. Prepare monthly statements for customers by copying the subsidiary ledger account.
q. Reconcile the monthly statements from vendors with the subsidiary accounts payable account.
r. Reconcile the bank account.

Required:

You are to divide the accounting-related duties a through r among Robert Smith, James Cooper, and Bill Miller. All of the responsibilities marked with an asterisk are assumed to take about the same amount of time and must be divided equally between the two employees, Smith and Cooper. Both employees are equally competent. Miller who is president of the company is not willing to perform any functions designated by an asterisk and a maximum of two of the other functions.

22. The Halpern Corporation became your audit client when its former CPA

died. You have completed your initial examination of Halpern Corporation's financial statements for the year ended and have prepared a draft of your auditor's report containing an unqualified opinion which was addressed to the board of directors. In addition, you have drafted a special report in letter form outlining deficiencies in the system of internal control noted in the course of your examination and your recommendations for the correction of these deficiencies.

When you reviewed the drafts of these reports with Halpern's president, he instructed you not to send the internal control letter. The president stated that he was aware the deficiencies existed and would give them his personal attention. Because he felt the board of directors should be concerned with major policy decisions and not with day-to-day management problems, he believed the board should not be burdened with such matters.

Required:

a. What factors would you consider before deciding whether or not you should send the internal control letter?
b. If you decide to send the internal control letter to Halpern Corporation, should it be sent to the board of directors or to the president? Discuss.

(AICPA adapted)

23. In connection with his examination of the financial statements of the Olympia Manufacturing Company, a CPA is reviewing procedures for accumulating direct labor hours. He learns that all production is by job order and that all employees are paid hourly wages, with time and a half for overtime hours.

Olympia's direct-labor-hour input process for payroll and job-cost determination is summarized in the accompanying flowchart.

Steps *A* and *C* are performed in timekeeping, step *B* in the factory-operating departments, step *D* in payroll audit and control, step *E* in data preparation (keypunch), and step *F* in computer operations.

Required:

For each input-processing step *A* through *F*:
a. list the possible errors or discrepancies that may occur.
b. cite the corresponding control procedure that should be in effect for each error or discrepancy.

(*Note:* Your discussion of Olympia's procedures should be limited to the input process for direct labor hours, as shown in steps *A* through *F* in the flowchart. *Do not discuss* personnel procedures for hiring, promotion, termination, and pay rate authorization. *In step* F *do not discuss* equipment, computer program, and general computer operational controls.)

Organize your answer for each input-processing step as follows:

Step	Possible Errors or Discrepancies	Control Procedures

(AICPA adapted)

24. The Y Company, a client of your firm, has come to you with a problem it would like you to solve.

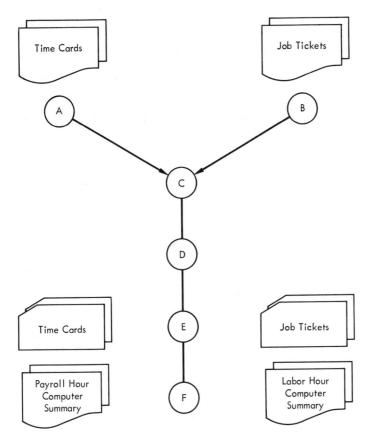

It has three clerical employees who must perform the following functions:

a. Maintain general ledger
b. Maintain accounts payable ledger
c. Maintain accounts receivable ledger
d. Prepare checks for signature
e. Maintain disbursements journal
f. Issue credits on returns and allowances
g. Reconcile the bank account
h. Handle and deposit cash receipts

Assuming that there is no problem as to the ability of any of the employees, the company requests that you assign the above functions to the three employees in such a manner as to achieve the highest degree of internal control. It may be assumed that these employees will perform no other accounting functions than the ones listed and that any accounting functions not listed will be performed by persons other than these three employees.

Required:

a. State how you would distribute the above functions among the three employees. Assume that, with the exception of the nominal jobs of the bank reconciliation and the issuance of credits on returns and allowances, all functions require an equal amount of time.

b. List four possible unsatisfactory combinations of the above-listed functions.   (AICPA adapted)

25. Lew Pherson and Vern Collier are friends who are employed by different CPA firms. One day during lunch they are discussing the importance of internal control in determining the amount of audit evidence required for an engagement. Pherson expresses the view that internal control must be carefully evaluated in all companies, regardless of their size, in basically the same manner. His CPA firm requires a standard internal control questionnaire on every audit as well as a flowchart of every transaction area. In addition, he says the firm requires a careful evaluation of the system and a modification in the evidence accumulated based on the strengths and weaknesses in the system.

Collier responds by saying he believes internal control cannot be adequate in many of the small companies he audits, therefore he simply ignores the evaluation of internal control and acts under the assumption of inadequate controls. He goes on to say, "Why should I spend a lot of time evaluating a system of internal control when I know it has all kinds of weaknesses before I start? I would rather spend the time it takes to fill out all those forms in testing whether the statements are correct."

Required:

a. Express in general terms the most important difference between the nature of the potential controls available for large and small companies.

b. Criticize the positions taken by Pherson and Collier, and express your own opinion about the similarities and differences that should exist in evaluating internal control for different-sized companies.

26. Recently, while eating lunch with your family at a local cafeteria, you observe a practice that is somewhat unusual. As you reach the end of the cafeteria line, an adding machine operator asks how many persons are in your party. He then totals the food purchases on the trays for all of your family and writes the number of persons included in the group on the adding machine tape. He hands you the tape and asks you to pay when you finish eating. Near the end of the meal, you decide you want a piece of pie and coffee so you return to the line, select your food, and again go through the line. The adding machine operator again goes through the same procedure, but this time he staples the second tape to the original and returns it to you.

When you leave the cafeteria, you hand the stapled adding machine tapes to the cash register operator, who totals the two tapes, takes your money, and puts the tapes on a spindle.

Required:

a. What internal controls has the cafeteria instituted for its operations?

b. How can the manager of the cafeteria evaluate the effectiveness of the control procedures?

c. How do these controls differ from those used by most cafeterias?

d. What are the costs and benefits of the cafeteria's system?

27. Internal auditing is a staff function found in virtually every large corporation. The internal audit function is also performed in many small companies

as a part-time activity of individuals who may or may not be called internal auditors. The differences between the audits by independent public accountants and the work of internal auditors are more basic than is generally recognized.

Required:

a. Briefly discuss the auditing work performed by the independent public accountant and the internal auditor with regard to
   (1) auditing objectives.
   (2) general nature of auditing work.
b. In conducting his audit, the independent public accountant must evaluate the work of the internal auditor. Discuss briefly the reason for this evaluation.
c. List the auditing procedures used by an independent public accountant in evaluating the work of the internal auditor.   (AICPA adapted)

28. Charting, Inc., a new audit client of yours, processes its sales and cash receipts documents in the following manner:

   a. *Cash receipts.* The mail is opened each morning by a mail clerk in the sales department. The mail clerk prepares a remittance advice (showing customer and amount paid) if one is not received. The checks and remittance advices are then forwarded to the sales department supervisor, who reviews each check and forwards the checks and remittance advices to the accounting department supervisor. The accounting department supervisor, who also functions as the credit manager, reviews all checks for payments of past due accounts and then forwards the checks and remittance advices to the accounts receivable clerk, who arranges the advices in alphabetical order. The remittance advices are posted directly to the accounts receivable ledger cards. The checks are endorsed by stamp and totaled. The total is posted to the cash receipts journal. The remittance advices are filed chronologically.

   After receiving the cash from the preceding day's cash sales, the accounts receivable clerk prepares the daily deposit slip in triplicate. The third copy of the deposit slip is filed by date, and the second copy and the original accompany the bank deposit.

   b. *Sales.* Salesclerks prepare the sales invoices in triplicate. The original and the second copy are presented to the cashier. The third copy is retained by the salesclerk in the sales book. When the sale is for cash, the customer pays the salesclerk, who presents the money to the cashier with the invoice copies.

   A credit sale is approved by the cashier from an approved credit list after the salesclerk prepares the three-part invoice. After receiving the cash or approved invoice, the cashier validates the original copy of the sales invoice and gives it to the customer. At the end of each day the cashier recaps the sales and cash received and forwards the cash and the second copy of all sales invoices to the accounts receivable clerk. The accounts receivable clerk balances the cash received with cash sales invoices and prepares a daily sales summary. The credit sales invoices are posted to the accounts receivable ledger, and then all invoices are sent to the inventory control clerk in the sales department for posting to the inventory control catalog. After posting, the inventory control clerk files all invoices numerically. The accounts receivable` clerk posts the daily sales summary to the cash receipts journal and sales journal and files the sales summaries by date.

The cash from cash sales is combined with the cash received on account, and this constitutes the daily bank deposit.

c. *Bank deposits.* The bank validates the deposit slip and returns the second copy to the accounting department where it is filed by date by the accounts receivable clerk.

Monthly bank statements are reconciled promptly by the accounting department supervisor and filed by date.

Required:

a. Flowchart the sales and cash receipts functions for Charting, Inc., using good form. Include the segregation of duties.
b. List the most important weaknesses in the system.
c. For each weakness, identify the type of error that is likely to occur.

(AICPA adapted)

29. The following are descriptions of systems of internal control for companies engaged in the manufacturing business:

(1) When Mr. Clark orders materials for his machine-rebuilding plant, he sends a duplicate purchase order to the receiving department. During a delivery of materials, Mr. Smith, the receiving clerk, records the receipt of shipment on this purchase order. After recording, Mr. Smith sends the purchase order to the accounting department, where it is used to record materials purchased and accounts payable. The materials are transported to the storage area by forklifts. The additional purchased quantities are recorded on storage records.

(2) Every day hundreds of employees clock in using time cards at Generous Motors Corporation. The timekeepers collect these cards once a week and deliver them to the tabulating machine department. There the data on these time cards are transferred to punch cards. The punched cards are used in the preparation of the labor cost distribution records, the payroll journal, and the payroll checks. The treasurer, Mrs. Webber, compares the payroll journal with the payroll checks, signs the checks, and returns the payroll checks to Mr. Strode, the supervisor of the tabulating department. The payroll checks are distributed to the employees by Mr. Strode.

(3) The smallest branch of Connor Cosmetics in South Bend employs Mary Cooper, the branch manager, and her sales assistant, Janet Hendrix. The branch uses a bank account in South Bend to pay expenses. The account is kept in the name of "Connor Cosmetics—Special Account." To pay expenses, checks must be signed by Mary Cooper or by the treasurer of Connor Cosmetics, John Winters. Ms. Cooper receives the canceled checks and bank statements. She reconciles the branch account herself and files canceled checks and bank statements in her records. She also periodically prepares reports of disbursements and sends them to the home office.

Required:

a. List the weaknesses in internal control for each of the above.
b. For each weakness, state the type of error(s) that is (are) likely to result. Be as specific as possible.

    c. How would you improve each of the three systems?   (AICPA adapted)

30. Western Meat Processing Company buys and processes livestock for sale to supermarkets. In connection with your examination of the company's financial statements, you have prepared the following notes based on your review of procedures:

    a. Each livestock buyer submits a daily report of his purchases to the plant superintendent. This report shows the dates of purchase and expected delivery, the vendor, and the number, weights, and type of livestock purchased. As shipments are received, any available plant employee counts the number of each type received and places a check mark beside the quantity on the buyer's report. When all shipments listed on the report have been received, the report is returned to the buyer.

    b. Vendor's invoices, after a clerical check, are sent to the buyer for approval and returned to the accounting department. A disbursement voucher and a check for the approved amount are prepared in the accounting department. Checks are forwarded to the treasurer for his signature. The treasurer's office sends signed checks directly to the buyer for delivery to the vendor.

    c. Livestock carcasses are processed by lots. Each lot is assigned a number. At the end of each day a tally sheet reporting the lots processed, the number and type of animals in each lot, and the carcass weight is sent to the accounting department where a perpetual inventory record of processed carcasses and their weights is maintained.

    d. Processed carcasses are stored in a refrigerated cooler located in a small building adjacent to the employee parking lot. The cooler is locked when the plant is not open, and a company guard is on duty when the employees report for work and leave at the end of their shifts. Supermarket truck drivers wishing to pick up their orders have been instructed to contact someone in the plant if no one is in the cooler.

    e. Substantial quantities of by-products are produced and stored, either in the cooler or elsewhere in the plant. By-products are initially accounted for as they are sold. At this time, the sales manager prepares a two-part form—one copy serves as authorization to transfer the goods to the customer and the other becomes the basis for billing the customer.

Required:

For each of parts *a* through *e* above, state

    a. what the specific internal control objective(s) should be at the stage of the operating cycle described.

    b. the control weaknesses in the present procedures, if any; and suggestions for improvements, if any.   (AICPA adapted)

31. Each of the following internal control procedures has been taken from a standard internal control questionnaire used by a CPA firm for evaluating controls in the payroll and personnel cycle.

Required:

    a. For each internal control procedure, identify the element(s) of internal control to which it applies (e.g., adequate documents and records or physical control over assets and records).

    b. For each procedure, identify one audit test the auditor could use to evaluate whether an existing control is effective.

Internal Control Procedure	Procedure Employed by Client		
	N/A	Yes	No

1. Approval of department head or foreman on time cards is required prior to preparing payroll.

2. All prenumbered time cards are accounted for before the preparation of checks begins.

3. Persons preparing the payroll do not perform other payroll duties (e.g., timekeeping, distribution of checks) or have access to other payroll data or cash.

4. All clerical operations in payroll are double-checked before payment is made.

5. All voided and spoiled payroll checks are properly mutilated and retained.

6. Personnel requires an investigation of an employment application from new employees. Investigation includes checking employee's background, former employers, and references.

7. Written termination notices are required, must properly document reasons for termination, and require approval of an appropriate official.

c. For each procedure, list a specific error that could result from the absence of the control.
d. For each procedure, identify one audit test the auditor could use to uncover errors resulting from the absence of the control if the errors exist.

6

Nature
of
Audit Tests

In this chapter there is a transition from the general concepts that apply to all aspects of the audit to the accumulation of evidence for specific transaction cycles. In making this transition, it is essential to understand certain terms and to have a thorough knowledge of basic evidence accumulation concepts. The following main topics are included in this chapter as a means of accomplishing the transition:

1. Types of audit tests
2. An integration of the different parts of the audit
3. A framework for determining audit procedures for tests of transactions
4. Timing of tests of transactions
5. A framework for determining audit procedures for direct tests of account balances

TYPES OF AUDIT TESTS

Auditing students often misunderstand the distinction between the terminology used in the professional literature for the purpose of discussing the important concepts of evidence accumulation and the terminology used by auditors in actually conducting audit tests. It is important to be able to distinguish between the two sets of terminology, and it is also necessary to understand the purpose of each type of test and the interrelationships of the different types of tests. Three types of audit tests are commonly discussed in the professional literature:

    1. Tests of overall reasonableness of financial statement balances
    2. Tests of compliance with the system of internal control
    3. Tests for substantive verification of financial statement balances

Five types of audit tests are commonly referred to in the actual conduct of audits:

    1. Analytical tests
    2. Observations
    3. Tests of transactions
    4. Direct tests of subsidiary account balances
    5. Tests of account inputs and outputs

Types of Tests—Professional Literature

Tests of Overall Reasonableness. These are the general tests discussed in Chapter 4, which include *ratios and trend analysis* for comparison with previous years and with industry standards. These tests are meant to aid the auditor in understanding the client's business better and in identifying areas where more intensive investigation may be needed. When the overall tests show a significant deviation from the auditor's expectations, follow-up with one of the other types of tests is necessary.

Compliance Tests. These tests are audit procedures designed to verify whether the client's controls are being applied in the manner described in the flowchart and internal questionnaire. If, after the tests, the auditor believes the client's controls are operating effectively, he is justified in placing reliance upon the system and thereby reducing the substantive tests. Compliance tests are concerned primarily with three aspects of the client's controls:

1. *The frequency with which the necessary control procedures were performed.* Before controls can be relied upon to reduce substantive testing, the prescribed procedures in the system must be consistently complied with. An example of a compliance test is the examination of a sample of duplicate sales invoices to determine whether each one has been initialed for the approval of credit.

2. *The quality of the performance of the control procedure.* Even if a control procedure has been performed, it may not necessarily have been done properly. Quality of performance of a procedure can be tested, for example, by discussing with the credit manager the criteria used in de-

ciding when credit sales should be approved and examining the details of approval documents for exceptions.

3. *The person performing the procedures.* The individual responsible for a control procedure must be independent of incompatible functions if the control is to be effective. This is accomplished by segregation of duties. An example is the segregation of duties between the handling of cash receipts and the recording of the transactions in the cash receipts journal and subsidiary accounts receivable ledger. Initials on documents can be inspected to determine who performed such procedures.

The client's control procedures can be conveniently divided into two types: those that leave a visual indication of having been performed (*an audit trail*) and those that do not. Examples of the former are the initials of an employee verifying the price and extensions on sales invoices, an internal auditor's initial indicating he has reviewed a bank reconciliation, and the signature of an authorized employee approving credit. The most likely control where no audit trail is available is the segregation of duties. An example is the opening of mail and the prelisting of cash receipts by an employee who does not prepare the cash receipts records.

When the auditor plans to rely upon a control that leaves an audit trail, it is usually tested for compliance by examining underlying documentation. For example, if the assistant credit manager approves sales returns and allowances, the auditor should discuss with him the criteria he uses to grant credit memos to determine if they are consistent with company policy and then test a sample of returns and allowances for missing approvals.

In testing compliance for the segregation of duties, documents and records are usually not available for the auditor's examination. In those instances it is necessary to make inquiries of personnel and observe the procedures as they are being performed to evaluate compliance. For example, a compliance test of the segregation of duties between the custody of cash and the recording of cash receipts can be accomplished by asking each person to describe his duties. During the audit the auditor should also observe who receives and deposits cash and who prepares cash receipts journal records.

Substantive Tests. A substantive test is a procedure designed to *test for dollar errors* directly affecting the fair presentation of financial statement balances. Such errors (often termed *monetary errors*) are a clear indication of the misstatement of the accounts. The only question the auditor must resolve is whether the errors are sufficiently material to require adjustment or disclosure. Examples of substantive tests are the comparison of a duplicate sales invoice with a shipping document to determine whether the quantity shipped equals the quantity billed, the footing of a duplicate sales invoice for accuracy, and the confirmation of customers' accounts receivable.

Relationship between Compliance and Substantive Tests

To better understand the nature of compliance and substantive tests, an examination of their differences is useful. Compliance tests differ from substantive tests in that an error in a compliance test is only an indication of the *likelihood* of errors affecting the dollar value of the financial statements. Compliance errors are material only if they occur with sufficient frequency to cause the auditor to believe there may be material dollar errors in the statements. Substantive tests should then be performed to determine whether *dollar errors have actually occurred.* As an illustration, assume the client's system requires an independent clerk to verify the quantity, price, and extension of each sales invoice, after which he must initial the duplicate invoice to indicate performance. A compliance audit procedure would be to examine a sample of duplicate sales invoices for the initials of the person who verified the quantitative data. If there are a significant number of documents without a signature, the auditor should follow this up with substantive tests. This can be done by extending the test of the duplicate sales invoices to include verifying prices, extensions, and footings or by increasing the sample size for the confirmation of accounts receivable. Of course, even though the compliance procedure is not operating effectively, the actual invoices may be correct. This will be the result if the person originally preparing the sales invoices did a conscientious and competent job.

There are two circumstances in which the auditor may decide not to perform compliance tests on a particular control in the system. The first is when he concludes that the *control procedure is not effective*; for example, because a person performing internal verification is incompetent or not independent. The justification for not testing is that there is no reason to test a control the auditor considers too ineffective to rely upon. The second is when the *audit cost required to test for compliance is greater than the cost savings from reduced substantive tests* that would result from relying upon the client's controls. An example is in the tests of sales invoices discussed in the preceding paragraph. The auditor could simply ignore the initials of the individual who had verified the calculations and act as if no internal verification had taken place. Naturally, substantive tests would have to be increased accordingly.

Even if the auditor's compliance tests yield good results, some substantive tests are necessary. It would be inappropriate, for example, to limit the testing of duplicate sales invoices to examining the initials of a person who has performed internal verification. The presence of the initials is some evidence of clerical accuracy, but additional assurance is needed. Even if a control procedure exists, errors are still possible if the procedure is performed improperly. The audit procedures, sample size, selection of the items for testing, and timing of substantive tests can be modified and reduced by compliance tests, but they cannot be eliminated.

Types of Tests—Conduct of the Audit

The preceding discussion of the three methods of verifying financial statement information is useful as a means of understanding the relationship between the review and evaluation of internal control and the rest of the audit, but it is an inadequate description of the way audits are actually conducted. There are specific audit procedures that are easily identified as tests of overall reasonableness, but there are few if any tests that are used solely for compliance or substantive testing. Instead, most other procedures accomplish both objectives simultaneously (commonly referred to as *dual-purpose tests*). The five types of tests actually used in conducting audits will now be examined.

Analytical Tests. These are the same as overall reasonableness tests previously discussed in this and other chapters.

Observations. These are the observations of activities in the client's organization to test compliance with the client's system of internal control. Such an observation could be a tour of the data-processing facility for the purpose of determining whether tapes and disks are properly safeguarded and programmers prohibited from operating the computer. Similarly, watching an individual do a bank reconciliation to determine who is doing it and when it is being performed is a test of the client's control procedures. Tracing a single transaction from its source to its final disposition by reference to documents as a test of the correctness of a flowchart or internal control questionnaire is also a form of observation.

Observation tests should be planned as carefully as any others, stressing specific objectives rather than a haphazard watching of activities. Since observations are meant to determine whether employees are complying with specific controls, such tests must be carried out systematically.

Tests of Transactions. The examination of underlying documentation and the performance of mechanical accuracy tests constitute the *testing of individual transactions* in the client's business. The primary purpose of tests of transactions is to verify the effectiveness of the client's system of internal control. This is compliance testing, but the procedures are also used for substantive testing. For example, assume an accounting clerk stamps a vendor's invoice after he has tested the document for clerical accuracy, proper classification in the purchases journal, and consistency with supporting documentation. A compliance test is performed by examining the invoice for the initials of the accounting clerk, and a substantive test is accomplished by actually performing the same procedures that were done by the clerk to determine if monetary errors exist. If the clerk's initials are on all the invoices, and the auditor believes the clerk is independent and competent, the substantive tests can be greatly reduced but they cannot be eliminated. In virtually all tests of transactions, some substantive testing is performed simultaneously with compliance testing *(dual-purpose tests)*.

Direct Tests of Subsidiary Account Balances. The ending balance of most balance sheet accounts is audited *directly* by *verifying the totals* making up the balance. For example, accounts receivable is made up of the subsidiary account balances of individual customers. The usual approach is to obtain a list of customers with the balance due from each customer at a point in time (*"a trial balance of accounts receivable"*), to reconcile the total with the general ledger and to directly confirm the balances with customers. The same approach is used for notes receivable, accounts payable, notes payable, and other accounts. Similarly, a list of inventory quantities is frequently obtained from the perpetual records, and a sample is counted by the auditor as a test of the accuracy of the perpetuals. These are all direct tests of subsidiary accounts. They are considered highly reliable and are used extensively in all audits.

Direct tests of subsidiary accounts are primarily concerned with monetary errors in accounts; they therefore can be considered primarily substantive tests. Yet, whenever an error is discovered in a test, the auditor investigates the cause of the error with special emphasis on the control breakdown that permitted the error. Thus these audit procedures are also compliance tests.

Tests of Account Inputs and Outputs. Another way to verify an account balance is by auditing the individual transactions which cause the balance to increase or decrease. Frequently such tests are closely related to the tests of subsidiary account balances. For example, in addition to confirming accounts receivable balances, it is possible to examine documents such as sales invoices and cash remittance advices in support of the debits and credits to the subsidiary account. The same concept applies to the verification of perpetual inventory records, individual notes receivable, and other accounts.

Besides verifying subsidiary balances, tests of account inputs and outputs are also frequently performed for directly testing an entire account balance, such as manufacturing equipment, repairs expense, and miscellaneous income. The transactions making up an account balance are verified by examining supporting documents; this procedure is called *account analysis*. Typically, the auditor obtains from the client a listing of the transactions making up the total balance in an account, foots it, and examines supporting documentation for a sample of transactions.

Tests of account inputs and outputs are similar to tests of transactions in that the form of the evidence is the same, but their purpose is to directly verify an account balance rather than to test the system of internal control. Hence input and output tests are primarily substantive tests, but they are secondarily tests of compliance.

Interrelationship of Types of Tests—Professional Literature and Conduct of the Audit

The discussion in the preceding section frequently referred to the purpose of each of the five types of tests auditors typically perform. It is important that auditors understand whether a particular test is being conducted to test the overall reasonableness of an account balance, to test compliance with the system, or to directly verify the balance in the financial statements. The matrix in Figure 6-1 summarizes the discussion.

FIGURE 6-1

Matrix of Types of Audit Tests—Professional Literature and Conduct of the Audit

Types of Tests—Conduct of the Audit	Overall reasonableness of financial statement balances	Compliance with the system of internal control	Substantive verification of financial statement balances
Analytical tests	P		
Observations		P	
Tests of transactions		P	S
Direct tests of subsidiary account balances		S	P
Tests of account inputs and outputs		S	P

P—Primary purpose of the test.
S—Secondary purpose of the test.

AN INTEGRATION OF THE DIFFERENT PARTS OF THE AUDIT

At this point it is appropriate to summarize the concepts discussed in previous chapters to facilitate an understanding of how the entire audit ties together in an integrated process. Figure 6-2, which is an expansion of Figure 3-3, is a summary diagram of the overview of the audit process. The most important concepts included in the diagram are now discussed briefly.

Obtain a General Understanding of the Client and its Circumstances. An essential part of every audit is to understand the background of the client, the motivations of management, and the nature of the busi-

FIGURE 6-2

OVERVIEW OF THE AUDIT PROCESS

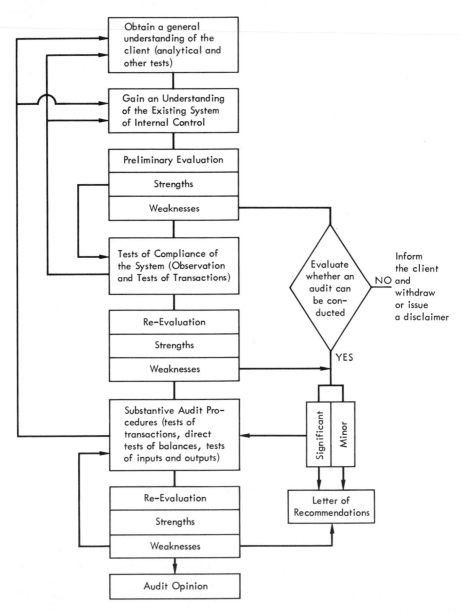

ness. This was studied in depth in Chapters 3 and 4. Chapter 3 includes an examination of the factors affecting the overall acceptable level of risk and the factors affecting the likelihood of error for a given client. A detailed review of these factors is given in Figure 3-3 on page 110. Chapter 4 focuses on the methods that auditors use to obtain an understanding of the client and its business and covers the following four topics:

1. Background information for the audit
2. Analytical tests
3. Understanding the client's legal obligations
4. Evaluation of the possibility of management's involvement in material fraudulent transactions

Gain an Understanding of the Existing System of Internal Control. The second standard of field work requires a thorough study of the existing system and an evaluation of its impact on audit evidence accumulation. To gain this understanding of the system, the auditor must know the reasons for reviewing it, the purposes of internal control, and the elements of internal control. The auditor obtains an understanding of the client's system by the review of records and documentation, discussions with client personnel, flowcharting, and internal control questionnaires. This information is essential to internal control review, but it is not by itself sufficient.

Preliminary Evaluation. Each major transaction cycle must be evaluated to determine significant strengths and weaknesses in the system. This is accomplished by identifying the controls that fulfill each of the seven internal control objectives for each cycle. Strengths represent the existence of adequate controls for a given objective, and weaknesses are any aspect of the system where errors are likely due to the absence of a control. There is no need to test the system for already perceived weaknesses, since such tests would only confirm what the auditor already knows. Instead, if the weaknesses are significant, the audit procedures should be modified to recognize the lack of controls. If the controls are so inadequate that the auditor cannot reasonably determine whether the statements are fairly presented, he should withdraw from the engagement or issue a disclaimer. If the auditor can conduct an audit, the client should be informed of all weaknesses discovered in the study of the system by the use of a management letter.

Tests of Compliance With the System. Each control that is to be relied upon to reduce direct tests of balances must be tested by observation or tests of transactions. The appropriate tests for controls in the sales and collection cycle are the subject of Chapter 8. Other cycles are studied at a later point.

Reevaluation. When the tests of the various controls have been completed, the results must be carefully analyzed to determine whether the system is operating as effectively as the auditor originally believed. Those controls that are operating satisfactorily can be relied upon, and as a result, the direct tests of account balances can be reduced. For those controls where the system is not operating effectively, the auditor cannot rely upon the system. In those circumstances, he must act as if the control did not exist and increase other tests accordingly.

Substantive Tests of Financial Balances. Substantive audit tests are based in part upon the auditor's evaluation of the strengths and weaknesses of the client's system after it has been tested for compliance. But it should be kept in mind that other variables also affect the nature of the tests. Considerations such as the overall level of assurance desired, the materiality of the balance in question, the first-year versus a subsequent-year audit, the results of previous audits, and other factors discussed in Chapter 3 must be considered.

The substantive tests include analytical tests for overall reasonableness, direct tests of subsidiary balances, tests of account inputs and outputs, and tests of transactions. Ordinarily, the substantive tests of transactions will already have been completed in conjunction with testing controls for compliance, but sometimes additional substantive procedures are considered necessary later in the audit.

Reevaluation. The results of the substantive tests also provide additional information about the system. If significant errors are found, it may be necessary to rechallenge the quality of internal controls and to perform additional tests to determine whether the financial statements are fairly presented. This step highlights the interrelationship of the different parts of the audit. The auditor constantly revises his opinion about the client's organization and system of internal control as more information is obtained. At the completion of the engagement, the auditor should have an excellent understanding of the client's system and the business in general.

Audit Opinion. After sufficient evidence has been accumulated to satisfy the auditor as to whether the financial statements are fairly presented, an audit opinion is given. The auditor can never be completely certain about the statements, but a satisfactory level of assurance considering the risk factors in the audit must be reached. If the auditor is satisfied that the statements are fairly presented, the standard short-form report discussed in Chapter 2 can be issued. Otherwise, one of the other types must be given.

A FRAMEWORK—TESTS OF TRANSACTIONS

A major decision the auditor must make in every audit is the appropriate audit procedures, sample size, items to be included in the sample for testing, and timing of the tests. One of the most important conclusions that has been reached in previous chapters is the need to adapt the audit program to the unique circumstances of a particular client. For this reason, we do not believe there is such a thing as a single audit program. In this section we are concerned with establishing a framework to aid in developing a tailor-made audit program for performing tests of transactions that will permit the auditor to consider the unique circumstances of the engagement.

The approach used in this text is to establish *detailed audit objectives* that are common to every transaction cycle and use these objectives as a point of departure for deciding on the audit tests in a particular engagement. The objectives used are identical to the seven internal control objectives discussed in Chapter 5. The same objectives are used because the purpose of performing tests of transactions is to determine whether the internal controls are effective. Thus they are relevant in determining the proper evidence to accumulate to evaluate the reliability of existing controls. These seven objectives for any given audit area are listed below, together with examples of the types of errors for which the auditor is searching in each objective:

Recorded Transactions are Valid. This objective deals with the possibility of invalid transactions being included in the records. Instances include the recording of a sale when no shipment took place, or a charge-off of an uncollectible account that has actually been paid.

Transactions are Properly Authorized. If a transaction takes place without proper authorization at the key points, an improper transaction may have occurred. Examples of transactions without proper authorization include the failure to authorize shipments and the acceptance of unauthorized sales returns and allowances.

Existing Transactions are Recorded. An error under this objective occurs whenever the client fails to record a transaction. An example is the shipment of goods without billing or inclusion in the accounting records. This objective is the opposite of the validity of the recorded transactions objective inasmuch as it deals with existing transactions not being recorded rather than recorded transactions not being valid.

Transactions are Properly Valued. Even though all transactions included in the records are authorized and valid, they may be stated at an incorrect amount. For the financial statements to be fairly stated, the individual transactions must be recorded at the correct amount. As an illustration, the quantities, prices, extensions, and footings on sales invoices must be correctly stated to meet this objective, and the amount of the sale must be correctly included in the sales journal and subsidiary ledgers.

Transactions are Properly Classified. This objective deals with the possibility of a transaction in the cycle being classified improperly. Examples of misclassifications include the recording of the disposal of a permanent asset as a sale, the recording of the receipt of loan proceeds as a collection of an outstanding account receivable, the recording of a collection of an account receivable as a cash sale, and the recording of a sale to a residential customer as a commercial sale.

Transactions are Recorded at the Proper Time. In addition to being correctly recorded, transactions must be recorded on a timely basis. The failure to record a transaction reasonably soon after its occurrence may result in including the amount in the wrong time period, especially if the transaction took place near the end of the accounting period. This is referred to as a *cutoff error*. The failure to record transactions on a timely basis can also result in the complete omission of the recording due to the loss or mishandling of the records.

Transactions are Properly Included in the Subsidiary Records and Correctly Summarized. Since the individual transactions are the source of the balances in the financial statements, they must be correctly summarized and posted to subsidiary records, the general ledger, and other reports. Although it is not difficult to perform tests to fulfill this objective, an audit is inadequate if it has not been done. A fraud error can be covered up in sales by underfooting the sales journal or posting the amounts in the journal to the general ledger incorrectly. Examples of unintentional errors are debiting a wrong general ledger account when the journals are posted or crediting a sales return to the wrong customer in the subsidiary ledger.

TIMING OF TESTS OF TRANSACTIONS

Ideally, the performance of tests of transactions should take place after the client's year-end. This permits the auditor to test the system for the entire year without any discontinuity between the tests of transactions and the direct tests of the balances. Since the direct tests of financial balances are based upon the results of the tests of transactions, they naturally take place even later in the audit.

However, it is not possible to follow this time schedule on many audits for several reasons. Some clients need their audits completed so soon after the end of the year that the tests of transactions and many other tests must be performed before the year-end in order to meet reporting deadlines. A closely related problem is the difficulty of basing the direct tests on the results of the tests of transactions if the auditor waits until the end of the year to perform both types of tests. Time pressures to complete the audit sometimes encourage auditors to develop the direct procedures independently of the results of the tests of transactions. Finally, the large number of clients with calendar-year financial statements makes it impractical for CPA firms to schedule their work loads to perform all tests after the year-end.

One solution is to partially test the system at one or more times during the year and then complete the tests after year-end. This approach is feasible and is frequently done for large clients. In fact, some clients are sufficiently large to justify having their auditors perform tests *continuously throughout the year*. For smaller clients it is possible, but expensive, to take this approach. The increased cost of testing the system at different points of time arises from discontinuity of starting the tests more than once, updating schedules, and familiarizing new staff on the audit with the work completed to date.

Another acceptable approach under some circumstances is to *limit the tests of the system to an interim date.* This method permits the auditor to complete the testing before the end of the year without having to test the system more than once. SAS 1 lists the following factors the auditor should consider in deciding whether the tests of the system can be limited to an interim period of less than twelve months:

1. *Results of the tests of the interim period.* If results indicate the reliability of the system is questionable, the system should not be relied upon without being tested for the remainder of the period. Naturally, if the expanded tests indicate the system is not reliable, the system should not be relied upon in determining the extent of direct tests of balances.

2. *Response to inquiries concerning the remaining period.* The most important inquiries should be directed at determining whether there were any significant changes in the system and accounting procedures during the remaining period. This information can be obtained from inquiries to management, observation of personnel changes, and examination of procedures manuals.

3. *Nature and amount of the transactions and balances involved.* If the transactions occurring between the completion of the compliance tests and the end of the year are atypical of the transactions for the year, this implies the need to test further. Such is the case with a highly seasonal business or with a firm that had several large or unusual transactions near the end of the year. A review of the journals for transactions taking place after the completion of the tests of the system should reveal unusual situations.

4. *Evidence of compliance within the remaining period that may be obtained from substantive tests performed by the independent auditor or from tests performed by internal auditors.* Evidence obtained through such tests as the pricing of inventory, cutoff tests for accounts payable, and confirmation of accounts receivable indicate both the adequacy of the system and the propriety of the ending balances. If these tests indicate satisfactory results, there is less need to test the remaining period specifically for the adequacy of the system. A review of the internal auditor's working papers where his results are satisfactory also has the effect of reducing the need to test the remaining period.

5. *Length of the remaining period.* When the time period between the interim testing and the balance sheet date is relatively short, it is less important to test the remaining period than when the time period is several months. Although it has not been stated in the professional literature, there is some consensus in the profession for requiring an interim test of no less than the first nine months of the year. If an interim test of a

lesser period is performed, it is necessary to complete the tests of the remaining period at a later date.

6. *Other matters the independent auditor considers relevant in the circumstances.* These include such considerations as the auditor's risk of exposure to legal sanction, the degree of familiarity with the client's operations, and the confidence the auditor has in the competence of personnel and integrity of management.

A FRAMEWORK—DIRECT TESTS OF FINANCIAL BALANCES

Once the tests of the system have been completed for a transaction cycle and their results evaluated, substantive tests of the related financial statement balances are performed. These substantive tests concentrate on the verification of the balance sheet accounts in the cycle, but income and expense accounts are also included. Tests of many balance sheet accounts relate to specific income statement accounts as well. For example, in testing accounts receivable, the auditor is also verifying sales and sales returns and allowances. However, it is also necessary to verify some of the income statement accounts directly.

In completing the tests of account balances, it is desirable to set up a framework similar to the one used for tests of transactions. This procedure facilitates approaching the audit of the account balance in a logical manner without specifying a required set of inflexible audit procedures for each account balance.

The framework used to test account balances is the use of *detailed objectives for direct tests of financial balances* in the same manner as was done for tests of transactions. The detailed objectives serve both as a guide to understanding what the auditor is trying to accomplish and as an aid in developing audit programs. The eight detailed objectives for the direct tests of financial balances are examined briefly at this point and are then applied specifically to the verification of individual accounts in subsequent chapters.

1. *Overall reasonableness.* Tests for overall reasonableness are intended to aid the auditor in evaluating whether the balances in the asset and related revenue accounts appear to include material errors. A great deal of skill is needed in applying overall reasonableness tests because the interpretation of the results is a highly subjective matter. For these tests the auditor should compare the individual balances of the current year with those of previous years, compute ratios, and perform other similar tests.

2. *Mechanical accuracy.* Tests for mechanical accuracy of balance sheet accounts include footing the client's schedules and lists and tracing the balances to the subsidiary and general ledgers.

3. *Existence.* The first part of the existence objective is to ascertain

whether all recorded amounts should be included. This is meant as a test of the validity and propriety of recorded amounts. The second part is to verify whether all amounts that should be included have actually been included.

4. *Ownership.* In addition to existing, most assets must be owned before it is acceptable to include them in the financial statements. An auditor should make specific tests to be sure recorded assets are owned. Naturally, this objective does not apply to the verification of liability and owner's equity accounts.

5. *Valuation.* The correct valuation of the individual balances making up the total account balance, including the arithmetic accuracy of all calculations, is one of the concerns in this objective. A second aspect of valuation as it relates to many asset balances is determining whether the overall balance is stated at its realizable value. For example, in accounts receivable, this requires the auditor to satisfy himself that the allowance for uncollectible accounts is reasonably stated, since it is a valuation account relating to accounts receivable.

6. *Classification.* Classification in balance sheet accounts involves determining whether amounts are separated as to short-term and long-term assets; amounts due from affiliates, officers, and directors are separated from amounts due from customers; and similar classification requirements.

7. *Cutoff.* In testing for cutoff, the objective is to determine whether transactions were recorded in the proper period. The transactions that are most likely to be misstated are those recorded near the end of the accounting period. It is proper to think of cutoff tests as a part of verifying either the balance sheet accounts or the selected revenue and expense accounts, but for convenience auditors usually perform them as a part of auditing the balance sheet accounts.

8. *Disclosure.* In fulfilling the disclosure objective, the auditor tests to make certain that all balance sheet and income statement accounts are correctly set forth in the financial statements and properly described in the body and footnotes of the statements.

Audit Procedures for Each Objective

A thorough understanding of the detailed audit objectives for direct tests of financial balances is essential to the development of adequate audit programs. If an auditor clearly understands the audit objectives already discussed in this chapter, it is relatively easy to develop a tailor-made audit program that takes into account the available evidence, the strengths and weaknesses in the internal control system, and the special circumstances in the audit.

In designing audit procedures to satisfy the audit objectives for any given account, several key points should be kept in mind:

   1. A given audit procedure is likely to fulfill more than one objective. The objectives are kept separate at this point to provide a

better understanding of the purpose of the procedures. This text often refers to the same audit procedure several times. This repetition does not mean the auditor will perform the procedure more than once, but rather that multiple objectives are met.

2. More than one procedure is frequently necessary to satisfactorily verify any given objective. The procedures tend to complement each other, but in some instances they may be substitutes.

3. The appropriate procedures for the audit of any audit area depend upon all of the circumstances of the audit discussed in previous chapters, but special emphasis is put on internal control.

4. It is relatively easy to combine the objectives and procedures into an audit program after the auditor has decided on the proper tests in a given audit area.

REVIEW QUESTIONS

1. Distinguish between a compliance test and a substantive test of transactions. Give two examples of each.

2. Distinguish between a compliance test and a substantive test of subsidiary account balances. Give two examples of each.

3. A considerable portion of the compliance and substantive tests of transactions are performed simultaneously as a matter of audit convenience. But the substantive tests of transaction procedures and sample size are in part dependent upon the results of the compliance tests. How can the auditor resolve this apparent inconsistency?

4. Evaluate the following statement: "Observations of people by an auditor are a waste of time. It is unreasonable to expect anyone to behave in a normal manner when they know the auditor is watching what they do. People will perform properly when the auditor is around and the auditor will make incorrect inferences about their normal behavior."

5. Explain what is meant by a dual purpose test. Give an example of one.

6. Explain the difference between a control procedure that leaves an audit trail and one that does not. Give one example of each. For each example, state a compliance procedure to test the effectiveness of the control.

7. Evaluate the following statement: "Tests of sales and collection transactions are such an essential part of every audit that I like to perform them as near the end of the audit as possible. By that time I have a fairly good understanding of the client's business and internal controls because confirmations, cutoff tests, and other procedures have already been completed."

8. State the relationship between the preliminary evaluation of an internal control system and tests of compliance.

9. In testing sales transactions using the framework developed in this chapter, explain the difference between these two objectives: "recorded transactions are valid" and "existing transactions are recorded." State one audit procedure that could be used to test each of these objectives.

10. An auditor is testing the purchases of raw material transactions by examining vendors' invoices, purchase orders, and receiving reports. Which of the documents would be the most important as a test of whether the recorded transaction is properly authorized? Which would be most important to test for the valuation objective? Which would be most important to test for the proper timing objective?

11. Explain how the calculation and comparison to previous years of the gross margin percent and the ratio of accounts receivable to sales is related to the confirmation of accounts receivable and other tests of the accuracy of accounts receivable.

12. List the circumstances under which it is acceptable to limit the tests of transactions to an interim date.

13. "Most of my clients have only two or three people in the entire office staff, including bookkeepers and secretaries; therefore, internal control is virtually nonexistent. My approach to auditing is not to rely on the system of internal control. I don't perform tests of transactions, but I compensate for it by extensively testing the ending balances in all balance sheet accounts." Evaluate these comments.

14. List the eight valuation objectives in the verification of the ending balance in inventory, and provide one useful audit procedure for each of the objectives.

15. Explain what is meant by a complementary and a substitutability relationship between overall reasonableness tests, compliance tests, and substantive tests.

DISCUSSION QUESTIONS AND PROBLEMS

16. Indicate whether each of the eleven audit procedures listed below is (1) an overall reasonableness test, (2) a compliance test, or (3) a substantive test. Also indicate whether it is (4) an analytical test, (5) an observation, (6) a test of transactions, (7) a direct test of subsidiary account balances, or (8) a test of account inputs and outputs.
    a. Foot the trial balance of accounts payable and compare the total with the general ledger.
    b. Examine vendor's invoices to verify the ending balance in accounts payable.
    c. Compare the balance in payroll tax expense with previous years. The comparison takes the increase in payroll tax rates into account.
    d. Discuss the duties of the cash disbursements bookkeeper with him and observe whether he has responsibility for handling cash or preparing the bank reconciliation.
    e. Confirm accounts payable balances directly with vendors.
    f. Account for a sequence of checks in the cash disbursements journal to determine whether any have been omitted.
    g. Examine the internal auditor's initials on monthly bank reconciliations as an indication of whether they have been reviewed.
    h. Examine vendor's invoices and other documentation in support of recorded transactions in the purchases journal.
    i. Multiply the commission rate by total sales and compare the result with commission expense.
    j. Examine vendor's invoices and other supporting documents to determine whether large amounts in the repair and maintenance account should be capitalized.
    k. Examine the initials on vendor's invoices that indicate internal verification of pricing, extending, and footing by a clerk.

17. The following are independent internal control procedures commonly found

in the purchases and cash disbursements cycle. Each control is to be considered independently.

a. At the end of each month an accounting clerk accounts for all pre-numbered receiving reports (documents evidencing the receipt of goods) issued during the month, and he traces each one to the related vendor's invoice and purchase journal entry. The clerk's tests do not include testing quantity or description of the merchandise received.

b. The cash disbursements bookkeeper is prohibited from handling cash. The bank account is reconciled by another person even though the bookkeeper has sufficient expertise and time to do it.

c. Before a check is prepared to pay for purchases by the accounts payable department, the related purchase order and receiving report are attached to the vendor's invoice being paid. A clerk compares the quantity on the invoice with the receiving report and purchase order, compares the price with the purchase order, recomputes the extensions, readds the total, and examines the account number indicated on the invoice to determine whether it is properly classified. He indicates his performance of these procedures by initialing the invoice.

d. Before a check is signed by the controller, he examines the supporting documentation accompanying the check. At that time he initials each vendor's invoice to indicate his approval.

e. After the controller signs the checks, his secretary writes the check number and the date the check was issued on each of the supporting documents to prevent their reuse.

Required:

a. For each of the internal control procedures, state the internal control objective(s) the control is meant to fulfill.

b. List one compliance procedure for each control procedure the auditor could perform to test the effectiveness of the control.

c. List one substantive test for each control the auditor could perform to determine whether financial errors are actually taking place.

18. For each of the following controls, identify whether the control leaves an audit trial, and list a compliance procedure the auditor can use to test the effectiveness of the control.

a. An accounting clerk accounts for all shipping documents on a monthly basis.

b. The bank reconciliation is prepared by the controller, who does not have access to cash receipts.

c. As employees check in daily by using time clocks, a supervisor observes to make certain no individual "punches in" more than one time card.

d. Vendor's invoices are approved by the controller after he examines the purchase order and receiving report attached to each invoice.

e. The cashier, who has no access to accounting records, prepares the deposit slip and delivers the deposit directly to the bank on a daily basis.

f. An accounting clerk verifies the prices, extensions, and footings of all sales invoices in excess of $300 and initials the duplicate sales invoice when he has completed the procedure.

g. All mail is opened and cash is prelisted daily by the president's secretary, who has no other responsibility for handling assets or recording accounting data.

19. Ron Blanch, CPA, spends considerable time evaluating internal control and performing compliance tests of the system. When he identifies controls in the system that can be relied upon to reduce the likelihood of errors, he tests the controls until he is confident no significant errors are possible. At that point he performs no additional tests of any kind, since he feels he has achieved an adequate level of assurance. In several audits he has performed no substantive tests of any kind in certain areas such as accounts payable and property, plant, and equipment because of extraordinary controls in the system. Blanch feels that this approach saves time on audits with good internal control, and it enables him to concentrate on helping the client improve the effectiveness of the system.

Required:

Evaluate Blanch's approach to conducting audits. Include a discussion of both the strengths and the weaknesses in his approach.

20. Jennifer Schaefer, CPA, follows the philosophy of performing interim tests of transactions on every December 31 audit as a means of keeping overtime to a minimum. Typically the interim tests are performed some time between August and November.

Required:

a. Evaluate her decision to perform interim tests of transactions.
b. Under what circumstances is it acceptable for her to perform no additional tests of transactions work as a part of the year-end audit tests?
c. If she decides to perform no additional testing, what is the effect on other tests she performs during the remainder of the engagement?

21. You are the in-charge accountant examining the financial statements of the Gutzler Company for the year ended December 31, 19X7. During late October 19X7, you, with the help of Gutzler's controller, completed an internal control questionnaire and prepared the appropriate memoranda describing Gutzler's accounting procedures. Your comments relative to cash receipts are as follows.

All cash receipts are sent directly to the accounts receivable clerk with no processing by the mail department. The accounts receivable clerk keeps the cash receipts journal, prepares the bank deposit slip in duplicate, posts from the deposit slip to the subsidiary accounts receivable ledger, and mails the deposit to the bank.

The controller receives the validated deposit slips directly (unopened) from the bank. He also receives the monthly bank statement directly (unopened) from the bank and promptly reconciles it.

At the end of each month, the accounts receivable clerk notifies the general ledger clerk by journal voucher of the monthly totals of the cash receipts journal for posting to the general ledger.

Each month, with regard to the general ledger cash account, the general ledger clerk makes an entry to record the total debits to cash from the cash receipts journal. In addition, the general ledger clerk on occasion makes debit entries in the general ledger cash account from sources other than the cash receipts journal, e.g., funds borrowed from the bank.

Required:

a. List the controls in the system for handling and recording cash.

b. List the weakness in the system.

c. For each control, list a compliance test that can be used to test the effectiveness of the system.

d. Considering Gutzler's internal control over cash receipts, list all other auditing procedures and reasons therefor which should be performed to obtain sufficient audit evidence regarding cash receipts. Do not discuss the procedures for cash disbursements and cash balances. Also do not discuss the extent to which any of the procedures are to be performed. Assume adequate controls exist to assure that all sales transactions are recorded. (AICPA adapted)

22. A large portion of the audit clients of Miller and Jordan, CPAs, have a December 31 year-end. The partners would like to do more interim testing on these engagements but most of the clients are small and have relatively weak systems of internal control. The clients have been asked to consider changing to a fiscal year-end, but with minor exceptions they have resisted the change. The effect on Miller and Jordan's professional practice is heavy peak loads during the period from January 1 to April 1 and significant idle time the rest of the year. How can the CPA firm reduce this problem and still meet the standards of the profession?

23. Three auditors are discussing concepts of evidence accumulation during lunch by comparing the extent to which evidence should be modified under difficult circumstances. One of the auditors took the position that every client should be audited in the same manner because, after all, every client gets the same audit opinion. The second auditor said that he believes the evidence should only depend on the risk of exposure to lawsuits and other possible sanctions against the auditor. He expressed the view that after the auditor sets his "level of confidence" the evidence should be the same for every audit. In other words, for a given "level of overall confidence" the evidence should not vary. The third auditor stated that he felt the "level of confidence" should be the same for each engagement, but the evidence should vary considerably depending on the circumstances of the engagement. He stated that the results of first year audit, the results of compliance and substantive tests of transactions, the reliability of the evidence, and other considerations in the engagement affect the combined amount of confidence the auditor should achieve.

Required:

a. Evaluate each of these auditors' positions.

b. State your own conclusions about whether the "level of confidence" should vary from audit to audit. How does this relate to overall reasonableness tests, compliance tests, and substantive tests?

c. State your conclusions about the need to consider the circumstances of the engagement. How does this relate to overall reasonableness tests, compliance tests, and substantive tests?

7

Working Papers

Working papers are the *written records kept by the auditor* of the evidence accumulated during the course of the audit, the methods and procedures followed, and the conclusions reached. They should include all the information the auditor considers necessary to adequately conduct his examination and provide support for his audit report. The purposes of the records, the types of working papers, and considerations in preparing working papers are the subject matter of this chapter.

PURPOSES OF WORKING PAPERS

The overall objective of working papers is to aid the auditor in providing reasonable assurance that an adequate audit was conducted in accordance with generally accepted auditing standards. In more specific terms, the purposes of the working papers as they pertain to the current year's audit include the following:

1. *Provide the basis for planning the audit.* If the auditor is to adequately plan the current year's audit, the necessary reference information must be available in the working papers to aid him in his decision making. The papers include such diverse planning information as the evaluation of internal control, a time budget for individual audit areas, the audit program, and the results of the preceding year's audit.

2. *Provide a record of the evidence accumulated and the results of the tests.* The working papers are the primary means of documenting that an adequate audit was conducted. If the need arises, the auditor must be able to demonstrate to commissions and courts that the audit was well planned and adequately supervised, the evidence accumulated was both competent and sufficient, and the audit report was proper considering the results of the examination.

Because of the increased litigation involving CPAs in recent years, the adequacy of working papers takes on an even greater importance. When lawsuits claim that an inadequate audit has been performed, the working papers of the CPA firm are normally subpoenaed as evidence in the trial. These papers become a critical element in defending any such lawsuit. They are the CPA firm's evidence of having performed the audit with due care and having complied with other professional and legal standards.

3. *Provide data for determining the proper type of audit report.* The working papers provide an important source of information to assist the auditor in deciding upon the appropriate audit report to issue in a given set of circumstances. The data in the papers are useful for evaluating the adequacy of audit scope and the fairness of the financial statements. In addition, the working papers contain information needed for the preparation of the financial statements.

4. *Provide the basis for review by supervisors and partners.* The working papers are the primary frame of reference used by supervisory personnel to evaluate whether sufficient competent evidence was accumulated to justify the audit report.

In addition to the purposes directly related to the current year's audit, the working papers can also serve as

1. The basis for preparing tax returns, filings with the SEC, and other reports
2. A source of information for issuing a management letter to the client for improving operations
3. A frame of reference for training personnel
4. An aid in planning and coordinating subsequent audits

CONTENTS AND ORGANIZATION

Each CPA firm establishes its own approach to preparing and organizing working papers, and the beginning auditor must adopt his firm's approach. The emphasis in the study of contents and organization in this text is on the general concepts common to all working papers.

The most critical requirement of working papers is their ability to stand on their own without reference to the oral comments of the auditors. Frequently, lawsuits or other situations requiring the use of the working papers do not occur until several years after the completion of the engagement. The personnel responsible for preparing the papers cannot be expected to remember what took place that long ago. Besides, they may no longer be employed by the firm. In deciding upon the contents and organization of the working papers, the auditor should act as if no one on the engagement would be available to defend the audit at a later date.

Figure 7-1 illustrates the contents and organization of a typical complete set of papers. A look at the contents indicates that they contain virtually everything involved in the examination. There is a definite logic to the type of working papers prepared for an audit and the way they are arranged in the files, even though different firms may follow somewhat different approaches. In Figure 7-1 the working papers start with the more general information such as corporate data in the permanent files and end with the financial statements and audit report. In between are the working papers supporting the tests described in the previous chapter. A discussion of the kinds of working papers prepared on a typical audit and the reasons for preparing them follows.

Permanent Files

Permanent files are intended to contain data of a *historical or continuing nature,* pertinent to the current examination. These files provide a convenient source of information about the audit that is of continuing interest from year to year. The permanent file typically includes the following:

1. *Extracts or copies of such company documents of continuing importance as the articles of incorporation, bylaws, bond indentures, and contracts.* The contracts are pension plans, leases, stock options, and so on. Each of these documents is of significance to the auditor for as many years as it is in effect.

2. *Analyses from previous years of accounts that have continuing importance to the auditor.* These include accounts such as long-term debt, stockholders' equity accounts, goodwill, and fixed assets. Having this information in the permanent file enables the auditor to concentrate on analyzing only the changes in the current year's balance while retaining the results of previous years' audits in a form accessible for review.

3. *Information related to the evaluation of internal control.* This includes organization charts, flowcharts, questionnaires, and other internal control information including enumeration of strengths and weaknesses in the system.

4. *The results of analytical testing from previous years' auditing.* Among these data are ratios and percentages computed by the auditor, and the total balance or the balance by month for selected accounts. This information is useful in helping the auditor decide whether there are

FIGURE 7-1

WORKING PAPER CONTENTS AND ORGANIZATION

STATEMENTS AND AUDIT REPORT
WORKING TRIAL BALANCE
ADJUSTING JOURNAL ENTRIES
LEGAL LETTERS/CONTINGENT LIAB.
B. OF D. MINUTES
AUDIT PROGRAMS
ANALYTICAL TESTS
ASSETS
LIABILITIES AND EQUITY
OPERATIONS
INTERNAL CONTROL EVAL.
TESTS OF TRANSACTIONS
PERMANENT FILES
WORKING PAPER CONTENTS & ORGANIZATION

unusual changes in the current year's account balance that should be investigated more extensively.

Analytical tests and internal control review are included in the current period working papers rather than in the permanent file by many CPA firms.

Audit Program

As explained in Chapter 1, an *audit program* is the list of audit procedures designed for each engagement to meet the evidence requirements of the audit. By maintaining a list of procedures in a separate file, the coordination and integration of all parts of the audit are enhanced. As the audit progresses, each auditor initials the program for the audit procedures he has performed and indicates the date of completion. The inclusion in the working papers of a well-designed audit program that has been completed in a conscientious manner is evidence of a high-quality audit.

General Information

Some working papers include current period information that is of a general nature rather than being designed to support specific financial statement amounts. This includes such items as abstracts or copies of minutes of the board of directors, abstracts of contracts or agreements not included in the permanent file, notes on discussions with the client, working paper review comments, and general conclusions.

Working Trial Balance

Since the basis for preparing the financial statements is the general ledger, the amounts included on that record are the focal point of the examination. As early as possible after the balance sheet date, the auditor obtains or prepares a listing of the general ledger accounts and their year-end balances. This schedule is the working trial balance.

The technique used by many firms is to have the auditor's working trial balance in the same format as the financial statements. Each line item on the trial balance is supported by a *lead schedule* containing the detailed accounts from the general ledger making up the line item total. Each detailed account on the lead schedule is in turn supported by appropriate supporting schedules evidencing the audit work performed and the conclusions reached. As an example, the relationship between cash as it is stated on the financial statements, the working trial balance, the lead schedule for cash, and the supporting working papers is presented in Figure 7-2. As the figure indicates, cash on the financial statements is the same as on the working trial balance and the total of the detail on the cash lead schedule. Initially, figures for the lead schedule were taken from the general ledger. The audit work performed resulted in an adjustment to cash which would be evidenced in the detail schedules and reflected in the lead schedule, the working trial balance, and the financial statements.

Indexing and Cross-Referencing

As a part of organizing and filing working papers, some type of indexing and cross-referencing system is necessary. A good indexing system both minimizes the time it takes for review and facilitates reference to underlying support when it is needed. One type of indexing is illustrated in Figure 7-2. The lead schedule for cash has been indexed as A-1, and the individual general ledger accounts making up the total cash on the financial statements are indexed as A-2 through A-4. The final indexing is for the schedules supporting A-3 and A-4. These supporting schedules are easy to relate to the appropriate working paper by using a consistent

FIGURE 7-2

RELATIONSHIP OF WORKING PAPERS TO FINANCIAL STATEMENTS

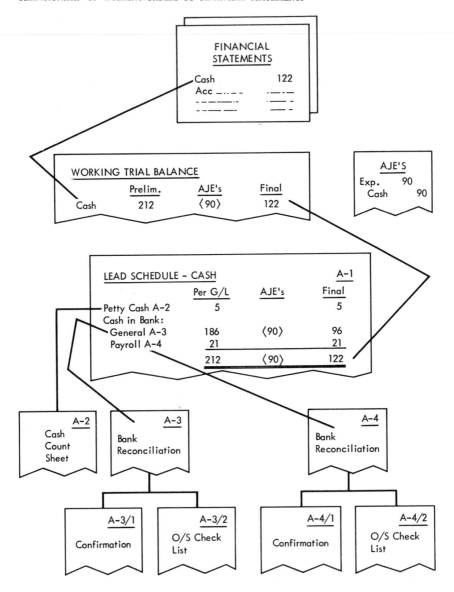

indexing system and indicating appropriate cross-references. Although indexing systems vary considerably for different CPA firms, a standard system is usually required for all audits of a given firm.

Adjusting and Reclassification Entries

When the auditor discovers material errors in the accounting records, he must make sure that the financial statements are corrected. For example, if the client has failed to properly reduce inventory for obsolete raw materials, an adjusting entry can be made by the auditor to reflect the realizable value of the inventory. Even though adjusting entries discovered in the audit are typically prepared by the auditor, they must be approved by the client because management is primarily responsible for the fair presentation of the statements. Each adjustment must be carefully documented in the working papers and given to the client by the end of the audit for entry in the general ledger. Figure 7-2 illustrates the adjustment of the general cash account for $90.

Reclassification entries are frequently made in the statements to properly present accounting information, even when the general ledger balances are correct. A common example is the reclassification for financial statement purposes of material credit balances in accounts receivable to accounts payable. Since the balance in accounts receivable on the general ledger reflects the accounts receivable properly from the point of view of operating the company on a day-to-day basis, the reclassification entry is not included in the client's general ledger.

Only those adjusting and reclassification entries that significantly affect the fair presentation of financial statements must be made. However, clients generally prefer to make all but negligible entries in order to have a more accurate set of financial statements at fiscal year-end. The determination of when an error should be adjusted is based upon *materiality*. The auditor should keep in mind that several immaterial errors that are not adjusted could result in a material overall misstatement when the errors are combined. It is common for auditors to summarize on a separate working paper all entries that have not been recorded as a means of determining their cumulative effect.

Supporting Schedules

The largest portion of working papers includes the detailed schedules prepared by auditors in support of specific financial amounts in the statements. Many different types of schedules are used. Use of the appropriate type of schedule for a given aspect of the audit is necessary to document the adequacy of the audit and to fulfill the other objectives of working papers. Following are the major types of supporting schedules:

1. *Analysis.* An analysis is designed to show the *activity in a balance sheet account* during the entire period under examination, tying together the beginning and ending balances. This type of schedule is normally

used for accounts such as marketable securities, notes receivable, allowance for doubtful accounts, property, plant, and equipment, long-term debt, and for all equity accounts. The common characteristic of these accounts is the significance of the activity in the account during the year. In most cases the working papers for analyses have cross-references to other working papers. An illustration of an analysis of the allowance for doubtful accounts is given in Figure 7-3. The analysis starts with the balance at the beginning of the year, which must agree with the ending balance from the preceding year, and works through the year's transactions to the ending balance. Each type of transaction has audit significance and is supported by another schedule.

2. *Trial balance or list.* This type of schedule consists of the *detail making up a year-end balance* of either a balance sheet or an income statement account. It differs from an analysis in that it includes only those items constituting the end-of-the-period balance. Common examples include trial balances or lists in support of trade accounts receivable, trade accounts payable, repair and maintenance expense, legal expense, and miscellaneous income.

3. *Comparison schedule.* For many revenue and expense accounts, a primary verification procedure is to *compare* the book amount with the preceding year's amount and budgeted amount in the manner described in Chapter 4 and to obtain and investigate reasons for significant variances. An illustration of a working paper of this type for general and administrative expenses is given in Figure 7-4. Although it is not included in the figure, an investigation and explanation of each significant variance is necessary.

An analysis, a trial balance or list, or a comparison schedule is typically included in the working papers in support of every material account in the general ledger. The remaining schedules discussed in this section are meant to support amounts included on one of these three schedules. For example, the working paper in Figure 7-3 refers to Schedule V-1, which would normally describe a test of reasonableness of the calculation of the provision for bad debts.

4. *Reconciliation of amounts.* A reconciliation *supports a specific amount* and is normally expected to tie the amount recorded in the client's records to another source of information. Examples include the reconciliation of bank balances with bank statements, the reconciliation of subsidiary accounts receivable balances with confirmations from customers, and the reconciliation of accounts payable balances with vendor's statements.

5. *Tests of reasonableness.* A test of reasonableness schedule, as the name implies, contains information that enables the auditor to evaluate whether the client's balance appears to include an error considering the circumstances in the engagement. Frequently, auditors test depreciation expense, the provision for federal income taxes, and the allowance for doubtful accounts by tests of reasonableness. Ratio and trend analysis of

FIGURE 7-3

ANALYSIS OF ALLOWANCE FOR DOUBTFUL ACCOUNTS

ABC Company, Inc.
Allowance for Doubtful Accounts

| Schedule C-6 Date |
| Prepared by DD 1/12/81 |
| Approved by JL 1/21/81 |

12/31/80

Balance 1/1/80	24000	PP
Provision for year	12072	V-1
Recoveries of accounts previously written off	567	C-6/2
	36639	
Write-offs for year	⟨9819⟩	C-6/3
Balance 12/31/80	26820	C-1
	①	

PP — Agrees with prior year's audit working papers.

① — Balance considered reasonable and adequate
to cover uncollectible items (C-6/4).

FIGURE 7-4

COMPARISON OF GENERAL AND ADMINISTRATIVE EXPENSES

ABC Company, Inc.
General and Administrative Expense
12/31/80

Schedule	*N-3*	Date
Prepared by	*DD*	*1/17/81*
Approved by	*JL*	*2/6/81*

Acct. No. 580

Sub-acct. No. and Description	Prior Year	Amount Current Year Budget	Amount Current Year Actual	Variance— Current Year Actual to— Prior Year	Variance— Current Year Actual to— Budget
581 Salaries	180000	205000	210000	30000	5000
582 Taxes	312800	331000	326982	14182	4018
583 Utilities	12644	12700	13216	522	516
584 Insurance	129620	128000	146812	17192	18812
585 Depreciation	2200	2300	2300	100	—0—
586 Supplies	4698	5000	4482	⟨216⟩	⟨518⟩
587 Tel. + Tel.	26640	28000	37877	11237	9877
588 Contributions	6000	6000	6000	—0—	—0—
589 Miscellaneous	7480	9000	19823	12343	10823
	682132	727000	767492	85360	40492

the type described in Chapter 4 is also frequently included in this type of working paper. An example of a reasonableness test for depreciation is given in Figure 7-5.

6. *Summary of procedures.* Another type of special purpose schedule *summarizes the results* of a specific audit procedure performed. Such schedules are particularly helpful to the reviewer because they generally give him a quick overview of a critical area. Important examples are the summary of the results of accounts receivable confirmation and the summary of inventory observations. The engagement partner can refer to such a schedule and determine, for example, that the coverage of inventories by actual observation was a certain percentage, such as 69 percent, and evaluate whether it is satisfactory.

7. *Examination of supporting documents.* A number of special purpose schedules are designed to *show detailed tests performed,* such as examination of documents during tests of transactions or cutoffs. These schedules show no totals, and do not tie into the general ledger because they document only the tests performed and the results found. The schedules must, however, state a definite positive or negative conclusion about the objective of the test. There are two schools of thought as to whether the details of all documents examined must be listed on these schedules. Many believe that only the exceptions found must be listed, and simply a statement as to scope and procedures will suffice regarding the others examined. Others believe that all items examined should be listed. An illustration of a list of exceptions type of schedule is included at the end of Chapter 9 in Figure 9-6 on page 305 for the verification of sales using statistical sampling.

8. *Informational.* This type of schedule contains information as opposed to audit evidence. These schedules include information for tax returns and SEC Form 10-K data, and data such as time budgets and the client's working hours, which are helpful in administration of the engagement.

9. *Outside documentation.* Finally, much of the content of the working papers consists of the outside documentation gathered by auditors, such as confirmation replies and copies of client agreements. Although not "schedules" in the real sense, these are indexed and interfiled and procedures are indicated on them in the same manner as the other schedules.

Client Assistance in Working Paper Preparation

The preparation of certain working papers by the client's employees is desirable as a means of *reducing the audit fee,* but a clear distinction must be made between preparation of working papers and accumulation of audit evidence. The client can assist the auditor by providing information and preparing schedules but the accuracy of the client-prepared schedules must be checked by the auditor. Common examples of working papers prepared by clients include the general ledger trial balance, trial

FIGURE 7-5

REASONABLENESS TEST FOR DEPRECIATION EXPENSE

ABC Company, Inc.
Over-all Test of Depreciation

Schedule _K-6_ Date
Prepared by _DD_ 2/2/82
Approved by _JL_ 2/10/82

12/31/81

Asset	Beginning Balance	Additions (Disposals) Net	Ending Balance	Average Rate	JR+Co. Estimate	Per Client
Buildings	462 000	238 284	700 284	5%	35 014	33 321
Mach+Equip.	331 290	41 253	372 543	10%	37 254	37 762
Furn+Fix.	129 767	5 873	135 640	10%	13 564	13 122
Autos	130 500	2 809	133 309	33⅓%	44 436	42 680
Lease Imp.	59 812	519	60 331	5%	3 016	3 118
					133 284	130 003
					130 003	
					3 281	

Net difference of $3,281 is not great. It is
probably due to the fact we assumed all net
additions received 6 mos. depreciation.

NOTE — See detailed tests K-6/1 through K-6/3.
Above assumption correct — total depreciation
expense is considered reasonable.

balances of accounts receivable and accounts payable, listings of current period additions to permanent assets, schedules of prepaid expenses, and lists of transactions making up selected revenue and expense accounts.

After a client-prepared working paper has been obtained and traced to the original source of the information, it is appropriate to treat it as if it had been prepared by the auditor. For example, assume the auditor receives a working paper from the client listing the current period acquisitions of manufacturing equipment. Typically, the auditor foots the working paper and traces the information to the general ledger and purchases journal to make sure the information on the schedule is accurate. The schedule is then used as the frame of reference to verify the recorded acquisitions by examining supporting documentation. As a part of the tests, the auditor makes notations on the working paper, draws conclusions about ·the reasonableness of the current period additions, and retains the working paper in his file.

Use of Tick Marks

Completed working papers must clearly indicate the audit work performed. This is accomplished in three ways: by a written statement in the form of a memorandum, by initialing the audit procedures in the audit program, and by notations directly on the working paper schedules. Notations on working papers are accomplished by the use of *tick marks,* which are *symbols* written adjacent to the detail on the body of the schedule. These notations must be clearly explained at the bottom of the working paper. For example, if the auditor has examined vendor's invoices and receiving reports in support of several fixed asset additions on a detailed schedule listing all fixed asset acquisitions, a tick mark (e.g., $\sqrt{}$) is used to indicate which additions were tested. At the bottom of the working paper, there must be an explanation of the tick mark (e.g., $\sqrt{}$—vendor's invoices and receiving reports were examined; no exceptions were found).

Many CPA firms use *standard tick marks,* which means that specific notations can only be used to indicate certain commonly performed procedures. The advantages of standard tick marks are the time saved by not having to explain the notations and the ease of review by superiors when everyone uses the same notation. An example of a standard tick mark is the use of the notation *TB* to indicate that a balance on a working paper has been traced to the trial balance.

Preparation of Working Papers

The proper preparation of schedules to document the audit evidence accumulated, the results found, and the conclusions reached is an important part of the audit. The auditor must recognize the circumstances requiring the need for a schedule and the appropriate design of schedules to be included in the files. Although the design depends on the objectives involved, working papers should possess certain characteristics:

1. Each working paper should be properly identified with such information as the client's name, the period covered, a description of the contents, the initials of the preparer, and the date of preparation, and it should be properly indexed and cross-referenced.
2. Each working paper should include sufficient information to fulfill the objectives for which it was designed. If the auditor is to properly prepare working papers, he must be clearly aware of his goals. For example, if a working paper is designed to list the detail and show the verification of support of a balance sheet account, such as prepaid insurance, it is essential that the detail on the working paper reconcile with the trial balance. In addition, the verification procedures should be indicated on the working paper.
3. All unanswered questions, exceptions, and inconsistencies existing in the working papers should be resolved and clearly explained.
4. The conclusions that were reached about the segment of the audit under consideration should be plainly stated.
5. The working papers should be sufficiently clear and self-explanatory to enable supervisory personnel to make an adequate review and evaluation without resorting to additional data to determine the reliability of the information.

Ownership of Working Papers

The working papers prepared during the engagement, including those prepared by the client for the auditor, are the *property of the auditor.* The only time anyone else, including the client, has a legal right to examine the papers is when they are subpoenaed by a court as legal evidence. At the completion of the engagement, working papers are retained on the CPA's premises for future reference. Many firms follow the practice of microfilming the working papers after several years to reduce storage costs.

Confidentiality of Working Papers

The need to maintain a confidential relationship with the client is expressed in Rule 301 of the Code of Professional Ethics, which states:

> A member shall not disclose any confidential information obtained in the course of a professional engagement except with the consent of the client.[1]

During the course of the examination, auditors obtain a considerable amount of information of a confidential nature, including officer salaries, product pricing and advertising plans, and product cost data. If auditors

---

[1] Code of Professional Ethics, p. 22.

divulged this information to outsiders or to client employees who have been denied access to the information, their relationship with management would be seriously strained. Furthermore, having access to the working papers would give employees an opportunity to alter information on the papers. For these reasons, care must be taken to protect the working papers at all times.

Ordinarily, the working papers can be provided to someone else only with the express permission of the client. This is the case even if a CPA sells his practice to another CPA firm. Permission is not required from the client, however, if the working papers are subpoenaed by a court or are used as part of a voluntary quality review program with other CPA firms.

REVIEW QUESTIONS

1. Select the one best response:
   Auditing working papers should not
   a. include any client-prepared papers or documents other than those prepared by the CPA or his assistant (s).
   b. be kept by the CPA after review and completion of the audit except for items required for the income-tax return or the permanent file.
   c. be submitted to the client to support the financial statements and to provide evidence of the audit work performed.
   d. by themselves be expected to provide sufficient support for the auditor's opinion.   (AICPA adapted)
2. List the purposes of working papers and explain why each purpose is important.
3. How can a CPA make the most effective use of the preceding year's audit programs in a recurring examination?   (AICPA adapted)
4. Define what is meant by a permanent file of working papers, and list several types of information typically included. Why doesn't the auditor include the contents of the permanent file with the current year's working papers?
5. Explain the purpose of a working trial balance. How does the use of lead schedules in the trial balance aid the auditor?
6. Distinguish between a reclassification entry and an adjusting entry. Give an example of each.
7. Distinguish between the following types of current period supporting schedules and state the purpose of each: analysis, trial balance, and comparison.
8. List the six types of schedules commonly used in support of an analysis, a trial balance, or a comparison schedule. State the purpose of each schedule.
9. Select the one best response:
   The actual operation of an internal control system may be most objectively evaluated by
   a. completing a questionnaire and flowchart related to the accounting system in the year under audit.
   b. review of the preceding year's audit workpapers to update the report of internal control evaluation.

c. selection of items processed by the system and determination of the presence or absence of errors and compliance deviations.

d. substantive tests of account balances based on the auditor's assessment of internal control strength. (AICPA adapted)

10. Explain why it is important for working papers to include each of the following: identification with the name of the client, description of the contents, period covered, initials of the preparer, date of the preparation, indexing and cross-referencing.

11. What type of working papers can be prepared by the client and used by the auditor as a part of the working paper file? When client assistance is obtained in preparing working papers, describe the proper precautions the auditor should take.

12. Define what is meant by a tick mark. What is the purpose of tick marks? What is a standard tick mark?

13. Why is it essential that the auditor not leave questions or exceptions in the working papers without an adequate explanation?

14. Who owns the working papers? Under what circumstances can they be used by other people?

15. A CPA sells his auditing practice to another CPA firm and includes all working papers as a part of the purchase price. Under what circumstances is this a violation of the Code of Professional Ethics?

16. Set up a working paper for Problem 29 on page 152. The working paper should include the client's name, the description of the working paper and other information of a "mechanical nature." In addition, the working paper should clearly identify the ratios you have calculated in a logical and understandable manner and the conclusion you have reached.

DISCUSSION QUESTIONS AND PROBLEMS

17. A major disagreement among CPA firms is whether it is legally advisable to keep review notes by supervisors as an internal part of the working papers.

Required:

a. What are the arguments in favor of maintaining the review notes in the working paper file?

b. What are the arguments in favor of destroying them?

18. An important part of every examination of financial statements is the preparation of audit working papers.

Required:

a. Discuss the relationship of audit working papers to each of the standards of field work.

b. You are instructing an inexperienced staffman on his first auditing assignment. He is to examine an account. An analysis of the account has been prepared by the client for inclusion in the audit working papers. Prepare a list of the comments, commentaries, and notations that the staffman should make or have made on the account analysis to provide an adequate working paper as evidence of his examination. (Do not include a description of auditing procedures applicable to the account.)

(AICPA adapted)

19. The preparation of working papers is an integral part of a CPA's examination of financial statements. On a recurring engagement a CPA reviews his audit programs and working papers from his prior examination while planning his current examination to determine their usefulness for the current engagement.

    Required:

    a. What are the purposes or functions of audit working papers?
    b. What records may be included in audit working papers?
    c. What factors affect the CPA's judgment of the type and content of the working papers for a particular engagement? (AICPA adapted)

20. In confirming accounts receivable on 12-31-X7, the auditor found fifteen discrepancies between the customer's records and the recorded amounts in the subsidiary ledger. A copy of all confirmations that had exceptions was turned over to the company controller to investigate the reason for the difference. He in turn had the bookkeeper perform the analysis. The bookkeeper analyzed each exception, determined its cause and prepared an elaborate working paper explaining each difference. Most of the differences in the bookkeeper's report indicated the errors were caused by timing differences in the client's and customer's records. The auditor reviewed the working paper and concluded that there were no material exceptions in accounts receivable.

    Two years subsequent to the audit it was determined that the bookkeeper had stolen thousands of dollars in the past three years by taking cash and overstating accounts receivable. In a lawsuit by the client against the CPA, an examination of the auditor's 12-31-X7 accounts receivable working papers, which were subpoenaed by the court, indicated that one of the explanations in the bookkeeper's analysis of the exceptions was fictitious. The analysis stated the error was caused by a sales allowance granted to the customer for defective merchandise the day before the end of the year. The difference was actually caused by the bookkeeper's theft.

    Required:

    a. What are the legal issues involved in this situation? What should the auditor use as a defense in the event he is sued?
    b. What was the CPA's deficiency in conducting the audit of accounts receivable?

21. James Garold, CPA, was engaged for several years by the Bond Corporation to make annual audits. As a result of a change in control, the corporation discontinued the engagement of Garold and retained another firm of accountants. The Bond Corporation thereupon demanded of Garold surrender of all working papers prepared by the accounting firm in making audits for the corporation. Garold refused on the ground that the working papers were their property. The corporation brought legal action to recover the working papers. State briefly what the law is, in general, as to ownership of accountants' working papers. (AICPA adapted)

22. Ron Horman, a CPA who has been practicing alone, decides to "sell his

practice" to Bloomquist. As a part of the transaction Bloomquist asks Horman to turn over to him all his files and working papers. One client does not want Bloomquist as his accountant and objects to the transfer of the files and working papers relating to his affairs.

Required:

Is the sale of the practice acceptable? Discuss the legal and ethical issues involved.   (AICPA adapted)
23. List the deficiencies in the working paper for the ABC Company in Figure 7-6. For each deficiency, state how the working paper could be improved.

FIGURE 7-6

NOTES RECEIVABLE WORKING PAPER

Schedule	Date
Prepared by cJD	1/21/82
Approved by PP	2/5/82

Acct. 110

	Maker					
	Apex Co.	Ajax, Inc.	J.J. Co.	P. Smith	Martin-Peterson	Tent Co.
Date:						
Made	6/15/80	11/21/80	11/1/80	7/26/81	5/12/80	9/3/81
Due	6/15/82	Demand	$200/mo.	$1000/mo.	Demand	$400/mo.
Face amount	5000<	3591<	13,180<	25,000<	2100<	12,000<
Value of Security	none⑨	none	24,000⑥	30,000⑦	none	10,000⑧
Notes:						
Beg. bal.	4000ᴾᵂᴾ	3591ᴾᵂᴾ	12,780ᴾᵂᴾ	—	2100ᴾᵂᴾ	—
Additions				25,000		12,000
Payments	<1000>	<3591>	<2400>	<5000>	<2100>	<1600>
End bal.						
① Current	3000✓	—	2400✓	12,000	—	4800
② Long-term	—	—	7980	8000	—	5600
③ Total	3000C	—0—	10,380C	20,000C	—0—	10,400C
	~	~	~	~	~	~
Interest:						
Rate	5%	5%	5%	5%	5%	6%
Pd. to date	none	paid	12/31/81	9/30/81	paid	11/30/81
Beg. bal.	104ᴾᵂᴾ	—0—ᴾᵂᴾ	24ᴾᵂᴾ	—0—	—0—ᴾᵂᴾ	—0—
④ Earned	175✓	102✓	577✓	468✓	105✓	162✓
Received	—0—	<102>	<601>	<200>	<105>	<108>
⑤ Accrued at 12/31/81	279	—0—	—0—	268	—0—	54
	~	~	~	~	~	~

<✓ — Tested
PWP — Agrees with prior year's working papers.
① Total of $22,200 agrees with working trial balance.
② Total of 21,584 agrees with working trial balance.
③ Total of $43,780 agrees with working trial balance.
④ Total of $1,589 agrees with miscellaneous income analysis in operations W/P.
⑤ Total of $601 agrees with A/R lead schedule.
(Over for remainder of legend.)

8

Audit
of the
Sales and Collection Cycle

OVERVIEW

This chapter presents information on the nature of the sales and collection cycle, primary internal control considerations for the cycle, and tests
of transactions procedures used for verifying sales, cash receipts, sales
returns and allowances, and the charge off of uncollectible accounts. The
intent in this chapter is to emphasize the methodology for deciding on
the appropriate evidence to accumulate for testing transactions in the
sales and collection cycle. An illustration of an audit program for sales and
cash receipts and how it was developed is included in Appendix B at
the end of the chapter. Audit procedures relating to the direct tests of
accounts receivable, allowance for uncollectable accounts, and bad debts
expense are the subject of Chapter 10.

The overall objective in the audit of the sales and collection cycle is to
evaluate whether the account balances affected by the cycle are fairly
presented in accordance with generally accepted accounting principles.
The following are typical accounts included in the sales and collection
cycle:

- Sales
- Sales Returns and Allowances
- Bad Debts Expense
- Trade Discounts Taken
- Trade Accounts and Notes Receivable

- Allowance for Uncollectible Accounts
- Cash in the Bank (debits for cash receipts)

The names and the nature of the accounts may of course vary depending upon the industry and client involved. There are differences in account titles for a service industry, such as medical clinics, a retail company, and an insurance company but regardless of the industry or account titles, the basic concepts are the same. To provide a frame of reference for understanding the material, a wholesale merchandising company is assumed for this chapter.

A brief summary of the way accounting information flows through the various accounts in the sales and collection cycle is illustrated by the use of T-accounts in Figure 8-1. This figure shows that with the exception of cash sales, every transaction and amount ultimately is included in the accounts receivable or allowance for doubtful accounts balances. For the purpose of simplicity the assumption is made that the same control procedures are used for both cash and credit sales.

For the most part, the audit of the sales and collection cycle can be performed independently of the audit of other cycles and subjectively combined with the other parts of the audit as the evidence accumulation process proceeds. The auditor must keep in mind that the concept of materiality requires him to consider the combination of errors in all parts of the audit before making a final judgment on the fair presentation in the financial statements. This is done by stopping at various times throughout the engagement and integrating the parts of the audit.

NATURE OF THE SALES AND COLLECTION CYCLE

Flow of Transactions

The sales and collection cycle involves the decisions and processes necessary for the transfer of the ownership of goods to customers after goods are made available for sale. It begins with a request for goods by a customer and ends with the conversion of material or service into an account receivable, and ultimately into cash.

The sales transaction cycle for a typical wholesale company is illustrated in Figure 8-2 with an *overview flowchart.* This type of flowchart is meant to aid readers in understanding the sales and collection function rather than to serve as a means of evaluating internal control. Therefore it does not include all documents in the system nor all internal controls. A detailed flowchart for evaluating internal control is illustrated in Figure 8-6 on page 254.

Documents and Records

Several important documents and records are typically used in the sales and collection cycle:

Customer order—a request for merchandise by a customer. It may be

FIGURE 8-1

ACCOUNTS IN THE SALES AND COLLECTION TRANSACTION CYCLE

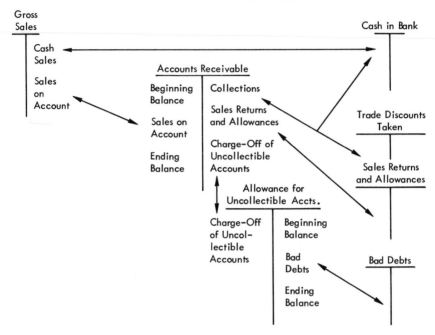

received by telephone, letter, a printed form that has been sent to prospective and existing customers, salesmen, or in other ways.

Sales order—a document for recording the description, quantity, and related information for goods ordered by a customer. This is frequently used to show credit approval and authorization for shipment.

Bill of lading or other shipping document—a document prepared at the time of shipment, indicating the description of the merchandise, the quantity shipped, and other relevant data. Formally, it is a written contract of the receipt and shipment of goods between the seller and the carrier. It is also used as a signal to bill the customer. The original is sent to the customer and one or more copies are retained.

Sales invoice—a document indicating the description and quantity of goods sold, the price including freight, insurance, terms, and other relevant data. It is the method of indicating to the customer the amount of a sale and due date of a payment. The original is sent to the customer and one or more copies are retained. It is also the basic document for recording sales in the accounting records.

Sales journal—a journal for recording sales. It usually indicates gross sales for different classifications, such as product lines, the entry to accounts receivable, and miscellaneous debits and credits. It is common to include only daily summaries in the journals. A copy of each day's duplicate sales invoices is retained, and these copies are totaled to equal

FIGURE 8-2

OVERVIEW FLOWCHART OF THE SALES AND COLLECTION
CYCLE OF A WHOLESALE COMPANY

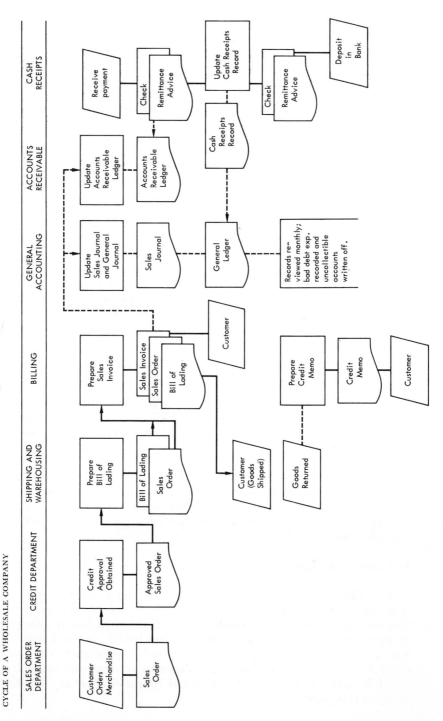

233

the total sales recorded in the journal. Totals of details in the journal are typically posted to the general ledger monthly.

Credit memo—a document indicating a reduction in the amount due from a customer because of returned goods or an allowance granted. It often takes the same general form as a sales invoice, but it supports reductions in accounts receivable rather than increases.

Sales returns and allowances journal—a journal that is basically the same as the sales journal for recording sales returns and allowances. Frequently the sales journal is designed to accommodate such transactions.

Remittance advice—a document that accompanies the sales invoice mailed to the customer and can be returned to the seller with the cash payment. It is used to indicate the customer name, the sales invoice number, and the amount of the invoice when the payment is received. If the customer fails to include the remittance advice with his payment, it is common for the person opening the mail to prepare one at that time. A remittance advice is used to permit the immediate deposit of cash and to improve control over the custody of assets.

Cash receipts journal—a journal for recording cash receipts from collections, cash sales, and all other cash receipts. It indicates total cash received, the credit to accounts receivable at the gross amount of the original sale, trade discounts taken, and other debits and credits. The daily entries in the cash receipts journal are supported by remittance advices.

Uncollectible account authorization forms—a document used internally, indicating authority to write an account receivable off as uncollectible.

Accounts receivable subsidiary ledger—a subsidiary ledger for recording individual sales, cash receipts, and sales returns and allowances for each customer. The total of the individual account balances in the subsidiary ledger equals the total balance of accounts receivable in the general ledger.

Monthly statement—a document sent to each customer indicating the beginning balance of accounts receivable, the amount and date of each sale, cash payments received, credit memos issued, and the ending balance due. It is, in essence, a copy of the customer's portion of the accounts receivable subsidiary ledger.

Functions in the Cycle

An understanding of the functions that take place in a typical client's organization for the sales and collection cycle is useful for understanding how an audit of the cycle is conducted. Students often find it difficult to envision which documents exist in any given audit area and how they flow through the client's organization. It is unlikely for anyone to understand the audit process without an understanding of accounting systems. The following functions for the sales and collection cycle are examined briefly at this point:

1. Processing customer orders
2. Granting credit
3. Shipping goods
4. Billing customers and recording sales
5. Processing and recording cash receipts
6. Processing and recording sales returns and allowances
7. Charging off uncollectible accounts receivable
8. Providing for bad debts

Processing Customer Orders. The request for goods by a customer is the starting point for the entire cycle. Legally, it is an offer to buy goods under specified terms. The receipt of a customer order results in the fairly immediate creation of a sales order and a sales invoice.

Granting Credit. Before goods are shipped, a properly authorized person must *approve credit* to the customer for sales on account. Weak practices in credit approval frequently result in excessive bad debts and accounts receivable that may be uncollectible. For most firms, an indication of credit approval on the sales order is the approval to ship the goods.

Shipping Goods. This critical function is the first point in the cycle where company assets are given up. Most companies recognize sales when goods are shipped. A shipping document is prepared at the time of shipment. This document, which is frequently a multicopy bill of lading, is essential to the proper billing of shipments to customers. Companies that maintain perpetual inventory records also update them by the use of shipping records.

Billing Customers and Recording Sales. Since the billing of customers is the means by which the customer is informed of the amount due for the goods, it must be done correctly and on a timely basis. The most important aspects of billing are to be sure all shipments made have been billed, no shipment has been billed more than once, and each one is billed for the proper amount. Billing at the proper amount is dependent upon charging the customer for the quantity shipped at the authorized price. The authorized price includes consideration of freight charges, insurance, and terms of payment. The proper recording of sales in the sales journal and the accounts receivable subsidiary ledger is also an important part of billing customers. Errors in any part of the billing process can result in significant errors in the financial statements.

Processing and Recording Cash Receipts. The preceding four functions are necessary for getting the goods into the hands of customers, properly billing them, and reflecting the information in the accounting records. The remaining functions involve the collection and recording of cash and the other means of reducing accounts receivable.

In processing and recording cash receipts, the most important concern is the possibility of the theft of cash. Theft can occur before receipts are entered in the records or at a later point in time. The most important consideration in the handling of cash receipts is that all cash must be recorded in the cash receipts journal and subsidiary ledger and deposited in the bank at the proper amount on a timely basis. Remittance advices are important for this purpose.

Processing and Recording Sales Returns and Allowances. When a customer is dissatisfied with the goods, the seller frequently accepts the return of the goods or grants a reduction in the charges. Returns and allowances must be correctly and promptly recorded in the sales returns and allowances journal as well as in the subsidiary record. *Credit memos* are normally issued for returns and allowances to aid in maintaining control and to facilitate record keeping.

Charging Off Uncollectible Accounts Receivable. Regardless of the aggressiveness of credit departments, it is not unusual if some customers do not pay their bills. When the company concludes that an amount is no longer collectible, it must be charged off. Typically, this occurs after a customer files bankruptcy or the account is turned over to a collection agency. Proper accounting requires an adjustment for these uncollectible accounts.

Providing for Bad Debts. The provision for bad debts must be sufficient to allow for the current period sales that the company will be unable to collect in the future. For most companies the provision represents a residual, resulting from management's year-end adjustment of the allowance for uncollectible accounts.

INTERNAL CONTROLS AND AUDIT
TESTS FOR SALES

All of the types of tests used in the conduct of the audit are used for for the sales and collection cycle, and it is important to keep their interrelationships in mind. First, *analytical tests* are used to consider overall fairness of the balances in the accounts affected by the cycle. Analytical tests should be performed sufficiently early in the audit so that they can be used as an aid in understanding the client and isolating problem areas for further investigation. On the other hand, it is desirable to wait until after the balance sheet date to do these tests so that the full year's financial information will be reflected in the ratios and trends. Since tests of the system are frequently performed on an interim basis, it is common to perform analytical tests after the tests of transactions but before most of the direct tests of financial balances. This practice is reflected in the text by including analytical tests as a part of direct tests of balances rather than as a part of tests of transactions.

Second, significant assurance of the fair presentation of accounts in the cycle is obtained through the *study and evaluation of internal control,* including *tests of transactions.* If the controls are good and compliance tests indicate the procedures are being followed, this is evidence of fair presentation. If substantive tests of transactions disclose no monetary errors, further evidence of fair presentation is obtained.

Finally, assurance is gained through *direct tests of financial balances* by the use of substantive procedures. These procedures are designed primarily to directly test the ending balance sheet accounts, but errors found in the balance sheet accounts will indicate the types of errors taking place in the recording of transactions.

For the two primary areas, sales and cash receipts, the audit procedures are studied in the tests of transactions framework discussed in Chapter 6. This approach is meant to facilitate an understanding of the concepts involved in performing the tests by concentrating on the objectives rather than procedures. The problem of how to determine the proper sample size for tests of the system is studied in Chapter 9, and the direct tests of the financial statement balances for the sales and collection transaction cycle are the subject of Chapter 10.

Summary of Objectives, Controls, and Tests for Sales Transactions

Figure 8-3 on pages 238 and 239 is a summary of the application of the concepts discussed in previous chapters to the audit of sales. This summary integrates internal control and audit objectives with key internal controls and tests of transactions. Its most important points are discussed in detail in the following pages.

Internal Control and Audit Objectives. The objectives are included in the framework developed in Chapter 6. Although certain controls and audit procedures satisfy more than one objective, it is convenient to consider each objective separately to facilitate a better understanding of the entire audit process.

Key Controls. The internal controls in sales are designed to achieve the seven objectives discussed in Chapter 6. If the controls necessary to satisfy any one of the objectives are inadequate, the likelihood of errors related to that objective are enhanced, regardless of the controls for the other objectives.

Compliance Tests. For each internal control there exists a related compliance test to verify its effectiveness. In most audits it is relatively easy to determine the nature of the compliance tests from the nature of the control. For example, if the internal control is to initial customer orders after they have been approved for credit, the compliance test is to examine the customer order for a proper initial.

Substantive Tests. In deciding on substantive tests of transactions, some procedures are commonly employed on every audit regardless of the circumstances, whereas others are dependent upon the adequacy of the controls and the results of compliance tests. We examine more

Figure 8-3

Summary of Objectives, Controls, and Tests for Sales Transactions

Internal Control and Audit Objectives	Key Internal Controls	Common Compliance Tests	Common Substantive Tests
Recorded sales are for shipments actually made to nonfictitious customers.	• Recording of sales is supported by authorized shipping documents and approved customer orders. • Sales invoices are prenumbered and properly accounted for. • Monthly statements are sent to customers; complaints receive independent follow-up.	• Examine copies of sales invoices for supporting bills of lading and customers' orders. • Account for integrity of numerical sequences of sales invoices. • Observe whether statements are mailed and examine customer correspondence files.	• Trace sales journal entries to bills of lading. • Trace shipments on bills of lading to entry of shipment in perpetual inventory records. • Trace sales journal entries to sales orders for credit approval and shipping authorization. • Trace credit entries in accounts receivable subsidiary ledger to valid source. • Review the sales journal, general ledger, and accounts receivable subsidiary ledger for large or unusual items.
Sales transactions are properly authorized.	• Specific or general authorization must occur, through proper procedures, at three key points: —Granting of credit before shipment takes place —Shipment of goods —Determination of prices and terms, freight and discounts.	• Examine documents for proper approval at these three points.	• Compare prices on sales invoices with authorized price lists or properly executed contracts.
Existing sales transactions are recorded.	• Shipping documents (e.g., bills of lading) are prenumbered and accounted for. • Sales invoices are prenumbered and accounted for.	• Account for integrity of numerical sequence of shipping documents. • Account for integrity of numerical sequence of sales invoices.	• Trace shipping documents to resultant sales invoice and entry into sales journal and accounts receivable ledger.

Summary of Objectives, Controls, and Tests for Sales Transactions—*(Cont.)*

Internal Control and Audit Objectives	Key Internal Controls	Common Compliance Tests	Common Substantive Tests
Recorded sales are for the amount of goods ordered and are correctly billed and recorded.	○ Internal verification of invoice preparation and posting by an independent person.	• Examine indication of internal verification on affected documents.	• Recompute information on sales invoices. • Trace entries in sales journal to sales invoices and posting to accounts receivable ledger. • Trace details on sales invoices to shipping records, price lists, and customers' orders.
Sales transactions are properly classified.	• Use of adequate chart of accounts. • Internal review and verification.	• Review chart of accounts for adequacy. • Examine indication of internal verification on affected documents.	• Examine documents supporting sales transactions for proper classification.
Sales are recorded on a timely basis.	• Procedures requiring billing and recording of sales on a daily basis as close to time of occurrence as possible. • Internal verification.	• Examine documents for unbilled shipments and unrecorded sales at any point in time. • Examine indication of internal verification on affected documents.	• Compare dates of recorded sales transactions with dates on shipping records.
Sales transactions are properly included in the subsidiary records and are correctly summarized.	○ Segregation of duties for recording of the sales journal and the accounts receivable ledger. • Regular monthly statements to customers. • Internal verification.	• Observe procedures. • Observe whether statements are mailed. • Examine indication of internal verification.	• Tests of clerical accuracy, e.g., footing journals and tracing postings to general ledger and accounts receivable ledger.

thoroughly some of the audit procedures employed when internal controls are inadequate in a later section.

Internal Controls and Compliance Tests

In this section we discuss the key internal controls and related tests of compliance included in Figure 8-3 in greater detail. For convenience they are discussed in terms of individual internal controls rather than internal control objectives.

Proper Record Keeping Procedures. Since each company has a somewhat unique system of originating, processing, and recording transactions, it may be difficult to evaluate whether its procedures are designed for maximum control; nevertheless, adequate record keeping procedures must exist before most of the internal control objectives can be met. Some companies, for example, automatically prepare a multicopy prenumbered sales invoice at the time a customer order is received. Copies of this document are used to approve credit, authorize shipment, record the number of units shipped, and bill customers. Under this system, there is almost no chance of the failure to bill a customer if all invoices are accounted for periodically. Under a different system, where the sales invoice is prepared only after a shipment has been made, the likelihood of the failure to bill a customer is much higher, unless some compensating control exists.

Proper compliance procedures for testing record keeping, including the adequacy of documents and the timeliness of recording, depend on the nature of the control being relied upon. For example, if the client requires that a duplicate sales invoice be attached to every shipping order to prevent failing to bill a customer for shipped goods, a useful compliance test is to account for a sequence of shipping orders and examine each one to make sure a duplicate sales invoice is attached.

Adequate Prenumbered Documents. The use of prenumbered documents is meant to prevent both the *failure* to bill or record sales and the occurrence of *duplicate* billings and recordings. Of course it doesn't do much good to have prenumbered documents unless they are properly accounted for. An example of the use of this control is where the billing clerk files a copy of all shipping documents in sequential order after each shipment is billed, with someone else periodically accounting for all numbers and investigating the reason for any missing documents.

A common compliance test for this control is to account for a sequence of various types of documents, such as duplicate sales invoices selected from the sales journal, watching for omitted and duplicate numbers, or invoices outside of the normal sequence. This test simultaneously provides evidence of both the "validity" and "failure to record" objectives.

Monthly Statements Are Mailed. The mailing of monthly statements by someone who has no responsibility for handling cash or preparing the sales and accounts receivable records is a useful control because it encourages a response from customers if the balance is improperly stated. For maximum effectiveness, all disagreements about the balance in the account should be directed to a designated official who has no responsibility for handling cash or recording sales or accounts receivable.

The auditor's observations of the mailing of statements by a properly designated person and the examination of customer correspondence files are useful compliance procedures for testing whether monthly statements have been sent to customers.

Proper Authorization. The auditor is concerned about authorization at *three key points*: credit must be properly authorized before a sale takes place; goods should be shipped only after proper authorization; and prices, including base terms, freight, and discounts, must be authorized. The first two of these controls are meant to prevent the loss of company assets by shipping to fictitious customers or those who will fail to pay for the goods. Price authorization is meant to make sure the sale is billed at the price set by company policy.

It is easy to test for compliance with the system for authorization by examining documents for proper approval of each of these three types.

Adequate Segregation of Duties. Proper segregation of duties within accounting is useful to prevent various types of errors, both fraudulent and unintentional. For example, if the sales register is prepared independently of the accounts receivable subsidiary records and the subsidiary record is reconciled with the control account periodically by someone independent of the persons preparing the records, an automatic cross-check exists. For the prevention of fraudulent errors, it is important that anyone responsible for recording the sales journal or subsidiary records be denied access to cash. It is also desirable to separate the credit-granting function from the sales function, since credit checks are intended to offset the natural tendency of sales personnel to optimize volume even at the expense of high bad debt write-offs.

The appropriate compliance tests for segregation of duties are ordinarily restricted to the auditor's observations of activities and discussions with personnel. For example, it is possible to observe whether the billing clerk also prepares the subsidiary ledger or has access to cash by opening incoming mail.

Internal Verification Procedures. The use of internal auditors or other independent persons for checking the processing and recording of sales transactions is essential for fulfilling each of the seven internal control objectives. The following are typical internal verification procedures for each objective.

The examination of internal auditors' reports and initials of independent persons on documents they have tested are examples of compliance procedures the external auditor can use.

Internal Control Objective	Example of an Internal Verification Procedure
1. Recorded sales are valid.	Account for a sequence of sales invoices and examine supporting documentation.
2. Sales are properly authorized.	Examine Dun and Bradstreet reports for customers to determine if credit was approved in accordance with company policy.
3. Existing sales transactions are recorded.	Account for a sequence of bills of lading and trace them to the sales journal.
4. Recorded sales are properly valued.	Compare quantity on sales invoices with shipping document records.
5. Recorded sales are properly classified.	Compare supporting documents for recorded sales with the chart of accounts.
6. Sales are recorded on a timely basis.	Examine Dun and Bradstreet reports for possession of the billing clerk to determine whether shipments that should already have been billed are included.
7. Sales transactions are properly included in the subsidiary records and correctly summarized.	Trace sales transactions from the sales journal to the subsidiary ledgers.

Substantive Tests of Sales Transactions

Determining the proper substantive tests of transactions procedures for sales is relatively difficult because they vary considerably depending on the circumstances. In subsequent paragraphs, the procedures frequently *not* performed are emphasized, since they are the ones requiring an audit decision. The substantive procedures are discussed in the same order in which they were included in Figure 8-3. It should be noted that some procedures fulfill multiple objectives.

Recorded Sales Are Valid. For this objective, the auditor is concerned with the possibility of *two types of errors:* sales being included in the journals for which no shipment was made and, alternatively, shipments being made to fictitious customers and recorded as sales. As might be imagined, the inclusion of invalid sales is rare, but the potential consequences are significant.

The appropriate substantive tests for detecting invalid transactions depend upon where the auditor believes the errors are likely to take place. Normally, the auditor tests for invalid sales only if he believes a control weakness exists; therefore, the nature of the tests depends upon the nature of the weakness. As a test of recorded sales for which there were no actual shipments, the auditor can trace from selected entries in the sales journal to make sure a related copy of the bill of lading and other supporting documents exist. If the auditor is also concerned about the possibility of a fictitious duplicate copy of a bill of lading, it may be necessary to trace the amounts to the perpetual inventory records as a test of whether inventory was reduced. A test of the possibility of a shipment to a fictitious customer is to examine the sales orders corresponding to a sales transaction entry in the sales journal for the existence of credit approval and shipping authorization. Another effective approach to auditing for invalid sales transactions is to trace the *credit* for the accounts receivable in the subsidiary ledger to its source. If the receivable was actually collected in cash or the goods returned, there must have originally been a valid sale. If the credit was for a bad debt charge-off or a credit memo, or if the account was still unpaid at the time of the audit, intensive follow-up by examining shipping and customer order documents is required, since each of these could indicate a fictitious sales transaction.

It should be kept in mind that *the ordinary audit is not primarily intended to detect fraud.* The preceding substantive tests should be necessary only if the auditor is particularly concerned about the occurrence of fraud errors due to inadequate controls.

In addition to detailed tests, overall reasonableness tests must be made to make sure there are no transactions that appear suspicious on the surface. Auditors typically test a small percentage of the population and therefore are unlikely to include unusual transactions in the sample. Overall review tests help the auditor find these transactions for further investigation. Examples of sales transactions frequently requiring further investigation are unusually large sales, the sale of a building or equipment, or sales to officers, directors, or affiliates. In addition, the auditor should review the general ledger and subsidiary records for unusual debits and credits or extraordinary amounts.

Sales Are Properly Authorized. It is normally necessary to test, by substantive procedures, whether the company's general credit, shipping, and pricing policies are being properly followed in the day-to-day operations. This is especially important with regard to the pricing of sales. Substantive pricing tests are done by comparing the actual price charged for different products, including freight and terms, with the price list authorized by management. If product prices are negotiated on an individual sale basis, the tests usually involve determining that the proper authorization by the sales manager or other appropriate official has occurred. Also, contracts which exist are examined, and in some cases, even confirmed directly with the customer. Procedures to test pricing are normally necessary regardless of the quality of the controls, but the sample size can be reduced if the controls are adequate.

Existing Sales Transactions Are Recorded. In many audits, no substantive transaction tests are made for this objective on the grounds that overstatements of assets are a greater concern in the audit of sales transactions than their understatement. If there are inadequate controls, as is likely in the case where no independent internal tracing from shipping documents to the sales journal takes place, substantive tests are necessary.

An effective procedure to test for unbilled shipments is to trace selected shipping documents from a file in the shipping department to related duplicate sales invoices, the sales journal, and accounts receivable subsidiary ledgers. To conduct a meaningful test using this procedure, the auditor must be confident that all shipping documents are included in the file. This can be done by accounting for a numerical sequence of the documents.

It is important that auditors understand the difference between tracing from source documents to the journals and tracing from the journals back to supporting documents. The former is a test for *omitted transactions*, whereas the latter is a test for *invalid transactions*.

Recorded Sales Are Properly Valued. The correct valuation of sales transactions concerns shipping the amount of goods ordered, correctly billing for the amount of goods shipped, and correctly recording the amount billed in the accounting records. Substantive tests to make sure that each of these aspects of valuation is correct are ordinarily conducted in every audit.

Typical substantive tests include recomputing information in the accounting records to verify whether it is proper. A common approach is to start with entries in the sales journal and compare the total of selected transactions with accounts receivable subsidiary ledgers and duplicate sales invoices. Prices on the duplicate sales invoices are normally compared with an approved price list, extensions and footings are recomputed, and the products listed on the invoices are compared with shipping records for description, quantity, and customer identification. Frequently, customer orders and sales orders are also examined for the same information.

The comparison of compliance and substantive tests for the valuation objective is a good example of the saving in audit time that can result when effective internal controls exist. It is obvious that the compliance test for this objective takes almost no time because it involves examining only an initial or other evidence of internal verification. Since the sample size for substantive tests can be reduced if this control is effective, there can be a significant saving from performing the compliance test due to its lower cost.

Recorded Sales Are Properly Classified. Charging the correct account is less of a problem in sales than in some other transaction cycles, but it is still of some concern. When there are cash and credit sales, it is important not to debit accounts receivable for a cash sale, or credit sales for collection of a receivable. It is also important not to classify sales of operating assets, such as buildings, as sales. For those companies using more than one sales classification, such as companies issuing segmented earnings statements, proper classification is essential.

It is common to test sales for proper classification as part of testing for valuation. The auditor examines supporting documents to determine the proper classification of a given transaction and compares this with the actual account to which it is charged.

Sales Are Recorded on a Timely Basis. It is important that sales be billed and recorded as soon after shipment takes place as possible to prevent the unintentional omission of transactions from the records and to make sure sales are recorded in the proper period. At the same time that substantive valuation procedures are being performed, it is common to compare the date on selected bills of lading or other shipping documents with the date on related duplicate sales invoices, the sales journal, and subsidiary ledgers. Significant differences indicate a potential cutoff problem.

Sales Transactions Are Properly Included in the Subsidiary Records and Correctly Summarized. The proper inclusion of all sales transactions in the accounts receivable subsidiary ledger is essential because the accuracy of these records affects the client's ability to collect outstanding receivables. Similarly, the sales journal must be correctly footed and posted to the general ledger if the financial statements are to be correct. In every audit, it is necessary to perform some clerical accuracy tests by footing the journals and tracing the totals and details to the general ledger and subsidiary records. Only the sample size is affected by the quality of the internal controls. Tracing from the sales journal to subsidiary records is typically done as a part of fulfilling other objectives, but footing the sales journal and tracing the totals to the general ledger is done as a separate procedure.

Summary

The association of compliance and substantive procedures with individual audit objectives as illustrated in Figure 8-3 is an effective means of developing audit procedures for testing sales. But the actual performance of the procedures can be done more efficiently by combining the procedures that are used for more than one objective and involve examining the same documents.

One of the auditor's objectives should be to structure his tests so that, as a whole, they will be performed as efficiently as possible. However, in combining procedures that serve multiple objectives, great care must be taken to assure that all objectives are being fulfilled by the procedures. The process of combining audit procedures is illustrated in the appendix at the end of the chapter.

AUDIT PROCEDURES FOR PROCESSING OF SALES RETURNS AND ALLOWANCES

The audit objectives and the client's methods of controlling errors are essentially the same for processing credit memos as the ones described for sales, with two important differences. The first relates to *materiality*. In many instances sales returns and allowances are so immaterial that they can be ignored in the audit altogether. The second major difference relates to *emphasis on objectives*. For sales returns and allowances, the primary emphasis is normally on testing the validity of recorded transactions as a means of uncovering any diversion of cash from the collection of accounts receivable that has been covered up by a fictitious sales return or allowance.

Naturally, the other objectives should not be ignored. But because the objectives and methodology for auditing sales returns and allowances are essentially the same as for sales, we will not include a detailed study of the area. The reader should be able to go through the same logic process used for sales to arrive at suitable controls, compliance tests to test the controls, and substantive tests to verify the amounts.

INTERNAL CONTROLS AND AUDIT TESTS FOR CASH RECEIPTS

The audit procedures for verifying cash receipts are developed around the same framework used for sales; i.e., considering internal control and audit objectives, key internal controls for each objective, compliance tests for each control, and substantive tests for each objective. As in all other audit areas, the compliance tests depend on the controls the auditor intends to rely upon to reduce substantive tests and the substantive tests depend on the results of the compliance tests and the other considerations in the audit. Thus it is inappropriate to think of a single audit program for cash receipts as being useful for all engagements.

Key internal controls, common compliance tests, and common substantive tests to satisfy each of the internal control and audit objectives for cash receipts are listed in Figure 8-4. Since this summary follows the same format as the previous one for sales, no further explanation of its meaning is necessary.

A detailed discussion of the internal controls, compliance tests, and substantive tests such as the one included for the audit of sales is not included for cash receipts. Instead, the audit procedures that are most likely to be misunderstood by students of auditing are explained in more detail.

An essential part of the auditor's responsibility in auditing cash receipts is the identifying of weaknesses in the system that enhance the likelihood of fraud. In expanding on Figure 8-4 the emphasis will be on those audit procedures that are designed primarily for the discovery of fraud. However, the reader should keep in mind throughout this discussion that the nonfraud procedures included in Figure 8-4 are the auditor's primary responsibility. Those procedures that are not discussed in the following paragraphs are omitted only because their purpose and the methodology for applying them should be apparent from their description.

Procedures Designed to Determine Whether All Cash Received Was Recorded

The most difficult type of cash defalcation for the auditor to detect is that which occurs *before the cash is recorded* in the cash receipts journal or other cash listing. For example, if a grocery store clerk takes cash and

Figure 8-4

Summary of Objectives, Controls, and Tests for Cash Receipts Transactions

Internal Control and Audit Objectives	Key Internal Controls	Common Compliance Tests	Common Substantive Tests
Recorded cash receipts are for funds actually received by the company.	• Separation of duties between handling cash and record keeping. • Independent reconciliation of bank accounts.	• Observation. • Observation.	• Trace from cash receipts journal to bank statements. • Proof of cash receipts. • Review the cash receipts journal, general ledger, and accounts receivable subsidiary ledger for large or unusual amounts.
Cash discounts are authorized.	• A policy on granting cash discounts must exist. • Approval of cash discounts.	• Discussion with management. • Examine remittance advice for proper approval.	• Examine remittance advices and sales invoices to determine whether discounts allowed are consistent with company policy.
Cash received is recorded in the cash receipts journal.	• Separation of duties between handling cash and record keeping. • Use of prenumbered remittance advices or a prelisting of cash. • Immediate endorsement of incoming checks. • Internal verification of the recording of cash receipts. • Regular monthly statements to customers.	• Discussion with personnel and observation. • Account for numerical sequence or examine prelisting. • Observation. • Observation • Examine indication of internal verification.	• Trace from remittances or prelisting to cash receipts journal.

Summary of Objectives, Controls, and Tests for Cash Receipts Transactions—*(Cont.)*

Internal Control and Audit Objectives	Key Internal Controls	Common Compliance Tests	Common Substantive Tests
Recorded cash receipts are deposited at the amount received.	• Same as objective 3 above. • Regular reconciliation of bank accounts.	• Same as above. • Review monthly bank reconciliations.	• Proof of cash receipts.
Cash receipts are properly classified.	• Use of adequate chart of accounts. • Internal review and verification.	• Review chart of accounts. • Examine indication of internal verification.	• Examine documents supporting cash receipts for proper classification.
Cash receipts are recorded on a timely basis.	• Procedure requiring recording of cash receipts on a daily basis. • Internal verification.	• Observe unrecorded cash at any point of time. • Examine indication of internal verification.	• Compare dates of deposits with dates in the cash receipts journal and prelisting of cash receipts.
Cash receipts are properly included in the subsidiary records and are correctly summarized.	• Segregation of duties for recording of the cash receipts journal and accounts receivable ledger. • Regular monthly statements to customers. • Internal verification.	• Observation. • Observation. • Examine indication of internal verification.	• Tests of clerical accuracy, e.g., footing journals and tracing postings to general ledger and accounts receivable ledger.

intentionally fails to register the receipt of cash on the cash register, it is extremely difficult to subsequently discover the theft. To prevent this type of fraud, internal controls such as those included in the third objective in Figure 8-4 are implemented by many companies. The type of control will of course depend on the type of business. For example, the controls for a retail store where the cash is received by the same person who sells the merchandise and rings up the cash receipts should be different from the controls for a company where all receipts are received through the mail several weeks after the sales have taken place.

It is normal practice to trace from *prenumbered remittance advices* or *prelists of cash receipts* to the cash receipts journal and subsidiary accounts receivable records as a *substantive* test of the recording of actual cash received. This test will only be effective if the cash was listed on a cash register tape or some other prelisting at the time it was received.

If the auditor is particularly concerned about weaknesses in the internal control system that could lead to fraudulently omitted cash receipts, there is an effective but time consuming approach that combines a part of the cash receipts tests with the audit of sales transactions. When the auditor traces a sales transaction to the debit in the customer's subsidiary ledger, he can also trace the subsequent *credit* that reduces the account receivable to its source. The credit must arise from cash received, sales returns and allowances, or accounts charged off as uncollectible. In testing the credits to the sales transactions, the auditor traces the cash receipts to the cash receipts journal, the sales returns and allowances to a properly authorized credit memo and the sales returns and allowances journal, and the accounts charged off to proper authorization. Any sales transactions not credited are still a part of accounts receivable and are tested as a part of the confirmation of the outstanding balances in accounts receivable. In this approach the auditor is looking for sales *without a valid credit* in the accounts receivable subsidiary ledger, which would be an indication of a possible defalcation. Of course, if an employee is able to omit the recording of a sale and subsequently takes the cash receipt from the customer before it is recorded, the procedure described here would be ineffective.

Proof of Cash Receipts

A useful audit procedure to test whether all recorded cash receipts have been deposited in the bank account is a proof of cash receipts. In this test the total cash receipts recorded in the cash receipts journal for a period of time, such as a month, are reconciled with the actual deposits made to the bank during the same time period. There may be a difference in the two due to deposits in transit and other items, but the amounts can be reconciled and compared. The procedure is not useful in discovering cash receipts that have not been recorded in the journals or time lags in making deposits, but it is useful in discovering recorded cash receipts that have not been deposited, unrecorded deposits, unrecorded loans, bank loans deposited directly into the bank account, and similar errors. A proof of cash receipts and cash disbursements is illustrated in Chapter 18 on page 586. This somewhat time-consuming procedure is ordinarily used only when the controls are weak. In rare instances where controls are extremely weak, the period covered by the proof of cash receipts may be the entire year.

Tests to Discover Lapping

Lapping, which is one common type of fraud, is the postponement of entries for the collection of receivables to *conceal an existing cash shortage*. The fraud is perpetrated by a person who records cash in both the cash receipts journal and subsidiary accounts receivable. He defers recording of the cash receipts from one customer and covers the shortages with receipts óf another customer. These in turn are covered from the receipts of a third customer a few days later. The employee must continue to cover the shortage through repeated lapping, replace the stolen money, or find another way to conceal the shortage.

This fraud can be detected by comparing the name, amount, and dates shown on remittance advices with cash receipts journal entries and related duplicate deposit slips. Since the procedure is relatively time consuming, auditors ordinarily perform the procedure only when there is specific concern with fraud because of a weakness in the system.

AUDIT PROCEDURES FOR CHARGING OFF AND RECORDING UNCOLLECTIBLE ACCOUNTS

Validity and *proper authorization* are the most important considerations the auditor should keep in mind in the verification of the write-off of individual uncollectible accounts. A major concern in testing accounts charged off as uncollectible is the possibility of the client's covering up a defalcation by charging off accounts receivable that have already been collected. The major control for preventing this type of error is proper authorization of the write-off of uncollectible accounts by a designated level of management only after the thorough investigation of the reason the customer has not paid.

Normally, the verification of the accounts charged off takes relatively little time. Typical procedures include the examination of approvals by the appropriate persons. For a sample of accounts charged off, it is also usually necessary for the auditor to examine correspondence in the client's files establishing their uncollectibility. In some cases the auditor will also examine Dun and Bradstreet and other credit reports. After the auditor has concluded that the accounts charged off by general journal entries are proper, selected items should be traced to the accounts receivable subsidiary ledger as a test of the records.

THE EFFECT OF THE RESULTS OF TESTS OF TRANSACTIONS ON THE REMAINDER OF THE AUDIT

The results of the compliance and substantive tests of transactions will have a significant effect on the remainder of the audit, especially on the direct tests of balances. The parts of the audit most affected by the tests of the sales and collection cycle transactions are the balances in *accounts receivable, cash, bad debts expense,* and *allowance for doubtful accounts.* Furthermore, if the results of the tests are unsatisfactory, it is necessary to do additional substantive testing for the propriety of sales, sales returns and allowances, charge-off of uncollectible accounts, and processing of cash receipts.

At the completion of the tests of transactions, it is essential to *analyze each compliance and substantive test exception* to determine its cause and the implication of the exception on the system and the audit of the affected accounts. The methodology and implications of exceptions analysis are explained more fully in Chapter 9.

The most significant effect of the results of the tests of the system in the sales and collection cycle is on the confirmation of accounts receivable. The type of confirmation, the size of the sample, and the timing of the test are all affected by the results of both compliance and substantive tests of transactions. The effect of the tests on accounts receivable, bad debts expense, and allowance for uncollectible accounts is considered in Chapter 10.

Appendix B:

Case Illustration

The concepts for testing the sales and collection cycle presented in this chapter are now illustrated by the case of the Hillsburg Hardware Company. A description of the system is followed by a preliminary evaluation of the system and, for each objective, the tests of the system a prudent auditor might consider appropriate for the circumstances.

The Hillsburg Hardware Company is a small wholesale distributor of hardware to independent, high-quality hardware stores in the southeastern part of the United States. This is the third year of the audit for this client, and there have never been any significant errors discovered in the tests. During the current year, two major changes have occurred. First, the chief accountant left the firm and has been replaced by Erma Swanson. There has also been some turnover of other accounting personnel. The overall assessment by management is that the accounting personnel are reasonably competent and highly trustworthy. The second major change is the financial condition of the client. In the past the client has been moderately profitable, but with the emergence of large discount hardware stores, sales volume has gradually declined and profits have been reduced. Several of Hillsburg's major customers have recently gone out of business due to this competition. To offset this, Hillsburg now sells to customers who would formerly not have been considered acceptable credit risks. The president, Rick Chulick, has been the chief operating officer for approximately ten years. He is regarded as a highly competent, honest individual who does a conscientious job. The following information is provided from the auditor's files:

1. *The organization chart and a flowchart of the system prepared for the audit.* This information is included in Figures 8-5 and 8-6. Sales returns and allowances for this client are too immaterial to include in the flowchart or to verify in the audit.

2. *Evaluation of internal controls and the related tests of transaction procedures for each objective.* An appropriate approach to evaluating a system of internal control and developing tests of transactions is included for sales in Figure 8-7 and cash receipts in Figure 8-8. A study of these two figures indicates the importance of isolating strengths (controls) and weaknesses (absence of controls) in the system. The compliance tests are designed to test the strengths and are shown separately from the substantive tests only to illustrate the differences in their nature.

3. *The strengths in the system and their effect.* These represent the controls the auditor is willing to rely upon to reduce substantive tests if the compliance tests indicate they are operating effectively. Figure 8-9 presents the strengths along with the effect of the strengths on specific errors, the compliance tests necessary to test the controls, and the effect on substantive tests if the controls are in fact operating effectively. The information for this figure is taken from Figures 8-7 and 8-8 to show the importance of strengths in designing tests of transactions.

4. *The weaknesses in the system and their effect.* These represent aspects of the system the auditor believes may result in significant errors because of the lack of adequate controls. The weaknesses are included in Figure 8-10, along with the effect of the weaknesses on specific errors and on audit procedures. The information for this figure is taken from Figures 8-7 and 8-8 to show the importance of weaknesses in designing tests of transactions.

5. *The analytical, compliance, and substantive procedures for sales, cash receipts, and charge-off of uncollectible accounts.* These audit procedures were developed after consideration of the strengths and weaknesses of the system and all other relevant factors of the audit. Figure 8-11 lists these procedures in the manner in which they are typically included in audit programs (the procedures are a summary of the ones listed in

Figures 8-7 and 8-8). Sample size and the particular items for inclusion in the sample are not included here, but they are considered in an extension of the case in the illustration in Appendix C at the end of Chapter 9.

FIGURE 8-5

HILLSBURG HARDWARE ORGANIZATION CHART—PERSONNEL

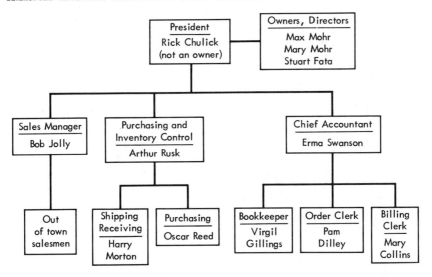

FIGURE 8-6

HILLSBURG HARDWARE—FLOWCHART OF SALES AND COLLECTIONS

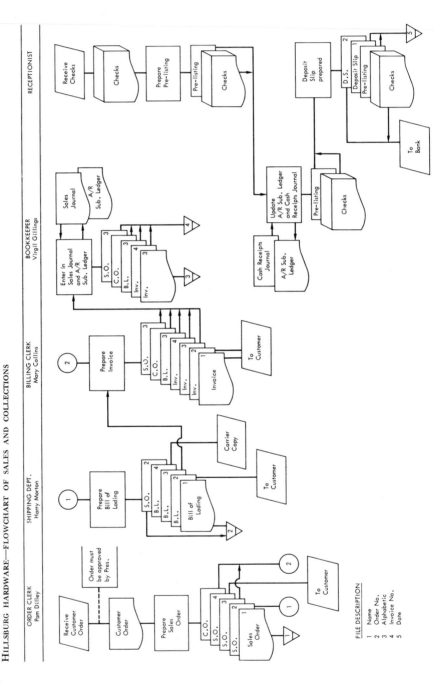

NOTES TO FIGURE 8-6:

1. All correspondence is sent to the president.
2. All sales order numbers are accounted for weekly by the accountant.
3. All bills of lading numbers are accounted for weekly by the accountant.
4. Sales amount recorded on sales invoice is based on standard price list.
5. Duplicate sales invoice is compared with bill of lading, and prices are checked daily by Pam Dilley and initialed before the original invoice is mailed to the customer.
6. Statements are sent to customers monthly.
7. Accounts receivable subsidiary ledger is reconciled with general ledger by the accountant on a monthly basis.
8. Sales invoices are recorded individually in the journal in the order they are received rather than sequentially.
9. Unpaid invoices are filed separately from paid invoices.
10. The sales journal, accounts receivable subsidiary ledger, and cash receipts journal are sent to the accountant on a monthly basis for posting to the general ledger.
11. The receptionist stamps incoming checks with a restrictive endorsement immediately upon receipt.
12. There are no cash sales.
13. Deposits are made at least weekly.
14. The bank account is reconciled by the accountant on a monthly basis.
15. All bad debts expense and charge-off of bad debts are approved by the president after being initiated by the chief accountant.

FIGURE 8-7

Hillsburg Hardware—Evaluation of Internal Controls and Tests of Transactions

Sales

Objective	Existing Controls	Weaknesses
1. Recorded sales are for shipments actually made to non-fictitious customers.	Pam Dilley examines underlying documents after billing.	Lack of internal verification for the possibility of sales invoices being recorded more than once.
2. Sales transactions are properly authorized.	Credit is approved by the president before shipment.	
3. Existing sales transactions are recorded.	Bills of lading are accounted for weekly by accountant to make sure they are billed.	Lack of internal verification that sales invoices are included in the sales journal (also see objective 3, weakness for cash receipts).
4. Recorded sales are for the amount of goods ordered and are correctly billed and recorded.	Internal verification of pricing, extension, and footings by Dilley.	
5. Sales transactions are properly classified.	None.	Not a problem, due to lack of cash sales.
6. Sales are recorded on a timely basis.	None.	Lack of control for test of timely recording.
7. Sales transactions are properly included in the subsidiary records and are correctly summarized.	a. Accountant reconciles subsidiary ledger with control account. b. Monthly statements are sent to customers.	No internal verification of footing the journal and posting totals to the general ledger.

FIGURE 8-7 (cont.)

Tests of Transactions		
Compliance	*Substantive*	*Comments*
a. Account for a sequence of duplicate sales invoices in the sales journal, observing for duplicate numbers. b. Examine underlying documents for indication of internal verification.	a. Trace recorded sales from the sales journal to the file of supporting documents, which includes a duplicate sales invoice, bill of lading, sales order, and customer order. b. Review the sales journal and ledger accounts for unusual transactions and amounts.	All procedures are done at year-end rather than at an interim date due to the weaknesses in the system. All procedures are done on a sample basis.
Examine customer order for proper credit approval.		This procedure is done as a part of 4c.
Account for a sequence of shipping documents.	a. Trace selected shipping documents to sales journal to be sure they are all included.	The detailed comparison of shipping documents with the journal is done as a part of objective 4.
Examine underlying documentation for indication of internal verification (see 1b above).	Select invoice numbers from the sales journal and trace to a. Duplicate sales invoice and test for total amount recorded in journal, date, customer name, and classification. Check pricing extension and footing. b. Bill of lading and test for customer name, product description, quantity, and date. c. Customer order and sales order and test for customer name, product description, quantity, and date.	All of these procedures can be conveniently performed at the same time along with those for objectives 1 and 5 because all support documents are attached to duplicate sales invoices.
	Done as a part of objective 4.	
	As a part of objective 4, compare dates on the bill of lading, duplicate sales invoice, and sales journal.	
a. Observe whether accountant reconciles subsidiary ledger with control account. b. Observe whether monthly statements are mailed.	a. Foot and crossfoot the sales journal, and trace totals to the general ledger. b. Trace selected invoices from the sales journal to the subsidiary ledger, and test for amount, date, and invoice number.	

FIGURE 8-8

Hillsburg Hardware—Evaluation of Internal Controls and Tests of Transactions

<table>
<tr><th colspan="3">*Cash Receipts*</th></tr>
<tr><th>*Objective*</th><th>*Existing Controls*</th><th>*Weaknesses*</th></tr>
<tr>
<td>1. Recorded cash receipts are for funds actually received by the company.</td>
<td>Accountant reconciles bank account.</td>
<td></td>
</tr>
<tr>
<td>2. Cash discounts are authorized.</td>
<td>Not applicable.</td>
<td></td>
</tr>
<tr>
<td>3. Cash received is recorded in the cash receipts journal.</td>
<td>a. Checks are stamped with a restrictive endorsement.
b. Statements are sent to customers monthly.</td>
<td>a. Prelisting of cash is not used to verify recorded cash receipts.
b. Receptionist handles cash after it is returned from cash receipts.
c. Bookkeeper has access to cash receipts and maintains accounts receivable records.</td>
</tr>
<tr>
<td>4. Recorded cash receipts are deposited at the amount received.</td>
<td>a. Statements are sent to customers monthly.
b. Accountant reconciles bank account.</td>
<td></td>
</tr>
<tr>
<td>5. Cash receipts are properly classified.</td>
<td>None.</td>
<td>Not a problem, due to lack of cash sales.</td>
</tr>
<tr>
<td>6. Cash receipts are recorded on a timely basis.</td>
<td>None.</td>
<td>Cash receipts are not deposited daily.</td>
</tr>
<tr>
<td>7. Cash receipts are properly included in the subsidiary records and are correctly summarized.</td>
<td>Accountant reconciles subsidiary ledger with control account.</td>
<td>No internal verification of footing the journal and posting totals to the general ledger.</td>
</tr>
</table>

FIGURE 8-8 (cont.)

Tests of Transactions		
Compliance	*Substantive*	*Comments*
Observe who performs the bank reconciliation.	a. Prepare a proof of cash receipts. b. Trace entries from the cash receipts journal to the bank statement, testing for amount and date of deposit. c. Review the cash receipts journal for unusual amounts. d. Review the accounts receivable subsidiary ledger for miscellaneous credits.	All procedures are done at year-end rather than at an interim date due to the weaknesses in the system. All procedures are done on a sample basis.
a. Observe whether a restricted endorsement is used on cash receipts. b. Observe whether monthly statements are mailed.	Compare prelisting of cash receipts with the cash receipts journal and with the duplicate deposit slip, testing for names, amounts, and date.	This procedure and those for 1a and 1b are normally performed together.
a. See 3a above. b. Observe whether accountant reconciles bank account.	The procedures for objectives 1 and 2 also fulfill these objectives.	
	Not tested.	
	Trace amounts from the cash receipts journal to the bank, testing for a delay in deposit.	Performed as a part of 1b above.
Observe whether accountant reconciles subsidiary ledger with control account.	a. Foot and crossfoot the cash receipts journal, and trace totals to the general ledger. b. Trace selected entries from the cash receipts journal to the subsidiary ledger, and test for amount and date. c. Trace selected credits from the subsidiary ledger to the cash receipts journal, and test for amount and date.	

Figure 8-9

Hillsburg Hardware—Strengths in the System and Their Effect

Strengths	Effect on Likely Errors	Compliance Tests Performed to Verify the Strengths (Effect on the Substantive Tests Is in Parentheses)
1. The accountant accounts for all bills of lading and traces them to sales invoices.	Reduces the likelihood of failing to bill shipments. An important control due to Weakness 1 in Figure 8-10.	Account for a series of bills of lading. (Due to Weakness 1, it will be necessary to trace from bills of lading to the duplicate sales invoices.)
2. Credit is approved by the president.	Reduces the likelihood of failing to follow company policy.	Examine credit approval on customer order. (Do not do any other tests of credit until balance sheets tests are done.)
3. The bank statement is reconciled by the accountant.	Reduces the likelihood of fraudulent errors.	Observation. (No effect until balance sheet tests are performed.)
4. The accountant reconciles the balance in the accounts receivable subsidiary ledger with the control accounts.	Reduces the likelihood of undetected errors in the subsidiary ledgers.	Observation and asking questions. (No effect until balance sheet tests are performed.)
5. The sales invoices are internally verified for pricing, extensions, and footings.	Reduces the likelihood of clerical errors.	Examination of duplicate invoices for initials. (Reduce substantive tests of invoices as well as confirmations.)
6. Statements are mailed to customers monthly, and all correspondence is sent directly to the president.	Reduces the likelihood of errors remaining undetected.	Observation and questions. (The effect is a reduction in all tests concerned with the overstatement of receivables. This includes pricing, extensions, footings, etc.)
7. Checks are stamped with a restrictive endorsement.	Reduces the likelihood of fraud.	Observation. (Reduction in tests for fraud.)

FIGURE 8-10

Hillsburg Hardware—Weaknesses in the System and Their Effect

Weaknesses	Effect on Likely Errors	Effect on Audit Procedures
1. The bookkeeper maintains the accounts receivable records and also has access to cash receipts.	Potential for fraud by the bookkeeper. Significantly offset by the lack of currency and restrictive endorsement.	Trace a larger sample than normal from the prelisting of cash receipts to the cash receipts journal. Test a larger sample than normal of the billing of shipments and the recording of invoices (as a test of omitting the invoice and theft of the check). It is not possible to test remittance advices because they are not retained. Instead trace the detail of the prelist of cash receipts to the duplicate deposit slip and the bank statement.
2. Cash receipts are not deposited daily.	Potential for loss of checks, and it enhances the likelihood of fraud in 1 above.	Trace a larger sample than normal from the prelisting of cash receipts to the cash receipts journal, and prepare a proof of cash.
3. Receptionist handles cash after it is returned from the A/R clerk.	A potential for fraud.	Trace a larger sample than normal from the prelisting of cash receipts to the bank statement.
4. The prelisting of cash is not used to verify cash receipts.	The failure to use this information enhances the likelihood of fraud in 1 above and unintentional loss of checks or other errors.	Trace a larger sample than normal from the prelisting of cash receipts to the cash receipts journal and bank statement.
5. There is no internal verification of the inclusion of all sales invoices in the sales journal.	There may be an intentional or an unintentional omission or duplicate recording of sales invoices. This weakness is enhanced by the recording of invoices in a manner other than sequential order. The likelihood of duplicate recording is partially offset by the president's receiving all correspondence from customers.	Account for a large sequence of duplicate sales invoices in the sales journal, watching for omissions and duplications. Due to the way the sales journal is organized, this procedure will have to be done with great care.
6. Lack of internal verification of footing and posting of journals.	Potential for fraud.	Foot and crossfoot journals, and trace the balances to the general ledger.

FIGURE 8-11

Hillsburg Hardware—Audit Program—Sales and Cash Receipts

Audit Procedures for Sales and Cash Receipts (Sample Size and the Items in the Sample Are Not Included)	Comments
General	All tests are done at year-end rather than at an interim date, due to the weaknesses in the system. All procedures are to be done on a test basis.
1. Perform analytical tests of the accounts in the cycle, and compare the results with industry trends and previous years.	
2. Test foot and crossfoot the journals, and trace the totals to the general ledger.	
3. Review the journals and the ledgers for unusual transactions and amounts.	
4. Review the subsidiary ledger for miscellaneous credits.	
Shipment of Goods	No further testing is done at this time. See procedure for the billing of customers 2c.
1. Account for a sequence of shipping documents.	
2. Trace selected shipping documents to a duplicate sales invoice for assurance that each one has been billed.	
Billing of Customers and Recording the Sales in the Records	
1. Account for a sequence of sales invoices in the sales journal.	
2. Trace selected duplicate invoice numbers from the sales journal to	
a. Accounts receivable subsidiary ledger, and test for amount, date, and invoice number.	
b. Duplicate sales invoice, and test for the total amount recorded in the journal, date, customer name, and classification. Check the pricing, extensions, footings, and evidence of internal verification by Pam Dilley on the duplicate sales invoice.	Procedures for 2b, 2c, and 2d can be conveniently performed at the same time because supporting documents are all attached to the duplicate sales invoices. Pricing of the sales invoice includes the basic price, terms, freight, etc.
c. Bill of lading, and test for customer name, product description, quantity, and date.	
d. Duplicate sales order, and test for customer name, product description, quantity, date, and approval by Pam Dilley.	
e. Customer order, and test for customer name, product description, quantity, date, and credit approval by Rick Chulick.	
Processing Cash Receipts and Recording the Amounts in the Records	These procedures are designed primarily for the internal control weakness of the bookkeeper's having access to checks.
1. Obtain the daily list of incoming cash receipts, and trace amounts to the cash receipts journal, testing for name, amount, date.	
2. Compare the daily list of incoming cash receipts with the duplicate deposit slip, testing for names, amounts, and dates. Trace the total to the bank statement, testing for dates and amounts.	
3. Prepare a proof of cash receipts.	
4. Trace from the cash receipts journal to entries in the subsidiary ledger, checking for date and amount.	

REVIEW QUESTIONS

1. Describe the nature of the following documents and records and explain their use in the sales and collection cycle: bill of lading, sales invoice, credit memo, remittance advice, monthly statement to customers.
2. Explain the importance of proper credit approval for sales. What effect do adequate controls in the credit function have on the auditor's evidence accumulation?
3. Distinguish between bad debts expense and the charge-off of uncollectible accounts. Explain why they are audited in completely different ways.
4. List the detailed audit objectives for the verification of sales transactions. For each objective, state one internal control the client can use to reduce the likelihood of errors.
5. State one compliance and one substantive test the auditor can use to verify the sales objective, "Recorded sales are stated at the proper amount."
6. List the most important duties that should be segregated in the sales and collection cycle. Expain why it is desirable that each of these duties be segregated.
7. Explain how prenumbered shipping documents and sales invoices can be useful controls for preventing errors in sales.
8. What three types of authorizations are commonly used in an internal control system for sales? For each authorization, state a substantive test the auditor could use to verify whether the control was effective in preventing errors.
9. Explain the purpose of footing and crossfooting the sales journal and tracing the totals to the general ledger.
10. What is the difference between the auditor's approach in verifying sales returns and allowances compared to sales? Explain the reasons for the difference.
11. Explain why auditors usually emphasize the detection of fraud in the audit of cash. Is this consistent or inconsistent with the auditor's responsibility in the audit? Explain.
12. List the detailed audit objectives for the verification of cash receipts. For each objective, state one internal control the client can use to reduce the likelihood of errors.
13. List several audit procedures the auditor can use to determine whether all cash received was recorded.
14. Explain what is meant by *proof of cash receipts,* and state its purpose.
15. Explain what is meant by *lapping,* and discuss how the auditor can uncover it. Under what circumstances should the auditor make a special effort to uncover lapping?
16. What audit procedures are most likely to be used to verify accounts receivable charged off as uncollectible? State the purpose of each of these procedures.
17. State the relationship between the confirmation of accounts receivable and the results of the tests of transactions.
18. Under what circumstances is it acceptable to perform tests of transactions for sales and cash receipts at an interim date?
19. Diane Smith, CPA, tested sales transactions for the month of March in an audit of the financial statements for the year ended December 31, 19X7. Based on the excellent results of both the compliance and the substantive tests, she decided to significantly reduce her direct tests of the financial balances at year-end. Evaluate this decision.

DISCUSSION QUESTIONS AND PROBLEMS

20. For each of the following questions, select the best response:
    a. The CPA tests sales transactions. One step is tracing a sample of sales invoices to debits in the accounts receivable subsidiary ledger. Based upon this step, he will form an opinion as to whether
       (1) Each sales invoice represents a valid sale
       (2) All sales have been recorded
       (3) All debit entries in the accounts receivable subsidiary ledger are properly supported by sales invoices
       (4) Recorded sales invoices have been properly posted to customer accounts
    b. For good internal control, the credit manager should be responsible to the
       (1) Sales manager
       (2) Customer-service manager
       (3) Controller
       (4) Treasurer
    c. For good internal control, the billing department should be under the direction of the
       (1) Controller
       (2) Credit manager
       (3) Sales manager
       (4) Treasurer
    d. The authorization for write-off of accounts receivable should be the responsibility of the
       (1) Credit manager
       (2) Controller
       (3) Accounts receivable clerk
       (4) Treasurer
    e. A CPA is examining the financial statements of a small telephone company and wishes to test whether customers are being billed. One procedure that he might use is to
       (1) Check a sample of listings in the telephone directory to the billing control
       (2) Trace a sample of postings from the billing control to the subsidiary accounts receivable ledger
       (3) Balance the subsidiary accounts receivable ledger to the general ledger control account
       (4) Confirm a representative number of accounts receivable
                                                                (AICPA adapted)
21. Items *a* through *h* are selected questions of the type generally found in internal control questionnaires used by auditors in evaluating controls in the sales and collection cycle. In using the questionnaire for a particular client, a yes response to a question indicates a possible strength in the system, whereas a no indicates a potential weakness.
    a. Are sales invoices independently compared to customers' orders for prices, quantities, extensions, and footings?
    b. Are sales orders, invoices, and credit memoranda issued and filed in numerical sequence and are the sequences accounted for periodically?

c. Are the selling function and sales register preparation independent of the cash receipts, shipping, delivery, and billing functions?

d. Are all COD, scrap, equipment, and cash sales accounted for in the same manner as charge sales and is the record keeping independent of the collection procedure?

e. Is the collection function independent of, and does it constitute a check on, the accounts receivable function and accounts receivable bookkeepers?

f. Are receivable subsidiary ledgers balanced regularly to control accounts by an employee independent of the detail posting functions?

g. Are cash receipts entered in books of original entry by persons independent of the mail-opening and receipts-listing functions?

h. Are receipts deposited intact daily on a timely basis?

Required:

a. For each of the above questions, state the internal control objectives being fulfilled if the control is in effect.

b. For each control, list a compliance procedure to test its effectiveness.

c. For each of the above questions, identify the nature of the potential financial errors.

d. For each of the potential errors in part *c,* list a substantive audit procedure to determine whether a material error exists.

22. The following errors or omissions are included in the accounting records of the Joyce Manufacturing Company:

a. A sales invoice was misadded by $1,000.

b. A material sale was unintentionally recorded for the second time on the last day of the year. The sale had originally been recorded two days previously.

c. Cash paid on accounts receivable was stolen by the mail clerk when the mail was opened.

d. Cash paid on accounts receivable that had been prelisted by a secretary was stolen by the bookkeeper who records cash receipts and accounts receivable. He failed to record the transactions.

e. A shipment to a customer was not billed due to the loss of the bill of lading.

f. Merchandise was shipped to a customer, but no bill of lading was prepared. Since billings are prepared from bills of lading, the customer was not billed.

g. A sale to a residential customer was unintentionally classified as a commercial sale.

Required:

a. For each error, state a control that should have prevented the error from occurring on a continuing basis.

b. For each error, state a substantive audit procedure that could uncover the error.

23. The following are commonly performed tests of transactions audit procedures in the sales and collection cycle:

a. Examine sales returns for approval by an authorized official.

b. Account for a sequence of shipping documents and examine each one to make sure a duplicate sales invoice is attached.

c. Account for a sequence of sales invoices and examine each one to make sure a duplicate copy of the shipping copy is attached.

d. Compare the quantity and description of items on shipping documents with the related duplicate sales invoices.

e. Trace recorded sales in the sales journal to the related subsidiary ledgers and compare the customer name, date, and amount for each one.

f. Review the prelisting in the cash receipts book to determine whether cash is prelisted on a daily basis.

g. Reconcile the recorded cash receipts on the prelisting of cash receipts with the cash receipts journal, and the bank statement for a one-month period.

Required:

a. Identify whether each audit procedure is a compliance or a substantive test.

b. State which of the seven detailed objectives each of the audit procedures fulfills.

24. For each of the following types of errors (parts *a* through *e*), select the control that should have prevented the error.

a. A manufacturing company received a substantial sales return in the last month of the year, but the credit memorandum for the return was not prepared until after the auditors had completed their field work. The returned merchandise was included in the physical inventory.

(1) Aging schedules of accounts receivable are prepared periodically.

(2) Credit memoranda are prenumbered, and all numbers are accounted for.

(3) A reconciliation of the trial balance of customers' ledgers with the general ledger control is prepared periodically.

(4) Receiving reports are prepared for all materials received, and such reports are numerically controlled.

b. The sales manager credited a salesman, Jack Smith, with sales that were actually "house account" sales. Later Smith divided his excess sales commissions with the sales manager.

(1) The summary sales entries are checked periodically by persons independent of sales functions.

(2) Sales orders are reviewed and approved by persons independent of the sales department.

(3) The internal auditor compares the sales commission statements with the cash disbursements record.

(4) Sales orders are prenumbered, and all numbers are accounted for.

c. A sales invoice for $5,200 was computed correctly but, in error, was posted as $2,500 to the sales journal and to the accounts receivable ledger. The customer remitted only $2,500, the amount on his monthly statement.

(1) Prelistings and predetermined totals are used to control postings.

(2) Sales invoice serial numbers, prices, discounts, extensions, and footings are independently checked.

(3) The customers' monthly statements are verified and mailed by a responsible person other than the bookkeeper who prepared them.

(4) Unauthorized remittance deductions made by customers or other matters in dispute are investigated promptly by a person independent of the accounts receivable function.

d. Copies of sales invoices show different unit prices for apparently identical items.

(1) All sales invoices are checked as to all details after their preparation.

(2) Differences reported by customers are satisfactorily investigated.

(3) Statistical sales data are compiled and reconciled with recorded sales.

(4) All sales invoices are compared with the customers' purchase orders.

e. The cashier diverted cash received over the counter from a customer to his own use and wrote off the receivable as a bad debt.

    (1) Aging schedules of accounts receivable are prepared periodically and reviewed by a responsible official.

    ● (2) Journal entries are approved by a responsible official.

    (3) Receipts are given directly to the cashier by the person who opens the mail.

    (4) Remittance advices, letters, or envelopes that accompany receipts are separated and given directly to the accounting department.

                                     (AICPA adapted)

25. The following sales procedures were encountered during the regular annual audit of Marvel Wholesale Distributing Company.

Customer orders are received by the sales order department. A clerk computes the dollar amount of the order and sends it to the credit department for approval. Credit approval is stamped on the order and returned to the sales order department. An invoice is prepared in two copies and the order is filed in the "customer order" file.

The customer copy of the invoice is sent to the billing department and held in the "pending" file awaiting notification that the order was shipped.

The shipping copy of the invoice is routed through the warehouse and the shipping department as authority for the respective departments to release and ship the merchandise. Shipping department personnel pack the order and prepare a three-copy bill of lading: the original copy is mailed to the customer, the second copy is sent with the shipment, and the other is filed in sequence in the bill of lading file. The invoice shipping copy is sent to the billing department.

The billing clerk matches the received shipping copy with the customer copy from the pending file. Both copies of the invoice are priced, extended, and footed. The customer copy is then mailed directly to the customer, and the shipping copy is sent to the accounts receivable clerk.

The accounts receivable clerk enters the invoice data in a sales accounts receivable journal, posts the customer's account in the subsidiary customers' accounts ledger, and files the shipping copy in the sales invoice file. The invoices are numbered and filed in sequence.

a. In order to gather audit evidence concerning the proper credit approval of sales, the auditor would select a sample of transaction documents from the population represented by the

    ● (1) Customer order file

    (2) Bill of lading file

    (3) Subsidiary customers' accounts ledger

    (4) Sales invoice file

b. In order to determine whether the system of internal control operated effectively to minimize errors of failure to post invoices to customers' accounts ledger, the auditor would select a sample of transactions from the population represented by the

    (1) Customer order file

    (2) Bill of lading file

    (3) Subsidiary customers' accounts ledger

    ● (4) Sales invoice file

c. In order to determine whether the system of internal control operated effectively to minimize errors of failure to invoice a shipment, the auditor would select a sample of transactions from the population represented by the

    (1) Customer order file

      ℓ (2) Bill of lading file
        (3) Subsidiary customers' accounts ledger
        (4) Sales invoice file
  d. In order to gather audit evidence that uncollected items in customers' accounts represented valid trade receivables, the auditor would select a sample of items from the population represented by the
        (1) Customer order file.
        (2) Bill of lading file
      ● (3) Subsidiary customers' accounts ledger
        (4) Sales invoice file   .   (AICPA adapted)

26. Your client is the Quaker Valley Shopping Center, Inc., a shopping center with thirty store tenants. All leases with the store tenants provide for a fixed rent plus a percentage of sales, net of sales taxes, in excess of a fixed dollar amount computed on an annual basis. Each lease also provides that the landlord may engage a CPA to audit all records of the tenant for assurance that sales are being properly reported to the landlord.

    You have been requested by your client to audit the records of the Bali Pearl Restaurant to determine that the sales totaling $390,000 for the year ended December 31, 19X7, have been properly reported to the landlord. The restaurant and the shopping center entered into a five-year lease on January, 19X7. The Bali Pearl Restaurant offers only table service. No liquor is served. During meal times there are four or five waitresses in attendance who prepare handwritten prenumbered restaurant checks for the customers. Payment is made at a cash register, manned by the proprietor, as the customer leaves. All sales are for cash. The proprietor also is the bookkeeper. Complete files are kept of restaurant checks and cash register tapes. A daily sales book and general ledger are also maintained.

Required:

  a. For purposes of this audit, which audit objectives are you primarily concerned with?
  b. List the auditing procedures that you would employ to verify the total annual sales of the Bali Pearl Restaurant. (Disregard vending machines sales and counter sales of chewing gum, candy, etc.)   (AICPA adapted)

27. The following auditing procedures are customarily applied in connection with the verification of cash balances or the testing of cash receipts transactions. Indicate a type of irregularity that could be expected to be disclosed by the application of each procedure and explain how the procedure would disclose the irregularity.
  a. Verification of the detail of deposit slips.
  b. Comparison of deposits as shown by the bank statement for several days prior to the end of the period under examination with receipts as shown by the cash book.
  c. Reconcilement of cash receipts by months as shown by the cash book with deposits as shown by the bank statements.   (AICPA adapted)

28. Jerome Paper Company engaged you to review its internal control system. Jerome does not prelist cash receipts before they are recorded and has other weaknesses in processing collections of trade receivables, the company's largest asset. In discussing the matter with the controller, you find he is chiefly interested in economy when he assigns duties to the fifteen office personnel. He feels the main considerations are that the work should be done by people who are most familiar with it, capable of doing it, and available when it has to be done.

The controller says he has excellent control over trade receivables because receivables are pledged as security for a continually renewable bank loan and the bank sends out positive confirmation requests occasionally, based on a list of pledged receivables furnished by the company each week.

Required:

a. Explain how prelisting of cash receipts strengthens internal control over cash.

b. Assume that an employee handles cash receipts from trade customers before they are recorded. List the duties which that employee should not do to withhold from him the opportunity to conceal embezzlement of the receipts. (AICPA adapted)

29. You have been asked by the board of trustees of a local church to review its accounting procedures. As a part of this review you have prepared the following comments relating to the collections made at weekly services and record keeping for members' pledges and contributions:

• The church's board of trustees has delegated responsibility for financial management and audit of the financial records to the finance committe. This group prepares the annual budget and approves major disbursements but is not involved in collections or record keeping. No audit has been considered necessary in recent years because the same trusted employee has kept church records and served as financial secretary for fifteen years.

• The collection at the weekly service is taken by a team of ushers. The head usher counts the collection in the church office following each service. He then places the collection and a notation of the amount counted in the church safe. Next morning the financial secretary opens the safe and recounts the collection. He withholds about $100 to meet cash expenditures during the coming week and deposits the remainder of the collection intact. In order to facilitate the deposit, members who contribute by check are asked to draw their checks to "cash."

• At their request a few members are furnished prenumbered predated envelopes in which to insert their weekly contributions. The head usher removes the cash from the envelopes to be counted with the loose cash included in the collection and discards the envelopes. No record is maintained of issuance or return of the envelopes, and the envelope system is not encouraged.

• Each member is asked to prepare a contribution pledge card annually. The pledge is regarded as a moral commitment by the member to contribute a stated weekly amount. Based upon the amounts shown on the pledge cards, the financial secretary furnishes a letter to requesting members to support the tax deductibility of their contributions.

Required:

Describe the weaknesses and recommend improvements in procedures for
a. Collections made at weekly services
b. Record keeping for members' pledges and contributions
Organize your answer sheets as follows:

Weakness	Recommended Improvement

(AICPA adapted)

30. You are auditing the Alaska Branch of Far Distributing Co. This branch has substantial annual sales which are billed and collected locally. As a part of your audit you find that the procedures for handling cash receipts are as follows:

Cash collections on over-the-counter sales and COD sales are received from the customer or delivery service by the cashier. Upon receipt of cash the cashier stamps the sales ticket "paid" and files a copy for future reference. The only record of COD sales is a copy of the sales ticket which is given to the cashier to hold until the cash is received from the delivery service.

Mail is opened by the secretary to the credit manager, and remittances are given to the credit manager for his review. The credit manager then places the remittances in a tray on the cashier's desk. At the daily deposit cutoff time the cashier delivers the checks and cash on hand to the assistant credit manager who prepares remittance lists and makes up the bank deposit which he also takes to the bank. The assistant credit manager also posts remittances to the accounts receivable ledger cards and verifies the cash discount allowable.

You also ascertain that the credit manager obtains approval from the executive office of Far Distributing Co., located in Chicago, to write off uncollectible accounts, and that he has retained in his custody as of the end of the fiscal year some remittances that were received on various days during the last month.

Required:

a. Describe the irregularities that might occur under the procedures now in effect for handling cash collections and remittances. (AICPA adapted)
b. Give procedures that you would recommend to strengthen internal control over cash collections and remittances.

31. The customer billing and collection functions of the Robinson Company, a small paint manufacturer, are attended to by a receptionist, an accounts receivable clerk, and a cashier who also serves as a secretary. The company's paint products are sold to wholesalers and retail stores.

The following describes *all* of the procedures performed by the employees of the Robinson Company pertaining to customer billings and collections:

a. The mail is opened by the receptionist who gives the customers' purchase orders to the accounts receivable clerk. Fifteen to twenty orders are received each day. Under instructions to expedite the shipment of orders, the accounts receivable clerk at once prepares a five-copy sales invoice form which is distributed as follows:

(1) Copy #1 is the customer billing copy and is held by the accounts receivable clerk until notice of shipment is received.
(2) Copy #2 is the accounts receivable department copy and is held for ultimate posting of the accounts receivable records.
(3) Copies #3 and #4 are sent to the shipping department.
(4) Copy #5 is sent to the storeroom as authority for release of the goods to the shipping department.

b. After the paint order has been moved from the storeroom to the shipping department, the shipping department prepares the bills of lading and labels the cartons. Sales invoice copy #4 is inserted in a carton as a packing slip. After the trucker has picked up the shipment, the customer's copy of the bill of lading and copy #3, on which are noted any undershipments, are returned to the accounts receivable clerk. The company does not "back order" in the event of undershipments; customers are expected to reorder the merchandise. The Robinson Company's copy of the bill of lading is filed by the shipping department.

c. When copy #3 and the customer's copy of the bill of lading are received by the accounts receivable clerk, copies #1 and #2 are completed by numbering them and inserting quantities shipped, unit prices, extensions, discounts, and totals. The accounts receivable clerk then mails copy #1 and the copy of the bill of lading to the customer. Copies #2 and #3 are stapled together.

d. The individual accounts receivable ledger cards are posted by the accounts receivable clerk by a bookkeeping machine procedure whereby the sales register is prepared as a carbon copy of the postings. Postings are made from copy #2 which is then filed, along with staple-attached copy #3, in numerical order. Monthly the general ledger clerk summarizes the sales register for posting to the general ledger accounts.

e. Since the Robinson Company is short of cash, the deposit of receipts is also expedited. The receptionist turns over all mail receipts and related correspondence to the accounts receivable clerk who examines the checks and determines that the accompanying vouchers or correspondence contains enough detail to permit posting of the accounts. The accounts receivable clerk then endorses the checks and gives them to the cashier who prepares the daily deposit. No currency is received in the mail, and no paint is sold over the counter at the factory.

f. The accounts receivable clerk uses the vouchers or correspondence that accompanied the checks to post the accounts receivable ledger cards. The bookkeeping machine prepares a cash receipts register as a carbon copy of the postings. Monthly the general ledger clerk summarizes the cash receipts register for posting to the general ledger accounts. The accounts receivable clerk also corresponds with customers about unauthorized deductions for discounts, freight or advertising allowances, returns, etc., and prepares the appropriate credit memos. Disputed items of large amount are turned over to the sales manager for settlement. Each month the accounts receivable clerk prepares a trial balance of the open accounts receivable and compares the resultant total with the general ledger control account for accounts receivable.

Required:

a. Discuss the internal control weaknesses in the Robinson Company's procedures related to customer billings and remittances and the accounting for these transactions. In your discussion, in addition to identifying the weaknesses, explain what could happen as a result of each weakness.

b. For each weakness, list one substantive audit procedure for testing the significance of the potential error. (AICPA adapted)

32. The Meyers Pharmaceutical Company, a drug manufacturer, has the following system for billing and recording accounts receivable:

a. An incoming customer's purchase order is received in the order department by a clerk who prepares a prenumbered company sales order form in which is inserted the pertinent information, such as the customer's name and address, customer's account number, quantity and items ordered. After the sales order form has been prepared, the customer's purchase order is stapled to it.

b. The sales order form is then passed to the credit department for credit approval. Rough approximations of the billing values of the orders are

made in the credit department for those accounts on which credit limitations are imposed. After investigation, approval of credit is noted on the
form.

c. Next the sales order form is passed to the billing department where a
clerk types the customer's invoice on a billing machine that cross-
multiplies the number of items and the unit price, then adds the automatically extended amounts for the total amount of the invoice. The
billing clerk determines the unit prices for the items from a list of billing
prices.

The billing machine has registers that automatically accumulate daily
totals of customer account numbers and invoice amounts to provide
"hash" totals and control amounts. These totals, which are inserted in a
daily record book, serve as predetermined batch totals for verification
of computer inputs.

The billing is done on prenumbered, continuous, carbon-interleaved
forms having the following designations:

(1) "Customer's copy."
(2) "Sales department copy," for information purposes.
(3) "File copy."
(4) "Shipping department copy," which serves as a shipping order. Bills
of lading are also prepared as carbon copy by-products of the invoicing procedure.

d. The shipping department copy of the invoice and the bills of lading are
then sent to the shipping department. After the order has been shipped,
copies of the bill of lading are returned to the billing department. The
shipping department copy of the invoice is filed in the shipping department.

e. In the billing department one copy of the bill of lading is attached to the
customer's copy of the invoice and both are mailed to the customer. The
other copy of the bill of lading, together with the sales order form, is
then stapled to the invoice file copy and filed in invoice numerical order.

f. A keypunch machine is connected to the billing machine so that punched
cards are created during the preparation of the invoices. The punched
cards then become the means by which the sales data are transmitted to
a computer for preparation of the sales journal, subsidiary ledger, and
perpetual inventory records.

The punched cards are fed to the computer in batches. One day's
accumulation of cards comprises a batch. After the punched cards have
been processed by the computer, they are placed in files and held for
about two years.

Required:

a. Flowchart the billing system as a means of understanding the system.
b. List the internal controls over sales for each of the seven internal control
objectives.
c. For each control, list a useful compliance test to verify the effectiveness
of the control.
d. For each audit objective for sales, list appropriate audit procedures, considering the system of internal control.
e. Combine the audit procedures from parts *c* and *d* into an efficient audit
program for conducting the audit. (The listed procedures should be
limited to the verification of the sales data being fed into the computer.

Do not carry the procedures beyond the point at which the cards are ready to be fed to the computer.) (AICPA adapted)

33. You are engaged in your first audit of the Licitra Pest Control Company for the year ended December 31, 19X8. The company began doing business in January 19X8 and provides pest control services for industrial enterprises. Additional information:

a. The office staff consists of a bookkeeper, a typist, and the president, Tony Licitra. In addition, the company employs twenty servicemen on an hourly basis who are assigned to individual territories to make both monthly and emergency visits to customers' premises. The servicemen submit weekly time reports which include the customer's name and the time devoted to each customer. Time charges for emergency visits are shown separately from regular monthly visits on the report.

b. Customers are required to sign annual contracts which are prenumbered and prepared in duplicate. The original is filed in numerical order by contract anniversary date, and the copy is given to the customer. The contract entitles the customer to pest control services once each month. Emergency visits are billed separately.

c. Fees for monthly services are payable in advance—quarterly, semi-annually, or annually—and are recorded on the books as "income from services" when the cash is received. All payments are by checks received by mail.

d. Prenumbered invoices for contract renewals are prepared in triplicate from information in the contract file. The original invoice is sent to the customer twenty days prior to the due date of payment, the duplicate copy is filed chronologically by due date, and the triplicate copy is filed alphabetically by customer. If payment is not received by fifteen days after the due date, a cancellation notice is sent to the customer and a copy of the notice is attached to the customer's contract. The bookkeeper notifies the servicemen of all contract cancellations and reinstatements and requires written acknowledgment of receipt of such notices. Mr. Licitra approves all cancellations and reinstatements of contracts.

e. Prenumbered invoices for emergency services are prepared weekly from information shown on serviceman's time reports. The customer is billed at 20 percent of the serviceman's hourly rate. These invoices, prepared in triplicate and distributed as shown above, are recorded on the books as "income from services" at the billing date. Payment is due thirty days after the invoice date.

f. All remittances are received by the typist, who prepares a daily list of collections and stamps a restrictive endorsement on the checks. A copy of the list is forwarded to the bookkeeper, who posts the date and amount received on the copies of the invoice in both the alphabetical and chronological files. After posting, the copy of the invoice is transferred from the chronological file to the daily cash receipts binder, which serves as a subsidiary record for the cash receipts book. The bookkeeper totals the amounts of all remittances received, posts this total to the cash receipts book, and attaches the daily remittance tapes to the paid invoices in the daily cash receipts binder.

g. The typist prepares a daily bank deposit slip and compares the total with the total amount shown on the daily remittance tapes. All remittances are deposited in the bank the day they are received. (Cash receipts from sources other than services need not be considered.)

Required:

a. List the audit procedures you would employ in the examination of the *income from services* account for 19X8. In developing the procedures, consider the strengths and weaknesses in the system of internal control.

(AICPA adapted)

9

Determining Sample Size
Using Attributes Sampling,
and Selecting the Items for Testing

Once the auditor has decided which procedures to select and when
they should be performed, it is still necessary to determine the proper
number of items to sample from the population and *which ones* to choose.
This chapter examines the process the auditor goes through in making
these two decisions for tests of transactions and the methodology followed
after the decisions are made. The sales and collection cycle is used as a
frame of reference for discussing these concepts. In the early part of the
chapter, the selection of items from the population by the use of *judgmental* and *random sampling* is examined. The remainder of the chapter
concerns the use of *attributes sampling* as it is applied to tests of transactions. The use of *variables sampling* is studied in Chapter 11.

THE NATURE OF THE PROBLEM

The difficulty facing the auditor in testing most populations is the
prohibitive *cost of testing the entire population*. There are a few audit
procedures, such as confirming bank balances and analyzing legal expense,
where it is typical to sample 100 percent of the population, but these are
exceptions. Once the decision has been made to test less than 100 percent
of the population, it becomes necessary to decide *how many* and *which
specific items* to test.

When a sample is obtained and audit procedures are performed on the sample items, the sample becomes a *representation* of the entire population. This is true regardless of the method used to select the sample. In using an audited sample to draw conclusions about the population, the auditor must evaluate the sample from four different standpoints:

1. A *quantitative* evaluation must be made to estimate the characteristics of interest about the total population. For example, in testing compliance with internal control, an estimate of the error rate of all transactions processed is made on the basis of the sample.
2. A *qualitative* evaluation must be made with respect to the system that generated any errors found. Regardless of the approach taken in the audit, the auditor must always determine the cause of the errors he finds and expand his procedures if follow-up is necessary.
3. An appraisal of the *effectiveness* of the audit procedures employed must be made. If the procedures used are not effective, the sample results will not represent competent evidential matter, no matter how large a sample is taken.
4. An appraisal of the *sampling risk* inherent in the sampling process must be made. There is always a risk that the quantitative conclusions about the total population drawn in number 1 above are wrong, unless 100 percent of the population is examined. Such is the nature of all sampling, whether it be judgmental or statistical. As will be discussed, when a judgmental sample is drawn, an intuitive evaluation is made of this risk. Under statistical sampling, the magnitude of this risk is measured and stated as part of the evaluation process.

JUDGMENTAL SAMPLING

A *judgmental sample* is the determination of the sample size and the selection of the individual items in the sample on the basis of sound reasoning by the auditor. It differs from statistical sampling primarily in the lack of objectivity in selecting the sample items and the inability to measure sampling risk.

The use of judgmental sampling is widespread even by those auditors who are strong advocates of statistical methods. There are many parts of every audit where statistical methods are not applicable, and most CPAs have clients where judgmental sampling is preferable because of cost considerations. Therefore it is important that auditors understand the characteristics of both statistical and judgmental sampling.

Regardless of the method of selecting the sample, the foremost consideration is the *need to make correct generalizations* about the population on the basis of the sample. Failure to do this is an indication of the lack of due care. Thus, in selecting a sample, the auditor is primarily concerned with its *representativeness* of the entire population, in terms of the characteristics of audit interest. This does not mean that the sample must be exactly the same as the population, but it should be approximately the same to be representative. For example, if the population contains significant errors, but the sample is almost free of errors, the sample is *nonrepresentative,* and likely to result in an improper audit decision. To improve the likelihood of a judgmental sample being a representative one for tests of transactions, there are several things the auditor should keep in mind:

1. In selecting items for examination, *each major type of transaction* in the cycle should be included in the sample. For example, in testing purchases of goods and services, it is inappropriate to test only raw materials purchases if the auditor is also interested in transactions such as advertising, repairs, and donations.
2. When different personnel are responsible for processing transactions during the accounting period, some *transactions prepared by each person* should be tested. If there is a change of accounting personnel during the year or if transactions at different locations are handled differently, the likelihood of a nonrepresentative sample is increased when the tests are restricted to the transactions prepared by only one of the employees.
3. When the auditor is testing for errors in amounts, *population items with large balances* should be tested more heavily than those with small balances. In compliance testing the auditor is interested in the adequacy of the controls, but for substantive tests the emphasis should be on testing larger dollar balances, since they are normally likely to contain any material errors.
4. The size of the sample should be modified to take into account the *circumstances of the audit.* For example, when the population size is large, the auditor's exposure to legal liability is high, and if internal controls are weak, the sample size for substantive tests of transactions should be larger than when these conditions do not prevail.
5. Tests of transactions should not be limited to interim testing when the internal controls are inadequate or when certain other conditions affect the auditor's timing of his tests.
6. Increasing the sample size cannot compensate for audit procedures that are ineffective. Careful selection of the proper audit procedures is always essential.

These six considerations are an important part of both judgmental and statistical sampling methods.

The most common approaches to selecting samples from accounting populations are *block sampling, haphazard selection,* and *random selection.* The first two are discussed briefly as a part of judgmental sampling, and the third is examined in more detail separately.

Block Sampling

A *block sample* is the selection of several items in sequence. Once the first item in the block is selected, the remainder of the block is chosen automatically. One example of a block sample is the selection of a *sequence* of 100 sales transactions from the sales journal for the third week of March. A total sample of 100 could also be selected by taking five blocks of 20 items each, ten blocks of 10, or fifty blocks of 2.

It is acceptable to use block samples for compliance testing only if a reasonable number of blocks is used. If few blocks are used, the probability of obtaining a nonrepresentative sample is too great, considering the possibility of such things as employee turnover, changes in the accounting system, and the seasonal nature of many businesses. The exact number has not been specified, but a "reasonable number" for most situations is probably at least nine blocks from nine different months.

Haphazard Selection

When the auditor goes through a population and selects items for the sample without regard to their size, source, or other distinguishing characteristics, he is attempting to select without bias. This is called a *haphazard sample.*

The most serious shortcoming of haphazard sampling is the difficulty of really remaining completely unbiased in selecting sample items. Due to the auditor's training and "cultural bias," certain population items are more likely to be included in the sample than others. For some auditors, sales to certain customers and sales journal entries at the top of the page are more likely to be included in a sample than sales to unknown customers and entries in the middle of the page. For other auditors, entries in the middle of the page or large amounts would be more likely to be selected.

Haphazard and block sampling are often useful and should not be automatically discarded as audit tools. In many situations the cost of unbiased or more complex selection methods outweighs the benefits obtained from using them. For example, assume the auditor wants to trace credits from the accounts receivable subsidiary ledger to the cash receipts journal and other authorized sources as a test for the possibility of fictitious credits in the subsidiary records. A haphazard or block approach is simpler and less costly than random selection in this situation and would be employed by most auditors. It is preferable to use random selection methods for selecting samples whenever it is feasible, but it is also necessary to consider the relationship between cost and benefit.

It is improper and a serious breach of due care to use *statistical measurement techniques* if the sample is selected by the haphazard, block or any other judgmental approach. Only *random selection* is acceptable when the auditor intends to evaluate a population statistically.

RANDOM SELECTION

Defined

A *random sample* is one in which every possible combination of elements (items) in the population has an equal chance of constituting the sample. The only way the auditor can be confident he has obtained a random sample is by adopting a formal methodology that is designed to accomplish this. Three methods of random selection are discussed in this book: *random number tables, computer terminals,* and *systematic sampling.* Each of these methods is commonly used in practice.

Requirements of Random Selection

In selecting a random sample, four important requirements are involved. These apply equally to tests of transactions and account balance testing and to each of the three methods of random selection. The requirements are as follows:

1. *The definition of the population must be consistent with the audit objectives.* It is valid to generalize only about the population from which the sample was taken. Hence it is critical that the auditor carefully define the population before the sample is selected. For instance, assume the auditor decides to test for the possibility of invalid sales. Due to the nature of the system of internal control, he decides to test the system for the entire year. It is inappropriate to take a random sample of items from only a few months to test for this objective, because the population of interest is the recorded sales for the entire year.

2. *The sampling unit must be defined.* A *sampling unit,* or *element,* is an individual item in the population. All sampling units sum to the population total. An example of a sampling unit is the individual sales invoice for a population of sales invoices or an individual customer balance for a list of accounts receivable. Naturally, the sampling unit selected must be consistent with the objective of the test. It makes no sense to select shipping documents as the sampling unit if the objective is to test for the validity of recorded sales.

3. *Every possible combination of sampling units must have an equal probability of constituting the sample.* There are two aspects of this requirement. The first is the possibility of a sampling unit's having no opportunity of being included. This can happen if some of the sampling units are inadvertently or intentionally excluded from the population. As an illustration, if the auditor is tracing from a file of unnumbered shipping documents as a test of unbilled shipments, it is not possible to determine whether all shipping documents have been included in the file. In fact, the missing documents may be the ones most likely to be in error. The auditor can avoid the problem of omitted sampling units by defining the sampling unit as a prenumbered document or a recorded line item in a journal or listing that totals to a population control total. The second aspect is the adoption of a proper methodology for random selection. This is necessary to ensure equal probability. The careful use of one of the three acceptable random sampling methods is meant to accomplish this.

4. *Once an item is selected, it must be pursued to a conclusion and included in the compilation of results.* It is inappropriate to discard a

randomly selected population item and replace it with another one. Similarly, it is necessary to perform the appropriate audit tests on each item in the sample to determine whether any sample items contain exceptions. When there are exceptions, the nature of each discrepancy must be investigated and included as a part of the generalization from the sample to the population. Even though any given sample item may seem unimportant by itself, when the evaluation of the population is made it will affect the audit conclusion reached.

Random Number Tables

A *random number table* is a listing of independent random digits conveniently arranged in tabular form to facilitate the selection of random numbers with multiple digits. An example of such a table, taken from the Interstate Commerce Commission "Table of 105,000 Random Decimal Digits," is included as Figure 9-1. This table has numbered lines and columns, with five digits in each column, as a convenience in reading the tables and documenting the portion of the table used.

The proper use of random number tables is important to ensure the selection of an unbiased sample. Four major steps are involved in the use of the tables:

1. *Establish a numbering system for the population.* Before a set of random numbers can be selected from the table, each item in the population must be identified with a *unique number.* This is usually not a problem, because many of the populations from which the auditor wants a random sample consist of prenumbered documents. When prenumbered records are not used, some type of numbering system must be developed. In rare instances the entire population may have to be renumbered, but ordinarily a simple approach can be devised to meet the objective. An illustration is the selection of a random sample of accounts receivable for confirmation from a trial balance that contains forty pages with up to ninety lines per page. The sampling unit can be defined as a line on the listing with an outstanding balance. The combination of page numbers and line numbers provides a unique identifying number for every line in the population.

2. *Establish correspondence between the random number table and the population.* Once the numbering system has been established for the population, correspondence is established by deciding upon the *number of digits* to use in the random number table and their *association with the population numbering system.* For example, assume the auditor is selecting a sample of one hundred duplicate sales invoices from a file of prenumbered sales invoices beginning with document number 3272 and ending with 8825. Since the invoices contain a four-digit number, it is necessary to use four digits in the random number table. If the first four digits of each five-digit set are used and the starting point in the random

FIGURE 9-1

RANDOM NUMBER TABLE

Item								
	(1)	(2)	(3)	(4)	(5)	(6)	(7)	(8)
1000	37039	97547	64673	31546	99314	66854	97855	99965
1001	25145	84834	23009	51584	66754	77785	52357	25532
1002	98433	54725	18864	65866	76918	78825	58210	76835
1003	97965	68548	81545	82933	93545	85959	63282	61454
1004	78049	67830	14624	17563	25697	07734	48243	94318
1005	50203	25658	91478	08509	23308	48130	65047	77873
1006	40059	67825	18934	64998	49807	71126	77818	56893
1007	84350	67241	54031	34535	04093	35062	58163	14205
1008	30954	51637	91500	48722	60988	60029	60873	37423
1009	86723	36464	98305	08009	00666	29255	18514	49158
1010	50188	22554	86160	92250	14021	65859	16237	72296
1011	50014	00463	13906	35936	71761	95755	87002	71667
1012	66023	21428	14742	94874	23308	58533	26507	11208
1013	04458	61862	63119	09541	01715	87901	91260	03079
1014	57510	36314	30452	09712	37714	95482	30507	68475
1015	43373	58939	95848	28288	60341	52174	11879	18115
1016	61500	12763	64433	02268	57905	72347	49498	21871
1017	78938	71312	99705	71546	42274	23915	38405	18779
1018	64257	93218	35793	43671	64055	88729	11168	60260
1019	56864	21554	70445	24841	04779	56774	96129	73594
1020	35314	29631	06937	54545	04470	75463	77112	77126
1021	40704	48823	65963	39359	12717	56201	22811	24863
1022	07318	44623	02843	33299	59872	86774	06926	12672
1023	94550	23299	45557	07923	75126	00808	01312	46689
1024	34348	81191	21027	77087	10909	03676	97723	34469
1025	92277	57115	50789	68111	75305	53289	39751	45760
1026	56093	58302	52236	64756	50273	61566	61962	93280
1027	16623	17849	96701	94971	94758	08845	32260	59823
1028	50848	93982	66451	32143	05441	10399	17775	74169
1029	48006	58200	58367	66577	68583	21108	41361	20732
1030	56640	27890	28825	96509	21363	53657	60119	75385

number table in Figure 9-1 is item 1000, column 1, the first invoice for inclusion in the sample is 3703. The next three numbers are *outside the range* of the population and are *discarded*. The next sample item is invoice 7804, and so forth.

3. *Establish a route for using the table.* The route defines which digits the auditor uses in a column and the method of reading the table. For a three-digit number, it is, for example, acceptable to use the first three digits, the middle three, or the last three. It is also acceptable to select numbers by reading vertically down columns or horizontally along rows. The route is an *arbitrary decision,* but it needs to be *established in advance* and *followed consistently.*

4. *Select a starting point.* Selecting a random starting point in the table is necessary only to eliminate the predictability of the sample. If the client has a copy of the random number tables used in selecting the random numbers and knows the starting point for their selection, he can

determine which items the auditor will be testing. It is acceptable to pick a starting point by simply using a *"blind stab"* into the table with a pencil. The number the pencil falls on is the first item included in the sample and the place from which the established route begins.

Special Considerations

A major problem in the use of random number tables occurs when there are a large number of *discards*. Discards increase the time it takes to select the sample and enhance the likelihood of making errors in using the table. Certain shortcuts can be used to reduce the discards, but care must be taken to avoid unequal probability of selection. An example is the selection of a random sample from a population of prenumbered shipping documents numbered from 14067 to 16859. If a five-digit number is used in the tables, only about three numbers out of one hundred are usable ($16,859 - 14,067 \div 100,000 = .028$). The discards can be greatly reduced by ignoring the first digit, which is common to all population items, and using a four-digit number in the table. The discards can be further reduced by carefully redefining the way the first digit in the four-digit random number is used. For example, 1 through 3 could be defined to produce a first digit *4*, 4 through 6 a first digit *5*, and 7 through 9 a first digit *6*. Thus, the random number 7426 from the table would be shipping document number 16426 in the population. This method reduces the discards to only about 10 percent, but it is fairly complicated and difficult to use.

Regardless of the method used in selecting a random sample, it is necessary to have *proper documentation*. This is beneficial as a means of rechecking and reviewing the selection of the numbers, expanding the sample if additional items are desired, and defending the methodology if the quality of the audit is questioned. *Minimum documentation* would include sufficient information in the working papers to permit the reproduction of the numbers at a later date. This includes the name and page number of the table, the correspondence between the population and the table used, the route, the starting point, and the sample size. Many auditors simply include in the working papers a copy of the table they used, with the random numbers identified. (For an example see Figure 9-5 on page 304.)

In selecting a random sample, there is a distinction between replacement and nonreplacement sampling. In *replacement sampling,* an element in the population can be included in the sample more than once if the random number corresponding to that element is selected from the table more than once; whereas in *nonreplacement sampling,* an element can be included only once. If the random number corresponding to an element is selected more than once in nonreplacement sampling, it is simply treated as a discard the second time. Although both selection approaches are consistent with sound statistical theory, auditors rarely use replacement sampling.

Computer Terminals

Most CPA firms now rent or have access to computer time-sharing programs which include programs for the selection of random numbers. The advantages of this approach over random number tables are *time saving, reduced likelihood of auditor error* in selecting the numbers, and *automatic documentation.*

In using computer terminals, it is still necessary for each population element to have a *unique identification number,* and *correspondence* must be established between the population numbers and the random numbers generated by the computer. There is no need for concern about discards in establishing correspondence because the computer can eliminate most types of discards.

For a typical computer program, it is necessary to input the smallest and largest numbers in the population sequence, the quantity of random numbers desired, and in some cases a random number to start the program. In addition, the auditor usually has the option of getting the list of random numbers in *selection order,* in *ascending numerical sequence,* or both. The input and output from a computer terminal are illustrated in Figure 9-2. In this illustration the auditor is selecting a sample of thirty shipping documents from the same prenumbered population sequence illustrated in the preceding section where the document numbers ranged from 14067 to 16859.

Systematic Selection

In systematic selection, the auditor calculates an *interval* and then methodically selects the items for the sample based on the size of the interval. The interval is determined by dividing the population size by the number of sample items desired. For example, if a population of sales invoices ranges from 652 to 3151 and the desired sample size is 125, the interval is 20 (3,151 − 652 ÷ 125). The auditor must now select a random number between 0 and 19 to determine the starting point for the sample. If the randomly selected number is 9, the first item in the sample is invoice number 661 (652 + 9). The remaining 124 items are 681 (661 + 20), 701 (681 + 20), and so on to the last item (3141).

The advantage of systematic sampling is its *ease of use.* In most populations a systematic sample can be drawn quickly, the approach automatically puts the numbers in sequential order, and documentation is easy.

A major problem with the use of systematic sampling is the possibility of *bias.* Because of the way in which systematic samples are selected, once the first item in the sample is selected, all other items are chosen automatically. This causes no problem if the characteristic of interest, such as compliance errors, are distributed randomly throughout the population; however, in many cases they are not. If compliance errors occurred at a

Figure 9-2

Random Selection by use of a computer terminal

```
..RUN (TRC900) SAMGEN

THIS PROGRAM GENERATES UP TO 1,000 SINGLE
   OR SETTED RANDOM NUMBERS.

FILE OPTION-YES OR NO? NO
QUIK OPTION-YES OR NO? NO

       ******** D A T A   I N P U T ********

(1) INPUT THE QUANTITY OF RANDOM NUMBERS
      TO BE GENERATED? 30
(2) ARE THE NUMBERS FORMATTED INTO SETS-YES OR NO? NO
(6) INPUT THE QUANTITY OF DIGITS IN THE LARGEST
      NUMBER? 5
(7) INPUT THE NUMBER OF RANGES OF VALUES
      TO BE GENERATED (MAX=50)? 1
(8) FOR EACH OF THE   1 RANGES INPUT THE
      LOWER (L) AND UPPER (U) LIMITS. SEPARATE SETS,
      IF ANY, WITH A HYPHEN (-).

      RANGE
      -----
      1 - 'L? 14067
          U? 16559

(9) PRINT SELECTION-INPUT 1 FOR NUMERICAL
      ORDER, 2 FOR SELECTION ORDER OR 3 FOR BOTH? 3

(10) DO YOU WANT TO CHANGE ANY INPUTS-YES OR NO? NO

     *****INPUT COMPLETE-DATA CHECK WILL BEGIN*****

(11) DO YOU WANT A LISTING OF RANGES SELECTED BEFORE
      DATA CHECK CONTINUES-YES OR NO? NO

(12) TOTAL COUNTED ITEMS =  2493
      REASONABLE-YES OR NO? YES

     **************DATA CHECK COMPLETE************
     ****RANDOM NUMBER GENERATION WILL BEGIN****

          ****GENERATION COMPLETE****

RANDOM NUMBERS-SELECTION ORDER
------------------------------
16258
15472
16159
15223
15390
15470
15592
14916
14297
15063
14249
16241
15701
14090
15100
16473
14199
14273
14775
15608
14224
15308
14682
15742
14431
16017
16225
15900
15674
14134
          ***SORTING***
```

```
RANDOM NUMBERS-NUMERICAL ORDER
------------------------------

SEQUENCE
SELECTED     RANDOM NUMBERS
--------     --------------
   14            14090
   30            14134
   17            14199
   21            14224
   11            14249
   18            14273
    9            14297
   25            14431
   23            14682
   19            14775
    8            14916
   10            15063
   15            15100
    4            15223
   22            15308
    5            15390
    6            15470
    2            15472
    7            15592
   20            15608
   29            15674
   13            15701
   24            15742
   28            15900
   26            16017
    3            16159
   27            16225
   12            16241
    1            16258
   16            16473


          ****RUN FINISHED****

ANOTHER RUN-YES OR NO ? NO
```

certain time of the month or with certain types of documents, a systematic sample would have a higher likelihood of failing to obtain a representative sample than would the two methods previously discussed. This shortcoming is sufficiently serious that some CPA firms do not permit the use of systematic sampling. Other firms require a careful examination of the way the population is listed to evaluate the possibility of a systematic error. In the opinion of the authors, *the use of systematic sampling is not advisable* unless the two other approaches discussed in this section are impractical.

Stratified Selection

In many situations an auditor will prefer not to obtain a simple random sample. Typically, this occurs when he believes certain segments or types of elements of the population differ significantly from the others with respect to the characteristic of audit interest. As an example, in the confirmation of accounts receivable, the auditor normally expects larger errors in accounts with large balances than in those with small balances. If there is a wide range of values in the accounts, it is inappropriate to select a random sample of the entire population without some consideration of the relative size of the items. This is accomplished through *stratification*: dividing the population into subpopulations and selecting a separate random sample from each stratum.

The most important aspect of stratification is deciding *the number of strata* needed and the *characteristics* which determine the elements to be included in each stratum. In composing the stratification design, each element in the population must be included in only one stratum, and all elements must appear in some stratum.

Population stratification is far less common for tests of transactions than for direct tests of account balances. In tests of transactions the primary concern is with the effectiveness of the system rather than with only certain types of transactions. Nevertheless, in some instances it will be desirable to test some types of transactions more extensively than others. This is the case, for example, when the control system is designed to treat certain types of transactions differently, such as any transaction over $100,-000 or those involving foreign customers. When statistical evaluation is being used, *different measurement techniques* are needed for stratified sampling than for simple unrestricted random sampling.

DETERMINATION OF SAMPLE SIZE USING ATTRIBUTES SAMPLING

Regardless of the method of determining the size of a sample, it must be large enough to enable the auditor to have a reasonable level of assurance that the conclusions he reached based on the sample are the same as they would have been if the entire population had been tested. The determination of whether a sample size is proper cannot be made independently of the nature of the audit tests, the exceptions found in the sample, and an analysis of the individual errors. Stated differently, the proper sample size cannot be determined until *after* the tests have been performed and evaluated. Any sample size determined before that point must be regarded as an *initial estimate* for planning. Depending upon the results of the tests, the initial estimate may be sufficient or may require revision.

Before it is possible to evaluate whether a sample size is sufficient for the circumstances, it is necessary to understand the decision-making process the auditor goes through. The determination of the sample size is such an integral part of the entire process of auditing that it is difficult to treat it as a separate problem. To maintain a proper perspective, the decision process for determining the number of items to test is considered as a part of the application of statistical sampling to tests of transactions procedures using *attributes estimation* (or *attributes sampling*). This is meant to aid in understanding not only the concepts of attributes sampling but also the decision-making process involved in determining a proper sample size for tests of transactions.

Attributes estimation in auditing is used to estimate the percentage of items in the population containing some characteristic or attribute of interest. In tests of transactions, the *attribute of interest* is usually a specific type of error and the auditor uses the rate of errors in the sample to estimate the population error rate. Since it is unreasonable to expect the population error rate to be exactly the same as that of the sample, the population error rate is expressed in terms of an *error rate interval*. This interval is a range of values which the auditor asserts has a reasonable probability of containing the true population rate. The formal mathematical measurements used allow him to attach a specific probability to the correctness of this assertion. Furthermore, the interval may be *one-sided* or *two-sided*. A two-sided interval gives upper and lower bounds of probable population error rate, which are generally referred to as the *upper precision limit* and *lower precision limit*. A one-sided interval generally specifies an upper bound only and represents the probable "worst likely error rate." This type of attributes estimate is the one most commonly used in tests of transactions.

In studying attributes sampling for tests of transactions, it is useful to separate the main steps and to study each one separately. The following steps provide an outline of the methodology for using attributes sampling:

1. State the objectives of the audit test.
2. Define the population.
3. Define the sampling unit.
4. Define the attributes of interest.
5. Specify the desired upper precision limit.
6. Specify the desired confidence level.

7. Estimate the population error rate.
8. Determine the initial sample size.
9. Randomly select the sample.
10. Perform the audit procedures.
11. Generalize from the sample to the population.
12. Perform error analysis.
13. Decide on the acceptability of the population.

State the Objectives of the Audit Test

The overall objectives of the test must be stated in terms of the particular transactions cycle being tested. Generally, the overall objective of tests of transactions is to test the controls in a particular cycle. In the test of the sales and collection cycle, the overall objective is usually to test the reliability of controls over sales or cash receipts.

Define the Population

The population represents the body of data about which the auditor wishes to generalize. The auditor can define the population to include whatever data he desires but he must *randomly sample from the entire population* as he has defined it and he may *generalize only about that population from which he has sampled.* For example, in performing tests of recorded sales transactions, the auditor generally defines the population as all sales invoices for the year. If the auditor randomly samples from only one month's transactions, it is invalid to draw statistical conclusions about the invoices for the entire year. It is important that the auditor carefully define the population in advance, consistent with the objectives of the audit tests. Furthermore, in some cases it may be necessary to define more than one population for a given set of audit objectives. For example, if the auditor intends to trace from shipping documents to sales invoices to test for unrecorded sales, and from sales invoices to shipping documents to test validity, there are two populations.

Define the Sampling Unit

The major consideration in defining the sampling unit is to make it consistent with the objectives of the audit tests. Thus, the definition of the population and the planned audit procedures usually dictate the appropriate sampling unit. For example, if the auditor wants to determine how frequently the client fails to fill a customer's order, the sampling unit must be defined as the customer's order. On the other hand, if the objective is to determine whether the proper quantity of the goods described on the customer's order is correctly shipped and billed, it is possible to define the sampling unit as the customer's order, the shipping document, or the duplicate sales invoice.

Define the Attributes of Interest

The auditor must carefully define the *characteristics (attributes)* being tested whenever attributes sampling is used. Unless a precise statement of what constitutes the attribute is made in advance, the staff person who performs the audit procedure will have no guidelines for identifying exceptions. The following is an example of five different attributes being tested as a part of one attributes sampling application:

1. A duplicate sales invoice is in the file.
2. A bill of lading and a customer order are attached to the duplicate sales invoice.
3. There is evidence that quantities, prices, and extensions were verified.
4. The amount on the duplicate sales invoice and the amount recorded in the sales journal are the same.
5. The quantity and the description on the duplicate sales invoice and the bill of lading are the same.

Each of these five attributes is verified for every item randomly selected for the sample. The absence of the attribute for any sample item is an error for that attribute.

Specify the Desired Upper Precision Limit

Even after a sample is audited, the exact population characteristics are still not known and cannot be stated. When attributes sampling is used, the results are stated in terms of the *upper and lower precision limits* as previously defined. As an example, assume an auditor took a random sample of two hundred sales invoices and found six errors when he compared shipping documents with sales invoices as a test of the correctness of the quantity and description in the billing of sales. The true, but unknown, population error rate is probably *not* exactly 3 percent. However, although the calculation is not shown here, it can be statistically determined that the true population error rate is likely to be within ± 2 percent of the sample error rate in this particular circumstance. This means the true population error rate is likely to be between 1 percent and 5 percent (3% ± 2%). In this example the sample error rate is 3 percent, the precision is 2 percent, the upper precision limit is 5 percent, and the lower precision limit is 1 percent.

Establishing the *desired* upper precision limit requires the auditor to make a professional judgment. It represents the error rate the auditor will permit in the population and still be willing to rely upon the controls in the system. The suitable upper precision limit is a question of *materiality* and is therefore affected by the *definition of the attribute* and the *importance of the attribute.* The upper precision limit the auditor will accept has a significant effect on the sample size. If the auditor requires an upper precision limit which is close to the sample error rate, a larger sample is needed than for a higher upper precision limit.

Specify the Desired Confidence Level

Whenever a sample is taken, there is always a risk that the quantitative conclusions about the population will be incorrect. This is always true unless 100 percent of the population is tested. As has been stated, this is the nature of both judgmental and statistical sampling.

When the auditor computes an upper precision limit on the basis of a statistical sample, there is still a chance that the true population error rate will exceed the computed value if the sample happens to be non-representative. In attributes testing, the confidence level is the statistical means of expressing the probability that the true population error rate does not exceed the stated upper precision limit. The confidence level, which is often referred to as *reliability,* is traditionally expressed as a percent. Referring to the foregoing example, assume that the auditor specifies the confidence level at 90 percent when the upper precision limit is an error rate of 5 percent. The auditor can now state in statistical terms that he is 90 percent confident that the true population error rate is 5 percent or less. Another way of saying this is that there is a *statistical risk* of 10 percent (100% − 90%) that the true population error rate exceeds 5 percent. The auditor must decide for himself if the desired reliability and upper precision limit are satisfactory to meet his audit objectives.

Choosing the appropriate confidence level in a particular situation is difficult, and the auditor must make this decision using his best judgment. Since the confidence level is a measure of the level of audit assurance the auditor desires, the important considerations affecting its choice are the *degree to which the auditor wishes to rely upon the system* and the *potential for adverse actions* against the client by the SEC, creditors, or other statement users. If the auditor plans to rely heavily upon the system as a basis for reducing substantive tests, a high level of assurance is desirable. Similarly, if the auditor feels the exposure to legal liability is great, it is desirable to set high confidence levels to minimize the likelihood of the true error rate's being greater than the computed results. There is general consensus in the profession that confidence levels used for tests of transactions should range from *90 to 95 percent.*

The auditor can establish different upper precision limit and confidence level requirements for different attributes of a particular audit test. For example, it is common for auditors to have different materiality and confidence level requirements for tests of credit approval than for tests of the existence of a bill of lading.

Estimate the Population Error Rate

In attributes sampling, an *advance estimate* of the population error rate is necessary to plan the appropriate sample size. If the estimated population error rate is low, a relatively small sample size will satisfy the auditor's desired upper precision limit. It is common to use the *results of the preceding year's audit* as information to help make this estimate; but if last year's results are not available or if they are considered unreliable, the auditor can take a small *preliminary sample* of the current year's population for this purpose. It is not critical that the estimates be absolutely correct because the current year's sample error rate is ultimately used to estimate the population characteristics.

Determine the Initial Sample Size

Four factors determine the initial sample size for attributes sampling: the *population size,* the *desired upper precision limit,* the *desired confidence level,* and the *advance estimate of the population error rate.* The population size is not a major factor in the early part of the following discussion and is examined later. The initial sample size is called an initial one because the errors in the actual sample must be evaluated before it is possible to decide whether the sample is sufficiently large to achieve the audit objectives.

When the three major factors affecting sample size have been determined, it is possible to compute an initial sample by using the *binomial distribution.* The concepts for the binomial distribution are straightforward, but the calculations are burdensome. Tables have been developed to overcome this and are included in Figure 9-3 for confidence levels of 90 and 95 percent. It should be kept in mind that these are "one-sided tables," which means that they represent the *upper* precision limit for the given confidence level.

Use of the tables. In using the tables to compute the initial sample size, three steps are required:

1. Select the table corresponding to the desired confidence level.
2. Locate the expected occurrence rate at the top of the table.
3. Read down the table in that column to the line that contains the desired upper precision limit. The left-hand column for that line contains the initial sample size to use. Interpolation for values not in the table is valid, but a minimum sample size of 50 items is required.

To illustrate the use of the table, assume an auditor is willing to rely upon the system of credit approval if the rate of missing credit approvals in the population (desired upper precision limit) does not exceed 6 percent at a 95 percent confidence level. On the basis of past experience, the sample error rate has been about 4 percent. Using the 95 percent confidence level table in Figure 9-3, the initial sample size is determined to be 400. (Occurrence rate is 4%; read down until 6 percent is reached in the table.)

Is this a large enough sample size for this audit? It is not possible to answer that question until after the tests have been performed. If the actual error rate in the sample turns out to be somewhat over 4 percent, but less than 6 percent, the auditor will be unsure of the adequacy of the controls. This will become apparent as we proceed.

Effect of Population Size. In the preceding discussion the size of the population was ignored in determining the initial sample size. It may seem strange to some readers, but statistical theory proves that in most types of populations where attributes sampling applies, the population size is only a *minor* consideration in determining sample size. This is true because representativeness is ensured by the random selection process. Once an adequate sample size is obtained to include a good cross-section of items, additional items are not needed.

The tables used by most auditors, including the tables in this text, are based upon infinite population sizes. It is possible to take the population size into effect in determining the initial sample size by making an adjustment called the *finite correction factor*. The finite correction factor has the effect of significantly reducing the sample size only when more than 10 percent of the population is included in the sample. The calculation is as follows:

$$n = \frac{n'}{1 + \dfrac{n'}{N}}$$

where n' = sample size before considering the effect of the
population size
N = population size
n = revised sample size after considering the effect of
the population size

As an example, assume the size of the population of sales orders in the previous problem to be 2,000. The revised sample size is computed as follows:

$$n = \frac{400}{1 + 400/2,000} = 333$$

If the population is 20,000 rather than 2,000, the revised sample size is 392, which is not significantly lower than the 400 shown in the table.

FIGURE 9-3

One-Sided Upper Precision Limits for Confidence Level of 90.0 Percent

Occurrence Rate

Sample Size	0.0	.5	1.0	2.0	3.0	4.0	5.0	6.0	7.0	8.0	9.0	10.0	12.0	14.0	16.0	18.0	20.0	25.0	30.0	40.0	50.0
50	4.5			7.6		10.3		12.9		15.4		17.8	20.1	22.7	24.7	27.2	29.1		39.8	50.0	59.9
100	2.3		3.3	5.2	6.6	7.8	9.1	10.3	11.7	12.7	14.0	15.0	17.3	19.6	21.7	24.0	26.1	31.4	36.6	46.9	56.8
150	1.5			4.4		6.9		9.3		11.6		13.9	16.1	18.4	20.5	22.7	24.8		35.2	45.5	55.4
200	1.1	1.9	2.6	4.0	5.2	6.4	7.6	8.8	10.0	11.0	12.2	13.3	15.5	17.7	19.8	22.0	24.0	29.3	34.5	44.4	54.4
250	.9			3.7		6.1		8.4		10.7		12.9	15.1	17.2	19.3	21.5	23.6		33.7	43.7	53.7
300	.8		2.2	3.5	4.7	5.9	7.0	8.2	9.3	10.4	11.5	12.6	14.7	16.9	19.0	21.1	23.2	28.2	33.2	43.2	53.2
350	.7			3.3		5.7		8.0		10.2		12.3	14.5	16.7	18.8	20.9	22.8		32.8	42.8	52.8
400	.6	1.3	2.0	3.2	4.4	5.6	6.7	7.8	8.9	10.0	11.1	12.2	14.3	16.5	18.5	20.5	22.5	27.5	32.5	42.5	52.5
450	.5			3.1		5.5		7.7		9.9		12.0	14.2	16.3	18.3	20.3	22.3		32.3	42.3	52.2
500	.5		1.8	3.1	4.2	5.4	6.5	7.6	8.7	9.8	10.9	11.9	14.1	16.1	18.1	20.1	22.1	27.1	32.1	42.1	52.0
550	.4			3.0		5.3		7.5		9.7		11.8	13.9	15.9	17.9	19.9	21.9		31.9	41.9	51.9
600	.4	1.1	1.7	2.9	4.1	5.2	6.3	7.4	8.5	9.6	10.7	11.7	13.7	15.7	17.7	19.7	21.7	26.7	31.7	41.7	51.7
650	.4			2.9		5.2		7.4		9.5		11.6	13.6	15.6	17.6	19.6	21.6		31.6	41.6	51.6
700	.3		1.7	2.9	4.0	5.1	6.2	7.3	8.4	9.5	10.5	11.5	13.5	15.5	17.5	19.5	21.5	26.5	31.5	41.5	51.5
750	.3			2.8		5.1		7.3		9.4		11.4	13.4	15.4	17.4	19.4	21.4		31.4	41.4	51.4
800	.3	1.0	1.6	2.8	3.9	5.0	6.1	7.2	8.3	9.3	10.3	11.3	13.3	15.3	17.3	19.3	21.3	26.3	31.3	41.3	51.3
850	.3			2.8		5.0		7.2		9.2		11.2	13.2	15.3	17.3	19.3	21.3		31.3	41.3	51.3
900	.3		1.6	2.7	3.9	5.0	6.0	7.1	8.2	9.2	10.2	11.2	13.2	15.2	17.2	19.2	21.2	26.2	31.2	41.2	51.2
950	.2			2.7		4.9		7.1		9.1		11.1	13.1	15.1	17.1	19.1	21.1		31.1	41.1	51.1
1000	.2	.9	1.5	2.7	3.8	4.9	6.0	7.1	8.1	9.1	10.1	11.1	13.1	15.1	17.1	19.1	21.1	26.1	31.1	41.1	51.1
1500	.2		1.4	2.5	3.6	4.7	5.7	6.7	7.7	8.7	9.7	10.7	12.7	14.7	16.7	18.7	20.7	25.7	30.7	40.7	50.7
2000	.1	.8	1.3	2.5	3.5	4.5	5.5	6.5	7.5	8.5	9.5	10.5	12.5	14.5	16.5	18.5	20.5	25.5	30.5	40.6	50.6
2500	.1		1.3	2.4	3.4	4.4	5.4	6.4	7.4	8.4	9.4	10.4	12.4	14.4	16.4	18.4	20.4	25.4	30.4	40.4	50.4
3000	.1	.7	1.3	2.4	3.4	4.4	5.4	6.4	7.4	8.4	9.4	10.4	12.4	14.4	16.4	18.4	20.4	25.4	30.4	40.4	50.4
4000	.1	.7	1.2	2.3	3.3	4.3	5.3	6.3	7.3	8.3	9.3	10.3	12.3	14.3	16.3	18.3	20.3	25.3	30.3	40.3	50.3
5000	.0	.7	1.2	2.3	3.2	4.2	5.2	6.2	7.2	8.2	9.2	10.2	12.2	14.2	16.2	18.2	20.2	25.2	30.2	40.2	50.2

FIGURE 9-3 (cont.)

One-Sided Upper Precision Limits for Confidence Level of 95.0 Percent

Occurrence Rate

Sample Size	0.0	.5	1.0	2.0	3.0	4.0	5.0	6.0	7.0	8.0	9.0	10.0	12.0	14.0	16.0	18.0	20.0	25.0	30.0	40.0	50.0
50	5.8			9.1		12.1		14.8		17.4		19.9	22.3	25.1	27.0	29.6	31.6		42.4	52.6	62.4
100	3.0		4.7	6.2	7.6	8.9	10.2	11.5	13.0	14.0	15.4	16.4	18.7	21.2	23.3	25.6	27.7	33.1	38.4	48.7	56.6
150	2.0			5.1		7.7		10.2		12.6		15.0	17.3	19.6	21.7	24.0	26.1		36.7	47.0	56.8
200	1.5	2.4	3.1	4.5	5.8	7.1	8.3	9.5	10.8	11.9	13.1	14.2	16.4	18.7	20.9	23.1	25.2	30.5	35.7	45.7	55.6
250	1.2			4.2		6.7		9.1		11.4		13.7	15.9	18.1	20.3	22.4	24.6		34.8	44.8	54.7
300	1.0		2.6	3.9	5.2	6.4	7.6	8.8	10.0	11.1	12.2	13.3	15.5	17.7	19.8	22.0	24.1	29.1	34.1	44.1	54.1
350	.9			3.7		6.2		8.5		10.8		13.0	15.2	17.4	19.5	21.7	23.6		33.6	43.6	53.6
400	.7	1.6	2.3	3.6	4.8	6.0	7.2	8.3	9.5	10.6	11.7	12.8	15.0	17.2	19.2	21.2	23.2	28.2	33.2	43.2	53.2
450	.7			3.5		5.9		8.2		10.4		12.6	14.8	16.8	18.9	20.9	22.9		32.9	42.9	52.9
500	.6		2.1	3.4	4.6	5.8	6.9	8.0	9.2	10.3	11.4	12.5	14.6	16.7	18.6	20.7	22.6	27.6	32.6	42.6	52.6
550	.5			3.3		5.7		7.9		10.1		12.3	14.4	16.4	18.4	20.4	22.4		32.4	42.4	52.4
600	.5	1.3	2.0	3.2	4.4	5.6	6.7	7.8	9.0	10.0	11.2	12.2	14.2	16.2	18.2	20.2	22.2	27.2	32.2	42.2	52.2
650	.5			3.2		5.5		7.7		10.0		12.1	14.1	16.1	18.1	20.1	22.1		32.1	42.1	52.1
700	.4		1.9	3.1	4.3	5.4	6.6	7.7	8.8	9.9	10.8	11.9	13.9	15.9	17.9	19.9	21.9	26.9	31.9	41.9	51.9
750	.4			3.1		5.4		7.6		9.8		11.8	13.8	15.8	17.8	19.8	21.8		31.8	41.8	51.8
800	.4	1.1	1.8	3.0	4.2	5.3	6.4	7.5	8.7	9.7	10.7	11.7	13.7	15.7	17.7	19.7	21.7	26.7	31.7	41.7	51.7
850	.4			3.0		5.3		7.5		9.6		11.6	13.6	15.6	17.6	19.6	21.6		31.6	41.6	51.6
900	.3		1.7	3.0	4.1	5.2	6.3	7.5	8.5	9.5	10.5	11.5	13.5	15.5	17.5	19.5	21.5	26.5	31.5	41.5	51.5
950	.3			2.9		5.2		7.4		9.4		11.4	13.4	15.5	17.4	19.5	21.4		31.5	41.5	51.5
1000	.3	1.0	1.7	2.9	4.0	5.2	6.3	7.4	8.4	9.4	10.4	11.4	13.4	15.4	17.4	19.4	21.4	26.4	31.4	41.4	51.4
1500	.2	.8	1.5	2.7	3.8	4.9	5.9	6.9	7.9	8.9	9.9	10.9	12.9	14.9	16.9	18.9	20.9	25.9	30.9	40.9	50.9
2000	.1	.8	1.4	2.6	3.7	4.7	5.7	6.7	7.7	8.7	9.7	10.7	12.7	14.7	16.7	18.7	20.7	25.7	30.7	40.7	50.7
2500	.1		1.4	2.6	3.6	4.6	5.6	6.6	7.6	8.6	9.6	10.6	12.6	14.6	16.6	18.6	20.6	25.6	30.6	40.6	50.6
3000	.1	.8	1.4	2.5	3.5	4.5	5.5	6.5	7.5	8.5	9.5	10.5	12.5	14.5	16.5	18.5	20.5	25.5	30.5	40.5	50.5
4000	.1	.7	1.3	2.4	3.4	4.4	5.4	6.4	7.4	8.4	9.4	10.4	12.4	14.4	16.4	18.4	20.4	25.4	30.4	40.4	50.4
5000	.1	.7	1.3	2.3	3.3	4.3	5.3	6.3	7.3	8.3	9.3	10.3	12.3	14.3	16.3	18.3	20.3	25.3	30.3	40.3	50.3

Effect of a Change in the Factors. In order to properly understand the concepts underlying statistical sampling in auditing, the reader should understand the effect of individually changing any of the four factors that determine sample size when the other factors remain unchanged. The following table illustrates the effect of increasing each of the four factors. A decrease of any of the factors will have the opposite effect.

Type of Change	Effect on Preliminary Sample Size
1. Increase the desired confidence level.	Increase
2. Increase the desired upper precision limit.	Decrease
3. Increase the estimate of the population error rate.	Increase
4. Increase the population size.	Increase

Randomly Select the Sample

After the auditor has computed the initial sample size for the attributes sampling application, he must choose the particular elements in the population to be included in the sample. It is essential that the selection be random whenever statistical sampling is used. This can be done by the use of random tables, computers, or systematic sampling, as previously discussed.

Perform the Audit Procedures

The audit procedures are performed in the same manner in statistical sampling as in judgmental sampling. The auditor examines each item in the sample to determine whether it is consistent with the definition of the attribute, and he maintains a record of all the errors found.

In performing the audit procedures, it is essential that the auditor avoid *nonsampling errors.* A nonsampling error occurs when the auditor fails to recognize the existence of an actual error in the sample items. This can result from many causes, including the lack of understanding of the objectives of the test, fatigue or boredom, carelessness, and deception on the part of the client by using fictitious documents or records. Nonsampling errors have the effect of understating the population error rate because of the omission of actual errors in the sample. For example, assume the auditor is comparing the quantity and description of merchandise shipped as they are stated on the shipping document with the corresponding data on the duplicate sales invoice for a sample of three hundred items. If the actual number of exceptions in the sample is nine, but the auditor unintentionally overlooks four of them because his mind wanders, a serious nonsampling error has occurred. Due to the auditor's failure to follow due care, an unacceptable population may be accepted.

A related consideration is the identification of types of *errors not defined as attributes* during planning. These must never be overlooked just because they were not expected. Unexpected errors usually result in the auditor's revising his initial definition of attributes or interest, and may even necessitate a revision of planned sample size.

Generalize from the Sample to the Population

After the auditor has completed his tests of the sample, he is in a position to generalize about the population. It would be wrong for him to conclude that the population error rate is exactly the same as the sample error rate; the odds of this being the case are just too low. Instead, he must *compute the upper precision limit* for the population error rate at the *confidence level he desires* based on the *actual sample results*. This is easily accomplished by using the same attributes sampling table that was used for determining the initial sample size.

To find the upper precision limit, it is necessary to know the error rate that was found in the sample, the actual sample size, the population size, and the desired confidence level. To illustrate, if the auditor has tested the random sample of four hundred items from the population of two thousand sales orders from the previous example and has determined that there are twelve missing credit approvals (3%), he can compute the upper precision limit for the population with the following steps:

1. Select the table corresponding to the desired confidence level.
2. Locate the actual error rate at the top of the table (occurrence rate).
3. Locate the actual sample size on the left side of the table. The intersection of the error rate and sample size is the computed upper precision limit at the desired confidence level. Again, it is appropriate to interpolate.

For the example in the preceding paragraph, the table in Figure 9-3 indicates a computed upper precision limit of 4.8 percent at a 95 percent confidence level (using the 95% confidence level table; a sample size of 400 and a 3.0 occurrence rate.) This result means the auditor can state with a 95 percent confidence level that the true population error rate does not exceed 4.8 percent. Stated another way, it means there is a 5 percent statistical risk (100% — 95%) of the true population error rate exceeding 4.8 percent. Does this result indicate that if 100 percent of the population were tested, the true error rate would be 4.8 percent? No, the true error rate is unknown, but there is only a 5 percent chance of the true rate being more than 4.8 percent. There is a 95 percent chance of it being 4.8 percent or less.

A useful way of looking at the statistical results is by a combination of the *point estimate of the error rate* and the *computed precision interval*. The point estimate of the population error rate is the same as the sample error rate; in this case 3 percent. The computed precision interval is 1.8 percent (4.8% — 3%). It represents a statistical measure of the inability to accurately measure the population error rate due to the restriction of the test to a sample. The combination of the two is the "worst likely error rate," which is called the computed upper precision limit, at the confidence level specified.

The *finite correction factor* can also be used to adjust the computed upper precision limit. This is done by multiplying the *computed precision interval* by $\sqrt{N-n}/N$ and adding the result to the sample error rate (N = population size; n = actual sample size). In the previous example the revised precision interval is approximately 1.6 percent (1.8% × $\sqrt{(2,000 - 400)}/2,000$). This means the revised computed upper precision limit is 4.6 percent (3.0% + 1.6%). The reduction in the computed upper precision limit is ordinarily not worth the effort to calculate it unless more than 10 percent of the population has been tested.

Perform Error Analysis

In addition to computing the upper precision limit for each attribute, it is necessary to *analyze the individual errors* to determine the breakdown in the internal control that caused them. The errors could have been caused by carelessness of employees, misunderstood instructions, intentional failure to perform procedures, or many other factors. The nature of an error and its cause have a significant effect on the qualitative evaluation of the system. For example, if all the errors in the tests of internal verification of sales invoices occurred while the person normally responsible for performing the tests was on vacation, this would affect the auditor's evaluation of the system and the subsequent investigation.

Decide on the Acceptability of the Population

It is important to distinguish between the *desired upper precision limit* and *confidence level* that were *chosen* by the auditor before the tests were performed and the *computed upper precision limit* and *confidence level* that *resulted* from the sample. The first set represents the *standards that were deemed necessary* by the auditor, and the second set is the *result that is objectively computed* on the basis of the sample.

Before the population can be considered acceptable, the computed upper precision limit determined on the basis of the actual sample results must be *less than or equal to* the desired upper precision limit when both are based upon the desired confidence level. In the example just given where the auditor had prespecified that he would accept a 6 percent population error rate at a 95 percent confidence level and the computed upper precision limit was 4.6 percent, the requirements of the sample have been met. In this case the control being tested can be relied upon to reduce the substantive tests as planned, provided a careful analysis of the cause of errors does not indicate the possibility of a significant problem in a particular aspect of the controls not previously considered.

When the computed upper precision limit fails to meet the planned requirements, it is necessary to take specific action. Four courses of action can be followed:

1. *Revise the upper precision limit or confidence level desired.* This alternative should be followed only when the auditor has concluded that the original specifications were too conservative. The relaxing of either the precision limit or the confidence level may be difficult to defend if the auditor is ever subject to review by a court or a commission. If these requirements are changed, it should be on the basis of well-thought-out reasons.

2. *Expand the sample size.* An increase in the sample size has the effect of decreasing the computed upper precision limit if the actual sample error rate does not increase. This can be demonstrated with the table in Figure 9-3 by keeping the sample error rate constant and observing the decrease in the computed upper precision limit for increases in sample size.

The decision of whether to increase the sample size until the computed upper precision limit is less than the desired upper precision limit must be made on the basis of the cost versus the benefits. If the sample is not expanded, it is necessary to perform additional substantive tests due to the unacceptability of the controls. The cost of the additional compliance testing must be compared with the additional cost of the substantive tests. Of course there is always a chance that an expanded attributes sample will continue to produce unacceptable results. Therefore, additional substantive tests will still be necessary. Another examination of Figure 9-3 will demonstrate that when the sample error rate is close to the desired upper precision limit, a large sample size is needed to satisfy the statistical requirements.

3. *Alter the substantive procedures.* Instead of expanding the sample in order to rely upon the controls, it is acceptable instead to perform additional substantive procedures. For example, if the compliance tests of the internal verification procedures for verifying the price, extension, and quantities on sales invoices indicate they are not being properly followed, the auditor may increase the substantive tests of the pricing, extension, and footing. An expansion of the confirmation of accounts receivable may also help to discover whether there are material errors.

4. *Write a management letter.* This action is desirable, in combination with one of the other three actions, regardless of the nature of the errors. When the auditor determines that the control system is not operating effectively, management should be informed.

In some instances it may be acceptable to limit the action to writing a management letter when the computed precision limit exceeds the required limit. This occurs if the auditor has no intention of relying on the control being tested or has already carried out substantive procedures to his own satisfaction as a part of the tests of transactions.

Other Considerations

In the preceding discussions, we bypassed several important considerations involving selecting the proper sample size and drawing conclusions about the results for the sake of better continuity. These topics are discussed at this time.

Distinction between Random Selection and Statistical Measurement. Auditors often do not understand the distinction between random selection and statistical measurement. It should now be clear that random selection is a part of statistical sampling but is not, by itself, statistical measurement. To have statistical measurement, it is necessary to mathematically generalize from the sample to the population.

It is acceptable to use random selection procedures without drawing statistical conclusions, but this practice is questionable if a reasonably large sample size has been selected. Whenever the auditor takes a random sample, regardless of his basis for determining the size of the sample, there is a *statistical measurement inherent in the sample*. Since there is little or no cost involved in computing the upper precision limit, we believe it should be done whenever it is possible. It would of course be inappropriate to draw a statistical conclusion unless the sample were randomly selected.

Need for Adequate Documentation. It is important that the auditor retain adequate records of the procedures performed, the methods used to select the sample and perform the tests, the results found in the tests, and the conclusions drawn. This is necessary as a means of *evaluating the results* of all tests when they are combined and as a basis for *defending the audit* if the need arises. An example of the type of documentation commonly found in practice is included in the appendix at the end of the chapter.

Need for Professional Judgment. A criticism occasionally levied against statistical sampling is that it embodies a reduction in the use of professional judgment. An examination of the thirteen steps given previously indicates how unwarranted this criticism is. To have a proper application of attributes sampling, it is necessary to use professional judgment in every one of the steps. For example, the selection of the initial sample size is dependent primarily upon the desired confidence level, the desired upper precision limit, and the estimated error rate. Each of these requires the exercise of high-level professional judgment. Similarly, the final evaluation of the adequacy of the entire application of attributes sampling, including the adequacy of the sample size, must also be based upon high-level professional judgment.

Use of Judgmental Sampling. The preceding discussion of attributes sampling should not be interpreted as a criticism of performing audit tests without the use of statistical sampling. First of all, a major portion of all audit tests must be performed outside of a statistical sampling context. This includes footing of journals, reviewing records, and having discussions with personnel. Second, in many instances the cost of performing random selection or testing a sufficient number of items to warrant a statistical inference exceeds the benefits of using a statistical approach.

The primary reason for not criticizing judgmental sampling, however, is the fact that in most instances it *does not differ* substantially from statistical methods. A careful examination of the steps in applying attributes sampling indicates that except for the degree of formality required, the methods are essentially the same for a judgmental or a statistical approach. The most important differences are in specifying the desirable upper precision limit, the confidence level, and the estimated error rate. In addition, there is a difference in the way the auditor generalizes from the sample to the population. Nevertheless, the same decisions that are made when the auditor uses statistical sampling must also be made, on a more intuitive basis, for judgmental sampling.

The most important advantage of attributes sampling for tests of transactions as compared with judgmental sampling is the requirement of *formally* specifying the auditor's judgments. We believe this encourages more careful and precise thinking about the *objectives* of the audit tests. We also believe the ability to determine the *results achieved* in terms of a computed upper precision limit and a confidence level is a significant benefit of attributes sampling.

Appendix C:
Case Illustration

To illustrate the concepts discussed in this chapter, the Hillsburg Hardware case from the appendix in Chapter 8 is extended to include the determination of sample size, the selection of items for testing, and the conclusions drawn on the basis of the results of the tests. The only parts of the tests of the sales and collection cycle included here are the tests of credit approval, the shipment of goods, the billing of customers, and recording the amounts in the records. It should be kept in mind that the procedures for Hillsburg Hardware were developed specifically for that client and would probably not be applicable for a different audit. The audit procedures for these tests are repeated at this time, along with comments to indicate the relationship of each procedure to attributes sampling.

In applying attributes sampling to the procedures for Hillsburg Hard-

Audit Procedures

Procedure	Comments

General

1. Perform analytical tests of the accounts in the cycle and compare the results with industry trends and preceding year.

   Random selection and statistical sampling are not applicable for the general steps. Advanced statistical techniques, such as regression analysis, could be applicable for analysis of the results of analytical tests.

2. Test foot and crossfoot the journals, and trace the totals to the general ledger (one month).

   Random selection and statistical sampling are not applicable for general procedures 2 to 4.

3. Review the journals and general ledger for unusual transactions and amounts.

4. Review the subsidiary ledger for miscellaneous credits.

Shipment of Goods

1. Account for a sequence of shipping documents.

   It is possible to do this by selecting a random sample and accounting for all customer orders selected. This requires a separate set of random numbers, since the sampling unit is different than for the other tests.

2. Trace selected shipping documents to a duplicate sales invoice for assurance that each one has been billed.

   No errors are expected, and a 2 percent error rate is considered acceptable at a 95 percent confidence level. A sample size of 200 is selected. The shipping documents are traced to the duplicate sales invoices. This is done for all 200 items. There are no exceptions for either number 1 or number 2. The results are considered acceptable. There is no further information about this portion of the tests in this illustration.

Billing of Customers and Recording the Sales in the Records

1. Account for a sequence of sales invoices in the sales journal.

   The audit procedures for billing and recording sales are the primary ones tested using attributes sampling for this case illustration. The attributes-sampling data sheet includes each of these procedures as attributes.

2. Trace selected duplicate sales invoice numbers from the sales journal to
   a. Accounts receivable subsidiary ledger, and test for amount, date, and invoice number.

Audit Procedures (Cont.)

Procedure	Comments
b. Duplicate sales invoice, and test for the total amount recorded in the journal, date, customer name, and classification. Check the pricing, extensions, footings, and evidence of internal verification by Pam Dilley on the duplicate sales invoice.	
c. Bill of lading, and test for customer name, product description, quantity, and date.	
d. Duplicate sales order, and test for customer name, product description, quantity, date, and approval by Pam Dilley.	
e. Customer order, and test for customer name, product description, quantity, date, and credit approval by Rick Chulick.	

ware, there are only two functions where statistical sampling is being used: the shipment of goods and the billing of customers. The emphasis is put on the billing of customers in the illustration because the duplicate sales invoice is the sampling unit for most of the audit procedures. In order to concentrate on the attributes sampling applications for the billing function, comments about the shipping function are restricted to the ones shown adjacent to the list of audit procedures. The reader should recognize, however, that the attributes sampling methodology followed for the shipping function would be essentially the same as the methodology illustrated for the billing function in the remainder of the case.

Objectives, Population, and the Sampling Unit

Most auditors use some type of preprinted form to document each attributes sampling application. An example of a commonly used form is given in Figure 9-4. The top part of the form includes a definition of (1) the objective, (2) the population, and (3) the sampling unit.

Define the Attributes of Interest

The attributes used in this application are taken directly from the audit program. The procedures that can be used as attributes for a particular application of attributes sampling depend upon the definition of the sampling unit. In this case all the procedures in the billing function can be included. The eight attributes used for this case are illustrated in Figure 9-4.

The definition of the attribute is a critical part of the use of attributes sampling. The decision as to which attributes to combine and which

FIGURE 9-4

HILLSBURG HARDWARE—STATISTICAL SAMPLING DATA SHEET—ATTRIBUTES

Client *Hillsburg Hardware*   Year end *12/31/7x*
Audit Area *Compliance Tests – Billing Function*   Pop. size *5,764*

Define the objective(s) *Examine duplicate sales invoices and related documents to determine if the system is functioning as intended and as described in the audit program.*

Define the population precisely (including stratification, if any) *Sales invoices for the period 11/1/7x to 12/31/7x. First invoice number = 3689. Last invoice number = 9452.*

Define the sampling unit, organization of population items, and random selection procedures *Sales invoice number, recorded in the sales journal sequentially; random number table.*

Description of Attributes	Planned Audit				Actual Results			
	Expect. error rate	Upr. prec. rate	Conf. level	Sample size	Sample size	Number of errors	Sample error rate	Upper precision limit
1. Existence of the sales invoice number in the sales journal.	0	2	95	150				
2. Amount and other data in the subsidiary ledger agree with sales journal entry.	1	4	95	150				
3. Amount and other data in the sales invoice agree with the sales journal entry.	1	4	95	150				
4. Evidence that pricing, extensions, and footings are checked (initials and correct amount).	1	4	95	150				
5. Quantity and other data on the bill of lading agree with the duplicate sales invoice.	1	4	95	150				
6. Quantity and other data on the sales order agree with the duplicate sales invoice.	1	6	95	50				
7. Quantity and other data on the customer order agree with the duplicate sales invoice.	2	8	95	50				
8. Credit is approved by Rick Chulick.	3	8	95	50				

Intended use of sampling results:

1. Effect on Audit Plan:

2. Recommendations to Management:

ones to keep separate is the most important aspect of defining the attributes. If all possible types of attributes, such as customer name, date, price, and quantity, are separated for each procedure, the large number of attributes makes the problem unmanageable. On the other hand, if all the procedures are combined into one or two attributes, greatly dissimilar errors are evaluated together. Somewhere in between, a reasonable compromise is needed.

Establishing the Desired Upper Precision Limits and the Desired Confidence Levels, Estimating Expected Error Rates, and Determining the Initial Sample Size

The upper precision limit for each attribute is decided on the basis of the auditor's judgment of what error rate is material. The failure to record a sales invoice would be highly significant, especially considering this particular system; therefore, as indicated in Figure 9-4, the lowest upper precision limit is chosen for attribute 1. The incorrect billing of the customer represents potentially significant errors, but no error is likely to be for the full amount of the invoice. As a result, a 4 percent desired upper precision limit is chosen for each of the attributes directly related to billing of shipments and recording the amounts in the records. The last three attributes have higher upper precision limits, since they are of less importance for the audit.

A confidence level of 95 percent is desired for all tests due to the change in personnel in the past year and the increased exposure to liability due to the declining profit.

The expected error rate is based upon previous years' results, modified upward slightly due to the change in personnel. The preliminary sample size for each attribute is determined from Figure 9-3 on the basis of the above considerations. This information is summarized for all attributes in Figure 9-4.

Random Selection

The random selection for the case is straightforward except for the need for a sample of 150 items for attributes 1 through 5 and only 50 items for attributes 6 through 8. This problem can be easily overcome by selecting a random sample of 50 for use on all eight attributes followed by another sample of 100 for the first five attributes. The documentation for the selection of the first fifty numbers is illustrated in Figure 9-5.

Perform the Audit Procedures and Generalize to the Population

The audit procedures that are included in the audit program and summarized in the attributes sampling data sheet must be carefully performed for every element in the sample. As a means of documenting the

FIGURE 9-5

HILLSBURG HARDWARE—RANDOM SAMPLE FOR TESTING SALES

Hillsburg Hardware
Random Sample for Testing Sales

	(1)	(2)	(3)	(4)	(5)	(6)
1036	77339	64605	4 82583	18 85011	00955	50 84348
1087	61714	57933	5 37342	26000	33 93611	93346
1088	15232	48027	15832	19 62924	11509	95853 End
1089	41447	34275	10779	20 83515	34 63899	30932
1090	23244	43524	16382	21 36340	35 73581	76780
1091	53460	83542	25224	22 70378	36 49604	14609
1092	53442	16897	6 61578	05032	37 81825	76822
1093	55543	19096	04130	23104	38 60534	44842
1094	18185	63329	02340	23 63111	39 41768	74409
1095	02372	45690	7 38595	23121	40 73818	74454
1096	51715	35492	8 61371	24 87132	41 81585	55439
1097	24717	16785	9 42786	25 86585	21858	39489
1098	78002	32604	10 87295	26 93702	99438	68184
1099	35995	08275	11 62405	27 43313	03249	74135
1100	29152	86922	31508	28 42703	42 59638	31226
1101	84192 Start	90150	02904	26835	17174	42301
1102	21791	24764	12 53674	30093	43 45134	24073
1103	63501	05040	13 71881	17759	44 91881	69614
1104	07149	1 69285	14 55481	24889	45 67061	06631
1105	59443	98962	15 74778	29 96920	46 65620	36794
1106	39059	2 58021	28485	30 43052	99001	44400
1107	73176	3 58913	22638	31 69769	21102	72292
1108	11851	09065	96033	02752	47 58232	56504
1109	37515	25668	16 55785	32 66463	48 52758	67588
1110	45324	00016	17 46818	04373	49 75360	87519

Population = 3689 to 9453.
Correspondence — First 4 digits in table.
Route — Read down to end of column; start at
top of the next column.
Sample size — 50, represented by sequential
numbers 1 to 50.

tests and providing information for review, it is common to include a worksheet of the results. Some auditors prefer to include a worksheet containing a listing of all of the elements in the sample, while others prefer to limit the documentation to identifying the errors. This latter approach is followed in the example (Figure 9-6).

At the completion of the testing, the errors are tabulated to determine the number of errors in the sample for each attribute. This enables the auditor to compute the sample error rate and determine the upper precision limit from the tables. This information is summarized in Figures 9-6 and 9-7.

FIGURE 9-6

HILLSBURG HARDWARE CO.—INSPECTION OF SAMPLE ITEMS FOR ATTRIBUTES

Hillsburg Hardware Co.

Prepared by MSW
Date 2/3/74

INSPECTION OF SAMPLE ITEMS FOR ATTRIBUTES

12/31/7x

Identity of Item Selected	Attribute Present										
Voucher No.	1	2	3	4	5	6	7	8	9	10	11
3679					X						
3859				X				X			
3990				X							
4071		X		X							
4270								X			
4222				X							
4331								X			
4513				X	X						
4676											
4681						X		X			
4859				X							
5367								X			
5578								X			
5802								X			
5823								X			
5963								X			
6157		X		X							
6229				X							
6311								X			
7188					X						
7536				X							
8182											
8351								X			
8517				X							
8713								X			
9361											
9370											
9545				X							
No. Errors	0	2	0	10	4	1	0	12			
Sample Size	150	150	150	150	150	50	50	50			

Figure 9-7

Hillsburg Hardware—Statistical Sampling Data Sheet—Attributes

Client *Hillsburg Hardware*
Audit Area *Compliance Tests – Billing Function*

Year end *12/31/7x*
Pop. size *5,764*

Define the objective(s) *Examine duplicate sales invoices and related documents to determine if the system is functioning as intended and as described in the audit program.*

Define the population precisely (including stratification, if any) *Sales invoices for the period 11/1/7x to 12/31/7x. First invoice number = 3689. Last invoice number = 9452.*

Define the sampling unit, organization of population items, and random selection procedures *Sales invoice number, recorded in the sales journal sequentially; random number table.*

Description of Attributes	Planned Audit				Actual Results			
	Expect. error rate	Upr. prec. rate	Conf. level	Sample size	Sample size	Number of errors	Sample error rate	Upper precision limit
1. Existence of the sales invoice number in the sales journal.	0	2	95	150	150	0	0%	2.0%
2. Amount and other data in the subsidiary ledger agree with sales journal entry.	1	4	95	150	150	2	1⅓	4.0
3. Amount and other data in the sales invoice agree with the sales journal entry.	1	4	95	150	150	0	0	2.0
4. Evidence that pricing, extensions, and footings are checked (initials and correct amount).	1	4	95	150	150	10	6⅔	11
5. Quantity and other data on the bill of lading agree with the duplicate sales invoice.	1	4	95	150	150	4	2⅔	6.0
6. Quantity and other data on the sales order agree with the duplicate sales invoice.	1	6	95	50	50	1	2	9.1
7. Quantity and other data on the customer order agree with the duplicate sales invoice.	2	8	95	50	50	0	0	5.8
8. Credit is approved by Rick Chulik.	3	8	95	50	50	12	24	35.9

Intended use of sampling results:

1. Effect on Audit Plan: *All controls tested can be relied upon as illustrated on working paper 7-6. Additional emphasis is needed in confirmation, allowance for uncollectible accounts, cut-off tests, and price tests.*

2. Recommendations to Management: *Each of the errors should be discussed with management. Specific recommendations are needed to correct the internal verification of sales invoices and to improve the approach to credit approvals.*

Figure 9-8

Hillsburg hardware—analysis of errors'

Hillsburg Hardware
ANALYSIS OF ERRORS

Prepared by

12/31/7x

Attribute	Number of Exceptions	Nature of Exceptions	Effect on the Audit and Other Comments
1	— 0 —		
2	2	Both errors were posted to the wrong account and were still outstanding after several months. The amounts were for $125.00 and $393.00.	Even though the upper control limit is equal to the desired limit, additional substantive work is needed, owing to the nature of the errors. Perform expanded confirmation procedures and review older uncollected balances thoroughly.
3	— 0 —	—	—
4	10	In 6 cases there were no initials for internal verification. In 2 cases the wrong price was used but the errors were under $10 in each case. In 1 case freight was not charged. In 1 case there was an extension error of $1,000. (Three of the last 4 errors had initials for internal verification.)	There is a lack of internal verification, and dollar errors appear to be occurring with excessive frequency. The internal verification cannot be relied upon. As a result test the 50 largest sales transactions for the year for proper price and expand the confirmation of accounts receivable.
5	4	In each case the date on the duplicate sales invoice was several days later than the shipping date.	Do extensive tests of the sales cut-off by comparing recorded sales to the shipping documents.
6	1	Just 106 items were shipped and billed though the sales order was for 112 items. The reason for the difference was an error in the perpetual records. The perpetuals indicated that 112 items were on hand, when there were actually 106. The system does not backorder for undershipments smaller than 25%.	No expansion of compliance or substantive tests. The system appears to be working effectively.
7	— 0 —	—	—
8	12	Credit was not approved. Four of these were for new customers. Discussed with Chulik, who stated his busy schedule did not permit approving all sales.	Expand the year-end procedures extensively in evaluating allowance for uncollectible accounts. This includes scheduling of cash receipts subsequent to year end and for all outstanding accounts receivable.

Error Analysis and Decision on the Acceptability of the Population

The final part of the application consists of analysis of the errors to determine their cause and drawing conclusions about each attribute tested. For every attribute where the computed upper precision limit exceeds the desirable limit, it is essential that some conclusion concerning follow up action be drawn and documented. The error analysis and conclusions reached are illustrated in Figure 9-8 and summarized at the bottom of the data sheet in Figure 9-7.

REVIEW QUESTIONS

1. Distinguish between a quantitative and a qualitative evaluation of a population and state the importance of each.
2. State what is meant by a representative sample and explain its importance in sampling audit populations.
3. In using judgmental sampling, what major considerations should be kept in mind to increase the likelihood of a representative sample?
4. Explain what is meant by block sampling and describe how an auditor could obtain five blocks of twenty sales invoices from a sales journal.
5. Compared with judgmental selection, what are the major advantages of random selection?
6. Why is the pursuit of every item in the sample essential when statistical sampling techniques are used?
7. Explain the difference between "sampling with replacement" and "sampling without replacement." Which method do auditors usually follow? Why?
8. Explain what is meant by a random number table. Describe how an auditor would select thirty-five random numbers from a population of 1,750 items by using a random number table.
9. Describe systematic sampling and explain how an auditor would select thirty-five numbers from a population of 1,750 items using this approach. What are the advantages and disadvantages of systematic sampling?
10. Describe what is meant by a sampling unit. Explain why the sampling unit for verifying the validity of recorded sales differs from the sampling unit for testing for the possibility of omitted sales.
11. Distinguish between the desired upper precision limit and the computed upper precision limit. How is each of them determined?
12. Distinguish between a "sampling error" and a "nonsampling error." How can each of them be reduced?
13. State the relationship between the following:
    a. Confidence level and sample size
    b. Population size and sample size
    c. Desired upper precision limit and sample size
    d. Expected error rate and sample size
14. Assume the auditor has selected 100 sales invoices from a population of 10,000 to test for an indication of internal verification of pricing and extensions. Determine the upper precision limit of the error at a 95 percent con-

fidence level if three exceptions existed in the sample. Explain the meaning of the statistical results in auditing terms.

15. Explain what is meant by error analysis and discuss its importance.
16. When the computed upper precision limit exceeds the desired upper precision limit, what courses of action are available to the auditor? Under what circumstances should each of these courses of action be followed?
17. Distinguish between random selection and statistical measurement. State the circumstances under which one can be used without the other.
18. List the decisions the auditor must make in using attributes sampling. State the most important considerations involved in making each decision.

DISCUSSION QUESTIONS AND PROBLEMS

19. You are now conducting your third annual audit of the financial statements of Elite Corporation for the year ended December 31, 19X7. You decide to employ unrestricted random number statistical-sampling techniques in testing the effectiveness of the company's internal control procedures relating to sales invoices, which are all serially numbered. In prior years, after selecting one representative two-week period during the year, you tested all invoices issued during that period and resolved all the errors which were found to your satisfaction.

    Required:

    a. Explain the statistical procedures you would use to determine the size of the sample of sales invoices to be examined.
    b. Once the sample size has been determined, how would you select the individual invoices to be included in the sample? Explain.
    c. Would the use of statistical sampling procedures improve the examination of sales invoices as compared with the selection procedure used in prior years? Discuss.
    d. Assume that the company issued fifty thousand sales invoices during the year and the auditor specified a confidence level of 95 percent with a desired upper precision limit of 4%. Does this mean that the auditor would be willing to accept the reliability of the sales invoice data if errors are found on no more than four sales invoices out of every ninety-five invoices examined? Discuss.   (AICPA adapted)

20. The following items apply to random sampling from large populations for attributes sampling. Select the most appropriate response for each question.

    a. A CPA wishes to determine the percentage of items in his client's inventory with annual sales of less than 50 percent of the units on hand at the inventory date. Which of the following exhibits the characteristic the CPA is measuring?

Item	Units in Inventory	Units Sold This Year
1. Firs	251	525
2. Furs	243	124
3. Friezes	198	98
4. Furzes	144	92

b. A CPA specifies that a sample shall have a confidence level of 90 percent. The specified confidence level assures him of
   (1) A true estimate of the population characteristic being measured
   (2) An estimate that is at least 90 percent correct
   (3) A measured precision for his estimate
   (4) How likely he can estimate the population characteristic being measured

c. If all other factors specified in a sampling plan remain constant, changing the specified confidence level from 90 percent to 95 percent would cause the required sample size to
   (1) Increase
   (2) Remain the same
   (3) Decrease
   (4) Become indeterminate

d. If all other factors specified in a sampling plan remain constant, changing the desired upper precision limit from 8 percent to 12 percent would cause the required sample size to
   (1) Increase
   (2) Remain the same
   (3) Decrease
   (4) Become indeterminate

e. If all other factors specified in a sampling plan remain constant, changing the estimated occurrence rate from 2 percent to 4 percent would cause the required sample size to
   (1) Increase
   (2) Remain the same
   (3) Decrease
   (4) Become indeterminate

f. In the evaluation of the results of a sample of a specified confidence level, the fact that the occurrence rate in the sample was 2 percent rather than the estimated occurrence rate of 4 percent would cause the computed upper precision limit to
   (1) Exceed the desired upper precision limit
   (2) Equal the desired upper precision limit
   (3) Be less than the desired upper precision limit
   (4) Cannot be determined from the information given   (AICPA adapted)

21. The following items apply to random sampling from large populations using attributes sampling. For each question, select the best response.

a. In a random sample of 1,000 records, a CPA determines that the rate of occurrence of errors is 2 percent. He can state that the error rate in the population is
   (1) Not more than 3 percent
   (2) Not less than 2 percent
   (3) Probably about 2 percent
   (4) Not less than 1 percent

b. From a random sample of items listed from a client's inventory count, a CPA estimates with 90 percent confidence that the error occurrence rate is between 4 percent and 6 percent. The CPA's major concern is that there is one chance in twenty that the true error rate in the population is
   (1) More than 6 percent
   (2) Less than 6 percent
   (3) More than 4 percent

       (4) Less than 4 percent

  c. If from a particular random sample a CPA can state with 90 percent confidence that the occurrence rate in the population does not exceed 20 percent, he can state that the occurrence rate does not exceed 25 percent with

       (1) 95 percent confidence

       (2) Greater reliability on his sample

       (3) The same reliability on his sample

       (4) Less reliability on his sample

  d. If a CPA wishes to select a random sample that must have a 90 percent confidence level and a desired upper precision limit of 10 percent, the size of the sample he must select will decrease as his estimate of the

       (1) Occurrence rate increases

       (2) Occurrence rate decreases

       (3) Population size increases

       (4) Reliability of the sample decreases

  e. If a CPA selects a random sample for which he specified a confidence level of 99 percent and an upper precision limit of 5 percent and subsequently changes the confidence level to 90 percent, the sample will produce an estimate that is

       (1) More reliable and more precise

       (2) More reliable and less precise

       (3) Less reliable and more precise

       (4) Less reliable and less precise

  f. If the result obtained from a particular sample will be critical, e.g., the CPA would not be able to render an unqualified opinion (unless every item in the population were examined), which of the following is the most important to the CPA?

       (1) Size of the population

       (2) Estimated occurrence rate

       (3) Desired upper precision limit

       (4) Desired confidence level

  g. Which of the following need not be known to evaluate the results of a sample for a particular attribute?

       (1) Occurrence rate in the population

       (2) Size of the sample

       (3) Desired confidence level

       (4) Occurrences in the sample   (AICPA adapted)

22. In each of the following independent problems, design an unbiased random sampling plan using the random number table in Figure 9-1. The plan should include defining the sampling unit, establishing a numbering system for the population, and establishing a correspondence between the random number table and the population. After the plan has been designed, select the first five sample items from the random number table for each problem. Use a starting point of item 1009, column 1, for each problem. Read down the table using the leftmost digits in the column. When you reach the last item in a column, start at the top of the next column.

  a. Prenumbered sales invoices in a sales journal where the lowest invoice number is 1 and the highest is 6211.

  b. Prenumbered bills of lading where the lowest document number is 21926 and the highest is 28511.

  c. Accounts receivable on 10 pages with 60 lines per page. Each line has a customer name and an amount receivable, except the last page, which has only 36 full lines.

d. Prenumbered invoices in a sales journal where each month starts over with number 1. (Invoices for each month are designated by the month and document number.) There are a maximum of 20 pages per month with a total of 185 pages for the year. All pages have 75 invoices, except for the last page for each month.

23. You desire a random sample of 80 sales invoices for the examination of supporting documents. The invoices range from numbers 1 to 9500 for the period January 1 through December 31. There are 128 pages of sales invoices numbered 1 through 128. Each page has 75 lines, but the last page in each month sometimes has a few less.

Required:

a. Design four different methods of selecting random numbers from the above population using a random number table or systematic sampling.
b. Which method do you consider the most desirable? Why?

24. The use of statistical sampling techniques in an examination of financial statements does not eliminate judgmental decisions.

Required:

a. Identify and explain four areas where judgment may be exercised by a CPA in planning a statistical sampling test.
b. Assume that a CPA's sample shows an unacceptable error rate. Describe the various actions that he may take based upon these findings.
c. A nonstratified sample of 80 accounts payable vouchers is to be selected from a population of 3,200. The vouchers are numbered consecutively from 1 to 3,200 and are listed, 40 to a page, in the voucher register. Describe four different techniques for selecting a random sample of vouchers for review. (AICPA adapted)

25. Lenter Supply Company is a medium-sized distributor of wholesale hardware supplies in the central Ohio area. It has been a client of yours for several years and has instituted an excellent system for the control of sales at your recommendation.

In providing control over shipments, the client has prenumbered "warehouse removal slips" that are used for every sale. It is company policy never to remove goods from the warehouse without an authorized warehouse removal slip. After shipment, two copies of the warehouse removal slip are sent to billing for preparation of a sales invoice. One copy is stapled to the duplicate copy of a prenumbered sales invoice, and the other copy is filed numerically. In some cases more than one warehouse removal slip is used for billing one sales invoice. The smallest warehouse removal slip number for the year is 14682 and the largest is 37521. The smallest sales invoice number is 47821 and the largest is 68507.

In the audit of sales, one of the major concerns is the effectiveness of the system in making sure all shipments are billed. The auditor has decided to use attributes sampling in testing the system.

Required:

a. State an effective audit procedure for testing whether shipments have been billed. What is the sampling unit for the audit procedure?

   b. Assuming the auditor expects no error in the sample but is willing to accept a maximum error rate of 3 percent, at a 90 percent confidence level, what is the appropriate sample size for the audit test?

   c. Design a random selection plan for selecting the sample from the population using the random number table. Select the first ten sample items from the table in Figure 9-1. Use a starting point of item 1013, column 3.

   d. Your supervisor suggests the possibility of performing other sales tests with the same sample as a means of efficiently using your audit time. List two other audit procedures that could conveniently be performed using the same sample and state the purpose of each of the procedures.

   e. Is it desirable to test the validity of sales with the random sample you have designed in part *c*? Why?

26. Mavis Stores had two billing clerks during the year. Snow worked three months and White worked nine months. As the auditor for Mavis Stores, Jones, CPA, uses attributes sampling to test clerical accuracy for the entire year, but due to the lack of internal verification, the system depends heavily upon the competence of the billing clerks. The quantity of bills per month is constant.

Required:

   a. Jones decided to treat the billing by Snow and White as two separate populations. Discuss the advisability of this approach, considering the circumstances.

   b. Jones decided to use the same confidence level, expected error rate, and desired upper precision limit for each population. Assuming he decided to select a sample of 200 to test Snow's work, approximately how large a sample is necessary to test White's?   (AICPA adapted)

27. The following questions concern the determination of the proper sample size in attributes sampling:

   a. For each of the columns numbered 1 through 7 determine the initial sample size needed to satisfy the auditor's requirements from the appropriate table in Figure 9-3. Wherever the sample size is more than 10 percent of the population, adjust it with the finite correction factor.

	1	*2*	*3*	*4*	*5*	*6*	*7*
Confidence level	90%	95%	95%	95%	95%	95%	95%
Desired upper precision limit	6%	6%	4%	6%	8%	6%	5%
Estimated population error rate	3%	3%	3%	3%	3%	3%	0%
Population size	1,000 -	100,000	6,000	1,000	500	500	1,000,000

   b. Using your understanding of the relationship between the above factors and sample size, state the effect on the initial sample (increase or decrease) of changing each of the following factors while the other three are held constant:

    (1) an increase in confidence level

    (2) an increase in the desired upper precision limit

(3) an increase in the estimated population error rate

(4) an increase in the population size

c. Compare your answers in part *b* with the results you determined in part *a*. Which of the four factors appears to have the greatest effect on the initial sample size? Which one appears to have the least effect?

d. Why is the sample size referred to as the initial sample size?

28. The following questions relate to determining the computed upper precision limit in attributes sampling:

a. For each of the columns numbered 1 through 8, determine the computed upper precision limit from the appropriate table in Figure 9-3. Wherever the sample size is more than 10 percent of the population, adjust the computed upper precision limit with the finite correction factor.

	1	2	3	4	5	6	7	8
Confidence level	90%	95%	95%	95%	95%	95%	95%	95%
Population size	5,000	5,000	5,000	50,000	500	900	5,000	500
Sample size	200	200	50	200	400	100	100	200
Number of error occurrences	4	4	1	4	8	10	0	4

b. Using your understanding of the relationship between the above four factors and the computed upper precision limit, state the effect on the computed upper precision limit (increase or decrease) of changing each of the following factors while the other three are held constant:

(1) a decrease in the confidence level

(2) a decrease in the population size

(3) a decrease in the sample size

(4) a decrease in the number of occurrences in the sample

c. Compare your answers in part *b* with the results you determined in part *a*. Which of the four factors appears to have the greatest effect on the initial sample size? Which one appears to have the least effect?

d. Why is it necessary to compare the computed upper precision limit with the acceptable upper precision limit?

29. For the examination of the financial statements of Mercury Fifo Company, Stella Mason, CPA, has decided to apply attributes sampling in the tests of sales transactions. Based upon her knowledge of Mercury's operations in the area of sales, she decides that the expected rate of error occurrence is likely to be 30 percent and that she would like to be 90 percent confident that the true error rate is not greater than 6 percent. Given this information, Mason selects a random sample of 150 sales invoices from the 5,000 written during the year and examines them for errors. She notes the following exceptions in her workpapers. There is no other documentation.

Invoice No.	*Comments*
5028	Sales invoice was originally footed incorrectly but was corrected by client before the bill was sent out.
6791	Voided sales invoice examined by auditor.

6810	Shipping document for a sale of merchandise could not be located.
7364	Sales invoice for $2,875 has not been collected and is six months past due.
7625	Client unable to locate the duplicate sales invoice.
8431	Check was dated three days later than the date entered in the sales journal.
8528	Customer order is not attached to the duplicate sales invoice.
8566	Billing is for $100 less than it should be due to a pricing error. No indication of internal verification is included in the invoice.
8780	Client unable to locate the duplicate sales invoice.
9169	Credit not authorized, but the sale was for only $7.65.
9974	Lack of indication of internal verification of price extensions and postings of sales invoice.

Required:

a. Which of the above stated exceptions are actually errors?
b. Explain why it is inappropriate to set a single accepted upper precision limit and expected rate of occurrence for the combined errors.
c. For each attribute as tested in the population, determine the computed upper precision limit assuming a 95 percent confidence level for each attribute. (You must decide which attributes should be combined, which should be kept separate, and which exceptions are actually errors, before you can determine the computed upper precision limit.)
d. State the appropriate error analysis for each of the errors in the sample.

30. In performing tests of transactions of sales for the Oakland Hardware Company, Ben Frentz, CPA, is concerned with the internal verification of pricing, extensions, and footings of sales invoices and the accuracy of the actual calculations. In testing sales using attributes sampling, a separate attribute is used for the compliance test (the existence of internal verification) and the substantive test (the actual accuracy of the calculation). Since the internal control is considered excellent, Frentz uses a 90 percent confidence level, a zero estimated population error rate, and a 5 percent desired upper precision limit for both attributes; therefore, the initial sample size is 50 items.

In conducting the tests, the auditor finds three sample items where there was no indication of internal verification on the sales invoice, but no sales invoices tested in the sample had a financial error.

Required:

a. Determine the computed upper precision limit for both the attributes, assuming a population of 5,000 sales invoices.
b. Compare the computed upper precision limit with the desired upper precision limit.
c. Discuss the most desirable course of action the auditor should follow in deciding upon the effect of the computed upper precision limit's exceeding the desired upper precision limit.

d. Which type of error analysis is appropriate in this case?

31. For the audit of Carbald Supply Company, Carole Wever, CPA, is conducting a test of sales for nine months of the year ended 12-31-X7. Included
among her audit procedures are the following:

   a. Foot and crossfoot the sales journal and trace the balance to the general
   ledger.
   b. Review all sales transactions for reasonableness.
   c. Select a sample of recorded sales from the sales journal and trace the
   customer name and amounts to duplicate sales invoices and the related
   shipping document.
   d. Select a sample of shipping document numbers and perform the following tests:
      (1) Trace the shipping document to the related duplicate sales invoice.
      (2) Examine the duplicate sales invoice to determine whether a copy of
      the shipping document, shipping order, and customer order are
      attached.
      (3) Examine the shipping order for an authorized credit approval.
      (4) Examine the duplicate sales invoice for an indication of internal
      verification of quantity, price, extensions, footings, and tracing the
      balance to the subsidiary ledger.
      (5) Compare the price in the duplicate sales invoice with the approved
      price list and the quantity with the shipping document.
      (6) Trace the balance in the duplicate sales invoice to the sales journal
      and subsidiary ledger for customer name, amount, and date.

   Required:

   a. For which of these procedures could attributes sampling be conveniently
   used?
   b. Considering the audit procedures Wever has developed, what is the most
   appropriate sampling unit for conducting most of the attributes-sampling
   tests?
   c. Set up an attributes-sampling data sheet similar to the one in Figure 9-4.
   For all compliance tests, assume an acceptable upper precision limit of
   3.5 percent and an expected population error rate of 1 percent. For all
   substantive tests, use 2.5 percent for the upper precision limit and a zero
   expected population error rate. Use a 90 percent confidence level for all
   tests.
   d. For the audit procedures not included in the attributes-sampling test in
   part *c,* describe appropriate judgmental sampling procedures to determine the items to include in the sample.

10

Completing the Tests in the Sales and Collection Cycle – Accounts Receivable

Chapter 10 is concerned with the analytical and direct tests of balances for the accounts in the sales and collection cycle and the relationship of these tests to the review and evaluation of internal control and tests of transactions. The detailed objectives for direct tests of financial balances presented in Chapter 6 are the frame of reference used to discuss the audit tests. Confirmation of accounts receivable, which is the most important direct test in the cycle, receives particular emphasis. The relationship between confirmations and tests of transactions and the factors affecting the auditor's confirmation decisions are the most important part of this discussion.

Before examining a methodology for completing the audit of the sales and collection cycle, a brief review of the tests of the cycle that were discussed in previous chapters is appropriate. These tests have a direct effect on the evidence needed to complete the audit of the cycle.

REVIEW OF THE TESTS OF THE SYSTEM

The overall objective in auditing the sales and collection cycle is to evaluate whether sales, sales returns and allowances, bad debts, accounts receivable, allowance for uncollectible accounts, and cash receipts are properly reflected in the financial records.

The emphasis to this point has been on understanding, evaluating, and testing the system of internal control. An understanding of the system comes about through flowcharting the client's sales and collection system, completing an internal control questionnaire, and tracing one or two transactions through the system from the customer's order to the collection of cash. The evaluation of internal control is accomplished by relating the seven objectives of internal control to the flowchart and internal control questionnaire for the purpose of identifying strengths and weaknesses in the system. The tests of transactions for the cycle include compliance tests to enable the auditor to evaluate the effectiveness of the controls and substantive tests to enable him to evaluate the correctness of the dollar amounts in the records.

In accumulating evidence for the sales and collection cycle, the importance of modifying the evidence for the circumstances of the audit cannot be overemphasized. The determination of the proper audit procedures, sample size, timing of the tests, and particular items to include in the sample can only be made after a careful analysis of the system and the other relevant factors in the engagement. The decision making involved in this process is one of the most important aspects of the study of auditing.

Audit Procedures. Compliance procedures for testing effectiveness need to be performed for those controls in the system the auditor intends to rely upon to reduce substantive tests. Whether or not to perform compliance tests is a cost-benefit question and should be decided on the basis of the cost to test the controls versus the savings if substantive tests are reduced.

Proper substantive procedures for testing the system depend upon the auditor's evaluation of internal control and the results of the compliance tests. Since some substantive procedures must always be performed to test whether transactions and balances are correctly recorded, it is convenient to carry out compliance and substantive tests of transactions simultaneously. If the compliance procedures indicate that the controls are inadequate, the substantive tests may need to be expanded.

Sample Size. Three major factors affect the number of sample items for tests of transactions: the error rate the auditor is willing to accept in the population, the error rate expected in the sample, and the risk the auditor is willing to take of obtaining a nonrepresentative sample. The first factor is a question of materiality, and the second one is based primarily on experience with the client in previous years. The risk factor is affected by the extent to which the auditor plans to rely on the system to reduce substantive tests and the overall level of assurance the auditor considers necessary. Population size has some effect on sample size, but it is generally not significant in transactions testing.

When the system of internal control is of high quality, the auditor can accept a lower confidence level for substantive tests of the system. In addition, the expected magnitude of errors is smaller when there are good controls. The combination of these two factors normally permits the auditor to reduce considerably the sample size for substantive tests.

Timing. Several factors determine whether the system should be tested at an interim date without a thorough test for the remainder of the year. These factors include the length of the untested time period, the results of the interim tests, discussions with the client about changes in the system, personnel changes, the nature of the transactions for the untested period, and the results of the preliminary substantive tests. Even when conditions are ideal, it is not possible to completely ignore the untested time period.

Items to Select for the Sample. In testing the system, it is essential to obtain a representative sample. Therefore, random selection is generally desirable, and it is a requirement when statistical methods are used. On the other hand, if the auditor observes unusual transactions or amounts, they should be investigated even if they are not included in the random sample. In addition, many auditors feel it is also important to review all large transactions.

DIRECT TESTS OF FINANCIAL BALANCES

After the auditor has completed the internal control evaluation and tests of transactions, it is appropriate to design and perform audit procedures for *analytical* and *direct tests* of the financial balances. Frequently a time lapse of several months occurs before the direct tests are performed when tests of transactions are conducted at an interim date. In many cases confirmation of accounts receivable also takes place before the balance sheet date, but some direct tests are always performed as of the balance sheet date.

Confirmation of accounts receivable is the most important audit procedure for direct tests of the sales and collection cycle. Confirmation is discussed briefly in studying the appropriate tests for each of the eight objectives of direct tests of balances, then in more detail in a separate section.

The direct tests of the cycle emphasize the fair presentation of accounts receivable and allowance for uncollectible accounts. The income statement accounts are not ignored in these tests, but they are verified more as a by-product of the balance sheet tests rather than directly. In analytical tests, income statement and balance sheet accounts are examined concurrently for reasonableness and receive equal attention.

Overall Reasonableness

There are two types of tests for overall reasonableness of accounts receivable: the *review of individual accounts receivable balances* for amounts deserving special attention, and *analytical tests*.

The individual accounts that typically deserve special attention are large balances, accounts that have been outstanding for a long period of time, and receivables from affiliated companies, officers, directors, and other related parties. The auditor should review the accounts receivable confirmation at the confirmation date and the balance sheet date to determine which accounts should be investigated further.

The following are examples of the major types of analytical tests for the sales and collection cycle:

1. Gross margin by product line
2. Sales returns and allowances as a percentage of gross sales by product line or segment
3. Trade discounts taken as a percentage of net sales
4. Bad debts as a percentage of gross sales
5. Days' sales in receivables outstanding
6. Aging categories as a percentage of accounts receivable
7. Allowance for uncollectible accounts as a percentage of accounts receivable
8. Comparison of individual customers' balances over a stated amount with their balances in the preceding year

Mechanical Accuracy

Most tests of accounts receivable and the allowance for uncollectible accounts are based on the *aged trial balance.* An aged trial balance is a listing of the balances in the subsidiary accounts receivable ledger at the balance sheet date. It includes the individual total balances outstanding and a breakdown of each balance by the length of time passed between the date of sale and the balance sheet date. An illustration of a typical aged trial balance is given in Figure 10-1.

Testing the information on the aged trial balance for mechanical accuracy is a necessary audit procedure. The total column and the columns depicting the aging must be footed, and the total on the trial balance must be reconciled with the general ledger. In addition, a sample of individual balances should be traced to the detailed subsidiary ledger or other supporting data to verify the customer name, balance, and proper aging. The extent of the testing for mechanical accuracy depends on the number of accounts involved and the degree to which the schedule has been verified by an internal auditor or other independent person before it is given to the auditor.

Existence

The most important tests for the existence *(validity)* of recorded accounts receivable are the confirmation of customers' balances, the examination of supporting documents evidencing the shipment of the goods, and the examination of subsequent cash receipts to determine whether the

FIGURE 10-1
AGED TRIAL BALANCE

ABC Company, Inc.
Accounts Receivable
Aged Trial Balance
12/31/75

Schedule _____
Prepared by *Olivest* 1/5   Date _____
Approved by _____

Account Number	Customer	Balance 12/31/7X	Aging based on invoice date				
			0–30 days	31–60 days	61–90 days	91–120 days	over 120
01011	Adams Supply	7329	4511	2818			
01044	Raymond, Inc.	1542	1542				
01100	Atwater Brothers	10519	10519				
01191	Beckman Bearings	4176	3676		500		
01270	Brown and Phillips	3000				3000	
01301	Christopher Plumbing	789					789
02733	Traveler's Equipment	2976	2976				
02742	Vanderbilt Parts and Maintenance	8963	8963				
09810	D.J.T.W. Co.	5111	1811	1700	1600		
09907	Zephyr Plastics	14300	9300	5000			
		229716	183773	26466	11466	6891	1100

accounts were collected. Normally, auditors do not examine shipping documents or evidence of subsequent cash receipts for any account in the sample that is confirmed, but these documents are used extensively as alternative evidence for nonresponses. The tests of transactions discussed in Chapters 8 and 9 are also useful in testing the validity of recorded transactions.

It is extremely difficult to test for omitted account balances in accounts receivable except by relying upon the self-balancing nature of the subsidiary accounts. For example, if the client decided to exclude an account receivable from the trial balance to deceive the auditor, the only likely way it will be discovered is by footing the accounts receivable trial balance and reconciling the balance with the control account in the general ledger. If all sales to a customer are omitted from the sales journal, the understatement of accounts receivable is almost impossible to uncover by direct tests of balances, but it can be revealed by tests of transactions for shipments made but not recorded.

Ownership

The ownership of accounts receivable ordinarily causes no audit problems because the receivables usually belong to the client, but in some cases a portion of the receivables may have been factored or sold at a discount. Generally, the client's customers are not aware of the existence of discounting; therefore, the confirmation of receivables will not bring it to light. A review of the minutes, discussions with the client, confirmation with banks, and the examination of correspondence files are usually sufficient to uncover instances where the receivables are not owned.

Valuation

Confirmation of the gross value of selected customers' balances is the most common direct test for valuation of accounts receivable. Tests of the debits and credits to particular customers' balances by examining supporting documentation for shipments and collections and tests of transactions of the type discussed in Chapter 8 are also helpful. The interrelationship of these tests is discussed in greater detail later in this chapter.

A second part of the valuation of accounts receivable is determining the *realizable value* of the outstanding balances; that is, the amount which will ultimately be collected. The client's estimate of the total amount that is uncollectible is represented by the allowance for uncollectible accounts. Although it is not possible to precisely predict the future, it is necessary for the auditor to evaluate whether the allowance is reasonable considering all of the available facts.

The starting point for the evaluation of the allowance for uncollectible accounts is to review the results of the tests of the system that are concerned with the client's credit policy. If the client's credit policy has remained unchanged and the results of the tests of credit policy and credit approval are consistent with those of the preceding year, the change in the balance in the allowance for uncollectible accounts should reflect only changes in economic conditions and sales volume. On the other hand, if the client's credit policy or the degree of compliance has significantly changed, great care must be taken to consider the effects of these changes as well.

A common way to evaluate the adequacy of the allowance is to examine carefully the noncurrent accounts in the aged trial balance to determine which ones have not been paid subsequent to the balance sheet date. The size and age of unpaid balances can then be compared with similar information from previous years to evaluate whether the amount of noncurrent receivables is increasing or decreasing over time. The examination of Dun and Bradstreet reports, discussions with the credit manager, and review of the client's correspondence file may also provide insights into the collectibility of the accounts. These procedures are especially important if a few large balances are noncurrent and are not being paid on a regular basis.

There are two pitfalls in evaluating the allowance by reviewing individual noncurrent balances in the aged trial balance. First, the current accounts are ignored in establishing the adequacy of the allowance even though some of these amounts will undoubtedly become uncollectible. Second, it is difficult to compare the results of the current year with those of previous years on such an unstructured basis. If the accounts are becoming progressively uncollectible over a period of several years, this fact could be overlooked. A way to avoid these difficulties is to establish the history of bad debt charge-offs over a period of time as a frame of reference for evaluating the current year's allowance. As an example, if historically a certain percentage of the total of each age category becomes uncollectible, it is relatively easy to compute whether the allowance is properly stated. If 2 percent of current accounts, 10 percent of 30- to 90-day accounts, and 35 percent of all balances over 90 days ultimately become uncollectible, these percentages can easily be applied to the current year's aged trial balance totals and the result compared with the balance in the allowance account. Of course the auditor has to be careful to modify the calculations for changed conditions.

After the auditor is satisfied with the allowance for uncollectible accounts, it is easy to verify bad debts expense. Let it be assumed that (1) the beginning balance was verified as a part of the previous audit, (2) the uncollectible accounts charged off were verified as a part of the tests of transactions, and (3) the ending balance in the allowance account has been verified by various means. Then bad debts expense is simply a residual balance that can be verified by a mechanical test.

Classification

It is normally relatively easy to evaluate the classification of accounts receivable by reviewing the aged trial balance for material receivables from affiliates, officers, directors, or other related parties. If there are notes receivable included with the regular accounts or accounts that are not properly classified as a current asset, these should also be segregated. Finally, if the credit balances in accounts receivable are significant, it is appropriate to reclassify them as accounts payable.

Proper Cutoff

Cutoff errors can occur for *sales, sales returns and allowances,* and *cash receipts.* They take place when current period transactions are recorded in the subsequent year or subsequent period transactions are recorded in the current year.

The objective of cutoff tests is the same regardless of the type of transaction, but the procedures vary. The objective is simply to verify whether the client has recorded transactions near the end of the year in the proper period. The cutoff objective is one of the most important in the cycle because errors in cutoff can significantly affect current period income. For example, the intentional or unintentional inclusion of several large, subsequent period sales in the current period and the exclusion of several current period sales returns and allowances can materially overstate net earnings. In determining the reasonableness of the cutoff, it is necessary to use a three-fold approach: first, decide on the appropriate *criteria for cutoff;* second, evaluate whether the client has established *adequate procedures* to ensure a reasonable cutoff; and third, *test* whether a reasonable cutoff was obtained.

Sales Cutoff. The criterion used by most clients for determining when a sale takes place is the *shipment of goods,* but some companies record invoices at the time title passes. The passage of title can take place before shipment (as in the case of custom-manufactured goods), at the time of shipment, or subsequent to shipment. For the proper measurement of current period income, the method must be in accordance with generally accepted accounting principles, and it must also be consistently applied.

The most important part of evaluating the client's method of obtaining a reliable cutoff is to determine the procedures in use. When a client issues prenumbered shipping documents sequentially, it is usually a simple matter to evaluate and test cutoff. Moreover, the segregation of duties between the shipping and the billing function also enhances the likelihood of recording transactions in the proper period. On the other hand, if shipments are made by company truck, the shipping records are unnumbered, and there is no independence between the shipping and the billing departments, it may be difficult, if not impossible, to be assured of an accurate cutoff.

When the client's records and procedures are adequate, the cutoff can usually be verified by obtaining the shipping document number for the last shipment made at the end of the period and comparing this number with current and subsequent period recorded sales. As an illustration, assume the shipping document number for the last shipment in the current period is 1489. All recorded sales before the end of the period should bear a shipping document number preceding number 1490. There should also be no sales recorded in the subsequent period for a shipment with a bill of lading numbered 1489 or lower. This can be easily tested by comparing recorded sales with the related shipping document for the last few days of the current period and the first few days of the subsequent period.

If the system is unusual or inadequate, it is necessary to carefully study and evaluate it before cutoff tests are determined. In extreme circumstances, physical observation of shipments and control of documents by the auditor during the period around year end may be required.

Sales Returns and Allowances. Generally accepted accounting principles require that sales returns and allowances be *matched with related sales* if the amounts are material. For example, if current period shipments are returned in the subsequent period, the proper treatment of the transaction is the inclusion of the sales return in the current period. (The returned goods would be treated as current period inventory.) For most companies, however, sales returns and allowances are recorded in the *period they occur,* under the assumption of approximately equal, offsetting errors at the beginning and end of the period. This is acceptable as long as the amounts are not significant.

When the auditor is confident that the client records all sales returns and allowances on a timely basis, the cutoff tests are simple and straightforward. The auditor can examine supporting documentation for a sample of sales returns and allowances recorded during several weeks subsequent to the closing date to determine the date of the original sale. If the amounts recorded in the subsequent period are significantly different from unrecorded returns at the beginning of the year, an adjustment must be considered. If the system for recording sales returns and allowances is evaluated as ineffective during the review and tests of the system, a larger sample is needed to verify cutoff.

Cash Receipts. For most audits a proper cash receipts cutoff is *less important* than either the sales or the sales returns and allowances cutoff because the improper cutoff of cash affects only the cash and the accounts receivable balances, and does not affect earnings. Nevertheless, if the misstatement is material, it could affect the fair presentation of these accounts, particularly when cash is a small or negative balance.

It is easy to test for a cash receipts cutoff error, which is frequently referred to as *"holding the cash receipts book open,"* by tracing recorded cash receipts to subsequent period bank deposits on the bank statement. If there is a delay of several days, this could indicate a cutoff error.

The confirmation of accounts receivable may also be relied upon to some degree to uncover cutoff errors for sales, sales returns and allowances, and cash receipts, especially when there is a long time span between the date the transaction took place and the recording date. However, when the cutoff error is for only a few days, the delays caused by the time it takes to deliver the mail confuse cutoff errors with normal reconciliation differences. For example, if a customer mails and records a check to a client for payment of an unpaid account on December 30 and the client receives and records the amount on January 2, the records of the two organizations will be different on December 31. This is not a cutoff error, but a *reconcilable difference* due to the delivery time; it will be difficult for the auditor to evaluate whether it is a cutoff error or a normal reconciling item if it is reported on a confirmation reply.

Adequate Disclosure

In addition to testing for the proper statement of the dollar amount in the general ledger, the auditor must also determine that the account balances resulting from the sales and collection cycle are properly disclosed in the financial statements. The disclosure problem is to decide whether the client has properly combined amounts and disclosed related information in the statements. To evaluate the adequacy of the disclosure, the auditor must have a thorough understanding of generally accepted accounting principles and disclosure requirements.

An important part of evaluating proper disclosure involves deciding whether material amounts requiring separate disclosure have actually been separated in the statements. For example, receivables from officers and affiliated companies must be segregated from accounts receivable from customers if the amounts are material. Similarly, under SEC requirements, it is necessary to separately disclose sales for different business segments. The proper aggregation of general ledger balances in the financial statements also requires combining account balances that are not relevant for external users of the statements. If all the accounts included in the general ledger were separately disclosed on the statements, most statement users would be more confused than enlightened.

As a part of proper disclosure, the auditor is also required to evaluate the adequacy of the *footnotes.* One of the major lawsuits in the history of the profession, the *Continental Vending* case, revolved primarily around the adequacy of the footnote disclosure of a major receivable from an affiliated company. The required footnote disclosure includes information about the pledging, discounting, factoring, and assignment of accounts receivable. Of course, in order to evaluate the adequacy of these disclosures, it is first necessary to know of their existence and to have complete information about their nature. This information is generally obtained in other parts of the audit by such procedures as examining the minutes, reviewing contracts and agreements, confirming the bank accounts, and discussing the existence of information requiring disclosure with management.

CONFIRMATION OF ACCOUNTS RECEIVABLE

One of the most important audit procedures used by auditors, the *confirmation of accounts receivable,* is the subject of the remainder of this chapter. Throughout this discussion the reader is urged to keep in mind that the primary purpose of accounts receivable confirmation is to satisfy the *existence, valuation,* and *cutoff* objectives.

AICPA Requirements

Only two audit procedures are formally required by the AICPA: the *confirmation of accounts receivable* and the *physical examination of inventory*. These two requirements are a direct result of the 1938 landmark legal case, *McKesson and Robbins,* in which a massive fraud involving fictitious accounts receivable and inventory was not uncovered in the audit. There was ample legal support to demonstrate that the confirmation of receivables and the physical observation of inventory would have brought the fraud to light, but at that time neither of these procedures was normally performed. Because of a strong reaction in the financial community, the membership of the AICPA voted in 1939 to require these two procedures whenever an unqualified report is issued.

In 1970 the requirement for confirmation was modified somewhat to permit an unqualified report even when accounts receivable are not confirmed when two conditions are met: first, the reason for not confirming the accounts must be that it is impractical or impossible to do so; second, the auditor must satisfy himself that accounts receivable is fairly stated by means of other auditing procedures. The modified requirement also specifically states that the auditor who fails to confirm accounts receivable has the burden of justifying the audit report he issues. The practical implication is that accounts receivable must be confirmed when the amount is material, except in unusual circumstances.

Relationship between Confirmation and Tests of Sales Transactions

The value of accounts receivable confirmation as evidence can be visualized more clearly by relating it to the compliance and substantive tests of transactions discussed in Chapters 8 and 9. If the beginning balance in accounts receivable can be assumed to be correct and a careful evaluation of the tests of the controls has been conducted, the auditor should be in an excellent position to evaluate the fairness of the ending balance in accounts receivable. (A review of Figure 8-1 on page 234 may help refresh your memory regarding this important concept.)

Confirmations are typically more effective than tests of transactions for discovering certain types of errors. These include invalid accounts, disputed amounts, and uncollectible accounts resulting from the inability to locate the customer. Although confirmations cannot ensure the discovery of any of these types of errors, they are more reliable than tests of transactions because confirmations are evidence obtained from an independent source, whereas tests of transactions rely upon internally created documents.

Confirmations are less likely to uncover omitted transactions and amounts than tests of the system for two reasons. First, in order to send a confirmation it is necessary to have a list of accounts receivable from which to select. Naturally, an omitted account will not be included in the population from which the sample is selected. Second, if an account with an omitted transaction is circularized, customers may ignore the confirmation or, alternatively, state that the amount is correct.

Clerical errors in billing customers and recording the amounts in the accounts can be effectively discovered by confirmation and tests of transactions. Confirmations are typically more effective in uncovering overstatements of accounts receivable than understatements, whereas tests of the system are effective for discovering both types.

The important concept in this discussion is the existence of both a *complementary* and a *supplementary* relationship between tests of sales transactions and confirmations. They are complementary in the sense that both types of evidence, when combined, provide a higher level of overall assurance of the fair presentation of sales, sales returns and allowances, and accounts receivable than can result from either type considered separately. The strengths of tests of transactions together with the strengths of confirmation result in a highly useful combination. The two types of evidence are supplementary in the sense that the auditor can obtain a given level of assurance by decreasing the tests of transactions if there is an offsetting increase in the confirmation of accounts receivable. The extent to which the auditor should rely upon the tests of transactions is dependent upon his evaluation of the effectiveness of the system. If he has carefully evaluated the controls, tested them for compliance, and concluded that the system is likely to provide correct results, it is appropriate to reduce the confirmation of accounts receivable. On the other hand, it would be inappropriate to bypass confirmation altogether.

Although the remaining sections in this chapter refer specifically to the confirmation of accounts receivable from customers, the concepts apply equally to other receivables such as notes receivable, amounts due from officers, and employee advances.

Confirmation Decisions

In performing confirmation procedures, the auditor must make four major decisions: the type of confirmation to use, the timing of the procedures, the sample size, and the individual items to select. Each of these is discussed along with the factors affecting the decision.

Type of Confirmation. Two common types of confirmations are used for confirming accounts receivable: *positive* confirmations and *negative* confirmations. A *positive* confirmation is a communication addressed to the debtor requesting him to confirm directly whether the balance as stated on the confirmation request is correct or incorrect. Figure 10-2 illustrates a positive confirmation. A *negative* confirmation is also a communication addressed to the debtor, but it requests a response only when he disagrees with the stated amount. Figure 10-3 illustrates a negative

Figure 10-2

Positive confirmation

ABC COMPANY, INC.
Middletown

January 5, 197Y

Middletown Supply Co.
19 South Main Street
Middletown

Gentlemen:

In connection with an examination of our financial statements, please confirm directly to our auditors

SMART & ALLEN
New York, New York

the correctness of the balance of your account with us as of December 31, 197X, as shown below.

This is not a request for payment; please do not send your remittance to our auditors.

Your prompt attention to this request will be appreciated. An envelope is enclosed for your reply.

____
Martin Abrams, Controller

No.______________

Smart & Allen
New York, New York

The balance receivable from us of $29,700 as of December 31, 197X is correct except as noted below:

____

____

____

____

Date________________________ By________________________

FIGURE 10-3

NEGATIVE CONFIRMATION

AUDITOR'S ACCOUNT CONFIRMATION

Please examine this statement carefully. If it does NOT agree with your records, please report any exceptions directly to our auditors

SMART & ALLEN

NEW YORK, NEW YORK

who are making an examination of our financial statements. An addressed envelope is enclosed for your convenience in replying.

Do not send your remittance to our auditors.

---

confirmation which has been attached to a customer's monthly statement with a gummed label.

A positive confirmation is *more reliable* evidence because the auditor can perform follow-up procedures if a response is not received from the debtor. With a negative confirmation, failure to reply must be regarded as a correct response even though the debtor may have ignored the confirmation request.

Offsetting the reliability disadvantage, negative confirmations are *less expensive* to send than positive confirmations, and thus more of them can be distributed for the same total cost. The determination of which type of confirmation to use is an auditor's decision, and it should be based on the facts in the audit. Positive confirmation should be used in the following circumstances:

1. Where there are a small number of large customers who account for a significant portion of total accounts receivable.
2. Where the auditor believes there may be disputed or inaccurate accounts. This would be the case when internal controls are considered inadequate or previous years' results are unsatisfactory.
3. Where the rules of certain regulatory agencies require them, such as those governing brokers and dealers in securities.

When the above conditions do not exist, it is acceptable to use negative confirmations, but negatives should not be used if the auditor believes the customer is likely to ignore the confirmation. Typically, when negatives are used, the auditor places great reliance upon the system as evidence of the fairness of accounts receivable. Negatives are often used for audits of hospitals, retail stores, and other industries where the receivables are due from the general public. In these cases far more reliance is placed on the tests of the system of internal control than on confirmations.

It is also common to use a combination of negatives and positives by sending the positives to accounts with large balances and negatives to those with small balances.

Timing. The most reliable evidence from confirmations is obtained when they are sent as close to the balance sheet date as possible, as opposed to confirming the accounts several months before year-end. This permits the auditor to directly test the accounts receivable balance on the financial statements without making any inferences about the transactions taking place between the confirmation date and the balance sheet date. On the other hand, as a means of completing the audit on a timely basis, it is frequently convenient to confirm the accounts at an interim date. This is permissible if the system of internal control is adequate and can provide reasonable assurance that sales, cash receipts, and other credits are properly recorded between the date of the confirmation and the end of the accounting period. Other factors the auditor is likely to consider in making the decision are the materiality of accounts receivable and the auditor's exposure to lawsuits because of the risk of client bankruptcy and similar risks.

If the decision is made to confirm accounts receivable prior to year-end, it is necessary to test the transactions occurring between the confirmation date and the balance sheet date by examining such internal documents as duplicate sales invoices, shipping documents, and evidence of cash receipts.

Sample Size. The considerations affecting the number of confirmations to send are essentially the same for judgmental as for statistical sampling:

1. The materiality of total accounts receivable. If accounts receivable is highly material relative to the other asset balances, a larger sample size is necessary than when it is immaterial.
2. The number of accounts receivable.
3. The distribution in the size of the accounts. If all the accounts are approximately the same size, fewer need to be confirmed than when their size is distributed over a wide range of values.
4. The results of the internal control evaluation and the tests of the system.
5. The results of the confirmation tests in previous years.
6. The likelihood of client bankruptcy and similar risks.
7. The type of confirmation being used. More confirmations are usually required for negative than for positive confirmation.

A discussion of these factors in the context of variables statistical sampling is given in Chapter 11.

Selection of the Items for Testing. Some type of *stratification is desirable* with most confirmations. A typical approach to stratification is to consider both the size of the outstanding balance and the length of time an account has been outstanding as a basis for selecting the balances for confirmation. In most audits the emphasis should be on confirming larger and older balances, since these are the ones that are most likely to include a significant error. But it is also important to sample some items from every material stratum of the population. In many cases the auditor selects all accounts above a certain dollar amount and selects a random sample from the remainder.

In selecting the items for confirmation, it is important that the auditor have complete *independence* in choosing the accounts to be confirmed. If the client dictates which accounts to select or refuses to grant permission to confirm certain accounts, the ability to operate independently is seriously threatened. On the other hand, clients do frequently request that certain accounts not be confirmed. Although this is undesirable and should be resisted, it is acceptable if the amounts are not material, the client's reasons appear valid, and it is possible to verify the balance in the accounts by other means. If the account balances that the client will not grant permission to confirm are material in relation to the financial statements as a whole, the standards of the profession do not permit the issuance of an unqualified opinion.

Maintaining Control

After the items have been selected for confirming, the auditor must maintain control of the confirmations until they are returned from the customer. If the client's assistance is obtained in preparing the confirmations, enclosing them in envelopes, or putting stamps on the envelopes, close supervision by the auditor is required. A return address must be included on all envelopes to make sure that undelivered mail is received by the CPA firm. Similarly, self-addressed return envelopes accompanying the confirmations must be addressed for delivery to the CPA firm's office. It is even important to mail the confirmations in a post-office box outside of the client's office. All of these steps are necessary to ensure an independent communication between the customer and the auditor.

When a confirmation request is returned as undelivered mail by the post office, it is necessary to carefully evaluate the reason why the request was not delivered. In most cases it represents a customer who has moved without paying his bill, but there is always the possibility of its being a fraudulent account. Even if it is a valid receivable, the existence of a large number of these accounts could indicate a serious collectibility problem which must be reflected in the allowance for uncollectible accounts.

Follow-up on Nonresponses

If the amounts are material, it is necessary to perform follow-up procedures for positive confirmations not returned by the customer. It is common to send second requests for confirmations and sometimes even third requests. Even with these efforts, some customers do not return the confirmation, so it is necessary to follow up with a method referred to as *alternative procedures.* The objective of alternative procedures is to determine by a means other than confirmation whether the nonconfirmed account was valid and properly stated at the confirmation date. For any positive confirmation not returned, the following documentation can be examined to verify the validity and valuation of individual sales transactions making up the ending balance in accounts receivable:

1. *Subsequent cash receipts.* Evidence of the receipt of cash subsequent to the confirmation date includes examining remittance advices, entries in the cash receipts records, or perhaps even subsequent credits in the accounts receivable subsidiary records. The examination of evidence of subsequent cash receipts is a highly useful alternative procedure because it is reasonable to assume that a customer would not make a payment unless it was a valid receivable. On the other hand, the fact of payment does not establish whether there was an obligation on the date of the confirmation. In addition, care should be taken to specifically match each unpaid sales transaction with evidence of its payment as a test for disputes or disagreements over individual outstanding invoices.

2. *Duplicate sales invoices.* These are useful in verifying the actual issuance of a sales invoice and the actual date of the billing.

3. *Shipping documents.* These are important in establishing whether the shipment was actually made and as a test of cutoff.

4. *Correspondence with the client.* Usually, the auditor does not need to review correspondence as a part of alternative procedures, but correspondence can be used to disclose disputed and questionable receivables not uncovered by other means.

The extent and nature of the alternative procedures depend primarily upon the materiality of the unconfirmed accounts, the types of errors discovered in the confirmed responses, the subsequent cash receipts of the unconfirmed accounts, and the auditor's evaluation of the system of internal control. It is normally desirable to account for all unconfirmed balances with alternative procedures even if the amounts are small, as a means of properly generalizing from the sample to the population.

Analysis of Differences

When the confirmation requests are returned by the customer, it is necessary to determine the reason for any reported differences. In many cases they are caused by timing differences between the client's and the customer's records. It is important to distinguish between these and *exceptions,* which represent misstatements of the accounts receivable balance. The most commonly reported types of differences on confirmations are as follows:

1. *Payment has already been made.* These typically arise when the customer has made a payment prior to confirmation date, but the client has not received the payment in time for posting before the confirmation date. Such instances should be carefully investigated to determine the possibility of a cash receipts cutoff error, lapping, or a theft of cash.

2. *Goods have not been received.* These typically result because the client records the sale at the date of shipment and the customer records the purchase when the goods are received. The lapse of time during which the goods are in transit is frequently the cause of differences reported on confirmations. These should be investigated to determine the possibility of the customer's not receiving the goods at all or the existence of a cutoff error on the client's records.

3. *The goods have been returned.* The client's failure to record a credit memo could result from timing differences or the improper recording of sales returns and allowances. Like other differences, these must be investigated.

4. *Clerical errors and disputed amounts.* The most likely case of the client's records being in error occurs when the customer states that there is an error in the price charged for the goods, the goods are damaged, the proper quantity of goods was not received, and so forth. These differences must be investigated to determine whether the client is in error and what the amount of the error is.

In most instances the auditor will ask the client to reconcile the difference and, if necessary, communicate with the customer to resolve any disagreements. Naturally, the auditor must carefully verify the client's conclusions on each significant difference.

Drawing Conclusions

When all differences have been resolved, including those discovered in performing alternative procedures, it is important to *reevaluate the system* of internal control. Each client error must be analyzed to determine whether it was consistent or inconsistent with the original evaluation of the strengths and weaknesses in the system. If a significant number of errors take place which are inconsistent with the strengths of the system, it indicates that the original evaluation of the system was incorrect. In such a case it is necessary to revise the evaluation and consider the impact of the revision on the audit.

It is also necessary to generalize from the sample to the entire population of accounts receivable. Even though the sum of the errors in the sample may not significantly affect the financial statements, the auditor must consider whether the population is likely to be materially misstated. This conclusion can be arrived at by using statistical sampling techniques or on a purely judgmental basis.

The final decision that must be reached about accounts receivable and sales is whether sufficient evidence has been obtained through analytical tests, tests of the system, cutoff procedures, confirmations, and other substantive tests to justify drawing conclusions about the fairness of the stated balance.

REVIEW QUESTIONS

1. Distinguish between direct tests of financial balances and tests of transactions for the sales and collection cycle. Explain how the tests of transactions affect the direct tests.
2. Cynthia Roberts, CPA, expresses the following viewpoint: "I do not believe in performing tests of transactions for the sales and collection cycle. As an alternative, I send a lot of negative confirmations on every audit at an interim date. If I find a lot of errors I analyze them to determine their cause. If the system is inadequate, I send positives at year-end to evaluate the amount of the errors. If the negatives result in minimal errors, which is often the case, I have found that the system is effective without bothering to perform tests of transactions, and the AICPA's confirmation requirement has been satisfied at the same time. In my opinion the best test of the system is to go directly to third parties." Evaluate her point of view.
3. List five analytical tests for the sales and collection cycle. For each test, describe an error that could be identified.
4. State the purpose of footing the total column in the client's trial balance, tracing individual customer names and amounts to the subsidiary ledger, and tracing the total to the general ledger trial balance. Is it necessary to trace each amount to the subsidiary ledger? Why?
5. Distinguish between valuation tests of gross accounts receivable and tests of the realizable value of receivables.
6. Explain why you agree or disagree with the following statement: "In most audits it is more important to carefully test the cutoff for sales than for cash receipts." Describe how you perform each type of test, assuming the existence of prenumbered documents.
7. Evaluate the following statement: "In many audits where accounts receivable is material, the requirement of confirming customer balances is a waste of time and would not be performed by competent auditors if it was not required by the AICPA. When the system of internal control is excellent and there are a large number of small receivables from customers who do not recognize the function of confirmation, it is a meaningless procedure. Examples are well-run utilities and department stores. In these situations tests of transactions are far more effective tests than confirmations."
8. Distinguish between a positive and a negative confirmation and state the circumstances when each should be used. Why do CPA firms frequently use a combination of positives and negatives on the same audit?
9. Under what circumstances is it acceptable to confirm accounts receivable prior to the balance sheet date?
10. State the most important factors affecting the sample size in confirmations of accounts receivable.
11. In Chapter 9 one of the points brought out was the need to obtain a representative sample of the population. How can this concept be reconciled with the statement in this chapter that the emphasis should be on confirming larger and older balances, since these are the most likely to contain errors?

12. Define what is meant by "alternative procedures" and explain their purpose. Which alternative procedures are the most reliable? Why?
13. Explain why the analysis of exceptions is important in the confirmation of accounts receivable, even if the errors in the sample are not material.
14. With regard to the sales and collection cycle, explain the relationship between flowcharts, preliminary evaluation, tests of compliance, and substantive tests.

DISCUSSION QUESTIONS AND PROBLEMS

15. For each of the following questions concerning the account balance in the sales and collection cycle, select the best response:
   a. In connection with his examination of the Beke Supply Company for the year ended August 31, 19X1, Derek Lowe, CPA, has mailed accounts receivable confirmations to three groups as follows:

Group Number	Type of Customer	Type of Confirmation
1	Wholesale	Positive
2	Current retail	Negative
3	Past-due retail	Positive

The confirmation responses from each group vary from 10 percent to 90 percent. The most likely response percentages are

(1) Group 1 90%   Group 2 50%   Group 3 10%
(2) Group 1 90%   Group 2 10%   Group 3 50%
(3) Group 1 50%   Group 2 90%   Group 3 10%
(4) Group 1 10%   Group 2 50%   Group 3 90%

   b. Of the following, the most common argument against the use of negative accounts receivable confirmations is that
   (1) The cost-per-response is excessively high.
   (2) Statistical sampling techniques cannot be applied to selection of the sample.
   (3) Recipients are more likely to feel that the confirmation is a request for payment.
   (4) The implicit assumption that no response indicates agreement with the balance may not be warranted.
   c. In connection with his review of key ratios, the CPA notes that Pyzi had accounts receivable equal to 30 days' sales at December 31, 19X0, and to 45 days' sales at December 31, 19X1. Assuming that there had been no changes in economic conditions, clientele, or sales mix, this change most likely would indicate
   (1) A steady increase in sales in 19X1.
   (2) An easing of credit policies in 19X1.
   (3) A decrease in accounts receivable relative to sales in 19X1.
   (4) A steady decrease in sales in 19X1.
   d. Balmes Company asks its CPA's assistance in estimating the proportion of its active 30-day charge account customers who also have an active in-

stallment credit account. The CPA takes an unrestricted random sample of one hundred accounts from the six thousand active 30-day charge accounts. Of the accounts selected, ten also have active installment credit accounts. If the CPA decides to estimate with 95 percent confidence, the estimate is that

(1) At most 10 percent of the active 30-day charge account customers also have active installment credit accounts.

(2) At least 10 percent of the active 30-day charge account customers also have active installment credit accounts.

(3) Between 7 percent and 13 percent of the active 30-day charge account customers also have active installment credit accounts.

(4) Between 4 percent and 16 percent of the active 30-day charge account customers also have active installment credit accounts.

e. The CPA learns that collections of accounts receivable during the first ten days of January were entered as debits to cash and credits to accounts receivable as of December 31. The effect generally will be to

(1) Leave both working capital and the current ratio unchanged at December 31.

(2) Overstate both working capital and the current ratio at December 31.

(3) Overstate working capital with no effect on the current ratio at December 31.

(4) Overstate the current ratio with no effect on working capital at December 31.

f. The return of a positive account receivable confirmation without an exception attests to the

(1) Collectibility of the receivable balance.

(2) Accuracy of the receivable balance.

(3) Accuracy of the aging of accounts receivable.

(4) Accuracy of the allowance for bad debts. (AICPA adapted)

16.a. What are the implications to a CPA if during his examination of accounts receivable some of a client's trade customers do not respond to his request for positive confirmation of their accounts?

b. Should the CPA send second requests? Why?

c. What auditing steps should a CPA perform if there is no response to a second request for a positive confirmation? (AICPA adapted)

17. In a properly planned examination of financial statements, the auditor coordinates his reviews of specific balance sheet and income statement accounts.

Required:

a. Why should the auditor coordinate his examinations of balance sheet accounts and income statement accounts in the sales and collection cycle? Discuss and illustrate by examples.

b. A properly designed audit program enables the auditor to determine conditions or establish relationships in more than one way.

c. Cite various procedures that the auditor employs that might lead to detection of each of the following two conditions:

(1) Inadequate allowance for doubtful accounts receivable

(2) Unrecorded sales commissions (AICPA adapted)

18. During the past few years your audit client, Commercial Dry Wall, has been in somewhat of an income slump, as competition for dry wall and newly

developed interior wall materials has been intensive. Losses have occurred because of the need to diversify and expand in different areas. In discussing the current year's audit, Brian Curtis, the controller, expresses dissatisfaction with the approach to auditing your firm and the profession as a whole takes in verifying financial statements. He feels the entire approach emphasizes only the overstatement of assets and the understatement of liabilities. His criticisms are especially intense in auditing accounts receivable, where the customer is likely to say nothing about understatements and respond to overstatements or even questionable items. He asserts that even the emphasis in the accounts normally selected for testing is on overstatements, since large balances and disputed amounts are frequently confirmed. After ranting on for about fifteen minutes, he talks about switching CPA firms to someone who is more interested in a balanced picture of overstatements and understatements, rather than only overstatements.

You feel an immediate response is necessary in this case, and you decide to restrict yourself to a discussion of accounts receivable. How would you answer him?

19. You have been assigned to the confirmation of accounts receivable for the Blank Paper Company audit. You have tested the trial balance and selected the accounts for confirming. Before the confirmation requests are mailed, the controller asks to look at the accounts you intend to confirm to determine whether he will permit you to send them.

He reviews the list and informs you that he does not want you to confirm six of the accounts on your list. Two of them are credit balances, one is a zero balance, two of the other three have a fairly small balance, and one balance is highly material. The reason he gives is that he feels the confirmations will upset these customers, because "they are kind of hard to get along with." He doesn't want the credit balances confirmed because it may encourage the customer to ask for a refund.

In addition, the controller asks you to send an additional twenty confirmations to customers he has listed for you. He does this as a means of credit collection for "those stupid idiots who don't know the difference between a CPA and a credit collection agency."

Required:

a. Is it acceptable for the controller to review the list of accounts you intend to confirm? Discuss.
b. Discuss the appropriateness of sending the twenty additional confirmations to customers.
c. Assuming the auditor complies with all the controller's requests, what is the effect on the auditor's opinion?

20. In your examination of the financial statements of the Kay Savings and Loan Association for year ended December 31, 19X5, you find a new account in the general ledger, Home Improvement Loans. You determine that these are unsecured loans not insured by any government agency, made on a discount basis to homeowners who are required to secure life insurance coverage provided by the association under a group life insurance policy for the outstanding amount and duration of the loan. Borrowers are issued coupon books which require monthly installment payments; however, borrowers may prepay the outstanding balance of the loan at any time in accordance with the terms of their loan contract. This account constitutes a material amount of the total assets of the association at December 31, 19X5.

Required:

a. Prepare an audit program for the examination of the new account, Home Improvement Loans.

b. During your examination of the Home Improvement Loans account the vice-president in charge of the loan department hands you a list of twenty-five accounts with balances from $300 to $8,000 representing approximately 40 percent of the total account balance. He states that confirmation requests are not to be prepared for these twenty-five accounts under any circumstances because the borrowers have requested "no correspondence."

   (1) Would you comply with the vice-president's request? Discuss.

   (2) Assuming you complied with the vice-president's request and did not send confirmation requests to the "no correspondence" accounts, what effect, if any, would this compliance have upon your auditor's short-form report? (AICPA adapted)

21. Maria Nolan, CPA, in examining the financial statements of the Quinn Helicopter Corporation for the year ended September 30, 19X7, found a material amount of receivables from the federal government. The governmental agencies replied neither to the first nor to the second confirmation requests, nor to a third request made by telephone.

Required:

a. How could Nolan satisfy herself as to the fairness of the receivables as of the balance at September 30, 19X7?

b. Assuming she was able to satisfy herself, what is the effect on the auditor's report? (AICPA adapted)

22. In connection with his examination of the financial statements of Houston Wholesalers, Inc., for the year ended June 30, 19X7, a CPA performs several cutoff tests.

Required:

a. (1) What is a cutoff test?

   (2) Why must cutoff tests be performed for both the beginning and the end of the audit period on initial engagements?

b. The CPA wishes to test Houston's sales cutoff at June 30, 19X7. Describe the steps that he should include in this test.

c. Describe steps the CPA should use to test cash receipts cutoff.

(AICPA adapted)

23. You have been assigned to the first examination of the accounts of the Chicago Company for the year ending March 31, 19X8. The accounts receivable were circularized at December 31, 19X7, and at that date the receivables consisted of approximately 200 accounts with balances totaling $956,750. Seventy-five of these accounts with balances totaling $650,725 were selected for circularization. All but 20 of the confirmation requests have been returned; 30 were signed without comments, 14 had minor differences which have been cleared satisfactorily, while 11 confirmations had the following comments:

a. We are sorry but we cannot answer your request for confirmation of our account as the PDQ Company uses an accounts payable voucher system.

b. The balance of $1,050 was paid on December 23, 19X7.

c. The above balance of $7,750 was paid on January 5, 19X8.

d. The above balance has been paid.
e. We do not owe you anything at December 31, 19X7, as the goods, represented by your invoice dated December 30, 19X7, number 25,050, in the amount of $11,550, were received on January 5, 19X8, on FOB destination terms.
f. An advance payment of $2,500 made by us in November 19X7 should cover the two invoices totaling $1,350 shown on the statement attached.
g. We never received these goods.
h. We are contesting the propriety of this $12,525 charge. We think the charge is excessive.
i. Amount okay. As the goods have been shipped to us on consignment we will remit payment upon selling the goods.
j. The $10,000, representing a deposit under a lease, will be applied against the rent due to us during 19X9, the last year of the lease.
k. Your credit dated December 5, 19X7, in the amount of $440 cancels the above balance.

Required:

What steps would you take to clear satisfactorily each of the above eleven comments?   (AICPA adapted)

24. You have examined the financial statements of the Heft Company for several years. The system of internal control for accounts receivable is very satisfactory. The Heft Company is on a calendar year basis. An interim audit, which included confirmation of the accounts receivable, was performed at August 31 and indicated that the accounting for cash, sales, sales returns and allowances, and receivables was very reliable.

The company's sales are principally to manufacturing concerns. There are about 1,500 active trade accounts receivable of which about 35 percent represent 65 percent of the total dollar amount. The accounts receivable are maintained alphabetically in five subledgers which are controlled by one general ledger account.

Sales are machine-posted in the subledgers by an operation that produces simultaneously the customer's ledger card, his monthly statement, and the sales journal. All cash receipts are in the form of customers' checks and are machine-posted simultaneously on the customer's ledger card, his monthly statement, and the cash receipts journal. Information for posting cash receipts is obtained from the remittance advice portions of the customers' checks. The bookkeeping machine operator compares the remittance advices with the list of checks that was prepared by another person when the mail was received.

Summary totals are produced monthly by the bookkeeping machine operations for posting to the appropriate general ledger accounts such as cash, sales, accounts receivable. Aged trial balances by subledgers are prepared monthly.

Required:

Prepare the additional audit procedures necessary for testing the balances in the sales and collection cycle. (Ignore bad debts and allowance for uncollectible accounts.)   (AICPA adapted)

25. The auditor for the Applegate Refrigeration Company has always been able to obtain cooperation from the credit manager in helping prepare confirmations in spite of his heavy responsibility for recording sales and cash

receipts, preparing all cash deposits, and handling the collection of slow-paying customers. The employees in the credit department type up the positive confirmation requests that have been indicated by the auditor on the accounts receivable trial balance and then return them to the auditor for mailing. The auditor compares the name and amount of the confirmation with the accounts receivable trial balance and mails the confirmations himself. Most of the confirmations for the 12-31-X8 audit were returned by the customers, and the auditor was able to satisfy himself that accounts receivable was fairly stated.

In late 19X9 it is determined that several accounts were fictitious or overstated at 12-31-X8. Due to the fraud the company is forced to file bankruptcy. Further investigation reveals that two of the incorrect accounts were positively confirmed on 12-31-X8. One confirmation was sent to a fictitious person at a post-office box number that was controlled by the credit manager. He simply put the incorrect address on the confirmation to make sure it would be sent to the post-office box. He then signed it as being correct and returned it as an ordinary confirmation. On the second confirmation, the credit manager had overstated the balance due from the customer by two thousand dollars. When the credit manager used the auditor's copy of the trial balance to prepare the confirmations, he reduced the customer's balance to the correct amount. Since the auditor had already footed the trial balance and traced the amounts to individual subsidiary ledgers, he did not discover the error.

Required:

a. List the ways in which the auditor has failed to follow due care in the conduct of the examination.
b. Do you believe that creditors of the client will be able to recover damages from the CPA firm in this case if they sue? Discuss.
c. How can the auditor avoid this type of problem when he obtains client assistance?

26. In the confirmation of accounts receivable for the Reliable Service Company, eighty-five positive confirmations and no negatives were mailed to customers. This represents 35 percent of the dollar balance of the total accounts receivable. For all non-responses second requests were sent, but there were still ten customers who had not responded. The decision was made to perform alternative procedures on the ten unanswered confirmation requests. An assistant is requested to conduct the alternative procedures and report to the senior auditor after he has completed his tests on two accounts. He prepared the following information for the working papers:

1. Confirmation request #9
   Customer name—Jolene Milling Co.
   Balance—$3,621 at 12-31-X7
   Subsequent cash receipts per the subsidiary ledger   1-15-X8—$1,837
        1-29-X8—$1,263
        2-6-X8—$1,429

2. Confirmation request #26
   Customer name—Rosenthal Repair Service
   Balance—$2,500 at 12-31-X7
   Subsequent cash receipts per the subsidiary ledger   2-9-X8—$ 500
   Sales invoices per the subsidiary ledger   9-1-X7—$4,200
   (I examined the duplicate sales invoice)

Required:

a. If you were called upon to evaluate the adequacy of the sample size, the type of confirmation used, and the percentage of accounts confirmed, what additional information would you need?

b. Discuss the need to send second requests and perform alternative procedures for nonresponses.

c. Evaluate the adequacy of the alternative procedures used for verifying the two nonresponses.

27. Your client took a complete physical inventory under your observation as of December 15 and adjusted the inventory control account (perpetual inventory method) to agree with the physical inventory. You have decided to accept the balance of the control account as of December 31, after reflecting transactions recorded therein from December 16 to December 31, in connection with your examination of financial statements for the year ended December 31.

Your examination of the sales cutoff as of December 15 and December 31 disclosed the following items not previously considered. What adjusting journal entries, if any, would you make for each of these items?

		Date		
Cost	Sales Price	Shipped	Billed	Credited to Inventory Control
$2,840	$3,690	12–14	12–16	12–16
3,910	5,020	12–10	12–19	12–10
1,890	2,130	1–2	12–31	12–31

(AICPA adapted)

28. You are considering using the services of a reputable outside mailing service for the confirmation of accounts receivable balances. The service would prepare and mail the confirmation requests and remove the returned confirmations from the envelopes and give them directly to you.

Required:

What reliance, if any, could you place upon the services of the outside mailing service? Discuss and state the reasons for your answer.

(AICPA adapted)

29. The following errors are commonly found in the sales and collection account balances:

a. Cash received from collections of accounts receivable in the subsequent period are recorded as current period receipts.

b. The allowance for uncollectible accounts is inadequate due to the client's failure to reflect depressed economic conditions in the allowance.

c. Several accounts receivable are in dispute due to claims of defective merchandise.

d. The pledging of accounts receivable to the bank for a loan is not disclosed in the financial statements.

e. Goods shipped and included in current period sales were returned in the subsequent period.

f. Several sales are not recorded due to the loss of shipping documents by the shipping department.

g. Uncollectible accounts are included in current period accounts receivable.

h. An accounts receivable bookkeeper who has access to cash is covering an embezzlement by lapping.

i. Long-term interest-bearing notes receivable from affiliated companies are included in accounts receivable.

j. The trial balance total does not equal the amount on the general ledger.

Required:

a. For each of these errors, list an internal control that should prevent the error.

b. List two audit procedures for each of these errors that the auditor can use to detect its existence.

30. You are a senior accountant on the staff of Marin and Matthews, certified public accountants. You are conducting the annual audit of the Never-Slip Corporation for the calendar year 19X9.

  You are now working on the audit of the accounts receivable and related allowance for bad debts accounts.

  All the data included in the client's general ledger and supporting schedules are summarized below.

General Ledger

Accounts Receivable

19X9		
Dec. 31	Balance	$184,064.20

Allowance for Uncollectible Accounts

19X9				19X9		
July 31	G.J.	$570.00		Jan. 1	Balance	$2,712.50
Oct. 31	G.J.	954.16		Dec. 31	G.J.	2,698.10

Bad Debts

19X9				19X9			
Dec. 31	G.J.	$2,698.10		Aug. 1	C.R.J.	$85.00

General Journal

July 31

Allowance for uncollectible accounts	$570.00	
Accounts receivable		$570.00
To charge off bad accounts (detail omitted)		

October 31

Allowance for uncollectible accounts	954.16	
Accounts receivable		954.16
Accounts charged off:		
Baker, J. A.	$110.00	
Dehner & Son	9.75	
Meek, Roger	350.00	
Wagner, James	494.41	
	$954.16	

December 31

Bad debts	2,698.10	
Allowance for uncollectible accounts		2,698.10
Annual charge based on ½% of net credit sales		

Cash Receipts Journal

On August 1 the $85 account of John Smith, previously charged off as of July 31, was collected in full. Credit was to bad debts.

Summary of Aging Schedule

The summary of the aged trial balance prepared by the client as of December 31, 19X9, was totaled as follows:

Under one month	$ 92,715.60
One to three months	58,070.15
Three to six months	29,126.89
Over six months	4,624.10
	$184,536.74

Credit balances:

Dabney Cleaners ..	$ 16.54—O.K.—Additional billing in January 19X0
Britting Cafeteria .	72.00—Should have been credited to Britt Motor Co.
Wehby & Son	384.00—Advance on a sales contract
	$472.54

Additional Information:

The accounts receivable clerk has access to cash, maintains accounts receivable subsidiary records, and approves the charge-off of uncollectible accounts receivable.

The auditor and the client have agreed on the following allowance for uncollectible account requirements:

It is agreed that ½ percent is adequate for accounts under one month.
Accounts one to three months are expected to require a reserve of 1 percent.
Accounts three to six months are expected to require a reserve of 2 percent.
Accounts over six months are analyzed as follows:

Definitely bad	$ 416.52
Doubtful (estimated 50% collectible)	516.80
Apparently good, but slow (estimated 90% collectible) ...	3,690.78
	$4,624.10

Required:

a. List the audit procedures you would consider necessary for the verification of bad debts, the charge-off of uncollectible accounts, and allowance for uncollectible accounts, assuming no testing has been done to this point.

b. Assuming you verify and are satisfied with the amounts charged off as uncollectible during the current year, what is the proper ending balance in allowance for uncollectible accounts?   (AICPA adapted)

11

The Use of Variables Sampling
in
Auditing

Both attributes sampling and variables sampling are valuable techniques in carrying out audit tests. However, there are significant differences in the application of these two methods. The first part of this chapter discusses these differences. The balance of the chapter presents the methods for handling one type of variables sampling, difference estimation, and then briefly discusses other types.

COMPARISON WITH ATTRIBUTES SAMPLING

Many of the basic concepts underlying attributes sampling apply to variables sampling as well. The auditor wants to generalize from a sample to the entire population but needs a method that takes into account the imperfection of sampling as opposed to testing the entire population. The two measures of this imperfection are the *precision interval* and the *confidence level*. Although the calculations for the two methods are different, the objectives and methodology are similar.

The major difference between the two methods is in the characteristic the auditor wants to measure. In *attributes sampling* the objective is to measure the *frequency of error* in the population. When attributes sampling is used in a compliance test, the statistical result obtained is a *computed upper precision limit at the desired confidence level;* this can also be stated as a "point estimate" plus a precision interval at the desired confidence level. For example, assume the auditor tests the percentage of duplicate sales invoices not supported by shipping documents by examining one hundred sales invoices from a population of ten thousand. If he found three invoices with no shipping documents attached, the point estimate of the error rate would be 3 percent, and the computed upper precision limit determined from the tables in Chapter 9 would be 7.6 percent at a 95 percent confidence level. Another way of stating this result is to say that it is a point estimate of 3 percent plus a precision interval of 4.6 percent at a 95 percent confidence level.

In *variables sampling,* as it is used in auditing, the objective is almost always to measure the *true dollar amount* of an account balance or some similar total. The computed result is stated in terms of *the dollar amount of the point estimate plus and minus the dollar amount of the precision interval at the confidence level desired.* It is common to calculate both *an upper and a lower limit* for variables sampling because an account balance can be understated or overstated. As an example, assume the auditor is confirming accounts receivable and computes the point estimate of the total balance as $1,470,000 with a $200,000 computed precision interval at a confidence level of 95 percent. This means the auditor estimates that, at a 95 percent confidence level, the true value of the accounts receivable to be between $1,270,000 and $1,670,000 ($1,470,000 ± $200,-000). At this early stage in the study of variables sampling, it is not possible for the reader to determine how these values are computed, but it is possible to observe that the results are stated in the same basic form as attributes.

Whenever it is feasible to use variables sampling for substantive tests, it is a more useful measurement device than attributes sampling because auditors are generally more interested in the monetary amount of errors than in the frequency of errors. As an illustration, assume the auditor could use either attributes or variables sampling in confirming accounts receivable. If attributes sampling is used, the statistical conclusion is stated in terms of the percentage of the accounts receivable that are in error regardless of the amount of the individual errors in the sample. In variables sampling, the auditor is measuring the correct dollar value of the accounts in the sample. Which of these is more useful? Variables sampling, because the correct dollar value of total accounts receivable is of primary interest to the auditor. As a result, attributes sampling is normally applied to tests of transactions and variables sampling is applied to direct tests of balances. The only time attributes sampling is used for direct tests of balances is when the cost of variables sampling is prohibitive or the method does not give useful results.

The major advantage of using variables sampling rather than judgmental sampling for measuring the dollar amount of errors or account balances is the *objectivity* of the results. At the completion of a test using variables sampling, the auditor can use his professional judgment in deciding whether he is satisfied with the potential error in the population considering the measurable statistical risk in the result.

DIFFERENCE ESTIMATION

There are several different types of variables-sampling techniques that may be applicable to auditing in different circumstances. One of these, *difference estimation* (without stratification), has been selected as a means of illustrating the concepts and methodology of variables sampling. In explaining the concepts, the steps in computing the *upper and lower confidence limits* for an estimate of the balance in accounts receivable are set forth and discussed.

In going through the steps of the illustration, the positive form of confirmation is used. The assumptions throughout are either that all confirmations were returned or that effective alternative procedures were carried out.[1] Hence the sample size is the number of positive confirmations mailed.

The objective of difference estimation for tests of accounts receivable is to measure the total amount of the *error* in the recorded account balance. Since a sample rather than the entire population is used, a range of values for the total error is calculated. Ultimately the auditor must decide whether the total error is too material to accept.

In discussing the steps for computing the statistical results in this section, no statistical formulas are included. Therefore the reader cannot be expected to know the source of the numbers used in the illustration. The purpose here is to provide a logical explanation of the meaning of the statistical conclusions before the formulas are introduced. Later in the chapter the formulas are included, but it is far more important to understand the auditing concepts in variables sampling than the statistical formulas. These are the steps for computing the results:

1. Take a random sample.
2. Determine the value of each error in the sample.
3. Compute the point estimate of the total errors.
4. Compute an estimate of the population standard deviation.
5. Compute the precision interval.
6. Compute the confidence limits.
7. Draw conclusions.

Take a Random Sample

The *sampling unit* is defined as the individual balance on the accounts receivable aged trial balance. The random sample is selected in the same

---

[1] The use of statistical sampling for the measurement of results obtained by positive confirmation is questioned by some auditors. If errors exist in the balances being confirmed, but the customer signs the confirmation and returns it without noting the exception, the statistical results do not accurately measure the errors in the population. Recent empirical studies indicate that this frequently occurs in accounts receivable confirmation. Virtually all auditors agree that it is not proper to statistically measure the results of negative confirmations because any sample items ignored by customers would automatically be treated as if they were correct.

manner as for attributes sampling, probably on the basis of page number and line number. The number of confirmations mailed is the sample size. The determination of sample size is discussed later in the chapter.

Determine the Value of Each Error in the Sample

For confirmations, the error is the *difference* between the confirmation response and the client's balance after the reconciliation of all timing differences and customer errors. For example, if a customer returns a confirmation and states the correct balance is $887.12, and the balance in the client's records is $997.12, the difference of $110 is an overstatement error if the auditor concludes the client's records are incorrect. For *non-responses,* the errors discovered by alternative procedures are treated identically to those discovered through confirmation. At the end of this step, there is an error value for each item in the sample, many of which are likely to be zero.

Compute the Point Estimate of the Total Errors

The *point estimate* is a direct extrapolation from the errors in the sample to the errors in the population. If the auditor sends one hundred confirmations from a population of one thousand accounts receivable and determines that the combined amount of the net errors in the sample is an overstatement of $4,600, the point estimate of the population error is an overstatement of $46,000 ($4,600 ÷ 100 = $46; $46 × 1,000 = $46,000).

It is unlikely, of course, for the actual, but unknown, error to be *exactly* the same as the point estimate. It is more realistic to estimate the error in terms of a *confidence interval determined by the point estimate plus and minus a computed precision interval.* For example, $46,000 ± $20,000 at a 95 percent confidence level would mean the auditor is 95 percent confident that the true error is an overstatement between $26,000 and $66,000. It should be apparent at this point that the calculation of the confidence interval is an essential part of variables sampling, and that the process used to develop it depends on the obtaining of a *representative sample.*

Now that an example has been given using variables sampling, it is appropriate to digress briefly to define, and to illustrate with the results of the example, the terminology used in difference estimation:

- *Point estimate*—A single estimate of the error in the population ($46,000) based on the average error in the sample ($46) times the population size (1,000).
- *Computed precision interval*—A statistical calculation that measures the inability to measure the exact amount of error in the population ($20,000). The precision interval must always be stated at a particular confidence level (95%).
- *Confidence interval*—The range of values representing the total

amount of error in the population at the stated confidence level ($26,000 to $66,000 at a 95% confidence level). The confidence interval is calculated from the point estimate and the precision interval ($46,000 ± $20,000).

- *Confidence limits*—The two values representing the bounds of the confidence interval. There is an upper confidence limit ($66,000) and a lower confidence limit ($26,000).

The bases for all four terms are the point estimate and the computed precision interval. The point estimate has already been explained, but the precision interval has not. To perform the calculation of the precision interval, it is necessary to first calculate an estimate of the population standard deviation.

Compute an Estimate of the Population Standard Deviation

The population *standard deviation* is a statistical measure of the *variability* in the values of the individual items in the population. If there is a large amount of variation in the values of population items, the standard deviation is larger than when the variation is small. For example, in the confirmation of accounts receivable, errors of $4, $14, and $26 have far less variation than the set $2, $275, and $812. Hence the standard deviation is smaller in the first set.

The standard deviation has a significant effect on the computed precision interval. As might be expected, the ability to predict the value of a population is better when there is a small rather than a large amount of variation in the individual values of the population.

A reasonable estimate of the value of the population standard deviation is computed by the auditor using a standard statistical formula applied to the sample. The size of the standard deviation estimate is determined solely by the characteristics of the auditor's sample results and is not affected by his professional judgment.

Compute the Precision Interval

The *precision interval* is calculated by a statistical formula. The results are a dollar measure of the inability to predict the true population error because the test was based on a sample rather than on the entire population. In order for the computed precision interval to have any meaning, it must be associated with a particular confidence level. A point estimate of the error of $46,000 plus or minus a computed precision of $20,000 at a confidence level of 95 percent has a completely different meaning than the same point estimate and computed precision at a 60 percent confidence level.

Four factors directly affect the size of the computed precision interval. To better understand the impact of each of these factors, it is assumed that the auditor has already calculated a precision interval of $20,000.

The four factors that affect the calculation and the effect of changing each factor are as follows:

1. *The standard deviation calculated on the basis of the sample.* When the standard deviation increases, the computed precision increases proportionately. For example, if the standard deviation is changed from $18 to $36, the computed precision of $20,000 increases to $40,000. An increase in the computed precision interval as a result of an increase in the standard deviation is a reasonable conclusion because a less precise measure of the population should be expected if the errors in the sample vary considerably. (The reader should recognize that an increase in the computed precision interval results in a less precise measure of the true population total value.)

2. *The population size.* An increase in the number of items in the population increases the computed precision somewhat more than proportionately. For example, if all of the other factors remained constant, the computed precision of $20,000 in a population of 1000 items would become $41,092 if the population were 2000 items.

It will be recalled that in attributes sampling the effect of the population size on the computed precision interval was very small, but in variables sampling a doubling of the population size results in approximately a doubling of the computed precision. The difference in the effect of the population size comes about because attributes-sampling conclusions are stated in terms of a population *error rate,* whereas the difference estimate conclusions are stated in terms of the *total value* of the error. Due to the importance of population size on the point estimate and the computed precision interval, a correct count of the total number of items in the population is essential for variables sampling.

3. *The sample size.* When the sample size is increased, the computed precision interval decreases if everything else stays constant. If every item in the population is tested, the computed precision interval becomes zero because the inability to predict has been eliminated. For small samples the computed precision interval is often too large to be useful.

The computed precision interval does not decrease proportionately with the increase in the sample size. In fact, to cut the computed precision interval in half, it is necessary to quadruple the sample size in most populations (i.e., there is a square root relationship). If the auditor desires to significantly reduce the computed precision interval, the additional cost is normally very high.

4. *The confidence level.* The concept of the confidence level is the same for variables sampling as it is for attributes. It is a statement of the probability that the true population value will actually fall within the limits of the confidence interval. When the desired confidence level is decreased, the precision interval also decreases. A low confidence level will provide a computed precision interval which is small; but, of course, there is a high risk of the true error lying outside the resultant confidence interval.

Compute the Confidence Limits

The *confidence limits,* which define the confidence interval, are calculated by combining the point estimate of the total errors and the computed precision interval at the desired confidence level (point estimate
± computed precision interval). As stated earlier, if the point estimate is
$46,000 and the computed precision interval is $20,000 at a 95 percent
confidence level, the *computed lower confidence limit* (LCL) is a $26,000
overstatement of accounts receivable and the *computed upper confidence
limit* (UCL) is a $66,000 overstatement. There is a 95 percent probability
of the true error being an overstatement between $26,000 and $66,000.
Another way of stating the same thing is to say there is a 2.5 percent
statistical risk that the true error is less than a $26,000 overstatement and
another 2.5 percent that it exceeds a $66,000 overstatement. In total there
is a 5 percent risk that the true value does not lie within the interval.

The statistical result can be demonstrated with the use of a *sampling
distribution* that depicts the *point estimate* of the population error, the
upper and lower confidence limits, and the *confidence level.* This distribution, shown in Figure 11-1, is based upon the assumption of a normal
distribution.

Draw Conclusions

The final decision the auditor must make in a variables sampling
application is whether the population is satisfactory. There are two
stages in the decision. The first is an *analysis of the individual client
errors* to determine their cause and to compare the errors discovered with
the weaknesses and strengths of the system. Error analysis was discussed
for accounts receivable in Chapter 10 and is performed in exactly the
same manner for judgmental and statistical sampling.

The second stage is an *evaluation of the total population error* (as
measured by the confidence interval) to decide whether it is so large that
the auditor believes the financial statements may be misstated by a

FIGURE 11-1

SAMPLING DISTRIBUTION

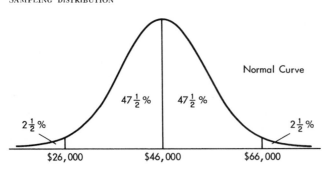

material amount. The materiality question must be decided on the basis of the size of the total error the auditor is willing to accept in accounts receivable and the risk he is willing to take of being wrong. The acceptable amount of error is called the *acceptable error (AE)*.

In deciding on the acceptability of the population, the auditor *compares both the computed upper confidence limit (UCL) and the computed lower confidence limit (LCL) with the acceptable error (AE)*. If the *absolute values* of both the UCL and the LCL are less than or equal to the AE, the population can be considered acceptable. *If either of the absolute values is greater than the AE, the population is not acceptable.* For example, in the previous illustration assume the auditor is willing to accept an error of $70,000 (AE = $70,000). Since the absolute values of the LCL and the UCL are $26,000 and $66,000 respectively, the population can be considered acceptable. If the AE had been $60,000 instead of $70,000, the population would not be acceptable. When the auditor compares the AE with the confidence limits, he is simply comparing the "worst likely value of the error in the population" with the total error he is willing to accept. If the "worst likely value" is larger than he can accept, he must take some action to correct the problem.

When the auditor decides that one or both of the computed confidence limits are not acceptable, there are several possible courses of action:

1. *Perform expanded audit tests in specific areas.* If an analysis of the errors indicates that most of the errors are of a particular type, it may be desirable to restrict the additional audit effort to the problem area. For example, if an analysis of the exceptions in confirmations indicates that most of the errors result from shipping cutoff, an extended search could be made of the year-end sales cutoff to be sure it is proper. However, great care must be taken to evaluate the cause of all errors in the sample before a conclusion is drawn about the proper emphasis in the expanded tests; there may be more than one problem area.

2. *Adjust the account balance.* When one of the computed confidence limits is larger than the auditor will accept, the client may be willing to adjust the book value. For example, in the case where the statistical results are $46,000 ± $20,000, if the client is willing to reduce the book balance by $46,000, the results are now 0 ± $20,000. The new computed lower confidence limit is an understatement of $20,000, and the upper confidence limit is a $20,000 overstatement. The client, however, may be unwilling to adjust the balance on the basis of a sample. Furthermore, if the computed precision interval exceeds the allowable error, an adjustment to the books cannot be made that will satisfy the auditor. This would be the case in the above example if the acceptable error were only $15,000.

3. *Increase the sample size.* When the auditor increases the sample size, the point estimate of the population remains approximately the same and the computed precision interval gets smaller *if* the number of errors and their amount and direction in the expanded sample are similar in nature to those in the original sample. When this occurs, the computed

lower confidence limit gets larger and the upper confidence limit gets smaller, which may satisfy the auditor's materiality standards. For example, assume the auditor will be satisfied if the true value of the error is less than $60,000 with a 5 percent risk of its exceeding that amount. If the upper confidence limit is $66,000 ($46,000 + $20,000), the population is not acceptable at this point. Now assume the sample size is increased and the number, amount, and direction of the errors in the additional sample are similar to those in the original sample. If the expanded sample produced a new confidence interval of $46,000 ± $13,000, which results in a computed upper confidence limit of $59,000, the population is now acceptable.

Increasing the sample enough to satisfy the auditor's materiality standards is often *costly*, especially when the confidence limits are well beyond the auditor's standards of acceptability. And even if the sample size is increased, there is no assurance of a satisfactory result. If the number, amount, and direction of the errors in the extended sample are proportionately greater or more variable than in the original sample, the results are still likely to be unacceptable. For accounts receivable confirmation it is also difficult to increase the sample size because the requests should be sent out near the end of the month being confirmed. By the time the auditor finds out the sample was not large enough, several weeks have usually passed. In spite of all of these difficulties, in many instances the auditor must extend the sample to obtain more information about the population. It is much more common to increase sample size in other audit areas where variables sampling is used than in confirming receivables, but even for confirmations it is occasionally necessary.

4. *Request the client to correct the population.* In some cases the client's records are so inadequate that a correction of the entire population is required before the audit can be completed. For example, in accounts receivable, the client may be asked to prepare the aging schedule again if the auditor concludes that it has significant errors. Whenever the client changes the valuation of some items in the population, it is of course necessary to audit the results again.

5. *Refuse to give an unqualified opinion.* If the auditor believes the recorded amount in accounts receivable, or any other account, is not fairly stated, it is necessary to follow at least one of the above alternatives or *qualify the audit opinion* in an appropriate manner. If the auditor believes there is a reasonable chance that the financial statements are materially misstated, it would be a serious breach of auditing standards to issue an unqualified audit report.

STATISTICAL CALCULATIONS

Now the calculations for the use of difference estimation can be shown. In studying these calculations, keep in mind that the objective is to estimate the true value of the errors in the population by computing a point estimate of the population errors and a computed precision interval at a particular confidence level. Each of the steps previously discussed is listed in the left-hand column of the following table. The statistical formula for each step is shown in the middle column, and an illustration of the calculation, using a new example, is shown on the right.

The statistical result is shown in graphical form in Figure 11-2. An examination of the figure shows there is a 50 percent risk of the true error exceeding a $9,040 overstatement, a 2.5 percent risk of it exceeding a $26,680 overstatement, a 2.5 percent risk of it exceeding a $7,600 understatement, and a 95 percent confidence level of the error being between a $7,600 understatement and a $26,680 overstatement.

It is relatively easy to calculate the same statistical results for the illustration at different confidence levels. All of the calculations are the same, but the confidence coefficient (Z) changes. Figure 11-3 shows the previous calculations for the confidence limits at 80 percent and 99 percent confidence levels.

The calculation of the statistical results of a difference estimate is actually less difficult and time consuming than it might appear to readers who are not familiar with statistical techniques. Nevertheless, the computations are sufficiently burdensome that many CPA firms now have computer time-sharing services and other computer techniques available to perform the calculations. Their use reduces the likelihood of mechanical errors in calculation, and it also allows the auditor to concentrate on understanding what he is doing rather than on performing the arithmetic involved.

Calculation of the Sample Size

The *preliminary estimate* of the sample size for difference estimates can be calculated by using the same basic formula as for computing the confidence interval. The formula AE = E* + API is used where AE = acceptable error in the population; E* = estimated point estimate of the population error; and API* = acceptable precision interval. The acceptable precision interval is the same as the computed precision interval except that the standard deviation (SD*) is an *advanced estimate,* based upon previous years' results or a preliminary sample rather than the

FIGURE 11-2

ERROR IN ACCOUNTS RECEIVABLE AT A 95% CONFIDENCE LEVEL

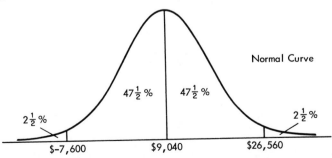

Steps	Statistical Formulas	Illustration
1. Take a random sample of size n	$n=$ sample size	100 accounts receivable are selected randomly from the aged trial balance containing 4,000 accounts.
2. Determine the value of each error in the sample		75 accounts are confirmed by customers, and 25 accounts are verified by alternative procedures. After reconciling timing differences and customer errors, the following twelve items were determined to be client errors (understatements):

Illustration (continued):

1.	12.75	7.	(.87)
2.	(69.46)	8.	24.32
3.	85.28	9.	36.59
4.	100.00	10.	(102.16)
5.	(27.30)	11.	54.71
6.	41.06	12.	71.56

Sum = 226.48

3. Compute the point estimate of the total errors

$$\bar{e} = \frac{\sum e_j}{n}$$

$$E = N\bar{e} \ or \ N\frac{\sum e_j}{n}$$

where e = average error in the sample
$\sum$ = summation
e_j = an individual error in the sample
n = sample size
E = point estimate of the total error
N = population size

Illustration:

$$e = \frac{226.48}{100} = 2.26$$

$$E = 4{,}000\,(2.26) = \$9{,}040$$

or

$$E = 4{,}000\,\frac{226.48}{100} = \$9{,}040$$

4. Compute the estimated population standard deviation of the errors from the sample

$$SD = \sqrt{\frac{\sum(e_j)^2 - n(\bar{e})^2}{n-1}}$$

where SD = standard deviation
e_j = an individual error in the sample

Illustration:

	e_j	e^2_j	(rounded to nearest dollar)
1.	13	169	
2.	(69)	4,761	
3.	85	7,225	

Steps	Statistical Formulas	Illustration
	n = sample size	4. 100 10,000
	e = average error in sample	5. (27) 729
		6. 41 1,681
		7. (1) 1
		8. 24 576
		9. 36 1,296
		10. (102) 10,404
		11. 55 3,025
		12. 72 5,184

$$227 \qquad 45,051$$

$$SD = \sqrt{\frac{45,051 - 100\,(2.26)^2}{99}}$$

$$SD = 21.2$$

5. Compute the precision interval for the estimate of the population of the errors at the desired confidence level

$$CPI = NZ \frac{SD}{\sqrt{n}} \sqrt{\frac{N-n}{N}}$$

where CPI = computed precision interval
N = population size
Z = confidence coefficient for the confidence level (CL); as follows:

CL	Z
80%	1.28
90%	1.64
95%	1.96
99%	2.58

SD = estimated population standard deviation
n = sample size
$\sqrt{\dfrac{N-n}{N}}$ = finite correction factor

$$CPI \text{ at } 95\% \ CL = 4,000 \cdot 1.96 \cdot \frac{21.2}{\sqrt{100}} \sqrt{\frac{4,000-100}{4,000}}$$

$$= 4,000 \cdot 1.96 \cdot \frac{21.2}{10} \cdot .99$$

$$= 4,000 \cdot 1.96 \cdot 2.11 = \$16,640$$

Steps	Statistical Formulas	Illustration
6. Compute the confidence limits at the CL desired	$UCL = E + CPI$ $LCL = E - CPI$ where UCL = computed upper confidence limit LCL = computed lower confidence limit E = point estimate of the total error CPI = computed precision interval at desired CL	$UCL = \$9,040 + \$16,640 = \$25,680$ $LCL = \$9,040 - \$16,640 = \$(7,600)$ The auditor can state with a 95% statistical confidence level that the true value of the error is between an understatement of \$7,600 and an overstatement of \$25,680.
7. Compare each of the computed confidence limits with the acceptable error		If the acceptable error (AE) is \$25,680 or more, the population can be considered acceptable. (The auditor is 95% confident that the true error does not exceed \$25,680.) An analysis of the individual errors is still necessary even if the computed results are satisfactory.

FIGURE 11-3

ERROR IN ACCOUNTS RECEIVABLE AT 80% AND 99% CONFIDENCE LEVELS

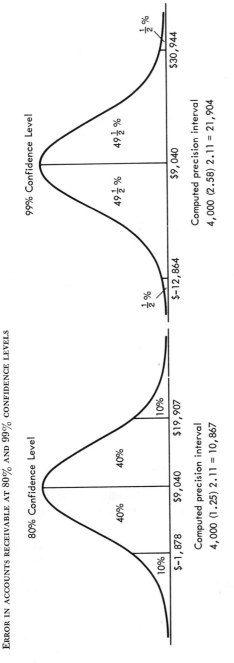

standard deviation (SD) calculated on the basis of the errors actually discovered. For convenience, the finite correction factor is ignored. If the auditor desires to include it, he may employ the same adjustment of the sample size for population size that was discussed in Chapter 9 for attributes sampling. The formula as modified now becomes:

$$API = AE - E^*$$
$$API = \frac{N \cdot Z \cdot SD^*}{\sqrt{n}}$$

If we solve the formula for n, the preliminary estimate of the sample size is:

$$n = \left(\frac{N \cdot Z \cdot SD^*}{AE - E^*} \right)^2$$

where:

n = preliminary estimate of the sample size
N = population size
Z = confidence coefficient
SD^* = advanced estimate of the standard deviation
AE = acceptable error in the population
E^* = estimated point estimate of the population error

As an illustration, assume the auditor decides he is willing to live with a total error in accounts receivable of $80,000 at a confidence level of 95 percent and allows for a $30,000 point estimate of total errors. The population size is 4,000 items, and the population standard deviation of the errors in the preceding year's audit was $100. What is the appropriate sample size?

$$n = \left[\frac{4,000 \cdot 1.96 \cdot 100}{80,000 - 30,000} \right]^2 = (15.7)^2 = 246$$

Will a sample size of 246 be large enough to meet the audit objectives? It is impossible to answer the question until the actual audit results are known. If the actual standard deviation exceeds $100 or the point estimate exceeds $30,000, the results are unlikely to be acceptable.

An examination of the formula indicates the effect on sample size of independently changing each of the factors in the formula. The relationships are as follows:

Type of Change	Effect of Factors on Preliminary Sample Size
1. Decrease the confidence level	Decrease
2. Decrease the acceptable precision interval	Increase
3. Decrease the estimate of the population standard deviation	Decrease
4. Decrease the population size	Decrease

The results are consistent with the conclusions reached in Chapter 9 when the four factors that affect attributes sampling were individually changed.

In this chapter we first discussed the calculation of the computed confidence limits on the basis of the actual sample and followed it with a determination of how to calculate the proper sample size. This was done to keep the discussion as simple as possible, but obviously in practice the calculation must be reversed. The auditor must estimate the proper sample size before he performs the audit tests, not afterward. The confidence limits are computed after the audit tests are performed.

Shortcomings of Difference Estimation

The *underlying assumptions* in any statistical sampling estimation technique must be satisfied before the statistical results can be considered reliable. In difference estimation, this is difficult to do in many auditing populations because the assumptions involve the *distribution of errors* throughout the population. When there are many population items with no errors or very small errors and a few large ones, or if all errors are in one direction, the underlying assumptions may not be satisfied. As an example, assume the auditor selects a sample of one hundred for confirmation from a population containing a few large errors, which, when combined, are material. If the sample of one hundred contains no errors, the auditor's calculations will indicate a point estimate of zero, a population standard deviation of zero, and a computed precision interval of zero at any confidence level chosen. This erroneous conclusion results from the use of difference estimation in a situation where the normal distribution assumption is not valid.

Difference estimation is a useful audit tool only when there are a relatively *large number of errors* in the population and they are not predominantly misstated in one direction. In these cases the technique is valuable for evaluating the significance of the errors and determining the adjustment in the financial statements needed to satisfy the auditor's materiality standards. Even when there are a large number of errors, unrestricted random sampling should ordinarily not be used if some of the errors are likely to be large and others small. *Stratified sampling* should be used in these situations.

When difference estimation is not an appropriate variables sampling tool, the auditor has several other useful alternatives, including *ratio estimation, mean-per-unit estimation,* and *dollar unit sampling.* These subjects, which also have their own strengths and weaknesses, are discussed briefly in the next section along with stratification. The basic concepts and methodologies for these techniques are similar to those discussed in difference estimation. Comparative details are not included here.

OTHER TECHNIQUES

Ratio Estimation

The *ratio estimate* is similar to the difference estimate inasmuch as both deal with the difference between the value of a population item as indicated on the client's records and the amount the auditor concludes is the correct balance. In the difference estimate, the auditor determines the point estimate of the error on the basis of the average error in the sample times the population size and computes a precision interval on the basis of the value of the individual errors in the sample. The ratio estimate projects the point estimate of the population error on the basis of the *net ratio of error* in the sample times the recorded total dollar amount of the population. For example, assume the auditor discovered twelve errors with a net overstatement of $226 in a random sample of one hundred items from a population of four thousand with a book value of $1,872,500. If the one hundred sample items had a book value of $39,-612, the point estimate of the population error is an overstatement of $10,673, that is ($226 ÷ $39,612) × $1,872,500. The precision interval is calculated on the basis of the ratio of error of each individual sample item in much the same manner as for difference estimates.

The ratio estimate is a more efficient estimation technique of the true error than the difference estimate if the size of the errors in the population is proportionate to the recorded value of the population items. If the size of the individual errors is independent of the recorded value, the difference estimate is generally more efficient. Since the former case seems likely to be true for many populations, the ratio estimate is often a better statistical sampling technique. Unfortunately, the same population distribution assumptions relating to difference estimation also apply to ratio estimates. Therefore, to be useful, ratio estimation should only be applied where the error rate is reasonably high and errors are not predominantly in one direction.

Mean-per-Unit Estimation

In *mean-per-unit estimation,* the auditor concentrates on the *audited value* rather than the error amount of each item in the sample. Except for the definition of what is being measured, the mean-per-unit estimate is calculated in exactly the same manner as the difference estimate. The *point estimate* of the audited value is the average audited value of each item in the sample times the population size. The *computed precision interval* is computed on the basis of the audited value of the sample items rather than the errors. When the auditor has computed the upper and lower confidence limits, a decision is made about the acceptability of the population by comparing these amounts with the recorded book value.

The main advantage of mean-per-unit estimation is that its effective use does not require a high error rate in the population. However, it suffers from being relatively inefficient. Therefore, whenever mean-per-unit estimation is used, extensive stratification is necessary to obtain reasonable precision. This generally requires use of the computer as an audit tool in designing the strata, selecting the sample, and computing the statistical results. When the population size is large and a computer is available, mean-per-unit estimation is often the most efficient and effective technique for conducting variables sampling.

Stratification

Stratified sampling is an extension of variables sampling in which all the elements in the total population are divided into two or more subpopulations. Each subpopulation is then independently tested and statistically measured in the manner described for variables estimation. After the results of the individual parts have been computed, they are combined into one overall population estimate in terms of a confidence interval. Subdividing or stratifying a population is not unique to statistical sampling, of course. Auditors have traditionally emphasized certain types of items when they are testing a population. For example, in confirming accounts receivable, it has been customary to place more emphasis on large accounts than on small ones. The major difference is that in statistical stratified sampling the approach is more objective and better defined than it is under most traditional stratification methods.

The purpose of stratified sampling is to *reduce the effect of skewness* in population distributions on samples thereby gaining efficiency. This is done by controlling overall sample mix through sampling selectively from each stratum. It is very important to define the strata so their items are as homogeneous as possible. For example, with difference estimation, the population should be divided into segments in such a manner as to make sure that errors of a similar size are included in the same strata. For example, a population of accounts receivable could be divided by including the large errors in the population in one stratum, the medium-sized errors in a second stratum, and the small errors (including the items with no errors) in a third stratum. The difficulty here is that the auditor must stratify the population before the sample is selected, and of course he does not know which population items include which size errors. Therefore the stratification must be based upon the auditor's professional judgment of where the different types of errors are likely to exist. For example, in accounts receivable, it may be reasonable to expect the large accounts to contain the large errors and the small ones to contain the small errors, even though this need not necessarily be true. For stratification with mean-per-unit estimation based on book values, the problem is less severe. In any case, if it turns out that the stratification is not reasonably consistent with the actual distribution of the value in the population, the computed confidence interval may not provide as precise an estimate of the total actual estimate of the population as desired.

Dollar Unit Sampling

In recent years a variables sampling technique has been developed which combines the concepts of attributes and variables estimation. Instead of defining the sampling unit as an individual accounts receivable balance, a sale to a customer, or a similar characteristic, it is defined as an individual dollar in an account balance. This method is referred to as *dollar unit sampling, cumulative monetary sampling,* or *sampling with probability proportional to size.* To illustrate, if there are four thousand accounts receivable with a book value of $1,872,500, the sampling unit is the individual dollar and the population size is 1,872,500. The auditor takes a random sample of the population of 1,872,500 and confirms the individual account balances which include the individual random dollars selected in the sample. The statistical results are calculated in a manner similar to attributes sampling, but the results are stated in terms of an upper confidence limit for dollar overstatement errors.

One significant feature of dollar unit sampling is its *automatic stratification* on the basis of dollar balances. Since the random sample is selected on the basis of individual dollars, an account with a large balance has a greater chance of being included than an account with a small one. In accounts receivable confirmation, an account with a $5,000 balance has a ten times greater probability of being included than one with a $500 balance.

There are also some difficulties in applying dollar unit sampling. In those situations where there are a large number of errors in a population, the sample size required to satisfy most auditors' allowable error standards is much higher than would be required with the three other variables sampling techniques. In addition, in many instances the difficulty of obtaining a random sample without the use of a computer makes dollar unit sampling a costly application. Nevertheless, this highly innovative technique has great potential as an audit tool and is likely to be more widely used as it becomes better understood by the profession.

In evaluating the four variables estimation techniques, it becomes apparent that *no single one is clearly superior* in every audit situation. Where there are large numbers of errors of approximately the same size in the population, either difference or ratio estimation is likely to be most suitable. On the other hand, when there are large populations with few errors, dollar unit sampling or stratified mean-per-unit estimation is more appropriate. It is necessary to understand which technique should be applied in a given situation if an auditor is to intelligently use statistical sampling as an audit tool.

AUDIT DECISIONS IN VARIABLES SAMPLING

Regardless of which method the auditor selects, two essential audit decisions must be made for every application of variables sampling: the *dollar amount of error the auditor is willing to accept* in the population and *the level of assurance the auditor needs that the statistical conclusions are correct.* These two decisions must be made for both judgmental and statistical sampling, but the existence of objective information often enables the auditor to make more meaningful decisions when statistical sampling is used.

The amount of error the auditor is willing to accept is a *materiality* question which must be based upon the factors discussed in Chapter 3. Major considerations affecting the total acceptable error are the amount of reported net earnings, the size of the total account balance being tested, and the expected amount of errors in other account balances in the audit. The amount of error the auditor is willing to accept (AE) is a major input in the determination of the proper sample size

$$n = \left(\frac{N \cdot Z \cdot SD^*}{AE - E^*} \right)^2$$

The level of assurance the auditor desires is a question of professional judgment concerning the *risk* he is willing to take that the true error is actually greater than the computed confidence limits. For example, at a 90 percent confidence level there is a 5 percent risk of the error's being greater than the UCL and a 5 percent risk of its being less than the LCL. The impact of the confidence level on a sample size can also be seen by examining the individual factors in the previous formula and observing the effect of Z.

In deciding upon the proper confidence level in variables sampling for a given audit test, the auditor must consider two things: the total *level of assurance he desires* and the *amount of assurance he has gained from other audit tests.* The total level of assurance the auditor desires for a particular audit area, such as accounts receivable, was discussed in Chapter 3. A relatively high level of assurance is necessary, for example, if the auditor believes there is considerable risk of a lawsuit or other adverse action because the company is listed with the SEC, profits have been declining rapidly, or the firm is in a highly cyclical business. When the opposite conditions exist, the level of assurance and therefore the confidence level can be correspondingly reduced.

The auditor should keep in mind that there are several sources for obtaining audit evidence about the fairness of an account balance other than the variables sampling test. In verifying accounts receivable, for example, other sources include the review of internal control, compliance and substantive tests of transactions, analytical tests, and cutoff tests. If the auditor obtains excellent results in each of these tests, it is reasonable to reduce the confidence level for confirmations to a fairly low level, such as 70 percent, because the overall level of assurance for accounts receivable will still be high. On the other hand, if the auditor desires a high level of overall assurance, but obtains relatively little assurance from the system of internal control and the other audit tests, it would be necessary to use a high confidence level, such as 95 percent, for confirmations. At this stage of the development of auditing theory, there are no effective methods for objectively combining the results of different audit tests into a meaningful level of assurance. Nevertheless, the factors affecting confidence level must always be considered.

REVIEW QUESTIONS

1. Distinguish between attributes sampling and variables sampling. When would each of these be a useful audit tool?
2. Explain why variables sampling is considered a more useful audit tool than attributes sampling when it is applicable.
3. Distinguish between difference estimation, mean-per-unit estimation, and ratio estimation. Give one example where each could be used.
4. Assume an auditor decided to select a random sample of accounts receivable for confirming from a sixty-page aged trial balance where each page is numbered. There are no more than seventy-five customer names per page, but the lines are not prenumbered. Describe how an auditor could obtain a random sample of one hundred accounts by using a random number table.
5. In using difference estimation, an auditor took a random sample of one hundred inventory items from a large population to test for proper pricing. Several of the inventory items were in error, but the combined net amount of the sample error was not material. In addition, a review of the individual errors indicated that no error was by itself material. As a result, the auditor did not investigate the errors or make a statistical evaluation. Explain why this practice is improper.
6. Distinguish between the point estimate of the total errors and the true value of the errors in the population. How can each be determined?
7. Evaluate the following statement made by an auditor: "On every aspect of the audit where it is possible, I calculate the point estimate of the errors and evaluate whether the amount is material. If it is, I investigate the cause and continue to test the population until I determine whether there is a serious problem. The use of statistical sampling in this manner is a valuable audit tool."
8. Distinguish between the following terms: confidence level, confidence limits, confidence interval, and computed precision interval. For the statistical statement "The population value of the errors is $50,000 \pm $16,000 with a reliability of 90 percent," calculate or identify the value for each of the four terms.
9. Define what is meant by the population standard deviation and explain its importance in variables sampling. What is the relationship between the population standard deviation and the required sample size?
10. An essential step in difference estimation is the comparison of each com-

puted confidence limit with the acceptable error. Why is this step so important and what should the auditor do if one of the confidence limits is larger than the acceptable error?

11. Define what is meant by a normal distribution in difference estimation and explain its importance in making auditing decisions.

12. Explain the circumstances under which a preliminary sample in variables sampling may not be large enough for the statistical requirements the auditor specifies.

13. Explain the circumstances where unrestricted difference estimation may not be a useful audit tool.

14. Define *stratified sampling* and explain its importance in auditing. How could an auditor obtain a stratified sample of thirty items from each of three strata in the confirmation of accounts receivable?

15. Explain how the methodology for calculating confidence limits using mean-per-unit estimation is the same as and different from difference estimation.

16. Define *dollar unit sampling* and explain its importance in auditing. How does it combine the features of attributes and variables estimation?

17. List the decisions the auditor must make in using variables sampling. What considerations influence the auditor in making each decision?

DISCUSSION QUESTIONS AND PROBLEMS

18. Each of the following ten items is concerned with the use of unrestricted random sampling without replacement for variables sampling. State whether each one is true or false.

   a. If the auditor wishes to use a table of random digits to select a random sample, he must first find a table conforming to the numbering employed by the items in the population he wishes to sample.

   b. If a usable number appears more than once in the table of random digits during the selection of the sample, the item should be included in the sample only once and another number selected from the table.

   c. A random sample of at least thirty items would have to be discarded if it produced one item disproportionately large in relation to the other items selected.

   d. The effect of the inclusion by chance of a very large or a very small item in a random sample can be lessened by increasing the size of the sample.

   e. The reliability specified by the auditor for a sample estimate expresses the degree of confidence that the true value will be within the computed confidence interval.

   f. The standard deviation is a measure of variability of items in the population.

   g. Variability of items in the population is a factor that usually causes the point estimate of the population, and its true value, to be different.

   h. It is necessary to determine the true standard deviation for a population in order to determine the size of the sample to be drawn from that population.

   i. The computed precision interval of the mean will always be less than the estimated standard deviation computed on the basis of a sample.

(AICPA adapted)

19. An audit partner is developing an office training program to familiarize his

professional staff with statistical decision models applicable to the audit of dollar-value balances. He wishes to demonstrate the relationship of sample sizes to population size and variability and the auditor's specifications as to precision and confidence level. The partner prepared the following table to show comparative population characteristics and audit specifications of two populations.

	Characteristics of Population 1 Relative to Population 2		Audit Specifications as to a Sample from Population 1 Relative to a Sample from Population 2	
	Size	Variability	Acceptable Precision Interval	Specified Confidence Level
Case 1	Equal	Equal	Equal	Higher
Case 2	Equal	Larger	Wider	Equal
Case 3	Larger	Equal	Narrower	Lower
Case 4	Smaller	Smaller	Equal	Lower
Case 5	Larger	Equal	Equal	Higher

In items (1) through (5) below you are to indicate for the specific case from the above table the required sample size to be selected from population 1 relative to the sample from population 2.

Your Answer Choice Should Be Selected From the Following Responses:

a. Larger than the required sample size from population 2.
b. Equal to the required sample size from population 2.
c. Smaller than the required sample size from population 2.
d. Indeterminate relative to the required sample size from population 2.

    (1) In case 1 the required sample size from population 1 is _____
    (2) In case 2 the required sample size from population 1 is _____
    (3) In case 3 the required sample size from population 1 is _____
    (4) In case 4 the required sample size from population 1 is _____
    (5) In case 5 the required sample size from population 1 is _____

(AICPA adapted)

20. During a professional development program at a CPA firm, an audit manager was instructing several younger staff members on how to calculate confidence intervals in the accounts receivable area by using difference estimation. As part of the discussion, he explained the importance of the population size in calculating the point estimate of the total error and the precision interval for the population. He ended his talk by informing the group that a 20 percent error in counting the number of accounts in the population would probably result in a misleading statistical calculation.

At that point one of the staff members raised his hand and stated that these conclusions were inconsistent with what he had learned about using attributes sampling. He also described how a statistics professor had explained to him when he was in college that the finite correction factor, which is affected by the population size, could frequently be ignored in variables sampling.

Required:

  a. Explain why the population size is far more important for making variables sampling calculations than it is for attributes sampling.

  b. Explain how the population size affects the statistical results in variables sampling in more ways than only the finite correction factor.

21. In auditing the valuation of inventory, the auditor, Claire Butler, decided to use difference estimation. She decided to select an unrestricted random sample of 80 inventory items from a population of 1,840 that had a book value of $175,820. Butler had decided in advance that she was willing to accept a maximum error in the population of $6,000 at a confidence level of 95 percent. There were eight errors in the sample and they were as follows:

	Audit Value	*Book Value*	*Sample Errors*
	$ 812.50	$ 740.50	$ (72.00)
	12.50	78.20	65.70
	10.00	51.10	41.10
	25.40	61.50	36.10
	600.10	651.90	51.80
	.12	0	(.12)
	51.06	81.06	30.00
	83.11	104.22	21.11
Total	$1,594.79	$1,768.48	$173.69

Required:

  a. Calculate the point estimate, the computed precision interval, the confidence interval, and the confidence limits for the population. Label each calculation.

  b. Should Butler accept the book value of the population? Explain.

  c. What options are available to her at this point?

22. The Cowslip Milk Company's principal activity is buying milk from dairy farmers, processing the milk, and delivering it to retail customers. You are engaged in auditing the retail accounts receivable of the company and determine the following:

  a. The company has fifty retail routes; each route consists of 100 to 200 accounts, the number that can be serviced by a driver in a day.

  b. The driver enters cash collections from the day's deliveries to each customer directly on a statement form in record books maintained for each route. Mail remittances are posted in the route record books by office personnel. At the end of the month the statements are priced, extended, and footed. Photocopies of the statements are prepared and left in the customers' milk boxes with the next milk delivery.

  c. The statements are reviewed by the office manager, who prepares a list for each route of accounts with 90-day balances or older. The list is used for intensive collection action.

  d. The audit program used in prior audits for the selection of retail accounts receivable for confirmation stated: "Select two accounts from each route, one to be chosen by opening the route book at random and the other as the third item on each list of 90-day or older accounts."

Your review of the accounts receivable leads you to conclude that statistical sampling techniques may be applied to this examination.

Required:

a. Since statistical sampling techniques do not relieve the CPA of his responsibilities in the exercise of his professional judgment, of what benefit are they to the CPA? Discuss.

b. Give the reasons why the audit procedure previously used for selection of accounts receivable for confirmation (as given in part *d* above) would not produce a valid statistical sample.

c. What are the audit objectives or purposes in selecting 90-day accounts for confirmation? Can the application of statistical sampling techniques help in attaining these objectives or purposes? Discuss.   (AICPA adapted)

23. You desire to evaluate the reasonableness of the book value of the inventory of your client, Draper, Inc., by using mean-per-unit estimation. You satisfied yourself earlier as to the inventory quantities. During the examination of the pricing and extension of the inventory, the following data were gathered using appropriate unrestricted random sampling with replacement procedures:

- Total items in the inventory (N)   12,700
- Total items in the sample (n)   400
- Total audited value of items in the sample ΣX_j \$38,400

- $\displaystyle\sum_{j=1}^{400}(X_j - X)^2$ 312,816

- Formula for estimated population standard deviation

$$SX_j = \sqrt{\dfrac{\displaystyle\sum_{j=1}^{j=n}(X_j - X)^2}{n-1}}$$

- Formula for estimated standard error of the mean $SE = \dfrac{SX_j}{\sqrt{n}}$

- Confidence level coefficient of the standard error of the mean at a 95% confidence level   ±1.96

Required:

a. Based on the sample results, what is the point estimate of the total value of the inventory? Show computations in good form where appropriate.

b. What statistical conclusion can be reached regarding the estimated total inventory value calculated in part *a* above at the confidence level of 95 percent? Present computations in good form where appropriate.

c. Independent of your answers to parts *a* and *b*, assume that the book value of Draper's inventory is \$1,700,000, and based on the sample results, the estimated point value of the inventory is \$1,690,000. The auditor desires a confidence level of 95 percent. Discuss the audit and statistical considerations the auditor must evaluate before deciding whether the sampling results support acceptance of the book values as a fair presentation of Draper's inventory.   (AICPA adapted)

24. In confirming accounts receivable with a recorded value of \$6,250,000 for

the Blessman Wholesale Drug Company, Gerald Bloomstad, CPA, has decided that if the total error in the account exceeds $60,000, he will consider the error material. He believes the point estimate of the error will approximate $20,000. He has decided to use unrestricted random sampling for difference estimation, and he believes a 90 percent confidence level is appropriate considering the circumstances of the engagement. Although Bloomstad doesn't know the standard deviation, he decides to estimate it a little bit high to make sure he doesn't undersample. The standard deviation is estimated at $22. There are 14,300 total accounts receivable in the trial balance.

Required:

a. Calculate the number of accounts receivable Bloomstad should confirm.
b. Assuming only 100 confirmation responses are received in the first and second requests, what should the auditor do at this point?
c. What would the sample size in part *a* have been if the estimated standard deviation was $32 instead of $22?
d. What would the sample size in part *a* have been if the allowable error were $80,000 and the expected point estimate were $20,000?
e. What would the sample size in part *a* have been if the allowable error were $90,000 and the expected point estimate were $50,000? Explain the relationship between your answers in *a* and *e*.

25. In testing the cash discounts on vendor's invoices the auditor did not expect to find any errors in the sample, and therefore he used attributes sampling techniques. Based upon the statistical requirements for the test, a sample size of 120 items was randomly selected and carefully tested. Much to the auditor's surprise, there were fifteen sample items where the client had failed to take the discount even though company policy clearly indicated one should have been taken. At this point, he decided to switch to variables estimation to measure the amount of the lost discounts.

Required:

a. Is it acceptable to change to variables estimation at this point? Explain.
b. If variables estimation is used, explain how the auditor should proceed. State in words the meaning of the confidence limits he will calculate in this case.

26. The following are five different sets of sample information from a population of 5,000 accounts receivable with a book value of $4,600,000. (In each situation, the net book value of the items in the sample exceeds the audit value.)

Situation	Sample Size	Total Net Error in the Sample	Population Standard Deviation Estimated from the Sample	Desired Confidence Level
1	100	1,000	25	95%
2	200	2,000	25	95%
3	200	2,000	50	95%
4	200	2,000	25	90%
5	200	1,000	25	95%

Required:

a. Using difference estimation, calculate the point estimate of the errors in the population, the computed precision interval, and the confidence limits for each of the five situations.

b. In general for a given population, state the effect on the computed upper confidence limit for each of the following (increase, decrease, no effect, or cannot determine from the information given):

   (1) An increase in the sample size (the average error in the sample, population standard deviation, and confidence level remain constant).

   (2) An increase in the average error in the sample (the sample size, population standard deviation, and confidence level remain constant).

   (3) An increase in the population standard deviation (the sample size, average error in the sample, and confidence level remain constant).

   (4) An increase in the confidence level (the sample size, average error in the sample, and population standard deviation remain constant).

   (5) An increase in the sample size and population standard deviation (the average error in the sample and confidence level remain constant).

   (6) An increase in the confidence level and the population standard deviation (the average error in the sample and sample size remain constant).

27. The following questions refer to the use of stratified sampling in auditing. For each one, select the best response.

   a. Mr. Murray decides to use stratified sampling. The basic reason for using stratified sampling rather than unrestricted random sampling is to

   (1) Reduce as much as possible the degree of variability in the overall population.

   (2) Give every element in the population an equal chance of being included in the sample.

   (3) Allow the person selecting the sample to use his own judgment in deciding which elements should be included in the sample.

   (4) Reduce the required sample size from a nonhomogeneous population.

   b. In an examination of financial statements, a CPA will generally find stratified sampling techniques to be most applicable to

   (1) Recomputing net wage and salary payments to employees.

   (2) Tracing hours worked from the payroll summary back to the individual time cards.

   (3) Confirming accounts receivable for residential customers at a large electric utility.

   (4) Reviewing supporting documentation for additions to plant and equipment.

   c. From prior experience, a CPA is aware that cash disbursements contain a few unusually large disbursements. In using statistical sampling, the CPA's best course of action is to

   (1) Eliminate any unusually large disbursements that appear in the sample.

   (2) Continue to draw new samples until no unusually large disbursements appear in the sample.

   (3) Stratify the cash-disbursements population so that the unusually large disbursements are reviewed separately.

   (4) Increase the sample size to lessen the effect of the unusually large
       disbursements.   (AICPA adapted)
28. In auditing the pricing and extension of raw material inventory, the auditor
    decided to select a sample of 140 inventory items as a test of the total. The
    decision was made to verify all of the largest 40 items because the recorded
    book value for these items was considerably larger than the others. A
    random sample was selected from the remainder of the population. Follow-
    ing is a summary of the population and the sample results:

Stratum	Popu- lation Size	Book Value	Sample Size	Book Value of the Sample Tested	Number of Errors	Net Dollar Value of the Errors
1	40	$ 745,000	40	$745,000	18	$89,750 (overstatement)
2	2,580	1,905,000	100	106,000	71	5,100 (overstatement)
Total	2,620	$2,650,000	140	$851,000	89	$94,850 (overstatement)

Required:

   a. Evaluate the decision to stratify the population in this situation.
   b. Using difference estimation, compute the point estimate of the total error
      in Stratum 2. (Hint: Calculate the point estimate in the same manner as
      you would for an unrestricted random sample.) What is the weakness of
      the point estimate for difference estimation as a measure of the actual
      error in the population?
   c. Using ratio estimation, compute the point estimate of the total error
      in the population. (Hint: Calculate the point estimate in the same man-
      ner as you would for an unrestricted random sample.) What is the weak-
      ness of the point estimate for ratio estimation as a measure of the actual
      error in the population?
   d. Compare the results of parts *b* and *c* and explain the reason for the
      difference.
29. In reviewing the results of a difference estimation calculation, an in-charge
    auditor, Roger Murphy, concluded that the confidence limits were larger
    than he could accept. In examining the details of the calculation, he de-
    termined that the point estimate of the population was nearly zero, but
    the standard deviation was large. He decided that there must be an error
    in the calculation, since it was impossible to get a small point estimate and
    a large standard deviation. His assistant, Lannell Tigg, expressed a dif-
    ferent viewpoint. She stated that the problem was simply the failure to
    take a sufficiently large sample size. Tigg ended her explanation by inform-
    ing Murphy that an increase in the sample size would automatically reduce
    the standard deviation and thereby reduce the confidence limits.

Required:

   a. Explain how it is possible to have a small point estimate in the popula-
      tion and a large standard deviation when difference estimation is used.

b. Was Tigg's explanation of the way to reduce the population standard deviation correct? Discuss.

30. Items (1) to (5) apply to an examination by Lee Melinda, CPA, of the financial statements of Summit Appliance Repair Company for the year ended June 30, 19X7. Summit has a large fleet of identically stocked repair trucks. It establishes the total quantities of materials and supplies stored on the delivery trucks at year-end by physically inventorying a random sample of trucks.

Melinda is evaluating the statistical validity of Summit's 19X7 sample. He knows that there were seventy-four trucks in the 19X6 required sample. Assumptions about the size, variability, precision interval, and confidence level for the 19X7 sample are given in each of the following five items. You are to indicate in each case the effect upon the size of the 19X7 sample as compared with the 19X6 sample. Each case is independent of the other four and is to be considered separately. *Your answer choice for each item (1) to (5) should be selected from the following responses:*

a. Larger than the 19X6 sample size
b. Equal to the 19X6 sample size
c. Smaller than the 19X6 sample size
d. Of a size that is indeterminate based upon the assumptions as given

(1) Summit has the same number of trucks in 19X7 but supplies are replenished more often, meaning that there is less variability in the quantity of supplies stored on each truck. The acceptable precision interval and confidence level remain the same.

Under these assumptions, the required sample size for 19X7 should be _____

(2) Summit has the same number of trucks; supplies are replenished less often (greater variability). Summit specifies the same precision interval but decides to change the confidence level from 95 percent to 90 percent.

Under these assumptions, the required sample size for 19X7 should be _____

(3) Summit has more trucks in 19X7. Variability and confidence level remain the same, but with Melinda's concurrence, Summit decides upon a wider acceptable precision interval.

Under these assumptions, the required sample size for 19X7 should be _____

(4) The number of trucks and variability remain the same, but with Melinda's concurrence, Summit decides upon a wider precision interval and a confidence level of 90 percent rather than 95 percent.

Under these assumptions, the required sample size for 19X7 should be _____

(5) The number of trucks increases, as does the variability of quantities stored on each truck. The confidence level remains the same, but the acceptable precision interval is narrowed.

Under these assumptions, the required sample size for 19X7 should be _____   (AICPA adapted)

31. For each of the following populations, the auditor has established an acceptable precision interval as a part of using difference estimation and has calculated actual statistical results after he conducted the audit tests:

Population	The Acceptable Precision Interval (at the Same Confidence Level as the Computed Precision Interval)	Point Estimate of the Population Error. Understated Book Value is ( )	Computed Precision Interval
1	$25,000	$6,000	$16,000
2	25,000	0	24,000
3	25,000	(14,000)	18,000
4	25,000	21,000	30,000
5	25,000	(12,000)	11,000

Required:

a. Determine which of the calculated results satisfy the acceptable precision interval the auditor set before the sample was selected.

b. For any result in part *a* that does not satisfy the acceptable precision interval, state the minimum adjustment in the client's book value, if any, that will make the sample result satisfactory.

c. What options does the auditor have for any sample result that does not satisfy the acceptable precision interval established by the auditor?

12

The Impact of EDP Systems
on
Auditing

There is no distinction between the audit concepts applicable to electronic data processing (EDP) and those applicable to manual systems. When computers or other aspects of EDP systems are introduced, generally accepted auditing standards and their interpretations, the Code of Professional Ethics, legal liability, and the basic concepts of evidence accumulation remain the same.

At the same time, the specific methods appropriate for implementing the basic auditing concepts do change with the introduction of EDP systems. An understanding of the impact of EDP on auditing becomes increasingly important as the use of computers by clients increases. In this chapter we study the way the conduct of an audit changes when an EDP system is a part of the client's preparation of financial records.

The first part of the chapter examines the impact of an EDP system on a typical client's organizational structure, its method of processing transactions, and its internal controls. The remainder of the chapter is devoted to a study of evaluating internal controls in an EDP system and auditing with and without the use of the computer.

IMPACT OF EDP ON AUDITING

The most important effect of EDP on auditing results directly from *changes in the client's organization* and the *information available* for auditors to examine. The major changes involved are considered in this section.

Changes in the Organizational Structure

The establishment of an EDP center generally brings the data-gathering and accumulation activities of different parts of the organization into one department. This change has the advantage of *centralizing data* and permitting *higher-quality controls* over operations. On the other hand, a frequent disadvantage of this change toward centralization is the *elimination* of the control provided by *division of duties* of independent persons who perform related functions and compare their results. As an illustration, in many manual systems different individuals prepare the sales journal and subsidiary records. The accuracy of their results is tested by comparing the subsidiary ledger with the total balance in the general ledger. Both these records will be prepared simultaneously by the computer with EDP.

The organizational structure also frequently changes by taking the record keeping function out of the hands of those who have custody of assets and putting it into the EDP center. This is a desirable change if it doesn't merely change the opportunity for defalcation from operating personnel to EDP personnel. The latter are in a position to take company assets for their own use if they also have the opportunity to prepare or process documents that result in the disposal of the assets. For example, if EDP personnel have access to documents authorizing the shipment of goods, in essence they have direct access to inventory.

The combining of functions in an EDP center generally causes more organizational problems than it solves. Auditors must use great care in evaluating inadequate segregation of duties for the possibility of both fraudulent and unintentional errors.

Changes in the Traditional Audit Trail

The *audit trail* is the accumulation of *source documents and records* maintained by the client which are the support for the transactions that occurred during the period. It includes such things as duplicate sales invoices, vendor's invoices, canceled checks, general and subsidiary ledgers, and all types of journals. Since the audit trail is a primary source of evidence used by auditors, it is important that an adequate trail be available for verification needs. Traditionally, every transaction should be supported by one or more visible source documents and a record in a journal and sometimes in a subsidiary ledger.

The effect of the computer on the audit trail depends on the level of sophistication of the system. When the computer is used only as an accurate high-speed calculator, the audit trail may not be affected, especially if management desires to maintain the traditional source documents and records. In highly integrated on-line systems, on the other hand, the traditional audit trail can be substantially eliminated unless specific provision is made for some detailed records. A common change that occurs in the audit trail is the *elimination or reduction of some source documents,* such as payroll time cards and inventory receiving reports. Even if they aren't eliminated, they are frequently filed in a manner that makes them difficult to retrieve for audit purposes. A second change in the system is the transfer of data and activities into a *form that is not visually observable* by the auditors. For example, the ledger summaries are included in master files in machine-readable form, the journals and records are not printed out but instead are retained on magnetic tapes or disks, and the methods of processing records are not observable because they are done by the computer.

Changes in the Method of Processing Transactions

The most important effect of the computer on the processing of transactions is that it provides *uniformity.* Once information is put into the system, the auditor can be confident it will be processed consistently with previous or subsequent information unless some aspect of the system itself is changed. This is important from an audit point of view because it means the system will process a particualr type of transaction consistently correctly or consistently incorrectly. As a result, the emphasis in auditing EDP systems for processing is likely to be on testing for unusual transactions and on testing for changes in the system over time rather than on testing a large sample of similar transactions.

The use of the computer also facilitates the inclusion of many different types of controls directly in the computer as a means of automatically detecting errors. It is possible to program automatic authorization controls such as credit limits for customers and price lists for products. It is also possible for the computer to review the reasonableness of a transaction within certain limits and the completeness of the information provided for a transaction. These procedures reduce the likelihood of errors.

Changes in the Approach to Auditing

The advent of EDP has challenged auditors to devise new methods for testing complex systems because of the loss of the audit trail. For a short time after audit trails began to disappear, auditors insisted upon extensive special printouts; but the high cost to clients forced auditors to think about alternative approaches.

The most important aspects of EDP that have affected auditing are the review and evaluation of internal control and the use of the computer in the conduct of audits. Both of these are discussed more extensively in subsequent sections of this chapter.

TYPES OF SYSTEMS

In discussing the impact of EDP systems on auditing methods, it is necessary to distinguish between different levels of complexity. In some instances the systems are so complex that the entire audit approach must be changed, whereas in others there is no significant change in any aspect of the audit. Four basic types of systems are discussed in this section: small systems, common systems, sophisticated systems, and unique systems. The characteristics and the audit implications of each type of system are briefly considered.

Small Systems

The primary function performed by a small computer system is the *sorting and manipulation* of input data and the *printing* of output reports. Transactions are easily traced in this type of system, and there is no loss of the audit trail. In a typical example of this type of system, shipping data, including the prices of the products, are keypunched and processed through the system along with accounts receivable detailed subsidiary ledgers. The output is a multicopy sales invoice for each sale, updated detailed subsidiary ledgers, and a sales journal.

The audit of this type of system is likely to require little training and background in EDP. Although it is unacceptable to completely ignore the computer installations because some of the controls involve EDP, for the most part this type of system can be viewed in the same manner as a manual system.

Common Systems

Common systems are characterized by the *batch processing mode*, the existence of *one central processing unit*, and the extensive use of *master files on magnetic tape* in processing. In this type of system the processing is usually restricted to calculations, extensions, summarizations, and similar activities. Typically, there is some loss of audit trail, but it is not significant. An example is the processing of shipping data where the only input is the customer number, the product number shipped, and the quantity shipped. The computer can automatically perform a credit check, price and extend the sales invoice, and update the accounts receivable master file of accounts receivable. Frequently, sales forecasts and production records can be simultaneously updated. Typically, the only loss of printed audit trail is the accounts receivable subsidiary ledger, but in some cases the detailed listing of sales invoices in the sales journal is also not available. However, this information is normally available in machine readable form.

The audit of a common system can be performed by auditors with limited specialized training in EDP auditing. Due to the large extent of a printed audit trail, the auditor has the option of performing some of the audit tests with or without the use of the computer. The decision can be made primarily on the basis of the auditor's experience and personal preference. Even though an audit trail exists, an active involvement in evaluating the EDP system is essential, since there are many opportunities for incompatible functions or other inadequate controls. Inasmuch as common systems represent the bulk of systems in use today, most of the discussion in this chapter is limited to this type.

Sophisticated Systems

In a sophisticated system, transactions are typically *initiated within the computer,* there is *extensive processing of data,* and there is *a substantial loss of audit trail.* Most of the *output is in machine readable language,* aside from exceptions and control totals. An example is the input of shipping documents by the shipping department on remote or on line teletype. All information in this system is processed by the computer and maintained in machine readable form.

Heavy reliance must be placed on internal control in the audit of a sophisticated system, and the system requires extensive testing with the use of the computer. Since many of these tests require EDP skills beyond the knowledge of most auditors, the auditor often must call upon *EDP specialists* within the CPA firm for assistance. Careful advance planning is an absolute necessity in auditing this type of system because many of the decisions about the documents and records the auditor will need and the approach the auditor intends to use in testing must be made before data are processed.

Unique Systems

Unique systems include such features as *highly complex processing,* a *network of processors and input and output devices,* and *on-line, real-time input* with inquiry from many points in the system covering widespread geographical locations. There is an *extensive loss of audit trail* and *automatic self-balancing.* The only *reporting is by exception,* and a common output is the actual finalized financial statement balances.

This highly complex computer operation requires extensive use of *high-level computer audit specialists.* Since this type of system presents a great opportunity for employee or management fraud, it must be carefully evaluated and controlled. In most instances where unique systems are employed, the auditor is involved with the client on a continuous basis. Computer processes and systems changes are often evaluated as they take place rather than subsequent to their installation. Also, extensive assistance is obtained from client EDP personnel and internal auditors.

AREAS OF ENGAGEMENT CONCERN

When a computer is used in the processing of financial data, five different areas of concern must be carefully considered as a part of the planning process before the bulk of the audit fieldwork is begun: evaluate internal accounting control, evaluate going-concern exposure, determine desirability of using computer-assisted audit techniques, evaluate potential for fraud, and make operating recommendations. Each area is introduced at this point, and the most important areas (evaluate internal accounting control and determine the desirability of using computer-assisted techniques) are subsequently discussed in more detail in the remainder of the chapter.

Evaluate Internal Accounting Control. As with all parts of the system, those involving computer processing must be described, understood, and evaluated as a basis for determining which audit procedures should be performed and which internal controls are to be relied upon.

Evaluate Going-Concern Exposure. In some industries the electronic data processing system plays such an integral role in a company's operations that a failure of the system could put the company out of business. In this type of situation the auditor must be particularly concerned with backup capabilities, recovery plans, and insurance. If these do not exist, the auditor must consider the need for disclosure and the possibility of qualifying his report as to the going-concern basis of the entity.

Determine Desirability Of Using Computer-Assisted Audit Techniques. Whether or not the auditor relies on and tests computer controls, it is often advantageous to use the computer as an audit tool. Significantly more information is often available in computer files than in related output reports. The major basis for deciding upon the extent to use the computer is the access to machine readable information and cost.

Evaluate Potential For Fraud. Although the professional literature, engagement letters, and letters of representation state that auditors' responsibility for fraud is limited, the auditor cannot ignore those situations where material fraud appears likely. Since the computer provides a vehicle through which the size of a defalcation can compound almost instantaneously, auditors must be particularly alert to those weaknesses in the client's EDP system that may provide opportunity for fraud, and make recommendations for their elimination. If the potential for material fraud is significant, expanded testing is necessary.

Make Operating Recommendations. Client expectations are much greater for the auditor making meaningful recommendations about operating efficiency in the computer area than for manual systems because many managements lack expertise in this area and rely upon the auditor to protect them.

INTERNAL CONTROLS IN AN EDP SYSTEM

The objectives of internal control do not change with the introduction of EDP, but the nature of certain of the basic elements may be somewhat different. The emphasis in this section is on the differences rather than on the similarities. The basic elements developed in Chapter 5 are repeated here as a starting point for the discussion of internal control in an EDP system:

1. Competent, trustworthy personnel with clear lines of authority and responsibility
2. Adequate separation of duties
3. Proper procedures for authorization
4. Adequate documents and records
5. Proper procedures for record keeping
6. Physical control over assets and records
7. Independent checks on performance

The types of controls in an EDP system can be conveniently classified into *general controls* and *application controls.* A general control relates to all parts of the EDP system and must therefore be evaluated early in the audit. Application controls, on the other hand, apply to a specific use of the system, such as for the processing of sales or cash receipts, and must be evaluated specifically for every audit area in which the client uses the computer. The following summary of the subparts of these two categories forms the basis for the subsequent discussion.

General Controls:

- The plan of organization and operation of the EDP activity
- The procedures for documenting, reviewing, testing, and approving systems and programs and changes therein
- Controls built into the equipment by the manufacturer (commonly referred to as "hardware controls")
- Controls over access to equipment and data files

Application Controls:

- Input controls
- Processing controls
- Output controls [1]

[1] Adapted from SAS 3, p. 3.

Plan of Organization

In a computer system it is not practical to segregate the recording function in a manner that produces the automatic cross-checks traditionally available in a manual system. In a manual system it is desirable to have one person record accounting information in the journals while a different person records the same data in the related subsidiary ledger, but in most EDP systems the functions of recording the journals, the subsidiary ledgers, and the general ledger are performed simultaneously by the computer. Since no organizational checks are available for EDP systems, different kinds of controls are needed over input, processing, and output to compensate for the inability to segregate the recording functions.

Even though segregation of the recording function is impractical, it is possible to have *segregation of duties within EDP* to reduce the likelihood of errors. The most important data-processing responsibilities that should be segregated are the following.

Systems Analyst. The systems analyst is responsible for the general design of the system. He sets the objectives of the overall system and the specific design of particular applications.

Programmer. Based upon the individual objectives specified by the systems analyst, the programmer develops special flowcharts for the application, prepares computer instructions, tests the program, and documents the results. It is important that the programmer not have access to input data or computer operation, since his understanding of the program can easily be used for his personal benefit.

Computer Operator. The computer operator is responsible for running data through the system in conjunction with the computer program. The operator follows the instructions set forth in the *program run book* which has been developed by the programmer.

Ideally, the operator should be prevented from having sufficient knowledge of the program to modify it immediately before or during its use. In several cases of recorded fraud, the operator had covered an embezzlement by temporarily changing the original program.

Librarian. The librarian is responsible for maintaining the computer programs, transactions files, and other important computer records. The librarian provides a means of important physical control over these records and releases them only to authorized personnel.

Data Control Group. The function of the data control group is to test the effectiveness and efficiency of all aspects of the system. This includes the adequacy of various types of controls, the quality of the input, and the reasonableness of the output. Inasmuch as control group personnel operate much like internal auditors, the importance of their independence is obvious.

Naturally, the extent of separation of duties depends heavily upon the size of the organization. In many small companies it is not practical to segregate the duties to the extent suggested. In these cases the audit evidence may require modification.

Procedures for Documenting, Reviewing, Testing, and Approving Systems and Programs and Changes Therein

The purpose of this general control area is to ensure that the client is adequately *controlling the computer programs* and other aspects of the system at all times. In concept these procedures are similar to those in a manual system.

The primary evidence the auditor reviews in this area is the *documentation standards manual,* which typically includes the systems documentation, the program documentation, and the run book documentation. The *systems documentation* sets forth the general objectives of an application and is used for broad planning. It includes the form of the input and output, testing procedures, authorizations, and similar items. The *program documentation* is the basis for developing the computer program and is much more specific. It should include the provisions for reviewing, testing, operating, and changing the computer program. The *run book documentation* is the basis for developing the operating instructions. It includes a description of the input, the detailed operating instructions, and a description of the output.

The documentation standards manual must be carefully reviewed by the auditor well in advance of the actual audit. It is the primary basis for the initial evaluation of the detailed procedures for any computer operation. In most instances an EDP audit specialist is needed to assist the regular auditor.

Hardware Controls

Hardware controls are built into the equipment by the manufacturer to *detect equipment failure.* There are a considerable number of possible specific hardware controls available in EDP systems.

From an internal control point of view, the independent auditor is *less* concerned about the adequacy of the hardware controls in the system than he is about the organization's methods of handling the errors that the computer identifies. The hardware controls are usually carefully designed by the manufacturer to adequately discover and report all machine failures. It is obvious, however, that unless the client's organization has made specific provision for handling machine errors, the output data will remain uncorrected.

Controls over Access to Equipment and Data Files

The auditor is interested in the client's means of *safeguarding the EDP records and files* to ensure that there is an adequate audit trail for the auditor's evidence accumulation needs and to permit advising the client about the potential loss of records that are important to the client's accounting and operating requirements.

The *physical safeguards* over records and files that are important in an EDP system are not significantly different from those that should exist in a manual accounting system. However, the compactness of EDP records and the possibility of erasing a large amount of information on some storage media make such records more vulnerable to accidental or intentional destruction, and thus it is essential that fire and security protection be provided by the use of adequate vaults and off-premises storage.

File protection rings are a useful safeguard against the erasure of information stored on magnetic tape. The presence *or* absence of the file protection ring permits the reading of information, but it cannot be erased when the ring is removed. Similarly, *internal and external file labels,* which are discussed in more detail shortly, are a means of protecting the information in files.

Input Controls

Input controls have to do with the application of a specific operation performed by EDP. They are of major importance in EDP systems, since the quality of the output depends upon the quality of the input. An *input error* is generally defined as any error in the data up to the time it is entered into the computer in machine readable form. The error can result from improper authorization, conversion into a machine readable form, lost data, added data, and other types of errors common to manual systems. The following are a few examples of input controls.

Keypunch Verifying. Having different operators check part or all of the original keypunching is a means of controlling errors from this source. The procedure consists of inserting the punched card into a *verifier* and rekeying data from the original documents. If the results do not match, the card is rejected. Since the operators are generally instructed to keypunch the information exactly as it is stated on the original documents, this control is useful only for detecting keypunch errors.

Check Digit. A check digit is a number that is a part of an *identification number*. It is used as a means of determining whether a recorded identification number is correct. As a highly oversimplified example of check digits, assume that salesmen identification numbers range from 1 to 9000. For the salesman with the identification number 3624, the number 15 (the summation of the four digits is the check digit in this example) could be added to the number for a new identification number of 362415. After this is done for each salesman, the computer can easily be programmed to determine whether the sum of the first four digits of each salesman identification number equals the last two digits. This is a useful control for detecting keypunch, machine, or programming errors. It is unnecessary to *keypunch verify* identification numbers if check digits are used.

Control Totals. Control totals are used to determine whether all the data that were put into the system were processed. Generally, the purpose of a control total is to make certain that no data are lost in handling or processing, but in some cases it is used to verify that the dollar amount is correct. A count or summation of a batch of input must be completed before the input goes into the system. After the data are processed the control total is compared with the final output. As an example, a batch of sales invoice documents might be footed before they are given to keypunching and then, after the information has been processed by the computer, the total can be compared with the output. In many cases the final comparison of the control total with the output total is performed by the computer.

Transmittal Controls and Route Slips. Both of these are forms used by organizations to help ensure that all batches of data are entirely processed. The *transmittal control* form is used to log the receipt of data, the date they are processed, and the release of the data. This control device is useful both for determining which data have been received but not processed and for isolating where unprocessed data are located. The *route slip* is attached to the file of data to inform the processing center of the proper path of processing and to provide a record of the actual processing performed.

Processing Controls

Processing controls are meant to check for reliability throughout a particular EDP application. The purpose is to test whether all transactions are recorded and processed properly and to be sure that no transactions are added. For the most part, these controls are programmed into the system as a part of designing a particular application. A few of these controls are as follows:

Tests For Valid Data. Data validity tests are performed to aid in determining whether inputs and outputs that should be included do in fact appear, as well as whether the information in question is correct. For example, it is possible to test each field to make sure that all fields actually have data. Similarly, a salesman's employee number can be compared with a master list to determine whether he sells the type of product included in the sales transaction being processed.

Crossfooting Tests. These are similar to those normally found in a manual accounting system. Individual categories are totaled independently by the computer and are then compared to make sure that they are equal to other related totals. Examples include crossfooting the individual categories in the sales journal or the payroll journal. If the totals are not equal, an error message is printed out.

Reasonableness Tests. These tests identify a total or transaction that exceeds some predesignated reasonable limit. One example of a reasonableness test consists of checking whether the recorded payroll hours worked by an employee who is paid on a weekly basis exceed a specified number, such as seventy hours. Other examples are reasonableness tests of each office employee's salary for the month, the maximum and minimum number of units of merchandise sold to a retail customer, and the maximum and minimum supplies expense for a given month. These controls are useful for controlling all kinds of large errors, including keypunch or program errors, loss of documents, and machine failures. Clearly, adequate reasonableness checks are important to the auditor as a means of preventing material errors.

File Label Controls. To ensure that the proper transaction or master file is used with the program being run, file labels that identify the file and summarize its contents are customarily used. An *internal file label* has the relevant information in machine language at both the beginning and the end of the file. The information at the beginning typically includes the file name, its identification number, and the reel number in a multi-reel file. At the end of the file there is usually the record count and the applicable control totals, as well as an indication that the record is the last item in the file. *External file labels* in a readable form aid operators, librarians, and other users to correctly identify the files. When magnetic tape or disks are used, the external label is attached directly to the tape reel or disk, whereas in a punched card file the information is normally written on the top of the file of cards.

Output Controls

Control over the reliability of output of an EDP system depends primarily on the *reliability of the input* and the *processing*. In addition, it is desirable to have a final review in the data processing department to check for obvious output errors such as incomplete output, control totals that do not reconcile, and missing information. It is also desirable to secure final *reasonableness tests* as a means of avoiding material errors. The *users* of the output are another potential source of control over errors in the output when they use the data for their information needs.

It is important that provisions be made for formal feedback from the users to the data processing center to help make certain that the cause of the errors is corrected.

An *error listing* is a common means of communicating errors that have been discovered in a data processing system. The system can be programmed to automatically report errors discovered during the processing of data (e.g., invalid data, control data differences, internal file label errors, and hardware malfunctions). Similarly, the procedures manual should require a manually prepared error listing whenever input or keypunch errors occur.

The error listing represents an essential method of controlling and evaluating the system for both the audior and the client. The client should use the error listing as a means of making certain that all errors are corrected; but even more important, it should be used as a means of correcting the cause and thus preventing future errors. Similarly, the auditor learns from the error listing the kinds of errors that are occurring in the system, as well as the corrective measures the client has taken to eliminate the cause.

EVALUATING INTERNAL CONTROL IN AN EDP SYSTEM

The objective of the review of internal control in an EDP system is the same as for a manual one: to aid in determining, on the basis of the adequacy of existing controls, the audit evidence that should be accumulated. Similarly, the technique of internal control evaluation for both EDP and non-EDP systems is to obtain information about the client's prescribed system, to evaluate its strengths and weaknesses, and to ascertain that the system is actually operating in accordance with the plan.

In obtaining information about the client's prescribed system and evaluating the system for strengths and weaknesses, the auditor is concerned with determining the existence and adequacy of the EDP controls that were enumerated in the preceding pages. Of course, it is also necessary to evaluate the non-EDP controls discussed earlier in the book, such as the separation of the custody over assets from the recording function.

It is common to start the internal control evaluation of an EDP system by obtaining preliminary information from three major sources: *flowcharts, EDP questionnaires,* and a study of the *error listings* generated by the system. The flowcharts and questionnaires have counterparts in non-EDP systems, but an error listing is unique to EDP systems. In most cases it is desirable to use all three approaches in evaluating internal control because they offer different types of information. The flowchart emphasizes the organization of the company and the flow of information throughout the system, whereas the internal control questionnaire emphasizes specific controls without relating individual controls to one another.

The error listing supports both these approaches by showing the actual errors that were reported by the EDP system. Ultimately, the auditor must use the information obtained to determine the most important strengths and weaknesses in the internal control system.

After the auditor obtains a preliminary understanding of the EDP system, he is in a position to decide upon the degree to which he plans to rely upon its controls. In doing this, he must also consider the related non-EDP controls and the total system affecting each application. Where controls in one segment, such as the EDP controls, are weak, he may determine that controls in the other segments are compensating, and vice-versa. Whenever the auditor feels that the total system cannot be relied upon, he will, of course, expand the substantive portion of the audit. This approach to internal control evaluation is the same as that discussed in Chapters 5 through 10.

If the auditor decides the system is potentially reliable, it is necessary to proceed with the evaluation by obtaining an in-depth understanding of the system. The procedures should include observations and interviewing of personnel, the performance of compliance tests, and investigating exceptions to prescribed controls and procedures.

As in manual systems, the auditor may decide not to rely upon the EDP controls even if they are adequate. This approach is followed if he believes the cost of an exhaustive study and test of the controls will exceed the reduction in the cost of the other procedures. When the auditor decides not to test the controls, they cannot be relied upon.

AUDITING AROUND THE COMPUTER

When the auditor relies completely on the non-EDP segment of a system, it is commonly referred to as auditing around the computer. Under this approach the auditor reviews internal control and performs tests of transactions and account balance verification procedures in the same manner as in non-EDP systems; there is no attempt to test the client's EDP controls or to use the computer to perform audit procedures.

To audit around the computer, the auditor must have access to sufficient source documents and a detailed listing of output in a readable form. This is possible only when all the following conditions are met:

1. The source documents are available in a nonmachine language.
2. The documents are filed in a manner that makes it possible to locate them for auditing purposes.
3. The output is listed in sufficient detail to enable the auditor to trace individual transactions from the source documents to the output and vice versa.

If any of these conditions does not exist, the auditor will have to rely upon computer-oriented controls and possibly use the computer for carrying out his procedures. Auditing around the computer is an acceptable and often desirable approach when the informational needs of the client's organization require it to maintain the necessary source documents and detailed output.

Complete reliance on manual controls, use of traditional techniques, and failure of the auditor to use the computer in carrying out audit procedures where the conditions allow it does not imply that he ignores the EDP installation. He continues to have a responsibility for a thorough review of the system of internal control to determine the weaknesses in the system as an aid in deciding on the appropriate audit procedures and the sample size necessary for each procedure. This includes both manual and EDP segments.

AUDITING WITH THE USE OF THE COMPUTER

There are two distinct ways in which the auditor uses the computer to perform audit procedures: (1) processing the auditor's test data on the client's computer system as a part of the review of internal control and (2) testing the records maintained by the computer as a means of verifying the client's financial statements.

Test Data Approach

The objective of the use of the test data approach is to determine whether the client's computer programs can correctly handle valid and invalid transactions as they arise. To fulfill this objective, the auditor develops different types of transactions that are processed under his own control using the client's computer programs on the client's EDP equipment. The auditor's test data must include both *valid and invalid transactions* in order to determine whether the client's computer programs will react properly to different kinds of data. Since the auditor has complete knowledge of the errors that exist in the test data, it is possible for him to check whether the client's system has properly processed the input. The auditor does this by examining the error listing and the details of the output resulting from the test data.

Test data are helpful in reviewing the client's system of processing data and its control over errors, but several difficulties must be overcome before this approach can be used. The major concerns are as follows:

1. *The test data must include all relevant conditions that the auditor desires to test.* The test data should provide for a test of the adequacy of all the controls discussed previously that are applicable to the client's program under review. Because considerable competence is required in developing data to test for all the relevant types of error that could occur, the assistance of an EDP specialist is generally required.

2. *The program tested by the auditor's test data must be the same pro-*

gram that is used throughout the year by the client. One approach the auditor can take to ensure that this condition is met is to run the test data on a surprise basis, possibly at random points throughout the year. This approach is both costly and time consuming. A more realistic method is to rely on the client's system of internal control over the use of the program and changes in the program.

3. *In some cases the test data must be eliminated from the client's records.* The elimination of the test data is necessary if the program being tested is for the updating of a master file such as the accounts receivable trial balance. It would not be proper to permanently include fictitious test transactions in a master file. There are feasible methods of eliminating the test data, but they generally require the assistance of an EDP specialist.

Auditor's Computer Program Approach

The second approach to auditing with the computer is for the auditor to run his own program on a controlled basis in order to verify the client's data recorded in a machine language. The auditor's computer program and the test data approach are complementary rather than mutually exclusive, in the same manner as are tests of transactions and direct balance verification. When the auditor uses test data he is evaluating the ability of the client's system to handle different types of transactions, whereas in the auditor's computer program approach the output of the system is being tested for correctness.

The auditor can potentially perform many different kinds of tests and other functions with a computer program if the client's data are in a machine language. These include:

1. *Verifying extensions and footings.* A computer program can be used to verify the accuracy of the client's computations by calculating the information independently. Examples include recalculating sales discounts taken and employees' net pay computations, footing an aging, and totaling the client's accounts receivable trial balance.

2. *Examining records for quality, completeness, consistency, and correctness.* In auditing a manual system, the auditor reexamines the accounting records for propriety as a matter of routine because they are visible and any inconsistencies or inaccuracies can be observed without difficulty. When auditing computerized records, the auditor's program can be instructed to scan all records for propriety in terms of specified criteria and print out the exceptions. Examples include reviewing accounts receivable balances for amounts over the credit limit and reviewing payroll files for terminated employees.

3. *Comparing data on separate files.* Where records on separate files should contain compatible information, a program can be used to determine if the information agrees or to make other comparisons. For instance, changes in accounts receivable balances between two dates can

be compared with details of sales and cash receipts on transaction files, and payroll details can be compared with personnel records.

4. *Summarizing or resequencing data and performing analyses.* Computer programs can be developed to change the format and aggregate data in a variety of ways. The ability to change the form of data allows the auditor to mechanically prepare analyses used in audit procedures and to simulate the client's data-processing systems to determine the reasonableness of recorded information. Examples include verifying accounts receivable aging, preparing general ledger trial balances, summarizing inventory turnover statistics for obsolescence analysis, and resequencing inventory items by location to facilitate physical observations.

5. *Comparing data obtained through other audit procedures with company records.* Audit evidence gathered manually can be converted to machine readable form (i.e., keypunched) and compared with other machine readable data. Examples include comparing confirmation responses with the subsidiary records and comparing creditor statements with accounts payable files.

6. *Selecting audit samples.* The computer can be programmed to select samples from any machine readable data in several different ways, including at random. It is also possible to use more than one criterion for sample selection, such as a 100 percent sample of high-dollar accounts receivable and random sampling of all other receivables.

7. *Printing confirmation requests.* After a sample has been selected, the auditor can have the data printed on confirmation request forms. This is a useful time-saving device for the preparation of confirmations.

The most serious problem in the use of computer programs for testing client data is to obtain a suitable program at a reasonable cost. Three approaches are available to auditors in selecting a computer program:

1. *Use the client's program.* This is an acceptable and economical alternative when the client already has a program that the auditor can use, such as for extensions of inventory and footing of totals. When this approach is followed, it is important to test the client's program for reliability before it is used.

2. *Use a program written by the auditor for the specific audit.* This approach is applicable when the client's programs are not available and when a generalized program is not feasible because of such problems as high processing cost or inaccessibility. A computer program written by the auditor fits the audit application for which it is being developed, but it has the disadvantage of high program development cost.

3. *Use a generalized program.* A generalized audit program is one developed by a CPA firm or other organization which can be used on different audits for most of the seven types of applications listed previously. The generalized program consists of a series of computer programs which together perform various data processing functions. These functions for the most part can be described as data manipulations. Generalized programs are a recent development in auditing that has

greatly increased the potential use of the computer for handling tasks. They have two important advantages. First, generalized programs are developed in such a manner that most of the audit staff can be quickly trained to use the program even though they have little formal EDP education. Second, generalized programs have a wide range of application, which can be made with a single program without having to incur the cost or inconvenience of developing an individualized program. The major disadvantages of generalized computer programs are the high initial cost of their development and their relatively inefficient processing speed.

The decision whether to use test data or auditor computer programs or to audit without the use of a computer must be made by the auditor on the basis of his professional experience. Sometimes the auditor is forced to use the computer to perform procedures due to the inaccessibility of source documents and detailed listing of output. Even if records are accessible, it may be desirable to perform tests with the computer if sufficient competent evidence can be accumulated at a reduced cost.

USE OF A GENERALIZED AUDIT PROGRAM

Since generalized audit programs (GAPs) are extensively used by CPA firms, it is important that students of auditing understand them. These programs are first explained in general terms, followed by an illustration of how they could be used.

Figure 12-1 contains a diagram of the GAP process for any application. The steps are as follows:

Objective Setting. The purpose of the test must be carefully specified in advance to achieve the desired results. The objective can be to foot a data file, select a random sample, or perform one or more of the other tasks previously described.

Application Design. The second step consists of three parts:

1. Identify and describe the client's data files and the pertinent information that might be accessed. This is necessary to extract data from the client's files.
2. Design the most useful format and contents of the auditor's GAP reports.
3. Develop a logical approach to extract and manipulate the data obtained from the client's records. This is done by the auditor with the use of a simple programming language.

Coding. The results of the application design are then coded on worksheets by the auditor in the simple GAP language. These are instructions telling the GAP what to do with the client's files to meet the audit objectives specified in step *a*.

FIGURE 12-1

THE GAP APPLICATION PROCESS

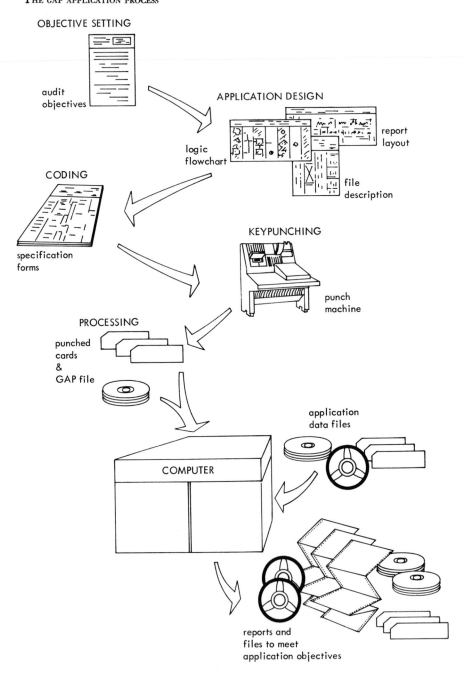

OBJECTIVE SETTING

audit
objectives

APPLICATION DESIGN

report
layout

logic
flowchart

file
description

CODING

specification
forms

KEYPUNCHING

punch
machine

PROCESSING

punched
cards
&
GAP file

application
data files

COMPUTER

reports and
files to meet
application objectives

Keypunching. The coded worksheets are keypunched, verified by the CPA's employees, and submitted to the computer, along with the GAP and the client's data files.

Processing. The processing phase consists of two stages. In the first stage, the GAP directs the computer to read the data file and to extract pertinent information. It is important to understand that all further processing takes place on the extracted information. The client's data file is no longer used and is removed from the process, thus ensuring that it will not be inadvertently changed or destroyed. Should it be necessary for the GAP to produce an intermediate output file, it is referred to as a work file. The second stage involves the functions required to produce the GAP reports. At the completion of the processing, the client's data files are returned to the client and the GAP file is returned to the CPA's office. Frequently the GAP coding instructions are retained for possible use on subsequent audits. The GAP reports are used for their intended audit purpose and retained in the working papers as documentation.

Illustration of the Use of a Generalized Audit Program for Accounts Receivable

The following is an illustration of a GAP application presented in terms of the steps given above.

Objective Setting.

1. Foot and crossfoot the accounts receivable master file and print the total and any crossfoot exceptions.
2. Determine if any balances are in excess of their credit limit and print a report of all exceptions.
3. Prepare and print an aging summary.
4. Randomly select accounts and print confirmations as follows:
   a. Positive confirmation of all accounts over $10,000 or over 90 days old
   b. Positive confirmation of 25 percent of all accounts between $1,000 and $10,000 not over 90 days old
   c. Negative confirmation of 5 percent of all others
5. Print a control listing of accounts selected for confirmation.
6. Select 5 percent of all accounts to trace to source documents for a test of aging.
7. Select and print a list of accounts for collectibility follow-up which are "for special handling."

Application Design. The client maintains accounts receivable on both a master file and a name and address file. The following is a list of the contents, noting whether the information was used in the application:

Accounts Receivable Master File

Element No.	Description of Contents	Used	Not Used
1	Division	X	—
2	Customer number	X	—
3	Credit limit	X	—
4	Salesman code	—	X
5	Cash discount percent	—	X
6	Date of last payment	X	—
7	Date of last purchase	X	—
8	Balance due	X	—
	Aging of balance due:		
9	Current	X	—
10	30 days	X	—
11	60 days	X	—
12	90 days	X	—
13	6 months	X	—
14	1 year	X	—

Name and Address File

Element No.	Description of Contents	Used	Not Used
1	Division	X	—
2	Customer number	X	—
3	Customer name	X	—
4	Street address	X	—
5	City and state	X	—
6	Zip code	X	—
7	Shipping location code	—	X
8	Customer type	—	X
9	Risk-rating code	X	—
	1 = no risk		
	2 = normal handling		
	3 = approval required when balance over 60 days		
	4 = special handling required for each purchase		

Coding. The objectives of this application were met by coding the various GAP functions to process the client's data files as follows:

1. The accounts receivable master file was read and the designated information was extracted. This was followed by extracting the name, address, and risk information from the name and address file.
2. The extracted information was next subjected to the following selection criteria:
   a. Add the aging fields within each record and subtract total from

balance due field. Place any difference in an aging overflow field and code the record for Report No. 1.

b. Foot aging and balance due fields for all records. The GAP prints such totals automatically.

c. Compare the balance due field with the credit limit field. If the balance exceeds the limit, code the record for Report No. 2.

d. Compare balance due with $10,000. If greater than $10,000, code the record for positive confirmation and Report No. 3.

e. Compare aging fields 90 days, 6 months, and 1 year with zero. If greater than zero, code the record for positive confirmation and Report No. 3.

f. Compare balance due with $1,000. If greater than $1,000 and not previously coded for positive confirmation, select 25 percent at random and code for positive confirmation and Report No. 3.

g. Compare balance due with $1,000. If less than $1,000 and not coded for positive confirmation, select 5 percent at random and code for negative confirmation and Report No. 4.

h. Select 5 percent of all accounts at random and code for Report No. 5.

i. Code any records with a risk rating equal to 4 and not selected for confirmation to Report No. 6.

Keypunching and Processing. After the codes were punched, they were processed with the GAP and the accounts receivable master file and the name and address file.

Reports. The following reports were printed:

- Report No. 1—all accounts where aging does not crossfoot (if any)
- Report No. 2—all accounts where balance is in excess of credit limit (if any)
- Report No. 3—accounts selected for positive confirmation and collectibility follow-up
- Report No. 4—accounts selected for negative confirmation
- Report No. 5—accounts for test of aging, showing all aging details, including dates of last payment and purchase
- Report No. 6—additional high-risk accounts selected for collectibility follow-up

In addition, positive and negative confirmations were printed.

AUDIT OF COMPUTER SERVICE CENTERS

Many clients now have their data processed at an independent computer service center rather than having their own computer. This is a logical approach for a business with an excessive volume of transactions for a manual system but inadequate volume to justify the cost of owning a computer.

In a computer service center operation, the client submits input data, and the service center processes the data for a fee and returns it to the client along with the agreed-upon output. Generally, the service center is responsible for designing the computer system and providing adequate controls to ensure that the processing is reliable.

The difficulty the independent auditor faces when a computer service center is used is in determining the adequacy of the service center's controls. The auditor cannot automatically assume the controls are adequate simply because it is an independent enterprise. If the client's service center application involves the processing of significant financial data, the auditor must consider the need to evaluate and test the service center's controls.

The extent of the review and testing of the service center should be based upon the same criteria the auditor follows in evaluating a client's own system. The depth of the review depends upon the complexity of the system and the extent to which the auditor intends to rely upon the system to reduce other audit tests. If the auditor concludes that active involvement with the service center is the only feasible way to conduct the audit, it may be necessary to perform an extensive review of the system, test the system by the use of test data and other compliance tests, and use the computer to perform tests of the type discussed in the preceding section. Extensive testing of this nature is unlikely in most audits, however, because most service center applications are reasonably simple. On the other hand, some review of the service center is usually done.

In recent years it has become increasingly common to have *one* independent auditor examine and test the system of internal control of the service center for the use of *all* customers and their independent auditors. The purpose of these independent reviews is to provide customers with a reasonable level of assurance of the adequacy of the service center's system and to eliminate the need for redundant audits by customers' auditors. If the service center has many customers and each customer requires a review of the service center records by its own independent auditor, the inconvenience to the service center can be substantial. When the service center's independent CPA firm completes the audit of the controls and records, a special report is issued indicating the scope of the audit and the conclusions. It is then the responsibility of the customer's auditor to decide upon the extent to which he wants to rely on the service center's audit report.

REVIEW QUESTIONS

1. Define what is meant by an audit trail and explain how the client's introduction of EDP can alter it. How does this change affect the auditor?
2. List the four types of EDP systems in the order of their complexity. What are the distinguishing characteristics of each of these systems?
3. Evaluate the following statement: "As EDP systems become more complex, the role of the traditional auditor declines. It is desirable that auditors in-

volved with EDP systems either become competent in specialized computer concepts or use computer audit specialists on the engagement."

4. In what ways is the potential for fraud greater in a highly complex EDP system than in a manual system?

5. List five specific internal controls that are equally applicable in a manual or an EDP system.

6. In what ways does the ideal segregation of duties for an EDP system differ from those found in a typical non-EDP system? List the major functions that should be segregated in an EDP system and explain why they should be segregated.

7. Distinguish between hardware controls and programmed controls and explain the purpose of each.

8. Distinguish between a file protection ring and a file label control and explain the purpose of each.

9. Explain why input controls are essential in an EDP system. Give three examples of input controls.

10. What is meant by processing controls? Give several examples of the type of errors they are meant to prevent.

11. Compare the methodology of evaluating a system of internal control in an EDP and a manual system.

12. Explain what is meant by auditing around the computer. Under what circumstances is it acceptable to follow this approach?

13. Explain what is meant by the test data approach to auditing with the computer. What are the major difficulties in using this approach?

14. List seven kinds of tests or other functions commonly performed by auditors' computer programs and give one specific example of each use.

15. Explain what is meant by a generalized audit program and discuss its importance as an audit tool.

16. Explain why it is unacceptable for an auditor to assume that an independent computer service center is providing reliable accounting information to an audit client. What can the auditor do to test the service center's system?

DISCUSSION QUESTIONS AND PROBLEMS

17. Select the best answer choice for the following:
    The detection and correction of errors in the processing of data should be the responsibility primarily of
    (1) The data-processing manager.
    (2) The machine operator.
    (3) An independent internal control group.
    (4) The independent public accountant.   (AICPA adapted)

18. The audit of the financial statements of a client that utilizes the services of a computer for accounting functions compels the CPA to understand the operation of his client's EDP system.
    a. The first requirement of an effective system of internal control is a satisfactory plan of organization. List the characteristics of a satisfactory plan of organization for an EDP department, including the relationship between the department and the rest of the organization.
    b. An effective system of internal control also requires an effective system of records control of operations and transactions (source data and its

flow) and of classification of data within the accounts. For an EDP system, these controls include input controls, processing controls, and output controls. List the characteristics of a satisfactory system of input controls. (Confine your comments to a batch-controlled system employing punched cards and to the steps that occur prior to the processing of the input cards in the computer.)   (AICPA adapted)

19. George Beemster, CPA, is examining the financial statements of the Louisville Sales Corporation, which recently installed an off-line electronic computer. The following comments have been extracted from Mr. Beemster's notes on computer operations and the processing and control of shipping notices and customer invoices:

> To minimize inconvenience Louisville converted without change its existing data-processing system, which utilized tabulating equipment. The computer company supervised the conversion and has provided training to all computer department employees (except keypunch operators) in systems design, operations, and programming.
>
> Each computer run is assigned to a specific employee, who is responsible for making program changes, running the program, and answering questions. This procedure has the advantage of eliminating the need for records of computer operations because each employee is responsible for his own computer runs.
>
> At least one computer department employee remains in the computer room during office hours, and only computer department employees have keys to the computer room.
>
> System documentation consists of those materials furnished by the computer company—a set of record formats and program listings. These and the tape library are kept in a corner of the computer department.
>
> The company considered the desirability of programmed controls but decided to retain the manual controls from its existing system.
>
> Company products are shipped directly from public warehouses, which forward shipping notices to general accounting. There a billing clerk enters the price of the item and accounts for the numerical sequence of shipping notices from each warehouse. The billing clerk also prepares daily adding machine tapes ("control tapes") of the units shipped and the unit prices.
>
> Shipping notices and control tapes are forwarded to the computer department for keypunching and processing. Extensions are made on the computer. Output consists of invoices (in six copies) and the daily sales register. The daily sales register shows the aggregate totals of units shipped and unit prices which the computer operator compares with the control tapes.
>
> All copies of the invoice are returned to the billing clerk. The clerk mails three copies to the customer, forwards one copy to the warehouse, maintains one copy in a numerical file, and retains one copy in an open invoice file that serves as a detail accounts receivable record.

Required:

Describe weakness in internal control over information and data flows and the procedures for processing shipping notices and customer invoices, and recommend improvements in these controls and processing procedures. Organize your answer as follows:

Weakness	Recommended Improvement
	(AICPA adapted)

20. You have been engaged by Central Savings and Loan Association to examine its financial statements for the year ended December 31.

   In January of the current year the association installed an on-line real-time computer system. Each teller in the association's main office and seven branch offices has an on-line input-output terminal. Customers' mortgage payments and savings account deposits and withdrawals are recorded in the accounts by the computer from data input by the teller at the time of the transaction. The teller keys the proper account by account number and enters the information in the terminal keyboard to record the transaction. The accounting department at the main office has both punched card and typewriter input-output devices. The computer is housed at the main office.

   In addition to servicing its own mortgage loans, the association acts as a mortgage servicing agency for three life insurance companies. In this latter activity the association maintains mortgage records and serves as the collection and escrow agent for the mortgagees (the insurance companies), who pay a fee to the association for these services.

   You would expect the association to have certain internal controls in effect because an on-line real-time computer system is employed. List the internal controls that should be in effect solely because this system is employed, classifying them as
   a. Those controls pertaining to input of information
   b. All other types of computer controls   (AICPA adapted)

21. Bill Goatly, CPA, has examined the financial statements of the Frey Manufacturing Company for several years and is making preliminary plans for the audit for the year ended June 30. During this examination, Goatly plans to use a set of generalized audit programs. Frey's EDP manager has agreed to prepare special tapes of data from company records for the CPA's use with the GAPs.

   The following information is applicable to Goatly's examination of Frey's accounts payable and related procedures:
   a. The formats of pertinent tapes are given below.
   b. The following monthly runs are prepared:
      (1) Cash disbursements by check number
      (2) Outstanding payables
      (3) Purchase journals arranged (1) by account charged and (2) by vendor
   c. Vouchers and supporting invoices, receiving reports, and purchase order copies are filed by vendor code. Purchase orders and checks are filed numerically.
   d. Company records are maintained on magnetic tapes. All tapes are stored in a restricted area within the computer room. A grandfather-father-son policy is followed for retaining and safeguarding tape files.

Required:

   a. Explain the grandfather-father-son policy. Describe how files could be reconstructed when this policy is used.
   b. Discuss whether company policies for retaining and safeguarding the tape files provide adequate protection against losses of data.
   c. Describe the controls that the CPA should maintain over

(1) Preparing the special tape

(2) Processing the special tape with the GAPs

d. Prepare a schedule for the EDP manager outlining the data that should be included on the special tape for the CPA's examination of accounts payable and related procedures. This schedule should show

(1) The client tape from which the item should be extracted

(2) The name of the item of data   (AICPA adapted)

22. The Meyers Pharmaceutical Company has the following system for billing and recording accounts receivable:

a. An incoming customer's purchase order is received in the order department by a clerk who prepares a prenumbered company sales order form in which is inserted the pertinent information, such as the customer's name and address, customer's account number, and quantity and items ordered. After the sales order form has been prepared, the customer's purchase order is stapled to it.

b. The sales order form is then passed to the credit department for credit approval. Rough approximations of the billing values of the orders are made in the credit department for those accounts on which credit limitations are imposed. After investigation, approval of credit is noted on the form.

c. Next the sales order form is passed to the billing department where a clerk types the customer's invoice on a billing machine that cross-multiplies the number of items and the unit price, then adds the automatically extended amounts for the total amount of the invoice. The billing clerk determines the unit prices for the items from a list of billing prices.

The billing machine has registers that automatically accumulate daily totals of customer account numbers and invoice amounts to provide "hash" totals and control amounts. These totals, which are inserted in a daily record book, serve as predetermined batch totals for verification of computer inputs. The billing is done on prenumbered, continuous, carbon-interleaved forms having the following designations:

(1) "Customer's copy"

(2) "Sales department copy" for information purposes

(3) "File copy"

(4) "Shipping department copy," which serves as a shipping order.

Bills of lading are also prepared as carbon copy by-products of the invoicing procedure.

d. The shipping department copy of the invoice and the bills of lading are then sent to the shipping department. After the order has been shipped, copies of the bill of lading are returned to the billing department. The shipping department copy of the invoice is filed in the shipping department.

e. In the billing department one copy of the bill of lading is attached to the customer's copy of the invoice and both are mailed to the customer. The other copy of the bill of lading, together with the sales order form, is then stapled to the invoice file copy and filed in invoice numerical order.

f. A keypunch machine is connected to the billing machine so that punched cards are created during the preparation of the invoices. The punched cards then become the means by which the sales data are transmitted to a computer. The punched cards are fed to the computer in batches. One day's accumulation of cards makes up a batch. After the punched cards have been processed by the computer, they are placed in files and held for about two years.

Required:

List the procedures that a CPA would employ in his examination of his selected audit samples of the company's

a. Typed invoices, including the source documents

b. Punched cards

(*Note:* The listed procedures should be limited to the verification of the sales data being fed into the computer. Do not carry the procedures beyond the point at which the cards are ready to be fed to the computer.)

(AICPA adapted)

23. In connection with his examination of the financial statements of the Olympia Manufacturing Company, a CPA is reviewing procedures for accumulating direct labor hours. He learns that all production is by job order and that all employees are paid hourly wages, with time and a half for overtime hours.

Olympia's direct labor hour input process for payroll and job-cost determination is summarized in the flowchart.

Steps *A* and *C* are performed in timekeeping, step *B* in the factory-operating departments, step *D* in payroll audit and control, step *E* in data preparation (keypunch), and step *F* in computer operations.

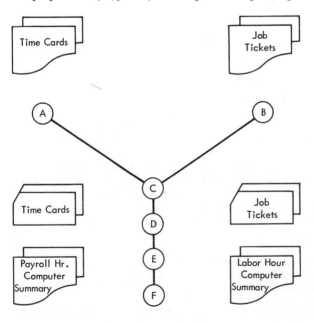

Required:

For each input-processing step *A* through *F*:
a. List the possible errors or discrepancies that may occur.
b. Cite the corresponding control procedure that should be in effect for each error or discrepancy.

Your discussion of Olympia's procedures should be limited to the input process for direct labor hours, as shown in steps *A* through *F* in the flowchart. *Do not discuss* personnel procedures for hiring, promotion, termination, and pay rate authorization. *In step* F *do not discuss* equ ,pment, computer program, and general computer operational controls. Organize your answer for each input-processing step as follows:

Step	Possible Errors or Discrepancies	Control Procedures
		(AICPA adapted)

24. You are conducting an audit of sales for the James Department Store, a retail chain store with a computerized sales system in which computerized cash registers are integrated directly with accounts receivable, sales, perpetual inventory records, and sales commission expense. At the time of sale the salesclerks keypunch the following information directly into the cash register:
- Product number
- Quantity sold
- Unit selling price
- Store code number
- Salesclerk number
- Date of sale
- Cash sale or credit sale
- Customer account number for all credit sales

The total amount of the sale, including sales tax, is automatically computed by the system and indicated on the cash register's visual display. The only printed information for cash sales is the cash register receipt, which is given to the customer. For credit sales, a credit slip is prepared and one copy is retained by the clerk and submitted daily to the accounting department.

A summary of sales is printed out daily in the accounting department. The summary includes daily and monthly totals by salesclerks for each store as well as totals for each of ninety-three categories of merchandise by store. Perpetual inventory and accounts receivable records are updated daily on magnetic tape, but supporting records are limited primarily to machine-readable records.

Required:

a. What major problems does the auditor face in verifying sales and accounts receivable?
b. How can the concept of test data be employed in this audit? Explain the difficulties the auditor would have to overcome in using test data.
c. How can a GAP be employed in this audit? List several tests that can be conducted using this approach.

d. The client is interested in installing several controls to automatically signal cash register operators when they have made an error. List four programmed controls the auditor could recommend to reduce the likelihood of these types of errors.

e. The client would also like to reduce the time it takes to keypunch the information into the cash register. Suggest several ways this could be accomplished, considering the information now being manually keypunched.

25. In the audit of Greenline Manufacturing Company for the year ended 12-31-X8, Roberta Bond, CPA, concluded that the lack of an audit trail for the property, plant, and equipment accounts precluded auditing that area in the traditional manner. As a result, the decision was made to use a generalized audit program in the verification of certain aspects of the accounts. The generalized audit program includes the following specific objectives:

a. Foot the file and print totals by major property category for cost of all assets, cost of current additions, and accumulated and current depreciation for both book and tax purposes.

b. Prepare a listing of all additions over $5,000 for vouching and inspection.

c. Prepare a listing of all disposals for detailed verification

d. Verify the calculations of depreciation expenses for both book and tax purposes.

The permanent asset master files for 12-31-X7 were saved by the client and include the same information as the 12-31-X8 files. Their contents are as follows:

Element No.	Description of Contents
1	Asset number
2	Description
3	Type code
4	Location code
5	Year of acquisition
6	Cost
7	Accum. Deprec.—beginning book
8	Depreciation—YTD book
9	Useful life
10	Tax depreciation method
11	Accum. Deprec.—beginning tax
12	Depreciation—YTD tax

(*Note:* All fixed assets use the straight-line method for book depreciation. Tax depreciation may be straight-line, double-declining balance, or sum-of-the-years' digits.)

Required:

a. Explain in detail how the information on the 12-31-X7 and 12-31-X8 master files should be used to fulfill the four audit objectives.

b. List the reports that will be generated by the GAP.

c. Explain what additional verification is necessary on each of these reports to satisfy the auditor that property, plant, and equipment is fairly stated.

13

Audit of
the Payroll and Personnel Cycle

The payroll and personnel cycle involves the employment and payment of all employees, regardless of classification or method of determining compensation. The employees include executives on straight salary plus bonus, office workers on monthly salary with or without overtime, salesmen on a commission basis, and factory and unionized personnel paid on an hourly basis. The cycle is important for several reasons. First, the salaries, wages, employer taxes, and other employer costs are a major expense in all companies. Second, labor is such an important consideration in the valuation of inventory in manufacturing and construction companies that the improper classification and allocation of labor can result in a material misstatement of net income. Finally, payroll is an area where occasionally large amounts of company resources are wasted because of inefficiency or are stolen through fraud.

As with the sales and collection cycle, the audit of the payroll and personnel cycle includes analytical tests, the evaluation of internal controls and tests of transactions, and direct tests of financial balances. Accordingly, the first part of this chapter deals with the nature of the cycle, including documents and records, and the primary functions and internal controls. The second part discusses analytical tests. The third part includes tests of transactions for the cycle related to key internal controls. Finally, the fourth part of the chapter focuses on the verification of the related liability and expense accounts with direct tests. These accounts include all salaries and wages expense accounts, employer pay-roll taxes and fringe benefits, and the liability for accrued wages, payroll taxes, and similar items connected with payroll.

The way in which accounting information flows through the various accounts in the payroll and personnel cycle is illustrated by T-accounts in Figure 13-1. In most systems the accrued wages and salaries account is used only at the end of an accounting period. Throughout the period, expenses are charged when the employees are actually paid rather than when the labor costs are incurred. The accruals for labor are recorded by adjusting entries at the end of the period for any earned but unpaid labor costs.

FIGURE 13-1

ACCOUNTS IN THE PAYROLL AND PERSONNEL CYCLE

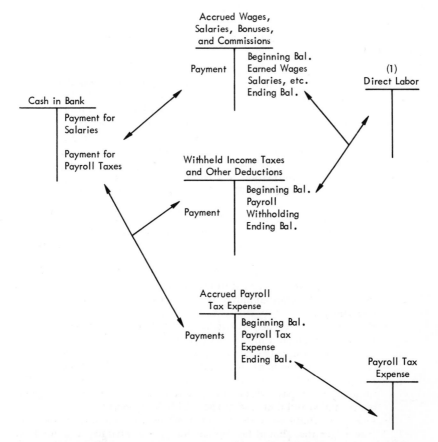

(1) Separate operating accounts for payroll also normally include officers' salaries and and bonuses, office salaries, sales salaries, and commissions and indirect manufacturing labor. These accounts have the same relationship to accrued wages and withheld taxes and other deductions that is shown for direct labor.

NATURE OF THE PAYROLL AND
PERSONNEL CYCLE

The payroll and personnel cycle begins with the hiring of personnel and ends with the payment to the employees for the services performed and to the government and other institutions for the withheld and accrued payroll taxes and benefits. In between, the cycle involves obtaining services from the employees consistent with the objectives of the company and accounting for the services in a proper manner. An overview flowchart of the payroll and personnel cycle for a typical small manufacturing company is shown in Figure 13-2.

Documents and Records

Various documents and records are of major importance in supporting the record flow used in the cycle:

- *Personnel records*—Records that include such data as the date of employment, personnel investigations, rates of pay, authorized deductions, performance evaluations, and termination of employment.
- *Deduction authorization form*—A form authorizing payroll deductions, including the number of exemptions for witholding of income taxes, U.S. savings bonds, and community fund.
- *Rate authorization form*—A form authorizing the rate of pay. The source of the information is a labor contract, authorization by management, or, in the case of officers, authorization from the board of directors.
- *Time card*—A document indicating the time the employee started and stopped working each day and the number of hours the employee worked. For many employees, the time card is prepared automatically by the use of time clocks. Time cards are usually submitted weekly.
- *Job time ticket*—A document indicating particular jobs on which a factory employee worked during a given time period. This form is used only where an employee works on different jobs or in different departments.
- *Payroll check*—A check written to the employee for services performed. The amount of the check is the gross pay less taxes and other deductions withheld. After the check is cashed and returned to the company from the bank, it is referred to as a canceled check.
- *Payroll journal*—A journal for recording payroll checks. It typically indicates gross pay, withholdings, and net pay. The journal is normally totaled and posted to the general ledger monthly.
- *Labor distribution*—A record summarizing the accounts in the general ledger that should be debited for payroll charges. The total on the labor distribution equals the total gross payroll in the payroll journal.
- *Earnings record*—A record maintained for each employee indicating

FIGURE 13-2

OVERVIEW OF PAYROLL AND PERSONNEL CYCLE

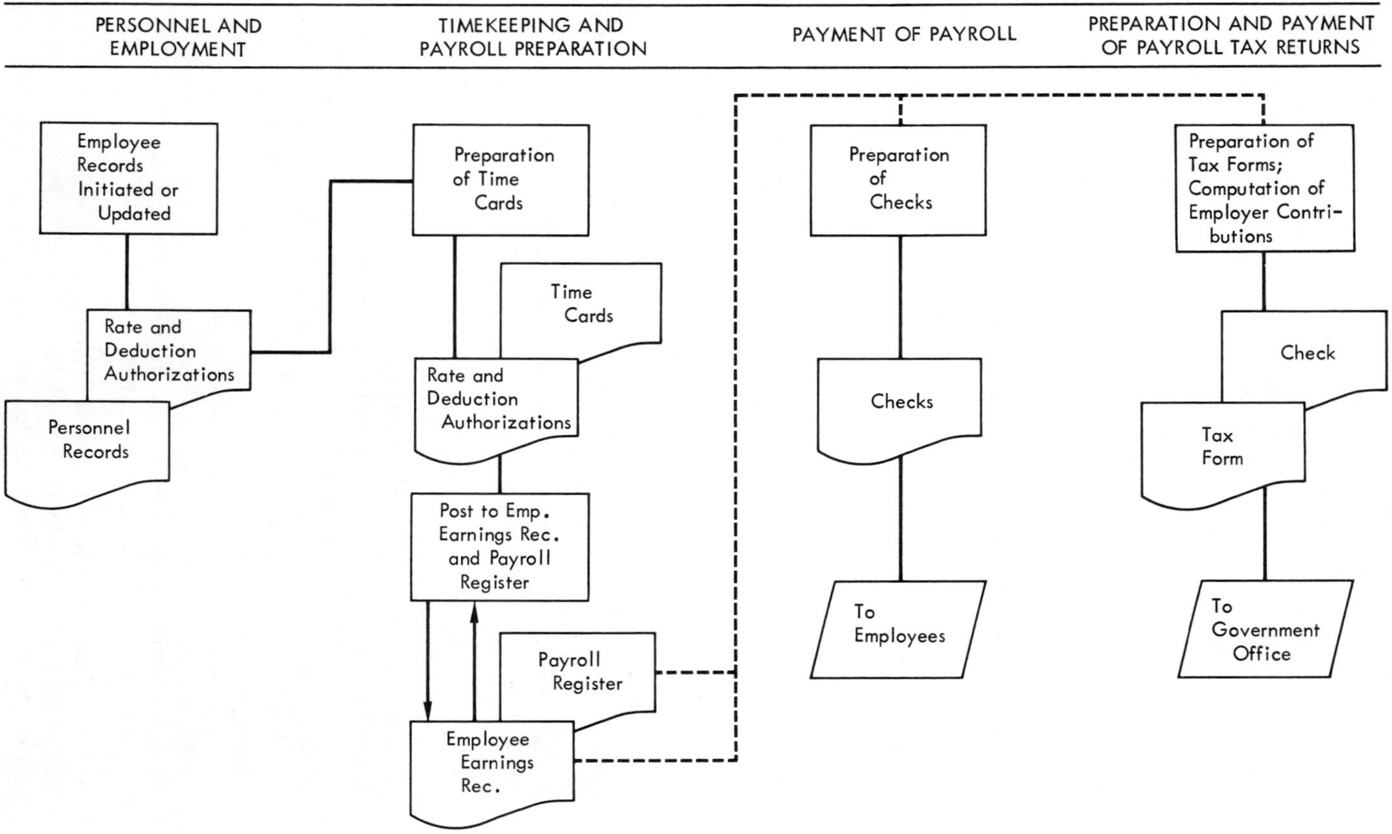

| PERSONNEL AND EMPLOYMENT | TIMEKEEPING AND PAYROLL PREPARATION | PAYMENT OF PAYROLL | PREPARATION AND PAYMENT OF PAYROLL TAX RETURNS |

the gross pay for each payment period, deductions from gross pay, net pay, check number, and date.

- *W-2*—A form issued for each employee summarizing the earnings record for the calendar year. The information includes gross pay, income taxes withheld, and FICA withheld. The same information is also submitted to the Internal Revenue Service and the State Commission of Income Taxation.
- *Payroll tax returns*—Tax forms submitted to local, state, and federal units of government for the payment of withheld taxes and the employer's tax. The nature and due date of the forms vary depending on the type of taxes. For example, federal withholding and social security payments are due monthly, and state unemployment taxes are due quarterly.

Functions in the Cycle and Internal Controls

Typically, four functions are accomplished through the payroll and personnel cycle. They are:

1. Personnel and employment
2. Timekeeping and payroll preparation
3. Payment of payroll
4. Preparation of payroll tax returns and payment of taxes

These functions are now examined in detail with regard to a typical manufacturing company where employees are required to maintain a record of the job on which they are working. The emphasis in this discussion is on the use of certain internal controls to prevent errors in providing data and to ensure the safety of assets.

Personnel and Employment. The personnel department plays the role of providing an independent source for interviewing and hiring qualified personnel. The department is also an independent source of records for the internal verification of wage information.

From an audit point of view, the most important internal controls in personnel involve the formal method of informing the timekeeping and payroll preparation personnel of the authorization of new employees, the authorization of initial and periodic changes in pay rates, and the termination date of employees no longer working for the company. As a part of these controls, segregation of duties is particularly important. No individual with access to time cards, payroll records, or checks should also be permitted access to personnel records. A second important control is the adequate investigation of the competence and trustworthiness of new employees. Frequently, an investigation of previous employment can uncover an unsatisfactory background.

Timekeeping and Payroll Preparation. This function is of major importance in the audit of payroll because it directly affects payroll expense for the period. It includes the preparation of time cards by employees, the summarization and calculation of gross pay, deductions, and net pay, the preparation of payroll checks, and the preparation of payroll records. There must be adequate controls to prevent errors in each of these activities.

Adequate control over the time on the time cards includes the use of a time clock or other method of making certain that employees are paid for the number of hours they worked. There should also be controls to prevent anyone from checking in for several employees or submitting a fictitious time card.

The summarization and calculation of the payroll can be controlled by well-defined policies for the payroll department, separation of duties to provide automatic cross-checks, reconciliation of payroll hours with independent production records, and independent internal verification of all important data. For example, payroll policies should require a competent independent person to recalculate actual hours worked, review for the proper approval of all overtime, examine time cards for erasures and alterations, and recheck pay rates and calculations.

Controls over the preparation of checks include preventing anyone who is responsible for preparing the checks from also having responsibility for summarizing the records or signing or distributing the checks. In addition, the checks should be prenumbered and recorded in the payroll journal on a timely basis.

When manufacturing labor affects inventory valuation, special emphasis should be put on controls to make sure labor is distributed to proper account classifications. There must also be an adequate system of recording job time tickets and other relevant payroll information in the cost accounting records. Independent internal verification of this information is an essential control.

Payment of Payroll. The actual signing and distribution of the checks must be properly handled to prevent their theft. The controls should include limiting the authorization for signing the checks to a responsible employee who does not have access to timekeeping or the preparation of the payroll, the distribution of payroll by someone who is not involved in the other payroll functions, and the immediate return of unclaimed checks for redeposit. If a check-signing machine is used to replace a manual signature, the same controls are required; in addition, the check-signing machine must be carefully controlled.

Most companies use an *imprest payroll account* to prevent the payment of unrecorded payroll transactions. An imprest payroll account is a separate payroll account in which a small balance is maintained. A check for the exact amount of each net payroll is transferred from the general account to the imprest account immediately before the distribution of the payroll. The advantages of an imprest account are that it limits the client's exposure to payroll fraud, allows the delegation of payroll check-signing duties, separates routine payroll expenditures from irregular expenditures, and facilitates cash management. It also simplifies the reconciliation of the payroll bank account if it is done at the low point in the payment cycle.

Preparation of Payroll Tax Returns and Payment of Taxes. The careful and timely preparation of all payroll tax returns is necessary to avoid penalties and criminal charges against the company. The most important control in the preparation of these returns is a well-defined set of policies that carefully indicate when each form must be filed. The independent verification by a competent individual is also an important control to prevent errors and potential liability for taxes and penalties.

ANALYTICAL TESTS

The use of analytical tests is as important in the payroll and personnel cycle as it is in every other cycle. The following types of analytical tests performed for the balance sheet and income statement accounts in the payroll and personnel cycle are useful for uncovering areas where additional investigation is desirable:

1. Compare the payroll expense account balance with those of previous years. Ideally, the previous years' balances should be adjusted for pay rate increases and increases in volume.
2. Compare direct labor ÷ sales with industry standards and those of previous years.
3. Compare commission expense ÷ sales with industry standards and those of previous years.
4. Compare payroll tax expenses ÷ salaries and wages with those of previous years. This comparison is not meaningful unless previous years' balances are adjusted for changes in the tax rate. It is also desirable to exclude officers' salaries from the calculation.
5. Compare accrued payroll taxes accounts with those of previous years.

TESTS OF TRANSACTIONS

Tests of transactions procedures are the *most important* means of verifying account balances in the payroll and personnel cycle. The emphasis on tests of transactions is due to the lack of independent third-party evidence, such as confirmation, for verifying accrued wages, withheld income taxes, accrued payroll taxes, and other balance sheet accounts. Furthermore, in most audits the amounts in the balance sheet accounts are small and can be verified with relative ease if the auditor is confident that the journals and payroll tax returns are properly prepared.

Even though the tests of transactions are the most important part of testing payroll, many auditors spend little time in this area. In many audits there is a minimal risk of material misstatements even though payroll is frequently a significant part of total expenses. There are three reasons for this: employees are likely to complain to management if they are underpaid, all payroll transactions are typically uniform and uncomplicated, and payroll transactions are extensively audited by federal and state governments for income-tax withholding, social security, and unemployment taxes.

Under certain circumstances auditors may extend their procedures considerably in the audit of payroll: (1) when payroll significantly affects the valuation of inventory and (2) when the auditor is concerned about the possibility of material fraudulent payroll transactions because of a weak system of internal control.

Relationship between Payroll and Inventory Valuation

In audits where the payroll is a significant portion of inventory, such as frequently occurs for manufacturing and construction companies, the improper account classification of payroll can significantly affect asset valuation for accounts such as work in process, finished goods, or construction in process. For example, the overhead charged to inventory at the balance sheet can be overstated if the salaries of administrative personnel are inadvertently or intentionally charged to indirect manufacturing overhead. Similarly, the valuation of inventory is affected if the direct labor cost of individual employees is improperly charged to the wrong job or process. When some jobs are billed on a cost-plus basis, revenue and the valuation of inventory are both affected by charging labor to incorrect jobs.

When labor is a material factor in inventory valuation, there should be special emphasis on testing the internal controls over proper classification of payroll transactions. Consistency from period to period, which is essential for classification, can be tested by reviewing the chart of accounts and procedures manuals. It is also desirable to trace job tickets or other evidence of an employee's having worked on a particular job or process to the accounting records that affect inventory valuation. For example, if each employee must account for all of his time on a weekly basis by assigning it to individual job numbers, a useful test is to trace the recorded hours of several employees for a week to the related job-cost records to make sure each has been properly recorded. It may also be desirable to trace from the job-cost records to employee summaries as a test for nonexistent payroll charges being included in inventory.

Tests for Fictitious Payroll

Although the auditor is not ordinarily responsible for the detection of fraud, he must extend his audit procedures when internal controls over payroll are inadequate. There are several ways employees can significantly defraud a company in the payroll area, but in this section the discussion is limited to tests for the two most common types of fictitious employees and fraudulent hours.

Fictitious Employees. The issuance of payroll checks for individuals who do not work for the company frequently results from the continuance of an employee's check after his employment has been terminated. Usually the person committing the fraudulent act is a payroll clerk, foreman, fellow employee, or perhaps the former employee himself. For example, under some systems a foreman could clock in daily for an employee and approve the time card at the end of the time period. If the foreman also distributes paychecks, considerable opportunity for fraud exists.

Certain procedures can be performed on canceled checks as a means of detecting fraud. A procedure used on virtually every payroll audit is to compare the names on canceled checks with time cards and with other records for authorized signatures and reasonableness of the endorsements. It is also common to scan endorsements on canceled checks for unusual or recurring second endorsements as an indication of a possible fictitious check. The examination of checks that are recorded as voided is also desirable to make sure they have not been fraudulently used.

A test for invalid employees is to trace selected transactions recorded in the payroll journal to the personnel department to determine whether the employees were actually employed during the payroll period. The endorsement on the canceled check written out to an employee can be compared with the authorized signature on the employee's withholding authorization forms.

A procedure that tests for proper handling of terminated employees is to select several files for employees that are terminated in the current year from the personnel records to determine whether each former employee received his termination pay in accordance with company policy. Continuing payments to terminated employees is tested by examining the payroll records in the subsequent period to ascertain that the employee is no longer being paid. Naturally, this procedure is not effective if the personnel department is not informed of terminations.

In some cases the auditor may request a surprise payroll payoff. This is a procedure in which each employee must pick up and sign for his check in the presence of a supervisor and the auditor. Any checks that have not been claimed must be subject to an extensive investigation to determine whether an unclaimed check is fraudulent. Surprise payoff is frequently expensive and in some cases may even cause problems with a labor union, but it may be the only likely means of detecting a fraud.

Fraudulent Hours. Because of the lack of available evidence, it is usually difficult for an auditor to discover if an employee records more time on his time card than he actually worked. One procedure is to reconcile the total hours paid according to the payroll records with an independent record of the hours worked, such as those often maintained by production control. Similarly, it may be possible to observe an employee clocking in more than one time card under a buddy approach. However, it is ordinarily easier for the client to prevent this type of fraud by adequate controls than for the auditor to detect it.

Internal Controls, Compliance Tests, and Substantive Tests

Following the same approach that was used in Chapter 8 for tests of sales and cash transactions, the internal controls, compliance tests, and substantive tests for each of the internal control and audit objectives are summarized in Figure 13-3. Again, the reader should recognize that:

1. The internal controls will vary from company to company; therefore, the auditor must evaluate the strengths and weaknesses of each system on the basis of the existing controls.
2. Controls the auditor intends to rely upon for reducing substantive tests must be tested with compliance tests.
3. The substantive tests will vary depending upon the quality of the internal controls and the other considerations of the audit, such as the effect of payroll on inventory.
4. The tests of transactions are not actually performed in the order given in Figure 13-3. The compliance and substantive tests are combined into dual-purpose tests and where appropriate are performed in as convenient a manner as possible.

The purpose of the controls and the meaning and methodology of audit tests that can potentially be used for payroll should be apparent from the descriptions in Figure 13-3. An extended discussion of these procedures is therefore not necessary.

Other Considerations

Three aspects of the payroll and personnel cycle and the related tests of transactions that were not included in the preceding summary also require consideration: preparation of payroll tax forms, payment of the payroll taxes withheld and other withholdings on a timely basis, and reimbursement of the payroll imprest account.

1. *Preparation of payroll tax forms.* The auditor should review the preparation of at least one of each type of payroll tax form the client is responsible for filing as a part of testing the system. There is a potential liability for unpaid taxes, penalty, and interest if the client fails to properly prepare the tax forms. The payroll tax forms are for such taxes as federal income and FICA withholding, state and city income withholdings, and federal and state unemployment.

A detailed reconciliation of the information on the tax forms and the payroll records may be necessary when the auditor believes that there is a reasonable chance the tax returns may be improperly prepared. Indica-

FIGURE 13-3

Summary of Tests of Payroll Transactions

Internal Control and Audit Objective	Key Internal Controls	Common Compliance Tests	Common Substantive Tests
Recorded payroll payments are for work actually performed by non-fictitious employees.	• Time cards are approved by foremen. • Time clock is used to record time. • Adequate personnel file. • Separation of duties between personnel, timekeeping, and payroll disbursements.	• Examine the cards for indication of approvals. • Examine time cards. • Review personnel policies. • Review organization chart, discuss with employees, and observe duties being performed.	• Compare canceled checks with payroll journal for name, amount, and date. • Examine canceled checks for proper endorsement. • Compare canceled checks with personnel records. • Review the payroll journal, general ledger, and payroll earnings records for large or unusual amounts.
Payroll transactions are properly authorized.	Specific or general approval is important at five points: • Authorization to work. • Hours worked, especially overtime. • Wage rate, salary, or commission rate. • Withholdings, including amounts for insurance and payroll savings. • Issuance of check.	• Examine personnel files. • Examine time cards for indication of approval. • Examine payroll records for indication of internal verification. • Examine authorizations in personnel file. • Examine payroll records for indication of approval.	• Compare time card with independent record of hours worked.
Existing payroll transactions are recorded.	• Payroll checks are prenumbered and accounted for. • Independent preparation of bank reconciliation.	• Account for a sequence of payroll checks. • Discuss with employees and observe reconciliation.	• Reconcile the disbursements in the payroll journal with the disbursements on the payroll bank statement. • Prove the bank reconciliation.

Internal Control and Audit Objective	Key Internal Controls	Common Compliance Tests	Common Substantive Tests
Recorded payroll transactions are for the amount of time actually worked and at the proper pay rate; withholdings are properly calculated.	• Internal verification of calculations and amounts.	• Examine indication of internal verification.	• Recompute hours worked from time cards. • Compare pay rates with union contract approval by board of directors or other source. • Recompute gross pay. • Check withholdings by reference to tax tables and authorization forms in personnel file. • Recompute net pay. • Compare canceled check with payroll journal for amount. .
Payroll transactions are properly classified.	• Adequate chart of accounts. • Internal verification of classification.	• Review chart of accounts. • Examine indication of internal verification.	• Compare classification with chart of accounts or procedures manual. • Review time card for employee department and job ticket for job assignment, and trace through to labor distribution.
Payroll transactions are recorded on a timely basis.	• Procedures require recording transactions as soon as possible after the payroll is paid. • Internal verification.	• Examine procedures manual. • Observe when recording takes place.	• Compare date of recorded check in the payroll journal with date on canceled checks and time cards. • Compare date on check with date the check cleared the bank.
Payroll transactions are properly included in the employee earnings record; they are properly summarized.	• Internal verification.	• Examine indication of internal verification.	• Test clerical accuracy, e.g., foot the payroll journal and trace postings to general ledger and employee earnings record.

tions of potential errors in the returns include the payment of penalties and interest in the past for improper payments, new personnel in the payroll department who are responsible for the preparation of the returns, the lack of internal verification of the information, and the existence of serious liquidity problems for the client.

2. *Payment of the payroll taxes withheld and other withholdings on a timely basis.* It is desirable to test whether the client has fulfilled its legal obligation in submitting payments for all payroll withholdings as a part of the payroll tests even though the payments are usually made from general cash disbursements. The withholdings of concern in these tests are such items as taxes, union dues, insurance, and payroll savings. The auditor must first determine the client's requirements for submitting the payments. The requirements are determined by reference to such sources as tax laws, union contracts, and agreements with employees. After the auditor knows the requirements, it is easy to determine whether the client has paid the proper amount on a timely basis by comparing the subsequent payment with the payroll records.

3. *Reimbursement of the payroll imprest account.* The periodic payment from the general cash account to the payroll account for net payroll is usually such a large amount that it should be tested for at least one payroll period. The major audit concern is the adequacy of the internal controls for making sure the check is prepared for the proper amount and deposited before payroll checks are handed out. The auditor should ascertain whether the amount of the canceled check paid from the general cash account equals the net payroll for the payroll period.

Analysis of Errors and Drawing Conclusions

Most payroll systems, in order to adequately control cash disbursed and to minimize employee complaints and dissatisfaction, are highly structured and well controlled. It is very common to use electronic data processing techniques to prepare all journals and payroll checks. In-house systems are often used, as are commercial outside service center systems. For factory and office employees, there are usually a large number of relatively homogeneous, small amount transactions. There are fewer executive payroll transactions, but they are also ordinarily consistent in timing, content, and amount. Thus, auditors seldom expect to find errors in testing payroll transactions. Occasionally, compliance errors occur, but most monetary errors are corrected by internal verification controls or in response to employee complaints. However, there are specific types of errors that give the auditor particular concern in auditing payroll transactions:

1. Classification errors in charging labor to inventory and job cost accounts. As previously indicated, these can result in misstated earnings.
2. Computational errors where electronic data processing is used. Recall

that one of the primary characteristics of the computer is processing consistency. If a calculation error is made for one item, it is probably also made on every other similar item.

3. Any errors that indicate possible fraud, particularly relating to the executive payroll.

Generally, the tests of transactions performed in the payroll cycle will utilize *attributes sampling* under a plan that assumes a zero error rate. Sample size should be large enough to give the auditor a reasonable chance of finding at least one error if an intolerable quantity of errors exist.

If classification errors are found through this procedure, the sample selected for attributes will often be used to then make a *variables estimate* of the total monetary error involved. Sample expansion is usually necessary, however, to achieve a precise enough estimate to conclude whether the total error is material in amount.

If a computational or possible fraud type error is found, specific investigation will be required to determine the facts that allowed such error to occur. Generally, further sampling and estimation are not done; rather, a *judgmental* approach based on the circumstances is taken.

If no errors are found, or if errors found are not alarming or unexpected, the auditor will conclude that the internal controls can be relied upon as planned and he will proceed with the direct tests of the affected accounts without modification.

DIRECT TESTS OF FINANCIAL BALANCES

Audit of Liability Accounts

The verification of the liability accounts associated with payroll, often termed *accrued payroll expenses,* ordinarily is straightforward if the system of internal control is operating effectively. When the auditor is satisfied that payroll transactions are being properly recorded in the payroll journal and the related payroll tax forms are being accurately prepared and promptly paid, the tests should not be time consuming.

The two major objectives in testing payroll-related liabilities are valuation and cutoff. The primary concern in both objectives is to make sure there are no understated or omitted accruals. The major liability accounts in the payroll and personnel cycle are now discussed.

Amounts Withheld from Employees' Pay. Payroll taxes withheld, but not yet disbursed, can be tested by comparing the balance with the payroll journal, the payroll tax form prepared in the subsequent period, and the subsequent period cash disbursements. Other withheld items such as union dues, savings bonds, and insurance can be verified in the same manner. If the system is operating effectively, cutoff and valuation can easily be tested at the same time by these procedures.

Accrued Salaries and Wages. The accrual for salaries and wages arises whenever employees are not paid for the last few days or hours of earned wages until the subsequent period. Salaried personnel usually receive all of their pay except overtime on the last day of the month, but frequently several days of wages for hourly employees are unpaid at the end of the year.

The correct cutoff and valuation of accrued salaries and wages depends on company policy, which should be followed consistently from year to year. Some companies calculate the exact hours of pay that were earned in the current period and paid in the subsequent period, whereas others compute an approximate proportion. For example, if the subsequent payroll results from three days' employment during the current year and two days' employment during the subsequent year, the use of 60 percent of the subsequent period's gross pay as the accrual is an example of an approximation.

Once the auditor has determined the company's policy for accruing wages and knows it is consistent with that of previous years, the appropriate audit procedure to test for cutoff and valuation is to recalculate the client's accrual. The most likely error of any significance in the balance is the failure to include the proper number of days of earned but unpaid wages.

Accrued Commissions. The same concepts used in verifying accrued salaries and wages are applicable to accrued commissions, but the accrual is often more difficult to verify because companies frequently have several different types of agreements with salesmen and other commission employees. For example, some salesmen might be paid a commission every month and earn no salary, while others will get a monthly salary plus a commission paid quarterly. In some cases the commission varies for different products and may not be paid until several months after the end of the year. In verifying accrued commissions, it is necessary to first determine the nature of the commission agreement and then test the calculations based on the agreement. It is important to compare the method of accruing commissions with previous years for purposes of consistency. If the amounts are material, it is also common to confirm the amount that is due directly with the employees.

Accrued Bonuses. In many companies the year-end unpaid bonuses to officers and employees are such a major item that the failure to record them would result in a material misstatement. The verification of the recorded accrual can usually be accomplished by comparing it with the amount authorized in the minutes of the board of directors.

Accrued Vacation Pay, Sick Pay, or Other Benefits. The consistent accrual of these liabilities relative to those of the preceding year is the most important consideration in evaluating the fairness of the amounts. The company policy for recording the liability must first be determined, followed by the recalculation of the recorded amounts.

Accrued Payroll Taxes. Payroll taxes such as FICA and state and federal unemployment taxes can be verified by examining tax forms prepared in the subsequent period to determine the amount that should have been recorded as a liability at the balance sheet date.

Audit of Expense Accounts

There are several accounts in the income statement that are affected by payroll transactions. The most important of these include officers' salaries and bonuses, office salaries, sales salaries and commissions, and direct manufacturing labor. There is frequently a further breakdown of costs by division, product, or branch. In addition, there may also be some fringe benefits such as medical insurance included in the expenses.

There should be relatively little additional testing of the income statement accounts in most audits beyond the analytical tests, tests of transactions, and related tests of liability accounts, which have already been discussed. Extensive additional testing should only be necessary when there are weaknesses in the system of internal control, significant errors are discovered in the liability tests, or major unexplained variances are found in the analytical tests. Nevertheless, some income statement accounts are often tested in the personnel and payroll cycle. These include:

Officers' Compensation. It is common to verify whether the total compensation of officers is the amount authorized by the board of directors because their salaries and bonuses must be included in the SEC's 10-K report and the federal income-tax return. Verification of officers' compensation is also warranted because some individuals may be in a position to pay themselves more than the authorized amount. The usual audit test is to obtain the authorized salary of each officer from the minutes of the board of directors and compare it with the related earnings record.

Commissions. Commission expense can be verified with relative ease if the commission rate is the same for each type of sale and the necessary sales information is available in the accounting records. The total commission expense can be verified by multiplying the commission rate for each type of sale by the amount of sales in that category. If the necessary information is not available, it may be necessary to test the annual or monthly commission payments for selected salesmen and trace those into the total commission payments. When the auditor believes it is necessary to perform these tests, they are normally done in conjunction with tests of accrued liabilities.

Payroll Tax Expense. Payroll tax expense for the year can be tested by first reconciling the total payroll on each payroll tax form with the total payroll for the entire year. Total payroll taxes can then be recomputed by multiplying the appropriate rate by the taxable payroll. The calculation is frequently time consuming because the tax is usually applicable on only a portion of the payroll and the rate may change part way through the year if the taxpayer's financial statements are not on a calendar year basis. The calculation is not worth the effort expended to obtain the information on most audits. When the auditor believes the test is necessary, it is ordinarily done in conjunction with tests of payroll tax accruals.

Total Payroll. A closely related test to the one for payroll taxes is the reconciliation of total payroll expense in the general ledger with the payroll tax returns and the W-2s. The objectives of the test are to determine whether payroll transactions were charged to a nonpayroll account or not recorded in the payroll journal at all. The audit objectives are certainly relevant, but it is questionable whether the procedure is useful in uncovering the type of error for which it was intended. Since the payroll tax records are usually prepared directly from the payroll journal, the errors, if any, are likely to be in both records. The procedure may be worthwhile in rare situations, but it is usually not necessary to perform it. Tests of transactions are a better means of uncovering these two types of errors in most audits.

REVIEW QUESTIONS

1. Explain the relationship between the payroll and personnel cycle and inventory valuation.
2. List five compliance tests that can be performed for the payroll cycle and state the purpose of each control being tested.
3. Explain why the percentage of total audit time in the cycle devoted to performing tests of transactions is usually far greater for the payroll and personnel cycle than for the sales and collection cycle.
4. Evaluate the following comment by an auditor: "My job is to determine whether the payroll records are fairly stated in accordance with generally accepted accounting principles, not to find out whether they are following proper hiring and termination procedures. When I conduct an audit of payroll I keep out of the personnel department and stick to the time cards, journals, and payroll checks. I don't care whom they hire and whom they fire, as long as they properly pay the ones they have."
5. Distinguish between the following payroll audit procedures and state the purpose of each: (1) trace a random sample of prenumbered time cards to the related payroll checks in the payroll register and compare the hours worked with the hours paid, and (2) trace a random sample of payroll checks from the payroll register to the related time cards and compare the hours worked with the hours paid. Which of these two procedures is typically more important in the audit of payroll? Why?
6. In auditing payroll withholding and payroll tax expense, explain why emphasis should normally be on evaluating the adequacy of the payroll tax return preparation procedures rather than the payroll tax liability. If the preparation procedures are inadequate, explain the impact this will have on the remainder of the audit.
7. List several analytical tests for the payroll and personnel cycle and explain

the type of error that might be indicated when there is a significant deviation in the comparison of the current year with previous years' results for each of the tests.

8. Explain the circumstances under which an auditor should perform audit tests primarily designed to uncover fraud in the payroll and personnel cycle. List five audit procedures that are primarily for the detection of fraud and state the type of fraud the procedure is meant to uncover.

9. Distinguish between an employee's earnings record, a W-2, and a payroll tax return. Explain the purpose of each.

10. List the supporting documents and records the auditor will examine in a typical payroll audit where the primary objective is to detect fraud.

11. List the five types of authorizations in the payroll and personnel cycle and state the type of error that is enhanced when each authorization is lacking.

12. Explain why it is common to verify total officers' compensation even when the test of transactions results in payroll are excellent. What audit procedures can be used to verify officers' compensation?

13. Explain what is meant by an imprest payroll account. What is its purpose as a control over payroll?

14. List several audit procedures the auditor can use to determine whether recorded payroll transactions are recorded at the proper amount.

15. Explain how attributes sampling can be used to test the payroll and personnel cycle.

16. For each of the following questions, select the best response:
    a. A factory foreman at Steblecki Corporation discharged an hourly worker but did *not* notify the payroll department. The foreman then forged the worker's signature on time cards and work tickets and, when giving out the checks, diverted the payroll checks drawn from the discharged worker to his own use. The most effective procedure for preventing this activity is to
       (1) Require written authorization for all employees added to or removed from the payroll.
       (2) Have a paymaster who has *no* other payroll responsibility distribute the payroll checks.
       (3) Have someone other than persons who prepare or distribute the payroll obtain custody of unclaimed payroll checks.
       (4) From time to time, rotate persons distributing the payroll.
    b. The CPA reviews Pyzi's payroll procedures. An example of an internal control weakness is to assign to a department supervisor the responsibility for
       (1) Distributing payroll checks to subordinate employees.
       (2) Reviewing and approving time reports for subordinates.
       (3) Interviewing applicants for subordinate positions prior to hiring by the personnel department.
       (4) Initiating requests for salary adjustments for subordinate employees.
    c. From the standpoint of good procedural control, distributing payroll checks to employees is best handled by the
       (1) Accounting department.
       (2) Personnel department.
       (3) Treasurer's department.
       (4) Employee's departmental supervisor.
    d. To minimize the opportunity for fraud, unclaimed salary checks should be

(1) Deposited in a special bank account.
(2) Kept in the payroll department.
(3) Left with the employee's supervisor.
(4) Held for the employee in the personnel department. (AICPA adapted)

DISCUSSION QUESTIONS AND PROBLEMS

17. Items *a* through *i* are selected questions typically found in internal control questionnaires used by auditors in evaluating controls in the payroll and personnel cycle. In using the questionnaire for a particular client, a yes response to a question indicates a possible strength in the system, whereas a no indicates a potential weakness.

a. Does an appropriate official authorize initial rates of pay and any subsequent change in rate?

b. Are written termination notices required that document reasons for termination?

c. Are formal records such as time clocks used for keeping time?

d. Is approval by a department head or foreman required for all time cards before they are submitted for payment?

e. Does anyone verify pay rates, overtime hours, and computations of gross payroll before payroll checks are prepared?

f. Does an adequate system exist for identifying jobs or products, such as work orders, job numbers, or some similar identification provided to employers to ensure proper coding of time records?

g. Are employees paid by checks prepared by persons independent of timekeeping?

h. Are employees required to show identification to receive paychecks?

i. Is a continuing record maintained of all unclaimed wages?

Required:

a. For each of the above questions, state the internal control objective(s) being fulfilled if the control is in effect.

b. For each control, list a compliance procedure to test its effectiveness.

c. For each of the above questions, identify the nature of the potential financial error(s) if the control is not in effect.

d. For each of the potential errors in part *c,* list a substantive audit procedure for determining whether a material error exists.

18. Following are some of the tests of transaction procedures frequently performed in the payroll and personnel cycle (each procedure is to be done on a sample basis):

a. Reconcile the monthly payroll total for direct manufacturing labor with labor cost distribution.

b. Examine the time card for the approval of a foreman.

c. Recompute hours on the time card and compare the total with the total hours for which the employee has been paid.

d. Compare the employee name, date, check number, and amounts on canceled checks with the payroll journal.

e. Trace the hours from the employee time cards to job tickets to make sure the total reconciles, and trace each job ticket to the job-cost record.

f. Account for a sequence of payroll checks in the payroll journal.

g. Select employees from the personnel file who have been terminated and determine whether their termination pay was in accordance with the union contract. As part of this procedure, examine two subsequent periods to determine whether the terminated employee is still being paid.

Required:

a. Identify whether each of the procedures is primarily a compliance or a substantive test.

b. State the purpose(s) of each of the procedures.

19. You are reviewing audit work papers containing a narrative description of the Tenney Corporation's factory payroll system. A portion of that narrative follows:

Factory employees punch time clock cards each day when entering or leaving the shop. At the end of each week the timekeeping department collects the time cards and prepares duplicate batch-control slips by department showing total hours and number of employees. The time cards and original batch-control slips are sent to the payroll accounting section. The second copies of the batch-control slips are filed by date.

In the payroll accounting section payroll transaction cards are keypunched from the information on the time cards, and a batch total card for each batch is keypunched from the batch-control slip. The time cards and batch-control slips are then filed by batch for possible reference. The payroll transaction cards and batch total card are sent to data processing where they are sorted by employee number within batch. Each batch is edited by a computer program which checks the validity of employee number against a master employee tape file and the total hours and number of employees against the batch total card. A detail printout by batch and employee number is produced which indicates batches that do not balance and invalid employee numbers. This printout is returned to payroll accounting to resolve all differences.

In searching for documentation you found a flowchart of the payroll system which included all appropriate symbols (American National Standards Institute, Inc.) but was only partially labeled. The portion of this flowchart described by the above narrative appears on page 426.

Required:

a. Number your answer 1 through 17. Next to the corresponding number of your answer, supply the appropriate labeling (document name, process description, or file order) applicable to each numbered symbol on the flowchart.

b. Flowcharts are one of the aids an auditor may use to determine and evaluate a client's internal control system. List advantages of using flowcharts in this context.

c. List several internal control strengths in the client's payroll system.

(AICPA adapted)

20. The following errors or omissions are included in the accounting records of Lathen Manufacturing Company:

a. Direct labor was unintentionally charged to job 620 instead of job 602 by the payroll clerk when he posted the labor distribution sheets. Job

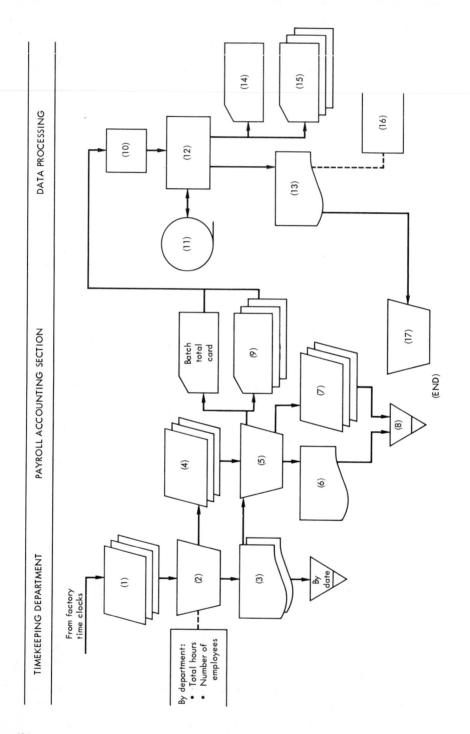

TIMEKEEPING DEPARTMENT   PAYROLL ACCOUNTING SECTION   DATA PROCESSING

From factory
time clocks

By department:
• Total hours
• Number of
  employees

(1)

(2)

(3)

By date

(4)

(5)

(6)

Batch
total
card

(9)

(7)

(8)

(17)

(END)

(10)

(11)

(12)

(13)

(14)

(15)

(16)

602 was completed and the costs were expensed in the current year, whereas job 620 was included in work in process.

b. Joe Block and Frank Demery take turns "punching in" for each other every few days. The absent employee comes in at noon and tells his foreman that he had car trouble or some other problem. The foreman doesn't know the employee is getting paid for the time.

c. The foreman submits a fictitious time card for a former employee each week and delivers the related payroll check to his house on the way home from work. They split the amount of the paycheck.

d. Employees frequently overlook recording their hours worked on job-cost tickets as required by the system. Many of the client's contracts are on a cost-plus basis.

e. The payroll clerk prepares a check to the same fictitious person every week, records the amount in the payroll journal, and submits it along with all other payroll checks for signature. When the checks are returned to him for distribution, he takes the check and deposits it in a special bank account bearing that person's name.

f. In withholding payroll taxes from employees, the payroll clerk deducts $.50 extra federal income taxes from several employees each week and credits the amount to his own employee earnings record.

g. The payroll clerk frequently forgets to record one or two checks in the payroll journal.

Required:

a. For each error, state a control that should have prevented the error from occurring on a continuing basis.

b. For each error, state a substantive audit procedure that could uncover the error.

21. In comparing total payroll tax expense with the preceding year, Merlin Brendin, CPA, observed a significant increase relative to the preceding year, even though the total number of employees had only increased from 175 to 195. To investigate the difference, he selected a large sample of payroll disbursement transactions and carefully tested the withholdings for each employee in the sample by referring to federal and state tax withholding schedules. In his test he found no exceptions; therefore, he concluded that payroll tax expense was fairly stated.

Required:

a. Evaluate Brendin's approach to testing payroll tax expense.

b. Discuss a more suitable approach for determining whether payroll tax expense was properly stated in the current year.

22. As part of the audit of McGree Plumbing and Heating, you have responsibility for testing the payroll and personnel cycle. Payroll is the largest single expense in the client's trial balance, and hourly wages make up most of the payroll total. A unique aspect of its business is the extensive overtime incurred by employees on some days. It is common for employees to work only three or four days during the week but to work long hours while they are on the job. McGree's management has found that this actually saves money, in spite of the large amount of overtime, because the union contract requires payment for all travel time. Since many of the employees' jobs require long travel times and extensive start-up costs, this policy is supported by both McGree and the employees.

You have already carefully evaluated and tested the payroll system and concluded that it contains no significant weaknesses. Your tests included tests of the time cards, withholdings, pay rates, the filing of all required tax returns, payroll checks, and all other aspects of payroll.

As part of the year-end tests of payroll, you are responsible for verifying all accrued payroll as well as accrued withheld payroll taxes. The accrued factory payroll includes the last six working days of the current year. The client has calculated accrued wages by taking 60 percent of the subsequent period's gross payroll and has recorded it as an adjusting entry to be reversed in the subsequent period.

Required:

List all audit procedures you would follow in verifying accrued payroll, withheld payroll taxes, and accrued payroll taxes.

23. You have been retained by the Ratliff Construction Company to verify the payroll expenses charged to Ratliff by a subcontractor retained on a series of cost-plus contracts over a two-year period. The management of Ratliff believes the subcontractor may have charged excessive costs to several jobs in the past few months and wants you to examine the subcontractor's records. Ratliff's contract permits the review and audit of all subcontractors' records as long as the cost is borne by Ratliff.

In examining the subcontractor's system, you observe that all charges to Ratliff are based on daily prenumbered job sheets prepared by each employee. Each day the employee fills out a job sheet that includes the employee's number, the jobs worked on, the hours worked for each job, and the date. At the end of each week the job sheets become the basis for preparing the payroll record. After the payroll is prepared, a copy is made of the daily job sheets as a basis for accumulating the total hours worked for any job. A copy of the employee's job sheets is inserted in a job folder for each project he worked on during the day. If he worked on more than one job, multiple copies of the job sheet are prepared and the hours for each job are circled before they are inserted. At the completion of a project, the total hours included in the job folder are totaled and multiplied by a standard labor rate. This becomes the basis for billing the prime contractor. The standard labor rate is the average of the union rate for all employees.

In reviewing the system, you observe that the subcontractor provides services for several subcontractors under several different types of arrangements. In some cases the company also acts as a prime contractor.

Required:

a. List the audit procedures you would perform in the verification of payroll in this situation and state the reason for performing each procedure.

b. What kind of audit report would you issue to Ratliff?

24. In the audit of Larnet Manufacturing Company, the auditor concluded that the system of internal control was inadequate because of the lack of segregation of duties. As a result, the decision was made to have a surprise payroll payoff one month before the client's balance sheet date. Since the auditor had never been involved in a payroll payoff, he did not know how to proceed.

Required:

a. What is the purpose of a surprise payroll payoff?

b. What other audit procedures can the auditor perform that may fulfill the same objectives?

c. Discuss the control procedures the auditor should require the client to observe when the surprise payroll payoff is taking place.

d. At the completion of the payroll payoff, there are frequently several unclaimed checks. What procedures should be followed for these?

25. The Kowal Manufacturing Company employs about fifty production workers and has the following payroll procedures.

The factory foreman interviews applicants and on the basis of the interview either hires or rejects the applicants. When the applicant is hired he prepares a W-4 form (Employee's Withholding Exemption Certificate) and gives it to the foreman. The foreman writes the hourly rate of pay for the new employee in the corner of the W-4 form and then gives the form to a payroll clerk as notice that the worker has been employed. The foreman verbally advises the payroll department of rate adjustments.

A supply of blank time cards is kept in a box near the entrance to the factory. Each worker takes a time card on Monday morning, fills in his name, and notes in pencil on the time card his daily arrival and departure times. At the end of the week the workers drop the time cards in a box near the door to the factory.

The completed time cards are taken from the box on Monday morning by a payroll clerk. Two payroll clerks divide the cards alphabetically between them, one taking the A to L section of the payroll and the other taking the M to Z section. Each clerk is fully responsible for her section of the payroll. She computes the gross pay, deductions, and net pay, posts the details to the employee's earnings records, and prepares and numbers the payroll checks. Employees are automatically removed from the payroll when they fail to turn in a time card.

The payroll checks are manually signed by the chief accountant and given to the foreman. The foreman distributes the checks to the workers in the factory and arranges for the delivery of the checks to the workers who are absent. The payroll bank account is reconciled by the chief accountant who also prepares the various quarterly and annual payroll tax reports.

Required:

a. List the most serious weaknesses in the system of internal control and state the errors that are likely to result from the weaknesses. In your audit of Kowal's payroll, what will you emphasize in your audit tests? Explain.

b. List your suggestions for improving the Kowal Manufacturing Company's system of internal control for the factory hiring practices and payroll procedures. (AICPA adapted)

26. During the first-year audit of Jones Wholesale Stationery you observe that commissions amount to almost 25 percent of total sales, which is somewhat higher than in previous years. Further investigation reveals that the industry typically has larger sales commissions than Jones and that there is significant variation in rates depending on the product sold.

At the time a sale is made, the salesman records his commission rate and the total amount of the commissions on the office copy of the sales invoice. When sales are recorded in the sales journal, the debit to sales commission expense and credit to accrued sales commission are also recorded. As part of recording the sales and sales commission expense, the accounts receivable clerk verifies the prices, quantities, commission rates, and all calculations on the sales invoices. When the sale is posted to the customer accounts receivable subsidiary ledger, the sales commission is posted to a salesman's commission ledger. On the fifteenth day after the end of the month the salesman is paid for the preceding month's sales commissions.

Required:

a. Develop an audit program to verify sales commission expense, assuming no audit tests have been conducted in any audit area to this point.
b. Develop an audit program to verify accrued sales commissions at the end of the year, assuming the tests you designed in part *a* resulted in no significant errors.

27. During your audit of the accounts of the Gelard Manufacturing Corporation, your assistant tells you that he has found errors in the computation of the wages of factory workers and he wants you to verify his work.

Your assistant has extracted from the union contract the following description of the systems for computing wages in various departments of the company. The contract provides that the minimum wage for a worker is his base rate, which is also paid for any "down time," time when the worker's machine is under repair or he is without work. The standard work week is 40 hours. The union contract also provides that workers be paid 150 percent of base rates for overtime production. The company is engaged in interstate commerce.

1. *Straight piecework.* The worker is paid at the rate of $.20 per piece produced.
2. *Percentage bonus plan.* Standard quantities of production per hour are established by the engineering department. The worker's average hourly production, determined from his total hours worked and his production, is divided by the standard quantity of production to determine his efficiency ratio. The efficiency ratio is then applied to his base rate to determine his hourly earnings for the period.
3. *Emerson Efficiency System.* A minimum wage is paid for production up to 66⅔ percent of standard output or "efficiency." When the worker's production exceeds 66⅔ percent of the standard output, he is paid at a bonus rate. The bonus rate is determined from the following table:

Efficiency	Bonus
Up to 66⅔%	0%
66⅔% – 79%	10%
80% – 99%	20%
100% –125%	45%

Your assistant has prepared the following schedule of information pertaining to certain workers for a weekly payroll selected for examination:

Worker	Wage Incentive Plan	Total Hours	Down Time Hours	Units Produced	Standard Units	Base Rate	Gross Wages per Books
Long	Straight piecework	40	5	400	—	$1.80	$ 82.00
Loro	Straight piecework	46	—	455*	—	1.80	91.00
Huck	Straight piecework	44	4	420†	—	1.80	84.00
Nini	Percentage bonus plan	40	—	250	200	2.20	120.00
Boro	Percentage bonus plan	40	—	180	200	1.90	67.00
Wiss	Emerson	40	—	240	300	2.10	92.00
Alan	Emerson	40	2	590	600‡	2.00	118.00

Includes 45 pieces produced during the 6 overtime hours.

†*Includes 50 pieces produced during the 4 overtime hours. The overtime, which was brought about by the "down time," was necessary to meet a production deadline.*

‡*Standard units for 40 hours production.*

Required:

a. Prepare a schedule comparing each individual's gross wages per books and his gross wages per your calculation. Computations of workers' wages should be in good form and labeled with the workers' names.

b. All the above errors, as well as others, were found in a weekly payroll selected for examination. The total number of errors was substantial. Discuss the courses of action you can take.

28. You are engaged in auditing the financial statements of Henry Brown, a large independent contractor. All employees are paid in cash because Brown believes this arrangement reduces clerical expenses and is preferred by his employees.

During the audit you find in the petty cash fund approximately $200, of which $185 is stated to be unclaimed wages. Further investigation reveals that Brown has installed the procedure of putting any unclaimed wages in the petty cash fund so that the cash can be used for disbursements. When the claimant to the wages appears, he is paid from the petty cash fund. Brown contends that this procedure reduces the number of checks drawn to replenish the petty cash fund and centers the responsibility for all cash on hand in one person inasmuch as the petty cash custodian distributes the pay envelopes.

Required:

a. Does Brown's system provide proper internal control of unclaimed wages? Explain fully.

b. Because Brown insists on paying salaries in cash, what procedures would you recommend to provide better internal control over unclaimed wages?

(AICPA adapted)

29. In many companies, labor costs represent a substantial percentage of total dollars expended in any one accounting period. One of the auditor's primary means of verifying payroll transactions is by a detailed payroll test.

You are making an annual examination of the Joplin Company, a medium-sized manufacturing company. You have selected a number of hourly employees for a detailed payroll test. The following worksheet outline has been prepared.

Column Number	Column Heading
1	Employee number
2	Employee name
3	Job classification
	Hours worked
4	Straight time
5	Premium time
6	Hourly rate
7	Gross earnings
	Deductions
8	FICA withheld
9	FIT withheld
10	Union dues
11	Hospitalization
12	Amount of check
13	Check and check number
14	Account number charged
15	Description of account

Required:

a. What factors should the auditor consider in selecting his sample of employees to be included in any payroll test?

b. Using the column numbers above as a reference, state the principal way(s) that the information in each column would be verified.

c. In addition to the payroll test, the auditor employs a number of other audit procedures in the verification of payroll transactions. List five additional procedures that may be employed.   (AICPA adapted)

30. The Generous Loan Company has one hundred branch loan offices. Each office has a manager and four or five subordinates who are employed by the manager. Branch managers prepare the weekly payroll, including their own salaries, and pay employees from cash on hand. The employee signs the payroll sheet signifying receipt of his salary. Hours worked by hourly personnel are inserted in the payroll sheet from time cards prepared by the employees and approved by the manager.

The weekly payroll sheets are sent to the home office along with other accounting statements and reports. The home office compiles employee earnings records and prepares all federal and state salary reports from the weekly payroll sheets.

Salaries are established by home office job-evaluation schedules. Salary adjustments, promotions, and transfers of full-time employees are approved by a home office salary committee based upon the recommendations of branch managers and area supervisors. Branch managers advise the salary committee of new full-time employees and terminations. Part-time and temporary employees are hired without referral to the salary committee.

Required:

a. Based upon your review of the payroll system, how might funds for payroll be diverted?

b. Prepare a payroll audit program to be used in the home office to audit the branch office payrolls of the Generous Loan Company.

(AICPA adapted)

14

Audit
of
the Acquisition and Payment Cycle

The third major transaction cycle discussed in this text is the acquisition of and payment for goods and services from outsiders. The acquisition of goods and services includes such items as the purchase of raw materials, equipment, supplies, utilities, repairs and maintenance, and research and development. The cycle does not include the acquisition and payment of employees' services or the internal transfers and allocations of costs within the organization. The former are a part of the payroll and personnel function, and the latter are audited as a part of the verification of individual assets or liabilities. The acquisition and payment cycle also excludes the acquisition and repayment of capital (interest-bearing debt and owner's equity), which are considered separately in Chapter 17.

The audit of the acquisition and payment cycle is studied in Chapters 14 and 15. In this chapter the basic format for discussing internal control cycles introduced in Chapter 8 and used again in Chapter 13 is repeated. The first part of the chapter deals with the nature of the acquisition and payment cycle, including documents and records, and primary functions and internal controls. The second part discusses tests of transactions for the cycle related to key internal controls. The third and final part covers direct tests of accounts payable, the major balance sheet account in the cycle. This last part gives special emphasis to the relationship between the tests of transitions and the direct tests performed. In Chapter 15 several other important balance sheet accounts which are a part of the acquisition and payment cycle are examined. These are manufacturing equipment, prepaid insurance, and accrued property taxes. The chapter also takes up direct tests of the income statement accounts included in the acquisition and payment cycle.

The large number and different types of accounts included in the acquisition and payment cycle distinguishes it from the other two previously studied cycles. For example, here are a few of the account titles the auditor is concerned with in a typical manufacturing company besides those indicated above:

- Raw material inventory
- Office supplies
- Rent
- Legal expense
- Fines and penalties
- Leasehold improvements
- Repairs and maintenance
- Insurance expense
- Officers' travel
- Accrued personal property taxes
- Retirement benefits
- Utilities

The way the accounting information flows through the various accounts in the acquisition and payment cycle is illustrated by T-accounts in Figure 14-1. To keep the illustration manageable, only the control accounts are shown for the three major categories of expenses used by most companies. For each control account, examples of the subsidiary expense accounts are also given.

Figure 14-1 shows that every transaction is either debited or credited to accounts payable. Because many companies make some purchases directly by check or through petty cash, the overview is an oversimplification. We assume that cash transactions are processed in the same manner as all others.

NATURE OF THE ACQUISITION AND PAYMENT CYCLE

The acquisition and payment cycle involves the decisions and processes necessary for obtaining the goods and services for operating a business. The cycle typically begins with the initiation of a purchase requisition by an authorized employee who needs the goods or services and ends with the payment for the benefits received. Although the discussion that follows deals with a small manufacturing company that makes tangible products for sale to third parties, the same principles apply to a service company, a government unit, or any other type of organization.

The *functions* and *flow of documents* for the acquisition and payment

FIGURE 14-1

ACCOUNTS IN THE ACQUISITION AND PAYMENT CYCLE

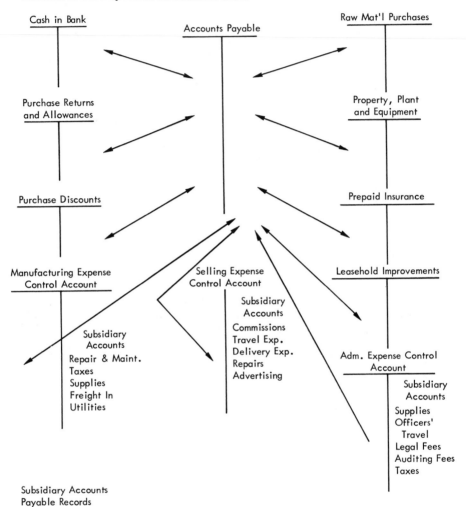

Subsidiary Accounts
Payable Records

Includes beginning balance, acquisitions,
payments, and the ending balance for each
customer. The total of all customer
balances equals the total in the accounts
payable control account.

cycle of a typical manufacturing company are illustrated in Figure 14-2.
The overview flowchart is meant to show how the information in Figure
14-1 is generated by a system. Many of the controls ordinarily integrated
into a system are not included at this point.

FIGURE 14-2

FLOWCHART OF THE ACQUISITION AND PAYMENT CYCLE

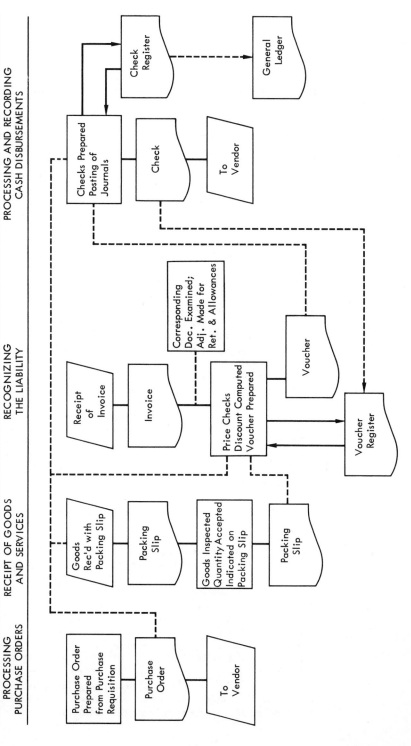

Documents and Records

To support the record flow in the acquisition and payment cycle, several important documents and records are used:

- *Purchase requisition*—A request for goods and services by an authorized employee. It may take the form of a request for such acquisitions as materials by a foreman or the storeroom supervisor, outside repairs by office or factory personnel, or insurance by the vice-president in charge of property and equipment.
- *Purchase order*—A document recording the description, quantity, and related information for goods and services the company intends to purchase. This document is frequently used to indicate authorization to procure goods and services.
- *Receiving report*—A document prepared at the time tangible goods are received which indicates the description of goods, the quantity received, the date received, and other relevant data. The receipt of goods and services in the normal course of business represents the date clients normally recognize the liability for an acquisition.
- *Vendor's invoice*—A document that indicates such things as the description and quantity of goods and services received, the price including freight, the cash discount terms, and the date of the billing. It is an essential document because it specifies the amount of money owed to the vendor for an acquisition.
- *Voucher*—A document frequently used by organizations to establish a formal means of recording and controlling acquisitions. Vouchers are the basis not only for recording acquisitions in the voucher register or purchase journal but also for making cash disbursements. Typically, the original copy of the voucher has a copy of the vendor's invoice, receiving report, and purchase order attached.
- *Voucher register*—A journal for recording the vouchers for the acquisition of goods and services. It usually includes several classifications for the most significant types of acquisitions, such as the purchase of inventory, repairs and maintenance, and supplies. There is also a column for miscellaneous debits and credits, and of course there must be a column for the credit to accounts payable. Individual transactions can be recorded in the voucher register, or several vouchers can be combined and recorded in summary form. When a voucher register is not used, the journal for recording acquisition transactions remains substantially unchanged, but it is called an *accounts payable journal* or *purchase journal*.
- *Check*—The means of paying for the acquisition when payment is due. After the check is signed by an authorized person, it is an asset. When cashed by the vendor and cleared by the client's bank, it is referred to as a canceled check.
- *Cash disbursements journal*—A journal for recording disbursements by check. It indicates the total cash paid, the debit to accounts payable at the amount for which the transaction being paid was recorded in the voucher register, the discounts taken, and other

debits and credits. The daily entries in the cash disbursements journal are supported by canceled checks.

- *Accounts payable subsidiary ledger*—A subsidiary ledger for recording the individual acquisitions, cash disbursements, and total balance due to each vendor. The total from the individual ledgers equals the total balance in accounts payable. Many companies do not maintain a formal accounts payable subsidiary ledger. These companies ordinarily pay on the basis of individual vouchers; therefore, the total of the unpaid vouchers equals the total accounts payable.
- *Vendor's statement*—A statement prepared monthly by the vendor indicating the beginning balance, acquisitions, payments to the vendor, and ending balance. These balances and activities are the vendor's representations of the transactions for the period and not the client's. Hence, except for disputed amounts and timing differences, the client's accounts, payable subsidiary ledger should be the same as the vendor's statement.

Functions in the Cycle and Internal Controls

A discussion of the primary functions in the acquisition and payment cycle will clarify what the auditor is trying to accomplish in the audit of the cycle. Four functions are involved:

1. Processing purchase orders
2. Receipt of goods and services
3. Recognizing the liability
4. Processing and recording cash disbursements

These functions are discussed in the order of their occurrence in a typical transaction cycle (see Figure 14-2). The emphasis is on the most important controls used to prevent errors in processing data and to ensure safety of assets.

Processing Purchase Orders. The request for goods or services by the client's personnel is the starting point for the cycle. The exact form of the request and the required approval depends upon the nature of the goods and services and the company policy.

Proper *authorization* for acquisitions is an essential part of this function because it ensures that the goods and services purchased are for authorized company purposes and it avoids the purchase of excessive or unnecessary items. Most companies permit general authorization for the purchase of regular operating needs such as inventory at one level and acquisitions of capital assets or similar items at another. For example, purchases of permanent assets in excess of a specified dollar limit may require board of director action; items purchased relatively infrequently, such as insurance policies and long-term service contracts, are approved by certain officers; supplies and services costing less than a designated amount are approved by foremen and department heads; and some types of raw materials and supplies are reordered automatically whenever they fall to a predetermined level. After the acquisition has been approved, there must be an *initiation of an order* to purchase the goods or services. An order is issued to a vendor for a specified item at a certain price to be delivered at or by a designated time. The order is usually in writing and is a legal document that is an offer to buy. For most routine items, a purchase order is used to indicate the offer.

It is common for companies to establish purchasing departments to ensure an adequate quality of goods and services at a minimum price. For good internal control, the purchasing department should not be responsible for authorizing the acquisition or receiving of the goods. All purchase orders should be prenumbered and should include sufficient columns and spaces to minimize the likelihood of unintentional omissions on the form when goods are ordered.

Receipt of Goods and Services. The receipt by the company of goods or services from the vendor is a critical point in the cycle because it is the point at which most companies first recognize the associated liability on their records. When goods are received, adequate control requires examination for description, quantity, timely arrival, and condition.

Most companies have the receiving department initiate a receiving report as evidence of the receipt and examination of the goods. One copy is normally sent to the storeroom and another to the accounts payable department for their information needs. To prevent theft and misuse, it is important that the goods be *physically controlled* from the time of their receipt until they are disposed of. The personnel in the receiving department should be independent of the storeroom personnel and the accounting department. Finally, the accounting records should transfer responsibility for the goods as they are transferred from receiving to storage and from storage to manufacturing.

Recognizing the Liability. The proper recognition of the liability for the receipt of goods and services requires *accurate and prompt* recording. The initial recording has a significant effect on the recorded financial statements and the actual cash disbursement; therefore, great care must be taken to include only valid company acquisitions at the correct amount.

The accounts payable department typically has the responsibility for verifying the propriety of acquisitions and for recording them in the voucher register or accounts payable journal. When the accounts payable department receives a vendor's invoice, a comparison should be made of the descriptions, prices, quantities, terms, and freight on the invoice with the information on the purchase order and, where applicable, the receiving report. Typically, extensions and footings are verified, an account distribution is entered on the invoice, and if a voucher system is used, the documents are assigned a voucher number. Next, the acquisition transaction is recorded in the voucher register as a liability and an expense or asset, and the amount is posted in the accounts payable subsidiary record.

An important control in the accounts payable department is to require that those personnel who record disbursements of cash *do not have access* to cash, marketable securities, and other assets. Adequate documents and records, proper procedures for record keeping, and independent checks on performance are also necessary controls in the accounts payable function.

Processing and Recording Cash Disbursements. For most companies, the vouchers are held by the accounts payable department until the time of payment. Payment is usually made by check in a multicopy format, with the original going to the payee, one copy filed with the voucher, and another filed alphabetically by payee. In most cases individual checks are recorded in the cash disbursements journal, but sometimes a numerical file of check copies is maintained which serves as a cash disbursements journal.

The most important controls in the cash disbursements function include the signing of checks by an individual with proper authority, separation of responsibilities for signing the checks and performing the accounts payable function, and careful examination of the supporting documentation by the check signer at the time the check is signed.

The checks should be prenumbered and printed on special paper, which makes it difficult to alter the name or amount. Care should be taken to physically control blank, voided, and signed checks before they are mailed. It is also important to have a method of canceling the supporting documents to prevent their reuse as support for another check at a later time. A common method is to write the check number on the supporting documents.

TESTS OF TRANSACTIONS

The most time-consuming accounts to verify by direct tests of financial balances in a typical audit are accounts receivable, inventory, permanent assets, accounts payable, and expense accounts. Of these five accounts, four are directly related to the acquisition and payment cycle. The net time savings can be dramatic if the auditor can reduce the direct tests in the accounts by spending time verifying the effectiveness of the acquisition system by tests of transactions. It should not be surprising, therefore, that tests of transactions for the acquisition and payment cycle receive a considerable amount of attention in well-conducted audits, especially when the client has effective controls.

The tests of transactions for the acquisition and payment cycle are divided into the two broad areas of *tests of acquisitions* and *tests of payments*. The acquisition tests concern three of the four functions discussed earlier in the chapter: processing purchase orders, receipt of goods and services, and recognizing the liability. The tests of payments concern the fourth function, processing and recording cash disbursements. The seven objectives previously used for other cycles provide the frame of reference for discussing the audit procedures for these two areas.

Tests for Verifying Acquisitions

Key internal controls, common compliance tests, and common substantive tests for each of the internal control and audit objectives are included in Figure 14-3. An assumption underlying the internal controls and audit procedures is the existence of a separate purchase journal for recording all acquisitions.

For each objective, the auditor must go through the same process of logic that has been discussed in previous chapters. First he must understand the system to determine which controls exist. After the auditor is aware of all existing controls for the objective, he can make a preliminary evaluation of the strengths and weaknesses of the system. At this point he must make a decision as to which strengths (controls) he intends to rely on to reduce substantive tests. These controls must be tested for compliance and evaluated for effectiveness. The substantive tests can be determined for the objective largely on the basis of this evaluation. After the auditor has developed the audit procedures for each of the objectives, the procedures can be combined into an audit program that can be efficiently performed.

In studying the summary in Figure 14-3, it is important to relate internal controls to audit objectives, compliance tests to internal controls, and substantive tests to audit objectives and strengths and weaknesses in the system. It should be kept in mind that the set of procedures for a particular audit engagement will vary with the internal controls and other circumstances.

Four of the seven audit objectives for acquisitions deserve special attention. A discussion of each of these four essential objectives follows:

Recorded Acquisitions Are for Goods and Services Received, Consistent with the Best Interests of the Client (Validity). If the auditor is satisfied that the controls are adequate for this objective, tests for improper and invalid transactions can be greatly reduced. Adequate controls are likely to prevent the client from including as a business expense or asset those transactions that primarily benefit management or other employees rather than the entity being audited. In some instances improper transactions are obvious, such as the acquisition of unauthorized personal items by employees or the actual embezzlement of cash by recording a fraudulent purchase in the voucher register. In other instances the propriety of a transaction is more difficult to evaluate, such as the payment of officers' memberships to country clubs, expense-paid vacations to foreign countries for members of management and their families, and management-approved illegal payments to officials of foreign countries. If the controls over improper or invalid transactions are inadequate, extensive examining of supporting documentation is necessary.

Existing Acquisitions Are Recorded. Failure to record the acquisition of goods and services received directly affects the balance in accounts payable. The auditor can rely on the system and thereby reduce the direct tests of accounts payable if he is confident that all acquisitions are recorded on a timely and accurate basis. Since the audit of accounts payable generally takes a considerable amount of audit time, the reliance on existing controls can significantly reduce audit costs.

When a client uses a perpetual inventory system, the tests of inventory can also be significantly reduced if the auditor believes the perpetuals are reliable. The controls over the acquisitions included in the perpetuals are normally tested as a part of the tests of transactions for acquisitions, and the controls over this objective play a key role in the audit. The inclusion of both quantity and unit costs in the inventory perpetual records permits a reduction in the tests of the physical count and the unit costs of inventory if the controls are operating effectively.

Acquisitions Are Correctly Valued. Since the valuation of many asset, liability, and expense accounts depends on the correct recording of transactions in the purchase journal, the extent of direct tests of many balance sheets and expense accounts depends on the auditor's evaluation of the effectiveness of the internal controls over the correct valuation of acquisition transactions. For example, if the auditor believes the permanent assets are correctly valued in the books of original entry, it is acceptable to vouch fewer current period acquisitions than if the controls are inadequate.

Acquisitions Are Correctly Classified. The auditor can reduce the direct tests of certain individual accounts if he believes the system is adequate to provide reasonable assurance of correct classification in the purchase journal. Although all accounts are affected to some degree by effective controls over classification, the two areas most affected are current period acquisitions of permanent assets and all expense accounts arising from the voucher register, such as repairs and maintenance, utilities, and advertising. Since vouching of current period permanent asset acquisitions for valuation and classification and verifying the classification of expense accounts are relatively time-consuming audit procedures, the saving in audit time can be significant.

Audit Procedures for Verifying Cash Disbursements

The basic format used for acquisitions is also used in Figure 14-4 for the internal controls and tests of transaction procedures for cash disbursements. The assumption underlying these controls and audit procedures is the existence of a separate cash disbursements and purchase journal. The comments previously made about the methodology and process for developing audit procedures for acquisitions apply equally to cash disbursements.

Once the auditor has decided on procedures, the acquisition and cash disbursements tests are typically performed concurrently. For example, for a transaction selected for examination from the purchase journal, the vendor's invoice and the receiving report are examined at the same time

Figure 14-3

Summary of Tests of Acquisitions

Internal Control and Audit Objectives	Key Internal Controls	Common Compliance Tests	Common Substantive Tests
Recorded acquisitions are for goods and services received, consistent with the best interests of the client (validity).	• Existence of purchase requisition, purchase order, receiving report, and vendor's invoice attached to the voucher. • Approval of acquisitions at the proper level. • Cancelation of documents to prevent their reuse. • Internal verification of vendor's invoices, receiving reports, purchase orders, and purchase requisitions.	• Examine documents in voucher for existence. • Examine indication of approval. • Examine indication of cancelation. • Examine indication of internal verification.	• Examine underlying documents for reasonableness and authenticity (vendor's invoices, receiving reports, purchase orders, and requisitions). • Trace inventory purchases to perpetual records. • Examine permanent assets acquired. • Review the purchases journal, general ledger, and accounts payable subsidiary records for large or unusual amounts.
Acquisition transactions are authorized.	• Approval of acquisitions at the proper level.	• Examine indication of approval.	• Examine supporting documentation for propriety.
Existing acquisition transactions are recorded.	• Purchase orders are prenumbered and accounted for. • Receiving reports are prenumbered and accounted for. • Vouchers are prenumbered and accounted for.	• Account for a sequence of purchase orders. • Account for a sequence of receiving reports. • Account for a sequence of vouchers.	• Trace from a file of receiving reports to the purchases journal. • Trace from a file of vouchers to the purchases journal.

Internal Control and Audit Objectives	Key Internal Controls	Common Compliance Tests	Common Substantive Tests
Recorded acquisition transactions are correctly valued.	• Internal verification of calculations and amounts.	• Examine indication of internal verification.	• Compare recorded transactions in the purchases journal with the vendor's invoice, receiving report, and other supporting documentation. • Recompute the clerical accuracy on vendor's invoices, including discounts and freight.
Acquisition transactions are properly classified.	• Adequate chart of accounts. • Internal verification of classification.	• Examine procedures manual and chart of accounts. • Examine indication of internal verification.	• Compare classification with chart of accounts by reference to vendor's invoices.
Acquisitions are recorded on a timely basis.	• Procedures require recording transactions as soon as possible after the goods and services have been received. • Internal verification.	• Examine procedures manual and observe whether unrecorded vendor's invoices exist. • Examine indication of internal verification.	• Compare dates of receiving reports and vendor's invoices with dates in the purchase journal.
Acquisition transactions are properly included in the accounts payable and inventory subsidiaries; they are properly summarized.	• Internal verification.	• Examine indication of internal verification.	• Test clerical accuracy, e.g., footing journals and tracing postings to general ledger and accounts payable and inventory subsidiaries.

Figure 14-4

Summary of Tests of Cash Disbursements

Internal Control and Audit Objectives	Key Internal Controls	Common Compliance Tests	Common Substantive Tests
Recorded cash disbursements are for goods and services actually received.	• Adequate segregation of duties between accounts payable and custody of signed checks. • Examination of supporting documentation before signing of checks by an authorized person. • Internal verification.	• Discuss with personnel and observe activities. • Discuss with personnel and observe activities. • Examine indication of internal verification.	• Trace the canceled check to the related purchases journal entry and examine for payee name and amount. • Examine canceled check for authorized signature, proper endorsement, and cancellation by the bank. • Review the cash disbursements journal, general ledger, and accounts payable subsidiary records for large or unusual amounts.
Recorded cash disbursement transactions are properly authorized.	• Approval of payment on supporting documents at the time checks are signed.	• Examine indication of approval.	• Examine supporting documents as a part of the tests of acquisitions.
Existing cash disbursement transactions are recorded.	• Checks are prenumbered and accounted for. • A bank reconciliation is prepared monthly by an employee independent of recording cash disbursements or custody of assets.	• Account for a sequence of checks. • Examine bank reconciliations and observe their preparation.	• Reconcile recorded cash disbursements with the cash disbursements on the bank statement (proof of cash disbursements).

Internal Control and Audit Objectives	Key Internal Controls	Common Compliance Tests	Common Substantive Tests
Recorded cash disbursement transactions are properly valued.	• Internal verification of calculations and amounts. • Monthly preparation of a bank reconciliation by an independent person.	• Examine indication of approval. • Examine bank reconciliations and observe their preparation.	• Compare canceled checks with the related purchase journal and cash disbursements journal entries. • Recompute cash discounts. • Prepare a proof of cash disbursements.
Cash disbursement transactions are properly classified.	• Adequate chart of accounts. • Internal verification of classification.	• Examine procedures manual and chart of accounts. • Examine indication of internal verification.	• Compare classification with chart of accounts by reference to vendor's invoices and purchase journal.
Cash disbursements are recorded on a timely basis.	• Procedures require recording of transactions as soon as possible after the check has been signed. • Internal verification.	• Examine procedures manual and observe whether unrecorded checks exist. • Examine indication of internal verification.	• Compare dates on canceled checks with the cash disbursements journal. • Compare dates on canceled checks with the bank cancelation date.
Cash disbursement transactions are properly included in the accounts payable subsidiary; they are properly summarized.	• Internal verification.	• Examine indication of internal verification.	• Test clerical accuracy, e.g., footing journals and tracing postings to general ledger and accounts payable subsidiary.

as the related canceled check. Thus the verification is speeded up without reducing the effectiveness of the tests.

Attributes Sampling for Tests of Acquisition and Payment Transactions

Due to the importance of tests of transactions for acquisitions and payments, the use of attributes sampling is common in this audit area. The approach to using attributes sampling for tests of acquisitions and payments is basically the same as for the tests of sales transactions discussed in Chapter 9. It should be noted, however, with particular reference to the most essential objectives presented earlier, that most of the important attributes in the acquisition and payment cycle have a direct monetary effect on the accounts. Further, many of the types of errors that might be found represent a misstatement of earnings and are of significant concern to the auditor. For example, there may be inventory cutoff errors, or direct misrecording of an expense amount. Because of this, the desired upper precision limit selected by the auditor in tests of many of the attributes in this cycle is relatively low. Since the amounts of individual transactions in the cycle cover a wide range, it is also common to segregate very large and unusual items and test them on a 100 percent basis.

ACCOUNTS PAYABLE

Accounts payable are *unpaid obligations* for goods and services received in the ordinary course of business. It is sometimes difficult to distinguish between accounts payable and accrued liabilities, but it is useful to define a liability as an accounts payable if the total amount of the obligation is *known and owed at the balance sheet date*. The accounts payable account therefore includes obligations for the acquisition of raw materials, equipment, utilities, repairs, and many other types of goods and services that were received before the end of the year. The great majority of accounts payable can also be recognized by the existence of vendor's invoices for the obligation. Accounts payable should also be distinguished from interest-bearing obligations. If an obligation includes the payment of interest, it should properly be recorded as a note payable, contract payable, mortgage payable, or bond.

Internal Controls

The effect of the client's internal controls in the acquisition and payment cycle on accounts payable tests can be illustrated by two examples. In the first example, assume the client has a highly effective system of recording and paying for acquisitions. The receipt of goods is promptly documented by prenumbered receiving reports; prenumbered vouchers are promptly and efficiently prepared and recorded in the voucher register and the accounts payable subsidiary ledger. Payments are also made promptly when due, and the disbursements are immediately recorded in the cash disbursements journal and the accounts payable subsidiary records. On a monthly basis, individual accounts payable subsidiary records are reconciled with vendor's statements, and the total is compared with the general ledger by an independent person. Under these circumstances, the verification of accounts payable should require little audit effort once the auditor concludes that the system is operating effectively. In the second example, assume the client defers recording acquisitions until cash disbursements are made, receiving reports are not used, and, because of a weak cash position, bills are frequently paid several months after their due date. When an auditor faces such a situation, there is a high likelihood of an understatement of accounts payable; therefore, under these circumstances, extensive direct tests are necessary to determine whether accounts payable is properly stated at the balance sheet date.

The most important controls over accounts payable have already been discussed as a part of the acquisition and payment cycle. In addition to those controls, it is important to have a monthly reconciliation of vendor's statements with recorded liabilities and subsidiary records with the general ledger. This should be done by an independent person.

Overall Audit Objectives

The overall audit objectives in the verification of accounts payable are to determine whether

1. All significant accounts payable incurred as of the balance sheet date are reflected in the statements at the proper amounts.
2. Liabilities are properly described and classified.

The auditor should recognize the difference in emphasis between the audit of liabilities and the audit of assets. When assets are being verified, attention is focused on making certain that the balance in the account is not overstated. The validity of recorded assets is constantly questioned and verified by confirmation, physical examination, and examination of supporting documents. The auditor should certainly not ignore the possibility of assets being understated, but the fact remains that the auditor is more concerned about the possibility of overstatement than understatement. The opposite approach is taken in verifying liability balances; that is, the main focus is on the discovery of understated or omitted liabilities.

The difference in emphasis in auditing assets and liabilities results directly from the *legal liability of CPAs*. If equity investors, creditors, and other users determine subsequent to the issuance of the audited financial statements that owner's equity was materially overstated, a lawsuit against the CPA firm is fairly likely. Since an overstatement of owner's equity can arise either from an overstatement of assets or from an understatement of liabilities, it is natural for CPAs to emphasize those two types of misstatements. The probability of a successful lawsuit against a CPA for failing to discover an understatement of owner's equity is far less likely.

Nevertheless, the auditing profession must avoid too much emphasis on protecting users from overstatements of owner's equity at the expense of considering understatements. If assets are consistently understated and liabilities are consistently overstated for large numbers of audited companies, the decision-making value of financial statement information is likely to decline. Therefore, even though it is natural for auditors to emphasize the possibility of overstating assets and understating liabilities, the uncovering of the opposite types of misstatements is also a significant responsibility.

Audit Tests of Accounts Payable

The same detailed audit objectives, with minor modifications, that were used as a frame of reference for verifying accounts receivable in Chapter 10 are also applicable to liabilities. The most obvious difference in verifying liabilities is the nonapplicability of the ownership objective. Ownership is an important part of verifying assets, but not of verifying liabilities. The second difference was discussed above: in auditing liabilities, the emphasis is on the search for understatements rather than for overstatements. The following is a discussion of the appropriate evidence accumulation for six of the eight detailed direct test audit objectives. In addition to the exclusion of ownership, disclosure is not discussed as there are no significant disclosure problems with accounts payable.

Mechanical Accuracy

The usual starting point for the tests of accounts payable is a *list of accounts payable* provided to the auditor by the client. Typical tests of the schedule include footing it and tracing the total to the general ledger. If the client has a subsidiary ledger for accounts payable that has been tested as part of the tests of the acquisition and payment cycle, it is common to trace a sample of vendors' names and balances from the list of accounts payable to the subsidiary ledger.

Overall Reasonableness

In most instances, analytical tests of expense account balances are more likely to reveal errors in accounts payable than are overall reasonableness tests directly applied to accounts payable. For example, the comparison of a total expense, such as repairs and maintenance, with that of the previous year may indicate the failure to include an unpaid repair in accounts payable. On the other hand, it is desirable to examine the list of outstanding accounts payable for the possibility of nonvendor accounts, interest-bearing liabilities, or other unusual items. It may also be desirable to compare the preceding year's accounts payable list with the current year's list to determine whether the vendors that had large balances at the beginning of the year were also included on the balance sheet date. It may be useful to compute ratios and compare the results with previous years as an indication of potential errors. For example, the auditor can compute the ratio of raw material purchases to accounts payable for raw materials, and accounts payable to total current liabilities.

Existence

In satisfying the existence objective, usually the auditor's emphasis is to determine whether the client has *omitted* accounts payable obligations from the accounts payable list. (The proper valuation of accounts payable is normally verified simultaneously, but for purposes of understanding the objectives, valuation is discussed as a separate objective.) The extent of tests to uncover unrecorded accounts payable, which is frequently referred to as the *search for unrecorded accounts payable,* depends heavily on the reliability of the system of internal control and the materiality of the potential balance in the account. The audit procedures that follow are typical tests:

1. *Examine underlying documentation for subsequent cash disbursements.* The purpose of this audit procedure is to uncover payments made in the subsequent accounting period that represent liabilities at the balance sheet date. The supporting documentation is examined to determine whether a payment was for a current period obligation. For example, if inventory was received prior to the balance sheet date, it will be so indicated on the receiving report. Frequently documentation for payments made in the subsequent period are examined for several weeks, especially when the client does not pay its bills on a timely basis. Any payment that is for a current period obligation should be traced to the accounts payable list to make sure it has been included as a liability.

2. *Examine underlying documentation for bills that still have not been paid several weeks after the end of the year.* This procedure is carried out in the same manner as the preceding one and serves the same purpose. The only difference is that it is done for unpaid obligations near the end of the examination rather than for obligations that have already been paid. For example, in an audit with a March 31 year-end, if the auditor examines the supporting documentation for checks paid until June 28, bills that are still unpaid at that date should be examined to determine whether they are obligations of the year ended March 31.

3. *Trace vendor's statements that show a balance due to the accounts payable list.* If the client maintains a file of vendor's statements, any statement indicating a balance due can be traced to the listing to make sure it is included as an accounts payable.

4. *Send confirmations to vendors with which the client does business.* Although the use of confirmations for accounts payable is less common

than for accounts receivable, it is often used to test for vendors omitted from the accounts payable list, omitted transactions, and misstated account balances. The sending of confirmations to active vendors for which a balance has not been included in the accounts payable list is a useful means of searching for omitted amounts. This type of confirmation is commonly referred to as *zero balance confirmation*. Additional discussion of confirmation of accounts payable is deferred until the end of the chapter.

5. *Trace receiving reports issued before year-end to related vendor's invoices.* All merchandise received before the end of the accounting period, indicated by the issuance of a receiving report, should be included as accounts payable. By tracing receiving reports issued at and before year-end to vendor's invoices and making sure they are included in accounts payable, the auditor is testing for unrecorded obligations.

In addition to the search for omitted accounts payable through the use of the five audit procedures just discussed, the auditor may also want to test for the *validity of recorded amounts*. Invalid accounts payable are uncovered using the same evidence that is used in searching for omitted amounts, but the starting point for performing the tests differs. In testing for omitted accounts, the auditor traces from evidence such as vendor's invoices, receiving reports, vendor's statements, and confirmations to the accounts payable list. In testing for invalid accounts, he traces from the accounts payable list to supporting documents such as vendor's invoices and receiving reports to make certain that the amounts should be included in accounts payable. The examination of a vendor's statement and the confirmation of amounts on the listing are also means for testing for validity. Because the auditor is primarily concerned about the understatement of liabilities, tests for omitted accounts ordinarily receive more attention than tests for invalid ones.

Valuation

The valuation of individual vendors' balances is accomplished by the same five steps that were discussed for existence, but the auditor is verifying the total amount of the liability to the vendor in addition to the existence of the liability. For example, in comparing the outstanding balance on a vendor's statement with the related balance on the accounts payable list, the existence objective is satisfied if the vendor's name is included in the list even though the amount may be wrong. On the other hand, the valuation objective is fulfilled only when the recorded amounts are determined to be correctly stated.

Classification

The auditor's primary concern in classification is that records clearly distinguish between accounts payable to vendors, notes payable, and liabilities to affiliates and other related parties. If there are long-term liabilities to vendors, they should be separated from current accounts payable regardless of whether or not they are interest bearing. It is also necessary to evaluate whether debit balances in accounts payable are sufficiently material to require reclassification as assets.

The auditor can evaluate the existence of any improper classifications by reviewing the list of accounts payable, examining the accounts payable subsidiary records, examining supporting documents, and discussing such matters with the client. An understanding of the nature of the client's business, including relationships with affiliates, is important in performing this review.

Cutoff

The five audit steps discussed under the existence objective are all concerned with ascertaining that accounts payable obligations are recorded in the proper period. This is a problem of cutoff. Since these procedures have already been discussed as a part of the existence objective, only two aspects of cutoff are enlarged upon here: the examination of receiving reports and the determination of the amount of inventory in transit.

In determining that the accounts payable cutoff is correct, *it is essential that the cutoff tests be coordinated with the physical observation of inventory.* For example, assume an inventory acquisition for $40,000 is received late in the afternoon of December 31, after the physical inventory is completed. If the acquisition is included in accounts payable and purchases, but excluded from inventory, the result is an understatement of net earnings of $40,000. On the other hand, if the acquisition is excluded from both inventory and accounts payable, there is an error in the balance sheet, but the income statement is correct. The only way the auditor will know which type of error has occurred is to coordinate cutoff tests with the observation of inventory.

The cutoff information for purchases should be obtained *during the physical observation* of the inventory. At this time the auditor should review the procedures in the receiving department to determine that all inventory received was counted, and he should record in his working papers the last receiving report number of inventory included in the physical count. During the year-end field work, the auditor should then test the accounting records for cutoff. He should trace receiving report numbers to the accounts payable records to verify that they are correctly included or excluded from accounts payable. For example, assume the last receiving report number representing inventory included in the physical count was 3167. The auditor should record this document number and subsequently trace it and several preceding numbers to their related vendor's invoice and to the accounts payable list or the accounts payable subsidiary records to determine that they are all included. Similarly, accounts payable for purchases recorded on receiving reports numbered larger than 3167 should be excluded from accounts payable.

When the client's physical inventory takes place before the last day of the year, it is still necessary to perform an accounts payable cutoff at the time of the physical count in the manner described in the preceding paragraph. In addition, the auditor must verify whether all acquisitions taking place between the physical count and the end of the year were added to the physical inventory and accounts payable. For example, if the client takes the physical count on December 27 for a December 31 year-end, the cutoff information is taken as of December 27. During the year-end field work, the auditor must first test to determine whether the cutoff was accurate as of December 27. After he is satisfied that the December 27 cutoff is accurate, the auditor must test whether all inventory received subsequent to the physical count, but before the balance sheet date, was added to inventory and accounts payable by the client.

Reliability of Vendor's Statements, Vendor's Invoices, and Confirmations

In deciding upon the appropriate evidence to accumulate for verifying accounts payable, it is essential that the auditor understand the relative reliability of the three primary types of evidence ordinarily used: vendor's invoices, vendor's statements, and confirmations.

Distinction between Vendor's Invoices and Vendor's Statements. In verifying the valuation of an account balance, the auditor should make a major distinction between vendor's invoices and vendor's statements. In examining vendor's invoices and related supporting documents, such as receiving reports and purchase orders, the auditor gets highly reliable *evidence of the valuation of individual transactions.* A vendor's statement is not as desirable as invoices for verifying individual transactions because a statement only includes the total amount of the transaction. The units acquired, price, freight, and other data are not included. On the other hand, a statement has the advantage of including the ending balance according to the vendor's records. Which of these two documents is better for verifying the correct balance in accounts payable? *The vendor's statement is superior for verifying accounts payable* because it includes the ending balance. The auditor could compare existing vendor's invoices with the client's list and still not uncover missing ones, which is the primary concern in accounts payable. Which of these two documents is better for testing acquisitions in tests of transactions? *The vendor's invoice is superior for verifying tests of transactions* because the auditor is verifying individual transactions and the invoice shows the details of the acquisitions.

Difference between Vendor's Statements and Confirmations. The most important distinction between a vendor's statement and a confirmation of accounts payable is the source of the information. A vendor's statement has been prepared by an independent third party, but it is in the hands of the client at the time the auditor examines it. This provides the client with an opportunity to alter a vendor's statement or not make particular statements available to the auditor. A confirmation of accounts payable, which normally is a request for an itemized statement sent directly to the CPA's office, provides the same information as the statement, but the information can be regarded as more reliable. In addition, confirmations of accounts payable frequently include a request for information about notes and acceptances payable as well as consigned inventory that is owned by the vendor but stored on the client's premises. An illustration of a typical accounts payable confirmation request is given in Figure 14-5.

Due to the availability of vendor's statements and vendor's invoices, which are both relatively reliable evidence because they originate from a third party, the *confirmation of accounts payable is less common than confirmation of accounts receivable*. If the client has an adequate system of internal control and vendor's statements are available for examination, confirmations are normally not sent. On the other hand, when the client's system is weak, when statements are not available, or when the auditor questions the client's integrity, it is desirable to send confirmation requests to vendors. The number of confirmations sent should depend upon the quality of the controls, the materiality of accounts payable, and the number of accounts outstanding. Due to the emphasis on understatements of liability accounts, the sample should include large accounts, active accounts, accounts with a zero balance, and a representative sample of all others.

In most instances where accounts payable are confirmed, it is done shortly after the balance sheet date. However, if the system of internal control is strong, it may be possible to confirm accounts payable at an interim date as a test of the quality of the system. Then if the confirmation indicates that the controls are ineffective, it is possible to design other audit procedures to test accounts payable at year-end.

When vendor's statements are examined or confirmations are received, there must be a *reconciliation* of the statement or confirmation with the accounts payable list. Frequently differences are caused by inventory in transit, checks mailed by the client but not received by the vendor at the statement date, and delays in processing the accounting records. The reconciliation is of the same general nature as that discussed in Chapter 10 for accounts receivable. The documents typically used to reconcile the balances on the accounts payable list with the confirmation or vendor's statement include receiving reports, vendor's invoices, and canceled checks.

REVIEW QUESTIONS

1. List five asset accounts, three liability accounts, and ten expense accounts included in the acquisition and payment cycle for a typical manufacturing company.
2. List one possible internal control for each of the seven internal control objectives for cash disbursements. For each internal control, list a compliance procedure to test the effectiveness of the control.

FIGURE 14-5

ACCOUNTS PAYABLE CONFIRMATION REQUEST

Roger Mead Inc.

January 15,1979

Roger Mead, Inc.
2116 Stewart Street
Waynewill, Kentucky 36021

Gentlemen:

Our auditors, Murry and Rogers, CPAs, are making an examination of our financial statements. For this purpose, please furnish them with the following information as of December 31, 1978:

(1) Itemized statements of our accounts payable to you showing all unpaid items;

(2) A complete list of any notes and acceptances payable to you (including any which have been discounted) showing the original date, dates due, original amount, unpaid balance, collateral and endorsers; and

(3) An itemized list of your merchandise consigned to us.

Your prompt attention to this request will be appreciated. An envelope is enclosed for your reply.

Yours truly,

____

3. Evaluate the following statement by an auditor concerning tests of acquisitions and payments: "In selecting the acquisitions and disbursements sample for testing, the best approach is to select a random month and test every transaction for the period. Using this approach enables me to thoroughly understand the system because I have examined everything that happened during the period. As a part of the monthly test, I also test the beginning and ending bank reconciliations and prepare a proof of cash for the month. At the completion of these tests I feel I can evaluate the effectiveness of the system."

4. What is the importance of cash discounts to the client and how can the auditor verify whether they are being taken in accordance with company policy?

5. What are the similarities and differences in the objectives of the following two procedures: (1) select a random sample of receiving reports and trace them to related vendor's invoices and purchase journal entries, comparing the vendor's name, type of material and quantity purchased, and total amount of the acquisition; and (2) select a random sample of purchases journal entries and trace them to related vendor's invoices and receiving reports, comparing the vendor's name, type of material and quantity purchased, and total amount of the acquisition.

6. If an audit client does not have prenumbered checks, what type of error has a greater chance of occurring? Under the circumstances, what audit procedure can the auditor use to compensate for the weakness?

7. What is meant by a voucher and a voucher register? Explain how their use can improve an organization's internal controls.

8. Explain why most auditors consider the receipt of goods and services the most important point in the acquisition and payment cycle.

9. Explain the relationship between tests of the acquisition and payment cycle and tests of inventory. Give specific examples of how these two types of tests affect each other.

10. Explain the relationship between tests of the acquisition and payment cycle and tests of accounts payable. Give specific examples of how these two types of tests affect each other.

11. The CPA examines all unrecorded invoices on hand as of February 29, 19X8, the last day of field work. Which of the following errors is most likely to be uncovered by this procedure?
    a. Accounts payable are overstated at December 31, 19X7.
    b. Accounts payable are understated at December 31, 19X7.
    c. Operating expenses are overstated for the twelve months ended December 31, 19X7.
    d. Operating expenses are overstated for the two months ended February 29, 19X8.   (AICPA adapted)

12. Explain why it is common for auditors to send confirmation requests to vendors with "zero balances" on the client's accounts payable listing, but uncommon to follow the same approach in verifying accounts receivable.

13. Distinguish between a vendor's invoice and a vendor's statement. Which document should ideally be used as evidence in auditing acquisition transactions and which for directly verifying accounts payable balances? Why?

14. It is less common to confirm accounts payable at an interim date than accounts receivable. Explain why.

15. In testing the cutoff of accounts payable at the balance sheet date, explain

why it is important that auditors coordinate their tests with the physical observation of inventory. What can the auditor do during the physical inventory to enhance the likelihood of an accurate cutoff?

DISCUSSION QUESTIONS AND PROBLEMS

16. For each of the following questions, select the one best response.
    a. In comparing the confirmation of accounts payable with suppliers and confirmation of accounts receivable with debtors, the true statement is that
       (1) Confirmation of accounts payable with suppliers is a more widely accepted auditing procedure than is confirmation of accounts receivable with debtors.
       (2) Statistical sampling techniques are more widely accepted in the confirmation of accounts payable than in the confirmation of accounts receivable.
       (3) As compared with the confirmation of accounts payable, the confirmation of accounts receivable will tend to emphasize accounts with zero balances at balance sheet date.
       (4) It is less likely that the confirmation request sent to the supplier will show the amount owed him than that the request sent to the debtor will show the amount due from him.
    b. As part of his search for unrecorded liabilities, a CPA examines invoices and accounts payable vouchers. In general this examination may be limited to
       (1) Unpaid accounts payable vouchers and unvouchered invoices on hand at the balance sheet date.
       (2) Accounts payable vouchers prepared during the subsequent period and unvouchered invoices received through the last day of field work whose dollar values exceed reasonable amounts.
       (3) Invoices received through the last day of field work (whether or not accounts payable vouchers have been prepared) but must include all invoices of any amount received during this period.
       (4) A reasonable period following the balance sheet date, normally the same period used for the cutoff bank statement.   (AICPA adapted)
17. Questions *a* through *h* are typically found in questionnaires used by auditors in evaluating internal controls in the acquisition and payment cycle. In using the questionnaire for a particular client, a yes response to a question indicates a possible strength in the system, whereas a no indicates a potential weakness.
    a. Is the purchasing function performed by personnel who are independent of the receiving and shipping functions and the payables and disbursing functions?
    b. Are all vendor's invoices routed directly to accounting from the mail room?
    c. Are all vouchers prenumbered and the numerical sequence checked by a person independent of voucher preparation?
    d. Are all extensions, footings, discounts, and freight terms on vendor's invoices checked for accuracy?
    e. Does a responsible employee review and approve the invoice account distribution before it is recorded in the purchases journal?

f. Are checks recorded in the cash disbursements journal as they are prepared?

g. Are all supporting documents properly canceled at the time the checks are signed?

h. Is the custody of checks after signature and before mailing handled by an employee independent of all payable, disbursing, cash, and general ledger functions?

Required:

a. For each of the above questions, state the internal control objective(s) being fulfilled if the control is in effect.

b. For each internal control, list a compliance procedure to test its effectiveness.

c. For each of the above questions, identify the nature of the potential financial error(s) if the control is not in effect.

d. For each of the potential errors in part *c*, list a substantive audit procedure that can be used to determine whether a material error exists.

18. Following are some of the tests of transactions procedures frequently performed in the acquisition and payment cycle. Each procedure is to be done on a sample basis.

a. Trace transactions recorded in the purchases journal to supporting documentation, comparing the vendor's name, total dollar amounts, and authorization for purchase.

b. Account for a sequence of receiving reports and trace selected ones to related vendor's invoices and purchases journal entries.

c. Review vouchers and supporting documents for clerical accuracy, propriety of account distribution, and reasonableness of expenditure in relation to the nature of the client's operations.

d. Examine documents in support of vouchers to make sure each voucher has an approved vendor's invoice, receiving report, and purchase order attached.

e. Foot the cash disbursements journal, trace postings of the total to the general ledger, and trace postings of individual purchases to the accounts payable subsidiary ledger.

f. Account for a numerical sequence of checks in the cash disbursements journal and examine all voided or spoiled checks for proper cancellation.

g. Prepare a proof of cash disbursements for an interim month.

h. Compare dates on canceled checks with dates on the cash disbursements journal and the bank cancellation date.

Required:

a. State whether each of the above procedures is primarily a compliance or a substantive test.

b. State the purpose(s) of each of the procedures.

19. The following errors or omissions are included in the accounting records of Westgate Manufacturing Company:

a. Telephone expense (account 2112) was unintentionally charged to repairs and maintenance (account 2121).

b. Purchases of raw materials are frequently not recorded until several weeks after the goods are received due to the failure of the receiving personnel to forward receiving reports to accounting. When pressure from a vendor's credit department is put on Westgate's accounting department, it searches for the receiving report, records the transactions in the purchases journal, and pays the bill.

c. The accounts payable clerk prepares a monthly check to Story Supply Company for the amount of an invoice owed and submits the unsigned check to the treasurer for payment along with related supporting documents which have already been approved. When he receives the signed check from the treasurer, he records it as a debit to accounts payable and deposits the check in a personal bank account for a company named Story Company. A few days later he records the invoice in the purchases journal again, resubmits the documents and a new check to the treasurer, and sends the check to the vendor after it has been signed.

d. The amount of a check in the cash disbursements journal is recorded as $4,612.87 instead of $6,412.87.

e. The accounts payable clerk intentionally excluded from the cash disbursements journal seven larger checks written and mailed on December 26th to prevent cash in the bank from having a negative balance on the general ledger. They were recorded on January 2 of the subsequent year.

f. Each month a fictitious receiving report is submitted to accounting by an employee in the receiving department. A few days later he sends Westgate an invoice for the quantity of goods ordered from a small company he owns and operates in the evening. A check is prepared, and the amount is paid when the receiving report and the vendor's invoice are matched by the accounts payable clerk.

Required:

a. For each error, state a control that should have prevented the error from occurring on a continuing basis.

b. For each error, state a substantive audit procedure that could uncover the error.

20. During your examination of the financial statements of the Gary Manufacturing Company for the year ended December 31, 19X8, you find that at January 1, 19X8, the company had installed the following punched-card processing system for recording raw material purchases:

a. Vendor's invoices are sent directly to the accounts payable department by the mail department.

b. All supporting documents to the invoices are accumulated in the accounts payable department and attached to the invoices. After being checked and cash discounts computed, the invoices are accumulated in batches and adding machine tapes prepared of the net invoice amounts to provide predetermined totals. Then the batches of invoices and tapes are sent to the tabulating department.

c. In the tabulating department keypunch operators prepare for each invoice an accounts payable punched card and one or more punched cards for the related debit distribution to several departmental inventories.

d. The invoice register is prepared by tab runs of the distribution cards and accounts payable cards. In this run, totals of distribution cards are compared by the tabulating machine with the amounts punched for the related accounts payable cards. Tab run subtotals by invoice batches are taken for checking to the predetermined totals.

e. The general ledger control account is posted monthly from the totals shown in the invoice register and all other journals.

f. By sorting, the distribution and accounts payable cards are separated. The distribution cards are filed for further processing. The accounts payable cards are sorted by due dates and tab runs prepared to determine cash requirements.

g. On the due dates the accounts payable cards are processed to prepare combined check and remittance statements.

h. At the end of the month the accounts payable cards in the unpaid file are tabulated for comparison with the general ledger control account.

Required:

a. List the audit procedures that you would employ in the examination of raw material purchases. In this part limit your discussion to procedures up to and including the preparation of the punched cards.

b. What audit procedures would you employ to satisfy yourself as to the reasonableness of the accounts payable balance at December 31, 19X8?

(AICPA adapted)

21. In testing cash disbursements for the Jay Klein Company, you have carefully reviewed the accounting system and evaluated the controls. The controls are reasonably good in the system, and no unusual audit problems have arisen in previous years.

Although there are not many personnel in the accounting department, there is a reasonable separation of duties in the organization. There is a separate purchasing agent who has responsibility for ordering goods and a separate receiving department for counting the goods when they are received and preparing receiving reports. There is a separation of duties between cash disbursements and accounts payable, and all information is recorded in the two journals independently. The controller reviews all supporting documents before signing the checks, and he immediately mails the check to the vendor. Check copies are used for subsequent recording.

All aspects of the system seem satisfactory to you, and you perform minimum tests of seventy-five transactions as a means of evaluating the system. In your tests you discover the following exceptions:

a. Two items in the purchases journal have been misclassified.

b. Three invoices had not been initialed by the controller, but there were no dollar errors evident in the transactions.

c. Five receiving reports were recorded at least two weeks later in the purchases journal than their date on the receiving report.

d. One invoice had been paid twice. The second payment was supported by a duplicate copy of the invoice. Both copies of the invoice had been marked "Paid."

e. One check amount in the cash disbursements journal was for $100 less than the amount stated on the vendor's invoice.

f. One voided check was missing.

g. Two receiving reports were missing from the voucher jacket for the invoice. One vendor's invoice had an extension error, and the invoice had been initialed that the amount had been checked.

Required:

a. What is the audit importance of each of these errors?

b. What follow-up procedures would you use to determine more about the nature of each error?

c. How would each of these errors affect the balance of your audit? Be specific.

d. How should each of the errors have been prevented by the client?

22. You are the staff accountant testing the combined purchases and cash disbursements journal for a small audit client. The system is regarded as reasonably good, considering the number of personnel.

The in-charge auditor has decided that a sample of eighty items should be sufficient for this audit because of the excellent controls. He gives you the following instructions:

a. All transactions selected must exceed $100.

b. At least fifty of the transactions must be for purchases of raw material because these transactions are typically material.

c. It is not acceptable to include the same vendor in the sample more than once.

d. All vendor's invoices that cannot be located must be replaced with a new sample item.

e. Both checks and supporting documents are to be examined for the same transactions.

f. The sample must be random, after modifications for the above instructions.

Required:

a. Evaluate each of these instructions for testing cash disbursements transactions.

b. Explain the difficulties of applying each of these instructions to attributes sampling.

23. During your audit of the Pientak Corporation for 19X7 you find that the corporation plans to install the following purchase order draft system for paying vendors:

a. The corporation will issue a draft in the form of a blank check attached to the purchase order for purchases. The purchase order draft (POD) form will combine a purchase order (upper half of form) with a blank check (lower half of form), and the two documents will be prenumbered with the same number and perforated so that the check can be easily detached.

b. The purchasing department will be responsible for the issuance, and the PODs will be valid for a period of ninety days from the date of issuance. Each of eight buyers will maintain a supply of PODs. The supply will be replenished as needed.

c. The cashier's department will maintain a log of the numbers of the PODs given to each buyer. Unissued PODs will be kept in a safe in the cashier's office. The POD form will consist of five parts, which will be distributed as follows:

(1) Copy #1 will be the purchase order and will be mailed to the vendor.

(2) Copy #2 will be sent to the receiving department.

(3) Copy #3 will be sent to the bookkeeping department.

(4) Copy #4 will be filed numerically in the purchasing department.

(5) Copy #5 will be kept by the buyer for follow-up purposes.

d. When the purchase order is issued, the buyer will enter the quantity, unit price, extended amount, and the total estimated amount of the order on the upper half of the POD form. The check will be made out in the vendor's name, dated and signed by the buyer. The original of the five-part form will then be mailed to the vendor.

e. The vendor will enter his invoice number, quantity, unit price, and total amount of goods to be shipped in the space provided on the check. When the goods are shipped, the vendor will enter the total amount of the shipment on the face of the check and present the completed check to the bank for payment. No partially filled orders will be accepted. Vendors who deliver a quantity less than that ordered must receive a new purchase order for additional quantities to be delivered.

f. The bank will honor the check if it has not matured, stamp it "Paid," and charge the amount to the corporation's general cash account. The bank will send the paid checks to the cashier's department daily. After reviewing the paid checks, the cashier's department will prepare an adding machine tape of the amounts and enter the total each day in the cash disbursements journal, debiting accounts payable. The paid checks will then be sent to the purchasing department.

g. When the goods are received, the receiving department will compare the quantity of items received with copy #2 of the POD, indicate the date the goods are received, initial copy #2, and route it to the purchasing department. The purchasing department will match the receiving department's copy #2 with the paid POD received from the cashier's department and enter the account distribution on the description section of the check. The extensions of unit prices multiplied by quantities entered by the vendor will be checked and the receiving department's copy #2 attached to the paid check and the documents sent to the bookkeeping department.

h. The bookkeeping department will charge the appropriate assets or expense accounts at the time the paid checks are recorded in the accounts payable register. The checks, together with the related receiving reports, will then be filed by vendor.

Required:

a. The treasurer of the corporation requests your aid in preparing a memorandum informing the bank of the new "POD" procedures. List the instructions that you would recommend be given to the bank regarding POD bank account and the payment of "POD" checks.

b. The internal control procedures within the corporation with regard to purchases in general are excellent. Suggest additional internal control measures needed for the use of purchase order drafts and verifications of paid and unpaid PODs. (AICPA adapted)

24. Each year near the balance sheet date when the president of Bargon Construction, Inc., takes a three-week vacation to Hawaii, he signs several checks to pay major bills during the period he is absent. Jack Morgan, head bookkeeper for the company, uses this practice to his advantage. Morgan makes out a check to himself for the amount of a large vendor's invoice, and since there is no purchases journal, he records the amount in the cash disbursements journal as a purchase to the supplier listed on the invoice. He holds the check until several weeks into the subsequent period to make sure the auditors do not get an opportunity to examine the canceled check. Shortly

after the first of the year when the president returns, Morgan resubmits the invoice for payment and again records the check in the cash disbursements journal. At that point, he marks the invoice "paid" and files it with all other paid invoices. Morgan has been following this practice successfully for several years and feels confident that he has developed a foolproof method.

Required:

a. What is the auditor's responsibility for discovering this type of embezzlement?
b. What weaknesses exist in the client's system of internal control?
c. What audit procedures are likely to uncover the fraud?

25. On January 11, 19X7, at the beginning of your annual audit of the Grover Manufacturing Company's financial statements for the year ended December 31, 19X6, the company president confides in you that an employee is living on a scale in excess of that which his salary would support.

The employee has been a buyer in the purchasing department for six years and has charge of purchasing all general materials and supplies. He is authorized to sign purchase orders for amounts up to $200. Purchase orders in excess of $200 require the countersignature of the general purchasing agent.

The president understands that the usual examination of financial statements is not designed, and cannot be relied upon, to disclose fraud or conflicts of interest, although their discovery may result. The president authorizes you, however, to expand your regular audit procedures and to apply additional audit procedures to determine whether there is any evidence that the buyer has been misappropriating company funds or has been engaged in activities that were a conflict of interest.

Required:

a. List the audit procedures that you would apply to the company records and documents in an attempt to
   (1) Discover evidence within the purchasing department of defalcations being committed by the buyer. Give the purpose of each audit procedure.
   (2) Provide leads as to possible collusion between the buyer and the suppliers. Give the purpose of each audit procedure.
b. Assume that your investigation disclosed that some suppliers have been charging the Grover Manufacturing Company in excess of their usual prices and apparently have been making kick backs to the buyer. The excess charges are material in amount.
   What effect, if any, would the defalcation have upon (1) the financial statements that were prepared before the defalcation was uncovered and (2) your auditor's report? Discuss.   (AICPA adapted)

26. Compare the confirmation of accounts receivable with the confirmation of accounts payable under the following headings:
a. Generally accepted auditing procedures. (Justify the differences revealed by your comparison.)
b. Form of confirmation requests. (You need not supply examples.)
c. Selection of accounts to be confirmed.   (AICPA adapted)

27. You were in the final stages of your examination of the financial statements of Ozine Corporation for the year ended December 31, 19X7, when you were consulted by the corporation's president who believes there is no point to your examining the 19X8 voucher register and testing data in support of 19X8 entries. He stated that (a) bills pertaining to 19X7 which were received too late to be included in the December voucher register were recorded as of the year-end by the corporation by journal entry, (b) the internal auditor made tests after the year-end, and (c) he would furnish you with a letter certifying that there were no unrecorded liabilities.

Required:

   a. Should a CPA's test for unrecorded liabilities be affected by the fact that the client made a journal entry to record 19X7 bills which were received late? Explain.
   b. Should a CPA's test for unrecorded liabilities be affected by the fact that a letter is obtained in which a responsible management official certifies that to the best of his knowledge all liabilities have been recorded? Explain.
   c. Should a CPA's test for unrecorded liabilities be eliminated or reduced because of the internal audit tests? Explain.
   d. Assume that the corporation, which handled some government contracts, had no internal auditor but that an auditor for a federal agency spent three weeks auditing the records and was just completing his work at this time. How would the CPA's unrecorded liability test be affected by the work of the auditor for a federal agency?
   e. What sources in addition to the 19X8 voucher register should the CPA consider to locate possible unrecorded liabilities?   (AICPA adapted)

28. Due to the small size of the company and the limited number of accounting personnel, the Dry Goods Wholesale Company initially records all acquisitions of goods and services at the time cash disbursements are made. At the end of each quarter when financial statements for internal purposes are prepared, accounts payable are recorded by adjusting journal entries. The entries are reversed at the beginning of the subsequent period. Except for the lack of a purchases journal, the controls over acquisitions are excellent for a small company. (There are adequate prenumbered documents for all acquisitions, proper approvals, and adequate internal verification wherever possible.)

   Before the auditor arrives for the year-end audit, the bookkeeper prepares adjusting entries to record the accounts payable as of the balance sheet date. A list of all outstanding balances is prepared, by vendor, on an accounts payable listing and is given to the auditor. All vendor's invoices supporting the list are retained in a separate file for the auditor's use.

   In the current year, the accounts payable balance has increased dramatically because of a severe cash shortage. (The cash shortage apparently arose from expansion of inventory and facilities rather than lack of sales.) Many accounts have remained unpaid for several months and the client is getting pressure from several vendors to pay the bills. Since the company had a relatively profitable year, management is anxious to complete the audit as early as possible so that the audited statements can be used to obtain a large bank loan.

Required:

    a. Explain how the lack of a purchases journal will affect the auditor's tests of transactions for acquisitions and payments.

    b. What should the auditor use as a sampling unit in performing tests of acquisitions?

    c. Assuming there are no errors discovered in the auditor's tests of transactions for acquisitions and payments, how will the existing system affect the verification of accounts payable?

    d. Discuss the reasonableness of the client's request for an early completion of the audit and the implications of the request from the auditor's point of view.

    e. List the audit procedures that should be performed in the year-end audit of accounts payable.

    f. State your opinion as to whether it is possible to conduct an adequate audit in these circumstances.

29. The Moss Company manufactures household appliances that are sold through independent franchised retail dealers. The electric motors in the appliances are guaranteed for five years from the date of sale of the appliances to the consumer. Under the guaranty defective motors are replaced by the dealers without charge.

    Inventories of replacement motors are kept in the dealers' stores and are carried at cost in the Moss Company's records. When the dealer replaces a defective motor, he notifies the factory and returns the defective motor to the factory for reconditioning. After the defective motor is received by the factory, the dealer's account is credited with an agreed fee for the replacement service.

    When the appliance is brought to the dealer after the guaranty period has elapsed, the dealer charges the owner for installing the new motor. The dealer notifies the factory of the installation and returns the replaced motor for reconditioning. The motor installed is then charged to the dealer's account at a price in excess of its inventory value. In this instance, to encourage the return of replaced motors, the dealer's account is credited with a nominal value for the returned motor.

    Dealers submit quarterly inventory reports of the motors on hand. The reports are later verified by factory salesmen. Dealers are billed for inventory shortages determined by comparison of the dealers' inventory reports with the factory's perpetual records of the dealers' inventories. The dealers order additional motors as they need them. One motor is used for all appliances in a given year, but the motors are changed in basic design each model year.

    The Moss Company has established an account, estimated liability for product guaranties, in connection with the guaranties. An amount representing the estimated guaranty cost prorated per sales unit is credited to the estimated liability account for each appliance sold, and the debit is charged to a provision account. The estimated liability account is debited for the service fees credited to the dealers' accounts and for the inventory cost of motors installed under the guaranties.

    The engineering department keeps statistical records of the number of units of each model sold in each year and the replacements that were made. The effect of improvements in design and construction is under continuous study by the engineering department, and the estimated guaranty cost per unit is adjusted annually on the basis of experience and improvements in design. Experience shows that, for a given motor model, the number of guaranties made good varies widely from year to year during the guaranty period, but the total number of guaranties to be made good can be reliably predicted.

Required:

a. Prepare an audit program to satisfy yourself as to the propriety of transactions recorded in the estimated liability for product guaranties account for the year ended December 31, 19X8.

b. Prepare the worksheet format that would be used to test the adequacy of the balance in the estimated liability for product guaranties account. The worksheet column headings should describe clearly the data to be inserted in the columns.   (AICPA adapted)

30. As part of the 6-30-X8 audit of accounts payable of Milner Products Company, the auditor sent twenty-two confirmations of accounts payable to vendors in the form of requests for statements. Four of the statements were not returned by the vendors, and five vendors reported balances different from the amounts recorded on Milner's accounts payable subsidiary ledgers. The auditor made duplicate copies of the five vendors' statements to maintain control of the independent information and turned the originals over to the client's accounts payable clerk to reconcile the differences. Two days later the clerk returned the five statements to the auditor with the following information on a working paper:

Statement 1	Balance per vendor's statement	$ 6,618.01
	Payment by Milner 6-30-X8	(4,601.01)
	Balance per subsidiary ledger	$ 2,017.00
Statement 2	Balance per vendor's statement	$ 9,618.93
	Invoices not received by Milner	(2,733.18)
	Payment by Milner 6-15-X8	(1,000.00)
	Balance per subsidiary ledger	$ 6,885,75
Statement 3	Balance per vendor's statement	$26,251.80
	Balance per subsidiary ledger	20,516.11
	Difference cannot be located due to the vendor's failure to provide details of its account balance	$ 5,735.69
Statement 4	Balance per vendor's statement	$ 6,170.15
	Credit memo issued by vendor on 7-15-X8	2,360.15
	Balance per subsidiary ledger	$ 3,810.00
Statement 5	Balance per vendor's statement	$ 8,619.21
	Payment by Milner 7-3-X8	(3,000.00)
	Unlocated difference not followed up due to minor amount	215.06
	Balance per subsidiary ledger	$ 5,834.27

Required:

a. Evaluate the acceptability of having the client perform the reconciliations, assuming the auditor intends to perform adequate additional tests.

b. Describe the additional tests that should be performed for each of the five statements that included differences.

c. What audit procedures should be performed for the nonresponses to the confirmation requests?

31. In confirming accounts payable at 12-31-X8, the following procedures are suggested to you for a client that has an excellent system of internal control and a history of prompt payment of all current liabilities.

a. Obtain a list of accounts payable at December 31, 19X8, from the client and

(1) Foot the list.

(2) Compare the total with the balance shown in the general ledger.

(3) Compare the amounts shown on the list with the balances in the accounts payable subsidiary ledger.

b. Selection of accounts to confirm.

(1) Select each account with a balance payable in excess of $2,000.

(2) Select a random sample of fifty other accounts over $100.

(3) Indicate the accounts to be confirmed on the accounts payable list, make a copy of the list, and give it to the accounts payable clerk along with instructions to type the vendor's name, address, and balance due on confirmations.

c. Compare the confirmations with the subsidiary ledger.

d. Have the client's controller sign each confirmation.

e. Have the accounts payable clerk insert the confirmations and return envelopes addressed to the CPA firm in the client's envelopes. The envelopes are also to be stamped and sealed by the clerk. This should all be done under the auditor's control.

f. Mail the confirmations.

Required:

Evaluate the procedures for confirming accounts payable.

32. The physical inventory for Ajak Manufacturing was taken on December 30, 19X8, rather than December 31 because the client had to operate the plant for a special order the last day of the year. At the time of the client's physical count, you observed that purchases represented by receiving report number 2631 and all preceding ones were included in the physical count, whereas inventory represented by succeeding numbers was excluded. On the evening of December 31, you stopped by the plant and noted that inventory represented by receiving report numbers 2632 through 2634 was received subsequent to the physical count, but prior to the end of the year. You later noted that the final inventory on the financial statements contained only those items included in the physical count. In testing accounts payable at December 31, 19X8, you obtain a schedule from the client to aid you in testing the adequacy of the cutoff. The schedule includes the following information that you have not yet resolved:

Information on the Vendor's Invoice

Receiving Report Number	Amount of Vendor's Invoice	Amount Presently Included in or Excluded from Accounts Payable *	Invoice Date	Shipping Date	FOB Origin or Destination
2631	$2,619.26	Included	12-30-X8	12-30-X8	Origin
2632	3,709.16	Excluded	12-26-X8	12-15-X8	Destination
2633	5,182.31	Included	12-31-X8	12-26-X8	Origin
2634	6,403.00	Excluded	12-16-X8	12-27-X8	Destination
2635	8,484.91	Included	12-28-X8	12-31-X8	Origin
2636	5,916.20	Excluded	1- 3-X9	12-31-X8	Destination
2637	7,515.50	Excluded	1- 5-X9	12-26-X8	Origin
2638	2,407.87	Excluded	12-31-X8	1- 3-X9	Origin

* All entries to record inventory purchases are recorded by the client as a debit to purchases and a credit to accounts payable.

Required:

a. Explain the relationship between inventory and accounts payable cutoff.

b. For each of the receiving reports, state the error in inventory or accounts payable if any exists and prepare an adjusting entry to correct the financial statements if an error exists.

c. Which of the errors in part *b* are most important? Explain.

33. You are provided with the following description of the accounting and internal control procedures relating to materials purchases by the Johnson Machinery Company, a medium-sized firm that builds special machinery to order:

> Materials purchase requisitions are first approved by the plant foreman, who then sends them to the purchasing department. A prenumbered purchase order is prepared in triplicate by one of several department employees. Employees account for all purchase order numbers. The original copy is sent to the vendor. The receiving department is sent the second copy to use for a receiving report. The third copy is kept on file in the purchasing department along with the requisition.
>
> Delivered materials are immediately sent to the storeroom. The receiving report, which is a copy of the purchase order, is sent to the purchasing department. A copy of the receiving report is sent to the storeroom. Materials are issued to factory employees subsequent to a verbal request by one of the foremen.
>
> When the mailroom clerk receives vendor's invoices, he forwards them to the purchasing department employee who placed the order. The invoice is compared with the purchase order on file for price and terms by the employee. The invoice quantity is compared with the receiving department's report. After checking footings, extensions, and discounts, the employee indicates approval for payment by initialing the invoice. The invoice is then forwarded to the accounting depart-

ment (voucher section) where it is coded for account distribution, assigned a voucher number, recorded in the voucher register, and filed by payment date due. The purchase order and receiving report are filed in the purchasing department.

On payment dates the voucher section requisitions prenumbered checks from the cashier. They are prepared, except for signature, and then returned to the cashier, who puts them through the check-signing machine. After accounting for the sequence of numbers, the cashier sends the checks to the bookkeeper, who makes entries in the cash disbursements journal. The checks are then forwarded to the voucher section where payment dates are entered in the voucher register. The checks are placed in envelopes and sent to the mailroom. The vouchers are subsequently filed in numerical order. At the end of each month an adding machine tape of unpaid invoices is prepared by a voucher clerk, and the total is compared with the general ledger balance. Any differences disclosed are investigated.

Required:

a. Prepare a flowchart for the acquisition and the payment system for Johnson Machinery Company.
b. List the controls in existence for each of the seven internal control objectives.
c. For each control in part *b,* list one compliance procedure for verifying its effectiveness.
d. List the most important weaknesses in the acquisition and payment system.
e. Design an audit program to test the system of internal control. The program should include, but not be limited to, the compliance tests from part *c* and procedures to compensate for the weaknesses in part *d.*

15

The Acquisition and Payment Cycle – Verification of Selected Accounts

An important characteristic of the acquisition and payment cycle is the large number of accounts involved. These include the following:

Cash in the bank	Rent payable
Inventory	Accrued professional fees
Supplies	Accrued property taxes
Leases and leasehold improvements	Income taxes payable
Land	Rent expense
Buildings	Property taxes
Manufacturing equipment	Income tax expense
Organization costs	Professional fees
Patents, trademarks, and copyrights	Cost of goods sold
Commercial franchises	Supplies
Prepaid rent	Fines and penalties
Prepaid taxes	Insurance expense
Prepaid insurance	Retirement benefits
Accounts payable	Utilities

Since the audit procedures for many of these accounts are basically similar, an understanding of the appropriate methodology for each account can be obtained by studying the following selected account balances:

- Cash in the bank—affected by all transaction cycles (Chapter 18)
- Inventory—represents tangible assets and is typically used up in one year (Chapter 16)

- Prepaid insurance—represents prepaid expenses (Chapter 15)
- Manufacturing equipment—represents long-lived tangible assets (Chapter 15)
- Accounts payable—represents specific liabilities where the amount and the date of the future payment date are known (Chapter 14)
- Accrued property taxes—represents estimated liabilities (Chapter 15)
- Operations accounts—included are several methods of verifying all accounts in this category (Chapter 15)

AUDIT OF MANUFACTURING EQUIPMENT

Property, plant, and equipment are assets that have expected lives of more than one year, are used in the business, and are not acquired for resale. The intention to use the assets as a part of the operation of the client's business and their expected life of more than one year are the significant characteristics that distinguish these assets from inventory, prepaid expenses, and investments.

Property, plant, and equipment can be classified as follows:

- Land and land improvements
- Buildings and building improvements
- Manufacturing equipment
- Furniture and fixtures
- Autos and trucks
- Leasehold improvements
- Construction of property, plant, and equipment in process

In this section the audit of *manufacturing equipment* is discussed as an illustration of an appropriate approach to the audit of all of the accounts in property, plant, and equipment. When there are significant differences in the verification of other types of property, plant, or equipment, these are briefly examined.

Overview of the Accounts

The accounts commonly used for manufacturing equipment are illustrated in Figure 15-1. The relationship of manufacturing equipment to the acquisition and the payment cycle is apparent by examining the debits to the asset account. Since the source of the debits in the asset account is the purchases journal, the current period's additions to manufacturing equipment have already been partially verified as part of the tests of the acquisition and payment cycle.

Audit Objectives

The objectives when auditing manufacturing equipment and the related depreciation and accumulated depreciation accounts are to determine whether:

1. Additions represent actual property installed or constructed that has been properly capitalized.
2. Costs and related depreciation for all significant retirements, abandonments, and disposals of property have been properly recorded.
3. The balances in the property accounts, including the amounts carried forward from the preceding year, are properly stated.
4. Depreciation has been accurately computed using a method that is acceptable and consistent with previous periods.
5. The balances in accumulated depreciation accounts are reasonable, considering expected useful lives of property units and possible net salvage values.

FIGURE 15-1

MACHINERY AND EQUIPMENT T-ACCOUNTS

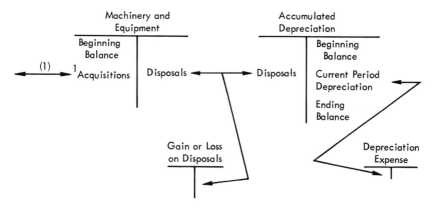

(1) Acquisitions of machinery and equipment arise from the acquisition and payment cycle. See Figure 14-1.

An Approach to Auditing Manufacturing Equipment

Manufacturing equipment is normally audited differently from current asset accounts for three reasons: there are usually fewer current period acquisitions of manufacturing equipment, the amount of any given acquisition is often material, and the equipment is likely to be kept and maintained in the accounting records for several years. Due to these differences, the emphasis in auditing manufacturing equipment is on the verification of current period acquisitions rather than on the balance in the account carried forward from the preceding year. In addition, the expected life of assets over one year requires a depreciation and accumulated depreciation accounts which is verified as a part of the audit of the assets.

Although the approach to verifying manufacturing equipment is dissimilar from that used for current assets, several other accounts are verified in much the same manner. These include patents, copyrights, catalog costs, and all property, plant, and equipment accounts.

In the audit of manufacturing equipment, it is helpful to separate the tests into the following categories:

- Analytical tests
- Verification of current year acquisitions
- Verification of current year disposals
- Verification of the ending balance in the asset account
- Verification of depreciation expense
- Verification of the ending balance in accumulated depreciation

Analytical Tests

As in all audit areas, the nature of the analytical tests depends upon the nature of the client's operations, but the following are illustrative of the type of ratio and trend analysis frequently performed.

Ratio or Trend	Use as It Relates to Manufacturing Equipment
1. Depreciation expense ÷ Gross manufacturing equipment cost	Possibility of a material error in computing depreciation
2. Accumulated depreciation ÷ Gross manufacturing equipment cost	Possibility of an error in accumulated depreciation
3. Monthly or annual comparison of repairs and maintenance, supplies expense, small tools expense, and similar accounts with previous years	Indication of expensing of a capital item or the increasing deterioration of the quality of the equipment
4. Gross manufacturing equipment cost ÷ Some measure of production	Possibility of idle equipment or equipment that has been disposed of

Verification of Current Year Acquisitions

The proper recording of current year additions is important because of the long-term effect the assets have on the financial statements. The failure to capitalize a permanent asset, or the recording of an acquisition at the improper amount, affects the balance sheet until the firm disposes of the asset. The income statement is affected until the asset is fully depreciated.

Due to the importance of current period acquisitions in the audit of manufacturing equipment, seven of the eight objectives for direct tests of balances are used as a frame of reference. (Disclosure is discussed in connection with the verification of ending balances.) Valuation and classification are the major objectives for this part of the audit.

Mechanical Accuracy. The starting point for the verification of current year acquisitions is normally a schedule obtained from the client of all purchases recorded in the general ledger during the year. A typical schedule lists each addition separately and includes the date of the acquisition, vendor, description, notation of new or used, life of the asset for depreciation purposes, depreciation method, cost, and investment credit.

The mechanical accuracy tests include footing the schedule and tracing the total to the manufacturing equipment general ledger account and tracing individual recorded additions to the subsidiary permanent asset ledger.

Overall Reasonableness. Beyond the ratio and trend analysis previously examined, other overall reasonableness tests include discussing the nature of manufacturing equipment additions with the plant superintendent, reviewing insurance coverage for unrecorded equipment, and reviewing the accounting records for potential additions that have been misclassified as another asset or expense.

Existence. The first part of the existence objective concerns the *validity and propriety of recorded additions.* In many audits sufficient evidence is obtained about this part of the objective during the tests of transactions in the acquisition and payment cycle; therefore, additional testing is unnecessary. If the auditor feels additional testing is necessary because of either the lack of adequate controls or the significance of the additions, vendor's invoices and receiving reports should be examined for approvals and the appropriateness of the acquisition for the client's business. It may also be desirable for the auditor to actually physically examine the assets acquired to make certain that they were received by the company, especially if the amounts are material.

The second part of the existence objective concerns the *failure to record* actual manufacturing equipment acquisitions. The failure to include additions to manufacturing equipment in the books of original entry is tested primarily through tests of acquisition and payment transactions and in the search for unrecorded liabilities. In auditing additions, there is more concern about the possibility of misclassifying a capital item as an expense or vice versa than the failure to record an addition in the journals. (Misclassifications are considered in the classification objective.) In the case of *leased equipment,* the auditor is concerned about the possibility of the need to capitalize the asset under the requirements of generally accepted accounting principles. The search for uncapitalized leases can be accomplished by examining lease and rent agreements for payments that are recorded as lease or rent expense.

Ownership. It is ordinarily unnecessary to verify the ownership of manufacturing equipment beyond examining vendor's invoices because ownership is apparent from the terms of the invoice, but for other property, plant, and equipment acquisitions additional verification is frequently necessary. For example, in verifying buildings or land acquisitions, it is common to examine property deeds, abstracts, tax bills, and similar evidence of ownership.

Valuation. Additional vouching besides what is done as a part of the tests of transactions is frequently considered necessary to verify the valuation of current period additions because of the complexity of many equipment transactions and the materiality of the amounts. It should ordinarily be unnecessary to examine supporting documentation for each addition, but it is normal to verify large and unusual transactions for the entire year as well as a representative sample of typical additions. The extent of the verification depends upon the auditor's willingness to rely on the client's internal controls over acquisitions and the materiality of the additions.

Tests for valuation of acquisitions are accomplished by comparing the charges on vendor's invoices with recorded amounts. The auditor must be aware of the client's capitalization policies to determine whether acquisitions are valued in accordance with generally accepted accounting principles and are treated consistently with those of the preceding year. For example, many clients automatically expense items that are less than a certain amount, such as $100. The auditor should be alert for the possibility of material transportation and installation costs, as well as the trade-in of existing equipment.

The auditor must also test by recalculation the client's calculations of the investment credit taken on qualified additions as a part of the valuation objective. The proper credit against the federal income tax for an acquisition depends on the federal tax laws governing the investment credit for the particular year under audit, the nature of the asset, its length of life, and whether the asset was acquired new as compared to used.

Classification. In conjunction with testing current period additions for existence and valuation, the auditor should also review recorded transactions for proper classification. In some cases, amounts recorded as manufacturing equipment should be classified as office equipment or as a part of the building. There is also the possibility that the client has improperly capitalized repairs, rents, or similar expenses.

The inclusion of transactions in repairs and maintenance expense, lease expense, supplies, small tools, and similar accounts that should properly be recorded as assets is a common client error. The error results from the lack of understanding generally accepted accounting principles and some clients' desire to avoid income taxes. The likelihood of these types of misclassifications should be evaluated in conjunction with the review of the controls in the acquisition and payment cycle. If the auditor concludes that they are highly likely, it may be necessary to vouch the larger amounts debited to the expense accounts. It is a common practice to do this as a regular part of the audit of the property, plant, and equipment accounts.

Cutoff. Cutoff tests for property accounts are not normally performed as a separate audit procedure. They are usually carried out for all accounts included in the acquisition and payment cycle as a part of the audit of accounts payable.

Verification of Current Year Disposals

Controls Over Disposals. The most important control over the disposal of manufacturing equipment is the existence of a formal system to inform management of the sale, trade-in, abandonment, or theft of recorded machinery and equipment. If the client fails to record disposals, the original cost of the manufacturing equipment account will be over-stated indefinitely, and the net book value will be overstated until the asset is fully depreciated. Another important control to protect assets from unauthorized disposal is a provision for authorization for the sale or other disposal of manufacturing equipment. Finally, there should be adequate internal verification of recorded disposals to make sure assets are correctly removed from the accounting records.

Audit Tests for Disposal. The two major objectives in the verification of the sale, trade-in, or abandonment of manufacturing equipment are the *existence* objective, which is concerned with the possibility of unrecorded disposals, and the *valuation* objective.

The starting point for verifying disposals is the client's schedule of recorded disposals. The schedule typically includes the date the asset was disposed of, the name of the person or firm acquiring the asset, the selling price, the original cost of the asset, the acquisition date, the accumulated depreciation of the asset, and the investment credit recapture, if any. Mechanical accuracy tests of the schedule are necessary, including footing the schedule, tracing the totals on the schedule to the recorded disposals in the general ledger, and tracing the cost and accumulated depreciation of the disposals to the manufacturing equipment subsidiary ledgers.

Because the failure to record disposals of manufacturing equipment no longer used in the business can significantly affect the financial statements, *the search for unrecorded disposals is essential.* The nature and adequacy of the controls over disposals affect the extent of the search. The following procedures are frequently used for verifying disposals:

1. Review whether newly acquired assets replace existing assets.
2. Analyze gains on the disposal of assets and miscellaneous income for receipts from the disposal of assets.
3. Review plant modifications and changes in product line, taxes, or insurance coverage for indications of deletions of equipment.
4. Make inquiries of management and production personnel about the possibility of the disposal of assets.

When an asset is sold or disposed of without having been traded in for a replacement asset, the *valuation* of the transaction can be verified by examining the related sales invoice and subsidiary property records. The auditor should compare the cost and accumulated depreciation in the subsidiary records with the recorded entry in the general journal and recompute the gain or loss on the disposal of the asset for comparison with the accounting records.

Two areas deserve special attention in the valuation objective. The first is the *trade-in of an asset for a replacement.* When trade-ins occur, the auditor should be sure the new asset is properly capitalized and the replaced asset properly eliminated from the records, considering the book value of the asset traded in and the additional cost of the new asset. The second area of special concern is the disposal of assets affected by the *investment credit recapture provisions.* Since the recapture affects the current year's income-tax expense and liability, the auditor must evaluate its significance. An understanding of the recapture provisions for the year the asset was acquired is necessary before the calculation can be made.

Verification of the Ending Balance in the Asset Account

Controls Over Existing Assets. The nature of the physical and accounting controls over existing assets determines whether it is necessary to verify manufacturing equipment acquired in prior years. Important controls include the use of a subsidiary ledger for individual fixed assets, adequate physical controls over assets that are easily movable (such as tools and vehicles), assignment of identification numbers to each plant asset, and periodic physical count of fixed assets and their reconciliation by accounting personnel. A formal system for informing the accounting department of all disposals of permanent assets is also an important control over the balance of assets carried forward into the current year.

Audit Tests. Typically the first step in the audit of the ending balance in manufacturing equipment is the *reconciliation* of the manufacturing equipment subsidiary ledger with the general ledger at the balance sheet date. The reconciliation is usually simply a matter of adding the individual subsidiary amounts to arrive at the ending total in the general ledger.

After reviewing the controls over existing assets and their related records, the auditor must decide whether it is necessary to verify the existence of individual items of manufacturing equipment included in the subsidiary ledger. If the auditor believes there is a high likelihood of significant missing permanent assets that are still recorded on the accounting records, an appropriate procedure is to select a sample from the subsidiary records and examine the actual assets. In rare cases the auditor may believe it is necessary that the client take a complete physical inventory of fixed assets to make sure they actually exist. If a physical inventory is taken, the auditor normally observes the physical count.

In ordinary circumstances, it is unnecessary to test the valuation of fixed assets recorded in prior periods because presumably they were verified in previous audits at the time they were acquired. However, the auditor should be aware that companies may occasionally have on hand manufacturing equipment that is no longer used in operations. If the amounts are material, the auditor should evaluate whether they should be written down to net realizable value or at least be disclosed separately as "nonoperating equipment."

A major consideration in verifying the ending balance in permanent assets is the possibility of existing *legal encumbrances*. A number of methods are available to determine if manufacturing equipment is encumbered. These include reading the terms of loan and credit agreements and mailing loan confirmation requests to banks and other lending institutions. Information with respect to encumbered assets may also be obtained through discussions with the client or confirmations with legal counsel. In addition, it is desirable to obtain information on possible liens by sending a "Request for Information under the Uniform Commercial Code" to the secretary of state or other appropriate officials of the state in which the company operates.

The *proper disclosure* of manufacturing equipment in the financial statements must be carefully evaluated to make sure generally accepted accounting principles are followed. Manufacturing equipment should include the gross cost and should ordinarily be separated from other permanent assets. Leased property should also be disclosed separately, and all liens on property must be included in the footnotes.

Verification of Depreciation Expense

Two major concerns are involved in auditing depreciation expenses: determining whether the client is following *a consistent depreciation policy* from period to period and whether the client's *calculations are accurate*. In determining whether the client is following a consistent depreciation policy there are five considerations: the useful life of current period acquisitions, the method of depreciation, the estimated salvage value, and the policy of depreciating assets in the year of acquisition and disposition. The client's policies can be determined by having discussions with the client and comparing the responses with the information in the auditor's permanent files.

In deciding on the reasonableness of the useful lives assigned to newly acquired assets, the auditor must consider a number of factors: the actual physical life of the asset, the expected life (taking into account obsolescence or the company's normal policy of upgrading equipment), and established company policies on trading in equipment. Occasionally, changing circumstances may necessitate a revaluation of the useful life of an asset and a change in the lives for depreciation purposes. When this occurs, a change in accounting estimate rather than a change in accounting principle is involved. The impact of this change on depreciation must be carefully evaluated.

A useful method of testing depreciation is to make a calculation of its overall reasonableness. The calculation is made by multiplying the undepreciated fixed assets by the depreciation rate for the year. In making these calculations, the auditor must of course make adjustments for current year additions and disposals, assets with different lengths of life, and assets with different methods of depreciation. The calculations can be made fairly easily if the CPA firm includes in the permanent file a breakdown of the fixed assets by method of depreciation and length of asset life. If the overall calculations are reasonably close to the client's totals and the system of internal control is adequate, detailed testing can be minimized.

In many audits it is also desirable to check the mechanical accuracy of depreciation calculations. This is done by recomputing depreciation expense for selected assets to determine whether the client is following a proper and consistent depreciation policy. To be relevant, the detailed calculations should be tied into the total depreciation calculations by footing the depreciation expense on individual subsidiary accounts and reconciling the total with the general ledger. If the client maintains its depreciation and amortization records on data-processing equipment, it may be desirable to consider using the computer in testing the calculations.

Verification of the Ending Balance in Accumulated Depreciation

Audit procedures to verify accumulated depreciation are usually limited to mechanical accuracy tests. The debits to accumulated depreciation are normally tested as a part of the audit of disposals of assets, whereas the credits are verified as a part of depreciation expense. If the auditor traces selected transactions to the subsidiary permanent asset ledger as a part of these tests and reconciles the total of the accounts with the general ledger, no additional testing should be required.

In some cases the life of manufacturing equipment may be significantly reduced due to such changes as reductions in customer demands for products, unexpected physical deterioration, or a modification in operations. Because of these possibilities, it is necessary to evaluate the adequacy of the allowances for accumulated depreciation each year to make sure the net book value exceeds the realizable value of the assets.

AUDIT OF PREPAID INSURANCE

Prepaid expenses, deferred charges, and intangibles are assets that vary in life from several months to several years. Their inclusion as assets results more from the concept of matching expenses with revenues than from their resale or liquidation value. The following are examples:

Prepaid rent	Organization costs
Prepaid taxes	Patents
Prepaid insurance	Trademarks
Deferred charges	Copyrights

Audit Objectives

The objectives in the verification of the prepaid expenses, deferred charges, and intangibles are to determine whether

1. The balances represent proper charges against future operations.
2. The additions represent charges to these accounts and are reflected at actual cost.
3. Amortizations or write-offs are reasonable under the circumstances.

In this section the audit of prepaid insurance is discussed as an account representative of this group because (1) it is found in most audits—virtually every company has some type of insurance; (2) it is typical of the problems frequently encountered in the audit of this class of accounts; and (3) the auditor's responsibility for the review of insurance coverage is an additional consideration not encountered in the other accounts in this category.

Overview of the Accounts

The accounts typically used for prepaid insurance are illustrated in Figure 15-2. The relationship between prepaid insurance and the acquisition and payment cycle is apparent in examining the debits to the asset account. Since the source of the debits in the asset account is the purchase journal, the payments of insurance premiums have already been partially tested as part of the tests of acquisition and payment transactions.

Internal Controls

The internal controls for prepaid insurance and insurance expense can be conveniently divided into three categories: controls over the acquisition and recording of insurance, controls over the insurance register, and controls over the charge-off of insurance expense.

Controls over the acquisition and recording of insurance are a part of the acquisition and payment cycle. The controls should include proper

FIGURE 15-2

PREPAID INSURANCE T-ACCOUNTS

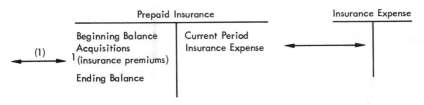

(1) Acquisitions of insurance premiums arise from the acquisitions and payment cycle. This can be observed by examining Figure 14-1.

authorization for new insurance policies and payment of insurance premiums consistent with those discussed in that cycle.

A record of insurance policies in force and the due date of each policy (*insurance register*) is an essential control to make sure the company has adequate insurance at all times. The control of the insurance register should include a provision for periodic review of the adequacy of the insurance coverage by an independent qualified person.

The detailed records of the information in the prepaid insurance schedule should be verified by someone independent of the person preparing them after they have been completed. A closely related control is the use of monthly "standard journal entries" for insurance expense. If a significant entry is required to adjust the balance in prepaid insurance at the end of the year, it indicates a potential error in the recording of the acquisition of insurance throughout the year or in the calculation of the year-end balance in prepaid insurance.

Audit Tests of Prepaid Insurance

Throughout the audit of prepaid insurance and insurance expense the auditor should keep in mind that the amount in insurance expense is a residual based upon the beginning balance in prepaid insurance, the payment of premiums during the year, and the ending balance. The only verification that is ordinarily necessary of the balance in the expense account is an analytical review and a brief test to be sure the charges to insurance expense arose from credits to prepaid insurance. Since the payments of premiums are tested as part of the tests of transactions and analytical review, the emphasis in the direct tests of insurance is on prepaid insurance.

In the audit of prepaid insurance, a schedule is obtained from the client or prepared by the auditor which includes each insurance policy in force, policy number, insurance coverage for each policy, premium amount, premium period, insurance expense for the year, and prepaid insurance at the end of the year. An example of a schedule obtained from the client for the auditor's working papers is given in Figure 15-3. The auditor's tests of prepaid insurance are normally indicated on the schedule.

Overall Reasonableness. A major consideration the auditor should keep in mind throughout the audit of prepaid insurance is the frequent *immateriality* of the beginning and ending balances. Furthermore, few transactions are debited and credited to the balance during the year, most of the transactions are small, and the transactions are usually simple to understand. Therefore the auditor can generally spend practically no time verifying the balance. When he plans not to verify the balance in detail, the analytical review becomes increasingly important as a means of identifying potentially significant errors. The following are commonly performed analytical tests of prepaid insurance and insurance expense:

1. Compare total prepaid insurance and insurance expense with previous years as a test of reasonableness.
2. Compute the ratio of prepaid insurance to insurance expense and compare it with previous years.
3. Compare the individual insurance policies and their coverage on the schedule obtained from the client with the preceding year's schedule as a test of the elimination of certain policies or a change in insurance coverage.
4. Compare the computed prepaid insurance balance on a policy-by-policy basis for the current year with that of the preceding year as a test of an error in calculation.
5. Review the *insurance coverage* listed on the prepaid insurance schedule with an appropriate client official or insurance broker for adequacy of coverage. The auditor cannot be an expert on insurance matters, but his understanding of accounting and the valuation of assets is certainly important in making certain a company is not underinsured.

For many audits, no additional tests need be performed beyond the review for overall reasonableness unless the tests indicate a high likelihood of a significant error or the internal control is considered inadequate. The remaining audit procedures should be performed only when there is a special reason for doing so. The discussion of these tests is organized around the audit objectives for performing direct tests of asset balances. For convenience of discussion, valuation and mechanical accuracy are combined and the order in which the objectives are discussed is different than that previously used.

Existence. The verification of the existence of the insurance policies in force can be tested in one of two ways: by referring to supporting documentation or by obtaining a confirmation of insurance information from the company's insurance agent. The first approach entails examining insurance invoices and policies in force. If these tests are performed, they should be done on a limited test basis. The sending of a confirmation to the client's insurance agent is a preferable approach because it is usually less time consuming than vouching tests, and it provides 100 percent confirmation. The use of confirmations for this purpose has grown rapidly in the past few years.

Ownership. The party who will receive the benefit if an insurance claim is filed is considered the owner. Ordinarily, the recipient named in the policy is the client, but when there are mortgages or other liens, the insurance claim may be payable to a creditor. The review of insurance policies for claimants other than the client is an excellent test of unrecorded liabilities and pledged assets.

Valuation and Mechanical Accuracy. The valuation of prepaid insurance involves verifying the total amount of the insurance premium, the length of the policy period, and the allocation of the premium to unexpired insurance. The amount of the premium for a given policy and

FIGURE 15-3

SCHEDULE OF PREPAID INSURANCE

ABC Company, Inc.
Prepaid Insurance

Schedule __F-2__ Date
Prepared by _Client/JL_ 1/20
Approved by _JR_ 1/25

12/31/7x

Insurer	Policy Number	Coverage	Term
Ever-ready Casualty Co.	IBB-79016 ②	Auto liability, collision, comprehensive, uninsured motorist — covers all autos owned and leased by the company.	6/1/7w-7x 6/1/7w-7y
Everystate Insurance	74-88-914 ②	Multi-peril — Headquarters and plant, including contents.	3/15/7w-7x ① 3/15/7w-7y ①
Standard Surety Co.	1 973 016 ②	Blanket Position Bond — $25,000	7/1/7w-7x
Commercial Bonding Co.	717-639 ②	Commercial Blanket Bond — $100,000	7/1/7x-7y

Reconciliation to Insurance Expense (General) Account:

Dependable Insurance	DIC-9161 ②	Personal property-Sales offices	1/1/7x-12/31/7x

Insurance expense

① Policy term is 3 years, expiring 3/14/7z; premium shown is annual portion. Annual premium is estimated, subject to annual review and adjustment. Premium is payable in monthly instalments under terms of contract. (See work paper section CC, Contracts Payable.)

② Reviewed and briefed policies; details of coverage in permanent file. Blanket Position Bond replaced by Commercial Blanket Bond on expiration.

③ Annual premium adjustment; traced to invoice and voucher.

④ Charged directly to expense; traced to invoice and voucher, premium paid 1/14/7x. Policy renewed 1/1/7y, premium paid 1/20/7y.

Figure 15-3 (cont.)

Annual Premium	Unexpired Premium 1/1/7x	Additions	Expense	Unexpired Premium 12/31/7x
6 300	2 625 LY		2 625	— ʜ
7 000	—	7 000	4 083	C 2 917 ʜ
12 600	2 625 LY	1 800 ③	4 425	— ʜ
15 100	—	15 000	11 954	C 3 146 ʜ
1 200	600 LY	—	600	— ʜ
800	—	800	400	C 400 ʜ
	5 850 ʜ LY	24 700 ʜ	24 087	6 463 ʜ GL
500			500	
			24 587 ʜ GL	

LY Agreed to last year's schedule of prepaid insurance in work papers.
ʜ Verified calculation / footing / cross-footing.
GL Agreed to general ledger.
C Unearned premium confirmed by broker; confirmation filed at F-2/1.

its time period can be verified simultaneously by examining the premium invoice or the confirmation from an insurance agent. Once these two have been verified, the client's calculations of unexpired insurance can be tested by recalculation. The schedule of prepaid insurance can then be footed and the totals traced to the general ledger to complete the mechanical accuracy tests.

Classification. The proper classification of debits to different insurance expense accounts should be reviewed as a test of the income statement. In some cases the appropriate expense account is obvious because of the type of insurance (such as insurance on a piece of equipment), but in other cases allocations are necessary. For example, fire insurance on the building may require allocation to several accounts, including manufacturing overhead. Consistency with previous years is the major consideration in evaluating classification.

Cutoff. Cutoff for insurance expense is normally not a significant problem because of the small number of policies and the immateriality of the amount. If the cutoff is checked at all, it is reviewed as a part of accounts payable cutoff tests.

Disclosure. In most audits, prepaid insurance is combined with other prepaid expenses and included as a current asset. The amount is usually small and is not a significant consideration to statement users.

AUDIT OF ACCRUED PROPERTY TAXES

Accrued liabilities are estimated unpaid obligations for services or benefits that have been received prior to the balance sheet date. Many accrued liabilities represent future obligations for unpaid services resulting from the passage of time but are not payable at the balance sheet date. For example, the benefits of property rental accrues throughout the year; therefore, at the balance sheet date a certain portion of the total rent cost that has not been paid should be accrued. If the balance sheet date and the termination of the rent agreement take place on the same date, any unpaid rent is more appropriately called rent payable than an accrued liability.

A second type of accrual is made up of those in which the amount of the obligation must be estimated due to the uncertainty of the amount due. An illustration is the obligation for federal income taxes when there is a reasonable likelihood that the amount reported on the tax return will be changed after an audit has been conducted by the Internal Revenue Service. The following are common accrued liabilities, including payroll-related accruals which were discussed as a part of Chapter 13:

Accrued officer bonuses   Accrued payroll taxes
Accrued commissions   Accrued pension costs

Accrued income taxes

Accrued interest

Accrued payroll

Accrued professional fees

Accrued rent

Accrued warranty costs

The verification of accrued expenses varies depending upon the nature of the accrual and the circumstances of the client. For most audits, accruals take little audit time, but in some instances accounts such as accrued income taxes, warranty costs, and pension costs are material and require considerable audit effort. To illustrate the audit of accruals, accrual property taxes are discussed in this section.

Overview of the Accounts

The accounts typically used by companies for accrued property taxes are illustrated in Figure 15-4. The relationship between the accrued property taxes and the acquisition and payment cycle is the same as for prepaid insurance and is apparent from examining the debits to the liability account. Since the source of the debits is the purchase journal, the payments of the property taxes have already been partially tested as a part of the tests of the acquisition and payment cycle.

As for insurance expense, the balance in property tax expense is a residual amount that results from the beginning and ending balances in accrued property taxes and the payments of property taxes. Therefore the emphasis in the tests should be on the property tax liability and property tax payments.

In verifying accrued property taxes, the most important considerations are the *inclusion of an accrual on each existing property* and the *consistent treatment and correct calculation of each accrual* from year to year.

The primary methods of testing for the inclusions of all accruals are (1) to perform the accrual tests in conjunction with the audit of current year property tax payments and (2) to compare the accruals with those of previous years. In most audits there are few property tax payments, but each payment is often material and therefore it is common to verify each one. First the auditor should obtain a schedule of property tax payments

FIGURE 15-4

ACCRUED PROPERTY TAXES

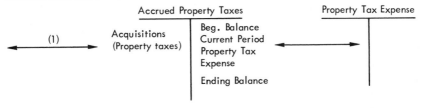

(1) Acquisitions of property taxes arise from the acquisition and payment cycle. This can be observed by examining Figure 14-1 in Chapter 14.

from the client and compare each payment with the preceding year's schedule to determine whether all payments have been included in the client-prepared schedule. It is also necessary to examine the permanent asset working papers for major additions and disposals of assets which may affect the property taxes accrual. If the client is expanding its operations, all property affected by local property tax regulations should be included in the schedule even if the first tax payment has not yet been made.

After the auditor is satisfied that all taxable property has been included in the client-prepared schedule, it is necessary to evaluate the reasonableness of the total amount of property taxes on each property being used as a basis to estimate the accrual. In some instances the total amount has already been set by the taxing authority, and it is possible to verify the total by comparing the amount in the schedule with the tax bill in the client's possession. In other instances the preceding year's total payments must be adjusted for the expected increase in property tax rates.

The auditor can verify the accrued property tax by recomputing the portion of the total tax applicable to the current year for each piece of property. The most important consideration in making this calculation is to use the same portion of each tax payment as the accrual that was used in the preceding year unless justifiable conditions exist for a change. After the accrual and property tax expense for each piece of property have been recomputed, the totals should be added and compared with the general ledger. In many cases property taxes are charged to more than one expense account. When this happens the auditor should test for proper classification by evaluating whether the proper amount was charged to each account.

A typical working paper showing the property tax expense, the accrued property taxes, and the audit procedures used to verify the balances is illustrated in Figure 15-5.

AUDIT OF OPERATIONS

Objectives

The audit of operations is meant to determine whether the income and expense accounts in the financial statements are fairly presented in accordance with generally accepted accounting principles. The auditor must be satisfied that each of the income and expense totals included in the income statement as well as net earnings is not materially misstated.

In conducting audit tests of the financial statements, the auditor must always be aware of the importance of the income statement to users of the statements. It is clear that many users rely more heavily on the income statement than the balance sheet for making decisions. Equity investors, long-term creditors, union representatives, and frequently even short-term creditors are more interested in the ability of a firm to generate profit than in the liquidity value or book value of the individual assets.

The overall objective of determining whether amounts in operations accounts are recorded in accordance with generally accepted accounting principles can be better achieved by evaluating whether each of the most important principles affecting net earnings has been observed by the client. Nine principles enumerated in the AICPA Accounting Research Study No. 4 are relevant to the audit of operations:

1. Sales, revenues and income should not be anticipated or materially overstated or understated. Accordingly, there must be proper cut-off accounting at the beginning and end of the period or periods.
2. Costs of sales and expenses should be appropriately matched against the periodic sales and revenues. It follows that there must be proper cutoff accounting for inventories and liabilities and for costs and expenses at the beginning and the end of the period or periods.
3. Appropriate charges should be made for depreciation and depletion of fixed assets and for amortization of other deferred costs.
4. Proper distribution of costs should be made as between fixed assets, inventories, maintenance and expenses. Direct costs are usually identifiable and common costs applicable to more than one activity should be distributed on appropriate cost incurrence bases such as time or use factors.
5. Contingency provisions and reserves should not be misused as a means of arbitrarily reducing income or shifting income from one period to another.
6. Nonrecurring and extraordinary gains and losses should be recognized in the period they occur, but should be shown separately from ordinary and usual operations.
7. There is a strong presumption that all gains and losses will be included in periodic income statements unless they are of such magnitude in relation to revenues and expenses from regular operations as to cause the statements to be misleading. (This requirement has been modified by Accounting Principles Board Opinion No. 9, which requires that all gains and losses are to be recognized in periodic income.)
8. Rental charges under material leases should be disclosed, and those which are in effect installment purchases of fixed assets should be capitalized.
9. If accounting principles in the determination of periodic results have not been consistently maintained, the effect of the change should be stated.

Considering the purposes of the statement of earnings, as well as the objectives of accounting for operations, the following two principles seem to have the greatest overall importance in conducting most audits:

1. The matching of periodic income and expense necessary for a proper determination of operating results

FIGURE 15-5

SCHEDULE FOR PROPERTY TAXES

ABC Company, Inc.
Property Tax Worksheet

Schedule	I-6	Date
Prepared by	PR	1/15
Approved by	GS	1/20

12/31/7x

Tax Bill No.	Area Code	Assessing Authority	Property	Assessed Value (1)	Total Tax (2)	Date Lien Payable (3)	Date Paid (4)	Period Covered
		West Coast Facilities						
526391	51	King County	Westside Warehouse	400,000	16,000	Jan. 1, 197x		197x
						Apr. 30, 1974		
						Oct. 31, 1974		
526392	51	King County	Headquarters Bldg.	250,000	10,000	Jan. 1, 197w		197w
						Apr. 30, 197x		
						Oct. 31, 197x		
						Jan. 1, 197x		197x
		Mid-West Facility						
17923	A	Minor County	Manufacturing Plant	2,000,000	23,000	Jul. 1, 197w	Jul. 1, 197w-7x	
					25,000	Jul. 1, 197x	Jul. 1, 197x-7y	
						Dec. 31, 197x		

(1) Assessed valuation is defined by the laws of both states as 50% of "true and fair value."

(2) Millage rates:
King County .0400 ($40 per $1,000)
Minor County .0115 ($11.50 per $1,000) for 197w-7x
.0125 ($12.50 per $1,000) for 197x-7y

(3) Laws of both states establish the lien date to be the same as the assessment date; assessment date for the West Coast state is statutorily defined as January 1, and for the Midwest state as July 1.

(4) Taxes are payable as follows:
West Coast state — one half no later than April 30 and the balance no later than October 31, for the preceding calendar year.
Midwest state — payable in full not later than December 31 following assessment date.

FIGURE 15-5 (cont.)

	Prepaid				Accrued		
Beginning Balance	Additions (6)	Expense	Ending Balance	Beginning Balance	Additions (6)	Payments	Ending Balance
—0—	16,000 ✓	16,000 ∧	—0— ✗	(5) —0—	16,000 ✓	—0—	16,000 ✗
				10,000			
						5,000 T	
						5,000 T	—0— ✗
—0—	10,000 ✓	10,000 ∧	—0— ✗	—0—	10,000 ✓		10,000 ✗
11,500		11,500 ∧	—0— ✗	—0—			—0— ✗
	25,000 ✓	12,500 ∧	12,500 ✗	—0—	25,000 ✓	25,000 T	—0— ✗
11,500 ⌃	51,000 ⌃	50,000 ⌃	12,500 ✗	10,000 ⌃	51,000 ⌃	35,000 ⌃	26,000 ✗
⌃ LY	⌃	⌃	⌃	⌃ LY	⌃	⌃	⌃

(5) Warehouse certified complete and accepted Dec. 22, 197w; inspected and valued by County in March 197x. Per state law (note 3), assessment date and lien date statutorily set at Jan. 1, 197x.

(6) Liability and deferred charge are recorded by company on the lien date. The deferred charge is amortized monthly, and the liability account relieved when instalments are paid.

LY Agreed to last year's workpapers.
✓ Agreed to county tax due notice (identified in left column).
∧ Agreed to amortization schedule and traced to standard journal entry.
T Traced to cancelled check and validated receipt.
⌃, ✗ Footed, cross-footed.

2. The consistent application of accounting principles for different periods

These two principles must be applied to the recording of individual transactions and to the combining of accounts in the general ledger for statement presentation. The client's failure to observe these principles could materially affect the comparability of results of operations and thus lead users to make erroneous inferences.

Approach to Auditing Operations

The audit of operations cannot be regarded as a separate part of the total audit process. A misstatement of an income statement account will most often equally affect a balance sheet account, and vice-versa. The audit of operations is so intertwined with the other parts of the audit that it is necessary to interrelate different aspects of testing operations with the different types of tests previously discussed. A brief description of these tests serves as a review of material covered in other chapters, but more important, it shows the interrelationship of different parts of the audit with operations testing. The parts of the audit directly affecting operations are as follows:

1. Analytical tests
2. Tests of transactions
3. Review of transactions with affiliates and interplant accounts
4. Analysis of account balances
5. Direct tests of balance sheet accounts
6. Tests of allocations

The emphasis in this section is on the operations accounts directly related to the acquisition and payment cycle, but the same basic concepts apply to the operations accounts in all other cycles.

Analytical Tests

Analytical tests were first discussed in Chapter 4 as a general concept and have been referred to in subsequent chapters as a part of particular audit areas. Analytical tests should be thought of as a part of the test of the fairness of the presentation of both balance sheet and income statement accounts. A few analytical tests and their effect upon operations in the acquisition and payment cycle follow.

Tests of Transactions

Compliance tests of internal controls and substantive tests of individual transactions both have the effect of simultaneously verifying balance sheet and operations accounts. For example, when an auditor concludes that the controls are adequate to provide reasonable assurance that transactions in the voucher register are valid, properly valued, correctly

FIGURE 15-6

Analytical Test	*Purpose in Relation to Operations*
1. Comparison of individual expenses with those of previous years	A possible overstatement or understatement of a balance
2. Comparison of individual asset and liability balances with those of previous years	A possible overstatement or understatement of a balance sheet account which would also affect an income statement account (e.g., a misstatement of inventory affects costs of goods sold)
3. Comparison of individual expenses with budgets	A possible misstatement of income statement accounts
4. Comparison of gross margin percent ratio with that of previous years	A possible misstatement of sales or cost of goods sold
5. Comparison of inventory turnover ratio with that of previous years	A possible misstatement of cost of goods sold
6. Comparison of prepaid insurance expense with that of previous years	A possible misstatement of insurance expense
7. Comparison of commission expense ÷ sales with that of previous years	A possible misstatement of commission expense
8. Comparison of individual manufacturing expenses ÷ total manufacturing expenses with those of previous years	A possible misstatement of individual manufacturing expenses

classified, and recorded in a timely manner, evidence exists as to the correctness of individual balance sheet accounts such as accounts payable and fixed assets, and income statement accounts such as advertising and repairs. On the other hand, inadequate controls and errors discovered through tests of transactions are an indication of the likelihood of misstatements in both the income statement and the balance sheet.

The evaluation of internal control and the related tests of transactions are the most important means of verifying many of the operations accounts in each of the transaction cycles. For example, if the auditor concludes after adequate tests that the system of internal control over acquisitions is reliable, the only additional verification of operating accounts such as utilities, advertising, and purchases should be cutoff tests. On the other hand, certain income and expense accounts are not verified at all by tests of transactions and others must be tested more extensively by other means. These are discussed as we proceed.

Review of Transactions with Affiliates and Interplant Accounts

The examination of underlying documents as a part of the tests of transactions is primarily designed to verify transactions with third parties, but transactions taking place with affiliates and subdivisions within the

client's organization are closely related. The possibility of improper recording and disclosing of transactions between closely interdependent
entities was discussed in Chapter 4, but it bears repeating as a part of the
verification of operations.

Transactions that are not conducted at arm's length may result in
either unwarranted detriment or benefit to the client. Assets purchased
or services obtained from affiliates by the client may be acquired at a
lower cost than their actual value. These bargain acquisitions could
suggest a superficial earning power than can be arbitrarily terminated in
the future. Similarly, a purchase at an unreasonably high cost may be
detrimental to the interests of existing stockholders, creditors, and other
statement users.

When a client deals with related parties, the auditor should determine
whether the transactions have been recorded at an amount equal to the
value of a similar exchange between independent, unrelated third parties.
In some cases the relationship between related parties is so close that an
affiliate must be considered a part of the same entity. For example, when
interplant transactions take place, they must be eliminated when the
combined statements are prepared if the amounts are material. If the
affiliate is not part of the same entity, the proper valuation of purchases
of inventory, services acquired from related parties, and other exchange
transactions must be carefully evaluated for propriety and reasonableness.
Usually all related party transactions are audited more extensively than
those with third parties.

Analysis of Account Balances

For some accounts the amounts included in the operations accounts
must be analyzed even though the three previously mentioned tests have
been performed. The meaning and methodology of analysis of accounts
will be described first, followed by a discussion of those occasions when
expense account analysis is appropriate.

Expense account analysis is the examination of underlying documentation of the individual transactions and amounts making up the total
of a particular expense account. The underlying documents are of the
same nature as those used for examining transactions as a part of tests of
acquisitions transactions and include such documents as invoices, receiving reports, purchase orders, and contracts.

Thus, expense account analysis is closely related to tests of transactions.
The major difference between the two is the degree of concentration on an
individual account. Since the test of transactions is meant to test the
effectiveness of the overall system, it constitutes a general review that
usually includes the verification of many different accounts. The analysis
of expense and other operations accounts consists of the examination of
the transactions in particular accounts to determine the propriety, classification, valuation, and other specific information about each account

analyzed. An audit working paper illustrating a typical approach to the analysis of an expense account is included in Figure 15-7.

In the following situations, expense account analysis of particular accounts may be appropriate even though tests of transactions have been performed:

1. *The analytical tests indicate there is a high likelihood of error in a particular account.* For example, if advertising expenses have increased dramatically in the current year, account analysis is frequently a useful way of determining the cause of the increase.

2. *The tests of transactions indicate there is a high likelihood of error in a particular account.* If several errors are discovered in one account during the tests of transactions, additional investigation by expense account analysis is often desirable.

3. *Certain accounts are likely to contain errors because it is difficult for the client to properly classify or value the transactions.* Some types of transactions require a reasonably high level of accounting skill for their classification and valuation to be properly determined. Accounts frequently analyzed for this purpose are rents and leases, repairs and maintenance, and gains and losses on the disposal of equipment or investments.

4. *The auditor knows that certain accounts are frequently subject to error.* Typical accounts in this category include miscellaneous expense, travel, and entertainment accounts.

5. *The analysis of certain accounts might disclose a contingency.* As an example, analysis of legal expenses may be necessary to determine whether a legal fee was for the defense against a lawsuit. Due to the potential economic significance of a lawsuit, it is an almost universal practice to analyze legal expenses 100 percent even when internal controls are excellent.

6. *Tax returns and the SEC require disclosure of certain information.* Examples include the breakdown of tax expense, officers' compensation and allowances, and each donation a company makes. It is often satisfactory to simply obtain the detailed information from the client without verifying it if other auditing procedures give the auditor confidence that the information is likely to be correct.

Direct Tests of Balance Sheet Accounts

Whenever an auditor verifies an asset or a liability account, the related revenue or expense account is also automatically tested. For example, sales are verified when accounts receivable are confirmed, and purchases and operating expenses are verified when the auditor searches for unrecorded liabilities at the balance sheet date. Similarly, when the auditor verifies the balance in prepaid insurance, insurance expense is also being tested.

FIGURE 15-7

EXPENSE ANALYSIS FOR LEGAL EXPENSE

| ABC Company, Inc.
General and Administrative Expenses | Schedule _V-10_ Date
Prepared by _GG_ _1/21_
Approved by _EW_ _1/28_ |

12/31/7x

Acct. 913 — Legal Expense

Paid to	For	Date	Amount
② Alexander J. Schweppe	Retainer — 12 months @ $500	Monthly ①	6000 ✓
" "	ABC vs. Carson — patent infringement suit	Apr. 14 Aug. 9	2800 ✓ 3109 ✓
② Smith, Todd & Ball	Consultation re: inquiry from Consumer Protection Bureau, State Attorney General's office	June 6 July 10	200 ✓ 200 ✓
③ L. Marvin Hall	Assistance in collecting overdue receivable from Star Mfg.	Nov. 10	105 ✓
			12414 G.L. ⋂

① Per minutes of meeting of Board of Directors 1/10/7x, Schweppe reappointed general counsel, with retainer.

② Attorney's letters requested { Received 1/23/7x; all matters listed are covered therein; letters filed in General Section of workpapers.

③ Attorney's letter not requested. Per phone conversation with Mr. Hall, 1/21/7x, he rarely represents the company, and his services have been limited to collection problems. The Star Mfg. matter was closed in October 197x, and he has not been involved in any other matters related to the company since that time.

✓ Examined statements and vouchers.
⋂ Footed.
GL Agreed to general ledger.

Cutoff tests, which are typically thought of as direct tests of balance sheet accounts, simultaneously affect both the income statement and the balance sheet. An example is when the auditor verifies the cutoff of sales as a part of the audit of accounts receivable. It doesn't matter whether cutoff tests are regarded as tests of operations or tests of the balance sheet —they affect both. The only reason for performing cutoff tests as a part of verifying balance sheet accounts is convenience.

Also, in many instances the expense account analysis as discussed above takes place as a part of the verification of the related asset. For example, it is common to analyze repairs and maintenance as a part of verifying fixed assets, rent expense as a part of verifying prepaid or accrued rent, and insurance expense as a part of testing prepaid insurance.

Tests of Allocations

Several expense accounts that have not yet been discussed are those arising from the internal allocation of accounting data. These include expenses such as depreciation, depletion, and the amortization of copyrights and catalog costs. The allocation of manufacturing overhead between inventory and cost of goods sold is an example of a different type of allocation that affects the expenses. Naturally, these accounts must be tested in some way during the course of the audit.

Allocations are important because they determine whether a particular expenditure is an asset or a current period expense. If the client fails to follow generally accepted accounting principles or fails to calculate the allocation properly, the financial statements can be materially misstated. The allocation of many expenses such as the depreciation of fixed assets and the amortization of copyrights is required because the life of the asset is greater than one year. The original cost of the asset is verified at the time of acquisition, but the charge-off takes place over several years. Other types of allocations directly affecting the financial statements arise because the life of a short-lived asset does not expire on the balance sheet date. Examples include prepaid rent and insurance. Finally, the allocation of costs between current period manufacturing expenses and inventory is required by generally accepted accounting principles as a means of reflecting all the costs of making a product.

In testing the allocation of expenditures such as prepaid insurance and manufacturing overhead, the two most important considerations are adherence to generally accepted accounting principles and consistency with the preceding period. The two most important audit procedures for allocations are tests for overall reasonableness and recalculation of the client's results. The most common way to perform these tests is as a part of the audit of the related asset or liability accounts. For example, depreciation expense is usually verified as part of the audit of property, plant, and equipment; the amortization of patents is tested as part of verifying new patents or the disposal of existing ones; and the allocations between inventory and cost of goods sold are verified as part of the audit of inventory.

REVIEW QUESTIONS

1. Explain the relationship between the tests of the system for the acquisition and payment cycle and those for the verification of property, plant, and equipment. Which aspects of property, plant, and equipment are directly affected by the tests of the system and which are not?

2. Explain why the emphasis in auditing property, plant, and equipment is on the current period acquisitions and disposals rather than on the balance in the account carried forward from the preceding year. Under what circumstances will the emphasis be on the balances carried forward?

3. What is the relationship between the audit of property accounts and the audit of repair and maintenance accounts? Explain how the auditor organizes the audit to take this relationship into consideration.

4. List and briefly state the purpose of all audit procedures that might reasonably be applied by an auditor to determine that all property and equipment retirements have been recorded on the books.

5. In auditing depreciation expense, what major considerations should the auditor keep in mind? Explain how each of these can be verified.

6. Explain the relationship between the tests of the system for the acquisition and payment cycle and those for the verification of prepaid insurance.

7. Explain why the audit of prepaid insurance should ordinarily take a relatively small amount of audit time if the client's system of internal control is effective.

8. Distinguish between the evaluation of the adequacy of insurance coverage and the verification of prepaid insurance. Explain which of these is more important in a typical audit.

9. What are the similarities and differences in verifying prepaid insurance and patents?

10. Explain the relationship between rent payable and the tests of the system for the acquisition and payment cycle. Which aspects of rent payable are not verified as a part of the tests of transactions?

11. How should the emphasis differ in verifying income taxes payable and accrued warranty expense?

12. In verifying accounts payable it is common to restrict the audit sample to a small portion of the population items, whereas in auditing accrued property it is common to verify all transactions for the year. Explain the reason for the difference.

13. Which documents will be used to verify prepaid property taxes and the related expense accounts?

14. List three expense accounts that are tested as part of the acquisition and payment cycle or the payroll and personnel cycle. List three expense accounts that are not directly verified as a part of either of these cycles.

15. What is meant by the analysis of expense accounts? Explain how expense account analysis relates to the tests of transactions that the auditor has already completed for the acquisition and payment cycle.

16. How would the approach for verifying repair expense differ from that used to audit depreciation expense? Why would the approach be different?

17. List the factors that should affect the auditor's decision as to whether or not to analyze a particular account balance. Considering these factors, list four expense accounts that are commonly analyzed in audit engagements.

18. Explain how cost of goods sold for a wholesale company could in part be verified by each of the following types of tests:
    a. Analytical tests
    b. Tests of transactions
    c. Review of transactions with affiliates
    d. Analysis of account balances
    e. Direct tests of balance sheet accounts
    f. Tests of allocations

DISCUSSION QUESTIONS AND PROBLEMS

19. For each of the following errors in property, plant, and equipment accounts, state an internal control the client could install to prevent the error from occurring and a substantive audit procedure the auditor could use to discover the error:
    a. The asset lives used to depreciate equipment are less than reasonable expected useful lives.
    b. Capitalizable assets are routinely expensed as repairs and maintenance, perishable tools, or supplies expense.
    c. Construction equipment that is abandoned or traded for replacement equipment is not removed from the accounting records.
    d. Depreciation expense for manufacturing operations is charged to administrative expenses.
    e. Tools necessary for the maintenance of equipment are stolen by company employees for their personal use.
    f. Acquisitions of property are recorded at the improper amount.
    g. A loan against existing equipment is not recorded in the accounting records. The cash receipts from the loan never reached the company because they were used for the down payment of a piece of equipment now being used as an operating asset. The equipment is also not recorded in the records.

20. In connection with a recurring examination of the financial statements of the Louis Manufacturing Company for the year ended December 31, 19X8, you have been assigned the audit of the manufacturing equipment, manufacturing equipment-accumulated depreciation, and repairs of manufacturing equipment accounts. Your review of Louis's policies and procedures has disclosed the following pertinent information:
    a. The manufacturing equipment account includes the net invoice price plus related freight and installation costs for all of the equipment in Louis's manufacturing plant.
    b. The manufacturing equipment and accumulated depreciation accounts are supported by a subsidiary ledger which shows the cost and accumulated depreciation for each piece of equipment.

c. An annual budget for capital expenditures of $1,000 or more is prepared by the budget committee and approved by the board of directors. Capital expenditures over $1,000 which are not included in this budget must be approved by the board of directors, and variations of 20 percent or more must be explained to the board. Approval by the supervisor of production is required for capital expenditures under $1,000.

d. Company employees handle installation, removal, repair, and rebuilding of the machinery. Work orders are prepared for these activities and are subject to the same budgetary control as other expenditures. Work orders are not required for external expenditures.

Required:

a. Cite the major objectives of your audit of the manufacturing equipment, manufacturing equipment–accumulated depreciation, and repairs of manufacturing equipment accounts. Do not include in this listing the auditing procedures designed to accomplish these objectives.

b. Prepare the portion of your audit program applicable to the review of 19X8 additions to the manufacturing equipment account.

(AICPA adapted)

21. The following types of internal controls are commonly employed by organizations for property, plant, and equipment:

a. Individual detailed subsidiary ledgers are maintained for each fixed asset.

b. Written policies exist and are known by accounting personnel to differentiate between capitalizable additions, freight, installation costs, replacements, and maintenance expenditures.

c. Purchases of permanent assets in excess of $20,000 are approved by the board of directors.

d. Wherever practical, equipment is labeled with metal tags and is inventoried in a systematic basis.

e. Depreciation charges for individual assets are calculated for each asset, recorded in individual subsidiary ledgers, and verified periodically by an independent clerk.

Required:

a. State the purpose of each of the above internal controls. Your answer should be in the form of the type of error that is likely to be reduced because of the control.

b. For each control, list one compliance procedure the auditor can use to test for the existence of the control.

c. List one substantive procedure for testing whether the control is actually preventing errors in property, plant, and equipment.

22. Hardware Manufacturing Company, a closely held corporation, has operated since 19X4 but has not had its financial statements audited. The company now plans to issue additional capital stock expected to be sold to outsiders and wishes to engage you to examine its 19X8 transactions and render an opinion on the financial statements for the year ended December 31, 19X8.

The company has expanded from one plant to three plants and has frequently acquired, modified, and disposed of all types of equipment. Fixed assets have a net book value of 70 percent of total assets and consist of land and buildings, diversified machinery and equipment, and furniture and fixtures. Some property was acquired by donation from stockholders. Depreciation was recorded by several methods using various estimated lives.

Required:

a. May you confine your examination solely to 19X8 transactions as requested by this prospective client whose financial statements have not previously been examined? Why?

b. Prepare an audit program for the January 1, 19X8, opening balances of the land, building, and equipment and accumulated depreciation accounts at Hardware Manufacturing Company. You need not include tests of 19X8 transactions in your program. (AICPA adapted)

23. You are engaged in the examination of the financial statements of the Ute Corporation for the year ended December 31, 19X7. The following schedules for the property, plant, and equipment and related allowance for depreciation accounts have been prepared by the client. You have checked the opening balances to your prior year's audit workpapers.

Ute Corporation

Analysis of Property, Plant, and Equipment and Related Allowance for Depreciation Accounts

Year Ended December 31, 19X7

Assets

Description	Final 12/31/X6	Additions	Retirements	Per Books 12/31/X7
Land	$ 22,500	$ 5,000		$ 27,500
Buildings	120,000	17,500		137,500
Machinery and equipment	385,000	40,400	$26,000	399,400
	$527,500	$62,900	$26,000	$564,400

Allowance for Depreciation

Description	Final 12/31/X6	Additions*	Retirements	Per Books 12/31/X7
Buildings	$ 60,000	$ 5,150		$ 65,150
Machinery and equipment	173,250	39,220		212,470
	$233,250	$44,370		$277,620

* *Depreciation expense for the year.*

Your examination reveals the following information:

a. All equipment is depreciated on the straight-line basis (no salvage value taken into consideration) based on the following estimated lives: buildings, 20 years; all other items, 10 years. The company's policy is to take one-half year's depreciation on all asset acquisitions and disposals during the year.

b. On April 1 the company entered into a ten-year lease contract for a die-casting machine with annual rentals of $5,000 payable in advance every April 1. The lease is cancelable by either party (sixty days' written notice is required) and there is no option to renew the lease or buy the equipment at the end of the lease. The estimated useful life of the machine is ten years with no salvage value. The company recorded the die-casting machine in the machinery and equipment account at $40,400, the present discounted value at the date of the lease, and $2,020, applicable to the machine, has been included in depreciation expense for the year.

c. The company completed the construction of a wing on the plant building on June 30. The useful life of the building was not extended by this addition. The lowest construction bid received was $17,500, the amount recorded in the buildings account. Company personnel were used to construct the addition at a cost of $16,000 (materials, $7,500; labor, $5,500; and overhead, $3,000).

d. On August 18, $5,000 was paid for paving and fencing a portion of land owned by the company and used as a parking lot for employees. The expenditure was charged to the land account.

e. The amount shown in the machinery and equipment asset retirement column represents cash received on September 5 upon disposal of a machine purchased in July 19X3 for $48,000. The bookkeeper recorded depreciation expense of $3,500 on this machine in 19X7.

f. Crux City donated land and building appraised at $10,000 and $40,000 respectively to the Ute Corporation for a plant. On September 1, the company began operating the plant. Since no costs were involved, the bookkeeper made no entry for the above transaction.

Required:

Prepare the formal adjusting journal entries that you would suggest at December 31, 19X7 to adjust the accounts for the above transactions. Disregard income-tax implications. The books have not been closed. Computations should be rounded off to the nearest dollar.   (AICPA adapted)

24. The following program has been prepared for the audit of prepaid real estate taxes of a client that pays taxes on twenty-five different pieces of property, some of which have been acquired in the current year:

a. Obtain a schedule of prepaid taxes from the client and tie the total to the general ledger.

b. Compare the charges for annual tax payments with property tax assessment bills.

c. Recompute prepaid amounts for all payments on the basis of the portion of the year expired.

Required:

a. State the purpose of each procedure.

b. Evaluate the adequacy of the audit program.

25. You have just commenced your examination of the financial statements of Vickey Corporation for the year ended December 31, 19X6. Analyses of the company's prepaid insurance and insurance expense accounts follow.

Vickey Corporation

Worksheet for Distribution of Insurance

For Year Ended December 31, 19X6

			Amount	
Date (19X6)	*Prepaid Insurance*	*Folio*	*Debit*	*Credit*
January 1	Balance forward		$ 5,550	
10	Premium on president's policy	CD	1,240	
14	Deposit on workmen's compensation policy for 19X6	CD	2,750	
31	Monthly amortization	JE		$ 410
April 1	Down payment on fire policy (April 1, 19X6, to April 1, 19X9)	CD	1,000	
	Total		$10,540	$ 410
	Insurance Expense			
January 10	Trip insurance on officers (inspection tour of dealers in December 19X5)	CD	$ 170	
31	Monthly amortization	JE	410	
February 21	Balance on workmen's compensation policy (per payroll audit for policy year ending December 31, 19X5) ..	CD	250	
April 10	Automobile collision policy (policy year April 1, 19X6 to April 1, 19X7)	CD	2,500	
June 10	Increase in fire policy (May 1, 19X6 to April 1, 19X9)	CD	590	
August 10	Fleet public liability and property damage policy (September 1, 19X6, to September 1, 19X7)	CD	3,780	
17	Check from insurance company for reduction in auto collision rate for entire policy year	CR		$ 120
October 1	Fire policy payment	CD	1,300	
19	Cost of repair to automobile damaged in a collision	CD	400	
	Total		$ 9,400	$ 120

Your examination also disclosed the following information:

a. Only one policy of those prepaid at January 1, 19X6, remained in force on December 31, and it will expire on March 31, 19X7. The policy was a 24-month policy and the total premium was $600.

b. Cash value of the life insurance policy on the life of the president increased from $1,110 to $1,660 during 19X6. The corporation is the beneficiary on the policy.

c. The corporation signed a note payable to an insurance company for the balance due on the fire insurance policy which was effective as of April 1. The note called for nine additional $1,000 semiannual payments plus interest at 6 percent per annum on the unpaid balance (also paid semi-annually).

d. An accrual dated December 31, 19X5, for $170 for insurance payable was included among accrued liabilities.

e. Included in miscellaneous income was a credit dated April 10 for $100 for a 4 percent dividend on the renewal of the automobile collision insurance policy. The insurance company is a mutual company. Also included in miscellaneous income was a credit dated November 2 for $350 for a check from the same insurance company for a claim filed October 19.

f. An invoice dated November 15 for $1,560 for employee fidelity bonds from November 15, 19X6, to November 15, 19X7, was not paid or recorded.

g. An invoice dated January 13, 19X7, for $2,800 for the 19X7 workmen's compensation policy was not recorded. The net amount of the invoice was $2,660 after a credit of $140 from the payroll audit for the year ended December 31, 19X6.

Required:

Prepare a worksheet to properly distribute all amounts related to insurance for 19X6. The books have not been closed for the year. The worksheet should provide columns to show the distribution to prepaid insurance, to insurance expense, and to other accounts. The names of other accounts affected should be indicated. Formal journal entries are not required.

(AICPA adapted)

26. You have assigned your assistant to the examination of the Cap Sales Company's fire insurance policies. All routine audit procedures with regard to the fire insurance register have been completed (i.e., vouching, footing, examination of canceled checks, computation of insurance expense and prepayment, tracing of expense charges to appropriate expense accounts, etc.). Your assistant has never examined fire insurance policies and asks for detailed instructions.

Required:

a. In addition to examining the policies for the amounts of insurance and premium and for effective and expiration dates, to what other details should your assistant give particular attention as he examines the policies? Give the reasons for examining each detail. (Confine your comments to fire insurance policies covering buildings, their contents, and inventories.)

b. After reviewing your assistant's working papers, you concur in his conclusion that the insurance coverage against loss by fire is inadequate and that if loss occurs the company may have insufficient assets to liquidate its debts. After a discussion with you, management refuses to increase the amount of insurance coverage.

(1) What mention will you make of this condition and contingency in your short-form report? Why?

(2) What effect will this condition and contingency have upon your opinion? Give the reasons for your position.   (AICPA adapted)

27. In examining the books of a manufacturing concern, you find on the December 31, 19X7, balance sheet the item "Costs of patents, $18,780."

Referring to the ledger accounts, you note the following items regarding one patent acquired in 19X1:

19X6 Legal costs incurred in defending the validity of the patent ..	$1,500
19X7 Legal costs in prosecuting an infringement suit	1,100
19X7 Legal costs (additional expenses) in the infringement suit	340
19X7 Cost of improvements (unpatented) on the patented device ...	900

There are no credits in the account and no allowance for amortization has been set up on the books for any of the patents. There are three other patents issued in 19X2, 19X3, and 19X4; all were developed by the staff of the client. The patented articles are presently very marketable but are estimated to be in demand only for the next few years.

Required:

    a. What auditing procedures of all the patents should be included in your work program and what details of patented articles should appear in the permanent file?

    b. Discuss the items included in the patent account both from accounting and from federal income tax standpoints.   (AICPA adapted)

28. As part of the audit of different audit areas, it is important to be alert for the possibility of unrecorded liabilities. For each of the following audit areas or accounts, describe a liability that could be uncovered and the audit procedures that could uncover it:

    a. Minutes of the board of directors' meetings

    b. Land and buildings

    c. Rent expense

    d. Interest expense

    e. Cash surrender value of life insurance

    f. Cash in the bank

    g. Officers' travel and entertainment expense

29. In connection with his examination of the financial statements of the Thames Corporation, a CPA is reviewing the federal income taxes payable account.

Required:

    a. Discuss reasons why the CPA should review federal income tax returns for prior years and the reports of internal revenue agents.

    b. What information will these reviews provide? (Do not discuss specific tax return items.)   (AICPA adapted)

30. With the approval of its board of directors, the Thames Corporation made a sizable payment for advertising during the year being audited. The corporation deducted the full amount in its federal income tax return. The controller acknowledges that this deduction probably will be disallowed because it relates to political matters. He has not provided for this disallowance in his federal income tax provision and refuses to do so because he fears that this will cause the revenue agent to believe that the deduction is not valid. What is the CPA's responsibility in this situation? Explain. (AICPA adapted)

31. While you are having lunch with a banker friend, you become involved in explaining to him how your firm conducts an audit in a typical engage-

ment. Much to your surprise, your friend is interested and is able to converse intelligently in discussing your philosophy of emphasizing the review and evaluation of internal control, analytical tests, tests of the system, and direct tests of balance sheet accounts. At the completion of your discussion, he says, "That all sounds great except for a couple of things. The point of view we take these days at our bank is the importance of a continual earnings stream. You seem to be emphasizing fraud detection and a fairly stated balance sheet. We would rather see you put more emphasis than you apparently do on the income statement."

Required:

How would you respond to your friend's comments?

32. You are examining the financial statements of a moderate-sized manufacturing corporation in connection with the preparation of financial statements to be issued with an unqualified opinion. There is some internal control, but the office and bookkeeping staff comprises only three persons. You have tested a random sample of acquisition transactions in detail and found no significant exceptions.

Required:

Submit a detailed audit program setting forth the steps you consider necessary in connection with the following expense accounts (the total of one year's charges in each account is set forth opposite each item):

Advertising	$60,000
Rent	8,000
Salesmen's commissions	39,000
Insurance	4,000

(AICPA adapted)

33. State what documents or evidence the auditor would examine in the verification of each of the following:
   a. Advertising expense, where advertising is placed through an agency
   b. Advertising expense, where advertising is placed directly in newspapers by the client
   c. Royalty expense
   d. Repair expense   (AICPA adapted)

34. Brian Day, a staff assistant, has been asked to analyze interest and legal expense as a part of the first-year audit of Rosow Manufacturing Company. In searching for a model to follow, Brian looked at other completed working papers in the current audit file and concluded that the closest thing to what he was looking for was a working paper for repair and maintenance expense account analysis. Following the approach used in analyzing repairs and maintenance, all interest and legal expenses in excess of $500 were scheduled and verified by examining supporting documentation.

Required:

   a. Evaluate Brian's approach to verifying interest and legal expense.
   b. Suggest a better approach to verifying these two account balances.

35. In performing tests of the acquisition and payment cycle for the Orlando Manufacturing Company, the staff assistant did a careful and complete job. Since the controls were evaluated as excellent before the testing began and

were determined to be operating effectively on the basis of the lack of errors in the tests of the system, the decision was made to significantly reduce the tests of expense account analysis. The audit senior decided to reduce but not eliminate the acquisition-related expense account analysis for repair expense, legal and other professional, miscellaneous, and utilities expense on the grounds that they should always be verified more extensively than normal accounts. The decision was also made to eliminate any account analysis for the purchase of raw materials, depreciation expense, supplies expense, insurance expense, and the current period additions to fixed assets.

Required:

a. List other considerations in the audit besides the effectiveness of the system of internal control that should affect the auditor's decision as to which accounts to analyze.
b. Assuming no significant problems were identified on the basis of the other considerations in part *a*, evaluate the auditor's decision of reducing but not eliminating expense account analysis for each account involved. Justify your conclusions.
c. Assuming no significant problems were identified on the basis of the other considerations in part *a*, evaluate the auditor's decision to eliminate expense account analysis for each account involved. Justify your conclusions.

16

Audit
of the
Inventory and Warehousing Cycle

Inventory takes many different forms, depending upon the nature of the operations of the business. For companies engaged in the retail or whole-sale business, the most important inventory is merchandise on hand available for sale. The inventory for hospitals includes food, drugs, and medical supplies. A manufacturing company has raw materials, purchased parts, and supplies for use in production, goods in the process of being manufactured, and finished goods available for sale. We have selected manufacturing company inventories for presentation in this text. However, most of the principles discussed apply to other types of businesses as well.

For the reasons given below, the audit of inventories is often the most complex and time-consuming part of the audit:

1. Inventory is generally a major item on the balance sheet, and it is often the largest item making up the accounts included in working capital.
2. The inventory is in different locations, which makes the physical control and counting of the inventory difficult. Companies must have their inventory accessible for the efficient manufacture and sale of the product, but this dispersal creates significant audit problems.
3. The diversity of the items in inventories creates difficulties for the auditor. Such items as jewels, chemicals, and electronic parts present problems of observation and valuation.

4. The valuation of inventory is also difficult due to such factors as obsolescence and the need to allocate manufacturing costs to inventory.
5. There are several acceptable inventory valuation methods, but any given client must apply a method consistent from year to year. Moreover, an organization may prefer to use different valuation methods for different parts of the inventory.

The physical flow of goods and the flow of costs in the inventory and warehousing cycle are shown in Figure 16-1 for a manufacturing company. The direct tie-in of the inventory and warehousing cycle to the acquisition and payment cycle and to the payroll and personnel cycle can be seen by examining the debits to the raw materials, direct labor, and manufacturing overhead T-accounts. The direct tie-in to the sales and collection cycle occurs at the point where finished goods are relieved (credited) and a charge is made to cost of goods sold. This close relationship to other transaction cycles in the organization is a basic characteristic of the audit of the inventory and warehousing cycle.

NATURE OF THE INVENTORY AND WAREHOUSING CYCLE

Functions in the Cycle and Internal Controls

The inventory and warehousing cycle can be thought of as comprising two separate but closely related systems, one involving the actual *physical*

FIGURE 16-1

FLOW OF INVENTORY AND COSTS
IN THE INVENTORY AND WAREHOUSING CYCLE

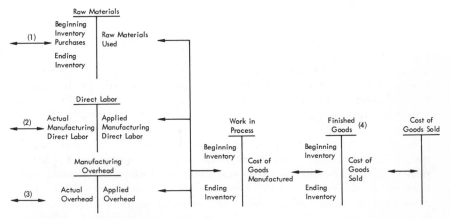

(1) Purchases arise from the acquisition and payment cycle.
(2) Actual costs arise from the payroll and personnel cycle.
(3) Actual costs arise from the acquisition and payment cycle, the payroll and personnel cycle, and the allocation of costs.
(4) Transfers to cost of goods sold arise from the sales and collection cycle.

flow of goods, and the other the *related costs.* As inventories move through the company, there must be adequate controls on both their physical movement and their related costs. A brief examination of the six functions making up the inventory and warehousing cycle will help in understanding these controls and the audit evidence needed to test their effectiveness.

Processing Purchase Orders. *Purchase requisitions* are used to request the purchasing department to place orders for inventory items. Requisitions may be initiated by stockroom personnel when inventory reaches a predetermined level, orders may be placed for the materials required to produce a particular customer order, or orders may be initiated on the basis of a periodic inventory count by a responsible person. Regardless of the method followed, the controls over purchase requisitions and the related purchase orders are evaluated and tested as part of the acquisition and payment cycle.

Receipt of New Materials. The receiving of the ordered materials is also part of the acquisition and payment cycle. Material received should be inspected for quantity and quality. The receiving department produces a *receiving report* which becomes a part of the necessary documentation before payment is made. After inspection, the material is sent to the storeroom and the receiving documents are typically sent to purchasing, the storeroom, and accounts payable.

Storage of Raw Materials. When material is received, it is stored in the stockroom until needed for production. Materials are issued out of stock to production upon presentation of a properly approved material requisition, work order, or similar document which indicates the type and quantity of material needed. This requisition document is used to post perpetual inventory records and to make book transfers from the raw materials to work in process accounts.

Processing the Goods. The processing portion of the inventory and warehousing cycle varies greatly from company to company. The determination of the items and quantities to be produced is generally based on specific orders from customers, sales forecasts, predetermined finished goods inventory levels, and economic production runs. Frequently a separate production control department is responsible for the determination of the type and quantities of production. Within the various production departments, provision must be made to account for the quantities produced, control of scrap, quality controls, and physical protection of the material in process. The production department must generate production and scrap reports so that accounting can reflect the movement of materials in the books and determine accurate costs of production.

In any company involved in manufacturing, an adequate *cost accounting system* is an important part of the processing of goods function. A cost system is necessary to indicate the relative profitability of the various products for management planning and control and to value inventories for financial statement purposes. There are basically two types of cost systems, although many variations and combinations of these systems are employed: *job cost* and *process cost*. The main difference is whether costs are accumulated by individual jobs when material is issued and labor costs incurred (job cost), or whether they are accumulated by particular processes, with unit costs for each process assigned to the products passing through the process (process cost).

Cost system records consist of ledgers, worksheets, and reports which accumulate material, labor, and overhead costs by job or process as the costs are incurred. When jobs or products are completed, the related costs are transferred from work in process to finished goods on the basis of production department reports.

Storage of Finished Goods. As finished goods are completed by the production department, they are placed in the stockroom awaiting shipment. In companies with good internal controls, finished goods are kept under physical control in a separate limited access area. The control of finished goods is often considered part of the sales and collection cycle.

Shipment. Shipping of completed goods is an integral part of the sales and collection cycle. Any shipment or transfer of finished goods must be authorized by a properly approved shipping document. The controls for shipment have already been studied in previous chapters.

Summary. The physical movement and related documentation in a basic inventory and warehousing cycle is shown in Figure 16-2. The figure re-emphasizes the important point that the recording of costs and movement of inventory as shown in the books must correspond to the physical movements and processes.

Parts of the Audit of the Inventory and Warehousing Cycle

The overall objective in the audit of the inventory and warehousing cycle is to determine that raw materials, work in process, finished goods inventory, and cost of goods sold are fairly stated on the financial statements. The basic inventory and warehousing cycle can be divided into five distinct parts:

Acquisition of Raw Materials, Labor, and Overhead Costs and Recording the Amounts in the Accounting Records. This part of the inventory and warehousing cycle includes the first three functions in Figure 16-2: processing of purchase orders, receipt of new materials, and storage of raw materials. The controls over these three functions are evaluated and tested as a part of performing compliance and substantive tests of transactions in the acquisition and payment cycle and the payroll and personnel cycle. At the completion of the acquisition and payment

FIGURE 16-2

Basic Inventory and Warehousing Cycle

	Processing of Purchase Orders	Receipt of New Materials	Storage of Raw Materials*	Processing the Goods*	Storage of Finished Goods*	Shipment
Flow of Material and Goods	1. Purchase requested by production department 2. Order placed by purchasing department	1. Goods received and inspected by separate receiving department	1. Goods placed in stockroom	1. Material placed in production 2. Direct labor incurred in production 3. Overhead costs incurred	1. Finished goods transferred from production to stockroom	1. Goods removed from stockroom and shipped
Related Documentation	1. Production department issues purchase requisition 2. Purchasing department issues purchase order and sends copy to: a. Vendor b. Receiving department c. Production department d. Accounting	1. Receiving department sends receiving reports and inspection reports to: a. Perpetual inventory b. Purchasing c. Stockroom d. Accounting 2. Accounting matches receiving reports, purchase orders, and invoices and records purchase	1. Quantities compared with receiving report (receiving report may be sent to accounting at this point in some systems) 2. Entries made in perpetual inventory records	1. Material requisitions recorded by a. Perpetual inventory b. Cost accounting c. General accounting 2. Labor and overhead cost distributed to applicable jobs or processes in cost records and in total in the general ledger	1. Production reports sent to: a. Perpetual inventory b. Cost accounting 2. Costs transferred from work in process to finished goods account	1. Shipping documents sent to: a. Perpetual records b. Accounting 2. Cost of sales entry made based on quantities shipped

*Inventory counts are taken and compared with perpetual and book amounts at any stage of the cycle, being certain that cutoff for recording documents corresponds to the physical location of the items. A count must ordinarily be taken at least once a year.

cycle, the auditor should be satisfied that acquisitions of raw materials and manufacturing costs are correctly stated. Similarly, when labor is a significant part of inventory, the payroll and personnel cycle tests should verify the proper accounting for these costs.

Internal Transfers of Assets and Costs. Internal transfers include the fourth and fifth functions in Figure 16-2: processing the goods and storage of finished goods. These two activities are not related to any other transaction cycles and therefore must be evaluated and tested as part of the inventory and warehousing cycle. The accounting records concerned with these functions are referred to as the *cost accounting records*.

Shipment of Goods and Recording the Revenue and Costs. The recording of shipments and related costs, which is the last function in Figure 16-2, is part of the sales and collection cycle. Thus, the controls over the function are evaluated and tested as a part of auditing the sales and collection cycle. The tests of the system should include procedures to verify the accuracy of the perpetual inventory records.

Physical Observation of Inventory. Observing the client taking a physical inventory count is necessary to determine whether recorded inventory actually exists at the balance sheet date and is properly counted by the client. Inventory is the first audit area in the text where physical examination is an essential type of evidence used to verify the balance in an account. Physical observation is studied in this chapter.

Inventory Pricing and Compilation. The costs used to value the physical inventory must be tested to determine whether the client has correctly followed an inventory method that is in accordance with generally accepted accounting principles and is consistent with previous years. The audit procedures used to verify these costs are referred to as *price tests*. In addition, the auditor must verify whether the physical counts were correctly summarized, the inventory quantities and prices were correctly extended, and the extended inventory was correctly footed. These tests are called *compilation tests*.

The first and third parts of the audit of the inventory and warehousing cycle have already been studied in connection with the other cycles. The importance of the tests of these other cycles should be kept in mind throughout the remaining sections of this chapter.

AUDIT OF COST ACCOUNTING

The cost accounting systems of different companies vary more than most other systems because of the wide variety of items of inventory and the level of sophistication desired by management. For example, a company that manufactures an entire line of farm machines will have a completely different kind of cost system than a steel fabricating shop that makes and installs custom-made metal cabinets. And it should not be surprising that small companies whose owners are actively involved in the manufacturing process will need less sophisticated records than will large multiproduct companies.

Controls over the Cost Accounting Department

Cost accounting controls are those controls that are related to the physical inventory and the consequent costs from the point where raw materials are requisitioned to the point where the manufactured product is completed and transferred to storage. It is convenient to divide these controls into two broad categories: the physical control over raw materials, work in process, and finished goods inventory, and the controls over the related costs.

Almost all companies need physical control over their assets to prevent loss from misuse and theft. The use of physically segregated, limited access storage areas for raw material, work in process, and finished goods is one major control to protect assets. In some instances the assignment of custody of inventory to specific responsible individuals may be necessary to protect the assets. Approved prenumbered documents for authorizing movement of inventory also protects the assets from improper use. Copies of these documents should be sent directly to accounting by the persons issuing them, bypassing people with custodial responsibilities. An example of an effective document of this type is an approved material requisition for obtaining raw material from the storeroom.

Perpetual inventory records maintained by persons who do not have custody of or access to assets is another useful cost accounting control. Perpetual inventory records are important for a number of reasons: they provide a record of items on hand, which is used to initiate production or purchase of additional materials or goods; they provide a record of the use of raw materials and the sale of finished goods, which can be reviewed for obsolete or slow-moving items; and they provide a record that can be used to pinpoint responsibility for custody as a part of the investigation of differences between physical counts and the amount shown on the records.

Another important control in cost accounting is the existence of an adequate system that integrates production and accounting records for the purpose of obtaining accurate costs for all products. The existence of adequate cost records is important to management as an aid in pricing, controlling costs, and costing inventory.

Tests of the Cost Accounting System

In auditing the cost accounting system, the auditor is concerned with four aspects: physical controls over inventory, documents and records for transferring inventory, perpetual records, and unit cost records.

Physical Controls. The auditor's tests of the adequacy of the physical controls over raw materials, work in process, and finished goods must be restricted to observation and inquiry. For example, the auditor can examine the raw materials storage area to determine whether the inventory is protected from theft and misuse by the existence of a locked storeroom. The existence of an adequate storeroom with a competent custodian in charge also ordinarily results in the orderly storage of inventory. If the auditor concludes that the physical controls are so inadequate that the inventory will be difficult to count, he should expand his observation of physical inventory tests to make sure that an adequate count is carried out.

Documents and Records for Transferring Inventory. The auditor's primary concerns in verifying the transfer of inventory from one location to another are that the recorded transfers are valid, the transfers that have actually taken place are recorded, and the quantity, description, and date of all recorded transfers are accurate. As in all other systems, it is necessary to understand the client's accounting system for recording transfers before relevant tests can be performed. Once the system is understood, the tests can easily be performed by examining documents and records. For example, a procedure to test the validity and accuracy of the transfer of goods from the raw material storeroom to the manufacturing assembly line is to account for a sequence of raw material requisitions, examine the requisitions for proper approval, and compare the quantity, description, and date with the information on the raw material perpetual records. Similarly, completed production records can be compared with the perpetual records to be sure all manufactured goods were physically delivered to the finished goods storeroom.

Perpetual Records. The existence of adequate perpetual inventory records has a major effect on the *timing and extent* of the auditor's physical examination of inventory. For one thing, when there are reliable perpetual records it is frequently possible to test the physical inventory prior to the balance sheet date. An interim physical inventory can result in significant cost savings for both the client and the auditor, and it enables the client to get the audited statements earlier. Perpetual records also enable the auditor to reduce the extent of the tests of physical inventory because reliance can be put on this control.

Tests of the perpetual records for the purpose of reducing the tests of physical inventory or changing their timing are done through the use of documentation. Documents to verify the purchase of raw materials can be examined at the time the auditor is verifying acquisitions as part of the tests of the acquisition and payment cycle. Documents supporting the reduction of raw material inventory for use in production and the increase in the quantity of finished goods inventory when goods have been manufactured are examined as part of the tests of the cost accounting documents and records in the manner discussed in the preceding section. Support for the reduction in the finished goods inventory through the sale of goods to customers is ordinarily tested as part of the sales and collection cycle. Usually it is relatively easy to test the accuracy of the perpetual records after the auditor determines how the system is designed and decides to what degree he intends to rely on the system.

Unit Cost Records. Obtaining accurate cost data for raw materials, direct labor, and manufacturing overhead is an essential part of the cost accounting system. An adequate cost system must be integrated with production and accounting records in order to produce accurate costs of all products. The cost accounting system is pertinent to the auditor in that the valuation of ending inventory depends upon the proper design and use of the system.

In testing the inventory cost records, the auditor must first develop an understanding of how the system operates. This is frequently somewhat time-consuming because the flow of costs is usually integrated with other systems, and it may not be obvious how the system provides for the internal transfers of raw materials and for direct labor and manufacturing overhead as production is carried out.

Once the auditor understands how the system operates, the approach to internal verification involves the same concepts that were discussed in the verification of sales and purchase transactions. Whenever possible, it is desirable to test the cost accounting records as a part of the acquisition, payroll, and sales tests to avoid testing the records more than once. For example, when the auditor is testing purchase transactions as a part of the acquisition and payment cycle, it is desirable to trace the units and unit costs of raw materials to the perpetual records and the total cost to the cost accounting records. Similarly, when payroll cost data are maintained for different jobs, it is desirable to trace from the payroll summary directly to the job cost record as a part of testing the payroll and personnel cycle.

A major difficulty in the verification of inventory cost records is determining the reasonableness of cost allocations. For example, the assignment of manufacturing overhead costs to individual products entails certain assumptions that can significantly affect the unit costs of inventory and therefore the fairness of the inventory valuation. In evaluating these allocations, the auditor must consider the reasonableness of both the numerator and the denominator that result in the unit costs. For example, in testing overhead applied to inventory on the basis of direct labor dollars, the overhead rate should approximate total actual manufacturing overhead divided by total actual direct labor dollars. Since total manufacturing overhead is tested as part of the tests of the acquisition and payment cycle and direct labor is tested as part of the payroll and personnel cycle, determining the reasonableness of the rate is not difficult. On the other hand, if manufacturing overhead is applied on the basis of machine hours, the auditor must verify the reasonableness of the machine hours by separate tests of the client's machine records. A major consideration in evaluating the reasonableness of all cost allocations, including manufacturing overhead, is consistency with previous years.

PHYSICAL OBSERVATION OF INVENTORY

Prior to the late 1930s auditors generally avoided responsibility for determining either the physical existence or the accuracy of the count of inventories. The audit evidence for the inventory quantities was usually restricted to obtaining a certification from management as to the correctness of the stated amount. In 1938 the discovery of major fraud in the McKesson & Robbins Company caused a reappraisal by the accounting profession of its responsibilities relating to inventory. In brief, the financial statements for McKesson & Robbins at December 31, 1937, which were "certified to" by a major accounting firm, reported total consolidated assets of $87 million. Of this amount, approximately $19 million was subsequently determined to be fictitious: $10 million in inventory and $9 million in receivables. Due primarily to their adherence to generally accepted auditing practice of that period, the auditing firm was not held directly at fault in the inventory area. However, it was noted that if certain procedures, such as observation of the physical inventory, had been carried out, the fraud would probably have been detected. The following requirement exists for inventory observation as a result of the McKesson & Robbins fraud:

> . . . it is ordinarily necessary for the independent auditor to be present at the time of count, and, by suitable observation, tests, and inquiries, satisfy himself respecting the effectiveness of the methods of inventory-taking and the measure of reliance which may be placed upon the client's representations about the quantities and physical condition of the inventories.[1]

An essential point in the SAS 1 requirement is the distinction between the observation of the physical inventory and the responsibility for taking it. The client has responsibility for setting up the procedures for taking an accurate physical inventory and actually making and recording the counts. The auditor's responsibility is to evaluate and observe the client's physical procedures and draw conclusions about the adequacy of the physical inventory.

The requirement of physical examination of inventory is not applicable in the case of *inventory in a public warehouse.* The AICPA position on inventory stored in a public warehouse is summarized as follows in Statement on Auditing Standards No. 1:

> In the case of inventories which in the ordinary course of business are in the hands of public warehouses or other outside custodians, direct confirmation in writing from the custodians is acceptable provided that,

[1] SAS 1 (331.09).

where the amount involved represents a significant proportion of the current assets or the total assets, supplemental inquiries are made to satisfy the independent auditor as to the bona fides of the situation.[2]

The Committee on Auditing Standards recommends that the supplemental inquiries include the following steps, to the extent that the auditor considers them necessary in the circumstances:

a. Discussion with the owner as to the owner's control procedures in investigating the warehouseman, and tests of related evidential matter.
b. Review of the owner's control procedures concerning performance of the warehouseman, and tests of related evidential matter.
c. Observation of physical counts of the goods, wherever practicable and reasonable.
d. Where warehouse receipts have been pledged as collateral, confirmation (on a test basis, where appropriate) from lenders as to pertinent details of the pledged receipts.[3]

Controls over the Physical Count of Inventory

Regardless of the client's inventory record keeping method, there must be a periodic physical count of the inventory items on hand. The client can take the physical count at or near the balance sheet date, at a preliminary date, or on a cycle basis throughout the year. The last two approaches are appropriate only if an adequate perpetual inventory system exists.

In connection with the client's physical count of inventory, adequate control procedures include proper instructions for the physical count, supervision by responsible personnel, independent internal verification of the counts, independent reconciliations of the physical counts with perpetual records, and adequate control over count tags or sheets.

An important aspect of the auditor's evaluation of the client's physical inventory control procedures is complete familiarity with them before the inventory begins. This is obviously necessary to evaluate the effectiveness of the client's procedures, but it also enables the auditor to make constructive suggestions beforehand. If the inventory instructions do not provide adequate controls, the auditor must spend more time making sure the physical count is accurate.

Audit Decisions in Physical Observation

The auditor's decisions in the physical observation of inventory are of the same general nature as in any other audit area: selection of audit procedures, timing, determination of sample size, and selection of the items for testing. The selection of the audit procedures is discussed

2 SAS 1, p. 62.
3 *Ibid.*

throughout the section; the other three decisions are discussed briefly at this time.

Timing. The auditor decides whether the physical count can be taken prior to year-end primarily on the basis of the accuracy of the perpetual inventory records. When an interim physical count is permitted, the auditor observes it at that time and also tests the perpetual records for transactions from the date of the count to year-end. In instances where the perpetual records are highly reliable, it may be unnecessary for the client to count the inventory every year. Instead, the auditor can test the perpetual records to the actual inventory on a sample basis at a convenient time. When there are no perpetual records, and the inventory is material, a complete physical inventory must be taken by the client near the end of the accounting period and tested by the auditor at the same time.

Sample size. Sample size in physical observation is usually impossible to specify in terms of the number of items because the emphasis during the tests is on observing the client's procedures rather than on selecting particular items for testing. A convenient way to think of sample size in physical observation is in terms of the total number of hours spent on the observation rather than the number of inventory items counted. The most important determinants of the amount of time needed to test the inventory are the quality of the controls over the physical counts, the reliability of the perpetual records, the total dollar amount and the type of inventory, the number of different significant inventory locations, and the nature and extent of errors discovered in previous years. In some situations inventory is such a significant item that dozens of auditors are necessary to observe the physical count, whereas in other situations one person can complete the observation in a short time.

Selection of Items. The selection of the particular items for testing is an important part of the audit decision in inventory observation. Care should be taken to observe the counting of the most significant items and a representative sample of typical inventory items, to inquire about items that are likely to be obsolete or damaged, and to discuss with management the reasons for excluding any material items.

Physical Observation Tests

The same detailed objectives that have been used in previous sections for direct tests of balances provide the frame of reference for discussing the physical observation tests. However, before the detailed objectives are discussed, some comments that apply to all of the objectives are appropriate.

The most important part of the observation of inventory is determining whether the physical count is being taken in accordance with the client's instructions. To do this effectively, *it is essential that the auditor be present* while the physical count is taking place. When the client's employees are not following the inventory instructions, the auditor must either contact the supervisor to correct the problem or modify the physical observation procedures. For example, if the procedures require one team to count the inventory and a second team to recount it as a test of accuracy, the auditor should inform management if he observes both teams counting together.

Obtaining an adequate understanding of the client's business is even more important in physical observation of inventory than for most aspects of the audit because inventory varies so significantly for different companies. A proper understanding of the client's business and its industry enables the auditor to ask about and discuss such problems as inventory valuation, potential obsolescence, and existence of consignment inventory intermingled with owned inventory. A useful starting point for the auditor to familiarize himself with the client's inventory is a tour of the client's facilities, including receiving, storage, production, planning, and record-keeping areas. The tour should be led by a supervisor who can answer questions about production, especially about any changes in the past year.

Attention is now turned to the detailed audit objectives.

Existence. Throughout the observation of the client's counting, the auditor should be aware of any aspect of the physical examination that is likely to result in material errors. Examples include the omission of large sections of inventory, duplicate counting of inventory, and significant movement of inventory during the count. The auditor can test for omitted inventory by examining different types of inventory to be sure each type is tagged. For example, if an inventory of parts is stored in bins where each part is in a separate compartment, the auditor could examine several compartments to be sure that each has an inventory tag attached. Duplicate counting of inventory can be tested by observing whether there is more than one tag on a pile of inventory. If the auditor is concerned about the possibility of fraudulent counts, several tag numbers can be selected at random and the tags examined to be sure each one is attached to an item of inventory.

Ownership. The fact that the inventory exists on the client's premises is some evidence of ownership, but the auditor should be aware of the possibility that *consigned* or other nonowned inventory may be included in the inventory. Discussions with the client, an understanding of the client's operations, and alertness for inventory items set aside or specially marked are useful in discovering unowned inventory.

Valuation. There are four important aspects of valuation in physical observation.

1. *Test counts.* In addition to observing the taking of the physical inventory, it is also necessary to recount some of the client's counts to be sure they are correct. Some of the auditor's test counts can be rough estimates to be sure the count is reasonable, but some should also be

made to check the accuracy of the client's counts. The test counts should emphasize the most material items, but a representative sample of all types of inventory should also be included. In performing test counts it is important to examine the recorded counts for quantity, proper description including the stage of completion for work in process, and unit of count such as ounce, pound, or ton.

2. *Recording client counts for subsequent testing.* It is necessary to record some of the client's inventory counts in the working papers on *inventory count sheets* for two reasons: to obtain documentation that an adequate physical examination was made, and to test for the possibility that the client might change the recorded counts after the auditor leaves the premises. In listing inventory quantities on the count sheets, it is important to record them in a manner that will facilitate the subsequent tracing of the counts to the client's recorded inventory quantities. The tag number, description of the item, quantity, and unit of count should all be carefully recorded on the count sheet.

3. *Comparison of physical counts with perpetual records.* When the client has perpetual records, the auditor's inventory counts can be reduced if a comparison is made of the physical and perpetual records. Substantial agreement between the physical counts and the perpetual records is evidence of the accuracy of both the physical counts and the perpetual records.

4. *Obsolescence tests.* Throughout the physical observation, the auditor should be alert for obsolete inventory. Items that are damaged, rust or dust covered, or located in areas that seem inappropriate for the nature of the inventory should be investigated and discussed with management. It is also appropriate to ask the employees taking the physical counts about the condition, usefulness, and turnover of the inventory.

Classification. As the auditor is observing the physical inventory, care should be taken to make sure the description on the inventory tags is correct. It is necessary to examine the inventory and compare it with the recorded description to distinguish between raw materials, work in process, and finished goods, but it is also important to test for accurate part numbers on the tags, the correct description of the state of completion of work in process, and the adequate inclusion of notations about obsolescence and damaged goods.

Cutoff Information. An important part of obtaining a reasonable cutoff of sales and purchases is accomplished during the physical inventory observation. A correct cutoff of sales requires that finished goods inventory included in the physical count be excluded from sales. Similarly, finished goods inventory excluded from the physical count because the goods have been set aside for shipment or already shipped out must be recorded as a sale. For the sales cutoff, the last shipping document number used should be recorded in the working papers for subsequent follow-up. In addition, a review should be made of the shipping department to test for the possibility of shipments set aside for shipping and not counted or goods awaiting pickup by customers. When prenumbered shipping documents are not used, a careful review of the client's method of getting a proper sales cutoff is the first step in testing the cutoff. Second, an evaluation of the effectiveness of the client's method must be made, preferably well before the audit starts. Finally, the auditor should include a list of the most recent shipments in the working papers for subsequent follow-up.

For the purchases cutoff, goods not included in inventory must also be excluded from purchases. The last receiving report number representing inventory included in the physical count should be documented in the working papers. A review should also be made of the receiving department to make sure that all inventory has been properly included in the physical count.

The appropriate audit procedures to use for testing whether the client has properly recorded the cutoff in its records have already been discussed for sales in Chapter 8 and for purchases in Chapter 14.

Mechanical Accuracy. At the completion of the physical count, the client should account for all used and unused tag numbers to make sure no tags have been lost or intentionally omitted. The auditor should record the used and unused tag numbers in the working papers for subsequent follow-up as a means of determining whether the client has added or deleted tags after the auditor left the premises.

Overall Reasonableness. At the completion of the physical observation, the auditor should review and summarize the results to determine whether the client's physical inventory reflects the actual inventory on hand. The overall review includes two important phases:

1. *Follow-up of exceptions.* Any exceptions observed in any of the preceding steps should be carefully documented in the working papers. They should be discussed with the client to determine the cause of the errors and the potential significance of the results. In evaluating the exceptions, it should always be kept in mind that the errors in the population are much more relevant than the errors in the sample. If extensive errors occur, consideration should be given to expanding the physical observation.

2. *Review for large omissions and duplications.* After the client has completed its counting of the inventory, the auditor should make a tour of the facilities to make sure the inventory at all locations has been counted and properly tagged. The objective is to make certain that no significant inventory has been overlooked or counted twice.

Disclosure. Before the adequacy of financial statement disclosure can be evaluated, the physical count of inventory must be compiled, priced, extended, and totaled. Therefore tests of disclosure are not a part of the physical observation procedure.

AUDIT OF PRICING AND COMPILATION

An important part of the audit of inventory is to perform all of the procedures necessary to make certain the physical counts were properly priced and compiled. *Pricing* includes all the tests of the client's unit prices to determine whether they are correct. *Compilation* includes all the tests of the summarization of the physical counts, the extension of price times quantity, footing the inventory summary, and tracing the totals to the general ledger.

Controls over Pricing and Compilation

The existence of an adequate cost system that is integrated with production and accounting records is the most important control for ensuring that reasonable costs are used for valuing ending inventory. A closely related control is the use of a *standard cost system* that indicates variances in material, labor, and overhead costs and can be used to evaluate the production system. When standard costs are used, procedures must be designed to keep the standards updated for changes in production processes and costs. The review of unit costs for reasonableness by someone independent of the department responsible for developing the costs is also a useful control over valuation.

A control designed to prevent the overstatement of inventory through the inclusion of obsolete inventory is a formal system of review and reporting of obsolete, slow-moving, damaged, and overstated inventory items. The review should be done by a competent employee by reviewing perpetual records for inventory turnover and holding discussions with engineering or production personnel.

Compilation controls are needed to provide a means of ensuring that the physical counts are properly summarized, priced at the same amount as the unit records, correctly extended and totaled, and included in the general ledger at the proper amount. Important compilation controls are adequate documents and records for taking the physical count and proper internal verification. If the physical inventory is taken on prenumbered tags and carefully reviewed before the personnel are released from the physical examination of inventory, there should be little risk of error in summarizing the tags. The most important control over accurate determination of prices, extensions, and footings is internal verification by a competent independent person.

Pricing and Compilation Procedures

The eight detailed objectives for direct tests of balances are also useful in discussing pricing and compilation procedures. For ease of studying the subject matter, the order of discussing the objectives has been changed.

Overall Reasonableness. Many of the ratios affecting inventory and cost of goods sold have been discussed in previous chapters, but their repetition at this point illustrates the close relationship of this cycle to the other cycles in the audit. Several appropriate ratios and trends for comparison with prior years are as follows:

Ratio or Trend	*Indication of Error in Inventory*
1. Comparison of gross margin percentage with previous years	Possible overstatement or understatement of inventory
2. Comparison of inventory turnover (costs of goods sold ÷ average inventory) with previous years	Possible obsolescence of inventory
3. Comparison of unit costs of inventory with previous years	Possible significant overstatement or understatement of unit costs
4. Comparison of current year manufacturing costs with previous years (variable costs should be adjusted for changes in volume)	Possible misstatement of unit costs of inventory, especially direct labor and manufacturing overhead

Existence. The major consideration in the compilation tests is making sure the physical counts have been properly included in the final inventory listing. For every engagement, the auditor must determine that all physical counts have been included in the final inventory summary, no physical count has been included in the summary more than once, no inventory items have been added after the physical count was completed, and the quantity and descriptions on the counts have been correctly included in the summary.

It is not possible to specify the exact audit procedures that should be applied for compilation because of significant differences in clients' systems, but several general observations can be made:

1. The tag numbers that were used in the physical count and in the audit working papers at the time of the observation should be traced to the final inventory summary to make sure they are properly included. Similarly, the unused tag numbers should be traced from the working papers to the summary to make sure no tag numbers have been added.
2. The test counts recorded in the audit working papers at the time of the observation should be traced to the final inventory summary to make sure they are correctly included.
3. Inventory items included in the final inventory summary can be traced to the tags for quantity and description as a test of the validity and accuracy of recorded inventory. Similarly, the information on inventory tags can be traced to the final inventory summary to make sure the physical counts have been properly included. The extent to which this should be done depends upon the extent

of test counts traced, the quality of the client's system, and the results of previous years' tests.

Classification. The classification of inventory into raw materials, work in process, and finished goods must be tested for proper presentation on the financial statements. As part of the compilation, it is normal practice to trace from the auditor's recorded test counts and inventory tags to make sure the client has properly summarized the inventory. If the auditor is familiar with the client's operations, he may also be able to distinguish between raw material and finished goods inventory by reviewing the descriptions of the items in the summary.

Ownership. A portion of the tests of ownership, such as observation for consigned inventory and discussions with the client's personnel, are done as a part of the physical observation. As a part of pricing and compilation, it is appropriate to review contracts with suppliers and customers and have discussions with management to test for the possibility of consigned inventory or inventory owned by others that is in the client's shop for repair or some other purpose.

Valuation. The proper valuation (pricing) of inventory is often one of the most important and time-consuming parts of the audit. In performing pricing tests, three things about the clients method of pricing are of the utmost importance: the method must be in accordance with generally accepted accounting principles, the application of the method must be consistent from year to year, and the lower of cost or market must be considered. Because the method of verifying the pricing of inventory depends upon whether items are purchased or manufactured, these two categories are discussed separately.

Pricing purchased inventory. The primary types of inventory included in this category are raw materials, purchased parts, and supplies. As a first step in verifying the valuation of purchased inventory, it is necessary to clearly establish whether LIFO, FIFO, Weighted Average, or some other valuation method is being used. It is also necessary to determine which costs should be included in the valuation of a particular item of inventory. For example, the auditor must find out whether freight, storage, discounts, and other costs are included in the cost and compare the findings with the preceding year's audit working papers to make sure the methods are consistent.

In selecting specific inventory items for pricing, emphasis should be put on the larger dollar amounts and on products that are known to have wide fluctuations in price, but a representative sample of all types of inventory and departments should be included as well. Stratified variables sampling is commonly used in these tests.

The auditor should list the inventory items he intends to verify for pricing and request the client to locate the appropriate vendor's invoices for him. It is important that sufficient invoices be examined to account for the entire quantity of inventory for the particular item being tested, especially for the FIFO valuation method. Examining sufficient invoices is useful to uncover situations where clients value their inventory on the basis of the most recent invoice only and in some cases to discover obsolete inventory. As an illustration, assume the client's valuation of a particular inventory is $12.00 per unit for 1,000 units, using FIFO. The auditor should examine the most recent invoices for acquisitions of that inventory item made in the year under audit until the valuation of all of the 1,000 units is accounted for. If the most recent acquisition of the inventory item was for 700 units at $12.00 per unit and the immediately preceding acquisition was for 600 units at $11.30 per unit, the inventory item in question is overstated by $210.00 (300 × $.70).

When the client has perpetual inventory records that include unit costs of acquisitions, it is usually desirable to test the pricing by tracing the unit costs to the perpetual records rather than to vendor's invoices. In most cases the effect is to significantly reduce the cost of verifying inventory valuation. Naturally, when the perpetual records are used to verify unit costs, it is essential to test the unit costs on the perpetual records to vendor's invoices as a part of the tests of the acquisition and payment cycle.

In price-testing inventory, care should be taken to identify the error in each item tested regardless of size. Even though an error in a particular sample item may be small in itself, the total error may be material if the error is common throughout the entire population. In the previous example the $210 error is probably immaterial, but it may be an indication of a common error in pricing.

Lower of cost or market must also be considered in pricing inventory. The most recent cost of an inventory item as indicated on a vendor's invoice of the subsequent period is a useful way to test for the market replacement cost, but it is also necessary to consider the sales value of the inventory item and the possible effect of rapid fluctuation of prices. As part of evaluating the lower of cost or market, it is also necessary to consider the possibility of obsolescence.

After the detailed price testing of purchased inventory is completed, it is desirable to review the inventory prices for reasonableness. Whenever possible, the prices should be compared with the preceding year and with standard costs, or simply examined for reasonableness on the basis of the auditor's knowledge of the value of the inventory. In this review, particular emphasis should be put on the unit of measure. For example, if the unit cost is stated in tons and the units are stated in pounds, the result could be a significant misstatement.

Pricing manufactured inventory. The auditor must consider the cost of raw materials, direct labor, and manufacturing overhead in pricing work in process and finished goods. The need to verify each of these has the effect of making the audit of work in process and finished goods inventory more complex than the audit of purchased inventory. Nevertheless, such considerations as selecting the items to be tested, testing for the lower of cost or market, and evaluating the possibility of obsolescence also apply.

It is necessary to consider both the unit cost of the raw materials and the number of units required to manufacture a unit of output in pricing raw materials in manufactured products. The unit cost can be verified in the same manner as that used for other purchased inventory—by examining vendor's invoices or perpetual records. Then it is necessary to examine engineering specifications, inspect the finished product, or find a similar method to determine the number of units it takes to manufacture a particular product.

Similarly, the hourly costs of direct labor and the number of hours it takes to manufacture a unit of output must be verified while testing direct labor. Hourly labor costs can be verified by comparison with labor payroll or union contracts. The number of hours needed to manufacture the product can be determined from engineering specifications or similar sources.

The proper manufacturing overhead in work in process and finished goods is dependent upon the approach being used by the client. It is necessary to evaluate the method being used for consistency and reasonableness and to recompute the costs to determine whether the overhead is correct. For example, if the rate is based on direct labor dollars, the auditor can divide the total manufacturing overhead by the total direct labor dollars to determine the actual overhead rate. This rate can then be compared with the overhead rate used by the client to determine unit costs.

When the client has a *standard cost system,* an efficient and useful method of determining valuation is by the review and analysis of variances. If the variances in material, labor, and manufacturing overhead are small, it is evidence of reliable cost records.

Mechanical Accuracy. A part of the compilation tests is the verification of extensions and footings. In testing the price times the quantity, special attention should be given to the proper unit of measure, the decimal point, and transposition errors. Sight testing is appropriate for most extensions, but some should be checked for absolute correctness. Individual pages should be footed, and the total of all pages should be tied to the general ledger. The extent of these tests should depend on whether the extensions and footings have been internally verified by client personnel, the number of inventory items, and the results found in previous year's audits.

Cutoff. The major purpose of inventory cutoff tests is to make sure the client has recorded shipments of inventory consistently with the recording of sales, and receipts of raw materials consistently with the recording of accounts payable. If a shipment has been excluded from inventory because the goods have already been sold, it must be included as a sale. Similarly, if inventory has been included in the physical count, it cannot also be included as a sale. A corresponding relationship exists between inventory and accounts payable.

Inventory cutoff tests can be considered a part of inventory audit procedures or a part of the audit of sales, purchases, and accounts payable.

Since the emphasis in cutoff tests is the examination of supporting documentation, they are normally performed as a part of sales, purchases, and accounts payable. Appropriate methodology for these tests has already been discussed in previous chapters, but it is worthwhile to point out again that the cutoff tests in sales, purchases, and accounts payable depend heavily on the cutoff information obtained during the physical observation of inventory.

Disclosure. At the completion of the tests of inventory, the auditor must evaluate whether the disclosure in the financial statements is adequate. Generally, all inventories are included in current assets and are broken down by raw materials, work in process, and finished goods. Generally accepted accounting principles also require the inclusion of a brief description of the method used for determining cost. An example of a commonly used description is "at cost (first-in, first-out method) or market, whichever is lower."

If inventory is pledged as collateral, or if there are significant purchase or sales commitments, this information must be disclosed in the notes to the financial statements. Information about pledged assets is usually obtained as a part of auditing liabilities and commitments, which is discussed in Chapters 17 and 19.

AN INTEGRATION OF THE TESTS

The most difficult part of understanding the audit of the inventory and warehousing cycle is to grasp the interrelationship of the many different tests the auditor makes to evaluate whether inventory and cost of goods sold are fairly stated. The following summary endeavors to aid the reader in perceiving the audit of the inventory and warehousing cycle as a series of integrated tests. The summary is depicted graphically in Figure 16-3.

Tests of the Acquisition and Payment Cycle. Whenever the auditor verifies acquisitions as part of the tests of the acquisition and payment cycle, evidence is being obtained about the accuracy of raw materials purchased and all manufacturing overhead costs except labor. These acquisition costs either flow directly into cost of goods sold or become the most significant part of the ending inventory of raw material, work in process, and finished goods. In audits involving perpetual inventory systems, it is common to test these as a part of tests of transactions procedures in the acquisition and payment cycle. Similarly, if manufacturing costs are assigned to individual jobs or processes, they are usually tested as a part of the same cycle.

Tests of the Payroll and Personnel Cycle. When the auditor verifies labor costs, the same comments apply as for acquisitions. In most cases the cost accounting records for direct and indirect labor costs can be tested as part of the audit of the payroll and personnel cycle if there is adequate advance planning.

FIGURE 16-3

INTERRELATIONSHIP OF VARIOUS TESTS
IN AUDITING INVENTORY AND COST OF GOODS SOLD

OBJECTIVE: Determine whether there is a fair presentation on the
financial statements of raw materials, work in process,
finished goods, and cost of goods sold.

INTERRELATED TESTS:

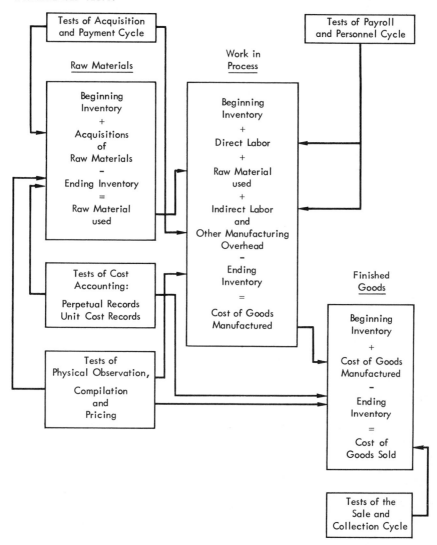

Tests of the Sales and Collection Cycle. Although there is a less
close relationship between the sales and collection and the inventory and
warehousing cycles than the two previously discussed, the relationship is

still important. Most of the audit testing in the storage of finished goods as well as the shipment and recording of sales takes place when the sales and collection cycle is tested. In addition, if a standard cost system is used, it may be possible to test the standard cost of goods sold at the same time that sales tests are performed.

Tests of Cost Accounting. Tests of cost accounting are meant to verify the controls affecting inventory that were not verified as part of the three previously discussed cycles. Tests are made of the physical controls, transfers of raw material costs to work in process, transfers of costs of completed goods to finished goods, perpetual records, and unit cost records.

Physical Inventory, Compilation, and Pricing. In most audits the underlying assumption in testing the inventory and warehousing cycle is that cost of goods sold is a residual of beginning inventory plus acquisitions of raw materials, direct labor, and other manufacturing costs minus ending inventory. When the audit of inventory and cost of goods sold is approached with this idea in mind, the importance of ending inventory becomes obvious. Physical inventory, compilation, and pricing are each equally important in the audit because an error in any one results in misstated inventory and cost of goods sold.

In testing the physical inventory, it is possible to rely heavily upon the perpetual records if they have been tested as a part of one or more of the previously discussed tests. In fact, if the perpetual records are considered reliable, the auditor can observe and test the physical count at some time during the year and rely upon the perpetuals to keep adequate records of the quantities.

When testing the unit costs, it is also possible to rely, to some degree, on the tests of the cost records made during the tests of transaction cycles. The existence of standard cost records is also useful for the purpose of comparison with the actual unit costs. If the standard costs are used to represent historical cost, they must be tested for reliability.

REVIEW QUESTIONS

1. For each of the following independent questions concerned with inventory controls, select the best response:
   a. In a company whose materials and supplies include a great number of items, a fundamental deficiency in control requirements would be indicated if
      (1) Perpetual inventory records were not maintained for items of small value.
      (2) The storekeeping function were to be combined with production and record keeping.
      (3) The cycle basis for physical inventory taking were to be used.
      (4) Minor supply items were to be expensed when purchased.
   b. For control purposes, the quantities of materials ordered may be omitted from the copy of the purchase order which is

(1) Forwarded to the accounting department.

(2) Retained in the purchasing department's files.

(3) Returned to the requisitioner.

(4) Forwarded to the receiving department.

c. Freije Refrigeration Co. has an inventory of raw materials and parts consisting of thousands of different items which are of small value individually but significant in total. A fundamental control requirement of Freije's inventory system is that

(1) Perpetual inventory records be maintained for all inventory items.

(2) The taking of physical inventories be conducted on a cycle basis rather than at year-end.

(3) The storekeeping function not be combined with the production and inventory record-keeping functions.

(4) Materials requisitions be approved by an officer of the company.

d. A CPA observes his client's physical inventory count on December 31, 19X1. There are eight inventory-taking teams, and a tag system is used. The CPA's observation normally may be expected to result in detection of which of the following inventory errors:

(1) The inventory takers forget to count all the items in one room of the warehouse.

(2) An error is made in the count of one inventory item.

(3) Some of the items included in the inventory had been received on consignment.

(4) The inventory omits items on consignment to wholesalers.

(AICPA adapted)

2. Give the reasons why inventory is often the most difficult and time-consuming part of many audit engagements.

3. Explain the relationship between the acquisition and payment cycle and the inventory and warehousing cycle in the audit of a manufacturing company. List several audit procedures in the acquisition and payment cycle that support your explanation.

4. State what is meant by cost accounting records and explain their importance in the conduct of an audit.

5. Many auditors assert that certain audit tests can be significantly reduced for clients with adequate perpetual records that include both units and cost data. What are the most important tests of the perpetual records the auditor must make before he can rely on them to reduce other audit tests? Assuming the perpetuals are determined to be effective, which tests can be reduced?

6. Before the physical examination, the auditor obtains a copy of the client's inventory instructions and reviews them with the controller. In evaluating the adequacy of inventory procedures for a small manufacturing company these deficiencies are identified: Shipping operations will not be completely halted during the physical examination and there will be no independent verification of the original inventory count by a second counting team. Evaluate the importance of each of these deficiencies and state the effect of each one on the auditor's observation of inventory.

7. At the completion of an inventory observation, the controller requested the auditor to give him a copy of all recorded test counts to facilitate the correction of all discrepancies between the client's and the auditor's counts. Should the auditor comply with the request? Why?

8. What major audit procedures are involved in testing for the ownership of

inventory during the observation of the physical counts and as a part of subsequent valuation tests?

9. In the verification of the amount of the inventory, one of the CPA's concerns is that slow-moving and obsolete items be identified. List the auditing procedures that the CPA could employ to determine whether slow-moving or obsolete items have been included in inventory.

10. During the taking of physical inventory, the controller intentionally withheld several inventory tags from the employees responsible for the physical count. After the auditor left the client's premises at the completion of the inventory observation, the controller recorded nonexistent inventory on the tags and thereby significantly overstated earnings. How could the auditor have uncovered the misstatement, assuming there are no perpetual records?

11. Explain why a proper cutoff of purchases and sales is heavily dependent on the physical inventory observation. What information should be obtained during the physical count to make sure cutoff is accurate?

12. Define what is meant by compilation tests. List several examples of audit procedures to verify compilation.

13. List the major overall reasonableness tests for inventory. For each test, explain the type of error that could be identified.

14. Included in the 12-31-X7 inventory of the Wholeridge Supply Company are 2,600 deluxe ring binders in the amount of $5,902. An examination of the most recent purchases of binders showed the following costs: 1-26-X8, 2,300 at $2.42 each; 12-6-X7, 1,900 at $2.28 each; 11-26-X7, 2,400 at $2.07 each. What is the error in valuation of the 12-31-X7 inventory for deluxe ring binders assuming FIFO inventory valuation? What would your answer be if the 1-26-X8 purchase was for 2,300 binders at $2.12 each?

15. The Ruswell Manufacturing Company applied manufacturing overhead to inventory at 12-31-X7 on the basis of $3.47 per direct labor hour. Explain how you would evaluate the reasonableness of total direct labor hours and manufacturing overhead in the ending inventory of finished goods.

16. Each employee for the Gedding Manufacturing Co., a firm using a job-cost system, must reconcile his total hours worked with the hours worked on individual jobs by the use of a "Job Time Sheet" at the time weekly payroll time cards are prepared. The Job Time Sheet is then stapled to the time card. Explain how you could test the direct labor dollars included in inventory as a part of the payroll and personnel tests.

17. Assuming the auditor properly documents receiving report numbers as a part of the physical inventory observation procedures, explain how he should verify the proper cutoff of purchases, including tests for the possibility of raw materials in transit, later in the audit.

DISCUSSION QUESTIONS AND PROBLEMS

18. The client's cost system is often the focal point in the CPA's examination of the financial statements of a manufacturing company.

Required:

a. For what purposes does the CPA review the cost system?

b. The Summerfield Manufacturing Company employs standard costs in its cost accounting system. List the audit procedures that you would apply to satisfy yourself that Summerfield's cost standards and related variance amounts are acceptable and have not distorted the financial statements. (Confine your audit procedures to those applicable to *materials*.)

(AICPA adapted)

19. Often an important aspect of a CPA's examination of financial statements is his observation of the taking of the physical inventory.

Required:

a. What are the general objectives or purposes of the CPA's observation of the taking of the physical inventory? (Do not discuss the procedures or techniques involved in making the observation.)

b. For what purposes does the CPA make and record test counts of inventory quantities during his observation of the taking of the physical inventory? Discuss.

c. A number of companies employ outside service companies who specialize in counting, pricing, extending, and footing inventories. These service companies usually furnish a certificate attesting to the value of the inventory.

Assuming that the service company took the inventory on the balance sheet date:

(1) How much reliance, if any, can the CPA place on the inventory certificate of outside specialists? Discuss.

(2) What effect, if any, would the inventory certificate of outside specialists have upon the type of report the CPA would render? Discuss.

(3) What reference, if any, would the CPA make to the certificate of outside specialists in his short-form report? (AICPA adapted)

20. Your audit client, Household Appliances, Inc., operates a retail store in the center of town. Because of lack of storage space, Household keeps inventory that is not on display in a public warehouse outside of town. The warehouseman receives inventory from suppliers and, on request from your client by a shipping advice or telephone call, delivers merchandise to customers or to the retail outlet.

The accounts are maintained at the retail store by a bookkeeper. Each month the warehouseman sends to the bookkeeper a quantity report indicating opening balance, receipts, deliveries, and ending balance. The bookkeeper compares book quantities on hand at month-end with the warehouseman's report and adjusts his books to agree with the report. No physical counts of the merchandise at the warehouse were made by your client during the year.

You are now preparing for your examination of the current year's financial statements in this recurring engagement. Last year you rendered an unqualified opinion.

Required:

a. Prepare an audit program for the observation of the physical inventory of Household Appliances, Inc. (1) at the retail outlet and (2) at the warehouse.

b. As part of your examination would you verify inventory quantities at the warehouse by means of

(1) A warehouse confirmation? Why?

(2) Test counts of inventory at the warehouse?·Why?

c. Since the bookkeeper adjusts books to quantities shown on the ware-

houseman's report each month, what significance would you attach to
the year-end adjustments if they were substantial? Discuss.

(AICPA adapted)

21. You encountered the following situations during the December 31, 19X7,
physical inventory of Latner Shoe Distributor Company:

a. Latner maintains a large portion of the shoe merchandise in ten warehouses throughout the eastern United States. This ensures swift delivery
service for its chain of stores. You are assigned alone to the Boston
warehouse to observe the physical inventory process. During the inventory count, several express trucks pulled in for loading. Although
infrequent, express shipments must be attended to immediately. As a
result, the employees who were counting the inventory stopped to assist
in loading the express trucks.

What should you do?

b. (1) In one storeroom of 10,000 items, you have test-counted about 200
items of high value and a few items of low value. You found no errors.
You also note that the employees are diligently following the inventory instructions.

Do you think you have tested enough items? Explain.

(2) What would you do if you counted 150 items and found a substantial number of counting errors?

c. In observing an inventory of liquid shoe polish, you note that a particular lot is five years old. From inspection of some bottles in an open
box, you find that the liquid has solidified in most of the bottles. What
action should you take?

d. During your observation of the inventory count in the main warehouse,
you found that most of the prenumbered tags that had been incorrectly
filled out are being destroyed and thrown away. What is the significance
of this procedure and what action should you take?

22. During the month of April, you are engaged to examine the balance sheet
of a new client as of March 31. The client manufactures steel castings and
forgings. A physical count of all inventories is made at the end of each
quarter of the fiscal year, and the company adjusts its inventory book
amounts to reflect the physical counts. As you were not engaged at the
time of the physical inventory on March 31, you request that the company
make another physical inventory count at the end of April in order that
you may observe and make test counts. The client agrees and another inventory is taken on April 30 which you witness.

Inventories of raw materials, work in process, and finished goods totaled
$125,000 at March 31. Total current assets amounted to $188,000, total
current liabilities were $186,000, and total assets were $450,000.

The company maintains perpetual inventory records of raw materials and
supplies but has no job-cost system or perpetual records of work in process
or finished goods. Production records are kept in the plant showing the tons
of castings poured each day, and sales records reflect the tons of castings
and forgings sold daily to various customers of the company.

Required:

What audit procedures would you use to satisfy yourself as to the *quantities*
on hand at the balance sheet date?   (AICPA adapted)

23. Late in December, 19X6, your CPA firm accepted an audit engagement at

Fine Jewelers, Inc., a corporation that deals largely in diamonds. The corporation has retail jewelry stores in several eastern cities and a diamond wholesale store in New York City. The wholesale store also sets the diamonds in rings and in other quality jewelry.

The retail stores place orders for diamond jewelry with the wholesale store in New York City. A buyer employed by the wholesale store purchases diamonds in the New York diamond market, and the wholesale store then fills orders from the retail stores and from independent customers and maintains a substantial inventory of diamonds. The corporation values its inventory by the specific identification cost method.

Required:

Assume that at the inventory date you are satisfied that Fine Jewelers, Inc., has no items left by customers for repair or sale on consignment and that no inventory owned by the corporation is in the possession of outsiders.
   a. Discuss the problems the auditor should anticipate in planning for the observation of the physical inventory on this engagement because of the
      (1) Different locations of the inventories.
      (2) Nature of the inventory.
   b. (1) Explain how your audit program for this inventory would be different from that used for most other inventories.
      (2) Prepare an audit program for the verification of the corporation's diamond and diamond jewelry inventories, identifying any steps that you would apply only to the retail stores or to the wholesale store.
   c. Assume that a shipment of diamond rings was in transit by corporation messenger from the wholesale store to a retail store on the inventory date. What additional audit steps would you take to satisfy yourself as to the gems that were in transit from the wholesale store on the inventory date? (AICPA adapted)
24. Items *a* through *h* are selected questions typically found in questionnaires used by auditors in evaluating internal controls in the inventory and warehousing cycle. In using the questionnaire for a particular client, a yes response to a question indicates a possible strength in the system, whereas a no indicates a potential weakness.
   a. Does the receiving department prepare prenumbered receiving reports and account for the numbers periodically for all inventory received, showing the description and quantity of materials?
   b. Is all inventory stored under the control of a custodian in areas where access is limited?
   c. Are all shipments to customers authorized by prenumbered shipping orders?
   d. Are detailed perpetual inventory records maintained for raw materials inventory?
   e. Are physical inventory counts made by someone other than storekeepers and those responsible for maintaining perpetual records?
   f. Is a standard cost system in effect for raw materials, direct labor, and manufacturing overhead?
   g. Is there a stated policy with specific criteria for writing off obsolete or slow-moving goods?
   h. Is the clerical accuracy of the final inventory compilation checked by a person independent of those responsible for preparing it?

Required:

a. For each of the above questions, state the purpose of the control.

b. For each control, list a compliance procedure to test its effectiveness.

c. For each of the above questions, identify the nature of the potential financial error(s) if the control is not in effect.

d. For each of the potential errors in part *c,* list a substantive audit procedure to determine whether a material error exists.

25. Following are audit procedures frequently performed in the inventory and warehousing cycle for a manufacturing company:

a. Compare the client's count of physical inventory at an interim date with the perpetual records.

b. Trace the auditor's test counts recorded in the working papers to the final inventory compilation and compare the tag number, description, and quantity.

c. Compare the unit price on the final inventory summary with vendor's invoices.

d. Read the client's physical inventory instructions and observe whether they are being followed by those responsible for counting the inventory.

e. Account for a sequence of raw material requisitions and examine each requisition for an authorized approval.

f. Trace the recorded additions on the finished goods perpetual records to the records for completed production.

g. Account for a sequence of inventory tags and trace each tag to the physical inventory to make sure it actually exists.

Required:

a. Identify whether each of the procedures is primarily a compliance or substantive test.

b. State the purpose(s) of each of the procedures.

26. Coil steel comprises one-half of the inventory of the Metal Fabricating Company. At the beginning of the year the company installed a system to control coil steel inventory.

The coil steel is stored within the plant in a special storage area. When coils are received a two-part tag is prepared. The tag is prenumbered and each part provides for entry of the supplier's name, receiving report number, date received, coil weight, and description. Both parts of the tag are prepared at the time the material is received and weighed and the receiving report prepared. The "A" part of the tag is attached to the coil, and the "B" part of the tag is sent to the stock records department with the receiving report. The stock records department files the tags numerically by coil width and gauge. The stock records department also maintains perpetual stock cards on each width and gauge by total weight; in a sense, the cards are a control record for the tags. No material requisitions are used by the plant, but as coils are placed into production, the "A" part of the tag is removed from the coil and sent to stock records as support of the production report which is the basis of entries on the perpetual inventory cards.

When the "A" part of the tag is received by the stock records department, it is matched with the "B" part of the tag and the "A" part is destroyed. The "B" part is stamped with the date of use, processed, and retained in a consumed file by width and guage. The coils are neatly stacked and arranged and all tags are visible.

The balance of the inventory is examined by standard procedures, and you are satisfied that it is fairly stated.

Physical inventories are taken on a cycle basis throughout the year. About one-twelfth of the coil steel inventories are taken each month. The coil steel control account and the perpetual stock cards are adjusted as counts are made. Internal control of inventories is good in all respects.

In previous years the client had taken a complete physical inventory of coil steel at the end of the year (the client's fiscal year ends December 31), but none is to be taken this year. You are engaged for the current audit in September. You audited the financial statements last year.

Required:

Assuming that you decide to undertake some preliminary audit work before December 31, prepare programs for
(1) The verification of coil steel quantities previously inventoried during the current year.
(2) Observation of physical inventories to be taken in subsequent months.
(AICPA adapted)

27. In connection with his examination of the financial statements of Knutson Products Co., an assembler of home appliances, for the year ended May 31, 19X7, Ray Abel, CPA, is reviewing with Knutson's controller the plans for a physical inventory at the company warehouse on May 31, 19X7.

Finished appliances, unassembled parts, and supplies are stored in the warehouse, which is attached to Knutson's assembly plant. The plant will operate during the count. On May 30 the warehouse will deliver to the plant the estimated quantities of unassembled parts and supplies required for May 31 production, but there may be emergency requisitions on May 31. During the count the warehouse will continue to receive parts and supplies and to ship finished appliances. However, appliances completed on May 31 will be held in the plant until after the physical inventory.

Required:

What procedures should the company establish to ensure that the inventory count includes all items that should be included and that nothing is counted twice? (AICPA adapted)

28. The following errors or omissions are included in the inventory and related records of Westbox Manufacturing Company:
   a. An inventory item was priced at $12 each instead of at the correct cost of $12 per dozen.
   b. In taking the physical inventory, the last shipments for the day were excluded from inventory and were not included as a sale until the subsequent year.
   c. The clerk in charge of the perpetual inventory records altered the quantity on an inventory tag to cover up the shortage of inventory caused by its theft during the year.
   d. Several inventory tags were lost after the auditor left the premises and were not included in the final inventory summary.
   e. In recording raw material purchases, the improper unit price was included in the perpetual records. Therefore the inventory valuation was

misstated because the physical inventory was priced by referring to the perpetual records.

f. During the physical count, several obsolete inventory items were included.

g. Due to a significant increase in volume during the current year and excellent control over manufacturing overhead costs, the manufacturing overhead rate applied to inventory was far greater than actual cost.

Required:

a. For each error, state a control that should have prevented the error from occurring.

b. For each error, state a substantive audit procedure that could be used to uncover the error.

29. Line-Rite Manufacturing Company, Inc., is a moderate-sized company manufacturing equipment for use in laying pipe lines. The company has prospered in the past, gradually expanding to its present size. Recognizing a need to develop new products, if its growth is to continue, the company created an engineering research and development section. During 19X7, at a cost of $70,000, this section designed, patented, and successfully tested a new machine which greatly accelerates the laying of small-sized lines.

In order to adequately finance the manufacture, promotion, and sale of this new product, it has become necessary to expand the company's plant and to enlarge inventories. Required financing to accomplish this has resulted in the company's engaging you in April 19X7 to examine its financial statements as of September 30, 19X7, the end of the current fiscal year. This is the company's initial audit.

In the course of your preliminary audit work you obtain the following information:

a. The nature of the inventory and related manufacturing processes do not lend themselves well to taking a complete physical inventory at year-end or at any other given date. The company has an inventory team which counts all inventory items on a cycle basis throughout the year. Perpetual inventory records, maintained by the accounting department, are adjusted to reflect the quantities on hand as determined by these counts. At year-end an inventory summary is prepared from the perpetual inventory records. The quantities in this summary are subsequently valued in developing the final inventory balances.

b. The company carries a substantial parts inventory which is used to service equipment sold to customers. Certain parts are also used in current production. The company considers any part to be obsolete only if it shows no usage or sales activity for two consecutive years. Parts falling into this category are reserved for fully. A reserve of $10,000 exists at present.

Your tests indicate that obsolescence in inventories might approximate $50,000. As part of your audit you must deal with each of the foregoing matters.

Required:

a. With respect to inventories, define the overall problem involved in this first audit.

b. Outline a program for testing inventory quantities.

c. Enumerate and discuss the principal problems involved in inventory obsolescence for the company, assuming the amount involved was significant with respect to the company's financial position.   (AICPA adapted)

30. On April 6, 19X7, fire completely destroyed the warehouse and all books and records of the Kramer Corporation, a wholesaler of office stationery. Kramer Corporation had a fire insurance policy on the inventory (in addition to insurance policies on other assets) which did not require the corporation to file a monthly inventory report. The Ecker Insurance Company retained you to audit the statement of the actual cash value of the inventory fire loss of $265,000 reported by Kramer Corporation.

The corporation began doing business on January 1, 19X6, and the financial statements for 19X6 were audited by the corporation's certified public accountant, who rendered an unqualified opinion. The CPA also prepared the corporation's income tax return for 19X6 and, with the president's permission, has granted you access to his copy of the tax return as well as to his workpapers relating to Kramer Corporation.

Required:

a. List the audit procedures you would apply to verify the amount of the inventory fire loss on April 6, 19X7, claimed by the insured.
b. Assume that you are satisfied with the results of your examination and you are now preparing your report.
   (1) Which, if any, of the generally accepted auditing standards pertaining to reporting would apply to this report? Discuss.
   (2) Describe the topics relating to your examination to which you should refer in your report. (AICPA adapted)

31. You are assigned to the December 31, 1976, audit of Sea Gull Airframes, Inc. The company designs and manufactures aircraft superstructures and airframe components. You observed the physical inventory at December 31 and are satisfied it was properly taken. The inventory at December 31, 1976, has been priced, extended, and totaled by the client and is made up of about 5,000 inventory items with a total valuation of $8,275,000. In performing inventory price tests you have decided to stratify your tests, and you conclude that you should have two strata: items with a total value over $5,000 and those with a value of less than $5,000. The book values are as follows:

	No. of Items	Total Value
More than $5,000	500	$4,150,000
Less than $5,000	4,500	4,125,000
	5,000	$8,275,000

In performing your pricing and extension tests, you have decided to test about 50 inventory items in detail. You selected 40 of the over $5,000 items and 10 of those under $5,000 at random from the population. You find all items to be correct except for some of the items *A* through *G* below which you believe may be in error. You have tested the following items, to this point, exclusive of *A* through *G*.

	No. of Items	Total Value
More than $5,000	36	$360,000
Less than $5,000	7	2,600

Sea Gull Airframes uses a periodic inventory system and values its inventory at lower of FIFO cost or market. You were able to locate all invoices needed for your examination. The seven inventory items in the sample you believe may be in error, along with the relevant data for determining the proper valuation, are shown below:

Inventory Items That Are Possibly in Error
(Amounts Are as Stated on Client's Inventory)

Description	Quantity		Price		Total
A. L37 Spars	3,000	meters	$8.00	meter	$24,000
B. B68 Metal formers	10,000	inches	1.20	foot	12,000
C. R01 Metal ribs	1,500	yards	10.00	yard	15,000
D. St26 Struts	1,000	feet	8.00	foot	8,000
E. Industrial hand drills	45	units	20.00	each	900
F. L803 Steel leaf springs	40	pairs	69.00	each	276
G. V16 Fasteners	5.50	dozen	10.00	dozen	55

Information for Pricing from Invoices

Voucher Number	Voucher Date	Date Paid	Terms	Receiving Report Date	Invoice Description
7-68	8-01-69	8-21-69	Net FOB dest.	8-01-69	77 V16 fasteners at $10 per dozen
11-81	10-16-76	11-15-76	Net FOB dest.	10-18-76	1,100 yards R01 metal ribs at $9.50 per yard; 2,000 feet St26 struts at $8.20 per foot
12-06	12-08-76	12-30-76	2/10, n/30 FOB S.P.	12-10-76	180 L803 steel leaf springs at $69 each
12-09	12-10-76	12-18-76	Net FOB dest.	12-11-76	45 industrial hand drills at $20 each; guaranteed for 4 years
12-18	12-27-76	12-27-76	2/10, n/30 FOB S.P.	12-21-76	4,200 meters L37 spars at $8 per meter
12-23	12-24-76	1-03-77	2/10, n/30 FOB dest.	12-26-76	12,800 inches B68 metal formers at $1.20 per foot
12-61	12-29-76	1-08-77	Net FOB dest.	12-29-76	1,000 yards R01 metal ribs at $10 per yard; 800 feet St26 struts at $8 per foot
12-81	12-31-76	1-20-77	Net FOB dest.	1-06-77	2,000 meters L37 spars at $7.50 per meter; 2,000 yards R01 metal ribs at $10 per yard

In addition, you noted a freight bill for voucher 12-23 in the amount of $200. This bill was entered in the freight-in account. Virtually all of the freight was for the metal formers.

This is the first time Sea Gull Airframes has been audited by your firm.

Required:

Review all information and determine the inventory errors of the seven items in question. State any assumptions you consider necessary to determine the amount of the errors.

32. The following calculations were made as of 12-31-X7 from the records of the Aladdin Products Supply Company, a wholesale distributor of cleaning supplies.

	19X7	*19X6*	*19X5*	*19X4*
Gross margin as percent of sales	26.4%	22.8%	22.7%	22.4%
Inventory turnover	56.1 days	47.9 days	48.3 days	47.1 days

Required:

List several logical causes of the changes in the two ratios. What should the auditor do to determine the actual cause of the changes?

33. In an annual audit at December 31, 19X7, you find the following transactions near the closing date:
   a. Merchandise costing $1,822 was received on January 3, 19X8, and the related purchase invoice recorded January 5. The invoice showed the shipment was made on December 29, 19X7, *FOB destination.*
   b. Merchandise costing $625 was received on December 28, 19X7, and the invoice was not recorded. You located it in the hands of the purchasing agent; it was marked *on consignment.*
   c. A packing case containing products costing $816 was standing in the shipping room when the physical inventory was taken. It was not included in the inventory because it was marked *Hold for shipping instructions.* Your investigation revealed that the customer's order was dated Dec. 18, 19X8, but that the case was shipped and the customer billed on January 10, 19X8. The product was a stock item of your client.
   d. Merchandise received on January 6, 19X8, costing $720 was entered in the purchase register on January 7, 19X8. The invoice showed shipment was made FOB supplier's warehouse on December 31, 19X7. Since it was not on hand at December 31, it was not included in inventory.
   e. A special machine, fabricated to order for a customer, was finished and in the shipping room on December 31, 19X7. The customer was billed on that date and the machine excluded from inventory, although it was shipped on January 4, 19X8.

Assume that each of the amounts is material.

Required:

   a. State whether the merchandise should be included in the client's inventory.
   b. Give your reason for your decision on each item above. (AICPA adapted)

34. A processor of frozen foods carries an inventory of finished products consisting of 50 different types of items valued at approximately $2 million. About $750,000 of this value represents stock produced by the company and billed to customers prior to the audit date. This stock is being held for the customers at a monthly rental charge until they request shipment, and is not separated from the company's inventory.

The company maintains separate perpetual ledgers at the plant office for both stock owned and stock being held for customers. The cost department also maintains a perpetual record of stock owned. The above perpetual records reflect quantities only.

The company does not take a complete physical inventory at any time during the year, since the temperature in the cold storage facilities is too low to allow one to spend more than fifteen minutes inside at a time. It is not considered practical to move items outside or to de-freeze the cold storage facilities for the purpose of taking a physical inventory. Due to these circumstances, it is impractical to test-count quantities to the extent of completely verifying specific items. The company considers as its inventory valuation at year-end the aggregate of the quantities reflected by the perpetual record of stock owned, maintained at the plant office, priced at the lower of cost or market.

Required:

a. What are the two principal problems facing the auditor in the audit of the inventory? Discuss briefly.
b. Outline the audit steps that you would take to enable you to render an unqualified opinion with respect to the inventory. (You may omit consideration of a verification of unit prices and clerical accuracy.)

(AICPA adapted)

35. As a part of your clerical tests of inventory for Martin Manufacturing, you have tested about 20 percent of the dollar items and have found the following exceptions:
a. *Extension Errors:*

Description	Quantity	Price	Extension as Recorded
Wood	465 board feet	$ .12 board feet	$ 5.58
Metal-cutting tools	29 units	30.00 each	670.00
Cutting fluid	16 barrels	40.00 barrel	529.00
Sandpaper	300 sheets	.95 per hundred	258.00

b. *Differences located in comparing last year's costs with the current year's costs on the client's inventory lists:*

Description	Quantity	This Year's Cost	Preceding Year's Cost
TA-114 Precision-cutting torches	12 units	$500.00 each	Unable to locate
Aluminum scrap	4,500 pounds	5.00 ton	$65.00 ton
Lubricating oil	400 gallons	6.00 gallon	4.50 barrel

c. *Test counts that you were unable to find when tracing from the test counts to the final inventory compilation:*

Tag No.	Quantity	Current Year Cost	Description
2958	15 tons	$75 ton	Cold rolled bars
0026	2,000 feet	2.25 foot	4″ aluminum stripping

d. *Page total, footing errors:*

Page No.	Client Total	Correct Total
14	$1,375.12	$1,375.08
82	8,721.18	8,521.18

Required:

a. State the amount of the actual error in each of the four tests. For any item where the amount of the error cannot be determined from the information given, state the considerations that would affect your estimate of the error.
b. As a result of your findings, what would you do about clerical accuracy tests of the inventory in the current year?
c. What changes, if any, would you suggest in internal controls and procedures for Martin Manufacturing during the compilation of next year's inventory to prevent each type of error?

36. You have been engaged for the audit of the Y Company for the year ended December 31, 19X7. The Y Company is engaged in the wholesale chemical business and makes all sales at 25 percent over cost.

Shown below are portions of the client's sales and purchases accounts for the calendar year 19X7:

Sales

Date	Reference	Amount	Date	Reference	Amount
12-31	Closing entry	$699,860	Balance forward		$658,320
			12-27	SI #965	5,195
			12-28	SI #966	19,270
			12-28	SI #967	1,302
			12-31	SI #969	5,841
			12-31	SI #970	7,922
			12-31	SI #971	2,010
		$699,860			$699,860

Purchases

Date	Reference	Amount	Date	Reference	Amount
Balance forward		$360,300	12-31	Closing entry	$385,346
12-28	RR #1059	3,100			
12-30	RR #1061	8,965			
12-31	RR #1062	4,861			
12-31	RR #1063	8,120			
		$385,346			$385,346

RR = *Receiving report.*
SI = *Sales invoice.*

You observed the physical inventory of goods in the warehouse on December 31, 19X7, and were satisfied that it was properly taken.

When performing a sales and purchases cutoff test, you found that at December 31, 19X7, the last receiving report that had been used was No. 1063 and that no shipments had been made on any sales invoices with numbers larger than No. 968. You also obtained the following additional information:

a. Included in the warehouse physical inventory at December 31, 19X7, were chemicals which had been purchased and received on receiving report No. 1060 but for which an invoice was not received until 19X8. Cost was $2,183.

b. In the warehouse at December 31, 19X7, were goods that had been sold and paid by the customer but which were not shipped out until 19X8. They were all sold on sales invoice No. 965 and were not inventoried.

c. On the evening of December 31, 19X7, there were two cars on the Y Company siding:

   (1) Car #AR38162 was unloaded on January 2, 19X8, and received on receiving report No. 1063. The freight was paid by the vendor.

   (2) Car # BAE74123 was loaded and sealed on December 31, 19X7, and was switched off the company's siding on January 2, 19X8. The sales price was $12,700 and the freight was paid by the customer. This order was sold on sales invoice No. 968.

d. Temporarily stranded at December 31, 19X7, on a railroad siding were two cars of chemicals en route to the Z Pulp and Paper Co. They were sold on sales invoice No. 966 and the terms were FOB destination.

e. En route to the Y Co. on December 31, 19X7, was a truckload of material which was received on receiving report No. 1064. The material was shipped FOB destination and freight of $75 was paid by the Y Co. However, the freight was deducted from the purchase price of $975.

f. Included in the physical inventory were chemicals exposed to rain in transit and deemed unsalable. Their invoice cost was $1,250, and freight charges of $350 had been paid on the chemicals.

Required:

a. Compute the adjustments that should be made to the client's physical inventory at December 31, 19X7.

b. Prepare the auditor's worksheet adjusting entries which are required as of December 31, 19X7.   (AICPA adapted)

37. Renken Company cans two food commodities which it stores at various warehouses. The company employs a perpetual inventory accounting system under which the finished goods inventory is charged with production and credited for sales at standard cost. The detail of the finished goods inventory is maintained on punched cards by the tabulating department in units and dollars for the various warehouses.

Company procedures call for the accounting department to receive copies of daily production reports and sales invoices. Units are then extended at standard cost, and a summary of the day's activity is posted to the Finished Goods Inventory general ledger control account. Next the sales invoices and production reports are sent to the tabulating department for processing. Every month the control account and detailed tab records are reconciled and adjustments recorded. The last reconciliation and adjustments were made at November 30, 19X7.

Your CPA firm observed the taking of the physical inventory at all locations on December 31, 19X7. The inventory count began at 4:00 P.M. and was completed at 8:00 P.M. The company's figure for the physical inventory is $331,400. The general ledger control account balance at December 31 was $373,900, and the final "tab" run of the inventory punched cards showed a total of $392,300.

Unit cost data for the company's two products are as follows:

Product	Standard Cost
A	$2.00
B	3.00

A review of December transactions disclosed the following:

a. Sales invoice #1301, 12-2-X7, was priced at standard cost for $11,700 but was listed on the accounting department's daily summary at $11,200.

b. A production report for $23,900, 12-15-X7, was processed twice in error by the tabulating department.

c. Sales invoice #1423, 12-9-X7, for 1,200 units of product A, was priced at a standard cost of $1.50 per unit by the accounting department. The tabulating department noticed and corrected the error but did not notify the accounting department of the error.

d. A shipment of 3,400 units of product A was invoiced by the billing department as 3,000 units on sales invoice #1504, 12-27-X7. The error was discovered by your review of transactions.

e. On December 27 the Memphis warehouse notified the tabulating department to remove 2,200 unsalable units of product A from the finished goods inventory, which it did without receiving a special invoice from the accounting department. The accounting department received a copy of the Memphis warehouse notification on December 29 and made up a special invoice which was processed in the normal manner. The units were not included in the physical inventory.

f. A production report for the production on January 3 of 2,500 units of product B was processed for the Omaha plant as of December 31.

g. A shipment of 300 units of product B was made from the Portland warehouse to Ken's Markets, Inc., at 8:30 P.M. on December 31 as an emergency service. The sales invoice was processed as of December 31. The client prefers to treat the transaction as a sale in 19X7.

h. The working papers of the auditor observing the physical count at the Chicago warehouse revealed that 700 units of product B were omitted from the client's physical count. The client concurred that the units were omitted in error.

i. A sales invoice for 600 units of product A shipped from the Newark warehouse was mislaid and was not processed until January 5. The units involved were shipped on December 30.

j. The physical inventory of the St. Louis warehouse excluded 350 units of product A that were marked "reserved." Upon investigation it was ascertained that this merchandise was being stored as a convenience for Steve's Markets, Inc., a customer. This merchandise, which has not been recorded as a sale, is billed as it is shipped.

k. A shipment of 10,000 units of product B was made on December 27 from the Newark warehouse to the Chicago warehouse. The shipment arrived on January 6 but had been excluded from the physical inventory.

Required:

Prepare a worksheet to reconcile the balances for the physical inventory, Finished Goods Inventory general ledger control account, and tabulating department's detail of finished goods inventory ("Tab Run").

The following format is suggested for the worksheet:

	Physical Inventory	*General Ledger Control Account*	*Tabulating Department's Detail of Inventory*
Balance per client	$331,400	$373,900	$392,300

(AICPA adapted)

17

Audit
of the Capital Acquisition
and Repayment Cycle

The final transaction cycle discussed in this text relates to the acquisition of capital resources in the form of interest-bearing debt and owner's equity and the repayment of the capital. The capital acquisition and repayment cycle also includes the payment of interest and dividends. The following are the major accounts in the cycle:

Notes payable	Paid-in capital in excess of par
Contracts payable	Donated capital
Mortgages payable	Retained earnings
Bonds payable	Appropriations of retained earnings
Interest expense	Treasury stock
Accrued interest	Dividends declared
Cash in the bank	Dividends payable
Capital stock—common	Proprietorship—capital account
Capital stock—preferred	Partnership—capital account

Four characteristics of the capital acquisition and repayment cycle significantly influence the audit of these accounts. First, *relatively few transactions* affect the account balances, but each transaction is often highly material in amount. For example, bonds are infrequently issued by most companies, but the amount of a bond issue is normally large. Due to their size it is common to verify each transaction taking place in the cycle for the entire year as a part of verifying the balance sheet accounts. It is not unusual to see audit working papers that include the beginning balance of every account in the capital acquisition and re- payment cycle and documentation of every transaction that occurred during the year. Second, the exclusion of *a single transaction could be material* in itself. Considering the impact of understatements of liabili- ties and owner's equity, which was discussed in Chapter 14, omission is a major audit concern. Third, *there is a legal relationship* between the client entity and the holder of the stock, bond, or similar ownership document. In the audit of the transactions and amounts in the cycle, the auditor must take great care in making sure that the significant legal requirements affecting the financial statements have been properly ful- filled and adequately disclosed in the statements. Fourth, there is *a direct relationship between* the *interest and dividends accounts and debt and equity.* In the audit of interest-bearing debt, it is desirable to simul- taneously verify the related interest expense and interest payable. This similarly holds true for owner's equity, dividends declared, and dividends payable.

The audit procedures for many of the accounts in the capital acquisi- tion and repayment cycle can best be understood by selecting representa- tive accounts for study. Therefore, this chapter discusses (1) the audit of notes payable and the related interest expense and interest payable to illustrate interest-bearing capital, and (2) common stock, paid-in capital in excess of par, retained earnings, and dividends.

NOTES PAYABLE

A *note payable* is a legal obligation to a creditor, which may be un- secured or secured by assets. Typically, a note is issued for a period of time somewhere between one month and one year, but there are also long-term notes of over a year. Notes are issued for many different pur- poses, and the pledged property includes a wide variety of assets, such as securities, inventory, and permanent assets. The principal and interest payments on the notes must be made in accordance with the terms of the loan agreement. For short-term loans a principal and interest pay- ment is usually required only when the loan becomes due, but for loans over ninety days the note usually calls for monthly or quarterly interest payments.

Overview of the Accounts

The accounts used for notes payable and related interest are shown in Figure 17-1. It is common to include tests of principal and interest payments as a part of the audit of the acquisition and payment cycle because the payments are recorded in the cash disbursements journal. But due to their relative infrequency, in many cases no capital transac- tions are included in the tests of transactions sample. Therefore, it is

FIGURE 17-1

NOTES PAYABLE AND THE RELATED INTEREST ACCOUNTS

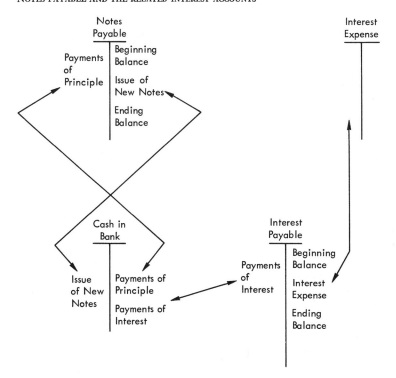

also normal to test these transactions as a part of the capital acquisition and repayment cycle.

Audit Objectives

The objectives of the auditor's examination of notes payable are to determine whether

1. Internal controls over notes payable are adequate.
2. The liability is properly valued, classified, and described for statement purposes.
3. Interest expense and interest payable are properly stated.
4. All significant disclosures have been included in the statements and footnotes.

Internal Controls

The most important controls over notes payable are (1) proper authorization for the issuance of new notes, (2) adequate controls over the repayment of principal and interest, and (3) proper record keeping procedures.

Responsibility for the issuance of new notes should be vested in the board of directors or high level management personnel. Generally, two signatures of properly authorized officials are required for all loan agreements. The amount of the loan, the interest rate, the repayment terms, and the particular assets pledged are all part of the approved agreement. Whenever notes are renewed, it is important that they be subject to the same authorization procedures as those for the issuance of new notes.

The periodic payments of interest and principal should be controlled as a part of the acquisition and payment cycle. At the time the note was issued, the accounting department should have received a copy of the note in the same manner in which it receives vendor's invoices and receiving reports. The accounts payable department should automatically issue checks for the notes when they become due, again in the same manner in which it prepares checks for acquisitions of goods and services. The copy of the note is the supporting documentation for payment.

Proper record keeping for notes includes the maintenance of subsidiary records and the maintenance of proper control over blank and paid notes by a responsible employee. Periodically the detailed note records should be reconciled with the general ledger and compared with the noteholders' records by an employee who is not responsible for maintaining the detailed records. At the same time, an independent person should recompute the interest expense on notes to test the accuracy and propriety of the record keeping. Paid notes should be canceled and retained under the custody of an authorized official.

Audit Tests of Notes Payable

The same audit objectives that have been used as a frame of reference for discussing all direct tests of financial balances in previous chapters are again used for notes payable. The most important objectives in the audit of notes payable are *existence, valuation, and disclosure*.

Mechanical Accuracy. The normal starting point for the audit of notes payable is a *schedule of notes payable and accrued interest* obtained from the client. A typical schedule is shown in Figure 17-2. The usual schedule includes detailed information of all transactions that took place during the entire year for principal and interest, the beginning and ending balances for notes and interest payable, and descriptive information about the notes, such as the due date of each note, the interest rate, and the assets pledged as collateral.

The mechanical accuracy tests of the schedule include footing the totals on the notes payable and interest schedule, tracing the balances to the general ledger, tracing the outstanding notes payable at the end of the period to the notes payable subsidiary ledgers, and tracing the beginning balances from the schedule to ending balances shown on the auditor's notes payable working paper relating to the preceding year.

When there are numerous transactions involving notes during the year, it may not be practical to obtain a schedule of the type shown in Figure 17-2. In that situation the auditor is likely to request that the client prepare a schedule of only those notes with unpaid balances at the end of the year. This would show a description of each note, its ending balance, and the interest payable at the end of the year, including the collateral and interest rate. The mechanical accuracy tests of this schedule should be the same as those illustrated in Figure 17-2, except that the auditor is likely to restrict sample size in the tracing the list of notes payable to the subsidiary ledger.

Overall Reasonableness. The most common test of overall reasonableness for notes payable is a test of interest expense. In most instances the auditor should be able to calculate the approximate interest expense by multiplying the average interest rate on notes by the average monthly balance outstanding in notes payable in the manner explained in Chapter 4. If the calculation is significantly different from the recorded interest expense on notes payable, it could be an indication of an error in interest calculations or a possible unrecorded note.

Existence. A major concern in the audit of notes payable is the possibility of the client's failing to include all notes payable as liabilities. The omission of a note payable could be intentional for the purpose of either making the financial statements appear more favorable or covering up a defalcation. But the omission could also result from unintentionally classifying a note as an account payable or failing to recognize the receipt of the borrowed cash.

The following audit procedures are useful for discovering unrecorded notes, but many of them should be used only when the internal controls over notes payable are weak:

1. Examine notes paid after year-end to determine whether they were liabilities at the balance sheet date.
2. Obtain a *standard bank confirmation* which includes specific reference to the existence of notes payable from all banks with which the client does business. Bank confirmations are discussed more fully in the next chapter.
3. Review the *bank reconciliation* for new notes credited directly to the bank account by the bank. On the bank reconciliation such a note should be indicated as a "reconciling item." Bank reconciliations are also discussed more fully in the next chapter.
4. Obtain confirmations from creditors who have held notes from the client in the past and are not currently included in the notes payable schedule. This is the same concept as a "zero balance" confirmation in accounts payable.
5. Obtain a standard confirmation for secured notes under the Uniform Commercial Code. Figure 17-3 is an example of this type of confirmation.

FIGURE 17-2

SCHEDULE OF NOTES PAYABLE AND ACCRUED INTEREST

ABC Company, Inc.
Notes Payable

Schedule *AA-4* Date
Prepared by *DB* *1/12/81*
Approved by *JL* *1/16/81*

12/31/80

Payee	Date Made	Due	Face Amount of Note	Description (Security)	Valuation	Balance at Beginning of Period
First National Bank	9/30/79	9/30/80	10 000	Investments	15 000	10 000
Second National Bank	9/30/80	9/30/81	10 000	Investments	16 000	
Third National Bank	10/31/80	10/31/81	10 000	Fixed Assets	22 000	
			30 000		53 000	10 000 ① ⑤

① – Traced to prior year audit workpapers.
② – Obtained copy of note included in permanent file.
③ – Examined cancelled note and check.
④ – Agreed to confirmation received from bank.
⑤ – Traced to general ledger.
⑥ – Recomputed expense; no differences noted.
⑦ – Cross footed
⑧ – Footed.

6. Analyze interest expense to uncover a payment to a creditor who is not included in the notes payable schedule. This procedure is automatically done if the schedule is similar to the one in Figure 17-2 because all interest payments are reconciled with the general ledger.
7. Examine paid notes for cancelation to make sure they are not still outstanding. They should be maintained in the client's files.
8. Review the minutes of the board of directors for authorized, but unrecorded notes.

The auditor is also concerned about the possibility of liabilities being included in the statements when such liabilities are not actually owed or were not authorized. The most common procedure for verifying the authenticity of recorded liabilities is by confirming the amount with the creditors, examining duplicate copies of the notes for authorization, and examining corporate minutes for the approval of the loans.

FIGURE 17-2 (cont.)

Notes,					*Interest*			
Additions	*Payments*	*Balance at End of Period*	*Rate Paid to*	*Accrued at Beginning of Period*	*Expense*	*Paid*	*Accrued at End of Period*
	10000③	—0—	④ 9½% *Maturity*	238	712⑥	950③	—0— ⑦
10000②		10000④	10% *Maturity*		250⑥		250⑦
10000②		10000④	10% *Maturity*		167⑥		167⑦
20000 ⑧	10000 ⑧	20000③⑦		238① ⑧	1129 ⑧	950 ⑧	417 ⑧

Valuation. The valuation of a note payable usually causes no
audit problems once the auditor is aware of its existence, because the
amount of the liability is set forth in the note. The examination of
duplicate notes and the confirmation of the balance is sufficient to satisfy
the valuation objective in most audits. However, in addition to verifying
the amount of the note, the auditor must also test the valuation of
accrued interest. To verify accrued interest, the auditor must determine
the *interest rate,* the *face amount of the note,* and the *date of the last
interest payment.* The first two items can be obtained and verified by
examining a duplicate copy of the note. The last interest payment date
can be obtained from the cash disbursements records. Alternatively, all
three items can be obtained by confirmation with the maker. After the
auditor is satisfied that the interest rate, face amount of the note, and
last interest payment date are correctly stated by the client, the accrued
interest can be verified by recalculation.

When a note payable does not include a stated interest rate, the
amount of interest to be paid is determined on the basis of the total
cash payments required to fulfill the note obligation minus the original
cash received from the creditor. For example, if a client receives cash of

FIGURE 17-3

STANDARD CONFIRMATION UNDER THE UNIFORM COMMERCIAL CODE

Uniform Commercial Code - REQUEST FOR INFORMATION OR COPIES - Form UCC 11

JULIUS BLUMBERG, INC. 80 EXCHANGE PLACE, N.Y.C. 10004

IMPORTANT - Read instructions on back before filling out form

REQUEST FOR COPIES OR INFORMATION. Present in DUPLICATE to Filing Officer.

1 Debtor (Last Name First) and Address	Party requesting information or copies: (Name and Address)	For Filing Officer, Date, Time, No. Filing Office

☐ INFORMATION REQUEST: ☐ COPY REQUEST:

Filing officer please furnish certificate showing if there is on file under the code as of_____, 19___ at_____ ____M., any presently effective financing statement filed pursuant to the UCC naming the above named debtor and any statement of assignment thereof, and if there is, giving the date and hour of filing of each such statement and the name(s) and address(es) of each secured party(ies) therein. Enclosed is uniform fee of $3.00.

Filing officer please furnish exact copies of each page of financing statements and statements of assignment listed below, at the rate of $1.00 each, which are on file with your office. Enclosed is $_____fee for copies requested. In case any of said statements contain more than one page the undersigned agrees to pay the sum of $1.00 for each additional page payable in advance.

Date_____(Signature of Requesting Party)_____

File No.	Date and Hour of Filing	Name(s) and Address(es) of Secured Party(ies) and Assignees, if any

CERTIFICATE: The undersigned filing officer hereby certifies that:

☐ the above listing is a record of all presently 'effective financing statements and statements of assignment which name the above debtor and which are on file in my office as of _____, 19___ at_____ ____M.

☐ the attached_____pages are true and exact copies of all available financing statements or statements of assignment listed in above request

COPY 1	Date	Signature of Filing Officer
9/65 STANDARD FORM NEW YORK STATE FORM UCC-11	APPROVED BY SECRETARY OF STATE OF NEW YORK	

$1,000 for a note and the provisions of the note require three payments of $400 each, the amount of the interest is $200. The *imputed interest rate* can be determined by reference to present value tables.

If a note is issued for assets other than cash, such as equipment, the original amount of the note may be difficult to verify. In this case the amount of the note must be calculated by first determining the correct imputed interest rate and then computing the present value of all cash repayments required by the client by the use of present value tables. The reasonableness of the client's imputed interest rate can be tested by comparing it with interest rates being paid on similar loans by the client or by similar companies.

Classification. The due date for each note must be determined by examining a duplicate copy of the note or by confirmation to determine whether any portion of the note comes due in more than a year from the balance sheet date. Amounts that do not become due for more than a year should be classified on the balance sheet as noncurrent liabilities. On the other hand, all installments on long-term loans that are due within a period of twelve months must be classified as current liabilities. The auditor should also examine the name of the maker to determine that notes payable to officers, directors, affiliates, and other related parties are clearly disclosed and not included with notes to third parties.

Cutoff. The recording of the notes payable in the proper period can be easily checked by the examination of a duplicate copy of the note or by confirmation. If the note is dated on or before the balance sheet date, it should be included as a current period liability.

Disclosure. The proper inclusion of notes payable in the balance sheet should follow the classification requirements discussed under the classification objective. However, an additional consideration is evaluating proper footnote disclosure. It is essential that the footnotes adequately describe the terms of notes payable outstanding and the assets pledged as collateral for the loans. If there are significant restrictions on the activities of the company required by the loans, such as compensating balance provisions or restrictions on the payment of dividends, these must also be disclosed in the footnotes. The auditor can determine the existence of this information by examining a copy of the note and by confirmation with the bank or other creditor.

OWNER'S EQUITY

A major distinction must be made in the audit of owner's equity between *publicly and closely held corporations.* In most closely held corporations there are few if any transactions during the year for capital stock accounts and there are typically only a few shareholders. The only transactions entered in the entire owner's equity section are likely to be the change in owner's equity for the annual earnings or loss and the declaration of dividends. The amount of time spent verifying owner's equity is frequently minimal for closely held corporations even though the auditor must test the existing corporate records.

For publicly held corporations the verification of owner's equity is more complex due to the larger numbers of shareholders and frequent changes in the individuals holding the stock. In this section the appropriate tests for verifying capital stock—common, paid-in capital in excess of par, retained earnings, and the related dividends in a publicly held corporation are discussed. The other accounts in owner's equity are verified in much the same way as these.

Overview of the Accounts

An overview of the specific owner's equity accounts discussed in this section is given in Figure 17-4.

Audit Objectives

The objectives of the auditor's examination of owner's equity are to determine whether

1. Internal controls over capital stock and related dividends are adequate.

FIGURE 17-4

OWNER'S EQUITY AND DIVIDENDS ACCOUNTS

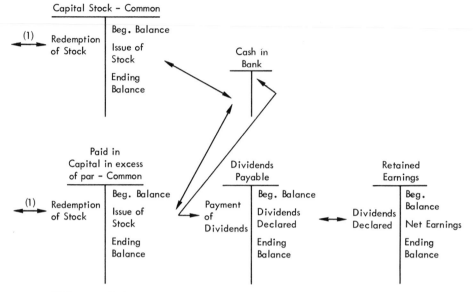

(1) Decrease Cash

2. The amounts of owner's equity are properly classified, described, and stated in accordance with generally accepted accounting principles and are not in conflict with requirements of the corporate charter or the articles of incorporation or with applicable statutes of the state of incorporation.

3. Transactions in capital stock and related owner's equity accounts are properly authorized and are recorded in accordance with generally accepted accounting principles.

4. Adequate disclsoure is made of owner's equity, including footnote disclosure.

Internal Controls

Several important internal controls are of concern to the independent auditor in owner's equity: proper authorization of transactions, proper record keeping, adequate segregation of duties between maintaining owner's equity records and handling cash and stock certificates, and the use of an independent registrar and stock transfer agent.

Proper Authorization of Transactions. Since each owner's equity transaction is typically material, many of these transactions must be approved by the board of directors. The following types of owner's equity transactions usually require specific authorization:

1. *Issuance of capital stock.* The authorization includes the type of the equity to issue (such as preferred or common stock), number of

shares to issue, par value of the stock, privileged condition for any stock other than common, and date of the issue.

2. *Repurchase of capital stock.* The repurchase of common or preferred shares, the timing of the repurchase, and the amount to pay for the shares should all be approved by the board of directors.

3. *Declaration of dividends.* The board of directors should authorize the form of the dividends (such as cash or stock), the amount of the dividend per share, and the record and payment dates of the dividends.

Proper Record Keeping and Segregation of Duties. When a company maintains its own records of stock transactions and outstanding stock, the controls must be adequate to make sure that the actual owners of the stock are recognized in the corporate records, the correct amount of dividends is paid to the stockholders owning the stock as of the dividend record date, and the potential for employee fraud is minimized. The proper assignment of personnel and adequate record-keeping procedures are useful controls for these purposes.

The most important procedures for preventing errors in owner's equity are (1) well-defined policies for preparing stock certificates and recording capital stock transactions, and (2) independent internal verification of information in the records. The client must be certain when issuing and recording capital stock that both the state laws governing corporations and the requirements in the corporate charter are being complied with. For example, the par value of the stock, the number of shares the company is authorized to issue, and the existence of state taxes on the issue of capital stock all affect issuance and recording.

A control over capital stock used by most companies is the maintenance of stock certificate books and a shareholder's ledger. A *capital stock book* is a record of the issuance and repurchase of capital stock for the life of the corporation. The record for a particular sales transaction includes such information as the certificate number, the number of shares issued, the name of the person to whom it was issued, and the issue date. When shares are repurchased, the capital stock book should include the canceled certificates and the date of their cancellation. A *shareholder's ledger* is the record of the outstanding shares at any point in time. The ledger acts as a check on the accuracy of the capital stock book and the balances in the general ledger and is used as the basis for the payment of dividends.

The disbursement of cash for the payment of dividends should be controlled in much the same manner as has been described in Chapter 13 for the preparation and payment of payroll. Dividend checks should be prepared from the capital stock book by someone who is not responsible for maintaining the capital stock records. After the checks are prepared, it is desirable to have an independent verification of the stockholders' names and the amount of the checks and a reconciliation of the total amount of the dividend checks with the total dividends authorized in the minutes. The use of a separate *imprest dividend account* is desirable to prevent the payment of a larger amount of dividends than was authorized.

Independent Registrar and Stock Transfer Agent. Any company whose stock is listed on a securities exchange is required to engage an *independent registrar* as a control to prevent the improper issue of stock certificates. The responsibility of an independent registrar is to make sure that stock is issued by a corporation in accordance with the capital stock provisions in the corporate charter and the authorization of the board of directors. The registrar is responsible for signing all newly issued stock certificates and making sure old certificates are received and canceled before a replacement certificate is issued when there is a change in the ownership of the stock.

Most large corporations also employ the services of a *stock transfer agent* for the purpose of maintaining the stockholder records, including records documenting transfers of stock ownership. The employment of a transfer agent not only serves as a control over the stock records by putting them in the hands of an independent organization, but reduces the cost of record keeping by the use of a specialist. Many companies also have the transfer agent disburse cash dividends to shareholders, thereby further improving internal controls.

Audit Tests of Capital Stock

The common stock and paid-in capital in excess of par accounts are so closely related that they are ordinarily verified at the same time. The audit procedures followed for auditing these two accounts depend primarily on the number and type of capital transactions in which the company has been involved in the current year. For example, the issuance of new capital stock for cash, the merger with another company through an exchange of stock, donated shares, and the purchase of treasury shares each require extensive auditing. The other factors affecting the audit procedures used for verifying capital stock are the existence of a registrar or transfer agent. The existence of these two controls not only decreases the likelihood of error but enables the auditor to rely on confirmation of certain information rather than verifying the information by other means. Regardless of the controls in existence, however, it is normal practice to verify all capital stock transactions and the ending balance in the account 100 percent because of the materiality of the amounts and the relative ease with which it can be done.

Usually the capital stock year-end balances and the transactions occurring during the year are audited simultaneously after the balance sheet date, but it is also acceptable to verify capital stock transactions at any time during the year. For example, if the client is involved in a major stock transaction where the valuation may be dependent upon the interpretation of generally accepted accounting principles such as in the case of a merger, it is common for the auditor to be asked his opinion about the proper accounting treatment of the transaction *before* the final agreement between the client and the third party is reached.

The same basic audit objectives for direct tests of balances that have been used in previous chapters also apply here. The most important objectives for capital stock and paid-in capital in excess of par are existence, valuation (which includes determining the number of shares outstanding), and disclosure. The other objectives can be conveniently discussed as a part of these three.

Existence. The starting point for the audit of capital stock is the recorded amounts in the client's general ledger. The auditor should trace all recorded capital stock transactions to authorizations in the minutes of the board of directors. It is also important to examine the minutes for the entire year to determine whether there are unrecorded capital stock transactions. Since the auditor should already have read the minutes early in the engagement and prepared excerpts of all information that is directly related to the financial statements, he can limit his examination of the minutes to an examination of the excerpts. Particular care should be taken to make sure the client has not failed to disclose a capital stock transaction that was approved near the end of the year.

Valuation. The correct valuation of capital stock transactions for cash can be readily verified by confirming the amount with the transfer agent and tracing the amount of the recorded capital stock transactions to cash receipts. (In the case of treasury stock the amounts are traced to the cash disbursements journal.) In addition, the auditor must verify whether the correct amounts were credited to capital stock and paid-in capital in excess of par by referring to the corporate charter to determine the par or stated value of the capital stock. When capital stock transactions are for stock dividends, acquisition of property for stock, mergers, or similar noncash transactions, the verification of valuation may be considerably more difficult. For these types of transactions the auditor must be certain that the client has correctly computed the amount of the capital stock issue in accordance with generally accepted accounting principles. For example, in the audit of a major merger transaction the auditor has to evaluate whether the transaction is a purchase or a pooling of interests. Frequently, considerable research is necessary to determine which accounting treatment is correct for the existing circumstances. After the auditor reaches a conclusion as to which method is appropriate, it is necessary to verify that the amounts were correctly computed.

The ending balance in the capital account is verified by first determining the number of shares outstanding at the balance sheet date. A confirmation from the transfer agent is the simplest way to obtain this information. When no transfer agent exists, the auditor must rely on examining the stock records and accounting for all shares outstanding in the stock certificate books, examining all canceled certificates, and accounting for blank certificates. After the auditor is satisfied that the number of shares outstanding is correct, the recorded par value in the capital account can be verified by multiplying the number of shares by the par value of the stock. The ending balance in the capital in excess of par account is a residual amount. It is audited by verifying the amount of recorded transactions during the year and adding them to or subtracting them from the beginning balance in the account.

A major consideration in the valuation of capital stock is verifying whether the number of shares used in the calculation of earnings per share is accurate. It is easy to determine the correct number of shares to use in the calculation when there is only one class of stock and a small number of capital stock transactions. The problem becomes much more complex when there are convertible securities, stock options, or stock warrants outstanding. A thorough understanding of APB 15 is important before the number of primary and fully diluted shares can be verified.

Disclosure. The most important sources of information for determining proper disclosure are the corporate charter, the minutes, and the auditor's analysis of capital stock transactions. The auditor should determine that there is a proper description of each class of stock, including such information as the number of shares issued and outstanding and any special rights of an individual class. The proper disclosure of stock options, stock warrants, and convertible securities should also be verified by examining legal documents or other evidence of the provisions of these agreements.

Retained Earnings and Dividends

The only transactions involving retained earnings for most companies are net earnings for the year and dividends declared. But there may also be corrections of prior period earnings, extraordinary items charged or credited directly to retained earnings, and the setting up or elimination of appropriations of retained earnings.

The starting point for the audit of retained earnings is an analysis of retained earnings for the entire year. The audit schedule showing the analysis, which is usually a part of the permanent file, includes a description of every transaction affecting the account.

The audit of the credit to retained earnings for net income for the year (or the debit for a loss) is accomplished by simply tracing the entry in retained earnings to the net earnings figure on the income statement. The performance of this procedure must of course take place fairly late in the audit after all adjusting entries affecting net earnings have been completed.

The emphasis in verifying decreases in retained earnings for dividends declared is on authorization and valuation. The authorization can be checked by examining the board of directors' minutes for the amount of the dividend per share and the dividend date. When the auditor examines the board of directors' minutes for dividends declared, he should be alert to the possibility of unrecorded dividends declared, particularly shortly before the balance sheet date. A closely related audit procedure is to review the permanent audit working paper file to determine if there are restrictions on the payment of dividends in bond indenture agreements or preferred stock provisions.

The valuation of a dividend declaration can be audited by recomputing the amount on the basis of the dividend per share and the number of shares outstanding. If the client uses a transfer agent to disburse dividends, the total can be traced to a cash disbursement entry to the agent and also confirmed.

When the client keeps its own dividend records and pays the dividends itself, the auditor can verify the total amount of the dividend by re-calculation and reference to cash disbursed. In addition it is necessary to verify whether the payment was made to the stockholders who owned the stock as of the dividend record date. The auditor can test this by selecting a sample of recorded dividend payments and tracing the payee's name on the canceled check to the dividend records to make sure the payee was entitled to the dividend. At the same time, the amount and the authenticity of the dividend check can be verified.

An important consideration in auditing debits and credits to retained earnings other than net earnings and dividends is determining whether the transactions should actually have been included. For example, prior period adjustments can be included in retained earnings only if they satisfy the requirements of APBs and the Financial Accounting Standards Board Statements. These would include such items as material non-recurring adjustments or a settlement of income taxes or litigation (APB 9) and special changes in the method of accounting for long-term construction contracts (APB 10).

After the auditor is satisfied that the recorded transactions are appropriately classified as retained earnings transactions, the next step is to decide whether they are properly valued. The audit evidence necessary to determine proper valuation depends on the nature of the transactions. If there is a requirement for an appropriation of retained earnings for a bond sinking fund, the correct amount of the appropriation can be determined by examining the bond indenture agreement. If there is a major loss charged to retained earnings because of a material nonrecurring abandonment of a plant, the evidence needed to determine the amount of the loss could include significant numbers of documents and records of the plant.

Another important consideration in the audit of retained earnings is evaluating whether there are any transactions that should have been included but were not. If a stock dividend was declared, for instance, the market value of the securities issued should be capitalized by a debit to retained earnings and a credit to capital stock. Similarly, if the financial statements include appropriations of retained earnings, the auditor should evaluate whether it is still necessary to have the appropriation as of the balance sheet date. As an example, an appropriation of retained earnings for a bond sinking fund should be eliminated by crediting retained earnings after the bond has been paid off.

The primary concern in determining whether retained earnings is correctly disclosed on the balance sheet is the existence of any restrictions on the payment of dividends. Frequently agreements with bankers, stockholders, and other creditors prohibit or limit the amount of dividends the client can pay. These restrictions must be disclosed in the footnotes to the financial statements.

REVIEW QUESTIONS

1. List four examples of interest-bearing liability accounts commonly found in balance sheets. What characteristics do these liabilities have in common? How do they differ?
2. Why are liability accounts included in the capital acquisition and repayment cycle audited differently from accounts payable?
3. It is common practice to audit the balance in notes payable in conjunction with the audit of interest expense and interest payable. Explain the advantages of this approach.
4. Which controls should the auditor be most concerned about in the audit of notes payable? Explain the importance of each of these controls.
5. Which overall reasonableness test is the most important in verifying notes payable? Which types of errors can the auditor uncover by the use of this test?
6. Why is it more important to search for unrecorded notes payable than for unrecorded notes receivable? List several audit procedures the auditor can use to uncover unrecorded notes payable.
7. What is the primary purpose of analyzing interest expense? Given this purpose, what primary considerations should the auditor keep in mind when doing the analysis?
8. Distinguish between the audit of transactions and direct tests of balances for liability accounts in the capital acquisition and repayment cycle.
9. List four types of restrictions long-term creditors often put on companies when granting them a loan. How can the auditor find out about each of these restrictions?
10. Describe what is meant by an imputed interest rate. How does an auditor determine whether the client's imputed rate is reasonable? What should be done in the audit of notes payable after the auditor is satisfied that the rate is reasonable?
11. What are the primary objectives in the audit of owner's equity accounts?
12. Evaluate the following statement: "The corporate charter and the bylaws of a company are legal documents; therefore, they should not be examined by the auditors. If the auditor wants information about these documents, an attorney should be consulted."
13. What are the major internal controls over owner's equity?
14. How does the audit of owner's equity for a closely held corporation differ from that for a publicly held corporation? In what respects are there no significant differences?
15. Describe the duties of a stock registrar and a transfer agent. How does the use of their services affect the effectiveness of the client's internal controls?
16. What kinds of information can be confirmed with a transfer agent?
17. Evaluate the following statement: "The most important audit procedure to verify dividends for the year is a comparison of a random sample of canceled dividend checks with a dividend list that has been prepared by management as of the dividend record date."
18. If a transfer agent disburses dividends for a client, explain how the audit of

dividends declared and paid is affected. What audit procedures are necessary to verify dividends paid when a transfer agent is used?

19. What should be the major emphasis in auditing the retained earnings account? Explain your answer.
20. Explain the relationship between the audit of owner's equity and the calculations of earnings per share. What are the main auditing considerations in verifying the earnings-per-share figure?

DISCUSSION QUESTIONS AND PROBLEMS

21. Items *a* through *f* are questions typically found in a standard internal control questionnaire used by auditors in evaluating internal controls for notes payable. In using the questionnaire for a particular client, a yes response indicates a possible strength in the system, whereas a no indicates a potential weakness.
    a. Are liabilities for notes payable incurred only after written authorization by a proper company official?
    b. Is a subsidiary ledger of notes payable maintained?
    c. Is the individual who maintains the notes payable subsidiary records someone other than the person who approves the issue of new notes or handles cash?
    d. Are paid notes canceled and retained in the company files?
    e. Is a periodic reconciliation made of the subsidiary records with the actual notes outstanding by an individual who does not maintain the subsidiary records?
    f. Are interest expense and accrued interest recomputed periodically by an individual who does not record interest transactions?

Required:

    a. For each of the above questions, state the purpose of the control.
    b. For each of the above questions, identify the type of financial statement error that could occur if the control were not in effect.
    c. For each of the potential errors in *b*, list an audit procedure the auditor can use to determine whether a material error exists.
22. The following are frequently performed audit procedures for the verification of bonds payable that were issued in previous years:
    a. Obtain a copy of the bond indenture agreement and review its important provisions.
    b. Determine that each of the bond indenture provisions has been met.
    c. Analyze the general ledger account for bonds payable, interest expense, and unamortized bond discount or premium.
    d. Test the client's calculations of interest expense, unamortized bond discount or premium, accrued interest, and bonds payable.
    e. Obtain a confirmation from the bondholder.
    f. Determine that each of the bond indenture provisions has been met.

Required:

    a. State the purpose of each of the above six audit procedures.
    b. List the provisions for which the auditor should be alert in examining the bond indenture agreement.

c. For each provision listed in *b*, explain how the auditor can determine whether its terms have been met.

d. Explain how the auditor should verify the unamortized bond discount or premium.

e. List the information that should be requested in the confirmation of bonds payable with the bondholder.

23. In making an audit of a corporation that has a bond issue outstanding, the trust indenture is reviewed and a confirmation as to the issue is obtained from the trustee.

Required:

List eight matters of importance to the auditor that might be found either in the indenture or in the confirmation obtained from the trustee. Explain briefly the reason for the auditor's interest in each of the items.

(AICPA adapted)

24. The Fox Company is a medium-sized industrial client that has been audited by your CPA firm for several years. The only interest-bearing debt owed by Fox Company is $200,000 in long-term notes payable held by the bank. The notes were issued three years previously and will mature in six more years. Fox Company is highly profitable, has no pressing needs for additional financing, and has excellent internal controls over the recording of loan transactions and related interest costs.

Required:

a. Describe the auditing that you think would be necessary for notes payable and related interest accounts in these circumstances.

b. How would your answer differ if Fox Company was unprofitable, had a need for additional financing, and had weak internal controls?

25. The ending general ledger balance of $186,000 in notes payable for the Sterling Manufacturing Company is made up of twenty-eight notes to eight different payees. The notes vary in duration anywhere from thirty days to two years, and in amount from $1,000 to $10,000. In some cases the notes were issued for cash loans; in other cases the notes were issued directly to vendors for the purchase of inventory or equipment. The use of relatively short term financing is necessary because all existing properties are pledged for mortgages. Nevertheless, there is still a serious cash shortage.

Record keeping procedures for notes payable are not good, considering the large number of loan transactions. There is no notes payable subsidiary ledger or independent verification of ending balances; however, the notes payable records are maintained by a secretary who does not have access to cash.

The audit has been done by the same CPA firm for several years. In the current year the following procedures were performed to verify notes payable:

a. Obtain a listing of notes payable from the client, foot the notes payable balances on the list, and trace the total to the general ledger.

b. Examine duplicate copies of notes for all outstanding notes included on the listing. Compare the name of the lender, amount, and due date on the duplicate copy with the listing.

c. Obtain a confirmation from lenders for all listed notes payable. The confirmation should include the due date of the loan, the amount, and the interest payable at the balance sheet date.

    d. Recompute accrued interest on the listing for all notes. The information for determining the correct accrued interest is to be obtained from the duplicate copy of the note. Foot the accrued interest amounts and trace the balance to the general ledger.

Required:

    a. What should be the emphasis in the verification of notes payable in this situation? Explain.

    b. State the purpose of each of the four audit procedures listed.

    c. Evaluate whether each of the four audit procedures was necessary. Evaluate the sample size for each procedure.

    d. List other audit procedures that should be performed in the audit of notes payable in these circumstances.

26. The Milfred Company is a medium-sized, closely held company that has been an audit client of Gordon and Coopers, CPAs, for several years. In the current year the senior on the audit, Rick Smith, CPA, compares interest expense with the amount in the preceding year and observes that the total has increased from $16,300 to $21,000. To Smith the increase seems large, especially since the company has not expanded in recent years.

    Smith decides to discuss this matter with the controller and is told that the increase is a result of higher interest rates and a greater number of loans outstanding. The controller informs Smith that short-term interest rates were 12 percent for the first six months and 15 percent thereafter. He also tells him that on May 29 the secured loan from the First National Bank for the building was refinanced and the interest rate went from 7.3 percent to 9.7 percent.

    The balances in the loan accounts as stated in the general ledger are as follows:

| | **Short-Term Loans** | | | | **Long-Term Secured Loan** | | |
	Dr.	*Cr.*	*Balance*		*Dr.*	*Cr.*	*Balance*
1-1-X7			$47,500	1-1-X7			$138,500
Jan.	$20,000	$31,700	59,200	Jan.	$427		138,073
Feb.	20,000	31,400	70,600	Feb.	435		137,638
Mar.	20,000	20,200	70,800	Mar.	444		137,194
Apr.	20,000	10,400	61,200	Apr.	454		136,740
May	20,000	2,500	43,700	May	465	$80,000	216,275
June	20,000	—	23,700	June	367		215,908
July	23,700	—	0	July	371		215,537
Aug.	—	—	0	Aug.	376		215,161
Sept.	—	12,700	12,700	Sept.	382		214,779
Oct.	20,000	33,700	26,400	Oct.	390		214,389
Nov.	20,000	29,200	35,600	Nov.	398		213,991
Dec.	20,000	40,600	56,200	Dec.	407		213,584

Required:

    a. Why should the auditor be concerned about an increase in interest expense?

    b. Perform overall reasonableness tests of interest expense to determine whether the interest expense of $21,000 is reasonable.

    c. What additional verification is appropriate in this situation?

27. The following covenants are extracted from the indenture of a bond issue. The indenture provides that failure to comply with its terms in any respect

automatically advances the due date of the loan to the date of noncompliance (the regular date is twenty years hence). Give any audit steps or reporting requirements you feel should be taken or recognized in connection with each one of the following:

a. "The debtor company shall endeavor to maintain a working capital ratio of 2 to 1 at all times, and, in any fiscal year following a failure to maintain said ratio, the company shall restrict compensation of officers to a total of $100,000. Officers for this purpose shall include Chairman of the Board of Directors, President, all vice presidents, Secretary, and Treasurer."

b. "The debtor company shall keep all property which is security for this debt insured against loss by fire to the extent of 100% of its actual value. Policies of insurance comprising this protection shall be filed with the trustee."

c. "The debtor company shall pay all taxes legally assessed against property which is security for this debt within the time provided by law for payment without penalty, and shall deposit receipted tax bills or equally acceptable evidence of payment of same with the trustee."

d. "A sinking fund shall be deposited with the trustee by semiannual payments of $300,000, from which the trustee shall, in his discretion, purchase bonds of this issue."   (AICPA adapted)

28. You were engaged to examine the financial statements of Ronlyn Corporation for the year ended June 30, 19X7.

On May 1, 19X7, the corporation borrowed $500,000 from the Second National Bank to finance plant expansion. The long-term note agreement provided for the annual payment of principal and interest over five years. The existing plant was pledged as security for the loan.

Due to unexpected difficulties in acquiring the building site, the plant expansion had not begun at June 30, 19X7. To make use of the borrowed funds, management decided to invest in stocks and bonds, and on May 16, 19X7, the $500,000 was invested in securities.

Required:

a. What are the audit objectives in the examination of long-term debt?

b. Prepare an audit program for the examination of the long-term note agreement between Ronlyn and Second National Bank. (AICPA adapted)

29. The Redford Corporation took out a twenty-year mortgage on 6-15-X8 for $2,600,000 and pledged its only manufacturing building and the land on which the building stands as collateral. Each month subsequent to the issue of the mortgage a monthly payment of $20,000 was paid to the mortgagor. You are in charge of the current year audit for Redford, which has a balance sheet date of December 31, 19X8. The client has been audited previously by your CPA firm, but this is the first time Redford Corporation has had a mortgage.

Required:

a. Explain why it is desirable to prepare a working paper for the permanent file for the mortgage. What type of information should be included in the working paper?

b. Explain why the audit of mortgage payable, interest expense, and interest payable should all be done together.

c. List the audit procedures that should ordinarily be performed to verify the issue of the mortgage, the balance in the mortgage and interest payable at 12-31-X8, and the balance in interest expense for the year 19X8.

30. Items *a* through *f* are common questions found in internal control questionnaires used by auditors in evaluating internal controls for owner's equity. In using the questionnaire for a particular client, a yes response indicates a possible strength in the system, whereas a no indicates a potential weakness.
    a. Does the company use the services of an independent registrar or transfer agent?
    b. Are issues and retirements of stock authorized by the board of directors?
    c. If an independent registrar and transfer agent are not used:
       (1) Are unissued certificates properly controlled?
       (2) Are canceled certificates mutilated to prevent their reuse?
    d. Are subsidiary ledgers and stock certificate books periodically reconciled with the general ledger by an independent person?
    e. Is an independent transfer agent used for disbursing dividends? If not, is an imprést dividend account maintained?
    f. Are all entries in the owner's equity accounts authorized at the proper level in the organization?

Required:

   a. For each of the above questions, state the purpose of the control.
   b. For each of the above questions, identify the type of potential financial statement errors if the control is not in effect.
   c. For each of the potential errors in *b*, list an audit procedure the auditor can use to determine whether a material error exists.

31. The following audit procedures are frequently performed by auditors in the verification of owner's equity:
    a. Review the articles of incorporation and bylaws for provisions relating to owner's equity.
    b. Review the minutes of the board of directors for the year for approvals related to owner's equity.
    c. Analyze all owner's equity accounts for the year and document the nature of any recorded change in each account.
    d. Account for all certificate numbers in the capital stock book for all shares outstanding.
    e. Examine the stock certificate book for any stock that was canceled.
    f. Recompute earnings per share.
    g. Review debt provisions and senior securities with respect to liquidation preferences, dividends in arrears, and restrictions on the payment of dividends or the issue of stock.

Required:

   a. State the purpose of each of these seven audit procedures.
   b. List the type of errors the auditors could uncover by the use of each audit procedure.

32. You are engaged in making the audit of a corporation whose records have not previously been audited by you. The corporation has both an independent transfer agent and a registrar for its capital stock. The transfer agent maintains the record of stockholders and the registrar checks that

there is no overissue of stock. Signatures of both are required to validate certificates.

It has been proposed that confirmations be obtained from both the transfer agent and the registrar as to the stock outstanding at the balance sheet date. If such confirmations agree with the books, no additional work is to be performed as to capital stock.

If you agree that obtaining the confirmations as suggested would be sufficient in this case, give the justification for your position. If you do not agree, state specifically all additional steps you would take and explain your reasons for taking them. (AICPA adapted)

33. The Rico Corporation is a medium-sized wholesaler of grocery products with 4,000 shares of stock outstanding to approximately twenty-five stockholders. Due to the age of several retired stockholders and the success of the company, management has decided to pay dividends six times a year. The amount of the bimonthly dividend per share varies depending upon the profits, but it is ordinarily between $5 and $7 per share. The chief accountant, who is also a stockholder, prepares the dividend checks, records the checks in the dividend journal, and reconciles the bank account. Important controls include manual check signing by the president and the use of an imprest dividend bank account.

The auditor verifies the dividends by maintaining a schedule of the total shares of stock issued and outstanding in the permanent working papers. The total amount of stock outstanding is multiplied by the dividends per share authorized in the minutes to arrive at the current total dividend. This total is compared with the deposit that has been made to the imprest dividend account. Since the transfers of stock are infrequent, it is possible to verify dividends paid for the entire year in a comparatively short time.

Required:

a. Evaluate the usefulness of the approach followed by the auditor in verifying dividends in this situation. Your evaluation should include both the strengths and the weaknesses of the approach.
b. List other audit procedures that should be performed in verifying dividends in this situation. Explain the purpose of each procedure.

34. Holmes Company has decided to declare a 10 percent stock dividend in the current year rather than having a cash dividend. There are 160,000 shares outstanding to approximately two thousand stockholders as of the date of the dividend. The stock was selling for $38½ per share on the date the dividend was declared, but it had dropped to $26 as of the balance sheet date. The par value of the stock is $20 per share. The company does not employ the services of a transfer agent.

Required:

a. What is the proper accounting treatment of the stock dividend?
b. What audit procedures should be used to verify the stock dividend? Describe the purpose of each procedure.

35. In 1956 Jack Harrigan and his brothers started a small manufacturing company as a sideline to their regular occupations. What began as a small informal partnership eventually became a successful business, and when the sons of two of the original partners entered the firm, the need to formalize the relationship became obvious to everyone concerned. After

lengthy discussions among themselves and with attorneys and CPAs, the decision was made to enter into a clearly defined partnership agreement rather than to incorporate. The partnership agreement was completed in 1971.

The firm has continued to operate successfully without internal difficulties since that time. Great care is taken by the firm to keep the affairs of the partnership entity and those of the individual partners completely separate. For example, if a personal transaction of a partner is paid by the partnership, his capital account is charged.

Your firm has audited the partnership entity for several years, and the individuals involved have concluded that the system of internal control is excellent. No unusual difficulties have been encountered in any year.

Required:

a. How does the fact that the business is a partnership rather than a corporation affect the audit of the capital acquisition and repayment cycle? (Be specific.)
b. How do the tests of transactions for each of the cycles other than the capital acquisition and repayment cycle differ when the client is a partnership rather than a corporation?
c. How do the direct tests of balances for each of the cycles other than the capital acquisition and repayment cycle differ when the client is a partnership rather than a corporation?

36. You are a CPA engaged in an examination of the financial statements of Pate Corporation for the year ended December 31, 19X9. The financial statements and records of Pate Corporation have not been audited by a CPA in prior years.

The stockholders' equity section of Pate Corporation's balance sheet at December 31, 19X9, follows:

Stockholders' equity:

Capital stock—10,000 shares of $10 par value authorized; 5,000 shares issued and outstanding	$ 50,000
Capital contributed in excess of par value of capital stock	32,580
Retained earnings	47,320
Total stockholders' equity	$129,900

Pate Corporation was founded in 19X1. The corporation has ten stockholders and serves as its own registrar and transfer agent. There are no capital stock subscription contracts in effect.

Required:

a. Prepare the detailed audit program for the examination of the three accounts comprising the stockholders' equity section of Pate Corporation's balance sheet. (Do not include in the audit program the verification of the results of the current year's operations.)
b. After every other figure on the balance sheet has been audited by the CPA, it might appear that the retained earnings figure is a balancing figure and requires no further verification. Why does the CPA verify retained earnings as he does the other figures on the balance sheet? Discuss.

(AICPA adapted)

37. You were engaged on May 1, 19X7, by a committee of stockholders to perform a special audit as of December 31, 19X6, of the stockholders' equity of the Major Corporation, whose stock is actively traded on a stock exchange. The group of stockholders who engaged you believe that the information contained in the stockholders' equity section of the published annual report for the year ended December 31, 19X6, is not correct. If your examination confirms their suspicions, they intend to use the report in a proxy fight.

Management agrees to permit your audit but refuses to permit any direct confirmation with stockholders. To secure cooperation in the audit, the committee of stockholders has agreed to this limitation and you have been instructed to limit your audit in this respect. You have been instructed also to exclude the audit of revenue and expense accounts for the year.

Required:

a. Prepare a general audit program for the usual examination of the stockholders' equity section of a corporation's balance sheet, assuming no limitation on the scope of your examination. Exclude the audit of revenue and expense accounts.

b. Describe any special auditing procedures you would undertake in view of the limitations and other special circumstances of your examination of the Major Corporation's stockholders' equity accounts.

(AICPA adapted)

18

Audit of Cash Balances in the Bank

The audit of cash balances is the last area studied in this text because the evidence accumulated for cash balances depends heavily on the results of the tests in all the various transaction cycles. For example, if the review and evaluation of internal control and audit tests of the acquisition and payment cycle lead the auditor to believe the controls over cash disbursements are excellent, it is appropriate to reduce the tests of the ending balance in cash. On the other hand, if the tests indicate the client's controls are inadequate, extensive year-end testing may be necessary.

TYPES OF CASH ACCOUNTS

It is important to understand the various types of cash accounts because the auditing approach differs between them. The following are the major types of cash accounts:

1. *General cash account.* The general account is the focal point of cash for most organizations because virtually all cash receipts and disbursements flow through the general cash account at some time. The disbursements for the acquisition and payment cycle are normally paid from this account, and the receipts of cash in the sales and collection fund are de-

posited in the account. In addition, the deposits and disbursements for all other cash accounts are normally made through the general account. Most small companies have only one bank account—the general cash account.

2. *Imprest payroll account.* As a means of improving control, many companies establish a separate imprest bank account for making payroll payments to employees. In an imprest payroll account, a fixed balance, such as $1,000, is maintained in a separate bank account. Immediately before each pay period one check is drawn on the general cash account to deposit the total amount of the net payroll in the payroll account. After all payroll checks have cleared the imprest payroll account, the bank account should have a $1,000 balance. The only deposits into the account are of the weekly and semimonthly payroll, and the only disbursements are paychecks to employees. For companies with many employees, the use of an imprest payroll account can improve internal controls and also reduce the time needed to reconcile bank accounts.

3. *Branch bank account.* For a company operating in multiple locations, it is frequently desirable to have a separate bank balance at each location. Branch bank accounts are useful for building public relations in local communities and permitting the centralization of operations at the branch level.

In some companies the deposits and disbursements for each branch are made to a particular bank account, and the excess cash is periodically sent to the main office general bank account. The branch account in this instance is much like a general account, but at the branch level.

A somewhat different type of branch account consists of one bank account for receipts and a separate one for disbursements. All receipts are deposited in the branch bank, and the total is transferred to the general account periodically. The disbursement account is set up on an *imprest basis,* but in a different manner than an imprest payroll account. A fixed balance is maintained in the imprest account, and the authorized branch personnel use these funds for disbursements at their own discretion as long as the payments are consistent with company policy. When the cash balance has been depleted, an accounting is made to the home office and a reimbursement is made to the branch account from the general account *after* the expenditures have been approved. The advantages of using an imprest branch bank account are the resulting controls over receipts and disbursements.

4. *Imprest petty cash fund.* A petty cash fund is actually not a bank account, but it is sufficiently similar to cash on deposit to merit inclusion. It is used for small cash purchases which can be paid more conveniently and quickly by cash than by check, or for the convenience of employees in cashing personal or payroll checks. An imprest cash account is set up on the same basis as an imprest branch bank account, but the expenditures are normally for a much smaller amount. Typical expenses include minor office supplies, stamps, and small contributions to local charities. Usually a petty cash account does not exceed $500 and may not be reimbursed more than once or twice each month.

5. *Savings accounts.* Excess cash accumulated during certain parts of

the operating cycle which will be needed in the reasonably near future is usually deposited in certificates of deposit or interest-bearing savings accounts. This money is not meant for use in the business until it is transferred back to the general cash account.

This chapter focuses on three types of accounts: the general cash account, the imprest payroll bank account, and the imprest petty cash fund. The others are similar to these and need not be discussed.

RELATIONSHIP BETWEEN CASH IN THE BANK AND THE TRANSACTION CYCLES

A brief discussion of the relationship between cash in the bank and the other transaction cycles serves a dual function: it clearly shows the importance of the tests of various transaction cycles to the audit of cash and it aids in further understanding the integration of the different transaction cycles. Figure 18-1 illustrates the relationship of the various transaction cycles, the focal point being the general cash account.

An examination of Figure 18-1 indicates why the general cash account is considered significant in almost all audits even when the ending balance is immaterial. The amount of cash *flowing* into and out of the cash account is frequently larger than for any other account in the financial statements. Furthermore, the susceptibility of cash to defalcation is greater than for other types of assets because most other assets must be converted to cash to make them usable.

An important distinction in the audit of cash should be made between verifying the client's reconciliation of the balance on the bank statement to the balance in the general ledger and verifying whether recorded cash in the general ledger correctly reflects all cash transactions that took place during the year. It is relatively easy to verify the client's reconciliation of the balance in the bank account to the general ledger, which is the primary subject of this chapter, but a significant part of the total audit of a company involves verifying whether cash transactions are properly recorded. For example, the following errors will each ultimately result in the improper payment of cash or the failure to receive cash, but none of them will normally be discovered as a part of the audit of the bank reconciliation:

1. Failure to bill a customer.
2. Billing a customer at a lower price than called for by company policy.
3. A defalcation of cash by interception of collections from customers before they are recorded. The account is charged off as a bad debt.
4. Duplicate payment of a vendor's invoice.
5. Improper payments of officers' personal expenditures.
6. Payment for raw materials that were not received.
7. Payment to an employee for more hours than he worked.
8. Payment of interest to a related party for an amount in excess of the going rate.

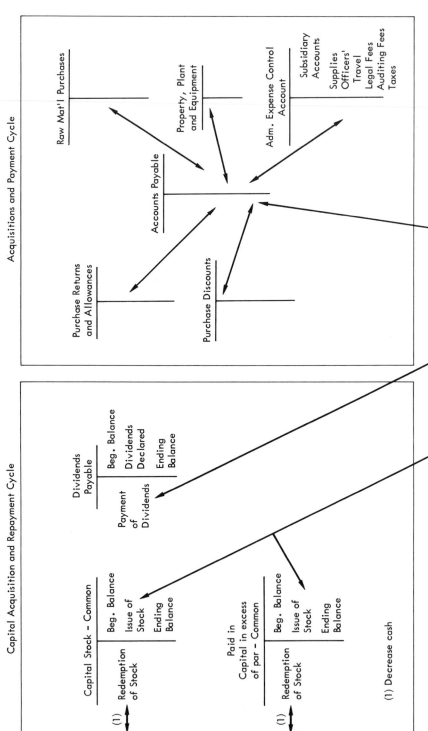

FIGURE 18-1

RELATIONSHIP BETWEEN CASH IN THE BANK AND THE TRANSACTION CYCLES

Acquisitions and Payment Cycle

Capital Acquisition and Repayment Cycle

Raw Mat'l Purchases

Property, Plant and Equipment

Adm. Expense Control Account

Subsidiary Accounts

Supplies
Officers'
Travel
Legal Fees
Auditing Fees
Taxes

Accounts Payable

Purchase Returns and Allowances

Purchase Discounts

Dividends Payable

Beg. Balance
Dividends Declared

Ending Balance

Payment of Dividends

Capital Stock - Common

Beg. Balance
Issue of Stock

Ending Balance

Redemption of Stock

(1)

Paid in Capital in excess of par - Common

Beg. Balance
Issue of Stock

Ending Balance

Redemption of Stock

(1)

(1) Decrease cash

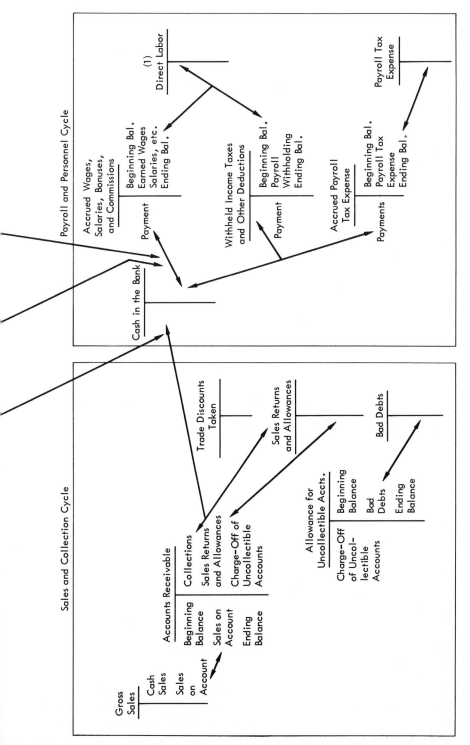

Payroll and Personnel Cycle

Direct Labor (1)

Accrued Wages, Salaries, Bonuses, and Commissions

	Beginning Bal.
Payment	Earned Wages Salaries, etc.
	Ending Bal.

Withheld Income Taxes and Other Deductions

	Beginning Bal.
Payment	Payroll Withholding
	Ending Bal.

Accrued Payroll Tax Expense

	Beginning Bal.
Payments	Payroll Tax Expense
	Ending Bal.

Payroll Tax Expense

Cash in the Bank

Sales and Collection Cycle

Gross Sales

| | Cash Sales |
| | Sales on Account |

Accounts Receivable

Beginning Balance	Collections
Sales on Account	Sales Returns and Allowances
	Charge-Off of Uncollectible Accounts
Ending Balance	

Trade Discounts Taken

Sales Returns and Allowances

Allowance for Uncollectible Accts.

Charge-Off of Uncol-lectible Accounts	Beginning Balance
	Bad Debts
	Ending Balance

Bad Debts

If these errors are to be uncovered in the audit, their discovery must come about through the tests of the systems that were discussed in the preceding chapters. The first three errors should be discovered as part of the audit of the sales and collection cycle; the next three errors should ordinarily be discovered as part of the acquisition and payment cycle; and the discovery of the last two errors should result from the payroll and personnel cycle and the capital acquisition and repayment cycle, respectively.

Entirely different types of errors are normally discovered as a part of the tests of a bank reconciliation. For example:

1. Failure to include a check that has not cleared the bank on the outstanding check list, even though it has been recorded in the cash disbursements journal.
2. Cash received by the client subsequent to the balance sheet date but recorded as cash receipts in the current year.
3. Deposits recorded in the cash book near the end of the year, deposited in the bank, and included in the bank reconciliation as a deposit in transit.
4. The existence of payments on notes payable that were debited directly to the bank balance by the bank but were not entered in the client's records.

The appropriate methods for discovering the preceding errors by testing the client's bank reconciliation will become apparent as we proceed. At this point it is important only that the reader distinguish between tests of transactions that are related to the cash account and tests that determine whether the book balance reconciles to the bank balance.

AUDIT OF THE GENERAL CASH ACCOUNT

The Auditor's Objectives

In testing the year-end balance in the general cash account, the auditor must accumulate sufficient evidence to evaluate whether

1. The cash balances as stated in the balance sheet represent cash on hand, in transit, or in the general cash account.
2. The cash is properly classified in the financial statements and adequate disclosure is made of restricted or committed funds and of cash not subject to immediate withdrawal.

Internal Controls

The controls over the year-end cash balances in the general account can be divided into two categories: *controls over the transaction cycles* affecting the recording of cash receipts and disbursements, and *independent bank reconciliations*.

The controls affecting the recording of cash transactions have been discussed in preceding chapters. For example, in the acquisition and payment cycle, major controls include the adequate segregation of duties between check signing and the accounts payable function, the signing of checks only by a properly authorized person, the use of prenumbered checks that are printed on special paper, adequate control of blank and voided checks, careful review of supporting documentation by the check signer before checks are signed, and adequate internal verification. If the controls affecting cash-related transactions are adequate, it is possible to reduce the audit tests for the year-end bank reconciliation.

Monthly reconciliation of the general bank account on a timely basis by someone independent of the handling or recording of cash receipts and disbursements is an essential control over the cash balance. The reconciliation is important to make sure the books reflect the same cash balance as the actual amount of cash in the bank after consideration of reconciling items; but even more important, the *independent* reconciliation provides a unique opportunity for an internal verification of cash receipts and disbursements transactions. If the bank statements are received unopened by the reconciler and physical control is maintained over the statements until the reconciliations are complete, the canceled checks, duplicate deposit slips, and other documents included in the statement can be examined by him without concern for the possibility of alteration, deletions, or additions. A careful bank reconciliation by competent client personnel includes the following:

1. Comparison of canceled checks with the cash disbursements journal for date, payee, and amount.
2. Examination of canceled checks for signature, endorsement, and cancellation.
3. Comparison of deposits in the bank with recorded cash receipts for date, customer, and amount.
4. Accounting for the numerical sequence of checks, and the investigation of missing ones.
5. Reconciliation of all items causing a difference between the book and bank balance and the verification of their propriety.
6. Reconciliation of total debits on the bank statement with the totals in the cash disbursements journal.
7. Reconciliation of total credits on the bank statement with the totals in the cash receipts journal.
8. Review of month-end interbank transfers for propriety and proper recording.
9. Periodic follow-up on outstanding checks and stop-payment notices.

The first four of these internal procedures are directly related to the tests of transactions that were discussed in previous chapters. The last five procedures are directly related to the reconciliation of the book and bank balance and are discussed in greater detail later.

Due to the importance of monthly reconciliation of bank accounts, another common control for many companies is to have a responsible employee review the monthly reconciliation as soon as possible after its completion. This review function is often performed by an internal auditor if the organization has such a function.

Audit Procedures for Year-End Cash

A major consideration the auditor must keep in mind in auditing the general cash balance is the possibility of fraud. The auditor must extend his audit procedures in the audit of year-end cash to determine the possibility of a material fraud when there are inadequate internal controls, especially the improper segregation of duties between the handling of cash and the recording of cash transactions in the journals. The study of cash in the following section assumes the existence of adequate controls over cash; therefore, fraud detection is not emphasized. At the completion of the study of typical audit procedures for the reconciliation of year-end cash, procedures designed primarily for the detection of fraud are examined.

In discussing the verification of year-end cash, we employ six of the eight detailed objectives that have been used in studying the audit of other asset balances. There is no discussion of the ownership and classification objectives, since they are not significant for cash in the bank. Also, because of their close relationship in the audit of year-end cash, the existence and valuation objectives are discussed together. These two objectives are the most important ones for cash and therefore receive the greatest attention.

Mechanical Accuracy. The starting point for the verification of the balance in the general bank account is to obtain a bank reconciliation from the client for inclusion in the auditor's working papers. Figure 18-2 depicts a bank reconciliation after it has been audited.

The mechanical accuracy tests of the bank reconciliation are usually limited to footing the totals on the bank reconciliation and tracing the book balance to the general ledger. The footing should include the outstanding checks and any other totals included on the reconciliation.

Overall Reasonableness. Tests of the reconciling items on bank reconciliations are normally accounted for on a 100 percent basis; therefore, there are few overall reasonableness tests to perform. The auditor should compare the reconciliation for each bank account with the one from the preceding year to make sure no significant item has been overlooked in the current year's reconciliation. In addition, the ending balance in cash can be compared with the balances in other months to see if there has been a significant change. The remainder of the overall reasonableness tests affecting cash are performed in other parts of the audit.

Existence and Valuation. The three major audit procedures involved in verifying the ending balance in the general bank account are

FIGURE 18-2

A WORKING PAPER FOR A BANK RECONCILIATION

ABC Company, Inc.
Bank Reconciliation

Schedule	A-2	Date
Prepared by	DED	1/10/7x
Approved by	SJO	1/18/7x

12/31/7x

Acct. 101 – General account, First National Bank

Balance per Bank		109,713	A-2/1
Add:			
Deposits in transit ①			
12/30	10,017		
12/31	11,100	21,117	
Bank service charges		—	
Bank charges for returned checks		—	
Deduct:			
Outstanding checks ①			
# 7,993	12/16	3,068	
8,007	12/16	9,763	
8,012	12/23	11,916	
8,013	12/23	14,717	
8,029	12/24	37,998	
8,038	12/30	10,000	⟨87,462⟩
Other reconciling items:			
Deposit to Payroll account credited			
to General account by bank, in error		⟨15,200⟩	A-3
Balance per books, before adjustments		28,168	
Adjustments:			
None		—	
Balance per books, adjusted		28,168	A-1

① Cut-off bank statement procedures completed by
    DED   1/10/7x

② Cut-off bank statement enclosures returned to
    client, acknowledged by   M. Smith   1/12/7x

all tests of the existence and valuation objectives: (1) receipt of a bank confirmation, (2) receipt of a cutoff bank statement, and (3) tests of the bank reconciliation.

Receipt of a bank confirmation. The direct receipt of a bank confirmation from every bank with which the client does business is necessary for every audit, except when there are an unusually large number of inactive accounts. If the bank does not respond to a confirmation request, the auditor must send a second request or ask the client to telephone the bank. As a convenience to auditors as well as to bankers who are requested to fill out bank confirmations, the AICPA has approved the use of a *standard bank confirmation* form. Figure 18-2 depicts a completed standard bank confirmation.

The importance of bank confirmations in the audit extends beyond the verification of the actual cash balance. Because of the multiple services offered by banks, the standard bank confirmation includes space for information of interest to the auditor besides specific information relating to the general cash account bank balance, such as

1. The balances in all bank accounts.
2. Restrictions on withdrawals. An example of a restriction is the bank's requirement of a compensating balance in the checking account.
3. The interest rate on interest-bearing accounts.
4. Information on liabilities to the bank for notes, mortgages, or other debt, including the amount of the loan, the date of the loan, its due date, interest rate, and the existence of collateral.
5. Contingent liabilities, open letters of credit, and similar items requiring disclosure in the financial statements.

After the bank confirmation has been received, the balance in the bank account confirmed by the bank should be traced to the amount stated on the bank reconciliation. Similarly, all other information on the reconciliation should be traced to the relevant audit working papers. In any case where the information is not in agreement, an investigation must be made of the difference.

Receipt of a cutoff bank statement. A cutoff bank statement is a partial period bank statement and the related canceled checks, duplicate deposit slips, and other documents included in bank statements, which is mailed by the bank directly to the CPA firm's office. The purpose of the cutoff bank statement is to verify the reconciling items on the client's year-end bank reconciliation with evidence that is inaccessible to the client. To fulfill this purpose, the auditor requests the client to have the bank send the statement for seven to ten days subsequent to the balance sheet date directly to the auditor.

Many auditors prove the subsequent period bank statement if a cutoff statement is not received directly from the bank. They perform the proof in the month subsequent to the balance sheet date by (1) footing all the canceled checks, debit memos, deposits, and credit memos; (2) checking to see that the bank statement balances when the footed totals are used;

FIGURE 18-3

STANDARD BANK CONFIRMATION

STANDARD BANK CONFIRMATION INQUIRY
Approved 1966 by
AMERICAN INSTITUTE OF CERTIFIED PUBLIC ACCOUNTANTS
AND
BANK ADMINISTRATION INSTITUTE (FORMERLY NABAC)

ORIGINAL
To be mailed to accountant

December 23 19 7X

Dear Sirs:

Your completion of the following report will be sincerely appreciated. **IF THE ANSWER TO ANY ITEM IS "NONE",
PLEASE SO STATE.** Kindly mail it in the enclosed stamped, addressed envelope direct to the accountant named below.

Report from

Yours truly, **ABC Company, Inc.**
(ACCOUNT NAME PER BANK RECORDS)

(Bank) First National Bank

By _A. L. Moore_
Authorized Signature

123 Financial Street

Bank customer should check here if confirmation of bank balance only (item 1) is desired.

Middletown

NOTE — If the space provided is inadequate, please enter totals hereon and attach a statement giving full details as called for by the columnar headings below.

Accountant — Smart & Allen

New York, New York

Dear Sirs:

1. At the close of business on __December 31__19 7X our records showed the following balance(s) to the credit of the above named customer. In the event that we could readily ascertain whether there were any balances to the credit of the customer not designated in this request, the appropriate information is given below.

AMOUNT	ACCOUNT NAME	ACCOUNT NUMBER	Subject to With-drawal by Check?	Interest Bearing? Give Rate
$ 109,713.11	General account	19751-974	Yes	No
1,000.00	Payroll account	19751-989	Yes	No

2. The customer was directly liable to us in respect of loans, acceptances, etc., at the close of business on that date in the total amount of $ 300,000 as follows:

AMOUNT	Date of Loan or Discount	Due Date	INTEREST Rate	INTEREST Paid To	DESCRIPTION OF LIABILITY, COLLATERAL, SECURITY INTERESTS, LIENS, ENDORSERS, ETC.
$ 150,000	12/9/7X	1/9/7X	10	N/A	General security agreement
90,000	12/16/7X	1/16/7X	10		
60,000	12/23/7X	1/23/7X	10		

3. The customer was contingently liable as endorser of notes discounted and/or as guarantor at the close of business of that date in the total amount of $ None , as below:

AMOUNT	NAME OF MAKER	DATE OF NOTICE	DUE DATE	REMARKS
$				

4. Other direct or contingent liabilities, open letters of credit, and relative collateral, were

None

5. Security agreements under the Uniform Commercial Code or any other agreements providing for restrictions, not noted above, were as follows (if officially recorded, indicate date and office in which filed):

UCC filing, Secretary of State, 1/12/7X, Capital City

Yours truly, (Bank) First National Bank

Date January 10 19 7X

By _Margaret Davis_ , V.P.
Authorized Signature

If the space provided is inadequate, please enter totals hereon and attach a statement giving full details as called for by the above columnar headings.

and (3) reviewing the items included in the footings to make sure they were canceled by the bank in the proper period and do not include any erasures or alterations. The purpose of this proof is to test whether the client's employees have omitted, added, or altered any of the documents accompanying the statement. It is obviously a test for intentional errors.

Tests of the bank reconciliation. The reason for testing the bank reconciliation is to verify whether the client's recorded bank balance is the same amount as the actual cash in the bank except for deposits in transit, outstanding checks, and other reconciling items. In testing the reconciliation, the cutoff bank statement provides the information for conducting the tests. Several major procedures are involved:

1. Trace the balance on the cutoff statement to the balance per bank on the bank reconciliation; a reconciliation cannot take place until these two are the same.
2. Trace checks included with the cutoff bank statement to the list of outstanding checks on the bank reconciliation and to the cash disbursements journal. All checks that cleared the bank after the balance sheet date which were included in the cash disbursements journal should also be included on the outstanding check list. If a check was included in the cash disbursements journal, it should be included as an outstanding check if it did not clear before the balance sheet date. Similarly, if a check cleared the bank prior to the balance sheet date, it should not be on the bank reconciliation.
3. Investigate all significant checks included on the outstanding check list that have not cleared the bank on the cutoff statement. The first step in the investigation should be to trace the amount of any items not clearing to the cash disbursements journal. The reason for the check's not being cashed should be discussed with the client, and if the auditor is concerned about the possibility of fraud, the vendor's accounts payable balance should be confirmed to determine whether the vendor has recognized the receipt of the cash in his records. In addition, the canceled check should be examined prior to the last day of the audit if it becomes available.
4. Trace the deposits in transit to the subsequent bank statement. All cash receipts not deposited in the bank at the end of the year should be traced to the cutoff bank statement to make sure they were deposited shortly after the beginning of the new year.
5. Account for other reconciling items on the bank statement and bank reconciliation. These include such items as bank service charges, bank errors and corrections, and unrecorded note transactions debited or credited directly to the bank account by the bank. These reconciling items should be carefully investigated to be sure they have been treated properly by the client.

Cutoff. Three aspects of cutoff concern the auditor in verifying the cash balance: cash receipts cutoff, cash disbursements cutoff, and the cutoff of bank transfers. The first two are discussed in this section, and cutoff of bank transfers is discussed subsequently under tests for kiting.

Cash receipts cutoff. An error in the cutoff of cash receipts occurs if the client *"holds open the cash receipts book"* as a means of improving the cash position on the financial statements. The error comes about by the client's recording cash receipts received subsequent to the balance sheet date in the current year's cash receipts journal. Typically, the error affects only cash and accounts receivable and not the income statement, but it can still be misleading to users if the amount is large. A common situation in which the client holds open the cash book is when it wants to increase the cash balance to prevent the inclusion of a negative cash balance on the balance sheet.

There are two useful audit procedures for detecting a cash receipts cutoff error. The first is to trace the deposits in transit to the cutoff bank statement to determine the date they were deposited in the bank account. Since the recorded cash will have to be included as deposits in transit on the bank reconciliation, the auditor can test for the number of days it took for the in-transit items to be deposited. If there is more than a two- or three-day delay between the balance sheet date and the subsequent deposit of all deposits in transit, there is an indication of a cutoff error. The second requires being on the premises at the balance sheet date and counting all cash and checks on hand and recording the amount in the working papers. When the bank reconciliation is tested, the auditor can check whether the deposits in transit equal the amount recorded.

Cash disbursements cutoff. The same type of cutoff problem discussed for cash receipts also exists for cash disbursements, but the objective of holding open the cash disbursements journal is to reduce accounts payable and thereby improve the current ratio. The simplest way to verify cash disbursements cutoff is to record the last check number used on the balance sheet date in the audit working papers. During the year-end field work, the disbursements journal can be examined to make sure the check number recorded in the working papers is the last one included. If the auditor is not on the client's premises on the balance sheet date to record the last check number, the canceled checks in the bank cutoff statement can be examined for the bank cancelation date. If a large number of checks cleared more than seven to ten days after the balance sheet date, the possibility of a cutoff error is likely. It is difficult to be certain of the existence of disbursement cutoff errors not only because of the time it takes for checks to arrive at the vendor's premises, but also because some vendors do not deposit cash receipts daily.

Disclosure. The cash classification on the balance sheet normally includes currency and undeposited checks, bank drafts, savings accounts, certificates of deposit, and demand deposits. Savings accounts and certificates of deposit should be separately disclosed unless the amounts are immaterial. If there are bank overdrafts, they should be included as liabilities rather than assets. In addition, cash available for general operations should be distinguished from cash restricted for special purposes. For example, cash deposited with a trustee for the payment of mortgage interest and taxes or the proceeds of a construction mortgage that is restricted to the payment of construction costs must be separately disclosed. The existence of these restrictions is determined by examining bank confirmations, reading the minutes, and examining agreements as a part of the tests of other assets or liabilities.

When there is an agreement between the bank and the client to maintain a minimum specified balance in the general checking account, the amount of the restricted balance should be segregated and described in a footnote. This is referred to as a *compensating balance*. Information on compensating balances can be obtained from bank confirmations, reading the minutes, and examining loan agreements between the bank and the client.

A practice followed by some companies to improve their cash and working capital position on the balance sheet is to make a long-term loan near the balance sheet date and repay it shortly after the end of the year. This is referred to as *window dressing*. The auditor can determine whether window dressing exists by reviewing loan transactions shortly before the end of the period and large repayments after the balance sheet date. If the auditor concludes that the purpose of the loan transactions was for window dressing rather than an actual need for cash to operate the company, the facts must be disclosed in a footnote.

Fraud-Oriented Procedures

It is frequently necessary for the auditor to extend his year-end audit procedures to test more extensively for the possibility of material fraud when the client's internal controls are weak. Many fraudulent activities are difficult if not impossible to uncover; nevertheless, the auditor is responsible for making a reasonable effort to detect fraud when he has reason to believe it may exist. The following procedures for uncovering fraud are discussed in this section: extended tests of the bank reconciliation, proofs of cash, and tests for kiting.

Extended Tests of the Bank Reconciliation. When the auditor believes the year-end bank reconciliation may be intentionally misstated, it is appropriate to perform extended tests of the year-end bank reconciliation. The purpose of the extended procedures is to verify whether all transactions included in the journals for the last month of the year were correctly included in or excluded from the bank reconciliation and to verify whether all items in the bank reconciliation were correctly included. Let us assume that the system of internal control is weak and the client's year-end is December 31. A common approach is to start with the bank reconciliation for November and compare all reconciling items with canceled checks and other documents in the December bank statement. In addition, all remaining canceled checks and deposit slips in the December bank statement should be compared with the December cash disbursements and receipts journals. All uncleared items in the November bank reconciliation and the December cash disbursements and receipts journals should be included in the client's December 31 bank reconciliation. Similarly, all reconciling items in the December 31 bank reconciliation should be items from the November bank reconciliation and December's journals that have not yet cleared the bank.

In addition to the tests just described, the auditor must also carry out procedures subsequent to the end of the year with the use of the bank cutoff statement. These tests would be performed in the same manner as previously discussed.

Proofs of Cash. Auditors frequently prepare a proof of cash when the client's internal controls over cash are not considered adequate. A proof of cash includes the following:

1. A reconciliation of the balance on the bank statement with the general ledger balance at the beginning of the proof-of-cash period.
2. A reconciliation of cash receipts deposited with the cash receipts journal for a period of time.
3. A reconciliation of canceled checks clearing the bank with the cash disbursements journal for a period of time.
4. A reconciliation of the balance on the bank statement with the general ledger balance at the end of the proof-of-cash period.

A proof of cash of this nature is commonly referred to as a four-column proof of cash—one column is used for each of the above types of information. A proof of cash can be performed for one or more interim months, the entire year, or the last month of the year. Figure 18-4 depicts a four-column proof of cash for an interim month.

The auditor uses a proof of cash to determine the following:

1. Whether all recorded cash receipts were deposited.
2. Whether all deposits in the bank were recorded in the accounting records.
3. Whether all recorded cash disbursements were paid by the bank.
4. Whether all amounts that were paid by the bank were recorded.

When the auditor does a proof of cash, he is combining tests of transactions and direct tests of balances. For example, the proof of the cash receipts is a test of recorded transactions, whereas the bank reconciliation is a test of the balance in cash at a point in time. The proof of cash is an excellent method of comparing recorded cash receipts and disbursements with the bank account and with the bank reconciliation. On the other hand, the auditor must recognize that the proof of cash disbursements is not useful for discovering checks written for an improper amount, invalid checks, or other errors where the dollar amount appearing on the cash disbursements records is incorrect. Similarly, the proof of cash receipts is not useful for uncovering the theft of cash receipts or the recording and deposit of an improper amount of cash.

Tests for Kiting. Embezzlers occasionally cover a defalcation of cash by a practice known as *kiting:* transferring money from one bank to another and improperly recording the transaction. Near the balance sheet

FIGURE 18-4

PROOF OF CASH

ABC Company, Inc.
Proof of Cash

Schedule_____	Date
Prepared by JG	7/15/7x
Approved by RP	7/17/7x

12/31/7x

Act. 101 — General account, First National Bank

		5/31/7x	Receipts	Disbursements	6/30/7x
Balance per Bank	①	121,782.12	627,895.20	631,111.96	118,565.36
Deposits in transit —					
5/31	②	21,720.00	<21,720.00>		
6/30	②		16,592.36		16,592.36
Outstanding checks —					
5/31	③	<36,396.50>		<36,396.50>	
6/30	③			14,800.10	<14,800.10>
NSF checks	④		<4,560.00>	<4,560.00>	
Bank debit memos	⑤			<120.00>	120.00
Payroll checks erroneously entered in Gen Disbursements Journal	⑥			1,621.48	<1,621.48>
To allow for effect of a cash disbursement recorded as a credit item in Cash Receipts Journal			8,500.00	8,500.00	
Sub-total, reconciling items		<14,676.50>	<1,187.64>	<16,154.92>	290.78
Balance per books		107,105.62	626,707.56	614,957.04	118,856.14
		GL	CR	CD	GL

① Per 6/30/7x bank statement
② Detailed listing filed below; traced to subsequent bank statements.
③ Outstanding-check list filed below; examined cancelled checks.
④ Detailed listing filed below; all NSF items were redeposited and had cleared as of 7/15/7x.
⑤ Safety deposit rentals; traced to recording via journal entry. Requested list of contents of safety deposit boxes.
⑥ Traced to journal entry correcting error.

date a check is drawn on one bank account and immediately deposited in a second account for credit before the end of the accounting period. In making this transfer, the embezzler is careful to make sure the check is deposited at a late enough date so that it does not clear the first bank until after the end of the period. Assuming the bank transfer is not recorded until after the balance sheet date, the amount of the transfer is recorded as an asset in both banks. Although there are other ways of perpetrating this fraud, each involves the basic device of increasing the bank balance to cover a shortage by the use of bank transfers.

A useful approach to testing for kiting, as well as for unintentional errors in recording bank transfers, is to list all bank transfers made a few days before and after the balance sheet date and trace each one to the accounting records for proper recording. For example, if a bank transfer is recorded in the current period as a disbursement, the auditor should examine the bank cancellation date on the check to see when it cleared. If the check cleared after the balance sheet date, it should be included as an outstanding check. Similarly, transfers deposited in the bank near the end of the year or included as deposits in transit can be traced to the cash receipts or disbursements journal to make sure they have been recorded in the journals in the proper period. For example, if a transfer was received by the bank and included as a deposit in transit on the bank reconciliation, kiting has probably occurred.

Even though audit tests of bank transfers are usually fraud oriented, they are often performed on audits where there are numerous bank transfers, regardless of the system of internal control. When there are numerous intercompany transfers, it is difficult to be sure each one is correctly handled unless a schedule of transfers near the end of the year is prepared and each transfer is traced to the accounting records and bank statements. In addition to the possibility of kiting, inaccurate handling of transfers could result in a misclassification between cash and accounts payable. The materiality of transfers and the relative ease of performing the tests make many auditors believe they should always be performed.

Summary. In designing audit procedures for uncovering fraud, careful consideration should be given to the nature of the weaknesses in the system of internal control, the type of fraud that is likely to result from the weaknesses, the potential materiality of the fraud, and the audit procedures that are most effective in uncovering the error. When the auditor is specifically testing for fraud, he should keep in mind that audit procedures other than direct tests of cash balances can also be useful. Examples of procedures that may uncover fraud in the cash receipts area include the confirmation of accounts receivable, tests for lapping, reviewing the general ledger entries in the cash account for unusual items, tracing from customer orders to sales and subsequent cash receipts, and examining approvals and supporting documentation for bad debts and sales returns and allowances. Similar tests can be used for testing for the possibility of fraudulent cash disbursements.

AUDIT OF THE PAYROLL BANK ACCOUNT

Tests of the payroll bank reconciliation should take only a few minutes if there is an imprest payroll account and an independent reconciliation of the bank account such as that described for the general account. Typically, the only reconciling items are outstanding checks, and for most audits the great majority clear shortly after the checks are issued. In testing the payroll bank account balances, it is necessary to obtain a bank reconciliation, a bank confirmation, and a cutoff bank statement. The reconciliation procedures are performed in the same manner as those described for general cash. Naturally, extended procedures are necessary if the controls are inadequate or if the bank account doesn't reconcile with the general ledger imprest cash balance.

The discussion in the preceding paragraph should not be interpreted as implying that the audit of payroll is unimportant. A review of Chapter 13 should remind the reader that the most important audit procedures for verifying payroll are tests of transactions, which are designed to test the controls. The most likely payroll errors will be discovered by those procedures rather than by checking the imprest bank balance.

AUDIT OF PETTY CASH

Petty cash is a unique account because it is frequently immaterial in amount, yet it is verified on most audits. The account is verified primarily because of the potential for defalcation and the client's expectation of an audit review even when the amount is immaterial.

Internal Controls Over Petty Cash

The most important control over petty cash is the use of an imprest fund that is the responsibility of *one individual*. In addition, petty cash funds should not be mingled with other receipts, and the fund should be kept separate from all other activities. There should also be limits on the amount of any expenditure from petty cash, as well as the total amount of the fund. The type of expenditure that can be made from petty cash transactions should be well defined by company policy.

Whenever a disbursement is made from petty cash, adequate controls require a responsible official's approval on a prenumbered petty cash form. The total of the actual cash and checks in the fund plus the total unreimbursed petty cash forms that represent actual expenditures should equal the total amount of the petty cash fund stated in the general ledger. Periodically, surprise counts and a reconciliation of the petty cash fund should be made by the internal auditor or other responsible official.

When the petty cash balance runs low, a check payable to the petty cash custodian should be made out on the general cash account for the reimbursement of petty cash. The check should be for the exact amount of the prenumbered vouchers that are submitted as evidence of actual expenditures. These vouchers should be verified by the accounts payable clerk and canceled to prevent their reuse.

Audit Tests for Petty Cash

The emphasis in verifying petty cash should be on testing petty cash transactions rather than the ending balance in the account. Even if the amount of the petty cash fund is small, there is potential for numerous improper transactions if the fund is frequently reimbursed.

An important part of testing petty cash is to first determine the client's procedures for handling petty cash by discussing the system with the custodian and examining the documentation of a few transactions. As a part of developing an understanding of the system, it is necessary to evaluate its strengths and weaknesses. Even though most petty cash systems are not complex, it is often desirable to use a flowchart and an internal control questionnaire, primarily for documentation in subsequent audits.

The tests of the system depend on the number and size of the petty cash reimbursements and the strengths and weaknesses of the system. When there are excellent controls and few reimbursement payments during the year, it is common for auditors not to test any further for reasons of immateriality. When the auditor decides to test petty cash, the two most common procedures are to count the petty cash balance and to carry out detailed tests of one or two reimbursement transactions. In such a case the primary procedures should include footing the petty cash vouchers supporting the amount of the reimbursement, accounting for a sequence of petty cash vouchers, examining the petty cash vouchers for authorization and cancellation, and examining the attached documentation for reasonableness. Typical supporting documentation includes cash register tapes, invoices, and receipts.

The petty cash tests can ordinarily be performed at any time during the year, but as a matter of convenience they are typically done on an interim date. If the balance in the petty cash fund is considered material, which is rarely the case, it should be counted at the end of the year. Unreimbursed expenditures should be examined as a part of the count to determine whether the amount of unrecorded expenses is material.

REVIEW QUESTIONS

1. Select the best response for each of the following multiple-choice questions:
    a. On December 31, 19X7, a company erroneously prepared an accounts payable voucher (Dr. cash, Cr. accounts payable) for a transfer of funds between banks. A check for the transfer was drawn January 3, 19X8. This error resulted in overstatements of cash and accounts payable at Decem-

ber 31, 19X7. Of the following procedures, the least effective in disclosing this error is review of the

(1) December 31, 19X7, bank reconciliations for the two banks.

(2) December 19X7 check register.

(3) Support for accounts payable at December 31, 19X7.

(4) Schedule of interbank transfers.

b. A CPA obtains a January 10 cutoff bank statetment for his client directly from the bank. Very few of the outstanding checks listed on his client's December 31 bank reconciliation cleared during the cutoff period. A probable cause for this is that the client

(1) Is engaged in kiting.

(2) Is engaged in lapping.

(3) Transmitted the checks to the payees after year-end.

(4) Has overstated its year-end bank balance.

c. The cashier of Baker Company covered a shortage in his cash working fund with cash obtained on December 31 from a local bank by cashing an unrecorded check drawn on the company's New York bank. The auditor would discover this manipulation by

(1) Preparing independent bank reconciliations as of December 31.

(2) Counting the cash working fund at the close of business on December 31.

(3) Investigating items returned with the bank cutoff statements.

(4) Confirming the December 31 bank balances.   (AICPA adapted)

2. Explain the relationship between internal control evaluation and tests of transactions for cash receipts, and the direct tests of cash balances.

3. Explain the relationship between internal control evaluation and tests of transactions for cash disbursements, and the direct tests of cash balances. Give one example where the conclusions reached about the controls in cash disbursements would affect the tests of cash balances.

4. Why is the monthly reconciliation of bank accounts by an independent person an important internal control over cash balances? Which individuals would generally not be considered independent for this responsibility?

5. Evaluate the effectiveness and state the shortcomings of the preparation of a bank reconciliation by the controller in the manner described in the following statement: "When I reconcile the bank account the first thing I do is to sort the checks in numerical order and find which numbers are missing. Next I determine the amount of the uncleared checks by referencè to the cash disbursements journal. If the bank reconciles at that point, I am all finished with the reconciliation. If it doesn't, I search for deposits in transit, checks from the beginning outstanding check list that still have not cleared, other reconciling items, and bank errors until it reconciles. In most instances I can do the reconciliation in twenty minutes."

6. How do bank confirmations differ from positive confirmations of accounts receivable? Distinguish between them in terms of the nature of the information confirmed, the sample size, and the appropriate action when the confirmation is not returned after the second request. Explain the rationale for the differences between these two types of confirmation.

7. Evaluate the necessity of following the practice described by an auditor: "In confirming bank accounts I insist upon a response from every bank the client has done business with in the past two years, even though the account may be closed at the balance sheet date."

8. Describe what is meant by a cutoff bank statement and state its purpose.

9. Why are auditors usually less concerned about the client's cash receipts cutoff than the cutoff for sales? Explain the procedure involved in testing for the cutoff for cash receipts.
10. What is meant by an imprest bank account for a branch operation? Explain the purpose of using this type of bank account.
11. Explain the purpose of a four-column proof of cash. List two types of errors it is meant to uncover.
12. When the auditor fails to obtain a cutoff bank statement, it is common to "prove" the entire statement for the month subsequent to the balance sheet date. How is this done and what is its purpose?
13. Distinguish between *lapping* and *kiting*. Describe audit procedures that can be used to uncover each of them.
14. Assume a client with excellent internal controls uses an imprest payroll bank account. Explain why the verification of the payroll bank reconciliation ordinarily takes less time than the tests of the general bank account even if the number of checks exceeds those written on the general account.
15. Distinguish between the verification of petty cash reimbursements and the verification of the balance in the fund. Explain how each of these is done. Which is more important?
16. Why is there a greater emphasis on the detection of fraud in direct tests of cash balances than for other balance sheet accounts? Give two specific examples that demonstrate how this emphasis affects the auditor's evidence accumulation in auditing year-end cash.
17. Explain why, in verifying bank reconciliations, most auditors emphasize the possibility of a nonexistent deposit in transit being included in the reconciliation and an outstanding check's being omitted rather than the omission of a deposit in transit and the inclusion of a nonexistent outstanding check.

DISCUSSION QUESTIONS AND PROBLEMS

18. When you arrive at your client's office on January 11, 19X7, to begin the December 31, 19X6, audit, you discover that the client had been drawing checks as creditors' invoices became due but not necessarily mailing them. Because of a working capital shortage, some checks may have been held for two or three weeks.

    The client informs you that unmailed checks totaling $27,600 were on hand at December 31, 19X6. He states that these December-dated checks had been entered in the cash disbursements book and charged to the respective creditors' accounts in December because the checks were prenumbered. Heavy collections permitted him to mail the checks before your arrival.

    The client wants to adjust the cash balance and accounts payable at December 31 by $27,600 because the cash account had a credit balance. He objects to submitting to his bank your audit report showing an overdraft of cash.

    Required:

    a. Prepare an audit program indicating the procedures you would use to satisfy yourself of the accuracy of the cash balance on the client's statements.

b. Discuss the acceptability of reversing the indicated amount of outstanding checks. (AICPA adapted)

19. Explain the objective(s) of each of the following audit procedures concerned with direct tests of general cash balances:

a. Compare the bank cancellation date with the date on the canceled check for checks dated on or shortly before the balance sheet date.

b. Trace deposits in transit on the bank reconciliation to the cutoff bank statement and the current year cash receipts journal.

c. Obtain a standard bank confirmation from each bank with which the client does business.

d. Compare the balance on the bank reconciliation obtained from the client with the bank confirmation.

e. Compare the checks returned along with the cutoff bank statement with the list of outstanding checks on the bank reconciliation.

f. List the check number, payee, and amount of all material checks not returned with the cutoff bank statement.

g. Review mintues of the board of directors, loan agreements, and bank confirmations for interest-bearing deposits, restrictions on the withdrawal of cash, and compensating balance agreements.

h. Prepare a four-column proof of cash.

20. William Green recently acquired the financial controlling interest of Importers and Wholesalers, Inc., importers and distributors of cutlery. In his review of the duties of employees, Green became aware of loose practices in the operation of the petty cash fund. You have been engaged as the company's CPA, and Green's first request is that you suggest a system of sound practices for operation of the petty cash fund. In addition to Green, who is the company president, the company has twenty employees, including four corporate officers. The petty cash fund has a working balance of about $200, and about $500 is expended by the fund each month.

Required:

Prepare a letter to Green containing your recommendations for good internal control procedures for operation of the petty cash fund. (Where the effect of the control procedure is not evident, give the reason for the procedure.) (AICPA adapted)

21. Following are errors an auditor might expect to find in the client's year-end cash balance (assume the balance sheet date is June 30):

a. A check was omitted from the outstanding check list on the June 30 bank reconciliation. It cleared the bank July 7.

b. A check was omitted from the outstanding check list on the bank reconciliation. It cleared the bank September 6.

c. Cash receipts collected on accounts receivable from July 1 to July 5 were included as June 29 and 30 cash receipts.

d. A loan from the bank on June 26 was credited directly to the client's bank account. The loan was not entered as of June 30.

e. A check that was dated June 26 and disbursed in June was not recorded in the cash disbursements journal, but it was included as an outstanding check on June 30.

f. A bank transfer recorded in the accounting records on July 1 was included as a deposit in transit on June 30.

g. The outstanding checks on the June 30 bank reconciliation were underfooted by $2,000.

Required:

    a. Assuming each of these errors was intentional, state the most likely motivation of the person responsible for making the error.

    b. What internal control procedure could be instituted for each of these errors to reduce the likelihood of occurrence?

    c. List an audit procedure the auditor could use to discover each error.

22. Following are errors an auditor might expect to find through tests of transactions or by direct tests of cash balances:

    a. The bookkeeper failed to record checks in the cash disbursements journal that were written and mailed during the first month of the year.

    b. The bookkeeper failed to record or deposit a material amount of cash receipts during the last month of the year. Cash is prelisted by the president's secretary.

    c. The cash disbursements journal was held open for two days after the end of the year.

    d. A check was paid to a vendor for a carload of raw materials that was never received by the client.

    e. A discount on a purchase was not taken even though the check was mailed before the discount period had expired.

    f. Cash receipts for the last two days of the year were recorded in the cash receipts journal for the subsequent period and listed as deposits in transit on the bank reconciliation.

    g. A check written during the last month of the year to a vendor was recorded in the cash disbursements journal twice to cover an existing fraud. The check cleared the bank and did not appear on the bank reconciliation.

Required:

    a. List an audit procedure to uncover each of the preceding errors.

    b. For each procedure in part *a*, state whether it is a direct test of cash balances or a test of transactions.

23. Discuss briefly what you regard as the more important deficiencies in the system of internal control in the following situation, and in addition include what you consider to be a proper remedy for each deficiency:

> The cashier of the Easy Company intercepted customer A's check payable to the company in the amount of $500 and deposited it in a bank account which was part of the company petty cash fund, of which he was custodian. He then drew a $500 check on the petty cash fund bank account payable to himself, signed it, and cashed it. At the end of the month while processing the monthly statements to customers, he was able to change the statement to customer A so as to show that A had received credit for the $500 check that had been intercepted. Ten days later he made an entry in the cash received book which purported to record receipt of a remittance of $500 from customer A, thus restoring A's account to its proper balance, but overstating cash in bank. He covered the overstatement by omitting from the list of outstanding checks in the bank reconcilement, two checks, the aggregate amount of which was $500.   (AICPA adapted)

24. The Patrick Company had poor internal control over its cash transactions. Facts about its cash position at November 30, 19X8, were as follows:

The cash books showed a balance of $18,901.62, which included undeposited receipts. A credit of $100 on the bank's records did not appear on the books of the company. The balance per bank statement was $15,550. Outstanding checks were: No. 62 for $116.25, No. 183 for $150.00, No. 284 for $253.25, No. 8621 for $190.71, No. 8623 for $206.80, and No. 8632 for $145.28.

The cashier abstracted all undeposited receipts in excess of $3,794.41 and prepared the following reconciliation:

Balance, per books, November 30, 19X8		$18,901.62
Add: Oustanding checks:		
8621	$190.71	
8623	206.80	
8632	145.28	442.79
		$19,344.41
Less: Undeposited receipts		3,794.41
Balance per bank, November 30, 19X8		$15,550.00
Deduct: Unrecorded credit		100.00
True cash, November 30, 19X8		$15,450.00

Required:

a. Prepare a supporting schedule showing how much the cashier abstracted.
b. How did he attempt to conceal his theft?
c. Taking only the information given, name two specific features of internal control which were apparently missing.   (AICPA adapted)

25. Referring to the bank confirmation on page 595, returned to Frick and Dayton for the Goodwell Corporation, answer the following questions:
    a. Why is the signature on the confirmation that of the controller of Goodwell instead of that of the auditor?
    b. What is the appropriate follow-up on each item included on the returned confirmation?
    c. If the confirmation had not been signed by a representative of the bank, what is the appropriate action on the part of the auditor?

26. On an audit with a September 30 balance sheet date, the auditor obtained the October bank statement from the client on November 26 during his year-end field work. In comparing the September checks clearing the bank in October with the year-end outstanding check list, the auditor observed that a check for $4,206 had not cleared. The auditor traced the check number and amount to the October 31 bank reconciliation to make sure it was included, and examined supporting documentation to test the propriety for the payment. The auditor concluded that the bank reconciliation was correct.

What had actually happened, however, was a defalcation by the bookkeeper. He forged a check to himself late in December for the amount owed on a purchase of merchandise. On October 2 he deposited the check in his personal account. He removed the canceled check from the bank statement when he received the checks from the bank for reconciliation.

STANDARD BANK CONFIRMATION INQUIRY
Approved 1966 by
AMERICAN INSTITUTE OF CERTIFIED PUBLIC ACCOUNTANTS
and
BANK ADMINISTRATION INSTITUTE (FORMERLY NABAC)

January 12, 19 77

Dear Sirs:

Your completion of the following report will be sincerely appreciated. **IF THE ANSWER TO ANY ITEM IS "NONE," PLEASE SO STATE.** Kindly mail it in the enclosed stamped, addressed envelope *direct* to the accountant named below.

Report from

Yours truly,

The Goodwell Corporation
(ACCOUNT NAME PER BANK RECORDS)

(Bank)   First National Bank

By *Arlo Roberts, Controller*
Authorized Signature

1126 Longsburn Street

Detroit, Michigan 48873

Bank customer should check here if confirmation of bank balances only (item 1) is desired.

☐

NOTE—If the space provided is inadequate, please enter totals hereon and attach a statement giving full details as called for by the columnar headings below.

Accountant   Frick and Dayton, CPAs
621 South 97 Street
Detroit, Michigan 48871

Dear Sirs:

1. At the close of business on December 31, 19 77 our records showed the following balance(s) to the **credit** of the above named customer. In the event that we could readily ascertain whether there were any balances to the credit of the customer not designated in this request, the appropriate information is given below.

AMOUNT	ACCOUNT NAME	ACCOUNT NUMBER	Subject to Withdrawal by Check?	Interest Bearing? Give Rate
$ 31,617.01	General Account	26-4116	Yes	No
8,361.07	Payroll Account	26-4118	Yes	No

2. The customer was directly liable to us in respect of loans, acceptances, etc., at the close of business on that date in the total amount of $51,621.17 , as follows:

AMOUNT	DATE OF LOAN OR DISCOUNT	DUE DATE	INTEREST Rate	INTEREST Paid to	DESCRIPTION OF LIABILITY, COLLATERAL, SECURITY INTERESTS, LIENS, ENDORSERS, ETC.
$ 10,000.00	10/1/76	6/1/77	8%	– –	Unsecured
41,621.17	4/1/73	4/1/78	7 3/4%	10/1/77	Mortgage—property of 1471 Lane Street Detroit, Michigan

3. The customer was contingently liable as endorser of notes discounted and/or as guarantor at the close of business on that date in the total amount of $30,000.00 as below:

AMOUNT	NAME OF MAKER	DATE OF NOTE	DUE DATE	REMARKS
$ 30,000	Fredrick Well Co.	4-1-75	12-1-76	Guarantor

4. Other direct or contingent liabilities, open letters of credit, and relative collateral, were

None

5. Security agreements under the Uniform Commercial Code or any other agreements providing for restrictions, not noted above, were as follows (if officially recorded, indicate date and office in which filed):

None

Date January 16, 19 77

Yours truly, (Bank) First National Bank

By *Ralph Dobson*
Authorized Signature

Additional copies of this form are available from the American Institute of CPAs, 666 Fifth Avenue, New York, N. Y. 10019

Since the bookkeeper knew the auditor would trace the uncleared check to the subsequent reconciliation, he included the check number and amount but reduced other outstanding checks from November by a corresponding amount. In late October the bookkeeper submitted a check for signature that was made out to the same vendor and included the invoice in the amount of $4,206 as support for the disbursement.

Required:

a. What weaknesses in the controls should have alerted the auditor to the possibility of fraud?
b. List four ways the auditor could have uncovered this defalcation.

27. XYZ operates sales divisions in several cities throughout the country. In addition to other activities the sales divisions are charged with the collection of local receivables; each division maintains a bank account in which all collections are deposited intact. Twice a week these collections are transferred to the home office by check; no other checks are drawn on this bank account. Except for cash receipts and cash disbursements books no accounting books are kept at the sales offices, but all cash records are retained by them in their files.

As part of your year-end audit you wish to include an audit of cash transfers between the sales divisions and the main office. It is intended that your representative will visit all locations.

Required:

a. What are the purposes of the audit of cash transfers?
b. Assuming that your representative has a full knowledge of audit procedures for regular cash collection to which he will attend at each location, design *only such additional specific* audit steps as he will be required to perform to audit the cash transfers from each sales division to home office.   (AICPA adapted)

28. In his examination of cash, the CPA is watchful for signs of kiting.

Required:

a. Define *kiting*.
b. List the CPA's audit procedures that would uncover kiting.
(AICPA adapted)

29. In the audit of the Regional Transport Company, a large branch that maintains its own bank account, cash is periodically transferred to the central account in Cedar Rapids. On the branch account's records, bank transfers are recorded as a debit to the home office clearing account and a credit to the branch bank account. Similarly, the home office account is recorded as a debit to the central bank account and a credit to the branch office clearing account. Gordon Light is the head bookkeeper for both the home office and the branch bank accounts. Since he also reconciles the bank account, the senior auditor, Cindy Marintette, is concerned about the weakness in the system of internal control.

As a part of the year-end audit of bank transfers, Marintette asks you to schedule the transfers for the last few days in 19X7 and the first few days of 19X8. You prepare the following list:

Amount of Transfer	Date Recorded in the Home Office Cash Receipts Journal	Date Recorded in the Branch Office Cash Disbursements Journal	Date Deposited in the Home Office Bank Account	Date Cleared the Branch Bank Account
$12,000	12-27-X7	12-29-X7	12-26-X7	12-27-X7
26,000	12-28-X7	1- 2-X8	12-28-X7	12-29-X7
14,000	1- 2-X8	12-30-X7	12-28-X7	12-29-X7
11,000	12-26-X7	12-26-X7	12-28-X7	1- 3-X8
15,000	1- 2-X8	1- 2-X8	12-28-X7	12-31-X7
28,000	1- 7-X8	1- 5-X8	12-28-X7	1- 3-X8
37,000	1- 4-X8	1- 6-X8	1- 3-X8	1- 5-X8

Required:

a. In verifying each bank transfer, state the appropriate audit procedures you should perform.
b. Prepare any adjusting entries required in the home office records.
c. Prepare any adjusting entries required in the branch bank records.
d. State how each bank transfer should be included in the 12-31-X7 bank reconciliation for the home office account before your adjustments in part *b*.
e. State how each bank transfer should be included in the 12-31-X7 bank reconciliation of the branch bank account before your adjustments in part *c*.

30. A surprise count of the Y Company's imprest petty cash fund, carried on the books at $5,000, was made on November 10, 19X7.

The company acts as agent for an express company in the issuance and sale of money orders. Blank money orders are held by the cashier for issuance upon payment of the designated amounts by employees. Settlement with the express company is made weekly with its representative who calls at the Y Company office. At that time he collects for orders issued, accounts for unissued orders, and leaves additional blank money orders serially numbered.

The count of the items presented by the cashier as composing the fund was as follows:

Currency (bills and coin)		$2,200
Cashed checks		500
Vouchers (made out in pencil and signed by recipient)		740
N.S.F. checks (dated June 10 and 15, 19X7)		260
Copy of petty cash receipt vouchers:		
Return of expense advance	$200	
Sale of money orders (#C1015–1021)	100	300
Blank money orders—claimed to have been purchased for $100 each from the Express Company (#C1022–1027)		600

At the time of the count there was also on hand the following:

Unissued money orders #C1028–1037
Unclaimed wage envelopes (sealed and amounts not shown)

The following day the custodian of the fund produced vouchers aggregating $400 and explained that these vouchers had been temporarily misplaced the previous day. They were for wage advances to employees.

Required:

a. Show the proper composition of the fund at November 10, 19X7.
b. State the audit procedures necessary for the verification of the items in the fund.

31. In connection with your audit of the ABC Company at December 31, 19X7, you were given a bank reconciliation by a company employee which shows:

Balance per bank	$15,267
Deposits in transit	18,928
	$34,195
Checks outstanding	21,378
Balance per books	$12,817

As part of your verification you obtain the bank statement and canceled checks from the bank on January 15, 19X8. Checks issued from January 1 to January 5, 19X8, per the books were $11,241. Checks returned by the bank on January 5 amounted to $29,219. Of the checks outstanding December 31, $4,800 were not returned by the bank with the January 15 statement, and of those issued per the books in January 19X8, $3,600 were not returned.

Required:

a. Prepare a schedule showing the above data in proper form.
b. Suggest four possible explanations for the condition existing here and state what your action would be in each case, including any necessary journal entries.   (AICPA adapted)

32. In connection with an audit you are given the following worksheet:

Bank Reconciliation

December 31, 19X7

Balance per ledger 12-31-X7		$17,174.86
Add:		
Collections received on the last day of December and charged to "cash in bank" on books but not deposited		2,662.25
Debit memo for customer's check returned unpaid (check is on hand but no entry has been made on the books)		200.00
Debit memo for bank service charge for December		5.50
		$20,142.61
Deduct:		
Checks drawn but not paid by bank (see detailed list below)	$2,267.75	
Credit memo for proceeds of a note receivable which had been left at the bank for collection but which has not		

been recorded as collected	400.00	
Check for an account payable entered on books as $240.90 but drawn and paid by bank as $419.00	178.10	2,945.85

Computed balance	$17,196.76
Unlocated difference	200.00

Balance per bank (checked to confirmation)	$16,996.76

Checks Drawn but Not Paid by Bank

No.	Amount
573	$ 67.27
724	9.90
903	456.67
907	305.50
911	482.75
913	550.00
914	366.76
916	10.00
917	218.90
	$2,267.75

Required:

a. Prepare a corrected reconciliation.

b. Prepare journal entries for items that should be adjusted prior to closing the books. (AICPA adapted)

33. Glatfelt Rural Electric Power Cooperative issues books of sight drafts to the foremen of its ten field crews. The foremen use the drafts to pay the expenses of the field crews when they are on line duty requiring overnight stays.

The drafts are prenumbered and, as is clearly printed on the drafts, are limited to expenditures of $300 or less. The foremen prepare the drafts in duplicate and send the duplicates, accompanied by expense reports substantiating the drafts, to the general office.

The draft duplicates are accumulated at the general office and a voucher is prepared when there are two or three draft duplicates on hand. The voucher is the authority for issuing a company check for deposit in an imprest fund of $5,000 maintained at a local bank to meet the drafts as they are presented for payment. The cooperative maintains a separate general ledger account for the imprest fund.

The audit of the voucher register and cash disbursements disclosed the following information pertaining to sight drafts and the reimbursement of the imprest fund:

a. Voucher #10524 dated 12-31-X7, paid by check #10524 dated 12-31-X7, for the following drafts:

Draft #	Date	Crew #	Explanation	Amount
6001	12-24-X7	3	Expenses, 12-22–12-24,	$160
2372	12-28-X7	6	Expenses, 12-26–12-28	310
5304	12-30-X7	7	Cash advance to foreman	260
			Voucher total	$730

b. Voucher #10531 dated 12-31-X7, paid by check #10531 dated 1-3-X8, for the following drafts:

Draft #	Date	Crew #	Explanation	Amount
4060	12-29-X7	1	Expenses, 12-27–12-29	$150
1816	1-3-X8	4	Expenses, 1-1–1-3	560
			Voucher total	$710

c. Voucher #23 dated 1-8-X8, paid by check #23 dated 1-8-X8, for the following drafts:

Draft #	Date	Crew #	Explanation	Amount
1000	12-31-X7	9	Expenses, 12-28–12-31	$270
2918	1-3-X8	10	Expenses, 12-28–12-31	190
4061	1-7-X8	1	Expenses, 1-4–1-6	210
			Voucher total	$670

d. All of the above vouchers were charged to Travel Expense.

e. Examination of the imprest fund's bank statement for December, the January cutoff bank statement, and accompanying drafts presented for payment disclosed the following information:

(1) Reimbursement check #10524 was not credited on the December bank statement.

(2) The bank honored draft #2372 at the established maximum authorized amount.

(3) Original 19X7 drafts drawn by foremen but not presented to the client's bank for payment by 12-31-X7 totaled $1,600. This total included all 19X7 drafts itemized above except #4060 and #2372, which were deducted by the bank in December.

(4) December bank service charges listed on the December bank statement but not recorded by the client amounted to $80.

(5) The balance per the bank statement at December 31, 19X7 was $5,650.

Required:

a. Prepare the auditor's adjusting journal entry to correct the books at December 31, 19X7. (The books have not been closed.) A supporting working paper analyzing the required adjustments should be prepared in good form.

b. Prepare a reconciliation of the balance per bank statement and the financial statement figure for the imprest cash account. The first figure in your reconciliation should be the balance per bank statement.

(AICPA adapted)

34. The following information was obtained in an audit of the cash account of Tuck Company as of December 31, 19X7. Assume that the CPA has satisfied himself as to the validity of the cash book, the bank statements, and the returned checks, except as noted.

a. The bookkeeper's bank reconciliation at November 30, 19X7.
   Balance per bank statement .... $ 19,400

Add deposit in transit		1,100
Total		$ 20,500

Less outstanding checks

	#2540	$140	
	1501	750	
	1503	480	
	1504	800	
	1505	30	2,300

Balance per books		$ 18,200

b. A summary of the bank statement for December 19X7.

Balance brought forward	$ 19,400
Deposits	148,700
	$168,100
Charges	132,500
Balance, December 31, 19X7	$ 35,600

c. A summary of the cash book for December 19X7 before adjustments.

Balance brought forward	$ 18,200
Receipts	149,690
	$167,890
Disbursements	124,885
Balance, December 31, 19X7	$ 43,005

d. Included with the canceled checks returned with the December bank statement were the following:

Number	Date of Check	Amount of Check	
#1501	November 28, 19X7	$ 75	This check was in payment of an invoice for $750 and was recorded in the cash book as $750.
#1503	November 28, 19X7	$580	This check was in payment of an invoice for $580 and was recorded in the cash book as $580.
#1523	December 5, 19X7	$150	Examination of this check revealed that it was unsigned. A discussion with the client disclosed that it had been mailed inadvertently before it was signed. The check was endorsed and deposited by the payee and processed by the bank even though it was a legal nullity. The check was recorded in the cash disbursements.

#1528	December 12, 19X7	$800	This check replaced #1504 that was returned by the payee because it was mutilated. Check #1504 was not canceled on the books.
——	December 19, 19X7	$200	This was a counter check drawn at the bank by the president of the company as a cash advance for travel expense. The president overlooked informing the bookkeeper about the check.
——	December 20, 19X7	$300	The drawer of this check was the Tucker Company.
#1535	December 20, 19X7	$350	This check had been labeled N.S.F. and returned to the payee because the bank had erroneously believed that the check was drawn by the Luck Company. Subsequently the payee was advised to redeposit the check.
#1575	January 5, 19X8	$10,000	This check was given to the payee on December 30, 19X7, as a postdated check with the understanding that it would not be deposited until January 5. The check was not recorded on the books in December.

e. The Tuck Company discounted its own 60-day note for $9,000 with the bank on December 1, 19X7. The discount rate was 6 percent. The bookkeeper recorded the proceeds as a cash receipt at the face value of the note.

f. The bookkeeper records customers' dishonored checks as a reduction of cash receipts. When the dishonored checks are redeposited they are recorded as a regular cash receipt. Two N.S.F. checks for $180 and $220 were returned by the bank during December. The $180 check was redeposited, but the $220 check was still on hand at December 31.

Cancellations of Tuck Company checks are recorded by a reduction of cash disbursements.

g. December bank charges were $20. In addition a $10 service charge was made in December for the collection of a foreign draft in November. These charges were not recorded on the books.

h. Check #2540 listed in the November outstanding checks was drawn in 19X5. Since the payee cannot be located, the president of Tuck Company agreed to the CPA's suggestion that the check be written back into the accounts by a journal entry.

i. Outstanding checks at December 31, 19X7, totaled $4,000 excluding checks #2540 and #1504.

j. The cutoff bank statement disclosed that the bank had recorded a deposit of $2,400 on January 2, 19X8. The bookkeeper had recorded this deposit on the books on December 31, 19X7, and then mailed the deposit to the bank.

Required:

Prepare a four-column proof of cash of the cash receipts and cash disbursements recorded on the bank statement and on the company's books for the month of December 19X7. The reconciliation should agree with the cash figure that will appear in the company's financial statements.

(AICPA adapted)

19

Completing the Audit

After the auditor has completed the tests in specific audit areas, it is necessary to summarize the results and perform additional testing of a more general nature. Summarization and general tests are an essential part of the audit because an overall evaluation of the combined results is performed during this phase. The following subjects are covered in discussing completion of the audit:

1. Review for contingent liabilities and commitments
2. Post-balance sheet review
3. Subsequent discovery of facts existing at the date of the auditor's report
4. Summarizing and drawing conclusions
5. Review for financial statement disclosures
6. Management representation letters
7. Working paper review
8. Management letters

REVIEW FOR CONTINGENT LIABILITIES AND COMMITMENTS

A *contingent liability* is a potential future obligation to an outside party for an unknown amount resulting from activities that have already taken place. The most important characteristic of a contingent liability is the uncertainty of the amount: if the amount were known, it would be included in the financial statements as an actual liability rather than a contingency.

The proper disclosure in the financial statements of material contingencies is through footnotes. A *footnote* should describe the nature of the contingency to the extent it is known and the opinion of legal counsel or management as to the expected outcome. The following is an illustration of a footnote related to pending litigation:

> As of December 31, 1978, the company is defendant in several lawsuits related to product liability. The aggregate amount of damages claimed is $10,000,000 in excess of product liability insurance coverage. Management and legal counsel believe that the company's liability for such excess, if any, should not be material in amount.

Certain contingent liabilities are of considerable concern to the auditor:

1. Pending litigation for patent infringement, product liability, or other actions
2. Income tax disputes
3. Product warranties
4. Notes receivable discounted
5. Guarantees of obligations of others
6. Unused balances in outstanding letters of credit

As each of these contingent liabilities are discussed, the reader should keep in mind that many of these potential obligations are ordinarily verified as an integral part of various segments of the engagement rather than at a point in time near the end of the audit. For example, unused balances in outstanding letters of credit may be tested as a part of confirming bank balances and loans from banks. Similarly, income-tax disputes can be checked as a part of analyzing income tax expense, reviewing the general correspondence file, and examining revenue agent reports. Even if the contingencies are verified separately, it is common to perform the tests well before the last few days of completing the engagement to ensure their proper verification. The tests of contingent liabilities near the end of the engagement are more of a review than an initial search.

General Audit Procedures

The appropriate audit procedures for testing contingencies are less well defined than the procedures that have already been discussed in other audit areas because the primary objective at the initial stage of the tests is to determine the *existence* of contingencies. As the reader knows from the study of other audit areas, it is more difficult to discover unrecorded transactions or events than to properly verify recorded information. Once the auditor is aware that contingencies exist, the evaluation of their materiality and the disclosure required can ordinarily be satisfactorily resolved.

The following are some of the audit procedures commonly used to search for contingent liabilities. The list is not meant to be all-inclusive, and each procedure is not necessarily performed on each audit.

1. Discuss with management the possibility of unrecorded contingencies. In these discussions the auditor must be specific in describing the different kinds of contingencies that may require disclosure. Naturally, discussions with management are not useful in uncovering the intentional failure to disclose existing contingencies, but if management has overlooked a particular type of contingency or does not fully comprehend accounting disclosure requirements, the discussion can be fruitful. At the completion of the audit, management is typically asked to make a written statement that it is aware of no undisclosed contingent liabilities as a part of the letter of representation.

2. Review current and previous years' internal revenue agent reports of income-tax settlements. The reports may indicate areas where disagreement over unsettled years are likely to arise. If a review has been in progress for a long time, there is an increased likelihood of an existing tax dispute.

3. Review the minutes of directors' and stockholders' meetings for indications of lawsuits or other contingencies.

4. Analyze legal expense for the period under audit and review invoices and statements from legal counsel for indications of contingent liabilities, especially lawsuits and pending tax assessments.

5. Obtain a confirmation from all major attorneys performing legal services for the client as to the status of pending litigation or other contingent liabilities. This procedure is discussed in more depth shortly.

6. Review existing working papers for any information that may indicate a potential contingency. For example, bank confirmations may indicate notes receivable discounted or guarantees of loans.

7. Obtain letters of credit in force as of the balance sheet date and obtain a confirmation of the used and unused balance.

Confirmation from Client's Legal Counsel

A major procedure auditors rely upon for discovering contingencies is a *letter of confirmation from the client's legal counsel* informing the auditor of pending litigation or any other information involving legal counsel that is relevant to financial statement disclosure. If a contingent liability actually exists, the auditor should also obtain the attorney's professional opinion of the expected outcome of the lawsuit and the likely amount of the liability, including court costs.

As a matter of tradition, many CPA firms analyze legal expense for the entire year and have the client send a standard attorney's letter to every attorney the client has been involved with in the current or preceding year, plus any attorney the firm occasionally engaged. In some cases this involves a large number of attorneys, including some who deal in aspects of law that are far removed from potential lawsuits.

Attorneys in recent years have become reluctant to provide certain information to auditors because of their own exposure to legal liability for providing incorrect or confidential information. The nature of the refusal of attorneys to provide auditors with complete information about contingent liabilities falls into two categories: the refusal to respond due to a lack of knowledge about matters involving contingent liabilities and the refusal to disclose information that the attorney regards as confidential between himself and his client. As an example of the latter situation, the attorney might be aware of a violation of a patent agreement which could result in a significant loss to the client if it were known. The inclusion of the information in a footnote could actually cause the lawsuit and therefore be damaging to the client.

When the nature of the attorney's legal practice does not involve contingent liabilities, his refusal to respond causes no audit problems. It is certainly reasonable for attorneys to refuse to make statements about contingent liabilities when they are not involved with lawsuits or similar aspects of the practice of law that directly affect the financial statements.

A serious audit problem does arise, however, when an attorney refuses to provide information that is within his jurisdiction and may directly affect the fair presentation of financial statements. If an attorney refuses to provide the auditor with information about material existing lawsuits or unasserted claims, the audit opinion would have to be modified to reflect the lack of available evidence. This requirement (SAS 12) has the effect of requiring management to give their attorneys permission to provide contingent liability information to auditors and to encourage attorneys to cooperate with auditors in obtaining information about contingencies.

The standard letter of confirmation from the client's attorney, which should be prepared on the client's letterhead and signed by one of the company's officials, should include the following:

1. A list, prepared by management, of material pending, threatened litigation, claims, or assessments about which the attorney has had significant involvement. An alternative is for the letter to request the attorney to prepare the list.
2. A list, prepared by management, of likely material unasserted claims and assertions with which the attorney has had significant involvement.
3. A request that the attorney furnish information or comment about the progress of each listed claim or assessment, the legal action the client intends to take, the likelihood of an unfavorable outcome, and an estimate of the amount or range of the potential loss.
4. A request for the identification of any unlisted pending or threatened legal actions or a statement that the client's list was complete.

5. A statement by the client informing the attorney of his responsibility to inform management whenever in the attorney's judgment there is a legal matter requiring disclosure in the financial statements. The letter of inquiry should also request that the attorney confirm directly to the auditor that he understands this responsibility.

6. A request that the attorney identify and describe the nature of any reasons for any limitations in this response.

An example of a typical standard letter that is now sent by the client to the attorney for return directly to the CPA's office is shown in Figure 19-1 on pages 610 and 611.

Evaluation of Known Contingent Liabilities

The auditor must evaluate the significance of the potential liability and the nature of the disclosure that is necessary in the financial statements if he concludes that there are contingent liabilities. The potential liability is sufficiently well known in some instances to be included in the statements as an actual liability. In other instances disclosure may be unnecessary if the contingency is highly remote or immaterial. Frequently the CPA firm obtains a separate evaluation of the potential liability from its own legal counsel rather than rely on management or management's attorneys. The client's attorney is an advocate for the client and frequently loses perspective in evaluating the likelihood of losing the case and the amount of the potential judgment.

Commitments

Closely related to contingent liabilities are commitments to purchase raw materials or to lease facilities at a certain price, agreements to sell merchandise at a fixed price, bonus plans, profit-sharing and pension plans, royalty agreements, and similar items. In a commitment the most important characteristic is the *agreement to commit the firm to a set of fixed conditions* in the future regardless of what happens to profits or the economy as a whole. In a free economy presumably the entity agrees to commitments as a means of bettering its own interests, but they may turn out to be less or more advantageous than originally anticipated. All commitments are ordinarily either described together in a separate footnote or combined with a footnote related to contingencies.

The search for unknown commitments is usually performed as a part of the audit of each audit area. For example, in verifying sales transactions the auditor should be alert for sales commitments. Similarly, commitments for the purchase of raw materials or equipment can be identified as a part of the audit of each of these accounts. The auditor should also be aware of the possibility of commitments as he is reading contracts and correspondence files, and inquiries should be made of management.

POST-BALANCE SHEET REVIEW

As a part of the verification of current period financial statements, the auditor has a responsibility to review transactions and events occurring after the balance sheet date to determine whether anything occurred that might affect the valuation or disclosure of the statements being audited. The auditing procedures employed to verify these transactions and events are commonly referred to as the review of *subsequent events* or *post-balance sheet review.*

The auditor's responsibility for reviewing for subsequent events is normally limited to the period beginning with the balance sheet date and ending with the date of the auditor's report. Since the date of the auditor's report corresponds to the completion of the important auditing procedures in the client's office, the subsequent events review should be completed near the end of the engagement. (When the auditor's name is associated with a registration statement under the Securities Act of 1933, his responsibility for reviewing subsequent events extends beyond the date of the auditor's report to the date the registration becomes effective.)

Types of Subsequent Events

Two types of subsequent events require consideration by management and evaluation by the auditor: those that have a direct effect on the financial statements and require adjustment and those that have no direct effect on the financial statements but for which disclosure is advisable.

1. *Those that have a direct effect on the financial statements and require adjustment.* These events or transactions provide additional information to management in determining the valuation of account balances as of the balance sheet date and to auditors in verifying the balances. For example, if the auditor is having difficulty in determining the correct valuation of inventory because of obsolescence, the sale of raw material inventory as scrap in the subsequent period should be used as a means of determining the correct valuation of the inventory as of the balance sheet date. The scrap value of the inventory would be entered in the accounting records as the carrying value of the inventory at the balance sheet date.

Such subsequent period events as the following require an adjustment of account balances in the current year's financial statements if the amounts are material:

1. The declaration of bankruptcy due to deteriorating financial condition of a customer with an outstanding accounts receivable balance.
2. The settlement of a litigation at an amount different from the amount recorded on the books.

Figure 19-1

Banergee Building Co.
409 Lane Drive
Buffalo, New York 10126

1-26-78

Bailwick & Bettle, attorneys
11216 - 5th Street N E
New York, New York 10023

Gentlemen:

Our auditor, Clarrett & Co., CPAs (1133 Broadway, New York, New York 10019) are making an examination of our financial statements for the fiscal year ended 12-31-77. In connection with their examination, we have prepared, and furnished to them, a description and evaluation of certain contingencies, including those attached, involving matters with respect to which you have been engaged and to which you have devoted substantive attention on behalf of the Company in the form of legal consultation or representation. These contingencies are regarded by the Company as material for this purpose. Your response should include matters that existed at 12-31-77 and during the period from that date to the date of the completion of their examination, which is anticipated to be on or about 2-13-78.

Please provide to our auditors the following information:

(1) An explanation, if any, you consider necessary to supplement the listed judgments rendered or settlements made involving the Company from the beginning of this fiscal year through the date of your reply.

Figure 19-1 (cont.)

-2-

(2) An explanation, if any, you consider necessary to supplement the listing of pending or threatened litigation, including an explanation of those matters as to which your views may differ from those stated and an identification of the omission of any pending or threatened litigation, claim, and assessment or a statement that the list of such matters is complete.

(3) An explanation, if any, you consider necessary to supplement the attached information concerning unasserted claims and assessments, including an explanation of those matters as to which your views may differ from those stated.

We understand that whenever, in the course of performing legal services for us with respect to a matter recognized to involve an unasserted possible claim or assessment that may call for financial statement disclosure, if you have formed a professional conclusion that we should disclose or consider disclosure concerning such possible claim or assessment, as a matter of professional responsibility to us, you will so advise us and will consult with us concerning the question of such disclosure and the applicable requirements of Statement of Financial Accounting Standards No. 5. Please specifically confirm to our auditors that our understanding is correct.

Please specifically identify the nature of and reasons for any limitation on your response.

Yours very truly,

Bangergee Building Co.

Clark Jones, Pres.

3. The disposal of equipment not being used in operations at a price below the current book value.
4. The sale of merchandise at a price below the cost included in the year-end inventory valuation.
5. The sale of investments at a price below recorded cost.

Whenever subsequent events are used to evaluate the amounts included in the statements, care must be taken to distinguish between conditions that existed at the balance sheet date and those that came into being after the end of the year. The subsequent information should not be incorporated directly into the statements if the conditions causing the change in valuation did not take place until subsequent to the year-end. For example, the sale of scrap in the subsequent period would not be relevant in the valuation of inventory for obsolescence if the obsolescence took place after the end of the year.

2. *Those that have no direct effect on the financial statements but for which disclosure is advisable.* Subsequent events of this type provide evidence of conditions that did not exist at the date of the balance sheet being reported on but are so significant that they require disclosure even though they do not require adjustment. Ordinarily these subsequent events can be adequately disclosed by the use of footnotes, but occasionally such an event may be so significant as to require *supplementing the historical statements* with statements that include the effect of the event as if it had occurred on the balance sheet date.

Following are examples of events or transactions occurring in the subsequent period that may require disclosure rather than an adjustment in the financial statements:

1. A decline in market value of securities held for temporary investment or resale.
2. The issuance of bonds or equity securities.
3. The acquisition of a business.
4. The settlement of litigation where the event that caused the lawsuit took place subsequent to the balance sheet date.
5. A decline in market value of inventory as a consequence of governmental action barring further sale of a product.
6. An uninsured loss of inventories as a result of fire.
7. A loss of an operating franchise.

Audit Tests

The audit procedures for the post-balance sheet review can be conveniently divided into two categories: procedures normally integrated as a part of the verification of year-end account balances, and those performed specifically for the purpose of discovering events or transactions that must be recognized in the current period.

The first category includes cutoff and valuation tests which are done as a part of the direct tests of financial balances. For example, subsequent period sales and purchases transactions are examined to determine whether the cutoff is accurate. Similarly, many valuation tests involving subsequent events are also performed as a part of the verification of account balances. As an example, it is common to test the collectibility of accounts receivable by reviewing subsequent period cash receipts. It is also a normal audit procedure to compare the subsequent period purchase price of inventory with the recorded cost as a test of lower of cost or market valuation. The procedures for cutoff and valuation have been discussed sufficiently in preceding chapters and are not repeated here.

The second-category tests are performed specifically for the purpose of obtaining information that must be incorporated into the current year's account balances or disclosed by a footnote.

These tests include the following:

1. *Discussions with management.* The nature of the discussion varies from client to client, but it normally includes inquiries about the existence of potential contingent liabilities or commitments, significant changes in the asset or capital structure of the company, the current status of items that were not completely resolved at the balance sheet date, and the existence of unusual adjustments made subsequent to the balance sheet date.

It is essential that the discussions with management about subsequent events be held with the proper client personnel to obtain meaningful answers. For example, discussing tax or union matters with the accounts receivable supervisor would not be appropriate. Most discussions should be held with the controller, the vice-presidents, and the president, depending on the information desired.

2. *Correspondence with attorneys.* Correspondence with attorneys, which was previously discussed, takes place as a part of the search for contingent liabilities. In obtaining confirmation letters from attorneys, the auditor must remember his responsibility for testing for subsequent events up to the date of the audit report. A common approach is to request the attorney to date and mail the attorney's letter as of the expected completion date for the field work.

3. *Review of internal statements prepared subsequent to the balance sheet date.* The emphasis in the review should be on changes in the business relative to the current year's results for the same period, particularly on major changes in the business or environment in which the client is operating. The statements should be discussed with management to determine whether they are prepared on the same basis as the current period statements, and there should be inquiries about significant changes in the operating results.

4. *Review of records of original entry prepared subsequent to the balance sheet date.* Journals and ledgers should be reviewed to determine the existence and nature of any transaction related to the current year.

If the journals are not kept up to date, the documents relating to the journals should be reviewed.

5. *Examination of minutes issued.* The minutes of stockholders' and directors' meetings subsequent to the balance sheet date must be examined for important subsequent events affecting the current period financial statements.

6. *Obtaining a letter of representation.* The letter of representation written by the client to the auditor formalizes statements the client has made about different matters throughout the audit, including discussions about subsequent events. Such letters are discussed shortly; an example is given in Figure 19-5.

Important Considerations in Post-Balance Sheet Reviews

Three major considerations should be kept in mind throughout the review for subsequent events: the nature and intensity should vary, depending on the conditions existing at the time of the review; the auditor must be familiar with the client and the industry; and careful follow-up and analysis is required in inquiries of management.

The post-balance sheet review must be conducted by an auditor who has been actively involved in the entire audit and understands the circumstances of the engagement. The importance of the performance of the review by an adequately experienced auditor was clearly shown in the 1968 case of *Escott* v. *Bar Chris Construction Corporation,* which revolved around inadequate disclosure of subsequent events. It was disclosed in the case that the staff person—an audit senior—used a written audit program and spent over twenty hours performing the subsequent audit review but failed to discover any of the material subsequent events. It was his first year as senior on an engagement, he was not a CPA, and he had had no previous experience in the industry. A major problem in the review was the senior's inability to recognize the symptoms of the deteriorating financial condition of the client.

Whenever the auditor discusses post-balance sheet events with management, there must be a careful follow-up to determine whether management's responses to questions are reasonable. For example, one of the criticisms of the audit in the *Bar Chris* case was that the senior on the engagement appeared to ask many of the right questions, but he neither looked at nor asked for any supporting documentation to verify the reasonableness of management's responses.

SUBSEQUENT DISCOVERY OF FACTS EXISTING AT THE DATE OF THE AUDITOR'S REPORT

If the auditor becomes aware *after the audited financial statements have been released* that some information included in the statements is materially misleading, he has an obligation to make certain that users who are relying on the financial statements are informed about the misstatements.[1] The most likely case in which the auditor is faced with this problem occurs when the financial statements are determined to include a material error subsequent to the issuance of an unqualified report. There are many possible causes of misstated statements, among them the inclusion of fictitious sales, the failure to write off obsolete inventory, or the omission of an essential footnote. Regardless of whether the failure to discover the error was the fault of the auditor, his responsibility remains the same.

The most desirable approach to follow when the auditor discovers the statements are misleading is to request that the client issue an immediate revision of the financial statements containing an explanation of the reasons for the revision. If a subsequent period's financial statements were completed before the revised statements could be issued, it is acceptable to disclose to users that new statements were completed before the revised statements could be issued and disclose the misstatements in the current statements. Whenever it is pertinent, the client should inform the Securities and Exchange Commission and other regulatory agencies of the misleading financial statements. The auditor has the responsibility for making certain that the client has taken the appropriate steps in informing users of the misleading statements.

If the client refuses to cooperate in disclosing the misstated information, the auditor must inform the board of directors of this fact. The auditor must also notify the regulatory agencies having jurisdiction over the client and each person who, to his knowledge, relies on the financial statements that the statements are no longer trustworthy. If the stock is publicly held, it is acceptable to request the Securities and Exchange Commission and the stock exchange to notify the stockholders.

It is important to understand that the subsequent discovery of facts requiring the recall or reissuance of financial statements does not arise from developments occurring after the date of the auditor's report. For example, if an account receivable is believed to be collectible after an adequate review of the facts at the date of the audit report, but the customer subsequently files bankruptcy, a revision of the financial statements is not required. The statements must be recalled or reissued only when information that would indicate that the statements were not fairly presented *already existed at the audit report date.*

In the previous section it was shown that the responsibility for post-balance-sheet review begins as of the balance sheet date and ends on the date of the completion of the field work. Any pertinent information discovered as a part of the review can be incorporated in the financial statements before they are issued. On the other hand, the auditor has

---

[1] The discussion in this section is more closely related to audit reports, which is the subject of the next chapter, than it is to completing the audit. However, many students of auditing confuse the examination of subsequent period events as a part of post-balance sheet review with the subsequent discovery of facts existing at the balance sheet date. The latter is studied at this point to eliminate the confusion.

no responsibility to search for subsequent facts of the nature discussed in this section, but if he discovers that issued financial statements are improperly stated, he must take action to correct them. The auditor's responsibility for reporting on improperly issued financial statements does not start until the date of the audit report. Typically, an existing material error is found as a part of the subsequent year's audit, or it may be reported to the auditor by the client.

SUMMARIZING AND DRAWING CONCLUSIONS

At the completion of the application of all the specific audit procedures for each of the audit areas, it is necessary to integrate the results into *one overall conclusion.* Ultimately, the auditor must decide whether sufficient audit evidence has been accumulated to warrant the conclusion that the financial statements are stated in accordance with generally accepted accounting principles, applied on a basis consistent with those of the preceding year. There are two important aspects of this conclusion. The first is *determining whether sufficient evidence has been obtained,* and the second is *deciding whether the existing evidence supports the auditor's opinion* that the statements are fairly stated. If the auditor has *not* obtained sufficient evidence to draw a conclusion about the fairness of the client's representations, additional evidence must be obtained or either a qualified opinion or a disclaimer of opinion must be issued. If the auditor believes that he *has* sufficient evidence, but it does not warrant a conclusion of fairly presented financial statements, they must be revised to the auditor's satisfaction or either a qualified opinion or an adverse opinion must be issued.

The final summarization of the adequacy of the evidence is a review by the auditor of the entire audit to determine whether all important aspects of the engagement have been adequately tested considering the circumstances of the engagement. A major step in this process is reviewing the audit program to make sure all parts have been accurately completed and documented. An important part of the review is to decide whether the audit program is adequate considering the problem areas that were discovered as the audit progressed. For example, if errors were discovered as a part of the tests of the sales system, the initial plans for the direct tests of accounts receivable may have been insufficient and should have been revised. As an aid in drawing final conclusions about the adequacy of the audit evidence, auditors frequently use *completing the engagement check lists.* These are reminders of aspects of the audit frequently overlooked. An illustration of part of a completing the engagement checklist is given in Figure 19-2.

An important part of evaluating whether the financial statements are fairly stated is summarizing the errors uncovered in the audit. Whenever the auditor uncovers errors that are in themselves material, the trial balance should be adjusted to correct the statements. It may be difficult

FIGURE 19-2

Completing the Engagement Checklist

	Yes	No
1. *Examination of prior year's working papers*		
a. Were last year's working papers and review notes examined for areas of emphasis in the current year audit?	_____	_____
b. Was the permanent file reviewed for items that affect the current year?	_____	_____
2. *Internal control evaluation*		
a. Has internal control been adequately reviewed?	_____	_____
b. Is the scope of the audit adequate in light of the weaknesses in the system?	_____	_____
c. Have all major weaknesses been included in a management letter?	_____	_____
3. *General documents*		
a. Were all current year minutes and resolutions reviewed, abstracted, and followed up?	_____	_____
b. Has the permanent file been updated?	_____	_____
c. Have all major contracts and agreements been reviewed and abstracted or copied to ascertain that the client complies with all existing legal requirements?	_____	_____

to determine the appropriate amount of the adjustment because the true value of the error is unknown; nevertheless, it is the auditor's responsibility to decide on the required adjustment. In addition to the material errors, there are often a large number of immaterial errors discovered which are not adjusted at the time they are found. It is necessary to combine individually immaterial errors to evaluate whether the combined amount is material. The auditor can keep track of the errors and combine them in several different ways, but many auditors use a convenient method known as an *unadjusted error worksheet* or *summary of possible adjustments*. It is relatively easy to evaluate the overall significance of several immaterial errors with this type of working paper. An example of a summary of possible adjustments is given in Figure 19-3.

REVIEW FOR FINANCIAL STATEMENT DISCLOSURES

A major consideration in completing the audit is to determine whether the disclosures in the financial statements are adequate. Throughout the audit the emphasis in most examinations is on verifying the accuracy of the balances in the general ledger by testing the most important accounts on the auditor's trial balance. Another important task is to make sure the account balances on the trial balance are correctly aggregated

FIGURE 19-3

UNADJUSTED ERROR WORKSHEET

ABC Company, Inc.
Summary of Possible Adjustments

Schedule __A-3__ Date
Prepared by _PR_ __1/28__
Approved by _GS_ __1/31__

12/31/7x

Workpaper Source				Total Amount	Current Assets
B-32	Unreimbursed petty cash vouchers			480	⟨480⟩
C-4					
C-4	Possible underprovision in allowance for doubtful accounts			4000	⟨4000⟩
C-8	Accounts receivable/Sales cutoff errors			600	600
D-2	Difference between physical inventory and book figures.			5200	5200
H-7/2	Unrecorded liabilities			4850	2000
V-10	Repairs expense items which should be capitalized			900	
	Totals				3,320

Conclusion:

The net effects of the above items are as follows:

Working capital $ ⟨2,440⟩
Total assets   6,070
Net income   ⟨610⟩

None of these aggregate effects or of the individual items has a material effect on the financial statements in total or with respect to the components they pertain to. On this basis, adjustment of any or all of the items is passed.

Paul Roberts
1/28

FIGURE 19-3 (cont.)

Non-current Assets	Current Liabilities	Non-current Liabilities	Equity	Sales and Revenues	Costs and Expenses	Federal Income Tax
			Possible Adjustments—Dr. ⟨Cr.⟩			
	240				480	⟨240⟩
	2000				4000	⟨2000⟩
	⟨300⟩			⟨600⟩		300
	⟨2600⟩				⟨5200⟩	2600
1850	⟨4350⟩				1000	⟨500⟩
900	⟨450⟩				⟨900⟩	450
2750	⟨5460⟩			⟨600⟩	⟨620⟩	610

and disclosed on the financial statements. Naturally, adequate disclosure includes consideration of all of the statements, including related footnotes.

The auditor actually prepares the financial statements from the trial balance in many small audits and submits them to the client for approval. Performing this function may seem to imply that the client has been relieved of responsibility for the fair representation in the statements, but that is not the case. The auditor acts in the role of adviser when he prepares the financial statements, but *management retains the final responsibility for approving the issuance of the statements.*

The review for the adequacy of disclosure in the financial statements at the completion of the audit is not the only time the auditor is interested in proper disclosure. Unless he is constantly alert for disclosure problems, it is impossible to adequately perform the final disclosure review. For example, as part of the examination of accounts receivable, the auditor must be aware of the need to separate notes receivable and amounts due from affiliates from trade accounts due from customers. Similarly, there must be a segregation between current and noncurrent receivables and a disclosure of the factoring or discounting of notes receivable if such is the case. An important part of verifying all account balances is determining whether generally accepted accounting principles were properly applied on a basis consistent with that of the preceding year. The auditor must carefully document this information in the working papers to facilitate the final review.

As part of the final review for financial statement disclosure, many CPA firms require the completion of a *financial statement disclosure checklist* for every engagement. These questionnaires are designed to remind the auditor of common disclosure problems encountered on audits and also to facilitate the final review of the entire audit by a partner. An illustration of a partial financial statement disclosure checklist is given in Figure 19-4. Naturally, it is not sufficient to rely on a checklist as a replacement for the auditor's own knowledge of generally accepted accounting principles. In any given audit, some aspects of the engagement require a much deeper level of expertise about accounting than can be obtained from such a checklist.

MANAGEMENT REPRESENTATION LETTERS

In most CPA firms it is a common practice to obtain a *letter of representation,* which documents management's most important oral representations during the audit. The management representation letter in Figure 19-5 indicates that such a letter is prepared on the client's letterhead, addressed to the CPA firm, and signed by high-level corporate officials. Although the letter seems to imply that it originated from the client, it is common practice for the auditor to prepare the letter and request the client to type it on the company's letterhead and sign it.

FIGURE 19-4

FINANCIAL STATEMENT DISCLOSURE CHECKLIST WITH
REFERENCES TO AUTHORITATIVE ACCOUNTING LITERATURE

PROPERTY, PLANT, AND EQUIPMENT

1. Are the following disclosures included in the financial statements or notes? (APB 12, para. 5)
   (a) balances of major classes of depreciable assets at the balance sheet date
   (b) allowances for depreciation, by class or in total, at the balance sheet date
   (c) general description of depreciation methods for major classes of PP&E (APB 22, para. 13)
   (d) total amount of depreciation charged to expense for each year presented
   (e) basis of valuation (SAS 1, para. 430.02)
2. Are carrying amounts of property mortgaged and encumbered by indebtedness disclosed? (APB 50, para. 6)
3. Are details of sale and leaseback transactions during the period disclosed? (APB 5, para. 19)
4. Is the carrying amount of property not a part of operating plant (i.e., idle, or held for investment or sale) segregated?

The purpose of the letter of representation is twofold. First, it is a means of impressing upon management its responsibility for the representations in the financial statements. For example, if the letter of representation includes a reference to pledged assets and contingent liabilities, honest management may be reminded of its unintentional failure to adequately disclose the information. To fulfill this objective, the letter of representation should be sufficiently detailed to act as a reminder to management. In addition, the auditor should carefully review the letter with members of management to be sure they understand the meaning and implication of each statement. The second purpose of the letter is to document the responses from the client to inquiries about various aspects of the audit.

A representation letter is a written statement from a nonindependent source and therefore *cannot be regarded as reliable evidence.* Although the letter does provide minimal evidence of having asked management certain questions, its primary purpose is psychological and to protect the auditor from potential claims by management that it was unaware of its responsibility.

WORKING PAPER REVIEW

There are three primary reasons why it is essential that the working papers be thoroughly reviewed by another member of the audit firm at the completion of the audit. First, a considerable portion of most audits

FIGURE 19-5

MANAGEMENT REPRESENTATION LETTER

ABC COMPANY, INC.
Middletown

February 10, 197X

Smart & Allen
New York, New York

Gentlemen:

The following representations, made to the best of our knowledge and belief, are being provided to you in connection with your examination of the balance sheet of ABC Company, Inc. at December 31, 197X and of the related statements of earnings and changes in financial position for the year then ended.

GENERAL:

We understand that, as is customary, your examination was made in accordance with generally accepted auditing standards and accordingly included such tests of the accounting records and such other auditing procedures as you considered necessary in the circumstances for the purpose of expressing an opinion on the financial statements but did not include a detailed audit on the transactions. We also understand that such examination would not necessarily disclose all irregularities should there be any.

No events have occurred and no facts have been discovered since December 31, 197X, which would make the balance sheet at that date or the statements of earnings and changes in financial position for the year then ended materially inaccurate or misleading. No shortages or irregularities have been discovered that have not been disclosed to you and to our knowledge there is nothing reflecting unfavorably upon the honesty of members of our organization.

No charges are pending against the Company for alleged violations of federal, state, or local laws, which would have any material effect on the financial statements.

FIGURE 19-5 (cont.)

- Page 2 -

INVESTMENTS IN COMMON STOCK OF NON-SUBSIDIARIES:

Investments in the common stock of Small, Inc. and Little Company are accounted for on the equity basis of accounting because the Company has the ability to exercise significant influence over operating and financial policies. No events have occurred and no facts have been discussed with respect to such investees which would materially affect the financial statements of ABC Company or which would indicate that a permanent diminution in value of any such Company has occurred.

CASH IN BANKS:

Cash on deposit and certificates of deposit are not restricted under a legally enforceable or best efforts compensating balance agreement, on behalf of the Company or any other party.

RECEIVABLES:

Trade notes, acceptances and accounts receivable are valid receivables and do not include any amounts for goods shipped on consignment or approval. In our opinion, the allowance provided is sufficient to cover any losses and any special discounts that can be reasonably anticipated at this date.

INVENTORIES:

Inventories were determined under the direction of management by actual count, and are fairly stated on the basis of lower of cost (last-in, first-out) or market. Reasonable allowance has been made for slow-moving, obsolete, unsalable or unusable items. All inventories were the property of the Company and do not include any goods consigned to it, any merchandise billed to customers or any items for which the liability has not been provided on the books.

PROPERTY, PLANT, AND EQUIPMENT:

All property, plant, and equipment is owned with satisfactory title and is included in the balances; charges during the year are stated at cost and were actual additions; property disposed of or abandoned was removed from the accounts.

The provision for depreciation and amortization for the year was determined on a basis consistent with the preceding years, and we believe that the method used and lives assigned continue to

FIGURE 19-5 (cont.)

be appropriate to allocate the cost of these assets over their estimated useful lives. The accumulated depreciation, amortization and
obsolescence are adequate to state these assets at a net amount reasonably allocable to the utility to be obtained over their respective remaining lives.

PLEDGED OR ASSIGNED ASSETS:

Disclosure is made in the financial statements of all significant mortgages, assignments, pledges or other encumbrances of
assets.

DIRECT LIABILITIES:

The Company has the following Pension Plans:

Employee Pension/Profit-Sharing Plan
R.S.T.U. Local #39 Pension Trust.

We have no intention of terminating our plans, withdraw-
ing from the multi-employer plan or taking any other action which
would result in an effective termination of the plans. We know of
nothing which would result in the termination of our pension plans
or the multi-employer plan.

CONTINGENT AND OTHER POSSIBLE LIABILITIES:

The Company had no contingent or other possible liabilities
which have not been disclosed in the financial statements.

PURCHASE AND SALE COMMITMENTS:

At year end, there were no important unfilled contracts
for purchases in excess of normal requirements or at prices substantially in excess of market, or for sales at prices that are
expected to result in loss.

CAPITAL STOCK:

All capital stock issued, or reserved for options, warrants
or other future issuance, is disclosed in the financial statements.

MINUTES:

Minutes of meetings of stockholders and directors as ex-
hibited to you are complete and authentic records of all such meetings held during the period from January 1, 197X to February 10,
197 Y on the dates shown below:

FIGURE 19-5 (cont.)

- Page 4 -

January 22, 197X
February 20, 197X
March 8, 197X (Special Board Meeting)
March 9, 197X (Annual Stockholders' Meeting)
April 20, 197X
May 27, 197X
July 19, 197X
September 18, 197X
October 21, 197X
November 8, 197X (Special Board Meeting)
November 15, 197X
December 10, 197X
January 21, 197Y

Yours very truly,

Adam Smith
PRESIDENT

T. T. Emary
SENIOR V.P., FINANCE

Martin Abrams
CONTROLLER

February 10, 197X
DATE

is performed by audit personnel with less than four or five years' experience. These people may have sufficient technical training to conduct an adequate audit, but their lack of experience affects their ability to make sound professional judgments in complex situations. Second, the working papers should be reviewed to make sure the audit meets the CPA firm's standard of performance. Within any organization the performance quality of individuals varies considerably, but careful review by top-level personnel in the firm assists in maintaining a uniform quality of auditing. Third, a review of the working papers is needed to counteract the bias that frequently enters into the auditor's judgment. Even though auditors attempt to remain objective throughout the audit, it is easy to lose proper perspective on a long audit when there are complex problems to solve.

Except for a final "independent review" which will be discussed shortly, the review of the working papers must be conducted by someone who is knowledgeable about the client and the unique circumstances in the audit. It is not possible for an auditor to evaluate whether a particular audit is adequate without extensive knowledge of the client. As a result, the initial review of the working papers prepared by any given auditor is normally done by his immediate supervisor. For example, the least experienced auditor's work is ordinarily reviewed by the audit senior; the senior's immediate superior, who is normally a supervisor or manager, carefully reviews the senior's work and also reviews the papers of the inexperienced auditor less thoroughly; finally, the partner assigned to the audit must ultimately review all working papers, but he reviews those prepared by the supervisor or manager more thoroughly than the others.

The objectives of the review consist of determining whether the original purposes of the working papers have been met. The original purposes, as discussed in Chapter 7, are these:

1. They provide the basis for planning the audit.
2. They are a record of the evidence accumulated and the results of the tests.
3. They provide data for determining the proper type of audit report.
4. They provide the basis for review by supervisors and partners.
5. They provide information that facilitates the preparation of management letters and reports such as filings with the SEC and tax returns.
6. They are a useful frame of reference for training personnel.
7. They assist in planning and coordinating subsequent audits.

There are several considerations the auditor should keep in mind in reviewing working papers. These considerations are dealt with as separate topics in the following discussion, but they are ordinarily performed simultaneously by the reviewer.

Mechanical accuracy. Certain aspects of the working papers are of a mechanical nature; nevertheless, they must be reviewed by someone before the audit is completed. These include the proper identification of all working papers, the date each working paper was prepared, and the initials of the preparer. Similarly, auditor calculations must be accurate, balances on the working papers must tie out to the trial balance when appropriate, and all adjusting entries must be posted.

Adequacy of individual working papers. The reviewer should evaluate whether each working paper in the file fulfills the purpose for which it was intended. This part of the review can be especially useful as a means of training assistants in the proper preparation of working papers in accordance with the CPA firm's policy.

Adequacy of evidence. The most important and time-consuming part of the review is evaluating the adequacy of the evidence and the reasonableness of the conclusions. Each major audit area must be reviewed to determine whether sufficient competent evidence was accumulated considering the circumstances of the engagement. The reviewer must evaluate the adequacy of the audit procedures, the sample sizes, the selection of the particular items for testing, and the timing of the procedures for each of the major segments of the audit. As part of this evaluation, consideration should be given to areas where there was excessive auditing or improper emphasis as well as instances where insufficient testing was done.

Reasonableness of the conclusions. One of the important concepts emphasized throughout the text is the need to draw conclusions about the population on the basis of the sample. A major responsibility of the reviewer is to evaluate whether the conclusions were reasonable considering the information obtained in the sample.

Financial statement disclosures. The reviewer must evaluate the adequacy of the financial statements based upon the information included in the working papers. The review should be along the same lines as those performed by the auditor making the original decision as to the acceptability of the client's disclosures.

Legal defensibility. At the completion of the audit, the working papers are the auditor's documentation of the evidence accumulated and the conclusions reached. If the auditor is ever called upon to defend the quality of the audit, the working papers become primary evidence for both the prosecution and the defense. The best defense against a lawsuit is a well-conducted audit with adequate documentation. At the same time, the reviewer must always be aware of the possibility of the working papers' being used as legal evidence of an inadequate audit. Good reviewers make sure there are no unanswered questions, ambiguous conclusions, inconsistent evaluations, or other incriminating evidence in the working papers.

Independent Review

At the completion of larger audits, it is common to have the entire set of working papers reviewed by a completely independent reviewer who has had no experience on the engagement. This reviewer frequently takes an adversary position to make sure the conduct of the audit was adequate. The audit team must be able to justify the evidence they have accumulated and the conclusions they reached on the basis of the unique circumstances of the engagement.

MANAGEMENT LETTERS

The purpose of a management letter (letter of recommendations) is to inform the client of the CPA's recommendations for improving the client's business. The recommendations range from suggestions for the improvement of the system of internal control to suggestions for more efficient operations. The combination of the auditor's experience in various businesses and a thorough understanding gained in conducting the audit put the auditor in a unique position to provide management with assistance.

In writing management letters, the weaknesses in the system of internal control normally receive special attention for two reasons. First, the auditor should by now have an excellent understanding of the system as a result of evaluating and testing many facets throughout the audit. Second, if the auditor has knowledge of the system but fails to inform the client of significant weaknesses, he can be held legally liable for not recommending improvements in the system. Even if the recommendations are made orally, they should also be documented by including them in a formal letter.

Whenever the auditor writes a management letter, care must be taken to make sure the comments included in the letter are consistent with the performance of the audit. For example, if a management letter states that there is an area where errors are likely or the physical protection of assets is inadequate, the audit evidence should be reviewed to make sure it was properly modified to take the weakness into account.

There are no standard formats or approaches for writing management letters. Each letter should be developed to meet the style of the auditor and the needs of the client, consistent with the CPA firm's concept of management letters. An example of a management letter is shown in Figure 19-6.

REVIEW QUESTIONS

1. Select the best response for each of the multiple-choice questions:
   a. The audit step most likely to reveal the existence of contingent liabilities is
      (1) A review of vouchers paid during the month following the year-end.
      (2) Accounts payable confirmations.
      (3) An inquiry directed to legal counsel.
      (4) Mortgage-note confirmation.
   b. A principal purpose of a letter of representation from management is to
      (1) Serve as an introduction to company personnel and an authorization to examine the records.

FIGURE 19-6

MANAGEMENT LETTER

ABLE AND BAKER, CPAS
New York, New York

March 3, 197y

BOARD OF DIRECTORS
ABC FINANCIAL INDUSTRIES, INC.
 and SUBSIDIARIES
NEW YORK, NEW YORK

In connection with our examination of the consolidated financial statements of ABC Financial Industries, Inc. and Subsidiaries for the year ending December 31, 197x, we reviewed the companies' accounting procedures and system of internal control. While we believe the existing controls and procedures to be adequate in most respects, we noted the following areas in which we believe more effective internal control or increased efficiency is necessary. We recognize that certain of the recommendations may have been adopted prior to issuance of this letter.

GENERAL

The following recommendations will have little impact unless implemented as part of a sustained program for developing the overall financial potential of the organization. ABC Financial has reached a size and complexity that demands the full attention of a financially oriented person, and we strongly urge consideration be given to employing such an individual.

DATA PROCESSING AND SYSTEMS INTEGRATION

Systems design and program changes over the past two to three years have been made principally on a patchwork basis, with the result that newly implemented systems have not been fully integrated with existing systems, and program documentation has not been updated for all changes.

Thus, it is possible for the same information to be processed differently through two systems, or for data to be processed through one part of a system and not another with the result that general or control records are not in agreement with subsidiary records.

Documentation of many of the systems reviewed had not been updated during the last two years, and included references to programs no longer in use or files no longer maintained.

A thorough review of the data processing function should be undertaken, first, to define the systems and procedures as they now stand, including all reports produced and their distribution; second, to identify and prioritize needed revisions to the existing systems; and third, to integrate the systems and procedures to provide accurate data to the operations and production departments.

CONTRACTS RECEIVABLE

A significant portion of the business of the corporations centers around the installment contracts receivable from customers. We believe there are a number of methods in which the contracts and related procedures may be improved.

FIGURE 19-6 (cont.)

Controls over the initiation, processing, recording and follow-up on customer contracts have been generally lax and heavy reliance has been placed on the individual abilities of company personnel rather than a more formal business management system.

There is at present no effective means of assuring that all contract sales by the individual sales offices are reported to the finance subsidiary, or for ensuring prompt and thorough follow-up on such sales.

The following points should be considered as a framework for providing strength in this area:

1. Complete centralization of contract responsibility in the finance subsidiary.

2. Use of prenumbered contract forms, all of which must be accounted for.

3. Use of prenumbered receipt forms, accounted for in the same manner as contract forms.

4. Establishment of a requirement that all contracts be recorded and ultimate disposition noted in the records. This should be accomplished by adoption of a policy defining follow-up procedures and standard disposition methods.

5. Design, implementation, and enforcement of filing procedures which would provide adequate support for customer receivables.

Contract form –

Collection personnel are at times hesitant to attempt enforcement of the present contract and have adopted the policy of terminating collection action when a delinquent patron invites or threatens legal action. It therefore appears that a new contract form should be drafted with legal assistance to assure an enforceable agreement.

Collection agencies –

Contracts turned over to collection agencies during the past year appear to be providing little return to the companies, and in fact may work to their detriment. It appears that one or two persons against whom the collection agency has attempted to file suit or garnishment proceedings have been able to substantiate payment to a sales office for the alleged delinquency. Inasmuch as accounting procedures in effect at the time of processing these early contracts were somewhat lax, it would be difficult to defend against such claims. We recommend that you consider abandoning collection efforts on these contracts in light of the minimal return being received and the possibility that such action could result in unfavorable publicity.

We further recommend that definite policies be established with regard to conditions under which contracts will be turned over to collection agencies.

FIGURE 19-6 (cont.)

Sales policies and techniques –

Sales and collection data which we accumulated during our review indicated that the largest portion of uncollectible contracts arose from sales having one or more of the following characteristics:

1. Contract amount significantly larger than normal.

2. Contract payment period significantly longer than normal.

3. Down payment significantly lower than normal.

We believe sales personnel should concentrate on what might be considered a "normal" sale, avoiding programs of excessive terms or nominal down payments. The policy of encouraging accelerated cash payments should be continued.

The second major factor contributing to uncollectible contract balances is dissatisfaction on the part of the customer shortly after receipt of the merchandise. Collection personnel have encountered resistance from patrons to whom salespeople had apparently promised results other than those contained in the written agreement. We believe these problems could be minimized through establishment and enforcement of sales guidelines to avoid issuance of implied guarantees beyond those in the service agreement.

To assist in achieving the goals outlined above, we believe the present commission and bonus policies should be modified to include collections as a factor to provide an incentive for obtaining acceptable credit risks and down payments within established guidelines.

CASH RECEIPTS

The present system provides no assurance that all receipts are being deposited to company accounts. The use of "deposit only" type bank accounts in proximity to each sales office is a significant strength in this area, but should be augmented through the use of prenumbered receipt forms and strict enforcement of the requirement that receipts be deposited daily.

We noted also that the sales offices maintain records of customer payments paralleling those kept by the finance subsidiary. Comparison of these dual records revealed a number of discrepancies, and we believe there is little justification for maintaining both. Ostensibly, such records are kept at the sales office in order that services to persons delinquent in their accounts can be restricted; however, it appears that this could be achieved through periodic notification to the sales offices by the finance company, thus removing the accounting functions from the sales offices.

At the home office, control over receipts could be strengthened by more systematic review and control of bank deposit tickets.

CASH DISBURSEMENTS

It is sometimes the practice of corporate officers to carry a supply of checks on a corporation general bank account for use on an as-needed basis, with the result that these checks often remain unaccounted for over long periods. Use of an executive checking account on an imprest basis should be considered, if this practice is necessary.

FIGURE 19-6 (cont.)

Other procedures to be considered in the area of cash disbursements are the timely review of outstanding checks for removal of old or improper items; annotation of general ledger account distribution on paid invoices; and establishment of a log for control of transfers from the numerous deposit-only accounts and efficient utilization of funds in these accounts.

The list of authorized signers supplied by various banks includes two former employees. The list should be updated and the banks notified to preclude unauthorized access to cash.

PAYROLL

Controls over payroll disbursements appear to be generally adequate, except that preparation and distribution of payroll for the newly-opened Texas sales offices is performed by the same individual. This procedure could be strengthened by either requiring signature of the manager and the employee on the individual time slip, or sending the checks from the home office directly to the sales office managers for distribution.

We recommend that policies on commissions be formalized and that computations for each employee be made a part of the payroll record; current practice places the determination in the hands of the area supervisor, with little or no documentation available for support.

FACILITIES AND EQUIPMENT

At present, leasehold improvements and equipment are identified only by the vendor from whom acquired and, to a limited extent, by location. Major equipment items should be identified by location and information provided with respect to costs, dates of acquisition, and estimated lives.

We noted that the companies have an exclusive manufacturing agreement with a major equipment supplier. The document evidencing this agreement appears quite informal and we suggest that the situation be reviewed with your attorney to determine the advisability of redrafting the agreement.

OPERATING RESULTS, REPORTING, AND PLANNING

In light of the multistate expansion of operations, we believe that consideration should be given to centralization of common procedures for increased control and efficiency. This would involve the centralization of the financing and contract handling functions in the finance subsidiary and the development of standardized accounting techniques and documents for submission to the central accounting office.

In order to provide meaningful management operating reports, corporate expenses should be identified and recorded as direct charges to the appropriate sales offices, as costs of operations, or as general, administrative, and selling expenses. Sales and performance data should be accumulated, analyzed and applied in a comprehensive approach to management which includes cash forecasting and profit planning.

FIGURE 19-6 (cont.)

It is suggested that a series of operating reports be designed and implemented at the earliest possible date to permit effective management control. The specific nature of the reports will be dictated by the requirements of management, but, at a minimum, should measure actual against planned performance for:

1. Weekly – Gross sales for each location.

2. Biweekly – Collections and cash receipts for each location.

3. Monthly – Complete operating statements for each location.

4. Quarterly – Consolidated corporate financial statements.

OTHER

With regard to the newly formed finance company, we noted a tendency on the part of the collection personnel to exaggerate their intended actions in the event payments were not forthcoming, to make threats of collection which may not be enforceable, and in general, to make any statements to the patrons which they believed would exact payment from them. In light of the questions raised about the present contract, and the unfavorable publicity which could result from official or semiofficial investigation, we believe that every attempt should be made to ensure that the actions of collection personnel are within their authority and do nothing to discredit the organization.

We further noted the practice adopted by the collectors of requesting that patrons remit delinquent payments by special delivery to the attention of the individual collectors, and that such payments are often routed, unopened, directly to these collectors. This could result in a serious breach of controls regarding the handling of cash, and we recommend that all incoming mail be opened by an employee not associated with the collection or recordkeeping functions.

We would be pleased to discuss the above comments and recommendations further with you and to assist in their implementation.

Able and Baker
Certified Public Accountants

(2) Discharge the auditor from legal liability for his examination.

(3) Confirm in writing management's approval of limitations on the scope of the audit.

(4) Remind management of its primary responsibility for financial statements.

c. Three months subsequent to the date of his report, a CPA becomes aware of facts that existed at the date of his report and affect the reliability of the financial statements of a client whose securities are widely held. If the client refuses to make appropriate disclosure, the CPA should notify

(1) Regulatory agencies having jurisdiction over the client.

(2) All stockholders.

(3) All present and potential investors in the company.

(4) Stockholders and the financial press.

d. An example of an event occurring in the period of the auditor's field work subsequent to the end of the year being audited which normally would not require disclosure in the financial statements or auditor's report would be

(1) Decreased sales volume resulting from a general business recession.

(2) Serious damage to the company's plant from a widespread flood.

(3) Issuance of a widely advertised capital stock issue with restrictive covenants.

(4) Settlement of a large liability for considerably less than the amount recorded.

e. Assuming that none of the following have been disclosed in the financial statements, the most appropriate item for footnote disclosure is the

(1) Collection of all receivables subsequent to year-end.

(2) Revision of an employees' pension plan.

(3) Retirement of the president of the company and election of a new president.

(4) A material decrease in the advertising budget for the coming year and its anticipated effect upon income.

2. Distinguish between a contingent liability and an actual liability and give three examples of each.

3. In the audit of the James Mobley Company, you are concerned about the possibility of contingent liabilities resulting in income tax disputes. Discuss the procedures you could use for an extensive investigation in this area.

4. Explain why the analysis of legal expense is an essential part of every audit engagement.

5. During the audit of the Merril Manufacturing Company, Ralph Pyson, CPA, has become aware of four lawsuits against the client by having discussions with the client, reading corporate minutes, and reviewing correspondence files. How should Pyson determine the materiality of the lawsuits and the proper disclosure in the financial statements?

6. Distinguish between the two general types of subsequent events and explain how they differ. Give two examples of each type.

7. In obtaining confirmations from attorneys, Bill Malano attempts to obtain the confirmation request as early as possible after the balance sheet date. This approach enables him to make sure he has a signed letter from every attorney and to properly investigate any exceptions. It also eliminates the

problem of having a lot of unresolved loose ends near the end of the audit. Evaluate Malano's approach.

8. What major considerations should the auditor take into account in determining how extensive the post balance sheet review should be?

9. Distinguish between the subsequent events occurring between the balance sheet date and the date of the auditor's report, and the subsequent discovery of facts existing at the date of the auditor's report. Give two examples of each and explain the appropriate action by the auditor in each instance.

10. Miles Lawson, CPA, believes the final summarization is the easiest part of the audit if careful planning is followed throughout the engagement. He makes sure each segment of the audit is completed before he goes on to the next. When the last segment of the engagement is completed, he is finished with the audit. He believes this may take a little longer on each part of the audit, but he makes up for it by not having to do the final summarization. Evaluate Lawson's approach.

11. Compare and contrast the accumulation of audit evidence and the evaluation of the adequacy of the disclosures in financial statements. Give three examples where adequate disclosure could depend heavily upon the accumulation of evidence and three others where audit evidence does not normally significantly affect the adequacy of the disclosure.

12. Distinguish between a management representation letter and a management letter and state the primary purpose of each. List five items that might be included in the contents of each letter.

13. List the primary things the reviewer should consider in the review of working papers and explain the importance of each.

14. Distinguish between regular working paper review and independent review and state the purpose of each. Give two examples of important potential findings in each of these two types of review.

DISCUSSION QUESTIONS AND PROBLEMS

15. You are making an annual examination for the purpose of rendering an opinion regarding the financial statements for use in an annual report to stockholders. Answer the following questions concerning events subsequent to the date of the financial statements:
    a. What auditing procedures should normally be followed in order to obtain knowledge of subsequent happenings?
    b. What is the period with which the auditor is normally concerned with regard to post-balance sheet events?
    c. Give five different examples of events or transactions that might occur in the subsequent period.
    d. What is the auditor's general responsibility, if any, for reporting such events or transactions?
    e. In your report, how would you deal with each of the examples you listed in part c above? (AICPA adapted)

16. The following unrelated events occurred after the balance sheet date but before the audit report was prepared:
    a. The granting of a retroactive pay increase.
    b. Determination by the federal government of additional income tax due for a prior year.

c. Filing of an antitrust suit by the federal government.
d. Declaration of a stock dividend.
e. Sale of a fixed asset at a substantial profit.

Required:

a. Explain how each of the items might have come to the auditor's attention.
b. Discuss the auditor's responsibility to recognize each of these in connection with his report.   (AICPA adapted)
17. The philosophy of George Hatton, CPA, is to intensively audit transactions taking place during the current audit period, but to ignore subsequent transactions. He believes each year should stand on its own and be audited in the year in which the transactions take place. According to Hatton, "If a transaction recorded in the subsequent period is audited in the current period, it is verified twice—once this year and again in next year's audit. That is a duplication of effort and a waste of time."

Required:

a. Explain the fallacy in Hatton's argument.
b. Give six specific examples of information obtained by examining subsequent events that are essential to the current period audit.
18. In analyzing legal expense for the Boatsman Bottle Company, Bart Little, CPA, observes that the company has paid legal fees to three different law firms during the current year. In accordance with his CPA firm's normal operating practice, Little requests standard confirmation letters as of the balance sheet date from each of the three law firms.

On the last day of field work, Little notes that one of the confirmations has not yet been received. The second confirmation request contains a statement to the effect that the law firm deals exclusively in registering patents and refuses to comment on any lawsuits or other legal affairs of the client. The third attorney's letter states that there is an outstanding unpaid bill due from the client and recognizes the existence of a potentially material lawsuit against the client but refuses to comment further to protect the legal rights of the client.

Required:

a. Evaluate Little's approach to sending the confirmations and his follow-up on the responses.
b. What should Little do about each of the confirmations?
19. In an examination of the Marco Corporation as at 12-31-X7, the following situations exist. No entries in respect thereto have been made in the accounting records.
a. The Marco Corporation has guaranteed the payment of interest on the ten-year, first-mortgage bonds of the Newart Company, an affiliate. Outstanding bonds of the Newart Company amount to $150,000 with interest payable at 5 percent per annum, due June 1 and December 1 of each year. The bonds were issued by the Newart Company on December 1, 19X5, and all interest payments have been met by that company with the exception of the payment due December 1, 19X7. The Marco Corporation states that it will pay the defaulted interest to the bondholders on January 15, 19X8.
b. During the year 19X7 the Marco Corporation was named as a defendant

in a suit for damages by the Dalton Company for breach of contract. An adverse decision to the Marco Corporation was rendered and the Dalton Company was awarded $40,000 damages. At the time of the audit, the case was under appeal to a higher court.

c. On December 23, 19X7, the Marco Corporation declared a common stock dividend of 1,000 shares, par $100,000, of its common stock, payable February 2, 19X8, to the common stockholders of record December 30, 19X7.

Required:

a. Define *contingent liability*.
b. Describe the audit procedures you would use to learn about each of the above situations.
c. Describe the nature of the adjusting entries or disclosure, if any, you would make for each of these situations.   (AICPA adapted)

20. The field work for the 6-30-X7 audit of Tracy Brewing Company was finished 8-19-X7, and the completed financial statements, accompanied by the signed audit reports, were mailed 9-6-X7. In each of the highly material independent events (*a* through *i*), state the appropriate action (1 through 4) for the situation and justify your response. The alternative actions are as follows:

(1) Adjust the 6-30-X7 financial statements.
(2) Disclose the information in a footnote in the 6-30-X7 financial statements.
(3) Request the client to recall the 6-30-X7 statements for revision.
(4) No action is required.

The events are as follows:

a. On 12-14-X7 the auditor discovered that a debtor of Tracy Brewing went bankrupt on 10-2-X7. The sale had taken place 4-15-X7, but the amount appeared collectible at 6-30-X7 and 8-19-X7.
b. On 8-15-X7 the auditor discovered that a debtor of Tracy Brewing went bankrupt on 8-1-X7. The most recent sale had taken place 4-2-X6, and no cash receipts had been received since that date.
c. On 12-14-X7 the auditor discovered that a debtor of Tracy Brewing went bankrupt on 7-15-X7 due to declining financial health. The sale had taken place 1-15-X7.
d. On 8-6-X7 the auditor discovered that a debtor of Tracy Brewing went bankrupt on 7-30-X7. The cause of the bankruptcy was an unexpected loss of a major lawsuit on 7-15-X7 resulting from a product deficiency suit by a different customer.
e. On 8-6-X7 the auditor discovered that a debtor of Tracy Brewing went bankrupt on 7-30-X7 for a sale that took place 7-3-X7. The cause of the bankruptcy was a major uninsured fire on 7-20-X7.
f. On 5-31-X7 the auditor discovered an uninsured lawsuit against Tracy Brewing which had originated on 2-28-X7.
g. On 7-20-X7 Tracy Brewing settled a lawsuit out of court which had originated in 19X4 and is currently listed as a contingent liability.
h. On 9-14-X7 Tracy Brewing lost a court case which had originated in 19X6 for an amount equal to the lawsuit. The 6-30-X7 footnotes state that in the opinion of legal counsel there will be a favorable settlement.
i. On 7-20-X7 a lawsuit was filed against Tracy Brewing for a patent

infringement action which allegedly took place in early 19X7. In the opinion of legal counsel there is danger of a significant loss to the client.

21. In connection with his examination of Flowmeter, Inc., for the year ended December 31, 19X7, Hirsh, CPA, is aware that certain events and transactions that took place after December 31, 19X7, but before he issues his report dated February 28, 19X8, may affect the company's financial statements. The following material events or transactions have come to his attention:

  a. On January 3, 19X8, Flowmeter, Inc., received a shipment of raw materials from Canada. The materials had been ordered in October 19X7 and shipped FOB shipping point in November 19X7.

  b. On January 15, 19X8, the company settled and paid a personal injury claim of a former employee as the result of an accident which occurred in March 19X7. The company had not previously recorded a liability for the claim.

  c. On January 25, 19X8, the company agreed to purchase for cash the outstanding stock of Porter Electrical Co. The acquisition is likely to double the sales volume of Flowmeter, Inc.

  d. On February 1, 19X8, a plant by Flowmeter, Inc., was damaged by a flood resulting in an uninsured loss of inventory.

  e. On February 5, 19X8, Flowmeter, Inc., issued and sold to the general public $2 million in convertible bonds.

Required:

For each of the above events or transactions, indicate the audit procedures that should have brought the item to the attention of the auditor, and the form of disclosure in the financial statements including the reasons for such disclosures.

Arrange your answer in the following format.

Item No.	Audit Procedures	Required Disclosure and Reasons

(AICPA adapted)

22. Mel Adams, CPA, is a partner in a medium-sized CPA firm and takes an active part in the conduct of every audit he supervises. He follows the practice of reviewing all working papers of subordinates as soon as it is convenient, rather than waiting until the end of the audit. When the audit is nearly finished, Adams reviews the working papers again to make sure he hasn't missed anything significant. Since he makes most of the major decisions on the audit, there is rarely anything that requires further investigation. When he completes the review, he prepares a pencil draft of the financial statements, gets them approved by management, and has them typed and assembled in his firm's office. No other partner reviews the working papers because Adams is responsible for signing the audit reports.

Required:

  a. Evaluate the practice of reviewing the working papers of subordinates on a continuing basis rather than when the audit is completed.

  b. Is it acceptable for Adams to prepare the financial statements rather than make the client assume the responsibility?

    c. Evaluate the practice of not'having a review of the working papers by another partner in the firm.

23. Ron Morgan, CPA, has prepared a letter of representation for the president and controller to sign. It contains references to the following items:

    a. Inventory is fairly stated at the lower of cost or market and includes no obsolete items.

    b. All actual and contingent liabilities are properly included in the statements.

    c. All subsequent events of relevance to the financial statements have been disclosed.

Required:

    a. Why is it desirable to have a letter of representation from the client concerning the above matters when the audit evidence accumulated during the course of the engagement is meant to verify the same information?

    b. To what extent is the letter of representation useful as audit evidence? Explain.

    c. List several other types of information commonly included in a letter of representation.

24. In a management letter to the Cline Wholesale Company, Jerry Schwartz, CPA, informed management of its weak system in the control of inventory. He elaborated on how the system could result in a significant misstatement of inventory by the failure to recognize the existence of obsolete items. In addition, Schwartz made specific recommendations on how to improve the system and save clerical time by installing a computer system for the company's perpetual records. Management accepted the recommendations and installed the system under Schwartz's direction. For several months the system worked beautifully, but unforeseen problems developed when a master file was erased. The cost of reproducing and processing the inventory records to correct the error was significant, and management decided to scrap the entire project. The company sued Schwartz for failure to use adequate professional judgment in making the recommendations.

Required:

    a. What is Schwartz's legal and professional responsibility in the issuance of management letters?

    b. Discuss the major considerations that will determine whether he is liable in this situation.

25. Lancaster Electronics produces electronic components for sale to manufacturers of radios, television sets, and phonographic systems. In connection with his examination of Lancaster's financial statements for the year ended December 31, 19X7, Don Olds, CPA, completed field work two weeks ago. Mr. Olds is now evaluating the significance of the following items prior to preparing his auditor's report. Except as noted, none of these items have been disclosed in the financial statements or footnotes.

    1. Recently Lancaster interrupted its policy of paying cash dividends quarterly to its stockholders. Dividends were paid regularly through 19X6, discontinued for all of 19X7 in order to finance equipment for the company's new plant, and resumed in the first quarter of 19X8. In the annual report dividend policy is to be discussed in the president's letter to stockholders.

2. A ten year loan agreement, which the company entered into three years ago, provides that dividend payments may not exceed net income earned after taxes subsequent to the date of the agreement. The balance of retained earnings at the date of the loan agreement was $298,000. From that date through December 31, 19X7, net income after taxes has totaled $360,000 and cash dividends have totaled $130,000. Based upon these data the staff auditor assigned to this review concluded that there was no retained earnings restriction at December 31, 19X7.

3. The company's new manufacturing plant building, which cost $600,000 and has an estimated life of twenty-five years, is leased from the Sixth National Bank at an annual rental of $100,000. The company is obligated to pay property taxes, insurance, and maintenance. At the conclusion of its ten-year noncancelable lease, the company has the option of purchasing the property for $1. In Lancaster's income statement the rental payment is reported on a separate line.

4. A major electronics firm has introduced a line of products that will compete directly with Lancaster's primary line, now being produced in the specially designed new plant. Because of manufacturing innovations, the competitor's line will be of comparable quality but priced 50 percent below Lancaster's line. The competitor announced its new line during the week following completion of field work. Mr. Olds read the announcement in the newspaper and discussed the situation by telephone with Lancaster executives. Lancaster will meet the lower prices which are high enough to cover variable manufacturing and selling expenses but will permit recovery of only a portion of fixed costs.

Required:

For each item 1 to 4, discuss the additional disclosure in the financial statements and footnotes required for the fair presentation of financial statements.   (AICPA adapted)

26. In connection with your examination of the financial statements of Olars Mfg. Corporation for the year ended December 31, 19X6, your post-balance sheet-date review disclosed the following items:

a. January 3, 19X7: The state government approved a plan for the construction of an express highway. The plan will result in the appropriation of a portion of the land area owned by Olars Mfg. Corporation. Construction will begin in late 19X7. No estimate of the condemnation award is available.

b. January 4, 19X7: The funds for a $25,000 loan to the corporation made by Mr. Olars on July 15, 19X6, were obtained by him by a loan on his personal life insurance policy. The loan was recorded in the account "loan from officers." Mr. Olars's source of the funds was not disclosed in the company records. The corporation pays the premiums on the life insurance policy, and Mrs. Olars, wife of the president, is the beneficiary of the policy.

c. January 7, 19X7: The mineral content of a shipment of ore enroute on December 31, 19X6, was determined to be 72 percent. The shipment was recorded at year-end at an estimated content of 50 percent by a debit to raw material inventory and a credit to accounts payable in the amount of $20,600. The final liability to the vendor is based on the actual mineral content of the shipment.

d. January 15, 19X7: Culminating a series of personal disagreements between Mr. Olars, the president, and his brother-in-law, the treasurer, the
latter resigned, effective immediately, under an agreement whereby the
corporation would purchase his 10 percent stock ownership at book value
as of December 31, 19X6. Payment is to be made in two equal amounts
in cash on April 1 and October 1, 19X7. In December the treasurer had
obtained a divorce from his wife, who was Mr. Olars's sister.

e. January 31, 19X7: As a result of reduced sales, production was curtailed
in mid-January and some workers were laid off. On February 5, 19X7,
all the remaining workers went on strike. To date the strike is unsettled.

f. February 10, 19X7: A contract was signed whereby Mammoth Enterprises
purchased from Olars Mfg. Corporation all of the latter's fixed assets (including rights to receive the proceeds of any property condemnation),
inventories, and the right to conduct business under the name "Olars
Mfg. Division." The effective date of the transfer will be March 1, 19X7.
The sale price was $500,000 subject to adjustment following the taking
of a physical inventory. Important factors contributing to the decision
to enter into the contract were the policy of the board of directors of
Mammoth Industries to diversify the firm's activities and the report of
a survey conducted by an independent market appraisal firm which revealed a declining market for Olars products.

Required:

Assume that the above items came to your attention prior to completion
of your audit work on February 15, 19X7, and that you will render a short-
form report. For *each* of the above items:

a. Give the audit procedures, if any, that would have brought the item to
your attention. Indicate other sources of information that may have revealed the item.

b. Discuss the disclosure that you would recommend for the item, listing all
details that you would suggest should be disclosed. Indicate those items or
details, if any, that should not be disclosed. Give your reasons for recommending or not recommending disclosure of the items or details.

(AICPA adapted)

27. You have completed your audit of Carter Corporation and its consolidated
subsidiaries for the year ended December 31, 19X7, and were satisfied with
the results of your examination. You have examined the financial statements
of Carter Corporation for the past three years. The corporation is now preparing its annual report to shareholders. The report will include the consolidated financial statements of Carter Corporation and its subsidiaries and
your short-form auditor's report. During your audit the following matters
came to your attention:

a. The Internal Revenue Service is currently examining the corporation's
19X5 federal income tax return and is questioning the amount of a deduction claimed by the corporation's domestic subsidiary for a loss sustained
in 19X5. The examination is still in process, and any additional tax liability is indeterminable at this time. The corporation's tax counsel believes that there will be no substantial additional tax liability.

b. A vice president who is also a stockholder resigned on December 31, 19X7,
after an argument with the president. The vice president is soliciting
proxies from stockholders and expects to obtain sufficient proxies to gain

control of the board of directors so that a new president will be appointed. The president plans to have a footnote prepared which would include information of the pending proxy fight, management's accomplishments over the years, and an appeal by management for the support of stockholders.

Required:

Prepare the footnotes, if any, that you would suggest for the two items listed above.   (AICPA adapted)

20

Auditor's Reports

An audit report informs financial statement users of the extent to which the auditor has performed his evidence accumulation responsibilities and the results of his findings. Earlier in the text it was established that management, rather than the auditor, has the basic responsibility for the fairness of the representations in the financial statements. If the auditor believes the statements are not fairly stated in accordance with generally accepted accounting principles, and the client refuses to make revisions, the audit report informs users that the statements are not fairly stated. Similarly, if for any reason the auditor is unable to satisfy himself that the statements are fairly stated, the report informs users that the auditor lacks knowledge about the fairness of the financial statement presentation.

The only information about the audit that is normally available to statement users comes through the audit report, and therefore the wording must clearly communicate the auditor's message. Due to the need for unambiguous statements about the work performed and the results found, the profession has developed standard audit reports for different circumstances and well-defined rules for determining the appropriate type of report.

The basic requirements for issuing audit reports are derived from the Generally Accepted Standards of Reporting. They are included on page 38 in Chapter 2. The last standard is especially important because it requires an expression of opinion about the overall financial statements or a specific statement that an overall opinion is not possible, along with the reasons for not expressing an opinion. The standard also requires a clear-cut statement by the auditor of the nature of the examination and the degree to which the auditor limits his responsibility.

STANDARD UNQUALIFIED REPORT

A standard short-form audit report can be issued when certain conditions have been met. An example of the short-form report is included in Chapter 2, on page 41. An explanation of the five parts of the short-form report is also included in Chapter 2 (pp. 42–43). It is suggested that the section on short-form reports be reread at this time. In subsequent discussion, mention of a *standard scope paragraph* refers to the first paragraph in the short-form report and a *standard opinion* refers to the second paragraph. For purposes of convenience, the address, signature of the CPA firm, and date of the audit report are deleted from examples of short-form reports in the remainder of this chapter.

Requirements of the Standard Short-Form Report

The standard short-form report can be issued only under the following circumstances:

1. Sufficient evidence has been accumulated, and the auditor has conducted the engagement in a manner that enables him to conclude that the three standards of field work have been met.
2. The three general standards have been followed in all respects on the engagement.
3. The financial statements are presented in accordance with generally accepted accounting principles which are applied on a basis consistent with that of the preceding period.
4. There are no unusual uncertainties concerning future developments which cannot be reasonably estimated or satisfactorily resolved.

Modifications in the Wording of the Unqualified Report

In certain situations an unqualified report is issued, but the wording deviates from the standard unqualified opinion. It is important to distinguish between these reports and the qualified opinions discussed later in the chapter. The *unqualified report with modified wording* meets the criteria of a complete audit with satisfactory results and financial statements that are fairly presented, but the auditor feels it is important to provide additional information. In a *qualified report* the auditor either has not performed a satisfactory audit or is not satisfied that the financial statements are fairly presented.

The following are the most important causes of a modification in the wording of the unqualified short-form report:

1. *Reports involving the use of other auditors.* When the CPA relies upon a different CPA firm to perform part of the audit, which is common when the client has several widespread branches or subdivisions, the principal CPA firm can follow one of three alternatives: make no reference in its audit report; make reference in the report; or qualify its report. When the auditor makes reference to the other auditor in the report, it is called a *shared unqualified report.*

When the auditor decides to make no reference in the report, the standard wording is used. This form of the short-form report is acceptable if the principal auditor is able to satisfy himself as to the independence and professional reputation of the other auditor and is satisfied with the other auditor's examination.

A shared unqualified report is appropriate when it is impractical to review the work of the other auditor or when the portion of the financial statements audited by the other CPA is material in relation to the total. The following is an example of the relevant portion of a shared opinion that should not be construed as a qualification:

> We have examined the consolidated balance sheet of Big Company, Inc., and subsidiaries as of December 31, 19—, and the related consolidated statements of earnings, retained earnings and changes in financial position for the year then ended. Our examination was made . . . . We did not examine the financial statements of Little Company, which statements reflect total assets and revenues constituting 20% and 30% respectively of the related consolidated totals. These statements were examined by other auditors whose report thereon has been furnished to us and our opinion expressed herein insofar as it relates to the amounts included for Little Company is based solely upon the report of the other auditors.
>
> In our opinion, based on our examination and the report of other auditors referred to above, the aforementioned consolidated financial statements present fairly the financial position of Big Company, Inc., and subsidiaries as of December 31, 19—, and the results of their operations and changes in their financial position for the year then ended. . . .

The appropriate report when the principal auditor is unwilling to issue an unqualified report on the portion of the statements audited by another auditor is discussed later as a part of departures from unqualified reports.

2. *Reports on less than a full set of statements.* The auditor is frequently asked to report on one basic financial statement and not the others. A common example is a report on the balance sheet only. For this type of examination, it is acceptable to issue an unqualified report on the statement if the auditor has unrestricted access to all the information he needs and conducts the audit in accordance with generally accepted auditing standards.

3. *Departures from a promulgated accounting principle with which*

the auditor agrees. Rule 203 of the AICPA Code of Professional Ethics states that in unusual situations a departure from a published accounting principle promulgated by a body designated by the AICPA to establish accounting principles may not require a qualified or adverse opinion. However, to justify an unqualified opinion, the auditor must be satisfied and must state in the audit report that to have adhered to the published position would have produced a misleading result in that particular situation.

4. *Comments to emphasize certain points.* Under certain circumstances the CPA may wish to emphasize specific matters regarding the financial statements even though he intends to express an unqualified opinion. Normally, such explanatory information should be included in a separate middle paragraph in the report. The following are examples of explanatory information the auditor may feel should be expressed:

   a. The existence of significant related party transactions.
   b. Important events occurring subsequent to the balance sheet date.
   c. The description of accounting matters affecting the comparability of the financial statements with those of the preceding year.

CONDITIONS REQUIRING A DEPARTURE FROM AN UNQUALIFIED OPINION

A major responsibility of the auditor is to recognize when an unqualified report is no longer applicable. The following circumstances, which are summarized at this point and discussed in more detail subsequently, result in a departure from an unqualified report:

1. The scope of the auditor's examination has been significantly restricted by the client. If the client will not permit the auditor to confirm material receivables, physically observe inventories, or perform some other important procedure, it is unlikely that the auditor will be able to determine whether the statements are fairly presented.
2. The auditor has been unable to perform significant audit procedures or obtain essential information because of conditions beyond either the client's or the auditor's control. For example, when the engagement is not agreed upon until after the client's year-end, it may not be possible to physically observe inventories, confirm receivables, or perform other important procedures.
3. The financial statements have not been prepared in accordance with generally accepted accounting principles. For example, if the client insists upon using replacement costs for permanent assets or values inventory at selling price rather than historical cost, a modification of the unqualified opinion is required. When generally accepted accounting principles are referred to in this context, consideration of the adequacy of all informative disclosures, including footnotes, is important.

4. The accounting principles used in the financial statements have not been consistently applied. Even if the auditor recommends the change from one acceptable accounting principle, such as FIFO inventory valuation, to another one, such as LIFO, the audit report must make a specific reference to the change.
5. There are unusual uncertainties affecting the financial statements which cannot be reasonably estimated at the date of the auditor's report. There may be such things as significant unresolved lawsuits against the firm in excess of the insurance coverage or questions about the likelihood of the firm's being able to sell its products because of impending changes in state or federal laws.
6. The auditor is not independent with respect to the entity that is being audited.

At this point the various types of reports used by auditors to depart from the unqualified report are briefly discussed. Following this, each condition requiring a departure from an unqualified report is studied more thoroughly and associated with the appropriate types of audit reports.

AUDIT REPORTS OTHER THAN UNQUALIFIED

Three primary types of audit reports are issued under conditions that require a departure from an unqualified opinion: a *qualified report,* an *adverse opinion,* and a *disclaimer of opinion.*

In addition, *reports on unaudited financial statements* are frequently issued, which as the name implies are actually not audit reports. However, their frequency and close relationship to disclaimers of opinions justify inclusion at this point. Several types of *special audit reports* are also issued by CPAs for situations such as statements prepared on a cash basis, audits of specific aspects of a company's business other than financial statements, and reviews of internal control. Special reports are considered at the end of the chapter.

Qualified Report

A qualified report can result from the existence of one or more of the first five of the previously discussed six conditions requiring a departure from an unqualified opinion. (If the auditor is not independent, a disclaimer must always be issued.) *However, a qualified report can be used to disclose any of those five conditions only when the auditor believes the overall financial statements are fairly presented.*

Materiality is an essential consideration in the determination of whether a qualified report is appropriate for a given set of circumstances. If an exception is immaterial relative to the financial statement of the entity for the current period and is not expected to have a material effect in future periods, it is appropriate to issue an unqualified report. A common instance is the immediate expensing of office supplies rather than carrying the unused portion in inventory because the amount is insignificant. At the other extreme are situations in which the amounts are of such great significance that the overall financial statements are materially affected. In these circumstances it is necessary to issue a *disclaimer of opinion* or an *adverse opinion,* depending on the nature of the exception. Between these two extremes are situations in which the overall financial statements are fairly stated, but there is an exception material enough to require disclosure. A qualified opinion is appropriate in such a situation. It is obvious that a qualified opinion is far less severe than an adverse opinion or a disclaimer.

The auditor must make the decision, based upon his professional judgment, as to what constitutes immaterial, reasonably material, or pervasively material circumstances. Unfortunately, at the present time auditors do not have guidelines adequate enough so that reasonably uniform judgments can be assumed among different auditors.

A qualified report can take the form of a *qualification of both the scope and the opinion* or an *opinion qualification only.* The only time a scope and opinion qualification can be issued is when the auditor has not been able to accumulate all the evidence required by generally accepted auditing standards. Therefore the scope and opinion qualification is used only when the auditor's scope has been restricted by the client or when conditions exist that prevent the auditor from conducting a complete audit (Conditions 1 and 2). The use of a qualification of the opinion only is restricted to the following three situations:

1. The financial statements have not been prepared in accordance with generally accepted accounting principles (Condition 3).
2. The accounting principles used in the financial statements have not been consistently applied (Condition 4).
3. There are unusual uncertainties affecting the financial statements that cannot reasonably be estimated at the date of the auditors report (Condition 5).

Whenever an auditor uses a qualified opinion, he must use either the term "except for" or the term "subject to" in the opinion paragraph. The implication is that the auditor is satisfied with the overall financial statements "except for" or "subject to" a particular part of the financial statements. The only time a "subject to" qualification is used is when there are unusual uncertainties (Condition 5). In all other cases, the opinion in a qualified report must include the expression "except for" (Conditions 1 through 4). Examples of both of these qualifications are given later in the chapter. It is unacceptable to use these two phrases with any type of audit opinion other than a qualified.

The appropriate use of a qualified report can be summarized as follows:

**The Auditor is Satisfied that the Overall Financial Statements are
Fairly Stated, but There is a Material Exception**

Conditions Requiring a *Departure from an Unqualified Report*	*Nature of the Qualification*
Condition 1—Scope restricted by client.	Scope and opinion—*except for*
Condition 2—Scope restricted by conditions.	Scope and opinion—*except for*
Condition 3—Statements are not in accordance with GAAP.	Opinion only—*except for*
Condition 4—Inconsistent application of GAAP.	Opinion only—*except for*
Condition 5—Unusual uncertainties exist.	Opinion only—*subject to*

Adverse Opinion

When the auditor is convinced that the overall financial statements do not fairly present the financial position, results of operations, or changes in financial position in accordance with generally accepted accounting principles, he must issue an *adverse opinion*. The adverse opinion is used only when one or more of the client's statements are materially misstated as a result of failing to use generally accepted accounting principles (Condition 3). For example, the failure to include essential footnote information or the use of direct costing for inventory valuation would require an adverse opinion if either one led to material misstatement in the overall statements.

The distinction between an adverse opinion and a qualified opinion is entirely a matter of materiality. An adverse opinion is required if the exception is so material that the auditor believes the overall financial statements are not fairly presented, whereas a qualified opinion is appropriate if he believes the overall statements are fairly presented even though all requirements for fair presentation have not been met.

Adverse opinions are extremely rare in the profession because most clients prefer to revise their financial statements rather than have an adverse opinion included with the statements. In spite of their rarity, the requirement that the adverse opinion be used when the financial statements are materially misstated puts the auditor in a position of greater independence if the auditor and the client have a difference of opinion about the proper application of a particular accounting principle.

Disclaimer of Opinion

A *disclaimer of opinion* specifies that the auditor does not express an opinion on the financial statements. It is issued automatically when the auditor is not independent (Condition 6), but it is also used when the auditor lacks sufficient information about the financial statements to express an overall opinion. Any one of the following three circumstances requires a disclaimer of opinion if the amount is highly material:

1. The scope of the auditor's examination has been significantly restricted by the client (Condition 1).
2. The auditor has been unable to perform significant audit procedures or obtain essential information because of conditions beyond either the client's or the auditor's control (Condition 2).
3. The significance of uncertainties affecting the financial statements make it impossible to determine whether the financial statements are fairly presented (Condition 5).

A disclaimer of opinion is distinguished from an adverse opinion in that it is made on the basis of *lack of knowledge* on the part of the auditor, whereas in an adverse opinion the auditor must have knowledge that the financial statements are not fairly presented.

The distinction between a disclaimer of opinion and a qualified report resulting from a .scope limitation or from the existence of future uncertainties is *entirely a question of materiality*. A disclaimer of opinion is required if the scope limitation or the presence of the unusual uncertainty is so material that the auditor cannot determine if the overall financial statements are fairly presented. A qualified opinion can be issued if he believes that the scope limitation or the existence of unusual uncertainty must be disclosed but that the overall statements are fairly presented.

Reports on Unaudited Statements

When the CPA is associated with financial statements but no audit has been performed or the auditing procedures are insignificant, the CPA must issue a disclaimer of opinion for unaudited financial statements and clearly mark each page of the financial statements "unaudited." A common example is the CPA's being retained by the client to do routine services such as preparing the financial statements and the tax return rather than performing an audit. When all footnotes or other disclosures that the auditor considers necessary have been included in the statements, the following disclaimer is appropriate:

> The accompanying balance sheet of X Company as of December 31, 19—, and the related statement(s) of income and retained earnings and changes in financial position for the year then ended were not audited by us and accordingly we do not express an opinion on them.

If the CPA has knowledge that the financial statements are not fairly presented, the preceding disclaimer for unaudited statements is not satisfactory. For example, when the unaudited financial statements are for *internal purposes only* and lack the necessary footnotes or other disclosures that are believed important to external users, the auditor must include a disclaimer similar to that in the previous example and a sentence to the effect that the statements are for internal purposes only and therefore do not necessarily include all the information necessary for adequate disclosure. On the other hand, if the unaudited statements *are for external purposes* and are known to contain information that is not in accordance with generally accepted accounting principles, the auditor must include a statement in addition to the disclaimer for unaudited financial statements informing the reader of his reservations about the financial statements. If the client refuses to revise his statements or to permit such a statement in the disclaimer, the auditor must withdraw from the engagement.

The only exception to the requirement that an auditor must issue a disclaimer for unaudited statements occurs when the auditor merely types on plain paper or reproduces unaudited financial statements prepared by the client and submits the statements directly to the client.

In most cases the distinction between unaudited financial statements and a regular disclaimer of opinion of the type discussed in the preceding section is unambiguous because only an insignificant number of auditing procedures have been performed for unaudited financial statements. There are situations, however, in which the auditor has performed a considerable amount of work and it is unclear whether (a) the work performed is so limited that the financial statements should properly be labeled as "unaudited," or (b) the work performed was such as to constitute an audit, but the scope limitations are so severe as to require a normal disclaimer of an opinion. The appropriate opinion in a particular situation depends more on the *intention of the engagement* and the *nature of the tests* than on the amount of time spent on them. The engagement is considered to be for unaudited statements if the auditor has spent most of his time performing bookkeeping work or preparing accounting entries rather than evaluating and testing the system of internal control or performing independent verification procedures such as confirmations with outsiders.

Summary

The requirements for the appropriate auditor's opinion for the six conditions requiring a deviation from the short-form report are summarized in Figure 20-1. Observe that more than one type of audit report is applicable for each condition requiring a deviation, except when the auditor is not independent. The deciding factor in determining the proper type of audit report for any given condition other than independence is the materiality of the amount in question. The determination of materiality is a judgment question requiring a high degree of professional competence.

TYPES OF REPORTS FOR CONDITIONS REQUIRING A DEVIATION FROM UNQUALIFIED REPORTS

It is now appropriate to turn to a more detailed discussion, including illustrations of the proper audit reports, for each of the six conditions requiring a deviation from an unqualified report.

FIGURE 20-1

Summary of the Proper Audit Report for Each Condition Requiring a Deviation from an Unqualified Report at Different Levels of Materiality

Conditions Requiring a Deviation from an Unqualified Report	The Amounts are Immaterial	The Amounts are Material, but They do not Overshadow the Overall Statement		The Amounts are so Material that the Overall Fairness of the Statements is in Question		No Significant Evidence was Accumulated
	Unqualified	Qualified Scope and Opinion	Qualified Opinion Only	Adverse	Disclaimer	Unaudited
Auditing related The scope of the examination has been restricted by the client.	✓	✓			✓	✓
The scope of the examination has been restricted by conditions.	✓	✓			✓	✓
Accounting related The financial statements have not been prepared in accordance with generally accepted accounting principles.	✓		✓	✓		
The accounting principles have not been consistently applied.	✓		✓			
Uncertainties Unusual uncertainties affect the financial statements.	✓		✓		✓	
Auditor related The auditor is not independent. (Disclaimer regardless of the materiality.)					✓	

The Scope of the Auditor's Examination Has Been Restricted by the Client

When clients impose restrictions on the auditor's scope, a qualified opinion, or a disclaimer of opinion, should be issued unless the restrictions are minor. Due to the potential effect of client restrictions on the independence of auditors, the AICPA has encouraged the use of a disclaimer of opinion whenever the materiality is in question. Two common restrictions imposed on the auditor's scope are the observation of physical inventory and the confirmation of accounts receivable, but other restrictions may also occur. An example of a disclaimer for a client restriction follows:

(SCOPE PARAGRAPH—QUALIFIED)
. . . and such other auditing procedures as we considered necessary in the circumstances, except that in accordance with your instructions we did not confirm accounts receivable, as of December 31, 19—.

(OPINION PARAGRAPH—DISCLAIMER)
Because accounts receivable at December 3, 19—, enters materially into the determination of financial position, results of operations, and changes in financial position, we do not express an opinion on the aforementioned financial statements taken as a whole.

The Scope of the Auditor's Examination Has Been Restricted by Conditions

A scope qualification and, depending on the materiality, either an opinion qualification or a disclaimer of opinion is necessary whenever conditions beyond the client's or the auditor's control prevent the auditor from performing procedures that he considers necessary. For example, if the auditor is unable to examine the client's recorded minutes because they are lost, it is necessary to issue a disclaimer of opinion, since the minutes often include vital information that cannot be found elsewhere. When the auditor cannot perform procedures he considers desirable, but he is able to satisfy himself with alternative procedures that the information being verified is fairly stated, an unqualified report is acceptable.

The most common case in which the auditor cannot carry out important procedures occurs when the engagement is agreed upon after the client's balance sheet date. The confirmation of accounts receivable, the physical examination of inventory, and other important procedures may not be possible under these circumstances.

For example, the following report would be appropriate for a company where the amounts were material but not pervasive if the auditor had not been on hand to observe inventory and could not satisfy himself by alternative procedures:

(SCOPE PARAGRAPH—QUALIFIED)

We have examined the balance sheet of X Company as of December 31, 19—, and the related statements of income and retained earnings for the year then ended. Our examination was made in accordance with generally accepted auditing standards, and accordingly included such tests of the accounting records and such other auditing procedures as we considered necessary in the circumstances, except as stated in the following paragraph.

(MIDDLE PARAGRAPH)

We did not observe the taking of physical inventories as of December 31, 19—, since this date was prior to our initial engagement as auditors for the company. The company's records do not permit adequate retroactive tests of inventory quantities.

(OPINION PARAGRAPH—QUALIFIED)

In our opinion, except for the effect of such adjustments, if any, as might have been disclosed had we been able to observe the physical inventory taken as of December 31, 19—, or to make retroactive tests, the statements present fairly . . .

When the amounts are so material that a disclaimer of opinion is required, the scope and middle paragraphs could remain the same, but the opinion paragraph might be as follows:

(OPINION PARAGRAPH—DISCLAIMER)

Because the inventories referred to in the preceding paragraphs enter materially into the determination of financial position and the results of operations, we are unable to express an opinion on the accompanying financial statements taken as a whole.

In the previous example, the auditor can issue an unqualified audit report even if it is not practical for him to be on hand during the count if he performs the necessary alternative procedures. These must ordinarily include tests of the client's perpetual records and examination of enough physical counts of the inventory at a different date to satisfy the auditor that the inventory was fairly stated at the balance sheet date.

The Financial Statements Have Not Been Prepared in Conformity with Generally Accepted Accounting Principles

When the auditor knows that the financial statements may be misleading because they were not prepared in accordance with generally accepted accounting principles, he must issue a qualified or an adverse opinion, depending on the materiality of the item in question. The opinion must clearly state the nature of the deviation from the accepted principles and the amount of the misstatement, if it is known. An example of a qualified opinion for the failure to capitalize leases follows:

(SCOPE PARAGRAPH—UNQUALIFIED)
(MIDDLE PARAGRAPH)

The Company has excluded from property and debt in the accompanying balance sheet certain lease obligations, which in our opinion should be capitalized in order to conform with generally accepted accounting principles. If these lease obligations were capitalized, property would be increased by $4,750,000, long-term debt by $4,200,000, and retained earnings by $550,000 as of December 31, 19—, and net income and earnings per share would be increased by $450,000 and $47, respectively, for the year then ended.

(OPINION PARAGRAPH—QUALIFIED)

In our opinion, except for the effects of not capitalizing certain lease obligations, as discussed in the preceding paragraph, the financial statements present fairly . . .

When the amounts are so material that an adverse opinion is required, the scope would still be unqualified, the middle paragraph could remain the same, but the opinion paragraph might be as follows:

(OPINION PARAGRAPH—ADVERSE)

In our opinon, because of the effects of the matters discussed in the preceding paragraph, the financial statements referred to above do not present fairly, in conformity with generally accepted accounting principles, the financial position of Billet Company as of December 31, 19—, or the results of its operations and changes in its financial position for the year then ended.

When the client fails to include information that is necessary for the fair presentation of financial statements in the body of the statements or in the related footnotes, it is the responsibility of the auditor to present the information in the audit report and issue a qualified or an adverse opinion. It is common to put this type of qualification in a middle paragraph and to refer to the middle paragraph in the opinion paragraph. An example of an audit report in which the auditor considered the financial statement disclosure inadequate follows:

(SCOPE PARAGRAPH—UNQUALIFIED)
(MIDDLE PARAGRAPH)

On January 15, 19—, the Company issued debentures in the amount of $3,600,000 for the purpose of financing plant expansion. The debenture agreement restricts the payment of future cash dividends to earnings after December 31, 19—.

(OPINION PARAGRAPH—QUALIFIED)

In our opinion, the accompanying financial statements, except for the omission of the information in the preceding paragraph, present fairly . . .

The Accounting Principles Used in the Financial Statements Have Not Been Consistently Applied

Whenever there is a change in accounting principles that has a material effect on the current year's statements or is expected to have a material effect in future years, it is necessary to report the change in the opinion *even if the change has been fully disclosed in the financial statements.* Assuming the accounting principle used in the current period's financial statements is generally accepted, it is sufficient to issue a qualified opinion. For example, if the client changed from the accelerated to the straight-line method of computing depreciation, the following wording is appropriate:

(SCOPE PARAGRAPH—UNQUALIFIED)
(OPINION PARAGRAPH—QUALIFIED)

. . . in conformity with generally accepted accounting principles applied on a basis consistent with that of the preceding year, except for the change (in which we concur) in depreciation methods as described in Note 6 to the financial statements.

If there were no footnotes in the financial statements explaining the nature of the above-mentioned change and the effect on the financial statements, the information must be included directly in the report rather than by reference to the footnotes. The inclusion of the auditor's expression of approval in the opinion is optional.

The auditor is required to issue either a qualified or an adverse opinion, depending on the materiality of the effect on the financial statements, when there is a change from a generally accepted accounting principle to one that lacks general acceptance.

The auditor must be able to distinguish between changes that affect consistency and those that may affect comparability but do not affect consistency. The following are changes that affect consistency and therefore require a qualified report if they are material:

1. Changes in accounting principles, such as a change from LIFO to FIFO inventory valuation.
2. Changes in reporting entities, such as the inclusion of an additional company in combined financial statements.
3. Corrections of errors in principle by changing from an accounting principle that is not generally acceptable to one that is generally acceptable, including correction of the resulting error.

Changes that do not affect consistency and therefore need not be included in the audit report as a consistency exception include the following:

1. Changes in an estimate, such as a decrease in the life of an asset for depreciation purposes.
2. Error corrections not involving principles, such as a previous year's mathematical error.
3. Variations in format and presentation of financial information.
4. Changes because of substantially different transactions or events, such as new endeavors in research and development or the sale of a subsidiary.

If those items that do not require a consistency exception because of their nature materially affect the comparability of financial statements, disclosure is required in the footnotes. A qualification for inadequate disclosure may be required if the client refuses to disclose the items properly.

Unusual Uncertainties Affecting the Financial Statements

A number of estimates are customarily made by management in the preparation of financial statements, including the useful lives of the depreciable assets, the collectibility of receivables, and the realizability of inventory and other assets. There is usually enough evidence so that these items are susceptible to reasonable estimation. Sometimes, however, the auditor encounters a situation in which the outcome of a matter cannot be reasonably estimated at the time the statements are being issued. These matters are defined as *"uncertainties."* Examples of such uncertainties include:

1. Recoverability of a deferred cost.
2. Income tax or litigation contingencies (collectible or payable).
3. Realizability of a significant receivable.
4. Continued availability of required financing.

There are also less specific situations in which the ability of the company to continue to operate as a *going concern* is open to question. For example, the existence of one or more of the following factors raises the question of uncertainty about the ability of a company to continue to operate:

1. The company's controls over operations are inadequate.
2. There are significant recurring operating losses.
3. The company has been unable to pay its debt obligations as they come due.
4. Serious shortages of liquidity are evidenced by the current liabilities exceeding the current assets.

The appropriate type of opinion to issue when either specific or general uncertainties exist depends on the materiality of the items in question. An unqualified opinion is appropriate if the uncertainty is immaterial. A qualified opinion, with the use of a "subject to" qualification, should be issued in those middle-ground situations where the financial statements are overshadowed by a material uncertainty. When the potential effect of the uncertainty is so pervasive that a subsequent adverse resolution of the uncertainty would require a radical change in the financial statements, the CPA firm *may issue a disclaimer but is not required to do so if a qualified opinion is issued and the uncertainty is adequately explained in a footnote.* Although SAS 2 does not require a disclaimer of opinion when highly material uncertainties exist, many CPA firms follow the policy of requiring them in extreme cases.

An illustration of a "subject to" opinion when there is an uncertainty due to existing litigation follows:

(SCOPE PARAGRAPH—UNQUALIFIED)
(MIDDLE PARAGRAPH)

As discussed in Note 3 to the financial statements, the Company is defendant in a lawsuit alleging infringement of certain patent rights and claiming royalties and punitive damages. The Company has filed a counter action, and preliminary hearings and discovery proceedings on both actions are in progress. Company officers and counsel believe the Company has a good chance of prevailing, but the ultimate outcome of the lawsuits cannot presently be determined, and no provision for any liability that may result has been made in the financial statements.

(OPINION PARAGRAPH—QUALIFIED)

In our opinion, subject to the effects of such adjustments, if any, as might have been required had the outcome of the uncertainty referred to in the preceding paragraph been known, the financial statements referred to above present fairly . . .

The following is an illustration of a disclaimer that is considered necessary because the validity of the going concern assumption is questionable and there are material uncertainties:

(SCOPE PARAGRAPH—UNQUALIFIED)
(MIDDLE PARAGRAPH)

The Company has sustained substantial losses from operations and, as described in the notes to the financial statements, the operations of the Company have been substantially reduced. The future of the Company as an operating business will depend upon its ability to operate profitably and the availability of such financing as may be required. It is not possible to determine the effect on the 19— financial statements referred to above because of the possible consequences of the following matters:

(a) The adequacy of the allowance for obsolescence of $2,000,000 on the plant, property, and equipment. (Note 6)

(b) The uncertainties arising from the contingent liabilities described in the notes to the financial statements.

(OPINION PARAGRAPH—DISCLAIMER)

Because it is impossible to determine the future operational activity of the Company and the effect of the material uncertainties referred to in the previous paragraphs, we are unable to and do not express an opinion on the accompanying consolidated financial statements for the year ended December 31, 19—.

The Auditor Is Not Independent

If the auditor has not fulfilled the independence requirements specified by the Code of Professional Ethics, which is quoted in full in Appendix A at the end of Chapter 2, he must disclaim an opinion on the financial statements even though all the audit procedures considered necessary in the circumstances were performed. The following report is recommended by the Committee on Auditing Procedures of the AICPA when the auditor is not independent:

We are not independent with respect to XYZ Company, and the accompanying balance sheet as of December 31, 19—, and the related statements of income and retained earnings and the statement of changes in financial position for the year then ended were not audited by us. Accordingly, we do not express an opinion on them.

The lack of independence overrides any other scope limitations. Therefore, no other reason for disclaiming an opinion should be cited. The above report is even used when the auditor has performed bookkeeping services for the client if he is not independent.

THE EXISTENCE OF MORE THAN ONE CONDITION REQUIRING EXCEPTION

Frequently auditors encounter situations involving more than one of the conditions requiring modification of the unqualified report. In these circumstances, the auditor should qualify his opinion for each condition unless the less significant exception has the effect of neutralizing the more serious exception. For example, if there is a scope limitation and a situation where the auditor was not independent, the scope limitation should not be revealed. In the following situations more than one exception should be included in the report:

1. The auditor is not independent and the auditor knows the company has not followed generally accepted accounting principles.

2. The auditor issues a qualified opinion because of a scope limitation and he has knowledge of a contingent liability concerning litigation that may cause bankruptcy if an adverse ruling is given.
3. The statements are unaudited and the auditor knows they do not conform to generally accepted accounting principles.
4. There is a deviation in the statements' preparation in accordance with generally accepted accounting principles and another accounting principle was applied on a basis that was not consistent with that of the preceding year.

NEGATIVE ASSURANCES

It is inappropriate to include in the audit report any additional comments that counterbalance the auditor's opinion. For example, the use of such terminology as "However, nothing came to our attention that would lead us to the question of the fairness of the presentations" as a part of a disclaimer of opinion is inappropriate and a violation of the standards of reporting. Statements of this kind, which are referred to as *negative assurances,* tend to confuse readers about the nature of the auditor's examination and the degree of responsibility he is assuming. The use of negative assurances in letters to underwriters, which is beyond the scope of this text, is an exception to the requirement.

LONG-FORM REPORTS

A typical long-form report includes the financial statements associated with a short-form report plus additional information likely to be useful to management and other statement users. The profession has intentionally refrained from defining or restricting the appropriate supplementary information included so as to enable auditors to individualize each long-form report to meet the needs of statement users. However, several standard types of information are commonly included in the additional information section of a long-form report. For example, it is normal to find detailed comparative statements supporting the control totals on the primary financial statements for accounts such as cost of goods sold, operating expenses, and miscellaneous assets. Other customary types of information include statistical data for past years in the form of ratios and trends, a schedule of insurance coverage, and specific comments on the changes in the financial statements that have taken place. The supplemental information is not restricted to the foregoing, nor would the above items appear in all cases.

It is important that the auditor clearly distinguish between his responsibility for the primary financial statements and his responsibility for additional information. Usually, the auditor has not performed a sufficiently detailed audit to justify an opinion on the additional information, but in some instances he may be confident that the information is fairly presented. The profession's reporting standards require the auditor to make a clear statement about the degree of responsibility he is taking for the additional information.

When long-form reports are issued to some users and only the basic financial statements on the same audit are issued to others, the auditor should exercise special care to assure himself that the long-form report does not include information that might support a claim that there is inadequate disclosure in the short-form report. For example, if the supplementary comments contain exceptions, reservations, or material disclosures not appearing in the short-form report, there is a basis for potential legal claims against the auditor for inadequate disclosure from those users who have received only the short-form report.

SPECIAL REPORTS

Many kinds of special reports exist in auditing because CPA firms do not restrict their practice to the verification of financial statements prepared in accordance with generally accepted accounting principles. Examples include reports for organizations that do not follow generally accepted accounting principles because of government or association restrictions, reports that relate only to certain aspects of the financial statements such as the determination of profit-sharing bonuses and compliance with bond indentures, and special studies. A few of the special reports are briefly examined here.

Cash Basis Statements

In preparing any special report, the auditor must make certain the statements clearly delineate the nature of the information being presented as well as the basis on which they have been prepared. The auditor has a responsibility to include in his report an expression of opinion regarding the fairness of the information being presented or an indication that no opinion can be given. If there is any possibility of users' mistakenly believing the information was prepared in accordance with generally accepted accounting principles, it is essential that the auditor insert in his report a qualified or an adverse opinion. For example, if statements prepared on a cash basis are clearly labeled in a manner such that users will not interpret them as statements prepared on the accrual basis, the following audit opinion is acceptable:

(SCOPE PARAGRAPH—UNQUALIFIED)
(OPINION PARAGRAPH—CASH BASIS)

In our opinion, the accompanying statements present fairly the assets and liabilities of the XYZ Company, at ———, 19—, arising from cash transactions, and the revenues collected and expenditures made by it during the year then ended, on a basis consistent with that of the preceding year.

When the auditor believes misleading inferences may be drawn from the cash basis report, he should insert a middle paragraph in the report making it clear that the statements present neither the financial position nor the results of operations. The preceding cash basis opinion can then follow the middle paragraph. On the other hand, if the statements are on a modified accrual basis, it is necessary to issue an adverse or a qualified opinion.

Debt Compliance Letters

Clients occasionally enter into contracts that require them to provide the lender with a report from a CPA as to the existence or nonexistence of some condition. For example, borrowing arrangements may require maintenance of a certain dollar amount of working capital at specified points in time and an independent accountant's report as to the compliance with the requirement.

Whenever the auditor becomes involved in debt compliance letters, three considerations are of paramount importance: first, he should not report on matters he is not qualified to evaluate; second, the report should limit the scope to the particular compliance items he tested; and third, the report must be an expression of opinion rather than a statement of fact. Some of the provisions of a debt compliance letter the auditor is normally in a position to verify are whether principal and interest payments were made when they were due, whether the proper limitations were maintained on dividends, working capital, and debt ratios, and whether the accounting records were adequate for conducting an ordinary audit. On the other hand, determining whether the client has properly restricted its business activity to the requirements of an agreement or evaluating if it has title to pledged property are legal questions that the CPA is not qualified to answer. Furthermore, the Code of Professional Ethics prohibits the auditor from practicing as an attorney in these circumstances.

Following is an example of a report including a limitation of the scope of the compliance review and expressing an opinion rather than a fact:

> We have examined the consolidated financial statements of the XYZ Company and subsidiaries as of December 31, 19—, and have reported thereon in a separate audit report dated March 17, 19—.
>
> In connection therewith, we have reviewed Section 1 and 8 of the Note Agreement between the ABC Insurance Company and XYZ Company dated October 15, 19—. In making such examination, as independent accountants, we obtained no knowledge of the existence of any condition or event that in our opinion constituted a default under the terms of Section 1 or 8 of the aforementioned note agreement. The purpose and scope of our examination was such that it would not neces-

sarily disclose all defaults, if any, which may exist with respect to the Note Agreement with ABC Insurance Company.

Forecasts

The AICPA Code of Professional Ethics specifically prohibits opinions on the accuracy of forecasts of any kind, but forecasts may be prepared and presented to the client. Whenever the CPA assists in preparing forecasts, the underlying assumptions should be specifically stated and a disclaimer of opinion such as the following must be attached to the forecast:

> Since projections are based on assumptions about circumstances and events that have not yet taken place, they are subject to the variations that may arise as future operations actually occur. Accordingly, we cannot give assurance that the projected results will actually be attained.

REVIEW QUESTIONS

1. Select the best response for each of the following questions:
   a. Parnell, CPA, accepted the audit engagement of Treacy Manufacturing, Inc. During the audit, Parnell became aware that he did not have the competence required for the engagement. What should he do?
      (1) Disclaim an opinion.
      (2) Issue a "subject to" opinion.
      (3) Suggest that Treacy engage another CPA to perform the audit.
      (4) Rely on the competence of client personnel.
   b. The CPA who regularly examines Viola Corporation's financial statements has been asked to prepare projected income statements for the next five years. If the statements are to be based upon the corporation's operating assumptions and are for internal use only, the CPA should
      (1) Reject the engagement because the statements are to be based upon assumptions.
      (2) Reject the engagement because the statements are for internal use.
      (3) Accept the engagement provided full disclosure is made of the assumptions used and the extent of the CPA's responsibility.
      (4) Accept the engagement provided Viola certifies in writing that its statements are for internal use only.
   c. The date of the CPA's opinion on the financial statements of his client should be the date of
      (1) Closing of the client's books.
      (2) Receipt of client's letter of representation.
      (3) Completion of all important audit procedures.
      (4) Submittal of the report to the client.
   d. When an auditor issues a qualified opinion because of an uncertainty, the reader of the auditor's report should conclude that
      (1) The auditor was not able to form an opinion on the financial statements taken as a whole.
      (2) The uncertainty occurred after the balance sheet date but prior to the audit report date.

(3) There were no audit procedures possibly available to the auditor by which he could obtain satisfaction concerning the uncertainty.

(4) The ability of the company to continue as a "going concern" is questionable.

e. When a CPA has been engaged to prepare unaudited financial statements for his client:

(1) The CPA must perform the basic accepted auditing standards necessary to determine that the statements are in conformity with generally accepted accounting principles.

(2) The CPA is performing an accounting service rather than an examination of the financial statements.

(3) The financial statements are representations of both the management and the CPA.

(4) The CPA may prepare the statements from the books but may not assist in adjusting and closing the books.   (AICPA adapted)

2. Explain why auditor's reports are important to users of financial statements.

3. List the five parts of an unqualified audit report and explain the meaning of each part. How do the parts compare with those found in a qualified report?

4. Distinguish between a standard unqualified report and an unqualified report with a modification in the wording. Provide two examples of the latter.

5. The management of Charlotte Building Company has made the decision to reduce the depreciable life of equipment because of the introduction of a new type of machine by the industry during the past year. Since there has been no change in accounting principles, the auditor believes a qualified opinion is not required in this situation, but he would like to include a middle paragraph in the audit report. Write the middle paragraph and the opinion paragraph for the unqualified report.

6. List the six conditions requiring a departure from an unqualified opinion and give one specific example of each of those conditions.

7. Distinguish between an opinion qualified as to scope only and one with a scope and an opinion qualification.

8. Distinguish between an "except for" and a "subject to" qualified opinion and give one specific example of each.

9. Distinguish between a qualified opinion, an adverse opinion, and a disclaimer of opinion and explain the circumstances under which each is appropriate.

10. Select the best response for each of the following:

a. A CPA will issue an adverse auditor's opinion if

(1) The scope of his examination is limited by the client.

(2) His exception to the fairness of presentation is so material that an "except for" opinion is not justified.

(3) He did not perform sufficient auditing procedures to form an opinion on the financial statements taken as a whole.

(4) Such major uncertainties exist concerning the company's future that a "subject to" opinion is not justified.

b. An auditor will express an "except for" opinion if

(1) The client refuses to provide for a probable federal income tax deficiency that is material.

(2) The degree of uncertainty associated with the client company's future makes a "subject to" opinion inappropriate.

    (3) He did not perform procedures sufficient to form an opinion on the consistency of application of generally accepted accounting principles.

    (4) He is basing his opinion in part upon work done by another auditor.

c. John Greenbaum, CPA, provides bookkeeping services to Santa Fe Products Company. He also is a director of Santa Fe and performs limited auditing procedures in connection with his preparation of Santa Fe's financial statements. Greenbaum's report accompanying these financial statements should include a

    (1) Detailed description of the limited auditing procedures performed.

    (2) Complete description of the relationships with Santa Fe that imperil Greenbaum's independence.

    (3) Disclaimer of opinion and a statement that financial statements are unaudited on each page of the financial statements.

    (4) Qualified opinion because of his lack of independence together with such assurance as his limited auditing procedures can provide.

d. A CPA was unable to observe the physical inventory that his client conducted on the balance sheet date. The CPA satisfied himself as to inventory quantities by other procedures. These procedures included making some physical counts of the inventory a week later and applying appropriate tests to intervening transactions. In his report on the financial statements, the CPA

    (1) Must disclose the modification of the scope of his examination and express a qualified opinion.

    (2) Must disclose the modification of the scope of his examination but may express an unqualified opinion.

    (3) May omit reference to any modification of the scope of his examination and express an unqualified opinion.

    (4) May omit reference to modification of the scope of his examination only if he describes the circumstances in an explanatory paragraph or his opinion paragraph.

e. In forming his opinion concerning the consolidated financial statements of Juno Corporation, a CPA relies upon another auditor's examination of the financial statements of Hera, Inc., a wholly-owned subsidiary whose operations constitute 30 percent of Juno's consolidated total. Hera's auditor expresses an unqualified opinion on that company's financial statements.

    The CPA examining Juno Corporation may be expected to express an unqualified opinion but refer to the report by the other auditor if

    (1) He concludes, based upon a review of the other auditor's professional standing and qualifications, that he is willing to assume the same responsibility as though he had performed the audit of Hera's financial statements himself.

    (2) He is satisfied with the audit scope for the subsidiary, based upon his review of the audit program, but his inquiries disclose that the other auditor is not independent or lacks professional standing.

    (3) He is satisfied with the other auditor's professional standing but concludes, based upon a review of the audit program, that the audit scope for the examination of Hera's financial statements was inadequate.

    (4) He is satisfied with the other auditor's professional reputation and audit scope but is unwilling to assume responsibility for the other

auditor's work to the same extent as though he had performed the work himself.

f. If a principal auditor decides that he will refer in his report to the examination of another auditor, he is required to disclose the
   (1) Name of the other auditor.
   (2) Nature of his inquiry into the other auditor's professional standing and extent of his review of the other auditor's work.
   (3) Portion of the financial statements examined by the other auditor.
   (4) Reasons why he is unwilling to assume responsibility for the other auditor's work.

g. A CPA conducting his first examination of the financial statements of Apollo Corporation is considering the propriety of reducing his work by consulting with the predecessor auditor and reviewing the predecessor's working papers. This procedure is
   (1) Acceptable.
   (2) Required if the new auditor is to render an unqualified opinion.
   (3) Acceptable only if the CPA refers in his report to his reliance upon the predecessor auditor's work.
   (4) Unacceptable because the CPA should bring an independent viewpoint to a new engagement.

h. An auditor's unqualified short-form report
   (1) Implies only that items disclosed in the financial statements and footnotes are properly presented and takes no position on the adequacy of disclosure.
   (2) Implies that disclosure is adequate in the financial statements and footnotes.
   (3) Explicitly states that disclosure is adequate in the financial statements and footnotes.
   (4) Explicitly states that all material items have been disclosed in conformity with generally accepted accounting principles.

                                                                 (AICPA adapted)

11. How does the auditor's opinion differ between scope limitations caused by client restrictions and limitations resulting from conditions beyond the client's control? Under which of these two would the auditor be most likely to issue a disclaimer of opinion? Explain.

12. Explain the difference between a disclaimer of opinion and a disclaimer for unaudited financial statements. Under what circumstances might the auditor have a difficult time deciding which one is appropriate?

13. Discuss why the AICPA has such strict requirements on audit opinions when the auditor is not independent.

14. Define what is meant by *negative assurance* and explain why it should not be used.

15. Under what circumstances can an auditor conduct an audit of forecast financial statements?

DISCUSSION QUESTIONS AND PROBLEMS

16. Your CPA firm has been asked to audit the local church, of which you are a member, as a public service for no fee. You are assigned to conduct the audit and conclude after a complete audit that the statements are fairly presented on a cash basis.

Required:

    a. Under what circumstances might you be considered not independent?

    b. Assuming you are independent, write the audit opinion you should use.

17. For each of the following, state the appropriate type of audit report to issue (unqualified, qualified, disclaimer, or adverse):

    a. Subsequent to the close of Holly Corporation's fiscal year, a major debtor was declared bankrupt due to a series of events. The receivable is significantly material in relation to the financial statements, and recovery is doubtful. The debtor had confirmed the full amount due to Holly Corporation at the balance sheet date. Since the account was good at the balance sheet date, Holly Corporation refuses to disclose any information in relation to this subsequent event. The CPA believes that all accounts were stated fairly at the balance sheet date.

    b. Kapok Corporation is a substantial user of electronic data-processing equipment and has employed an outside service bureau to process data in years past. During the current year Kapok adopted the policy of leasing all hardware and expects to continue this arrangement in the future. This change in policy is adequately disclosed in footnotes to Kapok's financial statements, but uncertainty prohibits either Kapok or the CPA from assessing the impact of this change upon future operations.

    c. The financial statements of Reid Corporation for the year ended December 31, 19X6, were accompanied by an unqualified opinion. Reid wishes unaudited financial statements prepared for the three months ended March 31, 19X7.

    d. The president of Lowe, Inc., would not allow the auditor to confirm the receivable balance from one of its major customers. The amount of the receivable is material in relation to Lowe's financial statements. The auditor was unable to satisfy himself as to the receivable balance by alternative procedures.

    e. Sempier Corporation issued financial statements that purported to present its financial position and results of operations but omitted the related statement of changes in financial position (the omission is not sanctioned by APB 19).   (AICPA adapted)

18. As part of his examination of the financial statements of the Marlborough Corporation for the year ended March 31, 19X7, Mario Romito, CPA, is reviewing the balance sheet presentation of a $1,200,000 advance to Franklin Olds, Marlborough's president. The advance, which represents 50 percent of current assets and 10 percent of total assets, was made during the year ended March 31, 19X7. It has been described in the balance sheet as "miscellaneous accounts receivable" and classified as a current asset.

Mr. Olds informs the CPA that he has used the proceeds of the advance to purchase 35,000 shares of Marlborough's common stock in order to forestall a takeover raid on the company. He is reluctant to have his association with the advance described in the financial statements because he does not have voting control and fears that this "will just give the raiders ammunition."

Mr. Olds offers the following four-point program as an alternative to further disclosure:

    1. Have the advance approved by the board of directors. (This can be done expeditiously because a majority of the board members are officers of the company.)

2. Prepare a demand note payable to the company with interest of 7.5 percent (the average bank rate paid by the company).
3. Furnish an endorsement of the stock to the company as collateral for the loan. (During the year under audit, despite the fact that earnings did not increase, the market price of Marlborough common rose from $20 to $40 per share. The stock has maintained its $40-per-share market price subsequent to year-end.)
4. Obtain a written opinion from the company attorney supporting the legality of the company's advance and the use of the proceeds.

Required:

a. Discuss the proper balance sheet classification of the advance to Mr. Olds and other appropriate disclosures in the financial statements and footnotes. (Ignore SEC regulations and requirements, tax effects, creditors' restrictions on stock repurchase, and the presentation of common stock dividends and interest income.)
b. Discuss each point of Mr. Olds's four-point program as to whether it is desirable and as to whether it is an alternative to further disclosure.
c. If Mr. Olds refuses to permit further disclosure, what is the effect on the auditor's report? Discuss.
d. In his discussion with the CPA, Mr. Olds warns that the raiders, if successful, will probably appoint new auditors. What consideration should the CPA give to this factor? Explain. (AICPA adapted)

19. You are engaged in the examination of the financial statements of Rapid, Inc., and its recently acquired subsidiary, Slow Corporation. In acquiring Slow Corporation during 19X7, Rapid exchanged a large number of its shares of common stock for 90 percent of the outstanding common stock of Slow Corporation in a transaction that was accounted for as a pooling of interests. Rapid is now preparing its annual report to shareholders and proposes to include in the report combined financial statements for the year ended December 31, 19X7, with a footnote describing its exchange of stock for that of Slow Corporation.

Rapid also proposes to include in its report the financial statements of the preceding year as they appeared in Rapid's 19X6 annual report along with a five-year financial summary from Rapid's prior annual reports, all of which have been accompanied by your unqualified auditor's opinion.

Required:

a. Discuss the objectives or purposes of the standard of reporting that requires the auditor's report to state whether generally accepted accounting principles have been consistently observed over the past two periods.
b. Describe the treatment in the auditor's report of interperiod changes having a material effect on the financial statements arising from
(1) A change to an alternative generally accepted accounting principle.
(2) Changed conditions that necessitate accounting changes but do not involve changes in the accounting principles employed.
(3) Changed conditions unrelated to accounting.
c. (1) Would the financial reporting treatment proposed by Rapid for the 19X7 annual report be on a consistent basis? Discuss.

(2) Describe the auditor's report that should accompany the financial statements as proposed by Rapid for inclusion in the annual report.

(AICPA adapted)

20. Charles Burke, CPA, has completed field work for his examination of the Willingham Corporation for the year ended December 31, 19X7, and is now in the process of determining whether to modify his report. Two independent, unrelated situations have arisen.

(1) In September 19X7 a lawsuit was filed against Willingham to have the court order it to install pollution-control equipment in one of its older plants. Willingham's legal counsel has informed Burke that it is not possible to forecast the outcome of this litigation; however, Willingham's management has informed Burke that the cost of the pollution-control equipment is not economically feasible and that the plant will be closed if the case is lost. In addition, Burke has been told by management that the plant and its production equipment would have only minimal resale value and that the production that would be lost could not be recovered at other plants.

(2) During 19X7 Willingham purchased a franchise amounting to 20 percent of its assets for the exclusive right to produce and sell a newly patented product in the northeastern United States. There has been no production in marketable quantities of the product anywhere to date. Neither the franchisor nor any franchisee has conducted any market research with respect to the product.

Required:

In deciding the type-of-report modification, if any, Burke should take into account such considerations as the following:

- Relative magnitude
- Uncertainty of outcome
- Likelihood of error
- Expertise of the auditor
- Pervasive impact on the financial statements
- Inherent importance of the item

Discuss Burke's type-of-report decision for each situation in terms of the above and other appropriate considerations. Assume that each situation is adequately disclosed in the notes to the financial statements. Each situation should be considered independently. In discussing each situation, ignore the other. It is not necessary for you to decide the type of report that should be issued. (AICPA adapted)

21. Following are three independent, unrelated auditor's reports. The corporation being reported on, in each case, is profit oriented and publishes general-purpose financial statements for distribution to owners, creditors, potential investors, and the general public. Each of the three reports contains deficiencies.

AUDITOR'S REPORT I

We have examined the consolidated balance sheet of Belasco Corporation and subsidiaries as of December 31, 19X7, and the related consolidated statements of income and retained earnings and changes in financial position for the year then ended. Our examination was made in accordance with generally accepted auditing standards and therefore included such tests of the accounting records and such other auditing procedures as we considered necessary in the circumstances. We did not examine the financial statements of Seidel Company, a major consolidated subsidiary. These statements were examined by other auditors whose reports thereon have been furnished to us, and our opinion expressed herein, insofar as it relates to Seidel Company, is based solely upon the reports of the other auditors.

In our opinion, except for the reports of the other auditors, the accompanying consolidated balance sheet and consolidated statements of income and retained earnings and changes in financial position present fairly the financial position of Belasco Corporation and subsidiaries at December 31, 19X7 and the results of its operations and the changes in its financial position for the year then ended, in conformity with generally accepted accounting principles applied on a basis consistent with that of the preceding year.

AUDITOR'S REPORT II

The accompanying balance sheet of Jones Corporation as of December 31, 19X7, and the related statements of income and retained earnings and changes in financial position for the year then ended, were not audited by us; however, we confirmed cash in the bank and performed a general review of the statements.

During our engagement, nothing came to our attention to indicate that the aforementioned financial statements do not present fairly the financial position of Jones Corporation at December 31, 19X7, and the results of its operations and the changes in its financial position for the year then ended, in conformity with generally accepted accounting principles applied on a basis consistent with that of the preceding year; however, we do not express an opinion on them.

AUDITOR'S REPORT III

I made my examination in accordance with generally accepted auditing standards. However, I am not independent with respect to Mavis Corporation because my wife owns 5 percent of the outstanding common stock of the company. The accompanying balance sheet as of December 31, 19X7, and the related statements of income and retained earnings and changes in financial position for the year then ended were not audited by me; accordingly, I do not express an opinion on them.

Required:

For each auditor's report, describe the reporting deficiencies, explain the reasons therefor, and briefly discuss how the report should be corrected. Each report should be considered separately. When discussing one report, ignore the other two. Do not discuss the addressee, signatures, and date. Also do not rewrite any of the auditor's reports. Organize your answer sheet as follows:

Report No.	Deficiency	Reason	Correction

(AICPA adapted)

22. About two years ago you were engaged to conduct an annual audit of Pierson Company. This was shortly after the majority stockholders assumed control of the company and discharged the president and several other corporate officers. A new president canceled a wholesaler's contract to distribute Pierson Company products. The wholesaler is a Pierson Company minority stockholder and was one of the discharged officers. Shortly after you commenced your initial audit, several lawsuits were filed against Pierson Company by the wholesaler. Pierson Company filed countersuits.

None of the suits has been decided. The principal litigation is over the canceled contract, and the other suits are claims against the company for salary, bonus, and pension fund contributions. Pierson Company is the plaintiff in suits totaling approximately $300,000 and defendant in suits totaling approximately $2 million. Both amounts are material in relation to net income and total assets. Pierson's legal counsel believes that the outcome of the suits is uncertain and that all the suits are likely to be "tied up in court" for an extended time.

You were instructed by the board of directors each year to issue an audit report only if it contained an unqualified opinion. Pierson Company refuses to provide for an unfavorable settlement in the financial statements because legal counsel advised the board of directors that such a provision in the financial statements could be used against Pierson by the opposition in court. The pending litigation was fully disclosed in a footnote to the financial statements, however.

You did not issue a report on the completion of your audit one year ago, and you have now completed your second annual audit. The scope of your audits was not restricted in any way, and you would render unqualified opinions if there were no pending litigations. You have attended all meetings of the stockholders and the directors and have answered all questions addressed to you at these meetings. You were promptly paid for all work completed to the current date. The board of directors of Pierson Company invited you to deliver to them an audit report containing an unqualified opinion or to attend the annual meeting of the stockholders one week hence to answer questions concerning the results of your audit if you are unwilling to render an unqualified opinion.

Required:

    a. Discuss the issues raised by the fact that the CPA attended the stockholders' and directors' meetings and answered all questions addressed to him. Do not consider the propriety of his failure to issue a written audit report.

    b. Should a CPA issue his audit report promptly after he has completed his examination? Why?

    c. Write the auditor's opinion you would render on Pierson Company's financial statements for the year just ended.   (AICPA adapted)

23. You are completing an examination of the financial statements of the Hilty Manufacturing Corporation for the year ended December 19X7. Hilty's financial statements have not been examined previously. Hilty's controller has given you the following draft of proposed footnotes to the financial statements.

The Hilty Manufacturing Corporation

Notes to Financial Statements

Year Ended December 31, 19X7

Note 1. Because we were not engaged as auditors until after December 31, 19X7, we were unable to observe the taking of the beginning physical inventory. We satisfied ourselves as to the balance of physical inventory at December 28, 19X7, by alternative procedures.

Note 2. With the approval of the commissioner of Internal Revenue, the company changed its method of accounting for inventories from the first-in, first-out method to the last-in, first-out method on January 1, 19X7. In the opinion of the company the effects of this change on the pricing of inventories and cost of goods manufactured were not material in the current year but are expected to be material in future years.

Note 3. The investment property was recorded at cost until October 19X7 when it was written up to its appraisal value. The company plans to sell the property in 19X8, and an independent real estate agent in the area has indicated that the appraisal price can be realized. Pending completion of the sale, the amount of the expected gain on the sale has been recorded in a deferred credit account.

Note 4. The stock dividend described in our May 24, 19X7, letter to stockholders has been recorded as a 105-for-100 stock split. Accordingly, there were no changes in the stockholders' equity account balances from this transaction.

Note 5. For many years the company has maintained a pension plan for certain employees. Prior to the current year pension expense was recognized as payments were made to retired employees. There was no change in the plan in the current year, but upon the recommendation of its auditor, the company provided $64,000, based upon an actuarial estimate, for pensions to be paid in the future to current employees.

Required:

For each of Notes 1 through 5, discuss
a. The adequacy and needed revisions, if any, of the financial statements or the note.
b. The necessary disclosure in or opinion modification of the auditor's report, assuming the revisions mentioned in part *a*, have been made.

(AICPA adapted)

24. Independent certified public accountants customarily issue two types of auditor's reports in connection with an examination of financial statements: a so-called short-form auditor's report in connection with financial statements intended for publication, and a so-called long-form auditor's report for the purposes of management and other parties.

Required:

a. Outline in *general terms* the kinds of materials that are commonly included in a long-form report other than those commonly included in a short-form report.

b. Does the auditor assume the same degree of responsibility for other data in the long-form report that he assumes for individual items in the customary basic financial statements (balance sheet and statements of income, retained income, and capital)? State the reasons for your answer.

(AICPA adapted)

25. You are newly engaged by the James Company, a New England manufacturer with a sales office and warehouse located in a western state. The James Company audit must be made at the peak of your busy season when you will not have a senior auditor available for travel to the western outlet. Furthermore, the James Company is reluctant to bear the travel expenses of an out-of-town auditor.

Required:

a. Under what conditions would you, the principal auditor, be willing to accept full responsibility for the work of another auditor?
b. What would be your requirements with respect to the integrity of the other auditor? To whom would you direct inquiries about the other auditor?
c. What reference, if any, would you make to the other auditor in your report if you were
   (1) Assuming full responsibility for his work?
   (2) Not assuming responsibility for his work?   (AICPA adapted)

26. The following draft of an auditor's report has been submitted for review:

> To: Eric Jones, Chief Accountant
>   Sunshine Manufacturing Co.
>
> We have examined the balance sheet of the Sunshine Manufacturing Co. for the year ended August 31, 19X7, and the related statements of income and retained earnings. Our examination included such tests of the accounting records and such other auditing procedures as we considered necessary in the circumstances except that, in accordance with your instructions, we did not count the buyers' cash working fund.
>
> In our opinion, subject to the limitation on our examination discussed above, the accompanying balance sheet and statements of income and earned surplus present fairly the financial position of the Sunshine Manufacturing Co. at August 31, 19X7, and the results of its operations for the year then ended.
>
> Frank George & Co.
> August 31, 19X7

It has been determined that

a. Except for the omission of the count of the buyers' cash working fund, there were no scope restrictions placed on the auditor's examination.
b. Sunshine Manufacturing has been in continuous operation since 1942, but its financial statements have not previously been audited.

Required:

a. Assuming that Frank George & Co. was able to perform alternative auditing procedures to satisfactorily substantiate the buyers' cash working fund and purchases through the fund, identify and discuss the deficiencies in the auditor's report.
b. Assuming that Frank George & Co. was unable to satisfactorily substan-

tiate the buyers' cash working fund and purchases through the fund by alternative auditing procedures, discuss the appropriateness of the opinion qualification proposed by Frank George & Co.'s report.

c. Discuss the potential consequences to the CPA of issuing a substandard report or failing to adhere in his examination to generally accepted auditing standards.   (AICPA adapted)

27. The financial statements of the Modern Manufacturing Company for the fiscal year ended September 30, 19X7, are presented below. The president of the company has requested you to make this year's examination and render a short-form audit report on the statements. The report would be addressed to the board of directors, and no restrictions would be placed on the scope of your audit work.

During the course of the audit you learn that inventories of finished products and work in process are stated at material cost alone, without including either labor or manufacturing overhead; that this practice has been followed for both tax and financial accounting purposes since the inception of the company in 1946; and that the elements of cost in the inventories should have been as follows for the beginning and end of the fiscal period:

| | Finished Goods September 30 | | Work in Process September 30 | |
	19X7	19X6	19X7	19X6
Materials	$88,000	$75,000	$34,000	$31,000
Labor	55,000	52,000	16,000	14,000
Overhead	28,000	24,000	17,000	16,000
	$171,000	$151,000	$67,000	$61,000

Except for the company's inventory methods, the statements are found to be acceptable in all respects.

Through an examination of the previous auditor's working papers, you have been able to satisfy yourself as to the correctness of the physical count and materials cost of the opening inventory.

Required:

Prepare an audit report addressed to the board of directors, such as is justified in the circumstances set forth above. Do not submit financial statements or notes to financial statements.   (AICPA adapted)

28. You have been engaged by the board of directors of the Products Company, a medium-sized manufacturer, to examine its balance sheets as of December 31, 19X6, and the related statement of income and retained earnings for the year then ended. You have made a similar examination for the preceding year. At the conclusion of your examination you will be expected to issue a short-form report relating to the financial statements.

In conducting your examination you encounter the following situations:

a. In response to a request for positive confirmation of its outstanding balance, one of the company's customers, a large mail-order concern whose balance represents almost one-half of total accounts receivable and 20

Modern Manufacturing Company

Balance Sheet

September 30, 19X7

Assets			*Liabilities and Stockholders' Equity*		
Current Assets			Current Liabilities		
Cash	$12,000		Trade accounts payable	$29,000	
Accounts receivable (net)	22,000		Salaries and wages	5,500	
Inventories, at material cost			Taxes, other than taxes on		
(first-in, first-out) or mar-			income	8,000	
ket, whichever lower	146,000		Taxes on income	13,000	
Prepaid expenses	6,000				
Total current assets	$186,000		Total current liabilities	$55,500	
Property, plant, and equip-			Stockholders' Equity		
ment (net)	158,000		Common stock, par value $100		
			a share, authorized, issued		
			and outstanding 2,000		
			shares	200,000	
			Retained earnings	88,500	
	$344,000			$344,000	

Modern Manufacturing Company

Statement of Income and Retained Earnings

Year Ended September 30, 19X7

Net sales of manufactured product	$750,000	
Cost of materials, including freight	300,000	
Gross profit on sales	$450,000	
Operating expenses	385,000	
Earnings from operations	$ 65,000	
Other deductions, less other income	22,000	
Earnings before taxes on income	$ 43,000	
Taxes on income (federal $12,000, state $1,000)	13,000	
Net earnings	$ 30,000	
Retained earnings—September 30, 19X6	58,500	
Retained earnings—September 30, 19X7	$ 88,500	

percent of total current assets, replies that its records are not maintained in a manner permitting confirmation.

b. It is the company's practice to store most of its finished goods in public warehouses from which shipments to customers are made. At December 31, 19X6, the date of the examination of inventory quantities, the inventory in these warehouses is substantial in relation to the company's total assets. One warehouse alone, which is located in a distant city and which is operated by a company not known to you, holds one-third of the company's finished goods.

c. The company has advised you that it is the defendant in litigation brought by a competitor for patent infringement. Counsel for the company advises of the amount of the damages sought by the competitor which is in excess of the company's net worth. Counsel also states that in his opinion, judgment will be in favor of your client.

d. For the entire year under examination, the company, in accordance with your recommendation made last year, charged its expenditures for computer development costs to current expenses. Previously such expenditures, which are material in amount in relation to the company's operations, had been recorded as deferred charges. The amounts so recorded in previous years are being amortized over five-year periods.

Required:

Considering the specific facts in these four situations, and assuming that any additional audit procedures you recommend will result in substantiating the facts as presented, you are to *state* and *justify fully* for each situation:

a. The additional audit procedures, if any, that should be followed.

b. The disclosures, if any, that should be made in the financial statements or in footnotes thereto.

c. The qualifications, comments, or references, if any, you should include in the short-form report in addition to the items in part *b* above.

(AICPA adapted)

29. For each of the following independent situations, state the nature of the appropriate qualification in the audit report:

a. Subsequent to the date of the financial statements as part of his post-balance-sheet-date audit procedures, a CPA learned of heavy damage to one of a client's two plants due to a recent fire; the loss will not be reimbursed by insurance. The newspapers described the event in detail. The financial statements and appended notes as prepared by the client did not disclose the loss caused by the fire.

b. A CPA is engaged in the examination of the financial statements of a large manufacturing company with branch offices in many widely separated cities. The CPA was not able to count the substantial undeposited cash receipts at the close of business on the last day of the fiscal year at all branch offices.

As an alternative to this auditing procedure used to verify the accurate cutoff of cash receipts, the CPA observed that deposits in transit as shown on the year-end bank reconciliation appeared as credits on the bank statement on the first business day of the new year. He was satisfied as to the cutoff of cash receipts by the use of the alternative procedure.

c. On January 2, 19X7, the Retail Auto Parts Company received a notice from its primary supplier that effective immediately all wholesale prices would be increased 10 percent. On the basis of the notice, Retail Auto Parts revalued its December 31, 19X6, inventory to reflect the higher costs. The inventory constituted a material proportion of total assets; however, the effect of the revaluation was material to current assets but not to total assets or net income. The increase in valuation is adequately disclosed in the footnotes.

d. During 19X7 the research staff of Scientific Research Corporation devoted its entire efforts toward developing a new pollution-control device. All costs that could be attributed directly to the project involving the pollution-control device were accounted for as deferred charges and classified on the balance sheet at December 31, 19X7, as a noncurrent asset. In the course of its audit of the corporation's 19X7 financial statements, Anthony, CPA, found persuasive evidence that the research conducted to date would probably result in a marketable product. The deferred research charges are significantly material in relationship to both income and total assets.

e. For the past five years a CPA has audited the financial statements of a manufacturing company. During this period, the examination scope was limited by the client as to the observation of the annual physical inventory. Since the CPA considered the inventories to be of material amount and he· was not able to satisfy himself by other auditing procedures, he was not able to express an unqualified opinion on the financial statements in each of the five years.

The CPA was allowed to observe physical inventories for the current year ended December 31, 19X7, because the client's banker would no longer accept the audit reports. In the interest of economy, the client requested the CPA to not extend his audit procedures to the inventory as of January 1, 19X7.

f. During the course of his examination of the financial statements of a corporation for the purpose of expressing an opinion on the statements, a CPA is refused permission to inspect the minute books. The corporation secretary instead offers to give the CPA a certified copy of all resolutions and actions relating to accounting matters.

g. A CPA has completed his examination of the financial statements of a bus company for the year ended December 31, 19X7. Prior to 19X7 the company had been depreciating its buses over a ten-year period. During 19X7 the company determined that a more realistic estimated life for its buses was twelve years and computed the 19X7 depreciation on the basis of the revised estimate. The CPA has satisfied himself that the twelve-year life is reasonable.

The company has adequately disclosed the change in estimated useful lives of its buses and the effect of the change on 19X7 income in a note to the financial statements. (AICPA adapted)

30. Evaluate the following comments about unaudited financial statements: "When a CPA associates his name with unaudited financial statements, his only responsibility is to the client and that is limited to the proper summarization and presentation on the financial statements of information provided by the client. The opinion clearly states that the auditor has not conducted an audit and does not express an opinion on this fair presentation. If a user of the statement relies on unaudited financial statements, he does so at his own risk and should never be able to hold the CPA responsible for inadequate performance. The user should interpret the financial statements as if they had been prepared by management."

31. Following are the financial statements of the Young Manufacturing Corporation and the auditor's report of their examination for the year ended January 31, 19X7. The examination was conducted by John Smith, an individual practitioner who has examined the corporation's financial statements and has reported on them for many years.

Young Manufacturing Corporation

Statements of Condition

January 31, 19X7 and 19X6

	19X7	19X6
Assets		
Current assets:		
Cash	$ 43,822	$ 51,862
Accounts receivable, pledged—less allowances for doubtful accounts of $3,800 in 19X7 and $3,000 in 19X6 (see note)	65,298	46,922
Inventories, pledged—at average cost, not in excess of replacement cost	148,910	118,264
Other current assets	6,280	5,192
Total current assets	$264,310	$222,240
Fixed assets:		
Land—at cost	38,900	62,300
Buildings—at cost, less accumulated depreciation of $50,800 in 19X7 and $53,400 in 19X6	174,400	150,200
Machinery and equipment—at cost, less accumulated depreciation of $30,500 in 19X7 and $25,640 in 19X6	98,540	78,560
Total fixed assets	$311,840	$291,060
Total assets	$576,150	$513,300

	19X7	19X6
Liabilities and Stockholders' Equity		
Current liabilities:		
Accounts payable	$ 27,926	$ 48,161
Other liabilities	68,743	64,513
Current portion of long-term mortgage payable	3,600	3,600
Income taxes payable	46,840	30,866
Total current liabilities	$147,109	$147,140
Long-term liabilities:		
Mortgage payable	90,400	94,000
Total liabilities	$237,509	$241,140
Stockholders' equity:		
Capital stock, par value $100, 1,000 shares authorized, issued and outstanding	$100,000	$100,000
Retained earnings	238,641	172,160
Total stockholders' equity	$338,641	$272,160
Total liabilities and stockholders' equity	$576,150	$513,300

Young Manufacturing Corporation

Income Statements

For the Years Ended January 31, 19X7 and 19X6

	19X7	*19X6*
Income:		
Sales	$884,932	$682,131
Other income	3,872	2,851
Total	$888,804	$684,982
Costs and expenses:		
Cost of goods sold	$463,570	$353,842
Selling expenses	241,698	201,986
Administrative expenses	72,154	66,582
Provision for income taxes	45,876	19,940
Other expenses	12,582	13,649
Total	$835,880	$655,999
Net income	$ 52,924	$ 28,983

TO: Mr. Paul Young, President   March 31, 19X7
      Young Manufacturing Corporation

I have examined the balance sheet of the Young Manufacturing Corporation and the related statements of income and retained earnings.

These statements present fairly the financial position and results of operations in conformity with generally accepted principles of accounting applied on a consistent basis. My examination was made in accordance with generally accepted auditing standards, and accordingly included such tests of the accounting records and such other auditing procedures as I considered necessary in the circumstances.

                      (Signed) John Smith

Required:

List and discuss the deficiencies of the auditor's report prepared by John Smith. Your discussion should include justifications that the matters you cited are deficiencies. (Do not check the addition of the statements. Assume that the addition is correct.)   (AICPA adapted)

Index